SAP PRESS Books: Always on hand

Print or e-book, Kindle or iPad, workplace or airplane: Choose where and how to read your SAP PRESS books! You can now get all our titles as e-books, too:

▸ By download and online access
▸ For all popular devices
▸ And, of course, DRM-free

Convinced? Then go to **www.sap-press.com** and get your e-book today.

OData and SAP NetWeaver® Gateway

SAP PRESS is a joint initiative of SAP and Galileo Press. The know-how offered by SAP specialists combined with the expertise of the Galileo Press publishing house offers the reader expert books in the field. SAP PRESS features first-hand information and expert advice, and provides useful skills for professional decision-making.

SAP PRESS offers a variety of books on technical and business-related topics for the SAP user. For further information, please visit our website: *www.sap-press.com*.

Dave Haseman, Ross Hightower
Mobile Development for SAP
2013, 617 pp., hardcover
ISBN 978-1-59229-448-0

Tanmaya Gupta
Function Modules in ABAP: A Quick Reference Guide
2014, 977 pp., hardcover
ISBN 978-1-59229-850-1

Emmanuel Hadzipetros
Architecting EDI with SAP IDocs: The Comprehensive Guide (2nd Edition)
2014, 910 pp., hardcover
ISBN 978-1-59229-871-6

Thorsten Schneider, Eric Westenberger, Hermann Gahm
ABAP Development for SAP HANA
2014, 609 pp., hardcover
ISBN 978-1-59229-859-4

Carsten Bönnen, Volker Drees, André Fischer, Ludwig Heinz, and Karsten Strothmann

OData and SAP NetWeaver® Gateway

Galileo Press

Bonn • Boston

Galileo Press is named after the Italian physicist, mathematician, and philosopher Galileo Galilei (1564–1642). He is known as one of the founders of modern science and an advocate of our contemporary, heliocentric worldview. His words *Eppur si muove* (And yet it moves) have become legendary. The Galileo Press logo depicts Jupiter orbited by the four Galilean moons, which were discovered by Galileo in 1610.

Editor Kelly Grace Weaver
Copyeditor Julie McNamee
Cover Design Graham Geary
Photo Credit iStockphoto.com/8118049/© wbritten
Layout Design Vera Brauner
Production Kelly O'Callaghan
Typesetting SatzPro, Krefeld (Germany)
Printed and bound in the United States of America, on paper from sustainable sources

ISBN 978-1-59229-907-2
© 2014 by Galileo Press Inc., Boston (MA)
1st edition 2014

Library of Congress Cataloging-in-Publication Data
Bonnen, Carsten.
OData and SAP NetWeaver Gateway / Carsten Bonnen, Volker Drees, Andre Fischer, Ludwig Heinz, and K Strothmann.
pages cm
Includes bibliographical references and index.
ISBN 978-1-59229-907-2 (alk. paper) -- ISBN 1-59229-907-5 (alk. paper) -- ISBN 978-1-59229-908-9 (alk. paper) --
ISBN 978-1-59229-909-6 (alk. paper) 1. SAP NetWeaver Gateway. 2. Open Data Protocol. I. Title.
QA76.76.S27B66 2014
006.3'3--dc23
2013037971

Contents at a Glance

Dear Reader,

Editors, even SAP editors, often have a penchant for poetry. You may think that there isn't too much poetry in the business of enterprise software, and…well, okay, you wouldn't be wrong. However, one area where you're likely to find it—if you're paying attention—is in product naming.

Which brings me to SAP NetWeaver Gateway. *Gateway*. What a fantastic product name, no? The word promises something. It says: "Welcome!" It says: "Come in!" It says: "Right this way!" And, indeed, the product itself is a reflection of what the name suggests: an entrance to the different, open standards of OData. So come, O pioneers! Follow well in order. We debouch upon a newer, mightier world.

Poetry or not, we at SAP PRESS would be interested to hear your opinion of this book. What did you think about *OData and SAP NetWeaver Gateway*? How could it be improved? As your comments and suggestions are the most useful tools to help us make our books the best they can be, we encourage you to visit our website at *www.sap-press.com* and share your feedback.

Thank you for purchasing a book from SAP PRESS!

Kelly Grace Weaver
Editor, SAP PRESS

Galileo Press
Boston, MA

kelly.weaver@galileo-press.com
www.sap-press.com

Contents

Part I: Getting Started

4   Deployment Options, Installation, and Configuration   137

Part II: Service Creation

15

Foreword by Dr. Vishal Sikka

It was October 2008. I was sitting on a Lufthansa 747, and it was one of those rare moments of quiet just before take-off when phones and emails are silenced. There was a lot going on in the world at that time, but for those few minutes I was able to look around and appreciate the beauty and timelessness of the plane I was sitting in. It was incredible to me that a plane introduced decades ago could feel so new and modern.

It was on this flight that I wrote my first blog about *timeless software*, the notion that very old and long-lived software systems should also be new and modern and beautiful, that these systems can adapt to future business needs that we can't even imagine today. It is the same principle we see in a 747 that has stood the test of time, as a reliable and simultaneously beautiful example of design and engineering that has adapted to its changing users. It is the same principle that cities are both simultaneously new and old, modern and yet steeped in history and tradition.

I believe this is what was fundamentally lacking in software systems at that time: an understanding of how to build software systems that are simultaneously reliable and coherent and beautiful and simple in design over a long period of time. Systems must be able to adapt and bring new breakthrough innovation to users, while at the same time maintaining their integrity, without compromise. This breakthrough thinking came just before a massive transformation at SAP, a time of great introspection in the company that began with a personal challenge from Hasso Plattner to intellectually renew the company. This meant rethinking and renewing how we do everything—how we build software, how we deliver software, how we think about our customers, and more specifically how we think about users. It was an incredible time for SAP, a time when we were able to finally start breaking free of the limitations we had set for ourselves.

SAP NetWeaver Gateway was the first example of timeless software, and for that reason it gives me great pleasure to see this book published.

With SAP NetWeaver Gateway, we freed SAP applications from the confines of the desktop and enabled developers to access them from any environment, tool, or device. Developers could finally use the development tools of their choice to create new applications, without disrupting their existing IT landscapes. For SAP, this was truly a breakthrough. Later we would bring SAP HANA, which would completely transform the IT industry—but first there was SAP NetWeaver Gateway bringing unprecedented choice and openness. Developers who didn't know anything about SAP development languages could use industry standards to create new applications that connect directly to SAP software. Any developer could now build and deliver applications to take advantage of SAP application functionality and content for new uses, including new mobile, social, and business applications. With the launch of SAP NetWeaver Gateway, we had massively grown the extensibility and connectivity—the reach—of what users could do with our solutions.

This first edition of *OData and SAP NetWeaver Gateway* is your comprehensive guide to SAP NetWeaver Gateway. After reading this book, you will understand SAP NetWeaver Gateway, its scope, and its related principles, standards, and technologies. The practical exercises included in this reference guide enable you to implement your first SAP NetWeaver Gateway projects with ease. I continue to be amazed by the things developers who don't even know SAP programming languages have been able to do using SAP NetWeaver Gateway.

Five years after that 747 flight, we have seen many companies implementing SAP NetWeaver Gateway as a building block of timeless software. From this book and from talking to one another after reading it, I hope and I know you will discover many more inventive things to do with SAP NetWeaver Gateway.

Dr. Vishal Sikka
Executive Board Member, Products & Innovations, SAP AG

Foreword by Michael Reh

Having spent many years working for SAP in the Microsoft and IBM area, I learned one thing the hard way: If they are not interoperable, awesome products can easily become mediocre products in real life scenarios.

This was especially true for SAP and Microsoft. Users simply expect these companies to work together to an extent where their products integrate seamlessly. One reason for this expectation is the need for an intuitive user interface for casual users. And what product is more intuitive than the already well known one? This is why our customers wanted SAP data and processes available to the casual user by means of Microsoft products—more specifically, Microsoft Office products. It is with this knowledge that I drove and accompanied the launch of the first SAP NetWeaver Gateway powered product: Duet Enterprise, jointly developed by SAP and Microsoft.

However, in times like these, when there is a new mobile device available and a new technology trend on the horizon every other day, it is imperative to expand beyond specific interoperability scenarios to include other players, other devices, and other applications. What the customer really needs is a multi-channel access to his business data and processes. The amazing thing about SAP NetWeaver Gateway is that it offers exactly this. It leverages interoperability between virtually any end-user device and the SAP Business Suite; i.e., it implements multi-channel access.

As head of the PTU Information Worker Division, I had the opportunity to be one of the main drivers behind the product. The purpose of SAP NetWeaver Gateway is to consume SAP data and processes in an easy and standardized way. Since then, I have been continuously impressed with the progress the product has made and the scenarios we and our customers implemented with SAP NetWeaver Gateway. Adoption has simply been overwhelming.

With so many scenarios out there and so many customers, partners, and developers using SAP NetWeaver Gateway, the obvious next step was to produce a compendium that collects all relevant information on SAP NetWeaver Gateway in one book. I am delighted to see that this book is now published. To some it may be a pleasant read, to others it may be a source of invaluable information, to most—I am sure about this—it will be both.

Michael Reh
Executive Vice President, Frontline Technologies

Foreword by Stephan Herbert

In recent years, user interface technologies have been changing rapidly to keep up with contemporary trends. As smart phones gain more and more popularity, this pace has increased further still. Though it feels like iPhone 3 and Android 1.0 were released decades ago, it was actually relatively recently—in 2008. These releases mark a substantial shift in the anticipated user experience. Indeed, they shape the expectations that Generation Y place on today's business applications.

So the fundamental question was: How can SAP provide a fast-paced environment without compromising on reliable business functions? It was obvious to us that data retrieval and data manipulation needed to be decoupled from UI development. Further, this decoupling needed to be executed in a way that allowed UI developers to grasp the concept quickly, while also providing easy access to business data. These requirements could only be achieved through a standardized protocol that is supported by a variety of development environments. This would ensure that developers would not need to invest time and energy learning proprietary protocols or deciphering cryptic metadata they did not need to consume. It was at this time that OData emerged as a de facto protocol standard.

As we started decoupling data retrieval and manipulation from UI development, it became apparent that the diversity and quantity of new media would also increase the volume of data retrieval and require the simple administration of system access.

With these thoughts in mind, we started to develop SAP NetWeaver Gateway, which was released in November 2011. Customer adoption was overwhelming. In less than 24 months, over 7,000 customers started using SAP NetWeaver Gateway. As adoption grows further, the demand for knowledge about SAP NetWeaver Gateway and OData continues to rise. I am therefore delighted to see this book published, as it provides comprehensive insight into crucial topics such as OData and how to implement and consume OData services from an SAP system via SAP NetWeaver Gateway. It will serve every interested reader as a compendium, whether the reader is a developer who builds services or applications consuming them, or is simply interested in learning more and understanding SAP NetWeaver Gateway a bit better.

Stephan Herbert
Vice President of Gateway Unit

Introduction

Barely 20 years ago, we all started surfing the World Wide Web. Around the same time, we started using mobile phones on a regular basis. At that time, however, not many people thought about bringing those two technologies together. Even fewer people expected the combination to become as popular as it is today.

If you remember that time, you'll know that companies like Google didn't even exist. Amazon was not around yet, and everyday devices such as iPods, iPhones, or iPads weren't even invented. Even Nokia—for years to come one of the leading companies for mobile phones—was just getting started. When you remember—and we assume some of you do—the past 20 years, you can easily see how fast things move in the IT area.

So let's fast forward to today. In today's world, not only can you surf the web using your PC, you can also use your smartphone, tablet, phablet, TV, or gaming console—to name only a few. Because of this, we face the challenge of providing business applications that address a virtually endless number of consumption channels. Furthermore, to remain competitive, we see a necessity to implement social and technological trends alike.

This book is about a product that enables you to implement those trends for SAP Business Suite applications: SAP NetWeaver Gateway. The book takes you on a tour to learn everything you need to know about SAP NetWeaver Gateway. If you are new to SAP NetWeaver Gateway and its concepts, you should take this tour from Chapter 1 to Chapter 15 in one read. If you already understand some of the concepts and technologies involved, we did our best to allow you to take detours, start in the middle of things, and jump around if you like. To make the tour as convenient as possible for you, the book is structured not only in simple chapters but also into several overarching parts.

Part I: Getting Started

The first part of the book consists of four chapters that cover the basics of SAP NetWeaver Gateway. This is the recommended starting point if you want to be informed about SAP NetWeaver Gateway and its related concepts, such as OData.

Chapter 1 gives you a high-level introduction to SAP NetWeaver Gateway and explains the motivation behind the product. It then provides a basic positioning of the product in the context of other SAP products.

OData is the industry standard used by SAP NetWeaver Gateway. We introduce it in detail in **Chapter 2**.

Chapter 3 provides you with a solid introduction to the architecture of SAP NetWeaver Gateway, including its backend concepts and integration with other SAP interfaces.

Chapter 4 closes the first part of the book by discussing the deployment options of SAP NetWeaver Gateway as found today in real-life system landscapes.

Part II: Service Creation

If you are an experienced traveler and know your way around SAP NetWeaver Gateway and OData, you may have skipped the first part of the book completely. Then again, maybe you worked your way through the first part of the book and just learned about SAP NetWeaver Gateway and OData. No matter which is the case, in this second part, you'll learn everything you need to know about service creation for SAP NetWeaver Gateway.

Chapter 5 explains the end-to-end development tools and development cycle for creating SAP NetWeaver Gateway services. It introduces you to both main methods of service creation: service development and service generation. Chapter 5 is the basis for the other chapters in the second part of the book.

Service development is the topic of **Chapter 6**. In this chapter, you'll learn about service development in the backend with ABAP. The chapter takes a hands-on approach to show you how to develop OData services.

Chapter 7 is about the second method of creating services: service generation. It explains the backend-side generation of OData services.

Part III: Application Development

As there are two sides to every coin, SAP NetWeaver Gateway has two sides as well: provisioning (backend services and their development) and consumption (usage of backend services in applications). While the second part of our book focused on provisioning, the third part covers consumption. The different chapters take different angles and show the flexibility of SAP NetWeaver Gateway.

Chapter 8 is all about the SAP NetWeaver Gateway Productivity Accelerator (GWPA). GWPA is the main tool for SAP NetWeaver Gateway when it comes to consumption; that is, application development.

One of the most commonly asked questions about application development is how to build mobile applications. **Chapter 9** answers this question and walks you through some examples of mobile application development.

Chapter 10 is related to mobile application development, but takes a different, standards-based approach. In this chapter, you'll learn how to use OData service consumption with SAPUI5.

Chapter 11 is dedicated to social media applications. You'll learn how to develop applications that leverage the power of different social media—from Facebook to Weibo—in combination with OData and SAP NetWeaver Gateway.

In **Chapter 12**, we close Part III of the book with a look at the consumption of OData services from within enterprise applications such as Microsoft Excel and Microsoft SharePoint.

Part IV: Administration

The fourth part of the book is all about the administration of SAP NetWeaver Gateway. In addition to deploying SAP NetWeaver Gateway, it's important to understand how to roll out software, how to handle errors, and so on, as described in **Chapter 13**.

In theory, the topic of security could have been part of Chapter 13; however, it's so important that it has its own chapter. **Chapter 14** is all about the security of SAP NetWeaver Gateway, from authentication to authorization to single sign-on (SSO).

Part V: Roadmap

In the last part of the book, you'll find only one chapter; **Chapter 15** provides an outlook on future developments. It takes a deep look into the crystal ball when it comes to topics such as the Internet of Things and gamification, and it closes the fifth part—and the book—with a summary of changes in SAP NetWeaver 7.40 and SAP NetWeaver Gateway. (You will also find information about SAP NetWeaver 7.40 mentioned throughout the book wherever necessary, of course.)

In addition to all the information contained in this book, we have also provided text versions of the code samples we use. These are available for download at the book's page at *www.sap-press.com*.

Acknowledgments

With this book, you do not hold only the work of five authors in your hands. In addition to countless hours of writing, rewriting, and then rewriting again by the authors, there were many other people involved directly or indirectly. Those people invested hours of their time to read the chapters, comment, criticize, or—in the case of friends and family—endure the authors and their moods and nightshifts.

Forewords

First, we would like to extend a very special thanks to Vishal Sikka for his spontaneous willingness to honor our book with a foreword.

Big thank yous from all authors go to Michael Reh and Stephan Herbert for their great forewords, which completed the unique introduction to our book.

Management

On behalf of Ludwig Heinz, special thanks goes to Daniel Wagner, his manager at itelligence AG, and to the mobile topic leader at itelligence AG, Matthias Kumm.

On behalf of our SAP authors, special thanks goes to Pascal Gibert, general manager of P&I BIT Gateway consumption tools; Stephan Herbert, vice president of Gateway Unit; and Thomas Anton, line manager for SAP NetWeaver Gateway. They all believed in us and the book and supported us in this daring endeavor. Further thanks goes to Joav Bally, chief product manager for SAP NetWeaver Gateway, in supporting us during the creation of the book.

Additional special thanks go to Michael Reh, executive vice president of Frontline Technologies, for his support even during his vacation.

Colleagues and Special Contributors

Jürgen Kremer, architect for SAP NetWeaver Gateway, is mentioned first for a reason. He has strongly influenced the core part of this book and has significantly improved it with his feedback and ideas. Jürgen, we are very grateful for your excellent contribution.

We would like to thank (in alphabetical order): Martin Bachmann, Wayne Brown, Holger Bruchelt, Suma C V, Fahmi Cheikhrouhou, Suparna Deb, Silvia Dicke, Artur Gajek, Tobias Griebe, Duong-Han Tran, Ralf Handl, Ran Hassid, Wolfgang Hegmann, Andreas Hoffner, Christopher Kästner, Felix Köhl, Gerald Krause, Timo Lakner, Oliver Liemert, Hendrik Lock, Thomas Meigen, Tatjana Pfeifer, Genady Podgaetsky, Martin Raepple, Elisabeth Riemann, Carlos Roggan, Christoph Scheiber, Claudia Schmidt, Maximilian Schneider, Daniel Schön, Henrike Schuhart, Jin Shin, Jörg Singler, Frank Speidel, Matthias Tebbe, Olaf Tennie, Constantin von Teuffel, Jirong Wang, Martin Wegmann, Stefan Weitland, Chris Whealy, and Andrew Whitaker.

Special thanks goes to Elisabeth "Lizzie" Riemann for her excellent pictures of some of the authors. Everyone who knows the authors in real life knows what a terrific job she did.

Friends and Family

Very special, warm, and individual thanks are extended from:

- Ludwig Heinz to his girlfriend, Anna, who supported and encouraged him in spite of all the time it took him away from her.

- André Fischer to his wife, Natalie, and his sons, Lars and Timo, for whom he had less time when writing the book—especially during their summer vacation this year—and to his mother, Greta, for her support.

- Karsten Strothmann to his partner, Mira, for her patience and support during long hours of writing, and to his son, Yann Erik, for his contented and happy smile each time his daddy turned his attention to him after hours of having worked on this book.

- Volker Drees to his wife, Bettina, and their daughter, Sarah Felicitas, for supporting him in writing this book and accepting the fact that he had to invest many, many hours in it.
- Carsten Bönnen to his girlfriend, Susanne, who supported him throughout the writing of the book.

In Memoriam

Carsten Bönnen would like to acknowledge the involvement of the two bushi in his life in the creation of this book. Without them, this book would never have happened the way it did. They will never be forgotten.

Final Thanks...

Our final—yet very important—thanks goes to Kelly Grace Weaver, our editor, whose patience, foresight, and ongoing support did a great deal in making this book the best book it could be. Additional thanks goes out to all the SAP PRESS people involved in creating this book.

PART I
Getting Started

This chapter introduces SAP NetWeaver Gateway and explains how SAP NetWeaver Gateway addresses the challenges of building user interface-based business applications. In addition, the chapter positions SAP NetWeaver Gateway in the context of other SAP products.

1 Introduction to SAP NetWeaver Gateway

In May 2011, SAP launched SAP NetWeaver Gateway at SAPPHIRE NOW. If you're asking what SAP NetWeaver Gateway is, the short answer is that SAP NetWeaver Gateway is a technology that improves the reach of SAP business applications. It increases the range of SAP business applications not only in terms of end users but also with regard to the number of developers and addressable environments in general. With the help of SAP NetWeaver Gateway, SAP business applications, parts of those applications, or simply SAP data can be used by an application developer without prior knowledge of SAP in order to build—for example—a mobile application.

SAP NetWeaver Gateway launch

SAP NetWeaver Gateway is able to extend the reach of SAP business applications because it's an open, standards-based framework that can be used by developers to build user-friendly business applications. More technically, SAP NetWeaver Gateway is a RESTful interface based on Atom and OData for the ABAP technology platform, which in turn connects with the SAP Business Suite. SAP NetWeaver Gateway provides a standard-based, centralized interface to the SAP world.

REST and OData

But let's start at the beginning. The motivation for a product such as SAP NetWeaver Gateway is derived from the requirements and challenges that are now placed on modern business applications. In this chapter, we start by looking at the challenges for modern business applications to get a better understanding of what they are. We then consider SAP

NetWeaver Gateway as a solution for those challenges. After that, we briefly discuss the installation and deployment options for SAP Net-Weaver Gateway. Finally, we take a closer look at how SAP NetWeaver Gateway positions itself in the context of other related SAP products and how it integrates with those products.

SAP NetWeaver Gateway and User Interfaces (UIs)

As you'll see, we'll talk a lot about UIs and applications in this chapter. Although SAP NetWeaver Gateway isn't a UI technology, its capabilities enable developers to have more choices with respect to the UIs they want to use.

1.1 Modern Business Applications

The requirements for business applications have dramatically changed in recent years. In fact, the use of digital media in general is subject to significant changes and, as a result, applications are as well. These changes are observed not only in the private area (the consumer world) but also in the business environment (the enterprise world). End users have become accustomed to a certain way of dealing with digital media and applications, characterized by the constant use of interactive—often intuitive—surfaces for mobile devices, social networks, or almost any application on virtually any device (from mobile phones to televisions to classic PCs).

End user expectations

These experiences in the consumer world lead to expectations in the enterprise world as well. End users have come to expect the same behavior from their business applications as they do from their private applications. And as their use of private applications—especially digital media applications—increases, so will their expectations.

In the wake of this development, IT departments of companies around the world are facing great challenges. In this section, we'll take a look at some of the considerations they have to keep in mind for both the UIs and backend infrastructures of their applications.

1.1.1   User Interfaces

As user expectations change, so must the applications that users work with. Let's consider some of the biggest things to keep in mind when designing the UIs of business applications.

Business
application
requirements

Intuitiveness

An intuitive UI is essential for applications and digital media in general. In addition to promoting greater acceptance among end users, an intuitive UI increases the effectiveness of these applications. In a time where special knowledge is becoming increasingly important and where experts can be involved in IT processes faster and more easily than ever before, it's important to reduce the training needs for the applications that support the process. Training that is dedicated only to the operation of an application is ineffective and expensive. With an intuitive interface, the need for training can either be avoided in the best case (no training) or at least it can be cut down (shortened training).

Application design

There are other advantages to intuitive UIs as well. Experience shows that intuitive interfaces lead to fewer user errors. Those errors cost money, either as a direct result or through the need for additional process steps to identify and correct these errors. Even ignoring the fact that those errors may endanger enterprises in other ways, it's still mandatory to reduce them to a minimum.

Another point in favor of intuitive UIs is that they increase efficiency and effectiveness in using an application. This is especially true for subject matter experts. An intuitive interface can help those experts execute process steps faster and more effectively. For experts, every second saved on a screen is a huge win and, in the long run, saves the company money.

End-user acceptance of an application is also important to consider. The rollout of applications in a company is only the first step—the more important step is the actual use of the application by the end user. If the application isn't understood, it's often not used or not used to the desired extent. Directly or indirectly, this may impact business processes and eventually business success. Improving already rolled-out

End user
acceptance

applications to change that situation will cause additional and unnecessary costs.

Process integration

In this context, it's important to take into consideration that many processes now involve external participants. In the business environment, this may be partners or suppliers on one side or customers on the other. Particularly with a focus on the customer, an intuitive UI is mandatory, because acceptance of applications becomes a key differentiator. If a surface isn't intuitive for the end user—in this case, the customer—this may jeopardize the company's success. The best example for this is the current situation in the area of mobile devices, where the importance of intuitive interfaces can't be emphasized too strongly here. In the mobile world, the most successful devices are not those with the best technology but those with the most intuitive UI (in combination with a decent technology, of course). The same is true for business-to-consumer (B2C) business applications; an application that is not immediately understood is rejected by the customer, who will move on to another company providing the same services with a more intuitive UI.

Appeal

Success criteria

An appealing user interface is just as important—and not the same as!— an intuitive user interface. The surface design of an application relates directly to the end-user acceptance and thus the success of the application. It differs from an intuitive interface in that while an intuitive interface may be easy to use, it may still be perceived as ugly by the end user. This may sound irrelevant, but this makes the point even more important, because it's often underestimated or completely neglected. An appealing UI dramatically increases acceptance by the end user, especially in combination with an intuitive UI, and this is critical for the success of an application. This applies both to applications used within a company and those that are external-facing. While partners still have an intrinsic motivation in the business environment to use applications that are necessary for their business, this is only partly true for customers. In other words, a nonintuitive, nonappealing UI may hinder processes or, in the worst case, prevent sales.

> **Gamification**
>
> The importance of a good UI is emphasized by the recent trend known as *gamification*. For a bit more on this, see Chapter 15.

Business Orientation

Business orientation refers to an application's relevance to the business world, and it is something that is often not taken into account in the preparation of applications. Instead, technical constraints often determine the UI and functionality of an application. However, these issues aren't relevant for the casual user and the business user; for them, it doesn't matter whether an application is written in Xcode, Java, or C#; those users don't care whether the frontend was implemented using HTML5, Flash, or Silverlight. What is important to end users is the use of an error-free, reliable application running on their device and facilitating their activities.

Business user

In addition to reliability, design and adaptability of an application are important for business orientation. Business users want to access their data. This means they want to see only the data in applications that are relevant for them. How can this be implemented? By including end users in the development process. For this, there are a variety of approaches (e.g., design thinking) that can be used. Independent from the approach used, it's important to find a common language between the different people involved, for example, designers, backend and frontend developers, process experts, subject matter experts, and end users.

Innovation

Innovation is one of the key drivers of business success today. To effectively introduce innovation in a company, it's important that processes adapt rapidly to innovation. For IT departments, it's just as imperative to implement those processes rapidly.

Process adaptation

The aspect of innovation is relevant for business orientation as well and thus exists in the same context. Depending on the industry, the business world is changing with dramatic speed. Reflecting these changes in enterprises is only possible when the applications and processes involved can be changed easily, and innovations can be implemented quickly.

Both devices and technologies today come with a much shorter lifecycle than a few years ago—and to find a common denominator between them isn't easy. To illustrate the problem, consider the current strategy many companies are following today: bring your own device (BYOD). As the name suggests, this policy means that employees can bring their own devices, which are usually mobile phones or tablets, to use for work. It's easy to see that this multiplicity of devices is a big problem for IT departments, both when it comes to rolling out applications as well as to the maintenance and management (including security aspects) of the private devices.

Technology lifecycle

Availability

The reality of today's business world makes it increasingly important to expand the availability of data and applications. In an ideal world, the end user would have access to any data at anytime, anywhere, and from whatever device he chose to use.

The demand for availability is tightly linked to a major trend: the increase in mobilization in the business world. Employees can work from anywhere using different devices—ranging from mobile phones to tablets—and from specialized devices in production to classic PCs. To exacerbate the problem, specific process steps are often required for applications to be made available on different devices. For example, sales representatives will want to use the same applications on both mobile devices and regular PCs.

From a technology perspective, we see a move from technology for experts (e.g., SAPGUI) to more general approaches (e.g., HTML5) and casual user software (e.g., Microsoft Outlook).

SAPGUI to HTML5

In summary, end users prefer to have any data available at any time and at any place. As a result, there are requirements for a broad range of devices and technologies to be able to meet this demand.

Agility

In this context, agility refers to the adaptability of business applications and thus is closely related to innovation. If a process changes within a company, it's important that this new process is quickly available through the respective applications. Agility is important on another level as well—if certain aspects of an application don't work, users expect it to be fixed. For example, if a new application turns out to be too slow or complex for a sales representative in the field, users will expect rapid changes to address the issue.

Agility and innovation may initially sound very similar, and, in fact, the two have a lot in common. A look at details, however, shows where the two differ. Agility refers to that part of innovation that is about how flexible processes, applications, and technologies can be adapted to business needs. These needs aren't necessarily driven by innovation. They may simply reflect changed market needs—for example, new standards or laws—or changed end user requirements based on the business environment or usability demands.

Flexible processes

In addition, flexible processes are only one side of the coin. In an increasingly globalized world, processes often extend to a variety of people, departments, and even countries. The roles and profiles of the people involved have to be taken into account. While an experienced business expert can work with SAPGUI effectively and quickly, it's much harder for a casual user to do so. In addition, processes often require the use of devices that don't even support specific standard software.

Integration

Business processes often span several departments and potentially large numbers of employees. The profiles of the employees involved in a process can be very different though; from the casual user to the expert user, any role can be involved in the same process. Thus, the challenge is to involve all users with respect to their specific skills and available equipment.

To integrate all people who are involved in a process in an optimal way, it's desirable to allow the persons to stay within their familiar environments. For example, while for one user SAPGUI may be optimal, for the next user, it may be Microsoft Excel.

Backend hiding

In terms of backend systems, integration can also mean "hiding" backend systems. In other words, the end user doesn't have to—and most likely doesn't want to—know which backend system he is working on. For the end user, this simplifies the world; for the IT department, this approach allows changes to the infrastructure without having to roll out those changes to the end user. For the end user, the backend systems become a kind of black box. Changes in this black box aren't relevant to him as long as his frontend still runs smoothly.

Maintenance

Maintenance and support

The wealth of new requirements creates brand new challenges for IT departments in the area of maintenance. Various devices and applications must be maintained. At the same time, end users have higher expectations for maintenance and support. The variety of platforms to be supported requires additional maintenance, which costs money. While the already established platforms represent some security here, the introduction of new applications quickly becomes a problem in terms of maintenance. For IT departments, it's essential that these new applications represent as little additional effort in terms of maintenance as possible. So the task is to create new, flexible, and innovative applications that are also easily supported by IT departments.

Security

In the field of security, there are problems similar to those that come with maintenance. The variety of applications, devices, and technologies makes securing them increasingly difficult. Despite all of the flexibility and innovation, it's not acceptable for a company to risk the security of its own data or foreign data. Taking into consideration that—to ensure flexibility—data is often held both on-site and in the cloud, as well as in different and sometimes mobile devices, security is becoming increasingly important and poses an increasingly complex problem.

Depending on the market environment, security issues can easily lead to issues with a company's reputation, and thus have a direct impact on revenue. Even putting reputation aside, security issues such as data leakage can lead to reduced revenue (e.g., if strategic information reaches a competitor).

Reduced TCO

Considering that there are always new challenges and demands facing IT, you might expect that there is a bigger budget for the projects related to these challenges. However, the business reality is usually different; the budget is often the same or even less than before. In the long run, the introduction of new devices and applications is supposed to reduce the total cost of IT, or to generate greater business value that makes up for the costs involved. Despite all identified challenges, and despite the introduction of new technologies and processes, it's generally expected that total cost of ownership (TCO) must not rise, or must at least be below the expected profit (return on investment, ROI).

Budget considerations

Nondisruptiveness

Directly related to costs is the final point: nondisruptiveness. Nondisruptiveness affects all stakeholders, from decision makers to IT departments to end users. Decision makers expect a high—if not 100%—availability of business systems, because failure can mean stopped business and thus costs. The end user expects a similar high availability because otherwise he can't do his work. In turn, IT departments are accountable to the decision makers and end users, and must ensure nondisruptiveness as a consequence. Thus, a requirement of all involved stakeholders—from executive to end user—is the desire for zero downtime. The installation of new solutions, technologies, or applications must not lead to failures in the system or reduce application availability.

Zero downtime

The difference between availability (which we've already discussed) and nondisruptiveness may not be obvious, however, nondisruptiveness differs from availability in that it specifically refers to cases in which new applications, technologies, solutions, or processes are implemented. In our usage here, we define availability as the technical implementation of improvements in the availability of processes, and so on, while nondis-ruptiveness is concerned with the implementation of new technologies, and so on, without disturbing the ongoing operations.

Keep in mind that we are talking about enterprise software here. For the casual end user, a downtime of a system might be an annoyance, but is seldom critical in terms of financial security or success for enterprise software; however, downtime can be critical to the financial success and the survival of a company.

1.1.2   Infrastructures

Infrastructure

Today's business applications have more than just UI challenges—they also face infrastructure challenges. Figure 1.1 shows a typical abstracted infrastructure as found in most companies.

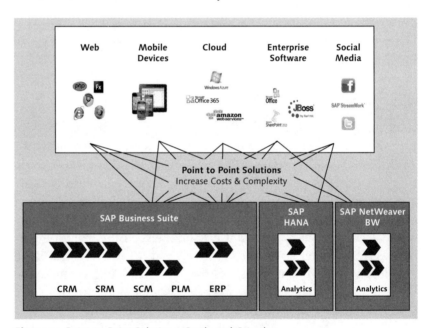

Figure 1.1 Point-to-Point Solutions: Costly and Complex

Point-to-point solutions

Note

As an example, Figure 1.1 focuses on SAP backend systems. However, these same types of infrastructure challenges exist even for non-SAP companies.

As you can see, business data is stored in one or more—often several—backend systems. The business processes exist in these systems or are mapped there, and access to the backend systems is usually realized using proprietary solutions or access methods (e.g., RFCs or web services). This infrastructure is complex, to say the least.

In an attempt to simplify this infrastructure, many backend systems now offer a web interface. A web interface already opens the backend systems to a wide range of devices. However, it just takes a look at one of the points mentioned before—integration—to realize that this won't be sufficient. The access methods and interfaces provided by the various backend systems can't be integrated easily because the content of the information provided via HTTP is—in contrast to HTTP as a protocol—not standardized.

A closer look at the infrastructure in Figure 1.1 reveals that in addition to the various backend systems, a variety of devices or channels have to be supported. Despite web enablement of the backend systems, this often leads to a point-to-point scenario in classic infrastructures with classic backend systems. In other words, each backend system must be approached individually. In addition to that, each channel comes with its own requirements; that is, access for each channel can't be realized in the same way. To support a channel, it's necessary to build an individual application for each channel. In a worst case scenario, that means it's necessary to create an individual application for each channel and each backend system. This approach, though not uncommon, is ineffective, expensive, and potentially insecure.

Classic infrastructure

To fully support the requirements of today's business applications, a solution that unifies access to the backend systems and abstracts the common aspects of the channels is much better. For that kind of solution, it's only necessary to implement channel-specific functionality and rely on common coding for the rest. An additional benefit of this approach is the availability and price of good developers. While backend experts are often scarce and expensive, developers for specific channels and technologies (e.g., Java developers, .NET developers) are more commonly available and less pricey.

Open standards   One approach to realize this is the use of open standards. Open standards that are implemented in systems or an intermediate layer allow abstraction of the specifics of the backend systems to an extent that the frontend developers only have to worry about the actual application development.

A second approach focuses particularly on the availability and the cost: cloud computing. Simplified cloud computing is the outsourcing of data and applications into the network. (We use the term *network* instead of *Internet* because it's possible to implement cloud computing in different network setups, not only the Internet.)

Cloud   Cloud computing is about using resources—either hardware or software—provided by or through the network. What makes the approach special is that the resources are provided as services. Accordingly, it's possible to distinguish between the following:

▸ **Infrastructure as a Service (IaaS)**
IaaS is the most basic form of cloud computing. In this case, the service provider offers only the infrastructure, without an operating system. Operating systems and software must be installed by the user of the service. A common approach in this area is to create complete system images and upload them to the cloud. The service provider in turn often uses virtual machines to operate the images.

▸ **Platform as a Service (PaaS)**
In this approach, the supplier also provides the operating system and additional software on-demand. Thus, the user no longer needs to worry about hardware or software and can concentrate on the actual task in the system.

▸ **Software as a Service (SaaS)**
Finally, this approach goes one step further. The service provider offers applications directly to the user. All tasks involved when it comes to maintenance of the application are with the service provider.

Public and   In addition to these three types of cloud computing, you can also distinguish between a public cloud and a private cloud. While the public cloud is usually an open cloud that is available on a public network—that is,
private cloud

the Internet—a private cloud exists within the confined spaces of a private network—for example, an enterprise. In general, it's also possible to implement a private cloud that can be accessed via the Internet; however, the private cloud is always implemented so that it's only accessible to a specific service user. The private cloud is especially important for implementing the security requirements of many companies.

> **Note**
>
> The subject of cloud computing is complex—entire books can and have been written about it. The information presented here is meant only as an introduction.

With all of the challenges and different options out there, it's essential to find a solution that works from the perspective of both the UI and the infrastructure.

1.2   SAP NetWeaver Gateway for Modern Business Applications

To briefly summarize the requirements discussed in the previous section, an intuitive and attractive UI for each application type is essential for a successful application. The supporting infrastructure should enable innovation and business orientation, while at the same time allowing high availability and flexibility. In addition, integration, maintainability, and security must be ensured. To top things off, the costs should be kept low, and changes to the infrastructure should happen without disruptions—this includes the rollout of processes and applications.

That description is exactly the goal of SAP NetWeaver Gateway. SAP NetWeaver Gateway provides an open, REST-based interface that implements simple access to SAP systems via the OData protocol. OData is widely used as an open protocol that was standardized in its most recent version, version 4, and is optimized for UIs and interaction. The OData standard was chosen by SAP for SAP NetWeaver Gateway because it is widely used, known, and easy to learn; members of the OASIS OData

REST and OData

Technical Committee responsible for development are companies such as IBM, CA, SAP, and Microsoft. (For more on OData, see Chapter 2.)

SAP NetWeaver Gateway provides simple, secure, and controlled access to SAP data via an open standard, abstracting the specifics of the SAP Business Suite systems. Refer back to the point-to-point solutions diagram that we showed in Figure 1.1, and now compare that to Figure 1.2, which shows SAP NetWeaver Gateway as a single solution that replaces all other point-to-point solutions.

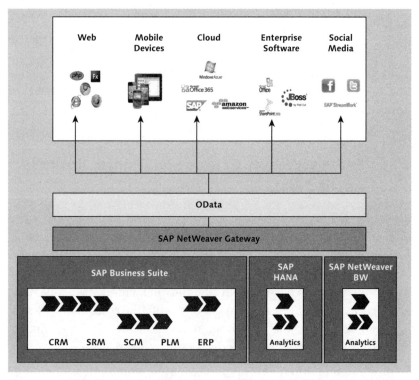

Figure 1.2 SAP NetWeaver Gateway: Solving the Point-to-Point Solution Problem

SAP NetWeaver Gateway layer

As shown in Figure 1.2, SAP NetWeaver Gateway is a layer between the channels (devices, applications, etc.) and the SAP Business Suite systems—more specifically, SAP NetWeaver ABAP-based systems. This layer allows you to mask the sometimes complex processes and data structures in the SAP Business Suite systems and present them to the outside world in a simplified way. In addition, SAP NetWeaver Gateway unifies access to SAP Business Suite data and processes via the OData protocol and thus opens the SAP world to virtually any developer who understands OData. Knowledge of SAP specifics isn't required.

By addressing non-SAP developers, SAP NetWeaver Gateway makes it possible to keep applications more flexible. For example, if an end user needs an application to access SAP data for Microsoft Office, a Microsoft developer can do the job without detailed knowledge of SAP. The applications can be implemented faster and better because it's now possible for the respective expert to build the application. This is especially important because UI technologies are evolving, so frontend applications change more frequently than backend processes.

> **Note**
>
> Control of the SAP Business Suite data and processes remain with the authorized persons who manage the SAP Business Suite systems. The rights and restrictions of the end user in the SAP Business Suite system are passed to the frontend application. Thus, it's neither intentionally nor accidentally possible for the application developer to gain or provide access to data that doesn't fall within the authorizations of the user.

Figure 1.3 shows the workflow for application creation with SAP NetWeaver Gateway. You start by setting up a project for each application, and the project team defines the scenario and the processes to be implemented. Such a project team may consist of a variety of experts, for example, a business process expert, a frontend developer, a backend developer, and probably a project manager and designer.

SAP NetWeaver Gateway workflow

With SAP NetWeaver Gateway, experts can speak in one language. It's not important to the frontend developer what the backend developer does in detail; in turn, the backend developer doesn't need to know the details of the frontend development. Discussions take place only on the data and processes level. Defined interfaces between the involved stakeholders facilitate discussions between the experts and reduce technology discussions to a minimum. This simplification and facilitation applies to all experts that are involved in a project. As shown in Figure 1.3, experts can then focus on their area of expertise. While the backend developer creates and exposes services to the frontend developer, the

SAP NetWeaver Gateway project interfaces

frontend developer can focus on the frontend creation. Using OData, the frontend used can be nearly any device and technology.

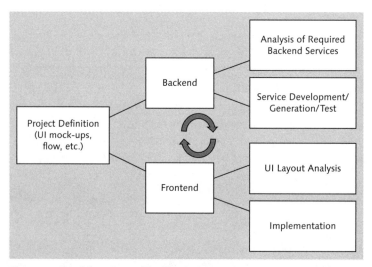

Figure 1.3 Workflow Exemplified for SAP NetWeaver Gateway Development

Project scalability The approach described here is only one approach. Due to the different configurations of SAP Business Suite systems, it's also possible that a single frontend developer builds applications for the existing data and services, which are already provided in the SAP Business Suite systems. This means development with SAP NetWeaver Gateway scales from individual developers to large project teams.

To summarize briefly, SAP NetWeaver Gateway provides a centralized interface for the SAP world (i.e., for all SAP NetWeaver ABAP-based backend systems) based on open industry standards. By supporting multichannel access instead of focusing only on the mobile channel, the use cases for SAP NetWeaver Gateway applications are vast.

> **Note**
>
> Other SAP technologies support OData as well, but may not use SAP NetWeaver Gateway yet. However, those products can be integrated into SAP NetWeaver Gateway scenarios through the use of OData.

So does SAP NetWeaver Gateway meet the requirements? Let's have a look at the list:

- ▶ **Intuitive, appealing UI**
  With SAP NetWeaver Gateway, the frontend developer has the opportunity to completely focus on the application to be developed and to devote maximum attention to the UI. By using specific—partially proprietary—tools for the specific channel, the user paradigm and experience of each channel can be implemented in an optimal way.

- ▶ **Innovation**
  With SAP NetWeaver Gateway application development, the implementation of new processes becomes more flexible. Innovation can be achieved more easily, and SAP NetWeaver Gateway reduces costs for the rollout. Changes need to be made only where change is really taking place. For example, if there is already an application for travel booking on an iPhone, it isn't necessary to touch the backend system to implement the same functionality for Microsoft Kinect. Only the frontend development for the new platform is required, and this frontend development can benefit from the already built applications for other channels.

- ▶ **Business orientation**
  With the flexibility in terms of channel (multichannel support) and developers, it's easy to develop applications that respect the requirements of the business reality the end user is living in. In certain scenarios, it might even be possible for the business process expert (BPX) to build the application.

- ▶ **Availability**
  Multichannel support increases the availability of data and processes. SAP NetWeaver Gateway ensures access to backend data and processes at almost any time.

Offline Scenarios

Offline scenarios pose special situations that have to be considered individually. We'll take a short look at offline scenarios in Appendix A.

► **Agility**
Development cycles can be shortened through the use of SAP NetWeaver Gateway. Accordingly, agility increases.

► **Integration**
Integration first takes place in the backend, which is now essentially one unit, instead of several. Then it takes place in the frontend, which profits from the use of standards. More specifically, each frontend that supports the standard can directly benefit from it. Frontends that don't understand or support the standard in any way normally can be integrated through individual applications.

► **Maintenance and security**
The security of data remains with the administrators of the backend systems, and the same applies to maintenance of the backend systems. Maintenance of the frontend systems is different, though, because it is dependent on the channel used. For specific needs in this area, SAP offers, for example, the SAP Mobile Platform, which allows remote maintenance of mobile applications.

► **Costs**
By shortening the development cycle and allowing the experts to focus on their respective areas of expertise, development costs can be reduced. In addition to already mentioned aspects, the main reason for this benefit is a reduction in friction between the different stakeholders. In addition, the implementation of SAP NetWeaver Gateway is relatively cheap and easy; if you are already an SAP customer, you may already have the relevant licenses. As we discuss in more detail in Chapter 4, SAP NetWeaver Gateway comes pre-installed with SAP NetWeaver 7.40, or can be implemented without disruption in an existing landscape.

► **Nondisruptiveness**
Finally, as you'll see in the next section, the installation and deployment for SAP NetWeaver Gateway is simple and nondisruptive.

In short: SAP NetWeaver Gateway is SAP's answer to developing business applications that provide the UIs and backend infrastructures required by today's modern users.

1.3 Installation and Deployment

If you want to use SAP NetWeaver Gateway in production and you already own the relevant licenses, you can download the SAP Net-Weaver Gateway package from the SAP Service Marketplace at *http://service.sap.com/swdc* by choosing INSTALLATION AND UPGRADES • BROWSE OUR DOWNLOAD CATALOG • SAP NETWEAVER AND COMPLEMENTARY PRODUCTS • SAP NETWEAVER GATEWAY • SAP NETWEAVER GATEWAY 2.0. Note that this is only necessary with SAP NetWeaver versions below 7.40 SP02; starting with this release, SAP NetWeaver Gateway doesn't have to be downloaded but is instead included. (However, for some scenarios, the download of additional plugins might be necessary. Those plugins can be found on the SAP Service Marketplace as well.)

SAP NetWeaver Gateway availability

SAP Developer Centers

If you simply want to test SAP NetWeaver Gateway as a developer or in any other function, you can access SAP NetWeaver Gateway easily through the SAP Developer Center for SAP NetWeaver Gateway: *http://developers.sap.com* • TOOLS & SDKs • SAP NETWEAVER GATEWAY. Using SAP Developer Centers—the center for SAP NetWeaver Gateway is only one among many—you can easily get access to SAP products. For SAP NetWeaver Gateway, you'll get access to an SAP NetWeaver Gateway installation without having to do any installation on your side. In addition, you'll get a free developer license to develop with SAP NetWeaver Gateway. In short, you're all set to get started with SAP NetWeaver Gateway development. The best thing about this scenario is that you can still use your own development environment.

After you have SAP NetWeaver Gateway downloaded or have it as part of SAP NetWeaver 7.40, you're ready for installation and deployment.

Note

This section provides only a brief overview of the installation and deployment process. For a detailed discussion, see Chapter 4.

1.3.1 Installation

Installation requirements

Table 1.1 and Table 1.2 list the requirements that must be met to operate SAP NetWeaver Gateway. The minimum hardware requirements are very easy to meet. This has two advantages: cost-effective systems for companies even after scaling, and easy installation (even for non-developers such as business experts).

Entity	Mimimum Requirement
Processor	Dual Core (two logical CPUs) with 2GHz
Main memory/RAM	8GB
Hard disk capacity	80GB

Table 1.1 Minimum Hardware Requirements for SAP NetWeaver Gateway

Entity	Requirement	
SAP NetWeaver Stack	The latest kernel patch for the corresponding SAP NetWeaver version has to be applied.	
	Core Components (GW_CORE and IW_FND)	▶ SAP NetWeaver 7.0 SPS25 ▶ SAP NetWeaver 7.01 SPS10 ▶ SAP NetWeaver 7.02 SPS07 ▶ SAP NetWeaver 7.03 SPS01 ▶ SAP NetWeaver 7.31 SPS01
	Core Component (SAP_GWFND) Comprises functional scope of IW_FND, GW_CORE, IW_BEP, and IW_HDB.	▶ SAP NetWeaver 7.40 SPS01

Table 1.2 Minimum Software Requirements

Entity	Requirement	
	Business Enablement Provisioning Component (IW_BEP)	▸ SAP NetWeaver 7.0 SPS18 ▸ SAP NetWeaver 7.01 SPS03 ▸ SAP NetWeaver 7.02 SPS06 ▸ SAP NetWeaver 7.03 SPS01 ▸ SAP NetWeaver 7.31 SPS01
	Content Adapter Components (IW_PGW) Screen Scraping Component (IW_SCS)	▸ SAP NetWeaver 7.0 SPS18 ▸ SAP NetWeaver 7.01 SPS03 ▸ SAP NetWeaver 7.02 SPS06 ▸ SAP NetWeaver 7.03 SPS01 ▸ SAP NetWeaver 7.31 SPS01 ▸ SAP NetWeaver 7.40 SPS01
	Content Adapter Component (IW_SPI)	▸ SAP NetWeaver 7.02 SPS06 ▸ SAP NetWeaver 7.03 SPS01 ▸ SAP NetWeaver 7.31 SPS01 ▸ SAP NetWeaver 7.40 SPS01
	Content Adapter Component (IW_HDB)	▸ SAP NetWeaver 7.02 SPS09 ▸ SAP NetWeaver 7.03 SPS01 ▸ SAP NetWeaver 7.31 SPS01
	Content Adapter Component (IW_GIL)	▸ SAP NetWeaver 7.01 SPS03 ▸ SAP NetWeaver 7.02 SPS06 ▸ SAP NetWeaver 7.03 SPS01 ▸ SAP NetWeaver 7.31 SPS01 ▸ SAP NetWeaver 7.40 SPS01
SAP WEB UIF	Core Component Version (IW_FND 250)	▸ SAP WEB UIF 7.01 SP01 ▸ SAP WEB UIF 7.31 SP00
	Optional Core Component (IW_FNDGC [for generic channel]*)	▸ SAP WEB UIF 7.46 SP00 ▸ SAP WEB UIF 7.47 SP00

Table 1.2 Minimum Software Requirements (Cont.)

Entity	Requirement	
SAP WEB UIF (Cont.)	Content Adapter Component (IW_GIL)	► SAP WEB UIF 7.0 SP03
		► SAP WEB UIF 7.01 SP00
		► SAP WEB UIF 7.31 SP00
		► SAP WEB UIF 7.46 SP00
		► SAP WEB UIF 7.47 SP00
SAP Backend	SAP Business Suite system	
* This component is only necessary if integration scenarios depending on the generic channel will be upgraded. In a fresh installation it's not necessary.		

Table 1.2 Minimum Software Requirements (Cont.)

1.3.2 Deployment

Embedded versus hub deployment

Two main deployment options are available for SAP NetWeaver Gateway: the hub deployment and the embedded deployment. However, the hub deployment can be subsequently split into two different deployment scenarios: development on the backend system and development on the hub itself. We'll discuss all three options next.

SAP NetWeaver 7.40

The deployment options for SAP NetWeaver Gateway normally include a decision about where to put which component of the product. However, this changes with SAP NetWeaver 7.40. SAP NetWeaver 7.40 includes SAP NetWeaver Gateway and installs SAP_GWFND as part of the standard installation. SAP_GWFND includes the functional scope of IW_BEP, GW_CORE, IW_FND, and IW_HDB.

Embedded Deployment

Embedded deployment means that the services are registered and published in the SAP Business Suite backend system. In terms of core components, we talk about IW_FND and GW_CORE for older versions, and IW_GWFND for SAP NetWeaver 7.40 or later.

The main benefit of embedded deployment is that the runtime overhead is reduced by one remote call. The main drawback is that if you use several SAP Business Suite systems, you'll have to configure SAP NetWeaver Gateway for every system. In addition, you can't use an embedded system as a hub for other backend systems; that is, routing and composition can't be used.

There are also some other drawbacks:

▶ An additional server is needed for SAP NetWeaver Gateway.

▶ Access to the backend is limited to remote-enabled interfaces, for example, RFCs, Business Application Programming Interfaces (BAPIs), SAP NetWeaver BW Easy Queries, Service Provider Interface (SPI) objects. These interfaces might not be optimal for usage on the hub.

▶ Generic Interaction Layer (GenIL) objects can't be accessed remotely, and there is no direct local access to metadata (Data Dictionary, DDIC) and business data.

As a word of caution, we don't recommend using an SAP Business Suite system with an embedded deployment of SAP NetWeaver Gateway as a hub system for an additional backend system. In that specific scenario, the version of the hub system may be lower than the version of the SAP NetWeaver Gateway backend components on the remote backend system. In many companies, there are strict policies about when to update which systems. This can lead to a situation in which the hub system can't be upgraded, while the backend system already is.

To avoid this situation, use either of the following:

▶ Embedded deployment for your SAP Business Suite systems

▶ Dedicated SAP NetWeaver Gateway hub systems with the latest release version of SAP NetWeaver Gateway

> **Note**
>
> For details on dependencies between IW_BEP and IW_FND, check SAP Note 1830198.

Hub Deployment: Development on the Backend System

The first option of hub deployment is used in situations where the services are deployed on the backend systems and only registered on the server. The server functionalities of SAP NetWeaver Gateway are only used on the dedicated server (hub). On the backend system, IW_BEP is deployed (or SAP_GWFND for SAP NetWeaver 7.40 or later).

The benefit of this hub deployment is that the system works as a single point of access to the backend systems. On this system, routing and composition of multiple systems is supported. Using this kind of hub system allows the system to be on a newer release, which enables the use of up-to-date functionality, for example, the latest authentication options or SAPUI5. In this scenario, security is improved because there is no direct access to the backend system. At the same time, the deployment allows direct access to local metadata (DDIC) and business data, which reduces runtime overhead.

> **Note**
>
> The hub system should not be an SAP Business Suite system; instead, it should be an SAP NetWeaver ABAP Application Server. This is true for both hub deployment options.

Hub Deployment: Development on the Hub

Development on the hub
The second option of hub deployment should be used in situations where either access to the backend system is restricted (that is, the backend system may not be touched) and development on the backend isn't possible. It should also be used on releases prior to SAP NetWeaver 7.40 when an installation of IW_BEP on the backend isn't allowed. In this form of hub deployment, server functionalities are only used on the SAP NetWeaver Gateway hub system, and—in contrast to the first option—service deployment takes place on the hub.

Benefits
The benefits of this hub deployment are that the backend systems don't have to be touched; that is, there is no need to install or upgrade SAP NetWeaver Gateway add-ons on the backend. In addition, services

developed by third-party developers don't need a deployment on the backend system.

> **Note**
>
> In this scenario, the developer is limited to functionality exposed by the backend through elements such as RFCs or BAPIs.

As you can see from the short overview on deployment of SAP NetWeaver Gateway, the deployment is—especially with SAP NetWeaver 7.40 or later—simple and not cost intensive. The different options allow an installation in nearly every setup or infrastructure. That said, the choice for a deployment largely depends on the requirements of the infrastructure in which SAP NetWeaver Gateway is installed. (Again, for a detailed discussion of an SAP NetWeaver Gateway deployment, see Chapter 4.)

> **Note**
>
> For further discussion of the pros and cons of embedded versus hub deployment, we recommend *http://help.sap.com/saphelp_gateway20sp06/helpdata/en/88/889a8cbf6046378e274d6d9cd04e4d/content.htm*.

1.4   SAP NetWeaver Gateway and Related Products

As of the time of this writing, SAP NetWeaver Gateway is the only product in the market that allows access to SAP Business Suite using REST and OData. However, although there is no direct competition, SAP NetWeaver Gateway does have a huge impact on many classic and brand-new scenarios involving SAP business systems. To better understand this, let's take a look at some related products and how they compare to SAP NetWeaver Gateway.

> **Note**
>
> The following comparison and positioning provides a basic understanding of SAP NetWeaver Gateway in the context of other SAP products. It's not an official SAP position and doesn't claim to be complete.

> **Gateway as a Service**
>
> This chapter doesn't cover Gateway as a Service (GWaaS). Being relatively new, we decided to discuss GWaaS in Chapter 15, which discusses the outlook for SAP NetWeaver Gateway.

1.4.1 Duet Enterprise

Product comparison

Before SAP NetWeaver Gateway was launched in 2011 at SAPPHIRE NOW, Microsoft together with SAP released a product that was already based on a predecessor of SAP NetWeaver Gateway: Duet Enterprise. Duet Enterprise was officially launched on February 1, 2011, and marked a new level of collaboration between Microsoft and SAP.

Microsoft interoperability

What is notable about Duet Enterprise is that it was not only released by Microsoft and SAP together, it was also co-developed by the two companies. The aim of Duet Enterprise was and is to improve the effectiveness and reach of IT and give teams and individuals in a company the opportunity to work better together. To achieve this goal, Duet Enterprise provides the technical basis for the integration of SAP applications into Microsoft SharePoint. In addition to this technical basis, Duet Enterprise comes with appropriate business content and tools to enable users and developers to find a simple introduction to the use of Duet Enterprise. This way, Duet Enterprise ensures easy and quick creation of solutions that fit seamlessly into processes and collaborative scenarios.

Particular attention is put on the possibilities to participate in SAP workflows and to access SAP reports. On the Microsoft side, a main focus, among others, is on the enrichment of MySite with SAP content such as HR information.

> **Note**
>
> Depending on the version of Duet Enterprise, it runs with Microsoft SharePoint 2010 or 2013. Earlier versions aren't supported. In the latest version of Duet Enterprise, Office 365 support was added. The support of the latest SharePoint versions allows an easy integration into Microsoft's Office (2010+) world.

With the launch of the standalone version of SAP NetWeaver Gateway, valid questions were raised about the positioning of the two products. Answering those questions is easier when you understand what Duet Enterprise does. To help with this understanding, Figure 1.4 shows the position of Duet Enterprise in the architecture.

SAP NetWeaver Gateway vs. Duet Enterprise

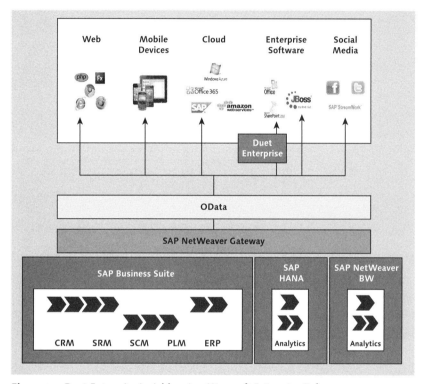

Figure 1.4 Duet Enterprise in Addressing Microsoft Enterprise Software

As you can see, Duet Enterprise is based on SAP NetWeaver Gateway and can be considered a kind of add-on because it takes care of the Microsoft-specific aspects of developing applications for the SAP Business Suite.

That said, it's possible to build applications for the Microsoft world with SAP NetWeaver Gateway only, but you'll miss out on the advantages that Duet Enterprise is offering, for example, built-in interoperability for the following:

Duet Enterprise benefits

59

- Offline support
- Application Lifecycle Management (ALM), transports
- Landscape management
- Authentication and security, single sign-on (SSO), user synchronization
- Monitoring and supportability (SAP Solution Manager)
- Business content

This built-in interoperability eliminates a lot of unnecessary work for the developer.

To sum up the previous considerations, Duet Enterprise is based on SAP NetWeaver Gateway and extends its functionality with relevant built-in functionalities that reduce the development time for applications in the SAP/Microsoft interoperability scenario. In other words, if you have SAP NetWeaver Gateway, you may not need Duet Enterprise anymore— but it will save you time and money if you are implementing projects that involve SAP and Microsoft technology and require them to interoperate.

1.4.2   SAP NetWeaver Portal

SAP NetWeaver Portal is SAP's enterprise portal and part of the SAP NetWeaver architecture. It works as a single point of access to all of your business information—SAP and non-SAP—through a simple web browser. SAP NetWeaver Portal is role-based and secure.

Integration platform
As an integration platform that supports different UI technologies, SAP NetWeaver Portal is a natural fit for SAP NetWeaver Gateway. As a complementary product, let's have a look at the benefits of using SAP NetWeaver Gateway with SAP NetWeaver Portal.

First, let's look at some of the requirements customers have today when it comes to SAP NetWeaver Portal:

- Introduction of new UIs
- Mobilization of existing content

▸ Central governance and management of SAP NetWeaver Gateway-based applications

▸ Creation of external facing web presence with information from SAP and non-SAP systems while taking advantage of the benefits of SAP NetWeaver Portal and SAP NetWeaver Gateway

To fulfill those requirements, the following key capabilities are offered:

SAP NetWeaver Portal capabilities

▸ Management of SAP NetWeaver Gateway applications based on existing roles using SAPUI5 iViews. (For more on this, we recommend: *http://help.sap.com/saphelp_nw73/helpdata/en/7d/f8218433ad454dad5 fddd189829fad/frameset.htm.*)

▸ Usage of SAP NetWeaver Portal as a central, scalable, and secure UI integration hub for SAP NetWeaver Gateway applications.

▸ Easy deployment of SAP NetWeaver Gateway applications to SAP NetWeaver Portal.

▸ Development of SAP NetWeaver Portal content by developers without traditional SAP skills via the integration of SAP NetWeaver Gateway data sources (see *http://help.sap.com/saphelp_nw73/helpdata/en/ c5/322d3d85c34704a8121864a31074bb/frameset.htm).*

To sum this up, SAP NetWeaver Gateway allows easy deployment of applications to SAP NetWeaver Portal. SAP NetWeaver Portal thus provides a role-based, secure, single point of access to these applications, while using existing, scalable infrastructure. Furthermore, SAP NetWeaver Gateway applications can leverage existing portal-based assets (e.g., documents, search, roles).

In short, SAP NetWeaver Gateway and SAP NetWeaver Portal in combination are a natural fit, and thus SAP NetWeaver Portal officially supports SAP NetWeaver Gateway services consumption since SAP NetWeaver 7.3 SP08.

1.4.3 SAP Mobile Platform

Although SAP Mobile Platform also allows access to SAP's business systems through mobile devices, it is different from SAP NetWeaver Gateway in a number of ways. Most notably, SAP NetWeaver Gateway allows multichannel access to the SAP Business Suite, which includes—but isn't limited to—access through mobile devices. In fact, as you can see from Figure 1.5, SAP Mobile Platform actually makes use of SAP NetWeaver Gateway.

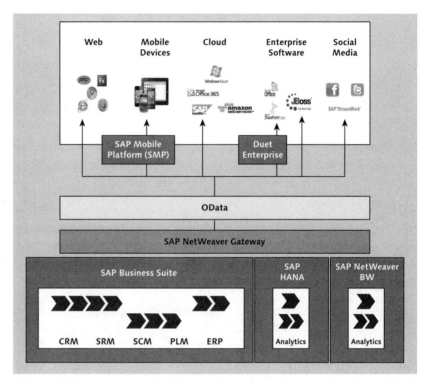

Figure 1.5 SAP Mobile Platform in the Big Picture

SAP Mobile Platform parts SAP Mobile Platform includes SAP Mobile Secure and the mobile client software development kits (SDKs). Together, SAP NetWeaver Gateway and SAP Mobile Platform provide complementary functionality based on their core purpose—multichannel and mobile support.

The recommended setup for mobile scenarios is the combination of SAP NetWeaver Gateway and SAP Mobile Platform. (This becomes much easier with SAP NetWeaver 7.40, because SAP NetWeaver Gateway is already part of the stack and only waiting to be activated.) Although the combination of the two products is recommend, they are separate for a reason: so that you can simply install or activate SAP

NetWeaver Gateway in your infrastructure and get started. You can build mobile applications connecting directly to SAP NetWeaver Gateway using mobile SDKs. This allows you to start small with SAP NetWeaver Gateway and grow slowly into an infrastructure using SAP NetWeaver Gateway and SAP Mobile Platform.

Keep in mind that the combination of SAP NetWeaver Gateway and the mobile SDKs is only recommended for simple deployments, proof of concepts (POCs), and test scenarios in general. In this setup, you won't have access to any of the more sophisticated functionalities of a mobile enterprise application platform (MEAP). There are no plans to extend SAP NetWeaver Gateway into a MEAP, so you won't find any such functionality in SAP NetWeaver Gateway.

Mobile enterprise application platform (MEAP)

1.4.4   SAP HANA

How does SAP HANA fit into this? How does SAP NetWeaver Gateway integrate with it? And more importantly why would we want SAP NetWeaver and SAP HANA to work together?

Before we start answering those questions, let's consider what SAP HANA is. SAP HANA converges database and application platform capabilities *in-memory* to transform transactions, analytics, text analysis, predictive, and spatial processing so businesses can operate in real time.

In-memory

Now let's have a look at what users expect. SAP HANA's calculation capabilities are one part of the equation; another part of the equation is easy provisioning of SAP Business Suite logic. In general, users expect a way to consume data from SAP HANA as well as data from the SAP Business Suite in a lighter and thus standard way. This is something that the combination of SAP NetWeaver Gateway and SAP HANA can offer. With the combination of those two technologies, it's possible to enrich SAP NetWeaver Gateway object property values with SAP HANA query results. In terms of access, it's possible to explore SAP HANA objects using SAP NetWeaver Gateway, while SAP NetWeaver Gateway allows easy provisioning of data in OData and enables transactional access to the SAP Business Suite.

Total cost of development (TCD)

As a result of these benefits, the combination of SAP NetWeaver Gateway and SAP HANA reduces the total cost of development (TCD) through standard access and provisioning in OData. When it comes to security, the separation of the SAP Business Suite from external consumers allows an enormous improvement and uses a secure infrastructure.

1.4.5 SAP NetWeaver Process Integration (PI)

System-to-system vs. system-to-user

SAP NetWeaver PI is an enterprise application integration (EAI) platform that is part of the SAP NetWeaver stack. Its main purpose is the exchange of information between different systems within a company and especially between a company and third parties (e.g., partners, suppliers). The main difference between SAP NetWeaver Gateway and SAP NetWeaver PI is in their uses cases; while SAP NetWeaver PI is focused on system-to-system communication, SAP NetWeaver Gateway is focused on system-to-user communication. That being said, it is possible to integrate the two products by using SAP NetWeaver PI as a central bus and keeping SAP NetWeaver Gateway close to the business systems. This can increase the system's overall performance and reduce TCO. For monitoring and supportability, SAP Solution Manager can be added to the mix to complete the picture.

> **Note**
>
> At the time of this writing a REST adapter for SAP NetWeaver PI is available through partners only.

1.4.6 SAP NetWeaver Business Warehouse (BW)

Analyzing data

SAP NetWeaver BW is one of SAP's business intelligence solutions, and part of the SAP NetWeaver technology platform. It can analyze huge amounts of data and present this data in an intuitive and easily readable way through reports. With the combination of SAP NetWeaver BW and SAP NetWeaver Gateway, it is possible to expose SAP NetWeaver BW data through lightweight consumption using OData, and also to create content in this scenario using SAP NetWeaver BW standard tools such as BEX Query Designer or through the multidimensional expressions

(MDX) interface. In addition, there are several benefits that can be achieved by combining the two products:

▶ **Total cost of development (TCD)**
In this scenario, content can be easily created without any coding at all, so it's possible to lower TCD dramatically.

▶ **Multichannel support**
SAP NetWeaver Gateway adds multichannel support, thus exposing existing SAP NetWeaver BW content to virtually any UI channel and broadening the reach of this existing content.

▶ **Consumption tools**
With SAP NetWeaver Gateway consumption tools, it's easily possible to create simple analytical applications on nearly any client.

▶ **Security**
Adding SAP NetWeaver Gateway means adding an additional middle layer and thus protecting the SAP NetWeaver BW system from direct (external) access.

1.5   Summary

In this first chapter, we outlined the challenges modern business applications face today. We took a look at the problem that enterprise applications face when it comes to accessing backend systems and introduced the classical point-to-point solution that is often implemented. After identifying the challenges and introducing the point-to-point approach, we showed how SAP NetWeaver Gateway can be a solution to those challenges and simplify the infrastructure for enterprise applications.

A close look at SAP NetWeaver Gateway revealed how it works in general and how it can be installed or used easily by everyone (e.g., through SAP Developer Centers). Finally, we took a look at the positioning in the market and eventually put SAP NetWeaver Gateway in the context of other SAP products. In the next chapter, we'll move past the basic introductory material and get into some technical details—specifically, we'll introduce you to the OData protocol in the context of SAP NetWeaver Gateway.

In this chapter, you'll learn all about OData—the underlying industry standard that SAP NetWeaver Gateway enables.

2   Introduction to OData

OData is a short and very memorable name for something big: a protocol that is here to open up the data silos of the IT world's big players and that will stay to change IT forever. In this chapter, you'll read about OData and its foundations (REST). You'll learn about the structure of an OData service and the operations and query options supported by OData. Finally, to show you the importance of this protocol for SAP, we'll provide a short overview of OData in SAP solutions.

In short, this chapter works as an OData jump-start to equip you with the OData background and basics needed for SAP NetWeaver Gateway.

2.1   OData and REST

Because OData is a REST-based protocol, we'll start this chapter with a brief introduction to both.

2.1.1   What Is REST?

A term that you frequently come across when talking about OData is the term *Representational State Transfer (REST)*. OData requests use the REST model, which was introduced in 2000 by Roy Fielding in his Ph.D. dissertation; Fielding used it to judge the architecture style of software architectures. An architecture is called RESTful if it complies with six architectural constraints:

Six architectural restraints

▶ **Client server architecture**
A uniform interface separates clients from servers, resulting in a separation of concern.

▶ **Statelessness**
No context is stored on the server between requests. Any request from a client contains all required information to service the request.

▶ **Cacheability**
Responses have to define themselves as cacheable or not cacheable to prevent clients from using stale or inappropriate data in response to additional, later requests.

▶ **Layered system**
A client can't tell whether it's connected directly to the end server or to a server along the way.

▶ **Uniform interface**
A uniform interface between clients and servers decouples the architecture.

▶ **Code on demand**
Servers can temporarily extend or customize the functionality of a client by transferring executable code. This constraint is actually optional.

These constraints must be followed for an architecture to be considered RESTful. How you handle the actual implementation is your own choice, as long as you fulfill the mentioned constraints.

REST commands   Each REST command is a request of one of the following types, informing the server from the client to perform one of the following operations on the server:

▶ GET
Get a single entry or a collection of entries.

▶ POST
Create a new entry.

▶ PUT
Update an existing entry.

▶ DELETE
Remove an entry.

▶ PATCH
Update single properties of an existing entity.

In a GET request, the response represents the retrieved data as an OData document. In POST and PUT, the client sends its data as an OData document in the request body. With POST, the server returns the created data in the response as an OData document. For DELETE, no document is exchanged.

POST, GET, PUT, and DELETE are supported by Create, Retrieve, Update, Delete (CRUD) interfaces on a server. An OData service might support all four interfaces, but this isn't mandatory. For instance, a service might only support data retrieval through a GET operation.

CRUD support

The most prominent example of a system that fully implements the principles of REST is the World Wide Web. This comes as no surprise because Fielding was a co-writer of the HTTP standard and wrote his dissertation in order to abstract the design principles from the concrete architecture of HTTP. A RESTful service takes advantage of the way the web works and benefits from its architecture.

> **Note**
>
> A common misconception is to think about REST as some kind of protocol, such as HTTP or SOAP. This is incorrect—REST is a development paradigm, not a protocol.

The key elements of a RESTful architecture are explained next.

URIs

A Uniform Resource Identifier (URI) identifies and locates a resource by the used access method (such as HTTP) and the location inside a network. The basic structure consists of an access method defining a scheme and a scheme-specific-part, which are separated by a colon:

<scheme>: <scheme-specific-part >

Every resource of a service that is important enough for a user to access has to have at least one URI. This URI can be bookmarked so that you can return to it later; you can also paste it in an email or a document. Through the OData protocol, entity sets or single entities are accessible via such URIs. The same is true for results of queries that use the query options of the OData protocol.

Links

HATEOAS   A server exposes a self-describing resource that can be manipulated by a client via a hypermedia link. The formal description of this concept is originally known as *Hypermedia as the Engine of Application State* (HATEOAS). If we take a closer look at what is behind this intimidating description, we see that it's all about links. Links are well known from HTML, where they allow you to navigate from one web page to another.

As a RESTful protocol, OData offers links that can either read or manipulate the resource itself or navigate to other connected resources. For example, when entering the URI

https://sapes1.sapdevcenter.com/sap/opu/odata/sap/ZGWSAMPLE_SRV/
SalesOrderCollection('0500000000')?sap-ds-debug=true

in your web browser, you'll find the links shown in Figure 2.1 in the payload of the returned Extensible Markup Language (XML).

```
<link title="SalesOrder" href="SalesOrderCollection('0500000000')" rel="edit"/>
<link title="BusinessPartner" type="application/atom+xml;type=entry"
href="SalesOrderCollection('0500000000')/BusinessPartner"
rel="http://schemas.microsoft.com/ado/2007/08/dataservices/related/BusinessPartner"/>
<link title="LineItems" type="application/atom+xml;type=feed"
href="SalesOrderCollection('0500000000')/LineItems"
rel="http://schemas.microsoft.com/ado/2007/08/dataservices/related/LineItems"/>
```

Figure 2.1 Links of an OData Entity Type

The first link is the self-link that allows the resource (in this case, the sales order) to be manipulated (read, updated, deleted). The two other links offer navigation to related entity sets, namely the business partner to whom this sales order belongs and the sales order line items.

Uniform Interface

HTTP verbs   One of the main features of RESTful services is that they use existing HTTP verbs against addressable resources identified in the URI. Conceptually, it's a way of performing database-style CRUD operations on resources by using HTTP verbs.

Stateless Communication

All RESTful services, including OData, use stateless communication. Stateless communication means that a client has to provide all information in a request so that it can be processed by the server. Session states held by the server do not exist—session information is stored on the client instead.

Multiple Representations of a Resource

Any RESTful server (such as SAP NetWeaver Gateway) can deliver different representations of a resource (such as XML or JavaScript Object Notation (JSON)). The advantage is that, for example, JSON can be more easily consumed by JavaScript clients.

XML or JSON

2.1.2   What Is OData?

The Open Data Protocol (OData) is a REST-based data access protocol released under the Microsoft Open Specification Promise (OSP) for querying and updating data. OData builds on broadly known and used industry standards such as Atom Publishing Protocol (AtomPub), XML, and JSON (JavaScript Object Notation), which makes it easier to understand and use. It's consistent with the way the web works and follows its core principles, allowing for a new level of data integration and interoperability across traditional platform and manufacturer boundaries. It's easy to understand and extensible, and provides consumers with a predictable interface for accessing a variety of data sources. In short, OData can be seen as Online Database Connectivity (ODBC) for the web. It opens up the silos of traditional IT and increases the value of data by allowing for easier and broader data access.

OData started back in late April of 2007 at the Microsoft MIX07 conference. An incubation project code-named Astoria was started to find a way to transport data across HTTP to architect and develop web-based solutions more efficiently. The project goal was to "enable applications to expose data as a data service that can be consumed by web clients within a corporate network and across the Internet." Even then, most of the core concepts of OData were used: HTTP, URIs to identify the various pieces of information reachable through a service, and the usage of

MIX07

simple formats such as XML or JSON for the representation of data exchanged in interactions.

MIX10 The next big milestone on the Microsoft side was the 2010 MIX Conference, where OData was officially announced by Doug Purdy of Microsoft during the keynote address. The name Open Data Protocol was chosen to indicate that the protocol is supposed to remain as open as possible, following the Open Data Philosophy. This school of thought follows the idea that certain data should be freely available to everyone to use and republish without restrictions from copyrights, patents, or other mechanisms of control. Microsoft first provided an OData SDK for download and announced that it would start to build OData support into a number of products, including SharePoint 2010 and Excel 2010. The OData protocol was consequently released under the OSP, which basically allows free usage of the protocol, inviting everyone to use it as a standard. This means that OData can be used freely without the need for a license or contract.

SAP NetWeaver Gateway In parallel, realizing a growing need for an easy-to-use non-ABAP developer access to its systems, SAP started to invest in SAP NetWeaver Gateway in 2009 as a means to enable large communities of developers outside the classic SAP development community.

OASIS Standard In 2012, Microsoft, Citrix, IBM, Progress Software, SAP, and WSO2 jointly submitted a proposal for the standardization of OData based on the OData V3 specification to OASIS—the Organization for the Advancement of Structured Information Standards. *OASIS* is a nonprofit, international consortium that drives the development, convergence, and adoption of open standards for the global information society. The consortium has more than 5,000 participants representing more than 600 organizations and individual members in 100 countries. Because the OData Technical Committee approved Committee Specification 01 version of OData Version 4.0 on August 14, 2013, OData might officially become for the IT industry what it unofficially already is—the generally accepted lingua franca used by the members of the IT industry for software interoperability across all platforms and borders.

Consumers and producers In the years since the announcement of Project Astoria at Mix '07, a rich ecosystem has developed around OData. This ecosystem is a growing community of data producers and consumers using the OData to exchange data. *OData consumers* are applications that consume data exposed using the OData protocol and can vary greatly in sophistication, from something as simple as a web browser to custom applications that take advantage of all of the features of the OData protocol. The most prominent OData consumer is probably Microsoft Excel. *OData producers* are services that expose their data using the OData protocol. Applications that expose OData include a number of household names such as Microsoft SharePoint 2010, IBM WebSphere, Microsoft Dynamics, as well as open-source projects such as Drupal or Joomla. On top of that, there is an ever growing number of live services that serve up information via OData to the public. You can, for example, browse Wikipedia via DBpedia. A detailed list of selected producers can be found on the OData website at *www.odata.org/ecosystem*.

The OData community knows that there is a problem—in this day of big data, there is an increasing amount of information coming from an increasing amount of sources that needs to be accessed on an increasing variety of devices (Figure 2.2).

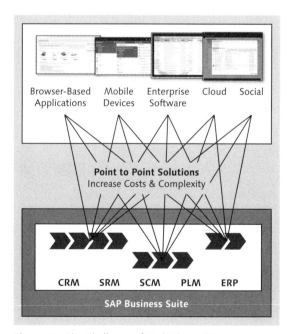

Figure 2.2 The Challenge of Multichannel Access

This problem needs a solution. As a web protocol for querying and updating data, as well as applying and building on web technologies such as HTTP, AtomPub, and JSON to provide access to information from a variety of applications, OData is that solution.

> **Note**
>
> Our focus in this book is specifically on OData with respect to SAP NetWeaver Gateway, so the information in this chapter provides only an introduction to OData's basic concepts, and then focuses specifically on OData and SAP NetWeaver Gateway. If you're looking for more general information on OData before you dive deeper into the book, we recommend spending some time on *www.odata.org*.

Abstract model and protocol

OData primarily defines two things: an abstract data model and a protocol that allows any client to access information exposed by any data source. As a result, OData allows mixing and matching providers and consumers following one of the fundamental OData ideas: that any client can access any data source. The obvious benefits of this are that it offers a simple and uniform way of sharing data on the protocol level, enables a broad integration across products and platforms, and basically only requires an HTTP stack to integrate with any OData producer.

Design principles

The OData protocol follows five design principles:

- **Data store variety**
  Select mechanisms that support diverse data stores. In particular, don't assume a relational data model.

- **Backwards compatibility**
  Clients and services that speak different versions of the OData protocol should interoperate, supporting everything allowed in lower versions.

- **REST principles**
  Adhere to these unless there is a good and specific reason not to.

- **Graceful degradation**
  It should be easy to build a very basic but compliant OData service, with additional work necessary only to support additional capabilities.

▶ **Simplicity**
Address the common cases and provide extensibility where necessary.

Using OData, structured data can be exchanged in both directions between a client and a server. A client uses an HTTP request on a server resource and receives a response. This request is placed by calling a service. A service defines the resources that can be accessed, the relevant HTTP operations, and the format of documents that represent those resources in requests. The representation is in an XML and/or JSON format.

High-level technical solution

There are four main building blocks of a technical OData implementation:

Building blocks of an OData implementation

▶ **OData data model**
The OData data model provides a generic way to organize and describe data.

▶ **OData protocol**
The OData protocol lets a client make requests to and get responses from an OData service. In essence, it's just HTTP-based RESTful CRUD interactions along with an OData-defined query language. Data sent by an OData service can be represented either in the XML-based format or in JSON.

▶ **OData client libraries**
The OData client libraries facilitate the creation of software that accesses data via the OData protocol. Using a specific client library (for example, from Microsoft) isn't strictly required, but it does make life a lot easier for developers. However, a developer is always free to create an OData client from scratch—it's just code.

▶ **OData services**
Finally, OData services are what implement the OData protocol and expose an endpoint that allows access to data. In effect, OData services use abstractions of the OData data model to translate data between its underlying form into the format sent to the client.

OData also offers a number of very intuitive URI conventions for navigation, filtering, sorting, and paging. This turns OData into a powerful query language—a *SQL light* for the web.

It's important to note that by using these building blocks in an OData implementation, any consumer sees only the data model provided by the OData service. The raw underlying data is wrapped and kept away from the consumer, keeping the internal data structure unexposed.

2.2 Structure of an OData Service

Building blocks of an OData service

Now that you have a little background, it's time to get an introduction to the technical details of OData. As you'll recall from the previous section, OData services are what implement the OData protocol and expose an endpoint that allows access to data. The structure of an OData service is comprised of the following building blocks:

► **Service document**
A service document represents a service by exposing all resources that can be accessed through the service, their URIs, names, and operations.

► **Service metadata document**
The service metadata document exposes all metadata of a service. It exposes the model, types, actions, relations, and detailed information of the semantics of the part of the model.

Elements of OData documents

Further, these two types of documents are in turn comprised of different elements:

► **Entity**
An entity is a potentially empty resource of zero or one content element(s). The content element contains one to many properties. At least one key field is required. Entities can be addressed individually by means of key values or as collections by means of query options.

► **Entity type**
An entity type describes a collection and has a name. In many cases, the names of the collection and the entity type are equal or related by some convention. Entity types have a structure defined by their properties and are also associated with a key, which is formed from a subset of the properties of the entity type. The entity key is needed to define associations between the entity types.

▶ **Entity set**
An entity set represents a potentially empty resource of entries. The cardinality is 0:many. Several entity sets can be based on the same entity type. For example, there might be a service that has the entity sets `EmployeeCollection`, `ContactCollection`, and `ManagerCollection`, which can all be based on the same entity type called `Person`. If an entity set is addressed by means of key values, the `GET_ENTITY` method of the entity set has to be implemented.

▶ **Property**
A property is a typed element that represents a primitive typed data element, structured data, or a link to another resource. Properties correspond to columns of a table.

▶ **Navigation property**
Entity types may include one or more *navigation properties*. A navigation property is a specific type of property containing a link that presents an association instance. These correspond to links that point to other tables and table entries, depending on the cardinality of the underlying association. The navigation property derives its name from the fact that it allows navigation from one entity (the entity type that declares the navigation property) to others (anything from 0). Similar to properties, navigation properties are specified in a separate element called `NavigationProperty`; this defines the navigation property name, the association being used, and the direction.

▶ **Association**
An association defines a relation between entity types. Recursive relations are allowed. Every association includes two association ends, which specify the entity types that are related and the cardinality rules for each end of the association.

The relationship between all of these elements is encapsulated in the *data model* of the OData service. The SAP NetWeaver Gateway Productivity Accelerator (GWPA) OData Model Editor (discussed in Chapter 8) allows developers to graphically model the entity relationship model of an OData service. Then the data model can be imported into the graphical OData modeler that is provided by SAP as part of GWPA, as shown in Figure 2.3.

Data model

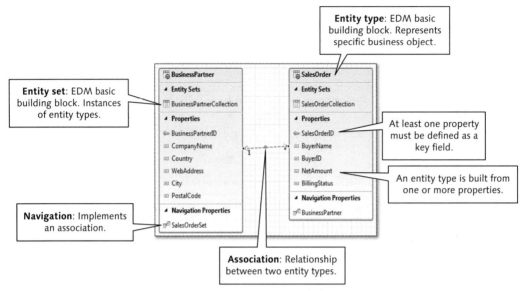

Entity type: EDM basic building block. Represents specific business object.

Entity set: EDM basic building block. Instances of entity types.

At least one property must be defined as a key field.

An entity type is built from one or more properties.

Navigation: Implements an association.

Association: Relationship between two entity types.

Figure 2.3 Entity Data Model Created with the GWPA OData Modeler

To explain all of these elements with respect to SAP, we'll use a sample service that has been built using the SAP NetWeaver Gateway Service Builder, which is the main tool for service creation in SAP NetWeaver Gateway. (We go into more detail about the Service Builder in Chapter 5.) The service provides access to demo data based on the SAP NetWeaver Enterprise Procurement Model (EPM), which is a frequently used demo scenario.

> **Note**
>
> The service in this section is available as part of the SAP Community Network (SCN) trial edition of SAP NetWeaver Application Server ABAP 7.4 that is available via SCN and via the demo system of the SAP NetWeaver Gateway Developer Center in SCN.

Sample data model

The sample service is based on the data model shown in Figure 2.4. This data model assumes that you want to expose a service to access business partners, sales orders, sales order line items, products, and the contacts of business partners.

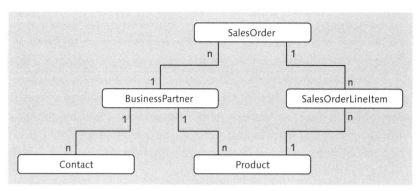

Figure 2.4 Data Model Sample Service ZGWSAMPLE_SRV

As we mentioned, there are two types of documents associated with each OData service: the *service document* and the *service metadata document*. In this section, we'll take a look at both of these for our sample service, and show you how the pieces and parts we described earlier are reflected in this example.

> **Note**
>
> This section is only an overview of OData services. We'll go into much more detail about all of this in Chapter 5, Chapter 6, and Chapter 7, where we provide detailed explanations of the steps involved in creating services.

2.2.1 Service Document

Let's explore the structure of an OData service by starting with the *service document*. The OData service document primarily lists all entity sets of an OData service. The service document is available at the service root URI and can be formatted either in Atom or JSON. The base URI of the service document is actually pointing to the service document itself. In our example, we'll call the root URI of the service document using the query parameter `sap-ds-debug=true`.

> **sap-ds-debug=true**
>
> Using the query parameter `sap-ds-debug=true`, the server responses of an SAP NetWeaver Gateway server are rendered as an HTML page with active links. No matter whether you choose XML or JSON as the output format, the

server response is rendered in a user-friendly manner that can be displayed in any browser. Another advantage of using this query parameter is that the user is able to follow all links in the server response, allowing for web-like navigation.

After you have access to the demo system provided by the SAP NetWeaver Gateway Developer Center, the service document of the sample service is accessible through the following URI:

https://sapes1.sapdevcenter.com/sap/opu/odata/sap/ZGWSAMPLE_SRV/

Entity sets Looking at the service document (Figure 2.5), we find one or more collection tags (`<app:collection>`) that define the relative URL and title of an individual collection or entity set, as shown in ❶. The service document contains a list of all entity types that can be accessed in this service. For each entity set, we find a relative link marked with *href* that points to the respective entity set. The sample service ZGWSAMPLE_SRV contains the five collections: `ProductCollection`, `BusinessPartnerCollection`, `ContactCollection`, `SalesOrderCollection`, and `SalesOrderLineItemCollection`.

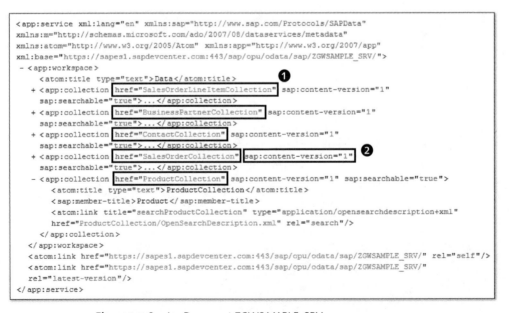

```
<app:service xml:lang="en" xmlns:sap="http://www.sap.com/Protocols/SAPData"
xmlns:m="http://schemas.microsoft.com/ado/2007/08/dataservices/metadata"
xmlns:atom="http://www.w3.org/2005/Atom" xmlns:app="http://www.w3.org/2007/app"
xml:base="https://sapes1.sapdevcenter.com:443/sap/opu/odata/sap/ZGWSAMPLE_SRV/">
 - <app:workspace>
    <atom:title type="text">Data</atom:title>        ❶
   + <app:collection href="SalesOrderLineItemCollection" sap:content-version="1"
       sap:searchable="true">...</app:collection>
   + <app:collection href="BusinessPartnerCollection" sap:content-version="1"
       sap:searchable="true">...</app:collection>
   + <app:collection href="ContactCollection" sap:content-version="1"
       sap:searchable="true">...</app:collection>
   + <app:collection href="SalesOrderCollection" sap:content-version="1"    ❷
       sap:searchable="true">...</app:collection>
   - <app:collection href="ProductCollection" sap:content-version="1" sap:searchable="true">
       <atom:title type="text">ProductCollection</atom:title>
       <sap:member-title>Product</sap:member-title>
       <atom:link title="searchProductCollection" type="application/opensearchdescription+xml"
       href="ProductCollection/OpenSearchDescription.xml" rel="search"/>
     </app:collection>
   </app:workspace>
   <atom:link href="https://sapes1.sapdevcenter.com:443/sap/opu/odata/sap/ZGWSAMPLE_SRV/" rel="self"/>
   <atom:link href="https://sapes1.sapdevcenter.com:443/sap/opu/odata/sap/ZGWSAMPLE_SRV/"
   rel="latest-version"/>
</app:service>
```

Figure 2.5 Service Document ZGWSAMPLE_SRV

You'll also notice that the service document contains some SAP-specific metadata, as shown in ❷. The annotations `sap:creatable`, `sap:updatable`, and `sap:deletable` state whether the collection allows adding, changing, or removing member resources. The annotation `sap:searchable` denotes whether the content of a collection can be searched using a Google-like search. Note that the SAP-specific annotations only show up in the service document and service metadata document if their value is set to a nondefault value. Default values are, for example, `true` for `creatable` and `false` for `searchable`. (For more details about this, we recommend *http://scn.sap.com/docs/DOC-44986*.)

SAP annotations

In our sample service, the `ContactCollection` and the `SalesOrderLineItemCollection` are marked as `sap:addressable="false"` (see Listing 2.1).

```
<app:collection sap:addressable="false"
sap:content-version="1" href="ContactCollection">
    <atom:title type="text">ContactCollection</atom:title>
    <sap:member-title>Contact</sap:member-title>
</app:collection>
```

Listing 2.1 Contact Collection Marked as `sap:addressable=false`

In this example, an exception is raised if a consumer tries to retrieve a list of contacts by sending an HTTP `GET` request to the `ContactCollection` or the `SalesOrderLineItemCollection`. (This is implemented via the code-based service implementation, which we discuss in more detail in Chapter 5 and Chapter 6.) This exception tells the consumer that the contacts can only be retrieved using the navigation property `Contacts` of the `BusinessPartner` entity while the `SalesOrderItems` can only be retrieved using the navigation property `LineItems` of the `SalesOrder` entity type.

By combining the base URI of the sample service ZGWSAMPLE_SRV *http://<host>:<port>/sap/opu/odata/sap/ZGWSAMPLE_SRV/* with the relative link *href="BusinessPartnerCollection"* that points to the collection `BusinessPartnerCollection`, the client is able to construct the absolute URI allowing him to retrieve the entries of the `BusinessPartner` collection. The URI that points to the business partner entity set of our sample service is the following:

Absolute URI

https://sapes1.sapdevcenter.com/sap/opu/odata/sap/ZGWSAMPLE_SRV/
BusinessPartnerCollection?sap-ds-debug=true

Entering this URI in a browser will deliver the XML response shown in
Figure 2.6. If you've accessed the service document using the query
parameter `sap-ds-debug=true`, you can browse the content of the service document by clicking the hyperlink (e.g., `BusinessPartnerCollec-
tion`).

```
<feed xmlns:d="http://schemas.microsoft.com/ado/2007/08/dataservices"
xmlns:m="http://schemas.microsoft.com/ado/2007/08/dataservices/metadata" xmlns="http://www.w3.org/2005/Atom"
xml:base="https://sapes1.sapdevcenter.com:443/sap/opu/odata/sap/ZGWSAMPLE_SRV/">
  <id>https://sapes1.sapdevcenter.com:443/sap/opu/odata/sap/ZGWSAMPLE_SRV/BusinessPartnerCollection</id>
  <title type="text">BusinessPartnerCollection</title>
  <updated>2013-12-10T13:55:28Z</updated>
- <author>
    <name/>
  </author>
  <link title="BusinessPartnerCollection" rel="self" href="BusinessPartnerCollection"/>
- <entry>
    <id>https://sapes1.sapdevcenter.com:443/sap/opu/odata/sap/ZGWSAMPLE_SRV/BusinessPartnerCollection('0100000000')</id>
    <title type="text">BusinessPartnerCollection('0100000000')</title>
    <updated>2013-12-10T13:55:28Z</updated>
    <category scheme="http://schemas.microsoft.com/ado/2007/08/dataservices/scheme" term="ZGWSAMPLE_SRV.BusinessPartner"/>
    <link title="BusinessPartner" rel="edit" href="BusinessPartnerCollection('0100000000')"/>
    <link title="SalesOrders" type="application/atom+xml;type=feed"
    rel="http://schemas.microsoft.com/ado/2007/08/dataservices/related/SalesOrders" href="BusinessPartnerCollection
    ('0100000000')/SalesOrders"/>
    <link title="Contacts" type="application/atom+xml;type=feed"
    rel="http://schemas.microsoft.com/ado/2007/08/dataservices/related/Contacts" href="BusinessPartnerCollection
    ('0100000000')/Contacts"/>
  - <content type="application/xml">
    - <m:properties>
        <d:BusinessPartnerID>0100000000</d:BusinessPartnerID>
        <d:BpRole>01</d:BpRole>
        <d:EmailAddress>do.not.reply@sap.com</d:EmailAddress>
        <d:PhoneNumber>0622734567</d:PhoneNumber>
        <d:FaxNumber/>
        <d:WebAddress>http://www.sap.com</d:WebAddress>
        <d:CompanyName>SAP</d:CompanyName>
        <d:LegalForm>AG</d:LegalForm>
        <d:CurrencyCode>EUR</d:CurrencyCode>
        <d:City>Walldorf</d:City>
        <d:PostalCode>69190</d:PostalCode>
        <d:Street>Dietmar-Hopp-Allee</d:Street>
        <d:Building>15</d:Building>
        <d:Country>DE</d:Country>
        <d:AddressType>02</d:AddressType>
        <d:AddressValStartDate>2000-01-01T08:00:00.0000000</d:AddressValStartDate>
        <d:AddressValEndDate>9999-12-31T08:00:00.0000000</d:AddressValEndDate>
        <d:CreatedBy>0000000033</d:CreatedBy>
        <d:CreatedAt>2013-11-24T13:24:37.0000000</d:CreatedAt>
        <d:ChangedBy>0000000033</d:ChangedBy>
        <d:ChangedAt>2013-11-24T13:24:37.0000000</d:ChangedAt>
      </m:properties>
    </content>
  </entry>
+ <entry>...</entry>
+ <entry>...</entry>
+ <entry>...</entry>
+ <entry>...</entry>
```

Figure 2.6 Result Query Entity Set BusinessPartnerCollection

Here's what you can see in the `BusinessPartnerCollection` entity set:

▶ The `<feed>` element defines a collection of zero or more `<entry>` elements. The content thus corresponds to a table.

▶ The `<entry>` element contains the data for one member of the feed's collection. Its content thus corresponds to a row of a table. Notice that each `<entry>` element contains one or more `<link>` elements.

▶ Each `<entry>` element always contains a self-reference, which is a `<link>` element marked with either `rel="self"` or `rel="edit"`. It contains the relative URL for reading the current entry from the collection.

▶ The primary key information of each entry is rendered into the response in brackets right after the name of the entity set. If the primary key consists of only one property, the value is provided right away without the property name (e.g., `BusinessPartnerCollection('0100000001')`). If the primary key consists of multiple properties, the primary key is provided by a comma-separated list of name/value pairs.

▶ Inside an `<entry>`, you find one or more `<properties>` tags that correspond to single table columns.

▶ The annotation `sap:searchable=true` denotes that the content of a collection can be searched. The `atom:link` with `rel="search"` points to an OpenSearch description document that describes how to do free-text (Google-like) search on the collection via the custom query option `"search="`.

▶ In the response, you find an additional relative link in each entry: *href="BusinessPartnerCollection('0100000000')/SalesOrders*. Following this link provides an XML response that lists the sales orders of the selected business partner. Such links are called *navigation properties*.

Now you're able to read, understand, and use an XML document for an entity set as a response from any OData service.

2.2.2 Service Metadata Document

As we defined earlier, the service metadata document exposes all metadata of a service, including the model, types, actions, relations, and $metadata

83

detailed semantics of the model (see Figure 2.7). The service metadata document URI can be constructed easily by appending the string *$metadata* to the service root URI. The service metadata document of the OData sample service is thus accessible via the following URI:

http://<host>:<port>/sap/opu/odata/sap/ZGWSAMPLE_SRV/$metadata

The purpose of the service metadata document is to enable consumers to discover the shape of an OData service, the structure of its resources, the known links between resources, and the service operations exposed. SDKs use this information to generate proxies that developers then use to access a service in their development environment of choice. This OData service information is encapsulated in the service metadata document via the *entity data model* for a given service. The entity data model describes the organization and relationship of the data resources that are modeled as entity types within a particular business scenario. For this, the service metadata document uses an XML language called the *Conceptual Schema Definition Language* (CSDL).

Figure 2.7 Service Metadata Document ZGWSAMPLE_SRV

Entity types   Figure 2.8 shows the `BusinessPartner` entity type contained in the service metadata document.

```
<EntityType sap:content-version="1" Name="BusinessPartner">
 - <Key>
        <PropertyRef Name="BusinessPartnerID"/>
   </Key>
   <Property Name="BusinessPartnerID" sap:label="Bus. Part. ID" MaxLength="10" Nullable="false" Type="Edm.String"/>
   <Property Name="BpRole" sap:label="Bus. Part. Role" MaxLength="3" Type="Edm.String"/>
   <Property Name="EmailAddress" sap:label="E-Mail Address" MaxLength="255" Type="Edm.String" sap:semantics="email"/>
   <Property Name="PhoneNumber" sap:label="Phone No." MaxLength="30" Type="Edm.String" sap:semantics="tel"/>
   <Property Name="FaxNumber" sap:label="Phone No." MaxLength="30" Type="Edm.String"/>
   <Property Name="WebAddress" sap:label="Description" MaxLength="255" Type="Edm.String" sap:semantics="url"/>
   <Property Name="CompanyName" sap:label="Company Name" MaxLength="80" Type="Edm.String"/>
   <Property Name="LegalForm" sap:label="Legal Form" MaxLength="10" Type="Edm.String"/>
   <Property Name="CurrencyCode" sap:label="Currency" MaxLength="5" Type="Edm.String" sap:semantics="currency-code"/>
   <Property Name="City" sap:label="City" MaxLength="40" Type="Edm.String" sap:semantics="city"/>
   <Property Name="PostalCode" sap:label="Postal Code" MaxLength="10" Type="Edm.String" sap:semantics="zip"/>
   <Property Name="Street" sap:label="Street" MaxLength="60" Type="Edm.String" sap:semantics="street"/>
   <Property Name="Building" sap:label="Building" MaxLength="10" Type="Edm.String"/>
   <Property Name="Country" sap:label="Country" MaxLength="3" Type="Edm.String" sap:semantics="country"/>
   <Property Name="AddressType" sap:label="Address Type" MaxLength="2" Type="Edm.String"/>
   <Property Name="AddressValStartDate" sap:label="Time Stamp" Type="Edm.DateTime"/>
   <Property Name="AddressValEndDate" sap:label="Time Stamp" Type="Edm.DateTime"/>
   <Property Name="CreatedBy" sap:label="Employee ID" MaxLength="10" Type="Edm.String"/>
   <Property Name="CreatedAt" sap:label="Time Stamp" Type="Edm.DateTime"/>
   <Property Name="ChangedBy" sap:label="Employee ID" MaxLength="10" Type="Edm.String"/>
   <Property Name="ChangedAt" sap:label="Time Stamp" Type="Edm.DateTime"/>
   <NavigationProperty Name="SalesOrders" ToRole="FromRole_Assoc_SalesOrder_BusinessPartner"
        FromRole="ToRole_Assoc_SalesOrder_BusinessPartner" Relationship="ZGWSAMPLE_SRV.Assoc_SalesOrder_BusinessPartner"/>
   <NavigationProperty Name="Contacts" ToRole="ToRole_Assoc_BusinessPartner_Contacts"
        FromRole="FromRole_Assoc_BusinessPartner_Contacts" Relationship="ZGWSAMPLE_SRV.Assoc_BusinessPartner_Contacts"/>
</EntityType>
```

Figure 2.8 Entity Type Definition: BusinessPartner

In our sample service, there are several entity sets; e.g., `SalesOrder-LineItemCollection`, `BusinessPartnerCollection`, and `ContactCollection` (Figure 2.9). The `EntityContainer` lists all of the entity sets belonging to one service.

Entity sets

```
<EntityContainer Name="ZGWSAMPLE_SRV" m:IsDefaultEntityContainer="true">
   <EntitySet sap:content-version="1" Name="SalesOrderLineItemCollection" sap:searchable="true"
       EntityType="ZGWSAMPLE_SRV.SalesOrderLineItem"/>
   <EntitySet sap:content-version="1" Name="BusinessPartnerCollection" sap:searchable="true"
       EntityType="ZGWSAMPLE_SRV.BusinessPartner"/>
   <EntitySet sap:content-version="1" Name="ContactCollection" sap:searchable="true"
       EntityType="ZGWSAMPLE_SRV.Contact"/>
```

Figure 2.9 Entity Set Definition: SalesOrderLineItemCollection, BusinessPartner-Collection, and ContactCollection

Associations between entity types are also part of the schema. They are listed one after the other in the metadata document (e.g., the association `Assoc_SalesOrder_BusinessPartner` between the entity types `BusinessPartnerCollection` and `ContactCollection`, as shown in Figure 2.10).

Associations

```
<Association sap:content-version="1" Name="Assoc_SalesOrder_BusinessPartner">
   <End Type="ZGWSAMPLE_SRV.SalesOrder"
       Role="FromRole_Assoc_SalesOrder_BusinessPartner" Multiplicity="*"/>
   <End Type="ZGWSAMPLE_SRV.BusinessPartner"
       Role="ToRole_Assoc_SalesOrder_BusinessPartner" Multiplicity="1"/>
</Association>
```

Figure 2.10 Association between the BusinessPartner Entity Type and the SalesOrder Entity Type

Navigation
properties

Finally, the BusinessPartner entity type has two navigation properties named Contacts and SalesOrders (Figure 2.11). The navigation property Contacts makes it possible to navigate from a BusinessPartner instance to all of the contacts that are defined in the backend system for this business partner. The navigation property SalesOrders, on the other hand, lets you navigate from a BusinessPartner instance to all sales orders that belong to this business partner.

```
<NavigationProperty Name="SalesOrders"
    ToRole="FromRole_Assoc_SalesOrder_BusinessPartner"
    FromRole="ToRole_Assoc_SalesOrder_BusinessPartner"
    Relationship="ZGWSAMPLE_SRV.Assoc_SalesOrder_BusinessPartner"/>
<NavigationProperty Name="Contacts" ToRole="ToRole_Assoc_BusinessPartner_Contacts"
    FromRole="FromRole_Assoc_BusinessPartner_Contacts"
    Relationship="ZGWSAMPLE_SRV.Assoc_BusinessPartner_Contacts"/>
</EntityType>
```

Figure 2.11 Navigation Properties of the BusinessPartner Entity Type

2.3   OData Operations

When discussing data access, people typically talk about CRUD or CRUD-Q (where the "Q" is for *query*) and indicate the operation to be executed. (Query is a kind of Read operation and therefore the "Q" is not always mentioned explicitly.) As already described in Section 2.1.1, OData uses the REST commands POST, GET, PUT, or DELETE, which map to CRUD. The OData protocol defines conventions for all of these CRUD operations, but it's not mandatory for every OData service to support all four operations. In this section, we'll explain each operation and give some context for their use.

2.3.1   Create

POST

The Create operation is to be used whenever you want to create data on the backend server. This is data that wasn't present before, for example, a new sales order or a new business partner. The related HTTP method is POST. If the Create operation is successful, you receive the HTTP 201 (created) response code, along with the entity that was created. Via the metadata, you can specify whether an entity set is creatable or not. This information is reflected in the metadata document and allows the consumer to act accordingly (e.g., if the application is of the type Player).

But there is no default handling of this annotation by the framework; instead, the service implementation has to handle it according to the metadata definition (see Chapter 5 and Chapter 6 for more details about service implementation).

2.3.2 Read

The `Read` operation is the most frequently used operation. Typically, applications primarily read data instead of updating data—for example, a lunch menu application that doesn't include any option to provide feedback about the menu provided. This data can be of any kind, such as customizing, master data, transaction data, and so on. The related HTTP method for the `Read` operation is `GET`. A successful read operation has the HTTP 200 (OK) status code.

GET

`Read` operations can be classified into two different kinds: `Query` and `Single Read`.

Query Operation

A `Query` operation is usually the entry point into an application. The purpose of a query is to read a set of entities. So the result of a query is always an entity set—irrespective of whether the result is empty (no entity), a single entity, or multiple entities. A `Query` operation is usually combined with a filter that reduces the number of results. An example of such a `Query` operation is the retrieval of a list of sales orders, optionally filtered by a certain sales area, a status, and/or a date.

Read a set of entities

Similar to the `Create` operation, you can control the `Query` operation via the metadata if an entity set can be directly read (`sap:addressable`). If an entity set isn't addressable, it may not be accessed via a `Query` operation. This is used if you only want to allow access via a navigation property. An example is not allowing a consumer to fetch the list of all sales orders in the system but just allowing access to the sales orders of a certain business partner by using the respective navigation property.

In the metadata definition of an entity set, you can also set the REQUIRES FILTER flag. This is supposed to enforce a consumer to provide a mandatory filter when accessing the entity set; that is, a consumer may not access the collection without a filter. Similar to the other metadata annotations, the SAP NetWeaver Gateway framework doesn't handle this. Instead, the service implementation needs to handle it accordingly (see Chapter 5 and Chapter 6 for more details about service implementation).

Single Read Operation

After you've fetched a set of entities, you can use the provided self-link to navigate to the details of the entities. For that, you can use the Single Read operation. The major difference to the Query operation is that you specify the primary key of the entity you want to read. So you're accessing an instance with the primary key versus querying for entities that might or might not result in a single unique instance.

The key information has to be passed in brackets right after the name of the collection. If the primary key consists of only a single property, the name of the property doesn't have to be provided. If the primary key consists of multiple properties, the property names have to be provided along with the values. But you don't need to worry about the concatenation of that information, because the self-links provided by the SAP NetWeaver Gateway server in the entity set already take care of it.

2.3.3 Update

Change an existing entity

The Update operation is used whenever you want to change an existing entity. As such, you have to provide the same key information as in the Single Read operation, explained earlier, to uniquely identify the entity you want to update.

PUT

The HTTP method for the Update operation is PUT. If the Update operation is successful, you receive the HTTP 204 (no content) status. You're intentionally not getting the entity back as part of the HTTP request, because the consumer typically knows the current state of the entity, and therefore the SAP NetWeaver Gateway server doesn't need to send it back.

Instead of PUT, it's possible to leverage the PATCH operation that allows you to perform a partial update. The PATCH method is supported by the framework and first calls the GETDETAIL method to retrieve all properties that won't be updated and then merges those values with the ones that are sent via the PATCH request before finally performing an update using the standard update method of an entity set.

Because the consumer knows the key of the entity, it is, of course, possible to perform a Single Read operation after the Update operation to fetch the updated entity. This might be required if the server, for example, does any calculation. It's not a good practice to misuse the Create operation for update requests just to receive the entity back as part of the response.

Similar to the other operations, there is an annotation in the metadata document that controls the ability to update an entity (Updatable).

2.3.4 Delete

Finally, the Delete operation is to be used whenever you want to delete an entity. Equal to the Update operation, you have to provide the primary key of the entity you want to erase. The related HTTP method is DELETE. A successful Delete operation has the HTTP 204 (no content) status code.

Via the sap:deletable annotation, you can specify whether entities of an entity set can be deleted or not. As before, the service implementation has to make sure that the actual operations are in line with the metadata definition (see Chapter 5 and Chapter 6 for more details about service implementation).

2.4 OData Query Options

OData specifies a simple yet powerful query language that allows a client to request arbitrary filtering, sorting, and paging. Via query string parameters, a client is able to express the amount and order of the data that an OData service returns.

Query options are essential to reducing or influencing the result set provided by the SAP NetWeaver Gateway server. In many cases, you don't want a huge collection to be returned as is (e.g., the list of all products in the backend system) if the result set isn't already filtered based on the user assignment (e.g., in an SAP CRM scenario, the service implementation probably only returns the business partners that are assigned to your user, not all existing business partners in the entire SAP CRM system).

In this short introduction, we're focusing on the most important query options only, as listed in Table 2.1.

Operation	Query Option
Filtering and projecting	$filter and $select
Sorting	$orderby
Client-side paging	$top, $skip and $inlinecount
Counting	$count
Inlining	$expand
Formatting	$format

Table 2.1 List of Most Important OData Query Options

We'll illustrate the different query options by querying the sample data set that contains a list of business partners (subset taken from the EPM sample content provided with SAP NetWeaver) as shown in Table 2.2.

BusinessPartner ID	CompanyName	LegalForm	City
100000000	SAP	AG	Walldorf
100000001	Becker Berlin	GmbH	Berlin
100000002	DelBont Industries	Ltd.	Wilmington, Delaware
100000003	Talpa	GmbH	Hannover
100000004	Panorama Studios	Inc.	Hollywood, California
100000005	TECUM	AG	Muenster
100000006	Asia High tech	Inc.	Tokyo

Table 2.2 Subset of Business Partners Contained in the SAP NetWeaver EPM Demo Data Model

BusinessPartner ID	CompanyName	LegalForm	City
100000007	Laurent	S.A.	Paris
100000008	AVANTEL	S.A.	Mexico City
100000009	Telecomunicaciones Star	S.A.	Buenos Aires
100000010	Pear Computing Services	Inc.	Atlanta, Georgia
100000011	Alpine Systems	AG	Salzburg
100000012	New Line Design	Ltd.	Manchester
100000013	HEPA Tec	GmbH	Bremen
100000014	Anav Ideon	Ltd.	Bismarck, North Dakota
100000015	Robert Brown Entertainment	Ltd.	Quebec
100000016	Mexican Oil Trading Company	S.A.	Puebla
100000017	Meliva	AG	Köln
100000018	Compostela	S.A.	Mendoza
100000019	Pateu	S.A.R.L.	Lyon
...	...	...	...
100000044	Sorali	AG	Karlsruhe

Table 2.2 Subset of Business Partners Contained in the SAP NetWeaver EPM Demo Data Model (Cont.)

Using this data set, we'll take a detailed look at all of the query options outlined in Table 2.1.

2.4.1 Filtering and Projecting ($filter and $select)

We'll start with the use case of filtering and projecting on a result set. A mobile application provides a list of business partners. Because not all properties of the entity set `BusinessPartnerCollection` can be displayed on the screen, only the properties `BusinessPartnerID` and

`CompanyName` are shown in the list. In addition, the user can limit the number of business partners by filtering the company names. A mockup screen of this application that is limiting the result by limiting the number of rows and columns retrieved is shown in Figure 2.12.

Figure 2.12 Mobile Application Using Filtering and Projecting

The subset is determined by selecting only the entries that satisfy the filter expression specified by the `$filter` query option and by limiting the number of properties being retrieved using the `$select` query option.

$filter The `$filter` system query option is one of the most important because it allows you to provide sophisticated filtering along with your service call. Similar to the other query options, you have to implement the filtering of your collection in the service implementation yourself; the framework provides no default filtering. Filters are translated by the framework—wherever possible—into corresponding `Select-Options` for easy handling in the ABAP code of the service implementation (see Chapter 5 and Chapter 6 for more details about service implementation).

The following HTTP request delivers the result shown in Figure 2.12:

https://sapes1.sapdevcenter.com/sap/opu/odata/sap/ZGWSAMPLE_SRV/
BusinessPartnerCollection?$filter=startswith(CompanyName,'S')

The result is a list of all companies whose company name starts with the letter "S" as shown in Table 2.3.

BusinessPartner ID	CompanyName	LegalForm	City
0100000000	SAP	AG	Walldorf
0100000041	South American IT Company	S.A.	Cordoba
0100000042	Siwusha	CJV	Shanghai
0100000044	Sorali	AG	Karlsruhe

Table 2.3 List of all Business Partners Whose Company Name Starts with "S"

Another example is to fetch a business partner from the `BusinessPartner` collection with the equal (=) operator using the property `BusinessPartnerID`. For example:

https://sapes1.sapdevcenter.com/sap/opu/odata/sap/ZGWSAMPLE_SRV/
BusinessPartnerCollection?$filter=BusinessPartnerID eq '0100000000'

The result is a list with just one entry, namely the business partner "SAP." You can also combine multiple filter statements with the logical operators `AND`, `OR`, and `NOT`. For example:

https://sapes1.sapdevcenter.com/sap/opu/odata/sap/ZGWSAMPLE_SRV/
BusinessPartnerCollection/$count?$filter=BusinessPartnerID eq
'0100000000' or BusinessPartnerID eq '0100000044'

The result of this is all business partners with the `BusinessPartnerID` = `'0100000000'` or `'0100000000'`, which are the business partners "SAP" and "Sorali."

The `$select` query option allows you to specify the properties you want to receive in the response. By default, the response contains all properties of the entity data model. In some situations, mainly for performance reasons, you might not want all fields to be retrieved or calculated on the backend and sent to the consumer via SAP NetWeaver Gateway. In such cases, you can use the `$select` query option to specify the exact

$select

93

properties you want. For example, the following HTTP request will result in the data shown in Table 2.4:

https://sapes1.sapdevcenter.com/sap/opu/odata/sap/ZGWSAMPLE_SRV/ BusinessPartnerCollection?$select=BusinessPartnerID,Company_Name

BP_Id	Company_Name
0100000000	SAP
0100000001	Becker Berlin
0100000002	DelBont Industries
0100000003	Talpa
0100000004	Panorama Studios
0100000005	TECUM
0100000006	Asia High tech
0100000007	Laurent
0100000008	AVANTEL
0100000009	Telecomunicaciones Star

Table 2.4 Result Set When Projecting via $select

In the service implementation, you can identify the properties that have been specified via the $select query option (see Chapter 5 and Chapter 6 for more details about service implementation). This allows the service developer to only fetch/calculate those fields that have actually been requested. If you're fetching your business data from an underlying RFC/BAPI module, there might not be a significant improvement by reducing the number of properties requested because the RFC/BAPI has to be executed anyway. An improvement can be achieved by fetching fewer fields/structures/tables, if the underlying RFC/BAPI supports this (i.e., if the underlying RFC/BAPI makes use of the ABAP feature to identify which interface fields have been requested using the IS SUPPLIED expression).

Even if you're not able to simplify the data retrieval in the backend, the SAP NetWeaver Gateway framework only sends back those properties that have been specified by the `$select` statement. So, in any case, you can at least reduce the amount of data that is transmitted over the wire by using the `$select` statement.

This query option can be applied to single entities as well as to feeds (collections).

2.4.2 Sorting ($orderby)

As the name implies, `$orderby` allows you to sort a result set based on properties of your data model. For each property, you can decide if you want the collection to be sorted as ascending (suffix `asc`) or descending (suffix `desc`). Ascending is the default sorting, so the appendix `asc` doesn't need to be provided explicitly along with the URI. Multiple properties have to be separated by commas, for example, if you want to first sort by using the property `City` and second by the property `CompanyName`. Note that navigation properties can't be used for sorting.

The framework doesn't perform the sorting itself. Instead, the sorting has to be done by the data provider implementation. As such, whatever sequence is returned by the related data provider method is kept and sent as a response back to the requestor. For example, the following HTTP request would result in the entire collection being sorted by `LegalForm` and `CompanyName` as shown in Table 2.5:

Sorted by data provider implementation

https://sapes1.sapdevcenter.com/sap/opu/odata/sap/ZGWSAMPLE_SRV/ BusinessPartnerCollection?$select=BusinessPartnerID,Company_Name, LegalForm&$orderby=LegalForm,CompanyName

BusinessPartner ID	CompanyName	LegalForm	City
0100000043	Danish Fish Trading Company	A/S	Copenhagen
0100000011	Alpine Systems	AG	Salzburg
0100000038	Bionic Research Lab	AG	Bühl
0100000017	Meliva	AG	Köln
0100000000	SAP	AG	Walldorf

Table 2.5 Business Partners Sorted by LegalForm and CompanyName

2.4.3 Client-Side Paging ($top, $skip, and $inlinecount)

Client-side paging is very often used in mobile applications where space to display results in lists is limited and where scrolling through result sets is cumbersome. In the example shown in Figure 2.13, the resulting list of business partners will be displayed on several pages if the number of retrieved business partners doesn't fit on one page, where only six entries can be displayed.

Flipping through pages

When flipping through the pages, the user should be informed how many entries have been found in total (see Figure 2.13, ❶). If, as in our example, the number of entries exceeds the number of entries found, the result should be shown on several pages. The user should be informed of which page he is currently on (see ❷) and through how many entries he has already navigated (see ❸).

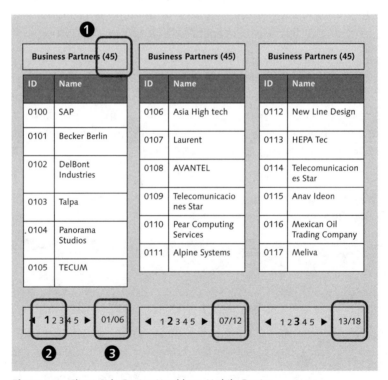

Figure 2.13 Client-Side Paging Used by a Mobile Device

For client-side paging, the client developer can use the following query options:

▸ `$top`

▸ `$skip`

▸ `$inlinecount`

The `$top` query option is typically used along with the `$skip` option, which we'll describe afterwards. Both together are used for client-side paging. `$top` specifies the number of entities you want to receive in your collection. If, for example, `$top=3` is provided, the data provider has to return only the first three entries of the result set.

Regarding performance, you should try to feed the `$top` value into, for example, the BAPI or RFC that you use for retrieving the data. Some function modules support the `maxrows` import parameter. Via the `maxrows` parameter, these function modules can reduce the set of data that is fetched from the database. This one is a perfect fit to provide the `$top` value, but don't forget that a `$skip` has been provided as well (in this case, `maxrows` typically is the sum of `$skip` and `$top`). For example, the following HTTP request retrieves the first six business partners of the `BusinessPartnerCollection` entity set (see Table 2.6):

https://sapes1.sapdevcenter.com/sap/opu/odata/sap/ZGWSAMPLE_SRV/ BusinessPartnerCollection?$select=BusinessPartnerID,CompanyName, LegalForm,City&$top=6

BP_Id	Company_Name	Legal_Form	City
100000000	SAP	AG	Walldorf
100000001	Becker Berlin	GmbH	Berlin
100000002	DelBont Industries	Ltd.	Wilmington, Delaware
100000003	Talpa	GmbH	Hannover
100000004	Panorama Studios	Inc.	Hollywood, California
100000005	TECUM	AG	Muenster

Table 2.6 First Six Business Partners Retrieved

$skip
As mentioned before, $skip and $top are usually used together for client-side paging. $skip defines the number of records (not pages) to be skipped at the beginning of the result set. If you provide, for example, $skip=2 as part of the URI, your result set won't contain record 1 and record 2, but will start as of record 3.

$skip and $top are handed over into the service implementation by the framework. The service implementation has to handle the query options. There is no default handling by the framework (see Chapter 5 and Chapter 6 for more details about service implementation).

If the function module used for the data retrieval doesn't contain a maxrows parameter, you should be careful when making use of $top and $skip. If you can't limit the amount of data that is read from the database table(s) for each "page" you query from the client, you might perform a lot of unnecessary read statements when paging through the result set. If you've implemented the data retrieval yourself (e.g., accessing your own Z-tables), you're usually more flexible in improving the $select statement (e.g., by using the up to x rows statement when accessing the database).

To access the third page of the collection, the following URI has to be issued by the client application as shown in Table 2.7:

https://sapes1.sapdevcenter.com/sap/opu/odata/sap/ZGWSAMPLE_SRV/ BusinessPartnerCollection?$select=BusinessPartnerID,CompanyName, LegalForm,City&$skip=12&$top=6

BusinessPartner ID	CompanyName	LegalForm	City
100000012	New Line Design	Ltd.	Manchester
100000013	HEPA Tec	GmbH	Bremen
100000014	Anav Ideon	Ltd.	Bismarck, North Dakota
100000015	Robert Brown Entertainment	Ltd.	Quebec

Table 2.7 Results for the Third Page Shown by the Mobile Application

BusinessPartner ID	CompanyName	LegalForm	City
100000016	Mexican Oil Trading Company	S.A.	Puebla
100000017	Meliva	AG	Köln

Table 2.7 Results for the Third Page Shown by the Mobile Application (Cont.)

The `$inlinecount` query option allows you to retrieve a count of the entities that match the filter criteria along with the response data itself. This is in contrast to `/$count` that only provides the count without the response data and which isn't a query option but a resource with its own URI.

The `$inlinecount` option has two values as shown in Table 2.8.

Option	Description
`$inlinecount=all-pages`	Provides a count of the number of entities identified by the URI
`$inlinecount=none`	Doesn't contain a count of the number of entities

Table 2.8 Options of Using $inlinecount

A consumer is typically able to count the entities retrieved itself. Nevertheless, `$inlinecount` has a significant value if it's combined with server- or client-side paging—as `$inlinecount` has to reflect the entire collection and not just the result of the current page (this is handled during service implementation). By this, a consumer application can display the total count of entities as well as (optionally) calculate the number of pages related to it (see Chapter 5 and Chapter 6 for more details about service implementation).

Refer to Figure 2.13, where you saw a mockup of an application that displays a list of business partners. It has a count (see ❶) of business partners (45) along with a page selector that initially shows the result of the first page, together with a total counter. In this example, the URI looks like the following:

https://sapes1.sapdevcenter.com/sap/opu/odata/sap/ZGWSAMPLE_SRV/
BusinessPartnerCollection?$select=BusinessPartnerID,CompanyName&
$inlinecount=allpages&$top=6

The SAP NetWeaver Gateway server "only" provides the first 6 entities as well as the total count of 45. The total number of pages is calculated by the consuming application.

The value for `$inlinecount` is sent by the server in the count tag `<m:count>48</m:count>` as shown in Figure 2.14.

```
<feed xmlns:d="http://schemas.microsoft.com/ado/2007/08/dataservices"
xmlns:m="http://schemas.microsoft.com/ado/2007/08/dataservices/metadata" xmlns="http://www.w3.org/2005/Atom"
xml:base="https://sapes1.sapdevcenter.com:443/sap/opu/odata/sap/ZGWSAMPLE_SRV/">
  <id>https://sapes1.sapdevcenter.com:443/sap/opu/odata/sap/ZGWSAMPLE_SRV/BusinessPartnerCollection</id>
  <title type="text">BusinessPartnerCollection</title>
  <updated>2013-08-03T19:14:46Z</updated>
- <author>
    <name/>
  </author>
  <link title="BusinessPartnerCollection" rel="self" href="BusinessPartnerCollection"/>
  <m:count>48</m:count>
- <entry>
    <id>https://sapes1.sapdevcenter.com:443/sap/opu/odata/sap/ZGWSAMPLE_SRV/BusinessPartnerCollection('0100000012')</id>
    <title type="text">BusinessPartnerCollection('0100000012')</title>
    <updated>2013-08-03T19:14:46Z</updated>
    <category scheme="http://schemas.microsoft.com/ado/2007/08/dataservices/scheme" term="ZGWSAMPLE_SRV.BusinessPartner"/>
    <link title="BusinessPartner" rel="edit" href="BusinessPartnerCollection('0100000012')"/>
  - <content type="application/xml">
    - <m:properties>
        <d:BusinessPartnerID>0100000012</d:BusinessPartnerID>
        <d:CompanyName>New Line Design</d:CompanyName>
        <d:LegalForm>Ltd.</d:LegalForm>
        <d:City>Manchester</d:City>
      </m:properties>
    </content>
  </entry>
+ <entry>...</entry>
+ <entry>...</entry>
```

Figure 2.14 Location of the Count Value in the HTTP Response to Using the $inlinecount Query Option

2.4.4 Counting ($count)

The `$count` request is used only to retrieve the number of entries in the collection. It doesn't provide anything else—just the number (simple scalar integer value).

2.4.5 Inlining ($expand)

$expand   The `$expand` query option comes into play whenever you want to read data from multiple entity types using just a single call to the SAP NetWeaver

Gateway server, instead of performing multiple calls sequentially or via a batch-request. A typical example for this, as shown in Figure 2.15, is the need to read a sales order header entity along with the collection of sales order line items associated to this order header (see ❶) in just a single call. Another example would be if you want to read a business partner alongside all sales order headers that belong to that business partner (see ❷), or, in an extreme scenario, if you want to retrieve all sales order headers together with all sales order line items of a business partner (see ❸).

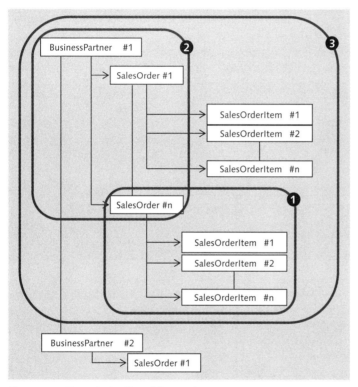

Figure 2.15 Example for Use of $expand

Because $expand happens along defined navigation routes, you have to define corresponding navigation properties in your model. In this example, we've defined a navigation property LineItems to navigate from the SalesOrderCollection entity set to the collection of related SalesOrderLineItem entities. The corresponding URI looks like the following:

Define navigation properties

https://sapes1.sapdevcenter.com/sap/opu/odata/sap/ZGWSAMPLE_SRV/
SalesOrderCollection('0500000011')?$expand=LineItems

The result set returned by the SAP NetWeaver Gateway server looks like that shown in Figure 2.16. The `SalesOrderLineItem` entities can be found in the section that is marked as `<m:inline>` ... `</m:inline>` (see ➋). In addition, the data for the sales order header data is retrieved (see ➊).

Figure 2.16 Response of an $expand Request

In a simplified way, the result can also be visualized as follows, where the entries that are returned inline are shown as indented list entries:

```
SalesOrder - Entity(SalesOrderID='123)
    SalesOrderItem - Entity(SalesOrderID= '123',Item='10')
```

```
SalesOrderItem - Entity(SalesOrderID= '123', Item='20')
SalesOrderItem - Entity(SalesOrderID= '123', Item='30')
SalesOrderItem - Entity(SalesOrderID= '123', Item='40')
```

Multiple expands are separated by commas. So if you also want to read the business partner information (navigation property `BusinessPartner` in a 1:1 relationship to the sales order), the URI is as follows:

http://<…>/sap/opu/odata/sap/ZGWSAMPLE_SRV/SalesOrderCollection ('0500000011')?$expand=BusinessPartner,LineItems

The result can be visualized as follows:

```
SalesOrder - Entity(SalesOrderID='123)
    BusinessPartner - Entity(PartnerID='0815')
    SalesOrderItem - Entity(SalesOrderID= '123', Item='10')
    SalesOrderItem - Entity(SalesOrderID= '123', Item='20')
    SalesOrderItem - Entity(SalesOrderID= '123', Item='30')
    SalesOrderItem - Entity(SalesOrderID= '123', Item='40')
    ...
```

The cardinality of the association assigned to the navigation property defines whether the result of the navigation is a feed/collection (in the above example, the feed of `SalesOrderItem` entities) or a single entry (in the above example, the `BusinessPartner` entity).

It's also possible to expand an expanded entity, which means that you can basically navigate along the entire relationship model, following the navigation properties. For example, you can navigate from a `Business-Partner` entity via the `SalesOrderCollection` to the `SalesOrderLine-ItemsCollection` as depicted earlier in Figure 2.15 (see ❸). To retrieve all sales orders of one business partner alongside all sales order line items, the consumer has to send the following URL to the server:

Nested expands

http://…/sap/opu/odata/sap/ZGWSAMPLE_SRV/BusinessPartnerCollection ('0100000000')?$expand=SalesOrders,SalesOrders/LineItems

The result can be visualized as followed:

```
BusinessPartner - Entity(BusinessPartnerID='123)
    SalesOrder  - Entity(SalesOrderID ='0815')
        SalesOrderItem - Entity(SalesOrderID= '0815',Item='10')
        SalesOrderItem - Entity(SalesOrderID= '0815',Item='20')
        SalesOrderItem - Entity(SalesOrderID= '0815',Item='30')
```

```
SalesOrder   - Entity(SalesOrderID='0816')
    SalesOrderItem - Entity(SalesOrderID= '0816',Item='10')
    SalesOrderItem - Entity(SalesOrderID= '0816',Item='20')
    SalesOrderItem - Entity(SalesOrderID= '0816',Item='30')
  ...
```

The $expand query option allows you to perform nested calls along the navigation properties of the entity data model. The SAP NetWeaver Gateway framework automatically executes the corresponding Get_Entityset/GET_ENTITY method of the related entity type. However, you need to consider the performance and the number of RFCs that have to be performed to retrieve the requested data.

GET_ENTITY_SET | In the first example, we performed an $expand of the sales order lines items for a single sales order. To retrieve the data of these two entity types (sales order header and sales order line item), the SAP NetWeaver Gateway framework performs the corresponding Get_Entityset/GET_ENTITY methods of the underlying service implementation independently of each other. In the given example, this may result in calling the identical RFC module twice, because the sales order header as well as the list of sales order line items is typically retrieved via a GET_DETAIL RFC function module (see Chapter 5 and Chapter 6 for more details about service implementation).

GET_EXPANDED_ENTITYSET | To avoid such inefficient calls, it's possible to implement a dedicated method in the service implementation that retrieves the result of an $expand statement with a single call (GET_EXPANDED_ENTITY/GET_EXPANDED_ENTITYSET). The implementation of that method is optional, but it should definitely be considered to avoid unnecessary backend calls and to improve performance.

2.4.6 Formatting ($format)

$format | The $format query option defines the format of an OData call as well as the expected response. The following two options are supported: XML and JSON. The default is XML. So if you don't add the $format query option, the SAP NetWeaver Gateway server automatically assumes $format=xml.

Let's look at the following example of a request that selects all business   XML
partners whose company name starts with an "S" and that only retrieves
the properties BusinessPartnerID and CompanyName from the Business-
PartnerCollection that we used earlier. Using the $format=xml query
option creates the result as shown in Figure 2.17, whereas the same
query result using the $format=json query option is depicted in Figure
2.18.

```xml
<feed xmlns:d="http://schemas.microsoft.com/ado/2007/08/dataservices"
xmlns:m="http://schemas.microsoft.com/ado/2007/08/dataservices/metadata" xmlns="http://www.w3.org/2005/Atom"
xml:base="https://sapes1.sapdevcenter.com:443/sap/opu/odata/sap/ZGWSAMPLE_SRV/">
  <id>https://sapes1.sapdevcenter.com:443/sap/opu/odata/sap/ZGWSAMPLE_SRV/BusinessPartnerCollection</id>
  <title type="text">BusinessPartnerCollection</title>
  <updated>2013-08-04T07:35:55Z</updated>
 - <author>
    <name/>
  </author>
  <link title="BusinessPartnerCollection" rel="self" href="BusinessPartnerCollection"/>
 - <entry>
    <id>https://sapes1.sapdevcenter.com:443/sap/opu/odata/sap/ZGWSAMPLE_SRV/BusinessPartnerCollection('0100000000')</id>
    <title type="text">BusinessPartnerCollection('0100000000')</title>
    <updated>2013-08-04T07:35:55Z</updated>
    <category scheme="http://schemas.microsoft.com/ado/2007/08/dataservices/scheme"
    term="ZGWSAMPLE_SRV.BusinessPartner"/>
    <link title="BusinessPartner" rel="edit" href="BusinessPartnerCollection('0100000000')"/>
   - <content type="application/xml">
     - <m:properties>
        <d:BusinessPartnerID>0100000000</d:BusinessPartnerID>
        <d:CompanyName>SAP</d:CompanyName>
      </m:properties>
    </content>
  </entry>
 + <entry>...</entry>
 + <entry>...</entry>
 + <entry>...</entry>
</feed>
```

Figure 2.17 Response Using the XML Format

```
{
 - d: {
  - results: [
    - {
      - __metadata: {
          uri: https://sapes1.sapdevcenter.com:443/sap/opu/odata/sap/ZGWSAMPLE_SRV/BusinessPartnerCollection
          ('0100000000'),
          type: "ZGWSAMPLE_SRV.BusinessPartner"
        },
        BusinessPartnerID: "0100000000",
        CompanyName: "SAP"
      },
    + {...},
    + {...},
    + {...}
    ]
  }
}
```

Figure 2.18 Response Using the JSON Format

The query result can also be retrieved using the `$format=JSON` query option.

As you can see, there is typically less overhead in a JSON-formatted request/response in contrast to an XML-formatted one. Therefore, it makes sense to use the JSON format whenever the consuming side is capable of handling this format.

Browser-Based Access

It's worth noting here how browsers handle the server responses in either XML or JSON. If you want to display the server responses in the JSON format, we recommend using either Firefox or Chrome, where you can install appropriate add-ons that perform a rendering in a user-friendly format.

If you're using Firefox, make sure that the JSONView add-on is installed. If it's not installed, choose TOOLS • ADDONS from the menu bar and search for the string JSONVIEW.

If you choose to retrieve the server response in XML format, which is the default format used by SAP NetWeaver Gateway, the SAP NetWeaver Gateway server returns XML with a MIME type of `application/atom+xml`. Most modern browsers interpret this as an Atom feed and format the results in the manner of a news feed. If the results are shown like a feed, details of the server response are suppressed that we want to explore here.

We recommend considering the query parameter `sap-ds-debug=true`, which is very helpful when testing your OData service with any browser. Adding this query parameter to the URL instructs the SAP NetWeaver Gateway hub to not only return plain XML or JSON, but to return a dynamically generated HTML page containing the result along with, for example, HTML navigation links.

2.5 OData in SAP Solutions

Because OData is extensible, you can enrich standard OData requests and responses with extra information. OData for SAP products is an OData extended by SAP to better fit business needs. It contains SAP-specific metadata that helps the developer to consume SAP business data, such as descriptions of fields that can be retrieved from the ABAP Data Dictionary.

The following are examples of OData for SAP applications:

▸ Human-readable, language-dependent labels for all properties (required for building UIs).

▸ Free-text search, within collections of similar entities, and across collections using OpenSearch.

▸ Semantic annotations, which are required for applications running on mobile devices to provide seamless integration with the contacts, calendar, and telephone functionalities. The client needs to know which OData properties contain a phone number, a part of a name or address, or something related to a calendar event.

Not all entities and entity sets will support the full spectrum of possible interactions defined by the uniform interface, so capability discovery helps clients avoid requests that the server can't fulfill. The metadata document tells whether an entity set is searchable, which properties may be used in filter expressions, and which properties of an entity will always be managed by the server.

As a result, the OData data format enhanced by SAP annotations makes SAP business information both human-readable and self-describing. The barrier for consuming SAP business data and functionality is lowered to where no specialized knowledge of an SAP system is required. Backend data is decoupled from the consumption in the frontend. A new group of developers with little to no SAP background can develop against SAP systems, needing minimal training. These developers are able to pick the technology of their choice to access SAP data and SAP functionality in a convenient way. In the end, this allows not only for the creation of new applications but also for the enrichment of already-existing applications with SAP data and functionality for a large number of target platforms and technologies.

SAP NetWeaver Gateway is the core of SAP's OData strategy. It provides OData access for multiple channels (Figure 2.19) and is regularly extended with additional OData features (Table 2.9).

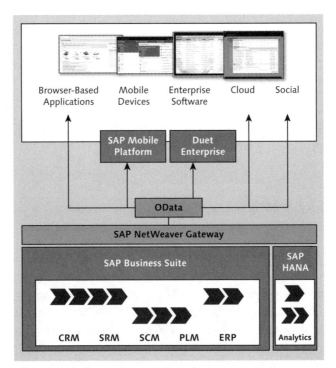

Figure 2.19 SAP NetWeaver Gateway Providing OData Access for Multiple Channels

OData Feature	Description	Availability in SAP NetWeaver Gateway 2.0
Atom	Atom is an XML-based document format that describes lists of related information known as feeds.	SP03
JSON	JSON is a lightweight data interchange format based on a subset of the JavaScript programming language standard.	SP03
OpenSearch description	The OpenSearch description document format can be used to describe a search engine so that it can be used by search client applications.	SP04

Table 2.9 Overview of Selected OData Features Supported by SAP NetWeaver Gateway

OData Feature	Description	Availability in SAP NetWeaver Gateway 2.0
HTTP status code	Defines HTTP status codes in exceptional cases via the service implementation.	SP05
CRUD	The HTTP `POST`, `GET`, `UPDATED`, and `DELETE` requests are performed on resources.	SP05
Read (media resources)	Reads the binary association of a media link entry. The media link entry can either point to an internal binary in a table, for example, or to an external link that must be set in the data provider.	SP03
CUD (media resources)	Create, update, and delete media resources are associated with a media link entry.	SP04
Batch handling	Batch requests allow the grouping of multiple operations into a single HTTP request payload.	SP04
Repeatable requests/idempotency	This is any kind of operation that can be repeated by providing a request ID. A repeated request is processed by the idempotency framework (fallback). This can be used to avoid multiple executions of a certain operation.	SP05
Deep insert	This is an operation to create an entity with deep data in an inlined format, for example, to create a parent/child relationship simultaneously.	SP03
Expand	A URI with an `$expand` system query option indicates that entries associated with the entry or collection of entries identified by the resource path section of the URI must be represented inline.	SP03

Table 2.9 Overview of Selected OData Features Supported by SAP NetWeaver Gateway (Cont.)

OData Feature	Description	Availability in SAP NetWeaver Gateway 2.0
Merge/patch	An update request sent via HTTP method `MERGE/PATCH` indicates that a subset of the entry's properties is sent to the server and should be merged with those fields that aren't present in the request.	SP05
Paging	The `$top` and `$skip` system query option identifies a subset of the entries in the collection of entries.	SP03
Filter	The `$filter` system query option identifies a subset of the entries in the collection of entries.	SP03
Order by	The `$orderby` system query option specifies an expression for determining what values are used to order the collection of entries.	SP03
Select (handled by OData client generically)	The `$links` option specifies that the response to the request contains the links between an entry and an associated entry or a collection of entries.	SP03
Skip token (server-driven paging)	The request response contains an `<atom:link rel="next">` element for partial representations of the collection of entries.	SP04
Multiorigin/multidestination (origin segment parameter)	A service may need to connect to multiple backend systems, and the backend calls are done in parallel.	SP05 (SAP-specific extension)

Table 2.9 Overview of Selected OData Features Supported by SAP NetWeaver Gateway (Cont.)

OData Feature	Description	Availability in SAP NetWeaver Gateway 2.0
XSRF token-based protection mechanism	The protection against XSRF attacks is ensured via a token-based exchange mechanism in the HTTP request/response header between the client and the server.	SP03 (SAP-specific extension)

Table 2.9 Overview of Selected OData Features Supported by SAP NetWeaver Gateway (Cont.)

Almost all OData provisioning and consumption at SAP is done using SAP NetWeaver Gateway, and a number of very diverse products and solutions base major or minor parts of their features and functionalities on OData via SAP NetWeaver Gateway (Figure 2.20). This includes both ABAP-based and non-ABAP solutions.

Both ABAP and non-ABAP solutions

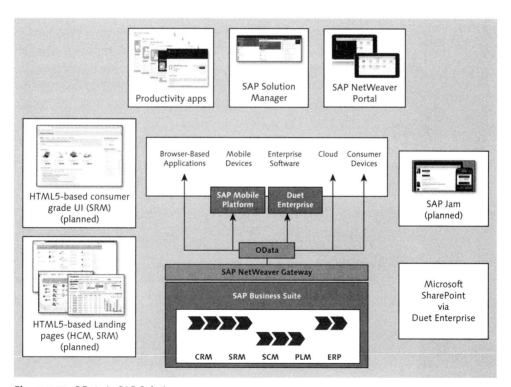

Figure 2.20 OData in SAP Solutions

In this section, we take a look at some of the diverse SAP solutions that benefit from OData.

2.5.1   Mobile Productivity Applications

Mobile has been very important for SAP for a while. SAP mobile applications can be downloaded using typical channels such as Android Market, Blackberry App World, iTunes, or Microsoft Marketplace. Applications target scenarios such as mobile HR support for managers (SAP ERP HCM Manager Insight), support for hospitals (SAP Electronic Medical Record), or access to customer financial profiles for sales reps (SAP Customer Financial Fact Sheet).

A significant amount of SAP's mobile applications use OData based on SAP NetWeaver Gateway for communicating with mobile devices, often in close collaboration with SAP Mobile Platform. The latter, for example, provides workflow notifications, allows for device-specific handling of push notifications, and provides a reverse proxy.

2.5.2   SAP Fiori

SAP Fiori is a collection of applications providing a simple, intuitive user experience across a number of selected SAP business transactions. These transactions have been selected by the frequency of usage and the business value for end users. SAP Fiori has a consistent design across all of the different supported transactions and, even more important, across all of the different interaction channels and platforms SAP Fiori targets—desktop, tablet, and mobile. So an SAP Fiori application is used the same way across devices and looks mostly the same, but with optimizations depending on the device that's being used to consume it.

SAPUI5/HTML5   SAP Fiori is based on SAP NetWeaver Gateway and OData for its SAP Business Suite connectivity. As a frontend technology, it relies on SAPUI5/HTML5. For a bit more information about SAP Fiori and SAPUI5, see Chapter 10.

2.5.3 SAP Jam

SAP Jam is an enterprise social network that combines the platform of
SuccessFactors Jam with features of SAP StreamWork. SAP Jam provides
the basis for social learning, onboarding, and other talent processes. It
improves these processes by allowing employees to more easily find the
content and experts to help them with their business needs. Furthermore, employees can discuss and learn from each other in communities.
Features such as simple video and screen capture, polling, activity feeds,
and public and private groups enable new approaches to doing business.
SAP Jam builds on the same profile and organization data available in
other SuccessFactors modules.

SuccessFactors

In a further step to open up to the outside world, SAP Jam allows for
OData provisioning and OData consumption:

▶ The OData-Jam API allows for easy OData provisioning. It offers easy
creation of social business applications using mashups between SAP
Jam and SAP NetWeaver Gateway.

▶ Business events and other business attributes can be consumed via
SAP NetWeaver Gateway and are then displayed in the SAP Jam feed.

2.5.4 SAP NetWeaver Portal

SAP NetWeaver Portal allows for the generation of basic UIs based on
OData. This is done using an Eclipse-based assistant that analyzes fields
and relations of an OData service and then supports the definition of a
basic application. The generated application is based on the *list detail
pattern*, which means that you can branch into details by starting from a
list of values.

In addition, it's possible to create iViews that display SAPUI5 applications in SAP NetWeaver Portal. These are based on the application integration iView template *com.sap.portal.appintegrator.sap*.

iViews

2.5.5 Duet Enterprise

Based on SAP's and Microsoft's jointly developed product, Duet Enterprise, the use of Microsoft SharePoint as a UI for SAP data has become

Microsoft
SharePoint

very straightforward and easy. Because Duet Enterprise is a product that has been jointly developed, a large number of processes that range across SAP and Microsoft system boundaries are supported. The relevant data is still stored in the SAP backend; however, Microsoft SharePoint can be used as the UI. The major advantage is the reduced training costs if users are used to working in a Microsoft SharePoint environment. Duet Enterprise uses OData and SAP NetWeaver Gateway as a basis.

2.5.6 SAP Solution Manager

SAP Solution Manager is one of the crucial components of an SAP environment. It offers support throughout the entire lifecycle of SAP solutions, from the business blueprint to the configuration to production processing. A one-stop shop approach with respect to tools, methods, and preconfigured contents is what makes it so unique. One of SAP Solution Manager's main goals is to allow for a timely reaction to problems. To achieve this, monitoring is essential. Using mobile applications either on Android or iOS, IT environments can now be monitored on the go. To allow for this mobile monitoring, SAP NetWeaver Gateway comes preinstalled with newer versions of SAP Solution Manager. The mobile application can either communicate directly using OData or, alternatively, if the SAP Mobile Platform is available, via the SAP Mobile Platform and then using OData to connect to SAP NetWeaver Gateway.

2.5.7 SAP HANA

SAP HANA is SAP's fastest selling product of all time. This in-memory data platform is deployable as an on-premise appliance or in the cloud. It's best suited for performing real-time analytics, and developing and deploying real-time applications. At the core of this real-time data platform is the SAP HANA database, which is fundamentally different from any other database engine in the market today.

SAP HANA allows for both real-time analytics and real-time applications. In respect to analytics, it supports operational reporting (real-time insights from transactional systems such as SAP ERP), data warehousing

(SAP NetWeaver BW on SAP HANA), and predictive and text analysis on big data. With respect to real-time applications, it's good for, for example, core process accelerators (transactional data is replicated in real time from SAP ERP into SAP HANA for immediate reporting, and then results can even be fed back into SAP ERP), planning and optimization applications (e.g., sales planning, cash forecasting), and sense and response applications that provide real-time insights in big data (e.g., smart meter applications).

All of this is possible due to SAP HANA's secret sauce: OLAP *and* OLTP. Other database management systems (DBMSs) on the market are typically either good at transactional workloads or analytical workloads, but not both. When transactional DBMS products are used for analytical workloads, they require you to separate your workloads into different databases (OLAP and OLTP). You have to extract data from your transactional system (SAP ERP), transform that data for reporting, and load it into a reporting database (SAP NetWeaver BW). The reporting database still requires significant effort in creating and maintaining tuning structures, such as aggregates and indexes, to provide even moderate performance. Due to its hybrid structure for processing transactional workloads and analytical workloads fully in-memory, SAP HANA combines the best of both worlds.

OLAP and OLTP

SAP HANA offers numerous possibilities for improving business processes, and the usage of OData enhances this potential. To allow for the most flexible consumption of information via OData, SAP HANA allows for two different models: the usage of SAP NetWeaver Gateway with SAP HANA integration, or usage of the native SAP HANA OData support via SAP HANA Extended Application Services (SAP HANA XS).

Integration of SAP NetWeaver Gateway with SAP HANA

Integration provides a basic integration framework for read-only scenarios based on the OData channel that expose SAP HANA information models as OData services. SAP HANA information models are used to create multiple views of transactional data and are the combination of attributes and measures. OData representations of SAP HANA information

SAP NetWeaver Gateway with SAP HANA

models can be used for analytical purposes. Following this implementation method, there are two main components as essential parts of the SAP HANA integration:

▶ The abstract SAP HANA database model provider extracts metadata out of the SAP HANA database repository and adapts it to the OData channel representation. Metadata retrieval implementation follows a kind of hybrid approach; there is a generic part as well as a specific implementation part. To name specific SAP HANA information models, developers need to reimplement the definition method of the ABAP code of the service implementation. (For more details on service implementation, see Chapter 5 and Chapter 6.)

▶ The generic SAP HANA database data provider delegates requests to the SAP HANA database. Only read scenarios are supported. Runtime data retrieval works generically without a special implementation of subclasses or configuration. Container structure and metadata data information about which data has to be retrieved will be received with the technical request context information.

With the help of the integration framework, the following information models can be exposed as OData services from the SAP HANA database:

▶ **Attribute views**
Attribute views are reusable dimensions or subject areas used for business analysis.

▶ **Analytic views**
Analytic views are multidimensional views or OLAP cubes. Using analytic views, you analyze values from a single fact table that is based on the related attributes from the data foundation and attribute views.

▶ **Calculation views**
Calculation views are used to create your own data foundation using database tables, attribute views, analytic views, and calculation views to address a complex business requirement.

The integration scenario is contained in the IW_HDB add-on, and, as of 7.40, it's part of the SAP_GWFND component, which is part of the standard.

SAP HANA XS Engine

SAP HANA Extended Application Services (SAP HANA XS) was introduced with SAP HANA SP5. The core concept of SAP HANA XS is to deeply embed a full-featured application server, web server, and development environment within the core parts of the SAP HANA database. This allows for outstanding performance and an access to SAP HANA core features. With SAP HANA XS, you can now build and deploy your application completely within SAP HANA, providing an opportunity for a lower cost of development and ownership. To facilitate creating applications, the SAP HANA Studio comes with all of the necessary tools.

The SAP HANA XS programming model allows for the ability to generate OData services from any existing SAP HANA table or view. The process is simple and straightforward. From within an SAP HANA project, create a service definition document (*xsodata*). Within this document, specify the name of the source table/view, an entity name, and optionally the entity key fields. XS OData services are great because they provide a large amount of functionality with minimal amounts of development effort. They currently come with a few limitations, however: only the OData service framework is read. On the other hand, they are quick. Upon activation, there is an executable service that is ready to test. The generated service supports standard OData parameters such as `$metadata` for introspection, `$filter`, `$orderby`, and so on. It also supports Atom/XML and JSON.

2.5.8 SAP-Certified Partner Solutions

One of the strengths of SAP NetWeaver Gateway is its openness, which is highly beneficial for SAP's large ecosystem. Many SAP partners have already developed SAP NetWeaver Gateway-based solutions or are in the process of doing so. For these solutions, SAP offers a certification. An overview of certified SAP NetWeaver Gateway-based partner solutions can be found on the SAP Partner Finder website (*www.sap.com/partners/directories/SearchSolution.epx*).

2.6   Summary

In this chapter, we've introduced you to OData, which is the underlying protocol that SAP NetWeaver Gateway enables. Although the chapter isn't meant to be a comprehensive discussion of the topic, you should now have a basic understanding of what it is and how it works. To close out our discussion, we'll leave you with some tips and tricks for working with OData.

Ten OData Dos and Don'ts

- *Do* think in REST terms.
- *Do* use the OData system query options $filter, $top, $skip, and $orderby.
- *Do* provide a usable set of filterable properties.
- *Do* make your properties concrete and readable.
- *Do* use the right data type for your properties.
- *Do* use media resources and media link entries instead of binary properties.
- *Do* follow links provided by the server; *don't* construct links in your client application.
- *Don't* invent your own custom query options.
- *Do* strive for high-quality services (e.g., in respect to usability and performance).
- *Don't* construct URIs in your client application; follow the links provided by the server.

This chapter explains the architectural concepts of SAP NetWeaver Gateway and provides a high-level look at its integration with other SAP interfaces. It lays the foundations for later chapters by introducing a certain part of the theoretical groundwork required for SAP NetWeaver Gateway development.

3   Architecture and Integration

SAP NetWeaver Gateway has a clear goal—to open up classic SAP systems to non-ABAP developers. Initially, the scope of SAP NetWeaver Gateway was limited to so-called "lightweight consumption" use cases. To achieve and facilitate these use cases, SAP NetWeaver Gateway provided a platform for provisioning and consumption of services and diverse tools for developing content to be consumed. Now, the definition of gateway principles and their implementation across SAP has broadened the usage of SAP NetWeaver Gateway by allowing for additional usage scenarios, such as analytical consumption.

Extended scope

On the following pages, you'll gain an understanding of the architectural concepts behind gateway principles, an overview of SAP NetWeaver Gateway's architecture, and information about what data sources SAP NetWeaver Gateway can use to integrate with your SAP systems.

3.1   Gateway Principles

At the beginning of enterprise software, systems had been designed as both monolithic and self-contained. With the evolution of enterprise software into a landscape of many systems for various purposes, the challenge of how to connect these systems into end-to-end processes and experiences became obvious. The multisystem landscape is a reality today and, in many cases, even desirable to separate different aspects of running businesses. However, the introduction of middle-tier layers in

Timeless software

enterprise landscapes for improved system connection also introduced high cost, complexity, proprietary solutions, and many silo-like approaches for exposing data to the middle tier and connecting systems to each other.

To ease the multisystem landscape complexity, SAP has created a set of principles for how enterprise software systems should be engineered: *timeless software principles*. Timeless software is a systematic and layered approach to how a system of record should be efficiently exposed and how it should interface with the overall system landscape, development tools, runtime engines, and the lifecycle of software.

Thereby, a differentiation was made between aspects that are local to a system and that adapt the behavior of a given system or platform (platform adaptation) and the needs of a given consumer and the necessary infrastructure to serve a specific consumer (consumer adaptation). This separation makes sense because in an ideal landscape, platform adaptation is coupled to a certain system of record and required once for every system. Consumer adaptation for a specific channel (e.g., mobile, portals, social, UIs, analytics) is required only once per landscape and not for every individual system.

SAP's gateway principles are a set of architectural concepts, methods, design patterns, and standards describing how an enterprise system should make its data and functions available for consumption. They aim to provide access to systems of record by multiple channels and for multiple consumers. Gateway principles are used as guidance for platform adaptation in systems of record and for enabling developers to build timeless applications on top of these platforms. Furthermore, they are applicable for different application domains (e.g., lightweight, analytical, or social consumption).

Elemental gateway principles include the following:

▶ **Openness**
Services can be consumed from any device and any platform, and can create any experience.

▶ **Timelessness**
Services work with almost any SAP Business Suite version.

▶ **Ease of consumption**
Application Programming Interfaces (APIs) are easy to consume, and no internal SAP knowledge is required for the consumption of services.

▶ **User focus**
User interaction scenarios are a main driver for the architecture.

▶ **Division of work**
Non-SAP developers can consume services without any ABAP skills; they can work on the client development almost fully independent of the SAP NetWeaver Gateway service development.

SAP NetWeaver Gateway in its current form is basically a result of the application of the gateway principles architectural concepts, design patterns, and standards for diverse application flavors.

3.2 Architecture

From a bird's eye view, SAP NetWeaver Gateway's architecture consists of three tiers: the SAP Business Suite tier, the SAP NetWeaver Gateway Server tier, and the consumer tier (Figure 3.1). Each tier serves a clearly defined purpose and bundles components needed to fulfill this purpose.

Three-tier architecture

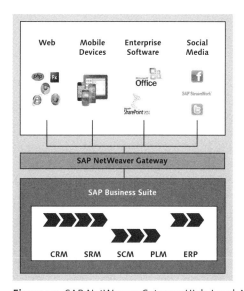

Figure 3.1 SAP NetWeaver Gateway High-Level Architecture

With this approach, lifecycles of the existing SAP Business Suite implementation and the client application environment are decoupled, and concerns are separated. As a result, the dependencies between systems are reduced to a minimum so that upgrades, updates, and deployments have no cross impact. The resulting outcome is a highly flexible landscape architecture that addresses a broad range of possible applications and scenarios.

Consumer tier

The consumer tier is where the actual consumption of SAP NetWeaver Gateway services takes place—with respect to consumption, this serves as the access point. Consumers are any UI-centric clients consuming OData protocol-compliant resources that are exposed by SAP NetWeaver Gateway. This exposure can either happen directly or indirectly, via additional infrastructure components (e.g., via SAP Mobile Platform). Typical consumers of SAP NetWeaver Gateway services include mobile devices, SAP/Microsoft Duet Enterprise, and SAPUI5/HTML5.

SAP NetWeaver Gateway tier

Not surprisingly, the SAP NetWeaver Gateway tier holds the major part of SAP NetWeaver Gateway functionalities and components—including the core components. It serves a number of purposes:

▶ It functions as the man in the middle between the backend and the consumer based on runtime components, metadata components, and the OData library.

▶ It provides tools for the development and creation of SAP NetWeaver Gateway services.

▶ It offers everything that is needed for operating an SAP NetWeaver Gateway landscape, such as logging, tracing, performance analysis tools, and globalization support.

SAP Business Suite tier

The SAP Business Suite tier is where business application data is located; it remains the system of record with to respect data. In addition, it holds the business logic of the SAP Business Suite, which means that for most applications, it holds by far the biggest part of the business logic. With respect to SAP NetWeaver Gateway-specific components, the SAP Business Suite tier basically consists of the add-on for business enablement and event provisioning: IW_BEP. As of SAP NetWeaver ABAP 7.40 SP02, the SAP Business Suite tier components are part of the software component SAP_GWFND and are included in SAP NetWeaver.

Concerning the technical implementation of this architecture, SAP NetWeaver Gateway consists of add-ons to the ABAP technology platform. These add-ons can be found on the SAP NetWeaver Gateway server tier and/or on the SAP Business Suite tier, depending on the specific deployment. Depending on the landscape setup and the usage scenario, this specific deployment can differ. As we briefly introduced in Chapter 1, there are basically two main deployment options: on a separate SAP NetWeaver Gateway system (hub deployment), and deployment embedded on the SAP Business Suite system (embedded deployment). In additional to these main options, a "mixed" deployment is possible. The specific landscape and usage scenario decides which deployment option to choose. (We'll go into more detail about this in Chapter 4.)

As we said, the major part of SAP NetWeaver Gateway lies in the middle tier. It's important to know, however, which SAP NetWeaver Gateway components can be found in the other tiers as well. Therefore, let's dig deeper and look more closely at the three tiers and their main components in detail, as shown in Figure 3.2. In Section 3.2.4, we'll also devote some time to explaining the add-on structure of SAP NetWeaver Gateway.

Detailed architecture

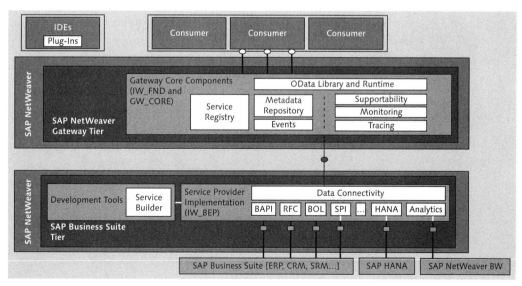

Figure 3.2 SAP NetWeaver Gateway Building Blocks

3.2.1   Consumer Tier

In the consumer tier, two kinds of components can be found—SAP NetWeaver Gateway consumers and integrated development environments (IDEs).

SAP NetWeaver Gateway Consumers

UI-centric clients   *SAP NetWeaver Gateway consumers* are components that consume SAP NetWeaver Gateway services. SAP NetWeaver Gateway is primarily designed to provide UI-centric clients (e.g., mobile, native, or web applications, such as SAPUI5/HTML5) access to business data. Clients can access SAP NetWeaver Gateway both directly and indirectly via additional infrastructure components. The SAP Mobile Platform is, for example, one of these additional infrastructure components for mobile scenarios. SAP/Microsoft Duet Enterprise is another one.

SAP NetWeaver Gateway consumers access REST API resources exposed by SAP NetWeaver Gateway via HTTP(S) using the OData protocol. In other words, there is actually not that much to know about SAP NetWeaver Gateway consumers—as long as a client technology can consume HTTP(S), it can consume SAP NetWeaver Gateway services. Also, if it can construct and parse XML, JSON, or ATOM, it can then process the data received. In fact, SAP doesn't make any recommendations or impose any restrictions on which client technology or even development language should be used for the consumption of an SAP NetWeaver Gateway service. Just make sure your client technology of choice has facilities for HTTP(S) communication and can construct and parse an XML or JSON document. Beyond that, SAP NetWeaver Gateway offers full freedom with respect to the client technology.

Integrated Development Environments

IDEs are used to develop SAP NetWeaver Gateway consumers. These development environments are standard and well-known environments such as Eclipse or Microsoft Visual Studio. Depending on the environment, SAP provides SAP NetWeaver Gateway-specific features and improvements that allow you to easily and quickly create applications that consume SAP NetWeaver Gateway services.

3.2.2   SAP NetWeaver Gateway Tier

The SAP NetWeaver Gateway tier consists of the core components (as we saw in Figure 3.2). Overall, this tier is the heart of SAP NetWeaver Gateway.

The center of the heart is the core components (Figure 3.3). This encompasses several central components: the runtime component, the OData library, and the metadata component. The *runtime* component contains an OData-specific runtime that efficiently processes OData requests and the functionality required to expose OData services. The OData library contains SAP-specific metadata that helps to consume SAP business data, such as descriptions of fields that can be retrieved from the ABAP Data Dictionary. The *metadata component* manages metadata within the SAP NetWeaver Gateway server. The SAP NetWeaver Gateway metadata primarily describes OData models that are exposed as OData service documents and OData service metadata documents. In particular, the metadata component exposes the standardized description of OData services by assembling OData service documents and service metadata documents. The data is then cached in the metadata cache.

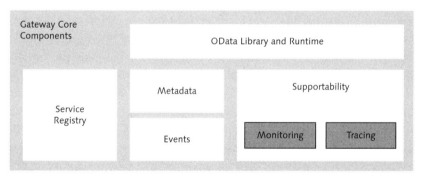

Figure 3.3 SAP NetWeaver Gateway Core Components

In addition to the central components, there are a number of other components that fall into the category of core components. The *service registry* is the data store that stores the linkage between an OData service and the actual implementation of this service, be it in the SAP Business Suite system or locally in SAP NetWeaver Gateway. Runtime services around *supportability, tracing, and monitoring* ensure a secure connection between consumers and SAP systems as well as the ability to monitor and trace messages from SAP NetWeaver Gateway components to the SAP Business Suite and back. Finally, *events* are supported to enable push scenarios (e.g., workflow scenarios where a component listens to business events in SAP systems and delivers a set of data descriptions of that event that can then be delivered to the consumer).

Generic Channel

In the initial releases of SAP NetWeaver Gateway, all development was done based on the *generic channel*. This channel was built on top of a generic framework that supported various exposure models. However, the OData channel was introduced with SAP NetWeaver Gateway 2.0 SP03, and is tailored and optimized to fit the OData protocol specifications. Today, the OData channel is the preferred and strongly recommended option; the generic channel shouldn't be used anymore. Therefore, this book solely focuses on the OData channel where development usually takes place in the SAP Business Suite tier. (We explain the OData channel in much more detail in Chapter 5.)

3.2.3   SAP Business Suite Tier

Business logic The SAP Business Suite tier, as you might expect, holds the data and business logic of SAP Business Suite. It consists of development tools and the service provider implementation. These are based on the add-on for SAP Business Suite enablement and event provisioning—IW_BEP— and additional add-ons such as IW_SPI or IW_GIL that have been built on top of IW_BEP to facilitate SAP Business Suite integration. IW_BEP is also needed for scenarios in which business events from the SAP Business Suite are being pushed to the SAP NetWeaver Gateway system (see Section A.2 of Appendix A), as well as for scenarios that are based on the OData channel.

Development Tools

Service Builder A set of design-time tools located in the SAP NetWeaver Gateway tier support the development of SAP NetWeaver Gateway services (Figure 3.4). They are very important because without them there would not be a lot to consume—at least not a lot of things that are suited for specific usage scenarios. (Most of the time, services are adjusted for a specific usage, if not generated or developed from scratch to perfectly fit the usage.) The SAP NetWeaver Gateway *Service Builder* (Transaction SEGW) is the main tool for service creation, and provides developers with tools to facilitate this throughout the entire development lifecycle of a service. The Service Builder provides an OData-compliant modeling environment for the creation and maintenance of SAP NetWeaver Gateway services without the need for programming. All development artifacts developers need to create a service are visualized, and wizards enable the creation of aggregated objects based on RFCs, Business Object Repository (BOR), and BAPIs. (For more details about the Service Builder, see Chapter 5.)

Figure 3.4 Tools for Service Development

Service Provider Implementation

The service provider implementation (Figure 3.5) provides connectivity to SAP Business Suite systems and can connect to a variety of SAP interfaces. This includes BAPIs and RFCs as well as SAP NetWeaver BW, Service Provider Interface (SPI), or SAP HANA. The service provider implementation is called by the runtime component or metadata component to access services from SAP Business Suite.

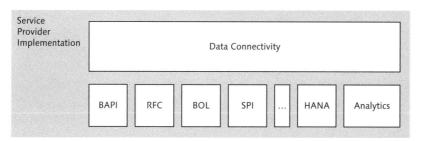

Figure 3.5 Service Provider Implementation

3.2.4   Add-On Structure

Add-ons   As we explained, SAP NetWeaver Gateway essentially consists of a set of add-ons to the ABAP technology platform. Having looked at the architecture and main components of SAP NetWeaver Gateway, it's now time to have a quick look at its add-on structure.

Mandatory vs. optional   The first thing to know is that there are mandatory and optional add-ons. The add-ons that are always required include, for example, the framework add-ons. An example for an optional add-on is the SPI add-on.

Cut and deployment   Second, it's important to understand that the add-ons are cut so that they combine several different components to allow for an easier deployment. On the other hand, the specific cut of the add-ons takes into account where the deployment happens (SAP NetWeaver Gateway or SAP Business Suite tier) and follows some logical grouping as well.

This results in two SAP NetWeaver Gateway tier add-ons (IW_FND and GW_CORE) and five SAP Business Suite tier add-ons (IW_BEP, IW_HDB, IW_PGW, IW_GIL, and IW_SPI). Furthermore, there are a few older add-ons that aren't recommended anymore (IW_CBS, IW_CNT, and IW_SCS) (Figure 3.6). Let's have a closer look at what these add-ons contain in respect to features and functionality (we're skipping the not recommended ones here).

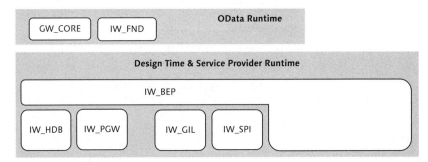

Figure 3.6 Functional View of Gateway Components

Here's what you should know about the framework components:

▶ GW_CORE contains the functionality required for the OData protocol.

▶ IW_FND, in which FND stands for foundation, holds the framework of the SAP NetWeaver Gateway server. This includes the runtime components, the metadata component, and the shared services such as monitoring, supportability, and security.

Here's what you should know about the SAP Business Suite enablement components:

▶ IW_BEP (Business Enablement Provisioning, BEP) holds the SAP Business Suite enablement and event provisioning.

▶ IW_HDB (SAP HANA) provides a business content adapter for SAP NetWeaver Gateway with SAP HANA that enables OData exposure of SAP HANA views via the ADBC (ABAP Database Connectivity) protocol.

▶ IW_PGW (process gateway) enables exposure for SAP NetWeaver Business Process Management (BPM) and process observer task exposure for SAP NetWeaver BPM and SAP Business Workflow (also called Unified Inbox).

▶ IW_GIL (GenIL) provides a generic OData adapter for content based on the Generic Interaction Layer (GenIL).

▶ IW_SPI (Service Provider Interface) provides a generic OData adapter for content based on the Service Provider Infrastructure (SPI).

Finally, you should know that what has been described is only half the story. There is another dimension to the add-on structure and that is the version of the underlying SAP NetWeaver. The preceding structure holds true for versions below SAP NetWeaver 7.40—but starting from SAP NetWeaver 7.40 SP02, there have been some changes to optimize the deployment (Figure 3.7).

Version effects

This optimization results primarily in two new components named IW_FNDGC and SAP_GWFND, which combine the four old add-ons IW_HDB, IW_BEP, IW_FND, and GW_CORE.

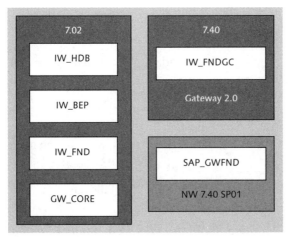

Figure 3.7 New Add-On Structure in SAP NetWeaver 7.40

3.3 Integration with Other SAP Interfaces

Reuse of data sources

As stated in the introduction to this chapter, SAP NetWeaver Gateway has the clear goal to open up classic SAP systems to non-ABAP developers. These classic SAP systems already have a number of ways of exposing data via different channels to the outside world. So the logical way to allow for a broad set of services to be available for easy reuse is to take what is already there as a basis. SAP NetWeaver Gateway therefore provides tools for easy generation of OData services from existing data sources in the SAP Business Suite system by reusing these generic data access options. As a result, developers can use data sources such as RFC/ BOR, SAP NetWeaver BW InfoCubes, MDX, Easy Query, and content built on the GenIL framework and the SPI framework for the creation of SAP NetWeaver Gateway services.

SAP standard concepts vs. add-ons

Technology-wise, in some cases, standard SAP concepts (e.g., RFCs or BOR) are used. In other cases, enabling the different generic data access options by SAP NetWeaver Gateway takes place with add-ons (e.g., SPI). These add-ons are either local add-ons that are deployed on the respective SAP Business Suite system (e.g., IW_GIL) or remote enabled add-ons (e.g., IW_SPI). Let's take a look at each of these options in a little more detail.

3.3.1 Remote Function Call (RFC)

A remote function call (RFC) is an SAP standard concept to call a function module running in a system different from the caller's system. The remote function can also be called from within the same system (as a remote call). The ability to call remote functions is provided by the RFC interface system. RFC allows for remote calls between two SAP systems or between an SAP system and a non-SAP system. RFCs consist of two kinds of interfaces, one for calling ABAP programs and one for calling non-ABAP programs. Because SAP NetWeaver Gateway targets opening up an ABAP system, the relevant kind of interfaces for this context are ABAP interfaces.

If an RFC function module is available, an SAP NetWeaver Gateway service can easily be exposed using the SAP NetWeaver Gateway development tools.

3.3.2 Business Object Repository (BOR)

SAP business objects and their BAPIs are managed within the Business Object Repository (BOR) in a structure based on the hierarchy of the SAP Business Suite business application areas. Every single SAP business object type and its methods are identified and described in the BOR. This description includes the SAP business object types, their SAP interface types, and their components, such as methods, attributes, and events. Business Application Programming Interfaces (BAPIs) are defined as the methods of SAP business object types. To the outside, the SAP business object reveals only its interface.

BAPIs

The BOR contains all SAP business object types, which makes it a perfect basis for generating SAP NetWeaver Gateway services. These can be easily built using the SAP NetWeaver Gateway development tools.

3.3.3 Service Provider Infrastructure (SPI)

The Service Provider Infrastructure (SPI) is an application- and UI-independent layer for business data exposure that is used across the entire SAP Business Suite. Examples include bill of material (BOM) in SAP Product Lifecycle Management (PLM), purchase requisition in Materials

Management (MM), and sustainability enhancements for vendors in Financial Accounting (FI).

SPI's main goal is to decouple the UI from the SAP Business Suite completely. It has no dependency on Web Dynpro or any other UI technology. Instead, it works as the backbone for different feeder technologies, such as Adobe Forms, and also offers a Floorplan Manager (FPM) integration.

Once again, this broad usage across the SAP Business Suite makes SPI a great source for SAP NetWeaver Gateway OData services. An SAP NetWeaver Gateway OData service can be easily created from an SPI object using the Service Builder.

3.3.4   SAP NetWeaver Business Warehouse (BW) InfoCubes

SAP NetWeaver BW, which is used for business intelligence, business planning, analytical services, and data warehousing, is an excellent source of high-quality analytical data.

Relational tables   InfoCubes are the central objects in SAP NetWeaver BW. An InfoCube is a set of relational tables arranged according to the star schema—a large fact table is surrounded by several dimension tables.

3.3.5   Multidimensional Expressions (MDX)

Query against an
OLAP database   Multidimensional expressions (MDX) is a language for querying and manipulating multidimensional data against an Online Analytical Processing (OLAP) database. MDX has been strongly moved forward by Microsoft and has become an accepted industry standard supported by a number of vendors, including SAP for SAP NetWeaver BW.

SAP NetWeaver Gateway provides an easy way of exposing SAP NetWeaver BW functionalities by using MDX. This exposure is done using the SAP NetWeaver Gateway Analytics Service Generator, which is part of the Service Builder. As the name clearly indicates, this is a generation-based process that doesn't require any coding.

3.3.6   Easy Query

Another way of exposing data from SAP NetWeaver BW is through Easy Query. Easy Query is a lot less complex than MDX and has been designed for simplicity and ease of consumption. Actually, all you have to do is to set a flag in the BEX Query Designer on the query level. The rest is done by the SAP NetWeaver BW system. Based on queries flagged as Easy Query and using SAP NetWeaver Gateway for access, it's possible to expose these as OData services.

3.3.7   Generic Interaction Layer (GenIL)

GenIL is a unifying interface between a client and integrated applications. A client (UI) can use the GenIL to access all APIs of the linked applications without recognizing the API details or the underlying data structures. This means the client doesn't have to be programmed for interaction with each individual application. Instead, it only needs to be programmed for the GenIL application.

APIs

GenIL as part of the Business Object Layer (BOL) is frequently used for the SAP Customer Relationship Management (SAP CRM) Web Client UI, but also in other SAP Business Suite applications such as SAP ERP Financials and SAP ERP Human Capital Management (SAP ERP HCM).

SAP NetWeaver Gateway allows for the generation of OData services that leverage GenIL. You're therefore able to leverage GenIL objects delivered by SAP and also custom build GenIL objects that have been built in these for OData service generation. The nodes, relations, and queries in the GenIL model are transformed to the corresponding entities in an OData model.

3.3.8   SAP HANA

SAP HANA is a platform for real-time analytics and applications. It enables organizations to analyze business operations based on large volumes and variety of detailed data in real time. In-memory computing, which enables analysis of very large, nonaggregated data in local memory, is the core technology underlying the SAP HANA platform. The advantages of light-speed data access and analysis can be easily leveraged with SAP NetWeaver Gateway and SAP HANA. A basic integration framework for read-only scenarios to expose SAP HANA information models as OData services allows for this. OData representations of SAP HANA information models can be used for analytical purposes.

Technically, this integration of SAP HANA and SAP NetWeaver Gateway is based on the OData channel approach, and two main components are the essential parts of this integration:

▶ The abstract SAP HANA model provider extracts metadata out of the SAP HANA DB repository and adapts it to the OData channel representation.

▶ The generic SAP HANA data provider delegates requests to the SAP HANA DB. In this case, only read scenarios are supported.

Attribute, analytic, and calculation views

With the help of the integration framework, three types of information models can be exposed as an OData service from the SAP HANA DB: attribute views, analytic views, and calculation views. (For more on the OData channel, see Chapter 5.)

3.3.9 SAP NetWeaver Business Process Management (BPM)

SAP NetWeaver BPM allows for controlling and automating business processes. It looks at a business from a process perspective rather than an organizational chart perspective and allows for modeling processes end to end. This is in fact extremely beneficial for both analyzing and modeling business processes. SAP NetWeaver BPM supports the entire business process lifecycle—from planning, implementation, and monitoring, right up to optimization.

3.3.10 SAP Business Workflow

SAP Business Workflow enables the design and execution of business processes within SAP application systems: Workflow processes are delivered as content in the SAP Business Suite. It is possible to enhance these SAP-provided workflows and create custom versions.

To allow SAP Business Workflow users to handle workflow items on any device or platform, SAP NetWeaver Gateway can expose SAP Business

Workflow tasks as OData RESTful services. This allows for a number of new business scenarios, such as workflow inboxes on mobile devices.

3.4 Summary

SAP NetWeaver Gateway's three-tier architecture follows gateway principles and timeless software principles and provides all of the flexibility needed for a wide range of possible use cases—from mobile scenarios to desktop applications to the Internet. At the same time, it offers all of the stability and reliability needed for business-critical use cases. Its main tier is the SAP NetWeaver Gateway tier, where most features and tools can be found. Still, parts of SAP NetWeaver Gateway may reside on the SAP Business Suite tier as well.

SAP NetWeaver Gateway comes with a set of tools that allow for the easy creation of SAP NetWeaver Gateway OData services using content and services already available via other SAP interfaces. This includes quite a number of SAP standard interfaces such as RFC, BOR, SPI, or GenIL.

In the next chapter, we'll round out Part I of the book with a discussion of SAP NetWeaver Gateway deployment, installation, and configuration.

This chapter discusses the methods of deploying SAP NetWeaver Gateway, including how to best install SAP NetWeaver Gateway, the necessary configuration steps for the chosen deployment method, and when to use which method.

4   Deployment Options, Installation, and Configuration

In this chapter, you'll learn the specifics about the different deployment options for SAP NetWeaver Gateway, including the advantages each method provides. We then look at preparations needed for a typical SAP NetWeaver installation and configuration process, followed by walking through a minimal installation and configuration in what we call a Quick Start Guide. Because this Quick Start Guide just addresses the absolute basics needed to have SAP NetWeaver Gateway up and running, we then present an overview of a standard installation and configuration process and look at selected steps in detail. The chapter closes by discussing the SAP NetWeaver Gateway best practices that are relevant during installation and configuration.

4.1   Introduction to SAP NetWeaver Gateway Deployment

There are basically two ways to look at the SAP NetWeaver Gateway deployment options: from the perspective of SAP NetWeaver Gateway, and from an architectural perspective. Both perspectives need to be taken into account to see the full picture. Because the deployment option chosen can have a major impact on performance, we highly

Deployment options

recommend selecting your option wisely, based on your system landscape and your intended use case.

In SAP NetWeaver Gateway 2.0, there are major differences with respect to deployment, depending on the underlying SAP NetWeaver version. With SAP NetWeaver 7.40, the add-on structure has been streamlined and further optimized for the OData channel, as compared to prior SAP NetWeaver versions.

Prior to SAP NetWeaver 7.40

Basic SAP NetWeaver Gateway functionalities, if running on releases prior to 7.40, are contained in different add-ons that have to be deployed separately. The SAP NetWeaver Gateway server or hub functionalities require that the add-ons GW_CORE and IW_FND be deployed on the server. IW_BEP has to be deployed on the SAP Business Suite systems for backend enablement (see Table 4.1).

	Core Components	Backend Enablement
7.31 and earlier	GW_CORE IW_FND	IW_BEP
As of 7.40	SAP_GWFND	SAP_GWFND

Table 4.1 SAP NetWeaver Version and Required SAP NetWeaver Gateway Add-Ons

From SAP NetWeaver 7.40

As of SAP NetWeaver 7.40 and higher, the software component SAP_GWFND is installed as part of the SAP NetWeaver 7.40 standard and includes the functional scope of IW_BEP, GW_CORE, IW_FND, and IW_HDB.

Table 4.2 shows the software components and optional add-ons of SAP NetWeaver Gateway with respect to SAP NetWeaver 7.40.

Name	Type	Version	Notes
SAP_ GWFND	ABAP	740	Installed as standard in systems based on SAP NetWeaver 7.40 and contains the following: ▶ Runtime components ▶ Metadata component ▶ Shared services, for example, monitoring ▶ OData libraries ▶ Business enablement provisioning ▶ Business content adapter for SAP NetWeaver Gateway with SAP HANA to enable exposure of SAP HANA views
IW_ FNDGC	ABAP	100	Optional. Only to be installed if generic channel services (outdated and not recommended) are still used.

Table 4.2 Software Components and Optional Add-Ons for SAP NetWeaver Gateway in SAP NetWeaver 7.40

From an architectural perspective, the big question is whether to go for a hub deployment or for an embedded deployment. More specifically:

Hub architecture vs. embedded deployment

▶ **Embedded deployment**
SAP NetWeaver Gateway core components IW_FND and GW_CORE are deployed in the SAP Business Suite system (or, alternatively, the SAP Business Suite system is based on release 7.40, where the software component SAP_GWFND is part of the standard).

▶ **Hub deployment**
SAP NetWeaver Gateway core components IW_FND and GW_CORE are deployed in an SAP NetWeaver Gateway hub system (or, alternatively, a 7.40 system is used as the hub system where the software component SAP_GWFND is part of the standard).

The hub deployment can be further split up into two suboptions, which actually leaves three deployment options. Each of these options has advantages and disadvantages. In this section, we'll discuss all three, compare them, and also discuss the scenario where you might use a mixed deployment that consists of both options.

4.1.1 Hub Deployment with Development in the SAP Business Suite System

In the case of hub deployment with development in the SAP Business Suite system (Figure 4.1), the SAP NetWeaver Gateway server functionalities are only used on a single dedicated server—the hub system. The SAP NetWeaver Gateway service is thus deployed on the SAP Business Suite systems (where either IW_BEP is deployed for systems prior to SAP NetWeaver 7.40, or the software component SAP_GWFND is deployed for SAP NetWeaver 7.40) and is then registered on the SAP NetWeaver Gateway server.

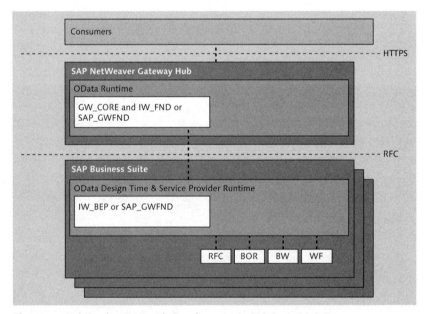

Figure 4.1 Hub Deployment with Development in SAP Business Suite

Deployment use cases

The following are the main use cases for this kind of deployment:

- Production scenarios with a medium-to-high load (e.g., used for the mobile applications delivered by the SAP Business Suite)
- Scenarios where development takes place in the SAP Business Suite system
- Scenarios where a developer needs to leverage all native interfaces and Data Dictionary (DDIC) structures in the SAP Business Suite systems

The hub deployment with development in the SAP Business Suite offers the following advantages:

▶ Support for routing and composition of multiple systems.

▶ Single point of access to multiple SAP Business Suite systems.

▶ More flexibility. Hub systems can be based on a newer release (SAP NetWeaver 7.31 or SAP NetWeaver 7.40) than any of the connected SAP Business Suite systems that supports additional authentication options (Kerberos, SAML browser protocol) and can be updated more frequently without too much overhead (service windows, regression tests).

The only disadvantage to this method is that an additional server is needed for SAP NetWeaver Gateway.

There are a few things to consider for the different SAP NetWeaver releases when deciding to go for this SAP NetWeaver Gateway deployment style. For SAP NetWeaver 7.0, 7.01, 7.02, 7.03, and 7.31, you should consider the following:

▶ The lifecycle of SAP NetWeaver Gateway content is dictated by the frequency of updates in the SAP Business Suite system.

▶ To enable communication between the SAP NetWeaver Gateway system and the SAP Business Suite system, you must install IW_BEP in the backend system.

For SAP NetWeaver 7.40, you should consider the following:

▶ The component SAP_GWFND is already installed as part of the standard SAP NetWeaver delivery.

▶ The lifecycle of SAP NetWeaver Gateway content is dictated by the frequency of updates in the SAP Business Suite system.

4.1.2 Hub Deployment with Development on the Hub

For hub deployment with development on the hub (Figure 4.2), the SAP NetWeaver Gateway server functionalities are only used on a dedicated server, the hub system. In contrast to the first option (hub deployment with development in the SAP Business Suite systems), this is where service deployment takes place. This option is used if either no development has to be performed on the SAP Business Suite systems or you cannot deploy the add-on IW_BEP in the SAP Business Suite (for releases prior to 7.40). In this specific case, the developer is limited to using the interfaces that are accessible via RFC in the SAP Business Suite systems.

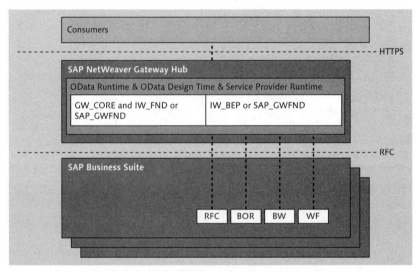

Figure 4.2 Hub Deployment with Development on the Hub

Example

In validated environments (e.g., the pharmaceutical industry), it's a very time-consuming process to change anything in the validated SAP Business Suite systems. Development for these systems is even more restricted. In these scenarios, deployment with development on the hub can be extremely beneficial for using new technologies without disrupting ongoing business-critical processes.

The hub can be located either behind or in front of the firewall. In addition, you can install the optional components for hub deployment in your SAP NetWeaver Gateway system.

Deployment use cases   The following are the main use cases for a hub deployment with development on the hub:

- Scenarios where no deployment of add-ons in the SAP Business Suite system is allowed or wanted.

- Scenarios where SAP NetWeaver Gateway add-ons can't be installed in the SAP Business Suite system for security, stability, or incompatibility (due to system release) reasons. In this case, this deployment option is mandatory.

- Proof of concept (POC) with SAP NetWeaver Gateway (no changes to existing infrastructure required).

- Scenarios where there are multiple SAP Business Suite systems.

- Scenarios where the SAP NetWeaver Gateway server is deployed in a demilitarized zone (DMZ).

The following are the advantages of hub deployment with development on the hub:

Advantages

- SAP NetWeaver Gateway capabilities need to be deployed only once within the landscape, which means there is no need to install (and upgrade) SAP NetWeaver Gateway add-ons in the SAP Business Suite system.

- Content can be deployed without touching the SAP Business Suite system, which means services developed by partners don't need any deployment on the SAP Business Suite systems.

- Routing and composition of multiple systems is supported.

- The lifecycle of consumer applications is decoupled from the SAP Business Suite system.

- Routing and connectivity with SAP Business Suite systems are managed centrally.

- Better security is provided because a request is validated at the dedicated box, and consequently potential attacks on the SAP NetWeaver Gateway system won't automatically affect the SAP Business Suite system.

- To enable external access and fulfill security requirements, you can locate the SAP NetWeaver Gateway system in a DMZ.

- The innovation speed of SAP NetWeaver Gateway and the connected SAP Business Suite systems are independent of each other.

▸ The lifecycle of SAP NetWeaver Gateway content is loosely coupled to the lifecycle of the SAP Business Suite system.

Disadvantages The following are the disadvantages of hub deployment with development on the hub:

▸ An additional server is needed for SAP NetWeaver Gateway.

▸ Access is limited to remote-enabled interfaces (RFC function modules, BAPIs, SAP NetWeaver BW Easy Queries, Service Provider Interface [SPI] objects).

▸ Remote-enabled interfaces might not be optimal (e.g., might not offer appropriate filter options).

▸ GenIL objects can't be accessed remotely.

▸ No direct local access to metadata (DDIC) and business data is provided, which means reuse of data is limited to remote access.

▸ OData services delivered by SAP as part of mobile applications or as part of SAP Fiori applications require the deployment of IW_BEP for releases prior to 7.40 on the SAP Business Suite system.

Release considerations There are a few things to consider for the different SAP NetWeaver releases when deciding to go for this SAP NetWeaver Gateway deployment style:

▸ For SAP NetWeaver releases 7.00, 7.01, 7.02, 7.03, and 7.31, you can install the component IW_BEP in each SAP Business Suite system. For SAP NetWeaver release 7.40 and higher, the core component SAP_GWFND is installed as standard and includes the functional scope of IW_BEP.

▸ There will be redundant deployment of metadata or ABAP Data Dictionary structures.

4.1.3 Embedded Deployment

For embedded deployment, the core components for SAP NetWeaver Gateway and any optional components are deployed together in the SAP Business Suite system (see Figure 4.3). For this deployment option, no additional SAP NetWeaver Gateway server is needed—only an SAP

Business Suite system. Development of SAP NetWeaver Gateway services takes place in the SAP Business Suite system.

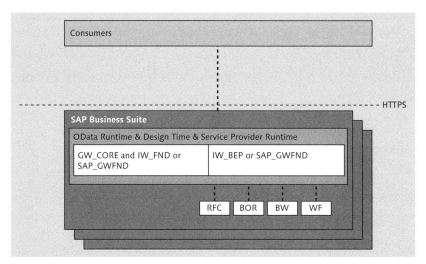

Figure 4.3 Embedded Deployment

The main use cases for an embedded deployment are:

Deployment use cases

▶ For POCs or production environments with a low load.

▶ Scenarios where developers need to leverage all native interfaces of the SAP Business Suite.

The embedded deployment method provides the following advantages:

Advantages

▶ Less runtime overhead, because you save on one remote call.

▶ Direct local access to metadata and business data.

▶ No content merge for different applications required.

▶ No additional, separate SAP NetWeaver Gateway system required, resulting in lower total cost of ownership (TCO) because there is one less system to maintain.

▶ Easy reuse of content in the SAP Business Suite system (e.g., you can reuse structures from the SAP Business Suite system and access local business logic).

The method has the following disadvantages:

▶ If multiple SAP Business Suite systems are used, SAP NetWeaver Gateway has to be configured on every single system.

▶ Routing and composition can't be used.

▶ The upgrade of add-ons in an SAP Business Suite system in larger companies is usually only possible once or twice a year (maintenance windows).

▶ The innovation speed of SAP NetWeaver Gateway and the SAP Business Suite system need to be synchronized.

▶ Devices need to be integrated with the SAP Business Suite system on a point-to-point basis.

▶ The lifecycle of SAP NetWeaver Gateway content is dictated by the frequency of updates in the SAP Business Suite system.

▶ Cross-system composition isn't advisable.

▶ A very high number of SAP NetWeaver Gateway service calls can have a performance effect and slow down the SAP Business Suite system. As a result, in a production system with a high number of service calls, this setup isn't advisable.

There is also one release consideration. As of SAP NetWeaver 7.40, the SAP_GWFND component is already installed as part of the standard SAP NetWeaver delivery. Due to that, embedded deployment is possible without any additional effort on every SAP Business Suite system running on top of SAP NetWeaver 7.40.

4.1.4 Comparison of Deployment Options

As you've seen so far, all three possible deployment options for SAP NetWeaver Gateway have advantages and disadvantages. To help you decide which option to use in your specific scenario, Table 4.3 summarizes and compares the major decision points.

	Embedded Deployment	Hub Deployment: Development on the Hub	Hub Deployment: Development on the SAP Business Suite System
Effort for Installation and Configuration	No additional server is required, and all activities take place in the SAP Business Suite system.	An additional server is required that needs to be ordered and set up. Typically, a trust relationship is set up between the hub and SAP Business Suite.	An additional server is required that needs to be ordered and set up. Typically, a trust relationship is set up between the hub and SAP Business Suite.
Performance	Puts additional load on the SAP Business Suite system; on the other hand, one remote call is saved.	SAP NetWeaver Gateway server takes the additional load.	SAP NetWeaver Gateway server takes the additional load.
Costs	No additional costs because the existing SAP Business Suite system is used.	Additional SAP NetWeaver Gateway server is needed.	Additional SAP NetWeaver Gateway server is needed.
Maintenance	SAP NetWeaver Gateway depends on the SAP Business Suite system maintenance schedule.	No dependencies between SAP NetWeaver Gateway and SAP Business Suite.	No dependencies between SAP NetWeaver Gateway and SAP Business Suite.

Table 4.3 Deployment Comparison

	Embedded Deployment	Hub Deployment: Development on the Hub	Hub Deployment: Development on the SAP Business Suite System
Development Effort/Limitations	Reuse structures from the SAP Business Suite system and use access to local business logic.	Access is limited to remote enabled interfaces (RFC function modules, BAPIs, SAP NetWeaver BW Easy Queries, SPI objects).	Full access, reusing structures from the SAP Business Suite system and accessing local business logic.
Recommended For	Playground and POCs; production systems only in case of limited load.	POC or production system usage; mandatory when no deployment of SAP NetWeaver Gateway add-ons in the SAP Business Suite is allowed.	Production system usage; usage in scenarios that use SAP Mobile Platform online applications or SAP Fiori.

Table 4.3 Deployment Comparison (Cont.)

4.1.5 Mixed Deployment Options

Combinations of deployment options

In real-world scenarios, deployment options often build on combinations of the three basic deployment options. Typically, these combinations address shortcomings or special situations in a bigger system landscape environment.

One example is a situation in which an embedded deployment is desired but not initially possible (e.g., because changes in backend systems are only possible during the maintenance windows). Therefore, a first setup includes an SAP NetWeaver Gateway hub deployment with development on the hub that connects to the SAP Business Suite system. This reduces the immediate system impact on the SAP Business Suite system. In a next step, the landscape complexity is then reduced after a piloting phase, meaning the SAP NetWeaver Gateway server is removed from the landscape and replaced by an embedded deployment on the SAP Business Suite system.

Another possible example is a combination of hub deployment and embedded deployment in a single-system landscape across several SAP Business Suite systems, which means that some SAP Business Suite systems use hub deployment, and some use embedded deployment. A system with embedded deployment can therefore also be used as a backend system in a hub deployment.

What should not be done is to use an SAP Business Suite system with embedded deployment as a hub system for additional SAP Business Suite systems (Figure 4.4). This might lead to a situation where the SAP NetWeaver Gateway release of the hub system is lower than the version of the SAP NetWeaver Gateway backend components of the remote SAP Business Suite system. (Such a situation can occur because it might not be possible to upgrade the hub system at the same time as the SAP Business Suite system.) In this case you will not be able to leverage new features of the higher version.

Combination to be avoided

To avoid such a situation, the recommended approach is to use one of the following two options:

Recommended deployment options

▶ Use the embedded deployment option for each of your SAP Business Suite systems.

▶ If you use a hub-based architecture, use a dedicated SAP NetWeaver Gateway hub system that should always run on the latest release of SAP NetWeaver Gateway.

Service Pack Level Equivalence in Mixed Environments

For mixed environments of SAP NetWeaver 7.40 and SAP NetWeaver Gateway 2.0 on top of NetWeaver 7.31 and earlier, you may wonder which SP level of SAP NetWeaver 7.40 is equivalent to which SP level of SAP NetWeaver Gateway running on a release prior to SAP NetWeaver 7.40. The answer to this question can be found in SAP Note 1942072: SAP NetWeaver Gateway 2.0 Support Package Stack Definition.

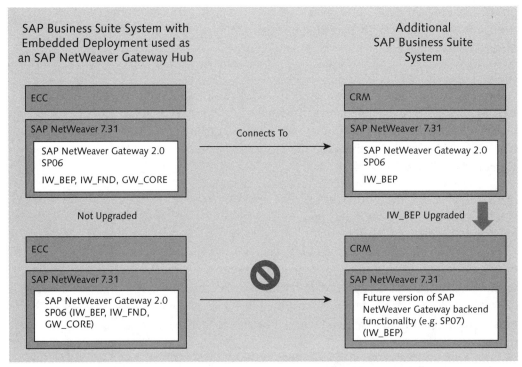

Figure 4.4 Potentially Problematic Upgrade Path Using an Embedded Deployment as Hub for Another Backend System

4.2 Preparing for Installation and Configuration

No matter what deployment option has been chosen, before you can start with the actual installation and configuration process, several preparation steps have to be executed. The first step for releases prior to 7.40 is to check whether you fulfill the installation prerequisites. In a next step, you need to get the software. Then it makes sense to note down important information that will be needed during the installation and configuration procedure.

Minimum
requirements

To run SAP NetWeaver Gateway, a number of prerequisites need to be fulfilled. This holds true in terms of both hardware and software. With respect to hardware, the minimum requirements for SAP NetWeaver Gateway are shown in Table 4.4.

Requirement	Specifications
Processor	Dual core or higher, 2GHz or higher
RAM	8 GB or higher
Hard disk capacity	80 GB primary or higher

Table 4.4 Hardware Requirements

With respect to software, the minimum requirements are a little more complicated; check the newest requirements in the SAP NetWeaver Gateway Installation Guide, because these prerequisites are specific for every single add-on. For the main components and SAP NetWeaver Gateway add-ons, the prerequisites (at the time of print) are shown in Table 4.5.

Further Resources

Installation prerequisites for SAP NetWeaver Gateway 2.0 SP06 can be found at:

http://help.sap.com/saphelp_gateway20sp06/helpdata/en/52/fc994f456a457 3957461be15520fe8/content.htm.

The SAP NetWeaver Gateway Installation Guide can be found at:

http://help.sap.com/saphelp_gateway20sp06/helpdata/en/c3/424a2657aa4c f58df949578a56ba80/frameset.htm.

Requirements	Specification	
SAP NetWeaver Stack	The latest kernel patch for the corresponding SAP NetWeaver version has to be applied.	
	Core Components GW_CORE and IW_FND	▸ SAP NetWeaver 7.0 SPS25
		▸ SAP NetWeaver 7.01 SPS10
		▸ SAP NetWeaver 7.02 SPS07
		▸ SAP NetWeaver 7.03 SPS01
		▸ SAP NetWeaver 7.31 SPS01

Table 4.5 Software Requirements

Requirements	Specification	
	Business Enablement Provisioning Component (IW_BEP)	▸ SAP NetWeaver 7.0 SPS18
		▸ SAP NetWeaver 7.01 SPS03
		▸ SAP NetWeaver 7.02 SPS06
		▸ SAP NetWeaver 7.03 SPS01
		▸ SAP NetWeaver 7.31 SPS01
	Core Component SAP_GWFND (remember, this comprises the functional scope of components IW_FND, GW_CORE, IW_BEP, and IW_HDB)	▸ SAP NetWeaver 7.40 SPS02
SAP Backend	SAP Business Suite system	

Table 4.5 Software Requirements (Cont.)

For additional information, check on the product availability matrix (PAM) for SAP NetWeaver Gateway at *http://service.sap.com/pam,* and search for SAP NetWeaver Gateway 2.0. Also check SAP Note 1569624 for SAP NetWeaver Gateway.

Download package
The SAP NetWeaver Gateway download package can be found on the SAP Service Marketplace in the SAP Software Download Center. Go to *http://service.sap.com/swdc,* and navigate to INSTALLATIONS AND UP-GRADES • BROWSE OUR DOWNLOAD CATALOG • SAP NETWEAVER AND COMPLEMENTARY PRODUCTS • SAP NETWEAVER GATEWAY • SAP NETWEAVER GATEWAY 2.0.

There you'll find the software under INSTALLATION AND UPGRADE and also the APPLICATION HELP that allows you to download the online documentation in plain HTML format. Alternatively, you can always work with the online documentation at *http://help.sap.com.*

Finally, before starting the actual configuration activities, a number of pieces of information need to be collected about the SAP NetWeaver Gateway host and the overall landscape (see Table 4.6). This will save time later and make things easier.

Required Information	Description
Fully Qualified Domain Name (FQDN)	Name of the SAP NetWeaver Application Server ABAP (AS ABAP) system or the load balancing device (for example, *server.domain.com*)
Administrator credentials	Login information of the administrator of the SAP NetWeaver AS ABAP to install and maintain the system
HTTP/HTTP(S) ports	HTTP and HTTP(S) port numbers of the central instance of the AS ABAP (for example, 8000 for HTTP and 8001 for HTTP(S))
SAP system	For each SAP system to which you want to connect the SAP NetWeaver Gateway server, the following information is required: ▸ System ID, system number ▸ Server name ▸ HTTP/HTTP(S) port ▸ Administrator credentials (i.e., user ID and password of an administrative user)

Table 4.6 Information Gathering

4.3 Quick Start Guide

The online documentation for SAP NetWeaver Gateway (*http:// help.sap.com/nwgateway*) explains all possible configuration options, many of which most people won't even need. Therefore, the idea behind this Quick Start Guide is to get you started quickly with some basic setup. After you have your basic setup running, you can then configure additional features and components as you like. Note that the Quick Start Guide is only valid for the embedded deployment option or for the option of hub deployment with development on the hub, which we've chosen for this guide.

Embedded deployment quick start

The Quick Start Guide gives you an easy-to-follow overview of the absolutely required steps to set up and configure SAP NetWeaver Gateway. After you've followed the steps, it leaves you with a working SAP

NetWeaver Gateway system that you can use as a playground environment or continue to configure to turn the very basic, absolutely minimal configuration into a fully usable production environment.

> **Important Notes**
>
> ▸ A sufficiently authorized user is required for this Quick Start Guide to work.
>
> ▸ This configuration is extremely basic, and only the absolutely required steps have been performed, so don't use this setup in a production environment without additional configuration (e.g., authorizations, security)! Full details can be found at *http://help.sap.com/saphelp_gateway20sp06/helpdata/en/4c/a670b0e36c4c01ae2b9a042056f9dc/frameset.htm*.

Remember, in the case of embedded deployment and hub deployment with development on the hub, the central components for SAP NetWeaver Gateway and any optional backend components are deployed together in the SAP Business Suite system or the hub system.

Setup and configuration steps

There are six steps needed to get your initial SAP NetWeaver Gateway setup running:

1. Deploy SAP NetWeaver Gateway add-ons.
2. Activate SAP NetWeaver Gateway.
3. Create the SAP system alias.
4. Create an SAP NetWeaver Gateway alias.
5. Activate node OPU.
6. Test your settings.

After you've performed these six steps, you should be able to develop a service on the embedded SAP NetWeaver Gateway system and publish it. Let's walk through these steps now.

4.3.1 Step 1: Deployment of the SAP NetWeaver Gateway Add-Ons

Transaction SAINT

In the first step, you deploy the three add-ons—GW_CORE, IW_FND, and IW_BEP—using Transaction SAINT, which is the SAP Add-On Installation Tool.

In a 7.40 system, this step can be skipped because the software component SAP_GWFND, which comprises all functionalities of GW_CORE, IW_FND, and IW_BEP, is already installed as part of the standard.

4.3.2   Step 2: Activate SAP NetWeaver Gateway

In the next step, you activate SAP NetWeaver Gateway by starting Transaction SPRO and navigating to the ACTIVATE OR DEACTIVATE SAP NETWEAVER GATEWAY node in the implementation guide (IMG) (Figure 4.5).

Activation in IMG

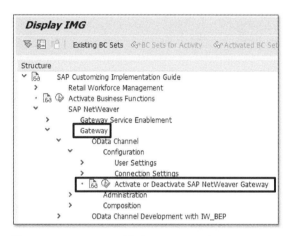

Figure 4.5 Activation of SAP NetWeaver Gateway

4.3.3   Step 3: Create an SAP System Alias

You now have to create a system alias entry that points from the hub system to the SAP Business Suite system. Because you've chosen an embedded deployment, you'll create a system alias entry LOCAL using the RFC destination NONE. To do so, go to MANAGE SAP SYSTEM ALIASES in the IMG (Figure 4.6). For this, you have to start Transaction SPRO and navigate to SAP NETWEAVER • GATEWAY • OData CHANNEL • CONFIGURATION • CONNECTION SETTINGS • SAP NETWEAVER GATEWAY TO SAP SYSTEM.

System alias

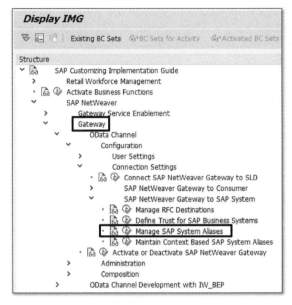

Figure 4.6 Create System Alias

This opens the maintenance view, in which you can fill in the values shown in Table 4.7.

Field	Value
SAP System Alias	LOCAL
Description	Local Gateway
Local GW	X
For Local App	(blank)
RFC Destination	NONE
Software Version	DEFAULT
System ID	The SID of your embedded system (i.e., SAP Business Suite)
Client	The client you're working in
WS Provider System	(blank)

Table 4.7 Change View Values

After you've entered the values, your screen should look like Figure 4.7.

Change View "Manage SAP System Aliases": Overview

New Entries

Manage SAP System Aliases

SAP System Alias	Description	Local GW	For Local App	RFC Destination	Software Version	System ID	Client	WS Provider System
LOCAL	Local Gateway	✓	☐	NONE	DEFAULT		800	

Figure 4.7 Example System Alias Creation

4.3.4   Step 4: Create an SAP NetWeaver Gateway Alias

The creation of an SAP NetWeaver Gateway alias is needed to have at least one entry for the SAP NetWeaver Gateway hub in the SAP NetWeaver Gateway Service Builder (Transaction SEGW) to allow for registering the services that you're going to develop.

SAP NetWeaver Gateway alias

To create an SAP NetWeaver Gateway alias, navigate to a different part in the IMG called SAP NETWEAVER GATEWAY SERVICE ENABLEMENT (Figure 4.8). This part contains the SAP NetWeaver Gateway hub-specific customizing settings. Enter the values shown in Table 4.8.

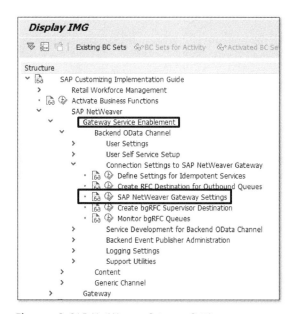

Figure 4.8 SAP NetWeaver Gateway Settings

Field	Value
DESTINATION SYSTEM	GW_HUB
CLIENT	The client you're working in
SYSTEM ALIAS	A unique name for the SAP NetWeaver Gateway host, for example, the SID
RFC DESTINATION	NONE

Table 4.8 Customizing Values

Your screen should now look like Figure 4.9.

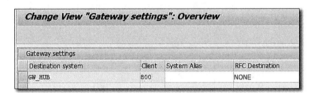

Figure 4.9 SAP NetWeaver Gateway Settings Overview

4.3.5 Step 5: Activate OPU Node

Transaction SICF In a freshly installed system, you now have to activate the OPU node using Transaction SICF (Figure 4.10).

Figure 4.10 Activate Node Using Transaction SICF

Next, a dialog pops up in which you need to confirm that all subnodes will be activated. To do this, click the YES button with the hierarchy symbol (Figure 4.11).

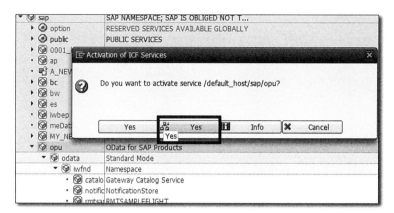

Figure 4.11 Confirmation of Internet Communication Framework Services Creation

Click the REFRESH icon. Now expand the OPU node again (see Figure 4.12), and check whether the changes have been successfully performed.

Virtuelle Hosts / Services	Documentation
▾ 🗔 default_host	VIRTUAL DEFAULT HOST
▾ 🌐 sap	SAP NAMESPACE; SAP IS OBLIGED
▸ ⊙ option	RESERVED SERVICES AVAILABLE G
▸ ⊙ public	PUBLIC SERVICES
▸ 🌐 0001_langes_feld	
· 🌐 ap	Application Platform
· 🖼 A_NEW_INTAL1	
▸ 🌐 bc	BASIS TREE (BASIS FUNCTIONS)
▸ 🌐 bw	BW
▸ 🌐 es	Enterprise Search
· 🌐 iwbep	Business Suite Enablement node fo
· 🌐 meData	meData synchronization Service
▸ 🌐 MY_NEW_TEST	DD
▾ 🌐 opu	OData for SAP Products
▾ 🌐 odata	Standard Mode
▸ 🌐 iwfnd	Namespace
▾ 🌐 sap	Namespace

Figure 4.12 Expanding the Node

4.3.6 Step 6: Test Your Settings

You can now test your settings by developing a simple service using the Service Builder (Transaction SEGW) (Figure 4.13).

Configuration verification

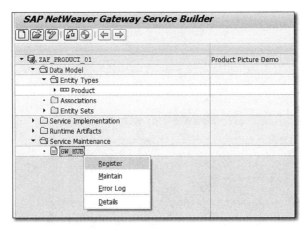

Figure 4.13 Expanding the Node for SAP NetWeaver Gateway Service Builder

As you can see in Figure 4.13, the name of the destination system of the SAP NetWeaver Gateway alias is shown in the SERVICE MAINTENANCE node in Transaction SEGW.

When selecting MAINTAIN in the context menu, Transaction /IWFND/ MAINT_SERVICE (Activate and Maintain Service) is started on the hub system (Figure 4.14). Note that the service has been registered for the LOCAL system alias that you've maintained in the process.

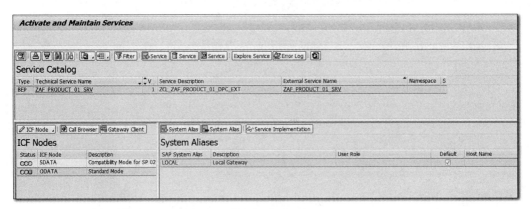

Figure 4.14 Activate and Maintain Services

4.4 Installation and Configuration in Detail

Needless to say, the configuration just discussed in the Quick Start Guide section is extremely basic and should by no means be used in a production environment without additional steps that are absolutely required for usage in a production system. And even for playground or POC systems, additional configurations are recommended and in some cases even needed.

Since only the absolutely required configuration steps were executed, and a number of important steps were dropped, the idea of this section is to provide you an overview of what you need to do for a full-blown installation and configuration of SAP NetWeaver Gateway, and to then dig deeper into some of the most important details. Again, a full SAP NetWeaver Gateway configuration guide can be found at *http://help.sap.com/nwgateway*.

The installation and configuration process of SAP NetWeaver Gateway consists of five phases (see Figure 4.15):

Process overview

1. The installation and configuration of the SAP NetWeaver Gateway add-ons (for systems prior to SAP NetWeaver 7.40)

2. The basic configuration of SAP NetWeaver Gateway

3. The OData channel configuration

4. The (optional) Business Enablement Provisioning (IW_BEP) configuration

5. Smoke testing the installation

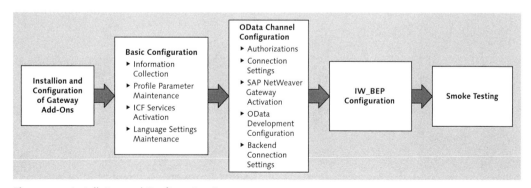

Figure 4.15 Installation and Configuration Process

Each of these phases can be further broken down into several steps. Let's now look into the details of these phases and steps.

4.4.1 Installing the SAP NetWeaver Gateway Add-Ons

Installation To install the required SAP NetWeaver Gateway add-ons, you must first download them. Because the downloaded installation packages have a compressed format, the initial step of the actual installation process is to unpack them into your local file system. Next, import the add-ons using the installation tool, Transaction SAINT. This step is only necessary for systems prior to SAP NetWeaver ABAP 7.40, because the 7.40 release contains the software component SAP_GWFND as part of the standard.

1. Call Transaction SAINT, and choose START.

2. Go to INSTALLATION PACKAGE • LOAD PACKAGES • FROM FRONT END to upload the installation files that you've previously downloaded from the Service Marketplace.

3. Select the add-on *<add-on> <add-on release>*, and choose CONTINUE. If all of the necessary conditions for importing the add-on have been fulfilled, the system displays the relevant queue. The queue consists of the add-on package and support packages and other add-on packages. To start the installation process, choose CONTINUE.

4. For more information, call Transaction SAINT, and choose INFO on the application toolbar.

5. The system prompts you to enter a password for each add-on component. These passwords can be found in the SAP NetWeaver Gateway Configuration Guide (*http://help.sap.com/nwgateway*).

4.4.2 Basic Configuration Settings

Configuration After you've installed the SAP NetWeaver Gateway components, you must configure your system. The steps for configuration include executing the basic customizing for SAP NetWeaver Gateway and describing system configuration activities.

Some tasks are mandatory, and others are optional and depend on specific use cases that you want to enable. With respect to the sequence, the mandatory basic configuration is the starting point after collecting the data needed for the configuration process. Then the OData channel configuration takes place.

Before starting the actual configuration activities, a number of pieces of information need to be collected about the SAP NetWeaver Gateway host and the overall landscape. (Refer back to Section 4.2 for details.)

Now that you've collected the required information, the configuration activities can begin. In a number of areas, settings need to be adjusted to SAP NetWeaver Gateway requirements with respect to values.

First, you need to use Transaction RZ10 to maintain the profile parameters with the values shown in Table 4.9.

Profile Parameter	Value
login/accept_sso2_ticket	1
login/create_sso2_ticket	2

Table 4.9 Profile Parameters

These two profile parameters are only activated after a system restart and are used to enable single sign-on (SSO) from and to the SAP NetWeaver Gateway system.

In the second step, Internet Communication Framework (ICF) services need to be configured. After the initial installation of an Application Server ABAP (AS ABAP), all ICF services are in an inactive state for security reasons. These services can be directly accessed via HTTP from the Internet. Therefore, unknowingly activated services represent a security risk, which can be mitigated by using suitable methods for restricting access.

Because multiple services can be executed when you call a URL, all relevant service nodes must be activated in a Transaction SICF tree. The URL path gets mapped to ICF subnodes (services) included in the URL. For example, if you want to activate the services for URL */sap/public/icman*, you have to activate the service tree default_host in Transaction SICF. Then, you have to activate services sap, public, and icman separately.

To activate a service, go to Transaction SICF, and select the required ICF service in the tree.

Service activation options
You then use one of the two options to activate the service: either the menu option (SERVICE/HOST • ACTIVATE) or the context menu (choose ACTIVATE SERVICE). You can either activate only a selected service node or the entire subtree (using the tree icon). The SAP NetWeaver Gateway services that need to be activated are shown in Table 4.10.

Service	Comments
/sap/public/opu	This service is needed for loading resources such as images.
/sap/opu/odata with all of its subnodes.	OData is the standard mode for all new applications. When creating a service, a new node is created automatically.
/sap/opu/sdata with the following subnodes: ▶ /sap/opu/sdata/iwcnt ▶ /sap/opu/sdata/iwfnd ▶ /sap/opu/sdata/sap	SData is the node used for existing applications. It's called compatibility mode for SP02. This is optional unless you're using scenarios based on the outdated generic channel.
If you want to use a web-based scenario, the following nodes on the target system need to be enabled: ▶ /sap/bc/srt/xip/sap ▶ /sap/bc/webdynpro/sap/saml2 ▶ /sap/public/bc ▶ /sap/public/bc/ur ▶ /sap/public/mysssocnt	Web-based scenarios here means that content is consumed via web services.

Table 4.10 Services to Be Activated

Language settings
In a third step, the language settings need to be checked and potentially adjusted. As for languages, the SAP NetWeaver Gateway system supports only the intersecting set of the languages of the connected SAP Business Suite backend systems. You can still make sure that your users

receive the appropriate language. Follow the specific logon language process for this.

Logon Language

For more information about logon languages, we recommend *http:// help.sap.com/saphelp_gateway20sp06/helpdata/en/85/81033c42663b34e10 000000a11402f/frameset.htm*.

4.4.3   OData Channel Configuration

In the next step, the OData channel configuration has to be maintained. This is a little more challenging due to dependencies on the specific SAP NetWeaver release. For example, where to find the configuration settings for the OData channel and the structure in the IMG can differ depending on the underlying SAP NetWeaver release, as described in the following list:

OData channel configuration

▶ **SAP NetWeaver releases 7.00 and 7.01**
   The OData channel configuration settings are available in the IMG in the system where software component IW_FND is deployed. In the SAP Reference IMG, navigate to SAP NETWEAVER • GATEWAY.

▶ **SAP NetWeaver releases 7.02 and 7.31**
   The OData channel configuration activities are listed in the IMG in the system where software component IW_FND is deployed. In the SAP Reference IMG, navigate to SAP NETWEAVER • GATEWAY • ODATA CHANNEL.

▶ **SAP NetWeaver release 7.40**
   If you use software component SAP_GWFND, IMG activities are available under SAP NETWEAVER • GATEWAY and SAP NETWEAVER • GATEWAY SERVICE ENABLEMENT.

In general, a number of steps need to be performed during the OData channel configuration. This includes setting the appropriate authorizations for users, configuring the connection settings for SAP NetWeaver Gateway to the SAP Business Suite system(s) (including RFCs and system aliases), activating SAP NetWeaver Gateway, setting up the OData channel service development on the SAP Business Suite system (and potentially on the hub system as well), and configuring the connection settings for the SAP Business Suite system to the SAP NetWeaver Gateway server. We walk you through these steps next.

Authorization Configuration

So the first task here is to set up an administrator role for SAP NetWeaver Gateway components and assign users to it. After that is done, you can set up one or several user roles and assign users to these as well. To do so, create your own roles or copy existing roles to new custom roles.

To facilitate things, SAP NetWeaver Gateway provides predefined roles as templates for developers, for administrators, and for support use cases. Support templates only have display authorizations and have been designed to be used by support colleagues.

Predefined role templates

The three most important kinds of templates are the framework templates (Table 4.11), the OData channel templates (Table 4.12), and the Business Enablement Provisioning templates (Table 4.13).

Further Resources

For more information about templates, we recommend *http://help.sap.com/saphelp_gateway20sp06/helpdata/en/c3/424a2657aa4cf58df949578a56ba80/frameset.htm*.

Template Name	Template for Role
/IWFND/RT_ADMIN	Framework administrator
/IWFND/RT_BOR_DEV	BOR developer
/IWFND/RT_DEVELOPER	Developer
/IWFND/RT_GW_USER	User
/IWFND/RT_TU_NOTIF	Technical user for notifications

Table 4.11 Framework Templates

Template Name	Template for Role
/IWBEP/RT_MGW_ADM	OData channel administrator
/IWBEP/RT_MGW_DEV	OData channel developer
/IWBEP/RT_MGW_USR	OData channel user
/IWHDB/RT_USER	OData channel SAP HANA integration user
/IWBEP/RT_SUB_USR	On-behalf subscription user

Table 4.12 OData Channel Templates

Template Name	Template for Role
/IWBEP/RT_BEP_ADM	Business Enablement Provisioning administrator
/IWBEP/RT_BEP_USR	Business Enablement Provisioning user

Table 4.13 Business Enablement Provisioning Templates

For creating the three most important roles, namely SAP NetWeaver Gateway developer, SAP NetWeaver Gateway administrator, and SAP NetWeaver Gateway user, only a few steps have to be performed.

Role creation steps

> **Further Resources**
>
> For more information on creating and assigning roles, we recommend *http://help.sap.com/saphelp_gateway20sp06/helpdata/en/c3/424a2657aa4cf58df949578a56ba80/frameset.htm*.

For the SAP NetWeaver Gateway developer, create a developer role based on the templates /IWFND/RT_DEVELOPER and /IWBEP/RT_MGW_DEV, which also contain the usual authorizations needed for ABAP development. For the SAP NetWeaver Gateway administrator, create a role for an administrator user with permissions and privileges for several tasks, including the following:

► Creating services
► Analyzing logs and identifying potential issues with the SAP NetWeaver Gateway landscape

- Installing, configuring, and maintaining SAP NetWeaver Gateway components and applications that run on top of SAP NetWeaver Gateway

- Configuring and maintaining users' data, including roles and user mapping

Finally, for SAP NetWeaver Gateway users, you must create roles specific to the user's required tasks. Either you can specify different authorizations for different user roles or have all authorizations bundled in a single user role. For more information, see Section 14.2 of Chapter 14.

Connection settings

Connecting SAP NetWeaver Gateway to the SAP Business Suite

In this step, the connection settings have to be maintained. This holds true in both possible directions—SAP NetWeaver Gateway to SAP Business Suite system(s) and SAP NetWeaver Gateway to consumers.

With respect to the connection settings for the consumers, you have to specify settings when using push flow. (For more details about push flow or notifications, see Appendix A.) After that has been done, you have to configure the SAP NetWeaver Gateway components and define how to interface with the backend system. These activities are again performed in the SAP Reference IMG using Transaction SPRO. Navigate to SAP NETWEAVER • GATEWAY • OData CHANNEL • CONFIGURATION • CONNECTION SETTINGS • SAP NETWEAVER GATEWAY TO SAP SYSTEM.

> **Further Resources**
>
> Detailed information on both how to configure the connection settings for SAP NetWeaver Gateway to consumers and how to configure the settings for SAP NetWeaver Gateway to SAP systems can be found at:
>
> *http://help.sap.com/saphelp_gateway20sp06/helpdata/en/c3/424a2657aa4c f58df949578a56ba80/frameset.htm*.

In the first step, you define the trust relationship between your SAP Business Suite system and the SAP NetWeaver Gateway host by using Transaction SM59 to configure the SAP Business Suite system to be the trusting system and the SAP NetWeaver Gateway host to be the trusted system.

Creating a Remote Function Call Destination on the SAP NetWeaver Gateway Host to the SAP System

A type 3 RFC connection from the SAP NetWeaver Gateway host to the SAP Business Suite system is the next thing to set up. To create one, go to Transaction SPRO, and open the SAP Reference IMG. Navigate to SAP NETWEAVER • GATEWAY • ODATA CHANNEL • CONFIGURATION • CONNECTION SETTINGS • SAP NETWEAVER GATEWAY TO SAP SYSTEM • MANAGE RFC DESTINATIONS. There you create the RFC of type 3. It's important to note that you've previously created a trust relationship between the SAP NetWeaver Gateway host and your SAP system.

Creating the SAP System Alias for Applications

In the next step, you need to specify where the SAP system alias should point. Depending on the specific scenario and your system landscape, you accordingly set up the system alias. This system alias is the result of the routing for an inbound request on SAP NetWeaver Gateway and can point to a remote or a local system. If that system alias is flagged as a local SAP NetWeaver Gateway instance, it means that the system that is responsible for processing (managing and storing) the data of an inbound request is the local SAP NetWeaver Gateway instance itself.

System alias creation

To configure the system alias, go to Transaction SPRO, and in the SAP Reference IMG, navigate to SAP NETWEAVER • GATEWAY • ODATA CHANNEL • CONFIGURATION • CONNECTION SETTINGS • SAP NETWEAVER GATEWAY TO SAP SYSTEM • MANAGE SAP SYSTEM ALIASES. After selecting CHOOSE NEW ENTRIES, enter the required information for the system alias. This information includes the system alias name, the RFC destination, and the software version, among other things. Check your system alias configuration using CHECK SAP SYSTEM ALIASES to ensure that everything functions properly. Although not mandatory, the system alias should also contain the SAP system ID of the system because it's needed to register an SAP NetWeaver Gateway service from within Transaction SEGW in that backend system.

Activating SAP NetWeaver Gateway

Global activation
Now it's time to activate SAP NetWeaver Gateway in your system. (It's always possible to deactivate it again. In that case, all SAP NetWeaver Gateway services stop running, and an error message is sent to any consumer that calls the services.) To activate SAP NetWeaver Gateway, go to Transaction SPRO, and open the SAP Reference IMG. Navigate to SAP NETWEAVER • GATEWAY • ODATA CHANNEL • CONFIGURATION • ACTIVATE OR DEACTIVATE SAP NETWEAVER GATEWAY, and then execute the activation.

Activating Services

The transaction for activating and maintaining services (Transaction /IWFND/MAINT_SERVICES) is used to maintain all registered services on the SAP NetWeaver Gateway server (hub system), to register and activate services, and to delete services. The main screen is divided into an upper and a lower part in which the upper part shows all registered services (SERVICE CATALOG), and the lower part shows the details of the selected service from the service catalog. The details are split into ICF nodes and system aliases.

Settings for OData Channel Service Development on the SAP Business Suite System

OData channel settings in SAP Business Suite
OData channel implementations retrieve data from a connected SAP Business Suite system. Both application logic and metadata are hosted there. All SAP NetWeaver Gateway services need to be registered in the backend before being ready for activation on the hub. On the SAP Business Suite system, both models and services need to be maintained (registered). This registration process takes place automatically when generating the runtime artifacts using the Service Builder.

> **Manual Registration of Services in the Backend**
>
> The registration process can also be started manually, if it hasn't been done during service development, using the Service Builder. If it's necessary to perform the registration process separately, you have to start Transaction SPRO,

and then navigate to SAP NETWEAVER • GATEWAY SERVICE ENABLEMENT • BACK-END ODATA CHANNEL • SERVICE DEVELOPMENT FOR BACKEND ODATA CHANNEL, and then choose either MAINTAIN MODELS or MAINTAIN SERVICES.

After a service has been defined in the SAP Business Suite system, it can be activated on the SAP NetWeaver Gateway system.

Connecting the SAP Business Suite System to the SAP NetWeaver Gateway Server

In this step, the system alias entries in the SAP Business Suite have to be maintained. The creation of an SAP NetWeaver Gateway alias is needed to have at least one entry for the SAP NetWeaver Gateway hub in the SAP NetWeaver Gateway Service Builder (Transaction SEGW) to allow for registering the services that you're going to develop.

Creating a Remote Function Call Destination from the SAP Business Suite System to the SAP NetWeaver Gateway Server

A type 3 RFC connection from the SAP Business Suite system to the SAP NetWeaver Gateway host is the next thing to set up. To create one, go to Transaction SM59. There you create the RFC of type 3. It's important to note that you've previously created a trust relationship between the SAP Business Suite system and your SAP NetWeaver Gateway host.

Maintaining SAP NetWeaver Gateway Settings in the SAP Business Suite System

To configure the settings for the SAP NetWeaver Gateway system in the SAP Business Suite system, go to Transaction SPRO, and, in the IMG, navigate to SAP NETWEAVER • GATEWAY SERVICE ENABLEMENT • BACKEND ODATA CHANNEL • CONNECTION SETTINGS TO SAP NETWEAVER GATEWAY • SAP NETWEAVER GATEWAY SETTINGS. Here you have to enter the values shown in Table 4.14.

Field	Value
DESTINATION SYSTEM	GW_HUB
CLIENT	Client in the SAP NetWeaver Gateway server where SAP NetWeaver Gateway has been activated
SYSTEM ALIAS	A unique name for the SAP NetWeaver Gateway server, for example, the SID
RFC DESTINATION	Enter the name of the RFC destination you have created beforehand

Table 4.14 SAP NetWeaver Gateway Settings: Customizing Values

4.4.4 Business Enablement Provisioning (BEP) Configuration

Business Enablement Provisioning (BEP) is a component that you enable in your existing SAP Business Suite system to handle the events and actions activated in the SAP system and to publish these events and actions through SAP NetWeaver Gateway. BEP provides functionality to expose data and events as OData-based REST services and is contained in the add-on IW_BEP (and, as of SAP NetWeaver 7.40, in the software component SAP_GWFND). You can use BEP to obtain and publish Business Object Repository (BOR) events without writing code, to obtain and send events for SAP Business Workflow, and to send events from your code.

To enable BEP, start by configuring its role templates. Next, you define an event and then the event subscription and notifications. Then the connection settings to the SAP NetWeaver Gateway landscape are specified. These settings are available both for BEP and the OData channel.

> **Further Resources**
>
> The detailed steps for configuring BEP can be found at:
>
> *http://help.sap.com/saphelp_gateway20sp06/helpdata/en/c3/424a2657aa4cf58df949578a56ba80/frameset.htm*

4.4.5 Smoke Testing

Now that we have finished the installation and configuration, it's important to verify that things work properly. This holds true for all relevant
areas—namely, service development, service consumption, and operations. In most cases, there is no need to check on every detail; a smoke
test is sufficient for POC and development systems. When a production
system is concerned, however, we recommend more detailed tests.
Depending on the business case, security topics should be specifically
tested. Also, before the go-live, an additional review of the system setup
and configuration should be performed.

Installation
verification

For smoke testing a POC or development system, we recommend the
following steps:

Smoke test
procedure

1. Use the SAP NetWeaver Gateway client using Transaction /IWFND/
   GW_CLIENT to call the CATALOG service that shows the service catalog
   (*/sap/opu/odata/IWFND/CATALOGSERVICE/ServiceCollection*).
2. Call one of the registered services, for example, RMT SAMPLE FLIGHT
   (*/sap/opu/odata/IWFND/RMTSAMPLEFLIGHT/TravelagencyCollection*).

If both of these services return usable data, this confirms that your SAP
NetWeaver Gateway installation works on a basic level. (It might be nec-
essary, however, to generate sample flight data by running the report
SAPBC_DATA_GENERATOR.)

For smoke testing a production system, the same basic steps just
described should be executed to confirm that service calls work and
return data. Also, a number of smoke tests should be executed to make
sure additional important SAP NetWeaver and SAP NetWeaver Gateway
features work. This includes, for example, basic security checks. Which
tests make sense depend on your specific setup. Potential tests include
the following:

Production
systems

▶ Call SAP NetWeaver Gateway services with different user roles and
  see whether the user can see the data he is supposed to see.
▶ Call SAP NetWeaver Gateway services with a user that isn't supposed
  to see data and check the result.

Additional tests recommended

As we've already stated, these are only smoke tests. We recommend appropriate tests to ensure your setup works as expected, especially in the performance and security areas.

To run test cases, it's possible to store them for the services you're interested in testing. This can be done using the SAP NetWeaver Gateway client, which offers the feature to store test cases in its test database. The handling of test cases using the SAP NetWeaver Gateway client is described in more detail in Chapter 13.

During quite a number of projects, best practices for SAP NetWeaver Gateway installation and configuration have evolved. In most cases, the official SAP documentation already reflects these lessons learned and points you in the right direction. Let's still have a look at the important best practices and where you can find information to give you additional background.

Deployment bottom line

With respect to deployment options, the bottom line is that you should only use an embedded SAP NetWeaver Gateway installation for a production environment in very exceptional cases; i.e., when there is either not a lot of load on the embedded environment or you're forced to use this setup for other reasons. The strong recommendation is to go for a separate SAP NetWeaver Gateway box to better scale and allow you to always keep the SAP NetWeaver Gateway version up to date.

On the other hand, if you're new to SAP NetWeaver Gateway and want to play around and learn or perform a simple POC, the embedded deployment makes things a lot easier and is the first pick for a straightforward and easy start.

Quick Sizer

When you look at sizing your landscape appropriately, SAP helps you with the Quick Sizer tool (*http://service.sap.com/quicksizing*). The Quick Sizer is a free web-based tool. It's highly recommended that you use this tool early in an SAP NetWeaver Gateway project, not only to make sure you have enough performance to handle all requests, but to do this in an economically smart way. You can find a document that specifically discusses SAP NetWeaver Gateway in the SAP NetWeaver document repository of the Quick Sizer tool.

A number of factors influence system performance, and this isn't limited to the obvious ones such as main memory or number and kind of CPUs. There are other factors specific to OData and SAP NetWeaver Gateway that you should take into account as well, and that can have a major impact. One example is the format of SAP NetWeaver Gateway service calls.

System performance

SAP NetWeaver Gateway 2.0 OData-compliant services implementing the JSON format have a lower overhead than those implementing the AtomPub format, when more than a hundred objects are retrieved. So for performance relevant calls that retrieve more than a hundred objects, the recommendation is to use JSON. When fewer than a hundred objects are retrieved, the overhead for both AtomPub and JSON is the same.

JSON vs. AtomPub

Concerning authorizations, the recommendation is to use SAP's role templates as much as possible to make your life easier.

Role templates

When talking about security, the main recommendation is to not directly expose your SAP NetWeaver Gateway system to the Internet, because this opens it up for attacks. Instead use a reverse proxy between the SAP NetWeaver Gateway and the outside world.

Reverse proxy

4.5   Summary

This chapter provided you with background on SAP NetWeaver Gateway's deployment options and an overview of how to perform the setup and configuration. To get you going quickly, a minimal configuration guide was introduced. Additional configuration details and best practices for SAP NetWeaver Gateway system configurations were provided to allow for a well-suited setup in more advanced system environments. With this and SAP's extensive standard documentation, you should be able to start setting up your own SAP NetWeaver Gateway system and tailor it to your specific needs while avoiding potential traps and taking advantage of SAP NetWeaver Gateway's extensive feature set.

With this, we conclude Part I of the book. In this next chapter, we dive into the heart of SAP NetWeaver Gateway: the service creation process.

PART II
Service Creation

This chapter explains the end-to-end cycle and the specific tools for creating SAP NetWeaver Gateway services, both for service development and for service generation.

5 Introduction to OData Service Creation

As you'll recall from Chapter 2, OData services are what implement the OData protocol and expose an endpoint that allows access to data. The number of OData services shipped with SAP NetWeaver Gateway is limited and will likely remain rather low because, by nature, OData services are granular and mostly tailored to individual use cases. More commonly, services are shipped as part of products such as SAP Fiori or SAP mobile solutions. A large amount of development time can go into building the right OData service, so understanding this process is essential.

Out-of-the-box OData services

The central interface that is used to define and implement services within SAP NetWeaver Gateway is the Service Builder (Transaction SEGW). After you've created a service in the Service Builder, it can be used directly in any interface. The Service Builder is a one-stop shop with respect to SAP NetWeaver Gateway service development and is supplemented by additional support tools. In certain cases, it even allows you to perform selected steps in third-party tools and then import the results (e.g., usage of an OData modeler for the model definition).

The main objective of this chapter is to give you an overview of the process of service creation, which we then discuss in more detail in Chapter 6 and Chapter 7. To achieve this, in Section 5.1, we give you a brief overview of the steps in the process for both types of service creation (service development and service generation). In Section 5.2, we look at the main tool involved in service creation: the SAP NetWeaver Gateway

Service Builder. We then complement this first look at the Service Builder with a quick look at some of SAP NetWeaver Gateway's other tools that support service creation and maintenance. This section will give you an idea of the tools that are available to assist with tasks during the service creation process. In Section 5.3, we then dig deeper into service creation and look in more detail at the three main steps in service creation: data model definition, service implementation, and service maintenance. Also, we look at additional service creation-related topics such as service redefinition and the reuse of existing SAP NetWeaver Gateway services in mashups to create OData services. Finally, we give you an introduction to the development paradigm used for service development: the OData channel (Section 5.4).

5.1   Service Creation Process Overview

Development
versus generation

In this section, we introduce you to the general steps in service creation. This explanation of the service creation process is somewhat simplified in an effort to explain it with distinct and sequential steps (a waterfall approach). In reality, some of the steps can also be performed out of order (an incremental approach). We'll go into a bit more detail about this at the end of this section, after presenting the simplified process.

There are two ways of creating OData services with SAP NetWeaver Gateway:

▶ **Service development**
The classic option is the code-based development of SAP NetWeaver Gateway services. This ABAP-based option is extremely flexible and allows you to develop highly efficient and specialized services, but it also requires some significant technical know-how.

▶ **Service generation**
The second way is the generation of SAP NetWeaver Gateway services. There are three main methods of service generation:

▷ RFC generation: Allows you to generate a service using a tool called the *RFC/BOR Generator.*

▷ Redefinition: Allows you to define a service based on an existing data source or an existing SAP NetWeaver Gateway service.

▸ Model composition: Allows for mashing up multiple existing services. The result is a new service that can be created without the need to change the existing services.

Of these two approaches, service generation is the quicker approach and requires a lot less effort. On the other hand, it's more limited, and thus is primarily recommended for developing very straightforward services. Service generation doesn't give you much optimization potential because, without custom coding, you are restricted to what the service generators offer. In most real-world situations, you'll want to opt for service development because the advantages are well worth the effort. Still, if you have a GenIL or Service Provider Interface (SPI) objects, analytical queries such as SAP NetWeaver BW Easy Queries, or a suitable RFC function module or Business Application Programming Interface (BAPI) and are aiming for a quick result, this might be an option for you. (We'll go into more detail about these specific options in Chapter 7, where we discuss service generation in detail.)

Whether you're using service development or service generation, you create an OData service by following the SAP NetWeaver Gateway service creation process. This process consists of three main phases: model definition, service implementation, and service maintenance. Depending on whether you go for development or generation, the individual phases of the service creation process can have different flavors. These flavors result in different tracks you take during the actual process.

Service creation process

Before you can start with this process, you have to complete the process of *service definition* as a prerequisite. This is the process of identifying what service to create and specifying its details. Ideally, you've done all of this together with the client developers so that you know exactly what data they require and how this works with the artifacts in the SAP Business Suite that will be the basis for your SAP NetWeaver Gateway service. After you have the service definition, you can start with the three development phases of the service creation process.

During the starting phase, *data model definition*, you define the model your service is based on. That is, you define the required artifacts such as entity types, entity sets, associations, and other components that your service will use (refer back to Chapter 2 for explanations of these

Data model definition phase

components). After data model definition, you must generate the repository objects and register them in the SAP Business Suite system so that you can proceed with the next main phase, which is the service implementation.

Service
implementation
phase In the *service implementation phase*, the operations that are supported by the service are implemented. Here the different tracks for service development and service generation come into play:

▶ For service development, operations that are supported by the service are implemented using ABAP coding.

▶ For service generation, there are three paths depending on the type of generation chosen:

   ▶ If you use RFC/BOR generation, service implementation takes place by mapping the OData model to the methods of the RFC function module or a Business Object Repository (BOR) object.

   ▶ If you use redefinition, there is no service implementation step. You only have to perform the model definition step, because the implementation of the service is generated based on the customizing that has been performed in the model definition step.

   ▶ If you use model composition, there is again no service implementation step. Instead, you include one or more existing services into a new model.

Service
maintenance phase The third phase of the service creation process, *service maintenance,* publishes the service so that it becomes visible in the service catalog of the SAP NetWeaver Gateway system. In effect, this means that the created OData service can then be consumed.

The three phases—data model definition, service implementation, and service maintenance—are depicted in Figure 5.1. Steps that are only performed in service development are marked with one color, and steps that are only executed in service generation are marked with a different color. Steps that have to be performed in both the development and generation of OData services in SAP NetWeaver Gateway are marked with both colors.

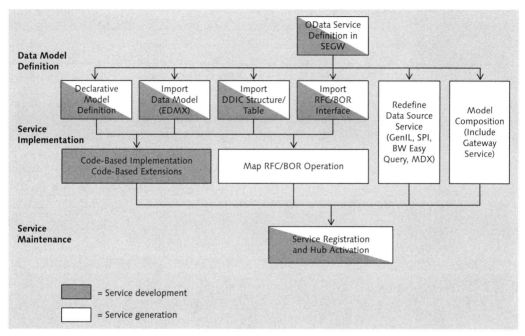

Figure 5.1 Service Creation Process

Although we clearly delineate the two methods of service creation (service generation and service development), it's actually possible to mix these in a way that suits you best. For example, you can create an OData service where one entity set is implemented using the RFC/BOR Generator (service generation), while a second entity set is implemented using code-based implementation (service development).

As we mentioned before, we've presented the service creation process in a very structured and clearly sequential way. This waterfall approach allowed you to easily understand what the different phases are for. In real-world projects, after you've understood how it works, you can adjust the sequence to what fits you best (within certain boundaries). The one exception to this rule is the service maintenance phase—this is almost always a one-time activity. As soon as a service is registered and activated (published), you don't have to touch these settings anymore, even if the implementation and/or model definition changes.

Incremental service creation process

183

> **Exception**
>
> The service publication is a one-time activity as long as you don't perform major changes. Registering the service for additional SAP Business Suite systems, for example, is such an activity in which you would have to go back to the service maintenance phase. Again, though, changes in the implementation of an already published service or in the data model can be used in the already published service without any further activities.

For all other phases, you'll typically always follow an incremental approach: you build a service—or part of it—execute and test it, and then go back and refine that same service until it fits all of your needs. During the creation of an OData service, you may change the model and/or the service implementation multiple times.

Furthermore, an approach often used in real-world projects is to perform the service implementation and the service maintenance in a different order. Performing the service maintenance with a service implementation stub before the actual service implementation allows you to browse metadata (service document and service metadata document), even if the service itself doesn't yet have any functionality. You've basically started with a service stub and can then fill this stub in an incremental way.

Figure 5.2 depicts the incremental service creation process. It's based on Figure 5.1 and adds incremental steps to the original process. These incremental steps are displayed by the solid line arrows that depict potential transitions among the three phases of data model definition, service implementation, and service maintenance. These phases are symbolized by the horizontal boxes. The dotted line stands for the one-time activity of service publication as part of the service maintenance phase.

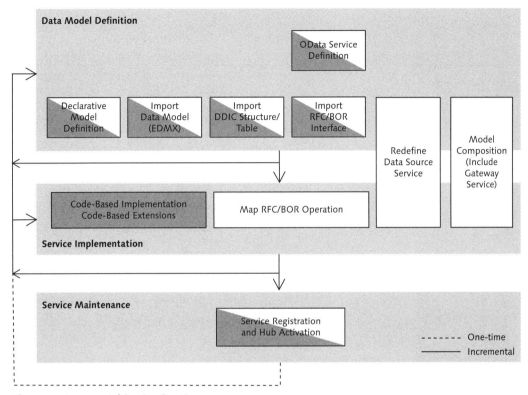

Figure 5.2 Incremental Service Creation

5.2   SAP NetWeaver Gateway Toolset

SAP NetWeaver Gateway provides a set of tools to address all needs from development to testing to operations. For now, we'll skip tools targeted at operating SAP NetWeaver Gateway and focus specifically on service creation-related tools. In this section, we'll take a look at SAP NetWeaver Gateway Service Builder—the central, one-stop development tool for SAP NetWeaver Gateway services—and the additional, well-integrated tools that support you during the SAP NetWeaver Gateway service creation process.

5.2.1 SAP NetWeaver Gateway Service Builder

Supports development lifecycle of an OData service

The Service Builder contains all relevant functions for modeling and development of OData services in SAP NetWeaver Gateway. This includes both code-based development of services and the generation of OData services. Also, it provides direct access to additional development-related functions such as service registration/activation and service validation. The Service Builder supports the entire development lifecycle of an OData service in SAP NetWeaver Gateway, and you can start it using Transaction SEGW (Figure 5.3).

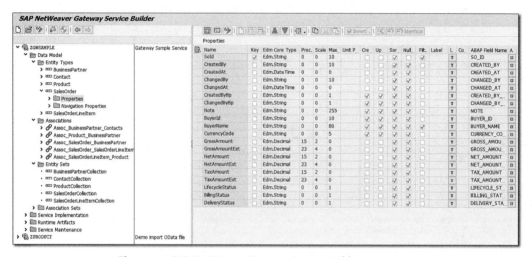

Figure 5.3 SAP NetWeaver Gateway Service Builder

Overall, the Service Builder addresses the needs of both experienced and less experienced developers, as well as nondevelopers. Whereas experienced developers can develop their own source code with maximum flexibility in their service implementation, they still can use the built-in OData modeler and other tools to simplify the development process. Less experienced developers will appreciate the possibility to use tools that allow generating OData services without having to write a single line of code.

The SAP NetWeaver Gateway Service Builder allows for centrally displaying and creating the definition of an OData service. This includes runtime artifacts (model provider class [MPC], data provider class [DPC], model, and service), OData artifacts (entity set, entity type, and properties), as well as used data sources and models.

The modeling environment follows a project-based approach, and all relevant data is consolidated in these projects. Development using the Service Builder is therefore organized in projects, and creating a project is the starting point of every service development using the Service Builder. Projects are used to bundle all artifacts that are needed for service development in one central place, thereby providing a means to organize the development process. The Service Builder allows the developer to open several projects at the same time as shown in Figure 5.4 (in this example, ZGWSAMPLE and ZPRODUCT).

Project-based development

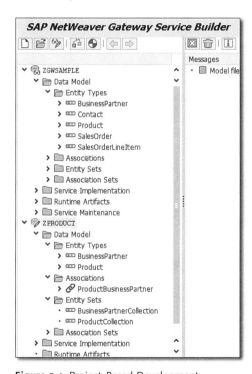

Figure 5.4 Project-Based Development

> **Note**
>
> From a technical system perspective, the Service Builder is used in a system where the Business Enablement Provisioning (BEP) component is installed,

which is typically an SAP Business Suite system (refer to Chapter 4 for a discussion of the different deployment options for SAP NetWeaver Gateway). The BEP component is delivered as add-on IW_BEP until SAP NetWeaver release 7.31. As of SAP NetWeaver release 7.40 SP02, the BEP component is included in SAP NetWeaver itself as part of component SAP_GWFND. As a result, it's possible to perform development of OData services using the Service Builder without additional effort in all systems after they run on top of SAP NetWeaver 7.40 SP02 or later.

Because the Service Builder is part of the BEP component that is typically (but not necessarily) installed on the SAP Business Suite system, you define the service model (model provider class, MPC) as well as the service logic (data provider class, DPC) on the same system where the BEP component is deployed. This is important to understand if it comes to referencing other ABAP Repository objects such as Data Dictionary (DDIC) elements (e.g., structures or data elements) that are required when calling, for example, an RFC or BAPI.

Comprehensive support for building OData services

The objective of the Service Builder is to provide comprehensive support for building OData services in a declarative way or by reusing existing business objects in the SAP Business Suite system. However, there are restrictions in what can be declared or generated. Advanced OData features may need to be implemented manually, and certain operations aren't available in a refined business object. The result of what you do in the Service Builder will always be ABAP classes, which are based on the OData channel programming model of SAP NetWeaver Gateway (covered in Section 5.4). You can always drill down to understand what is going on during service execution or tweak the code.

5.2.2 Beyond the Service Builder: Supporting Tools during the Service Creation Process

As stated, the main tool during the service creation process is the SAP NetWeaver Gateway Service Builder. At the same time, SAP NetWeaver Gateway provides a set of additional tools that are very useful during the development of SAP NetWeaver Gateway services. These tools allow, for example, for early testing of services or tracing what is happening when calling a service. As such, this section aims to briefly introduce you to some of the functionalities. For a more comprehensive description of the development support and administration toolset of SAP NetWeaver Gateway, see Chapter 13.

Integrated Test Environment

The SAP NetWeaver Gateway client can be used for both testing and troubleshooting and is a REST client built into SAP NetWeaver Gateway. It can be started from within SAPGUI using Transaction /IWFND/ GW_CLIENT. After you've created a service, you can use this tool for a first test, as shown in Figure 5.5.

Testing and troubleshooting

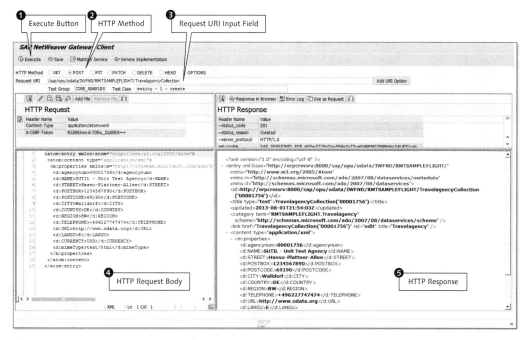

Figure 5.5 SAP NetWeaver Gateway Client: Create Request

First select an HTTP method such as GET, POST, DELETE, HEAD, or OPTIONS, as shown in ❷. Then enter the URI of your request into the REQUEST URI input field, as shown in ❸. It's also possible to set a certain HTTP header if needed. The body of an HTTP request can be entered either manually or uploaded from a file, as shown in ❹. In addition, it's possible to use the REQUEST function to create, for example, an update request based on the response (shown in ❺) of a read request that has been issued against the URI before. Finally, perform the HTTP request by choosing EXECUTE, as shown in ❶.

Test cases   A very useful feature of the SAP NetWeaver Gateway client is that test cases can be stored in a database. The test case shown in Figure 5.5 is one of more than 70 sample test cases that are delivered in test group CORE_SAMPLES for the standard test services TEA_TEST_APPLICA-TION and RMTSAMPLEFLIGHT. Note that the test cases of the CORE_SAMPLES test group have to be manually created from within the SAP NetWeaver Gateway client as shown in Figure 5.6.

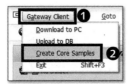

Figure 5.6 Create Core Samples from within the SAP NetWeaver Gateway Client

If you've saved a request as a test case, you can afterwards add or change the expected HTTP return code. A request can return multiple HTTP return codes that are valid (for example, 200, 401, 402, and 403). Therefore multiple statuses, including status ranges separated by a space, can be entered (for example: 201 401-403).

One or more test cases can then be run using the SAP NetWeaver Gateway client. The results are displayed in a table indicated by a traffic light icon together with the expected and actual HTTP return code.

Error Log

The error log is the second tool the developer will find very useful when it comes to troubleshooting. The error log can be called using Transaction /IWFND/ERROR_LOG in the SAP NetWeaver Gateway server system. There is also an SAP Business Suite system error log with a similar UI available that can be used to analyze errors that occurred in the SAP Business Suite system. The SAP Business Suite system error log can be started using Transaction /IWBEP/ERROR_LOG in the SAP Business Suite system.

The error log is tightly integrated with the SAP NetWeaver Gateway client, so it's possible to rerun a request sent by a consumer that led to errors. Do this by selecting REPLAY • GATEWAY CLIENT as shown in Figure 5.7.

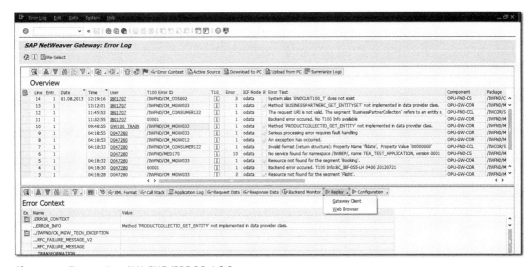

Figure 5.7 Transaction /IW_FND/ERROR_LOG

As another way to dig into potential problems, monitoring log entries can be generated for the system log and the application log of SAP NetWeaver Gateway. The system logs can be accessed using Transaction SM21. For the application log, use Transaction /IWFND/APPS_LOG.

Logging and tracing

Catalog Service

Each SAP NetWeaver Gateway system provides a CATALOG service that can be used to retrieve a list of all available services on SAP NetWeaver Gateway (Figure 5.8). The CATALOG service is an OData service, and the list of available services can be accessed via the following URL:

http://<server>:<port>/sap/opu/odata/iwfnd/CATALOGSERVICE/Catalog Collection

```
<?xml version="1.0" encoding="utf-8" ?>
- <app:service xml:base="http://▓▓▓▓▓▓▓▓▓▓▓▓/sap/opu/odata/iwfnd/CATALOGSERVICE/"
   xmlns:app="http://www.w3.org/2007/app" xmlns:atom="http://www.w3.org/2005/Atom"
   xmlns:m="http://schemas.microsoft.com/ado/2007/08/dataservices/metadata"
   xmlns:sap="http://www.sap.com/Protocols/SAPData">
   - <app:workspace>
      <atom:title>Data</atom:title>
      - <app:collection sap:creatable="false" sap:updatable="false" sap:deletable="false" sap:searchable="true"
         sap:content-version="1" href="ServiceCollection">
         <atom:title>ServiceCollection</atom:title>
         <sap:member-title>Service</sap:member-title>
         <atom:link href="ServiceCollection/OpenSearchDescription.xml" rel="search"
            type="application/opensearchdescription+xml" title="searchServiceCollection" />
      </app:collection>
      - <app:collection sap:content-version="1" href="CatalogCollection">
         <atom:title>CatalogCollection</atom:title>
         <sap:member-title>Catalog</sap:member-title>
      </app:collection>
   </app:workspace>
   <atom:link rel="self" href="http://▓▓▓▓▓▓▓▓▓▓▓▓/sap/opu/odata/iwfnd/CATALOGSERVICE/" />
   <atom:link rel="latest-version"
      href="http://▓▓▓▓▓▓▓▓▓▓▓▓/sap/opu/odata/iwfnd/CATALOGSERVICE/" />
</app:service>
```

Figure 5.8 Service Catalog: Service Document

OpenSearch   The CATALOG service supports OpenSearch. Developers or development tools are thus able to use a free text search allowing them to find services based on the service description that can be retrieved using the following URL:

http://<server>:<port>/sap/opu/odata/iwfnd/CATALOGSERVICE/Service Collection/OpenSearchDescription.xml

5.3 Steps in the Service Creation Process

In the opening parts of this chapter, we've introduced the SAP NetWeaver Gateway service creation process. To recap, this process consists of three phases: data model definition, service implementation, and service maintenance. You can take different tracks for creating your services depending on whether you go for service development or service generation. Now let's take a closer, more technical look at the different tracks and the individual steps in these tracks. Due to the various options for creating SAP NetWeaver Gateway services, you'll find it useful to refer back to Figure 5.1 throughout this section.

5.3.1 Data Model Definition in the Service Builder

The first phase of the service creation process is the data model definition phase. The goal of this phase is to use the Service Builder to create a data model that contains all information about the OData model of a service, such as entity types, complex types, properties, and associations. So, when developing an SAP NetWeaver Gateway service (service development) or when generating an SAP NetWeaver Gateway service using the RFC/BOR Generator (one specific type of service generation), the first main process step is to create a data model.

> **Note**
>
> When using the second method of service generation, which is to redefine an existing service, the data model isn't defined but rather *re*defined based on the existing business objects. For information about that kind of data model building, see Section 5.3.5.

There are several ways of defining a data model with the Service Builder, each of which addresses a specific use case.

The first option is the manual creation of the various components of an OData model, which is called a *declarative model definition*. Entity types, associations, and association sets in this approach are created manually.

Four options for defining an OData model

The second option is the import of data models in the EDMX format that have either been defined by the OData Model Editor of the SAP NetWeaver Gateway Productivity Accelerator (GWPA) or the entity data modeler provided by Microsoft Visual Studio. In addition, it's possible to import the service metadata document of an existing OData service.

The third and fourth options, which are much more convenient options for an ABAP developer, are to create entity types by reusing data models that already exist in the SAP Business Suite System. This can be done by the import of DDIC structures/tables or, alternatively, by the generation of new entity types based on an RFC/BOR interface.

Next, we'll discuss all four options in a bit more detail.

Declarative Data Model

A declarative data model is created manually using the Service Builder. This method is mainly used to create entity types based on manually created properties, which can be based on existing DDIC types. (To model

Entity types

an OData service from scratch in WYSIWYG style, alternative OData modeling tools, such as SAP NetWeaver Gateway Productivity Accelerator [see Chapter 8] and Microsoft Visual Studio, are better. However, in these cases, the model has to then be imported into the Service Builder.)

Import Data Model via EDMX

Using the import model option, the developer can import a complete OData model stored in an EDMX file, or a metadata document of an existing OData service, into the Service Builder. This includes the definition of entity types, entity sets, associations, and other components. You can import data model files that have been defined by graphical OData modeling tools, or service metadata files of an existing OData service.

> **Note**
>
> If you perform an import of a service metadata document or an EDMX file for an existing project into the Service Builder prior to SAP NetWeaver Gateway 2.0 SP07, the existing data model will be overwritten. With SP07, SAP provides the possibility to reimport data model files.

Import Data Model via DDIC

DDIC type support
To reduce the time required to create entity types and complex types in your data model and to leverage existing data structures in your SAP Business Suite system, you can import the following DDIC types into the Service Builder:

- Views
- Database tables
- Structures

> **Beautification**
>
> When creating an entity type from a DDIC type, the name of the entity type and the names of the properties of the entity type suggested by the Service Builder are derived from the original names of the DDIC type and its fields by removing the underscores and generating a name with camel case notation instead. For example, when using a structure such as BAPI_EPM_PRODUCT_HEADER, the Service Builder will propose the name BapiEpmProductHeader

for the entity type. The same naming convention for proposals is used for the property names of the generated entity type—so that instead of the original field name SUPPLIER_NAME, the field name of the generated entity type becomes SupplierName.

The name of the entity set and its properties should be easy to understand. This is because it's the entity set and the names of its properties that are visible to the consumer, and the names of the properties of an entity set are derived from the property names of the underlying entity type.

During the process of importing a DDIC structure or even afterward, the developer can start a process called *beautification*. Through this process, it's possible to reduce the number of properties of an entity type by simply removing single properties from it. In addition, it's possible to maintain the names of the properties of an entity type.

Reducing the number of properties to those that are absolutely necessary and maintaining the names that are visible to the outside world are important for creating services that are easy to consume. Publishing existing DDIC structures as is to the outside world is usually not very beneficial.

Beautification is discussed in more detail in Chapter 7, Section 7.2.1.

Import Data Model via RFC/BOR

Finally, the Service Builder also enables you to create entity types from function module parameters and BAPI parameters. A wizard is provided to guide you through the process. Using the interface of an RFC function module or a BOR interface is beneficial if they are being used to access the data in the SAP Business Suite system. Both code-based implementation and using the RFC/BOR Generator are possible with this approach.

Function module and BAPI parameters

5.3.2 Service Registration in the SAP Business Suite System

After the data model is defined, it must then be registered. Service registration in the SAP Business Suite manifests the data model definition phase's results. This means that the runtime objects required for an SAP NetWeaver Gateway service are generated using the Service Builder. For the convenience of the developer, the Service Builder also performs the necessary tasks to register the service in the SAP Business Suite.

Service Registration versus Service Maintenance

As you may recall from Section 5.1, the service maintenance phase of service creation involves activating and registering the service on the SAP NetWeaver Gateway server. This isn't to be confused with service registration in the SAP Business Suite system, which is a process that occurs after the data model definition. In this section, we're focusing on service registration in the SAP Business Suite system. In Section 5.3.4, we'll discuss service maintenance.

The difference between service registration and service maintenance is as follows:

▶ Service registration is an activity during service development that results in the creation of artifacts needed for development.

▶ Service maintenance is an activity during the deployment/operation of an SAP NetWeaver Gateway service. It activates the service for consumption.

Stub class creation

Based on the data model that has been created, the Service Builder generates a corresponding MPC and DPC, as well as extension classes. The MPC contains the coding that programmatically declares the data model being used by your service. The implementation of the service operations is performed in the DPC. The extension classes that have been generated by the Service Builder can be used to redefine methods of the generated base classes by custom code because the base classes are always regenerated when the model has been changed. (For more information on MPC and DPC, see Section 5.4.)

Service registration

To be used as a service, some configuration steps have to be performed; these steps are supported by the Service Builder (Figure 5.9). When generating a project for the first time, the developer has to specify the names of the MPC and its extension class and the DPC and its extension class. In addition, the developer has to specify the TECHNICAL MODEL NAME and the TECHNICAL SERVICE NAME. The latter becomes the external service name that is later used for publishing the service on the SAP NetWeaver Gateway.

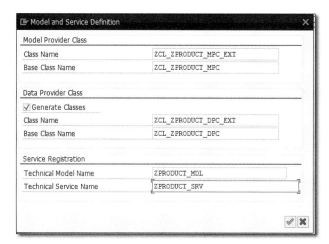

Figure 5.9 Model and Service Definition Using Service Builder

The MPC and the DPC are thus combined into an SAP NetWeaver Gateway service by means of configuration, not coding. These configuration steps are facilitated for you by the Service Builder when the project is generated for the first time. The model and service definition process is depicted in Figure 5.10. In addition to the MPC (covered in detail in Section 5.4.1) and the DPC (see Section 5.4.2), two additional repository objects for the model and the service are created as part of the registration process of a service in the SAP Business Suite.

MPC and DPC

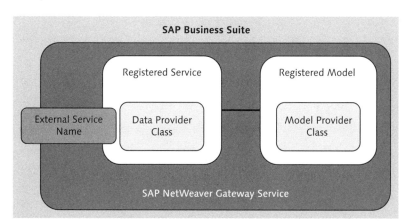

Figure 5.10 Register Service and Model

5.3.3 Service Implementation

During the service implementation phase of the service creation process, operations that are to be supported by the SAP NetWeaver Gateway services are implemented via ABAP code or via mapping of the methods of an RFC function module or BAPI on the properties of an OData model. Operations are executed on the defined data model during runtime and encompass CREATE, READ, UPDATE, DELETE, and QUERY methods (CRUD-Q methods).

It's important to note that the service implementation phase applies only to service development and to one of the service generation options: RFC/BOR generation. For service generation using redefinition, the service implementation step isn't necessary. This is because the implementation of the service will be generated based on the customizing that has been performed in the model definition step.

> **Note**
>
> We provide an introduction to service generation using redefinition in Section 5.3.5.

Next, we'll give you a brief overview of the service implementation phase for both scenarios where the phase is relevant: service development and service generation via mapping RFC/BOR interfaces.

Implementation for Service Development

Remember that during the service registration of the data model definition phase, a data provider extension class was created. Also during the service implementation phase, operations that are to be supported by the SAP NetWeaver Gateway services are being implemented.

To implement the supported SAP NetWeaver Gateway services using ABAP coding, you have to manually redefine the respective methods of the data provider extension class, which should remind you of the CRUD-Q operations:

- `<ENTITY_SET_NAME>_CREATE_ENTITY`
- `<ENTITY_SET_NAME>_GET_ENTITY`

- ► `<ENTITY_SET_NAME>_UPDATE_ENTITY`

- ► `<ENTITY_SET_NAME>_DELETE_ENTITY`

- ► `<ENTITY_SET_NAME>_GET_ENTITYSET`

Access to these methods is offered in a very convenient way by the Service Builder. This takes place by expanding the service implementation node as depicted in Figure 5.11. From there, you can navigate to the respective entry of an entity set, expanding all CRUD-Q methods of an entity set. Selecting GO TO ABAP WORKBENCH allows the developer to switch seamlessly to the class builder (Transaction SE24) to implement an operation.

Expand CRUD-Q methods

Figure 5.11 Code-Based Implementation

In addition, it might be necessary to redefine additional methods in the data provider extension class that aren't specific to an entity set such as the CRUD-Q methods mentioned earlier (if, for example, deep insert should be supported by the OData service).

Implementation for Mapping RFC/BOR interfaces

The process of implementation for mapping is different from that of service development. To start the mapping process, you have to select MAP TO DATASOURCE in the context menu of a CRUD-Q method of an entity set in the SERVICE IMPLEMENTATION folder (Figure 5.12). The built-in mapping tool of the Service Builder then allows defining relations between the interface parameters of a function module or BAPI and the properties of an entity set.

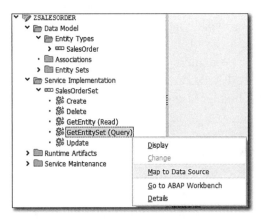

Figure 5.12 Mapping the Methods of an Entity Set to a Data Source

CRUD-Q

You can map the CREATE, READ, UPDATE, DELETE, and QUERY (CRUD-Q) methods of each entity set separately. The actual service implementation, that is, the coding in the CRUD-Q methods mentioned earlier, will be generated by the Service Builder based on the mapping you've performed. The Service Builder supports the developer by providing mapping proposals if the entity type has been created by importing a BOR or RFC interface. For example, as shown in Figure 5.13, the Service Builder suggested a mapping between the property SoId in the entity set SalesOrderSet and the property SO_ID of the export parameter SOHEADERDATA of the BAPI BAPI_EPM_SO_GET_LIST. This mapping can automatically be suggested because the entity type on which the entity set SalesOrderSet is based has been created by importing the interface parameter SOHEADERDATA.

If additional methods for the entity sets are mapped, the Service Builder checks the already existing mappings and derives proposals for them. If you, for example, started to map the Query operation (GET_ENTITYSET) of your entity set and now want to map the Read operation (GET_ENTITY), the Service Builder is able to provide a proposal for those properties that have already been mapped in the GET_ENTITYSET method.

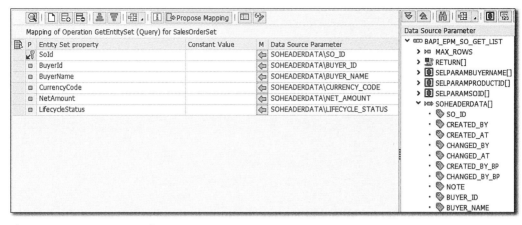

Figure 5.13 Mapping Proposals

5.3.4 Service Maintenance

The service maintenance phase primarily consists of the service activation and service registration step in the SAP NetWeaver Gateway system. For SAP NetWeaver Gateway to consume a service using an OData client, this service has to be activated. This activation takes place in the SAP NetWeaver Gateway server and makes the service ready for consumption.

The registration and activation of services in the hub is performed using Transaction /IWFND/MAINT_SERVICE (Activate and Maintain Service). Transaction /IWFND/MAINT_SERVICE is also used to maintain all activated services on the SAP NetWeaver Gateway server. Services have to be changed if they have been registered in several/additional connected SAP Business Suite systems, or they can simply be deactivated.

Activate and maintain service

Because the Service Builder is the one-stop-shop for service development, functionality has been added to the Service Builder that allows the developer to directly call the transaction for service maintenance from within the Service Builder. This is even possible for remote systems.

The developer can either select the list of SAP NetWeaver Gateway systems in the SERVICE MAINTENANCE node (Figure 5.14) or can click on the REGISTER button.

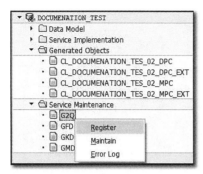

Figure 5.14 Registering a Service in the Hub from the SAP Business Suite

5.3.5 Service Generation via Redefinition

As explained in Section 5.1, redefinition is the process of generating a service based on an existing data source. This is done using a wizard and combines both the data model definition phase and the service implementation phase into the single phase of *redefinition*. The resulting generated service has to be registered and activated in the SAP NetWeaver Gateway server system (the service maintenance phase), and can then be consumed. The goal of redefinition is to allow for service creation with less effort.

Existing business objects

There are quite a number of existing business objects in an SAP system; SAP Customer Relationship Management (SAP CRM), SAP Product Lifecycle Management (SAP PLM), SAP Enterprise Asset Management (EAM), and SAP HANA—for example—all use a form of business object. Although these business object models have been designed for different use cases, all of them define objects, relations, actions, and queries similar to those that can be found in the OData protocol. It therefore comes as no surprise that a lot of these business objects can be used to generate OData services.

> **Note**
>
> On top of integrating existing SAP Business Suite business objects, it's also possible to integrate third-party OData services. This integration scenario is explained in Section 7.2.3 of Chapter 7, where the generation of services is explained in more technical detail.

The wizard for generating an OData Service using redefinition is almost identical for all integration scenarios. Selecting one of the options that are available (based on the installed add-on) starts a wizard that guides you through the following three steps:

Redefinition wizard

1. Select the business object.

2. Select artifacts of the data source (data model definition).

3. Generate runtime artifacts and service registration in the backend (service implementation).

In other words, the wizard starts with the data model definition part but automatically performs the steps that belong to the service implementation phase. After the service has been registered and implemented in the SAP Business Suite, it has to be activated in the SAP NetWeaver Gateway server.

The different integration scenarios described in this section are partly based on specific add-ons listed in Table 5.1. If these add-ons have been deployed to the SAP Business Suite system, the related context menu options in the Service Builder are visible as shown in Figure 5.15.

Most of the scenarios are also remote-enabled, which means that the business object that is to be consumed (for example, an SPI object) doesn't have to exist in the same system in which the BEP component is deployed. As a result, these scenarios can be implemented in the SAP NetWeaver Gateway server (assuming you are using hub deployment with development on the hub).

Name of Add-On	Integration Scenario	Remote-Enabled
IW_GIL	Generic Interaction Layer (GenIL)	
IW_SPI	Service Provider Interface (SPI)	X
IW_BEP	Analytical Queries	X
IW_HDB	SAP HANA	X
IW_BEP and IW_FND	OData Service (External)	X
IW_BEP	OData Service (SAP NetWeaver Gateway)	X

Table 5.1 Add-Ons for Generating a Service Based on an Existing Data Source

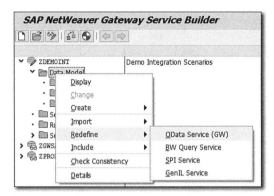

Figure 5.15 Context Menu Options to Create a Data Model Using Redefinition

Next, let's look at the different possible sources for suitable business objects in detail.

Generic Interaction Layer (GenIL)

Wrapper around existing business logic

Integration of GenIL with SAP NetWeaver Gateway offers the possibility of generating OData services based on existing GenIL components. GenIL is meant to be a wrapper around existing business logic. It provides access to all business objects via a unified interface for consuming application logic in the UI layer by using the *BOL API*. The BOL consists of two pieces:

▶ **GenIL**
The lower layer is a "dispatcher" that manages GenIL components and their models at runtime and distributes requests from above to the respective components implementing the requested objects.

▶ **BOL**
The stateful layer provides optimized performance by avoiding expensive repetitive access to the APIs and thus acts as a buffer for the UI.

While BOL was built for SAP CRM Web Client, the role of GenIL is different because it can be used for other integration scenarios as well. The consumption of SOAP-based web services using the Web Service tool that directly consumes GenIL is an example of such additional integration.

Similarly, SAP NetWeaver Gateway also allows you to generate OData services leveraging GenIL (as shown in Figure 5.16). The nodes, relations, and queries in the GenIL model are transformed to the corresponding entities in an OData model, as shown in Figure 5.17.

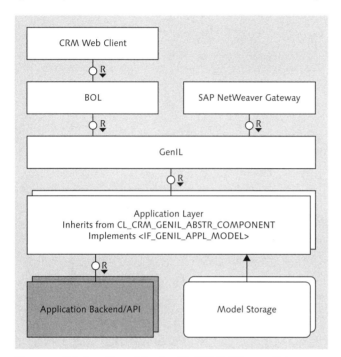

Figure 5.16 Integration of GenIL with SAP NetWeaver Gateway

Although BOL (and thus GenIL) are frequently used for SAP CRM Web Client, it has also been used in other SAP Business Suite applications such as SAP ERP Financials and SAP ERP Human Capital Management (HCM). The integration is contained in the IW_GIL add-on. This must be deployed locally on the SAP Business Suite System (for example, SAP CRM) on top of the BEP component.

> **Note**
>
> The GenIL integration scenario isn't remote enabled. To use services that are generated based on GenIL objects, the add-on IW_BEP component (SAP_GWFND starting from SAP NetWeaver release 7.40) has to be deployed on the SAP Business Suite system.

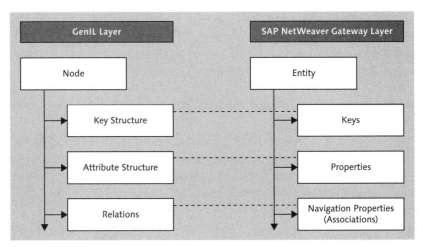

Figure 5.17 Mapping between the GenIL and OData Model

Service Provider Interface (SPI)

The Service Provider Interface (SPI) was originally developed for SAP PLM. SPI is a framework generated within the application layer that has different consumers. The framework is currently not only used by the applications for which it was originally developed, but also for various other applications within the SAP Business Suite.

SPI objects can be called remotely. As a result, it isn't mandatory to deploy the SAP NetWeaver Gateway IW_SPI add-on for SPI on the SAP Business Suite system. Because the add-on calls the RFC interface of the SPI layer, it can be deployed on the SAP NetWeaver Gateway server system. The IW_GIL add-on instead must be deployed locally on the SAP Business Suite system (for example, SAP CRM). The integration of SPI with SAP NetWeaver Gateway allows SPI application building blocks to be provisioned as OData services.

> **Further Resources**
>
> For more information about this topic, we recommend the following:
>
> ▶ SPI Wiki on SCN: *http://wiki.sdn.sap.com/wiki/display/SPI/Home*
> ▶ SAP Online Help: *http://help.sap.com/saphelp_crm70/helpdata/en/7c/ 0f77e9f297402aacb48ca7110c7f2a/frameset.htm*

Analytic Queries

Analytic queries are the main tools for consuming analytical data that is embedded in business applications such as the SAP Business Suite and in data warehouses such as SAP NetWeaver BW. While analytic queries in SAP Business Suite provide access to consistent operational data, analytic queries in the SAP NetWeaver BW hub offer access to consistent, highly aggregated data across the enterprise.

SAP NetWeaver Gateway and SAP NetWeaver BW integration allows you to publish SAP NetWeaver BW content as an OData service that has been defined using *multidimensional expressions* (MDX) or *SAP NetWeaver BW Easy Queries.* While the MDX approach can also be used for SAP NetWeaver BW systems starting with 7.0, the SAP NetWeaver BW Easy Query approach is only supported for release 7.30 and higher. SAP NetWeaver BW Easy Queries are, however, easier to understand and to handle.

SAP NetWeaver BW Easy Queries are analytic queries that meet certain criteria. For a given SAP NetWeaver BW Easy Query, an RFC module is created in the system. This is done automatically by the system, based on the available SAP NetWeaver BW query definition. Using this RFC, an SAP NetWeaver BW Easy Query interface can be defined as an OData service.

SAP NetWeaver
BW Easy Queries

To release an analytical query as an SAP NetWeaver BW Easy Query, you have to mark the corresponding checkbox in the query properties in BEx Query Designer (see Figure 5.18).

After this has been done and the query is saved, the generation of the RFC is triggered. General rules that apply for SAP NetWeaver BW Easy Queries are that characteristics are on the rows, key figures are on the columns, and free characteristics aren't mapped to OData.

Further Resources

More information about SAP NetWeaver BW Easy Queries can be found in SAP Online Help. Specifically, we recommend the following:

http://help.sap.com/saphelp_nw73/helpdata/en/b6/53d6c4e26a4504b8971c 6e690d2105/frameset.htm

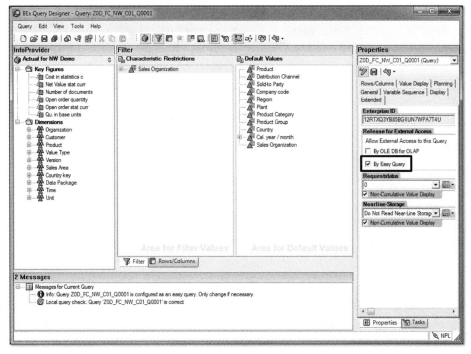

Figure 5.18 Define an Easy Query in the BEx Query Designer

Analytical annotations

Dimensions, dimension attributes, and measures are represented as properties of an entity type. The entity type representing the results of an MDX or an SAP NetWeaver BW Easy Query is annotated as `sap:semantics=aggregate`. Table 5.2 shows how SAP NetWeaver BW objects such as dimensions, dimension attributes, and measures are represented in OData. The table shows only the main annotations.

SAP NetWeaver BW Objects	OData Representation	SAP Annotation
Cube of Type Query	Entity Type	sap:semantics=aggregate
Dimension	Property	sap:aggregation-role=dimension
Dimension Attribute	Property	sap:attribute-for=<dimension name>
Measure	Property	sap:aggregation-role=measure

Table 5.2 Analytical Annotations

SAP HANA

SAP HANA is a high-performance, in-memory database. There are different integration scenarios available depending on the release of the SAP Business Suite system or the SAP NetWeaver BW system. With newer releases, these systems can run on top of SAP HANA; this means that SAP HANA replaces the relational database that was previously being used. These scenarios are called *SAP ERP on HANA*, *SAP CRM on HANA*, and *SAP NetWeaver BW on HANA*.

Older releases can also leverage the power of the SAP HANA database. In a side by side scenario, it's possible to copy data from these systems to SAP HANA in real time using the SAP Landscape Transformation replication service. This scenario is called *SAP NetWeaver Gateway with SAP HANA*.

Both the SAP on SAP HANA approach as well as the side-by-side approach store data in SAP HANA artifacts that can be published via SAP NetWeaver Gateway as an OData service. We've depicted both scenarios in Figure 5.19.

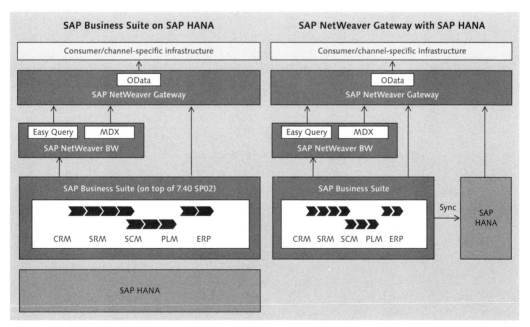

Figure 5.19 SAP HANA and SAP NetWeaver Gateway Integration Scenarios

SAP HANA views   With the help of the integration framework, it's possible to publish data from SAP HANA information models that are stored in a separate SAP HANA database as an OData service through SAP NetWeaver Gateway. The integration framework of SAP NetWeaver Gateway allows implementing read-only scenarios for the following SAP HANA objects:

- Attribute views
- Analytic views
- Calculation views

The connection between SAP NetWeaver Gateway and SAP HANA in an SAP NetWeaver Gateway with SAP HANA scenario is based on a secondary database connection that is maintained in Table DBCONN. The integration scenario isn't integrated into the Service Builder and requires code-based implementation of an MPC. This MPC must then be manually registered as a service together with a generic DPC.

ADBC interface   Because the ABAP Database Connectivity (ADBC) interface uses only one defined database user in Table DBCONN and single sign-on (SSO) isn't possible, the SAP HANA analytical privileges concept can't be used. As a workaround, additional authorization checks on the ABAP side have been implemented. The integration framework for SAP HANA is contained in the IW_BEP add-on for earlier versions of SAP NetWeaver, and starting from SAP NetWeaver 7.40 SP02, it's included in the SAP_GWFND component.

A more native integration can be achieved if the SAP Business Suite system runs on top of SAP NetWeaver AS ABAP 7.40, because this release has been optimized for SAP HANA. With SAP NetWeaver 7.40, new features have been added that allow easy consumption of existing SAP HANA artifacts in your ABAP code. Specifically, SAP HANA attribute views can now be accessed natively in ABAP applications using the new DDIC entity called *External View using Open SQL*. In addition, the modeling information from these new objects can be leveraged in the Service Builder. To do so, an external DDIC view can be imported as a data model with DDIC structures (as described earlier in the "Import Data Model via DDIC" section in Section 5.3.1).

External OData Service

OData Services Consumption and Integration (OSCI) is an additional integration scenario that aims at enabling consumption and integration of any OData service. With SP07 of SAP NetWeaver Gateway 2.0, this functionality is fully integrated with the Service Builder. In SP06, it has to be started using Transaction /IWBEP/OCI_SRV_GEN. The integration has to be implemented on the SAP NetWeaver Gateway server system, where the IW_BEP add-on also has to be deployed. The reason for this requirement is that, for the consumption of an OData service, you need the OData library—and this only resides on the SAP NetWeaver Gateway server. In addition, you also need IW_BEP for service development on the SAP NetWeaver Gateway server.

OSCI

As of SAP NetWeaver ABAP 7.40 SP02, this prerequisite will be fulfilled by any SAP NetWeaver ABAP system, because the software component SAP_GWFND comprises the required functionality described above.

OData Service (SAP NetWeaver Gateway)

The Service Builder allows you to generate a service based on an existing OData service in SAP NetWeaver Gateway. This integration scenario can be used to create a new service with the same interface as the original service, but with a changed behavior, which is accomplished by redefining methods in the new DPC extension class.

5.3.6 Service Generation via Model Composition

As discussed, it's also possible to mash up multiple existing services in SAP NetWeaver Gateway, which is called *model composition*. The result is a new service that can be created without the need to change the existing services. It's possible to redefine any SAP NetWeaver Gateway service irrespective of how it was created, which means that model composition can be used for older services that have been handcrafted, or any other service that has been built using the Service Builder. For example, it's possible to create a service in the Service Builder that includes the hand-crafted sample services GW_DEMO or RMTSAMPLEFLIGHT, even though these services were not built using the Service Builder.

A typical scenario for the use of model composition is to enhance services that have been generated from SAP NetWeaver BW, GenIL, SPI, SAP HANA, or external OData services. Think, for example, about a service that allows for creating a new purchase order and taking into account the purchase order history of your customer. The purchase order history can be retrieved using an appropriate SAP NetWeaver BW Easy Query, while a second service that creates new purchase orders can be created as well. A second scenario is the integration of data that is retrieved from SAP HANA or a third-party OData service with another SAP NetWeaver Gateway service.

> **Note**
>
> Model composition scenarios might require the implementation of the navigation via custom code on the hub.

Model composition is described in more detail in Section 7.3 of Chapter 7.

5.4 The OData Channel Development Paradigm

Now that we've discussed the basics of the different tracks of the SAP NetWeaver Gateway service creation process, let's look a little closer at the *the OData channel development paradigm*, which is a specific approach for service development. This introduction lays the theoretical foundation for Chapter 6, which goes into great detail about service development. The OData channel is part of the SAP NetWeaver Gateway basics if you plan on using service development.

The OData channel for SAP NetWeaver Gateway allows you to develop content by defining object models and registering a corresponding runtime DPC. The advantage of the OData channel paradigm is a certain freedom with respect to development; entire DDIC definitions and local interfaces of the SAP Business Suite can be used to develop SAP NetWeaver Gateway services. In addition, OData query options can be leveraged in the SAP Business Suite systems. This means that only data that has been requested by the client is selected from the SAP Business Suite system and sent back over the wire, which results in highly optimized services and major performance improvements due to a lower transferred data size.

SAP NetWeaver Gateway services with respect to the OData programming model consist of four components:

Four components of an SAP NetWeaver Gateway service

► The implementation of a *model provider class* (MPC) that provides the runtime representation of your model definition

► The implementation of a *data provider class* (DPC) that is called at runtime to perform data requests

► The *technical service name* that is used to register the service in the SAP Business Suite system

► The *technical model name* that is used to register the service in the SAP Business Suite system

The technical service name and technical model name are automatically generated with the MPC and DPC classes when generating a project using the Service Builder.

5.4.1 Model Provider Class

The MPC is an ABAP class that provides the runtime representation of your model definition; that is, the MPC defines the entity data model of a service. As such, all model information that you've defined in your project is generated into the MPC. As a consequence, you have to regenerate the MPC every time you change the model definition in your project. The MPC is important because everything you find in the service metadata document of an OData service published via SAP NetWeaver Gateway has programmatically been defined in the MPC.

Technically, the model definition is actually generated into two classes:

▸ The *base class* (with the suffix _MPC). Technically, the base class is derived from the /IWBEP/CL_MGW_PUSH_ABS_MODEL super class.

▸ The *extension class* (with the suffix _MPC_EXT). The extension class has the base class as the super class. The extension class is the class that will be registered via the technical model name. In the extension class, you can choose which methods to redefine and which methods to inherit from the base class.

In most cases, there is no need for a developer to touch the MPC that has been generated by the Service Builder. The exception to that rule is, for example, if you want to build SAP NetWeaver Gateway services with features that can't (yet) be modeled using SAP NetWeaver Gateway tools. In this case, the developer can redefine methods in the model provider extension class (see Figure 5.20).

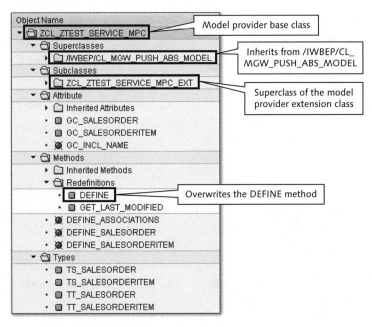

Figure 5.20 Model Provider Class

Model Provider Class Deep Dive

Usually there's no need for a developer to tap into the coding of the MPC being generated by the Service Builder. Let's still take a closer look at the methods being generated to get a better understanding of the underlying framework.

The `DEFINE` method in the MPC generated by the Service Builder contains calls to the entity type-specific `define_<entity_type>` methods and in addition a call to the `define_Association` method that creates the associations, association sets, referential constraints, and navigation properties.

The method `GET_LAST_MODIFIED` is the basis for a handshake between the SAP Business Suite and SAP NetWeaver Gateway to start a refresh of the cached metadata of the service on the SAP NetWeaver Gateway backend and the SAP NetWeaver Gateway server after the class has been changed. This method should not be changed manually.

In the entity type-specific `DEFINE` methods, the Service Builder generates the coding that creates the parts of the OData model that define the entity types and the entity sets that are based on entity type. The properties are created, and those properties that have been marked as a key field in the Service Builder are set as key fields in the coding:

```
lo_property = lo_entity_type->
create_property( iv_property_name = 'ProductID'
iv_abap_fieldname = 'PRODUCT_ID' ).
lo_property->set_is_key( ).
```

Finally, the entity type is bound to a DDIC structure, and one or more entity sets are created. Note that an entity type that is bound to an existing DDIC structure can leverage conversion exits as well as the labels of the data elements from the DDIC. The medium field label of a data element is used as `sap:label` by default:

```
...
lo_entity_type->
bind_structure( iv_structure_name   =
'BAPI_EPM_PRODUCT_HEADER' iv_bind_conversions = 'X' ).
...
lo_entity_set = lo_entity_type->
create_entity_set( 'Products' )
```

In the method `DEFINE_ASSOCIATION`, you can find the generated code that defines associations, association sets, referential constraints, and navigation properties of an OData model.

5.4.2 Data Provider Class and Data Provider Extension Class

The DPC is an ABAP class that provides all methods that are required to handle OData requests. It's called at runtime to perform these requests; essentially, we're talking about the runtime representation of your service implementation. For instance, a DPC executes CREATE, READ, UPDATE, DELETE, QUERY, and many more operations.

Again you can find an extension class (suffix _DPC_EXT) and a base class (suffix _DPC). The data provider extension class inherits from the DPC base class (see Figure 5.21). The DPC extension class is the class that is registered via the technical service name. So the extension class is the class that is executed in your OData service.

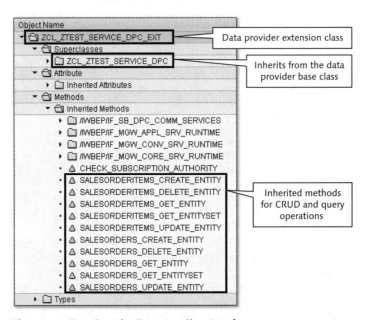

Figure 5.21 Data Provider Extension Class Interface

It's important to note that in the DPC, there are methods that are and are not specific to an entity set.

Entity set-specific methods

Data Provider Class Deep Dive

For each entity set, the Service Builder creates methods that are called by the framework if a CREATE, READ, UPDATE, or DELETE (CRUD) method is sent to this entity set. For an entity set called <ENTIYSET>, the methods created in the base class are shown in Table 5.3.

DPC Method Name	HTTP Verb	Target
<ENTITYSET>_CREATE_ENTITY	POST	Entity Set
<ENTITYSET>_DELETE_ENTITY	DELETE	Entity
<ENTITYSET>_GET_ENTITY	GET	Entity
<ENTITYSET>_GET_ENTITYSET	GET	Entity Set
<ENTITYSET>_UPDATE_ENTITY	UPDATE	Entity

Table 5.3 Entity Set-Specific CRUD Method Implementation in the DPC

There are additional methods available that apply not only for a single entity set but for all of them (nonentity set-specific methods). Examples of these methods are the methods handling $EXPAND statements, deep insert statements, or those that are called when a function import is performed. Let's take a closer look at these examples.

▶ GET_EXPANDED_ENTITY, GET_EXPANDED_ENTITYSET
  Handling of $expand statements is offered by the SAP NetWeaver Gateway framework out of the box in a generic way after you've modeled the appropriate navigation property and implemented the handling of navigation properties. There might be situations where you would instead handle $expand requests by a specific application implementation. Examples are certain BAPIs such as BAPI_EPM_SO_GET_LIST that, along with the header data, also retrieve line items. In this case, when retrieving the sales order header data for a certain sales order, the corresponding sales order items are also read. If the entity set is also called to expand the line items alongside the sales order header, this results in unnecessary database requests.

▶ CREATE_DEEP_ENTITY
  The counterpart of the $expand statement is the *deep insert* statement, which calls the CREATE_DEEP_ENTITY method. A typical example is the case where a sales order can only be created alongside at least one sales order item. In contrast to the $expand statement, there is no generic handling of a deep insert request. The developer has to implement this method.

▶ EXECUTE_ACTION
  The EXECUTE_ACTION method is a nonentity set-specific method as well. It's rather service semantic and is called if a function import into an OData service is called. Function imports allow you to execute functions that can

> read and/or write data. Function imports are suitable whenever the business scenario requires data to be read or changed that can't be modeled into an entity where you can use the CRUD-Q methods.

5.4.3 Technical Considerations with Respect to OData Channel Development

OData channel development can either take place on the SAP Business Suite system or on the SAP NetWeaver Gateway server, as shown in Figure 5.22. Both options are suited for certain use cases and have their advantages. Wherever you develop, the BEP component has to be installed there.

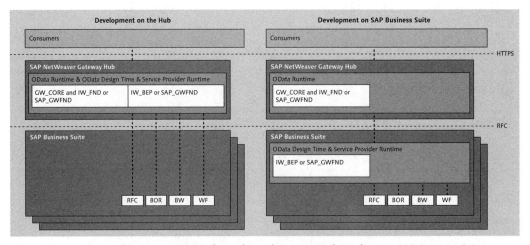

Figure 5.22 OData Channel Development on the Hub or on SAP Business Suite

5.5 Summary

Building OData services with SAP NetWeaver Gateway is done by following the SAP NetWeaver Gateway service creation process. This process is strongly supported and facilitated by the central SAP NetWeaver Gateway service creation tool: the SAP NetWeaver Gateway Service Builder. In this chapter, we introduced you to the tool and the process to establish a base of knowledge for the more technical step-by-step instructions in Chapter 6 and Chapter 7, which focus in detail on the processes of service development and service generation. In Chapter 6, you'll also be able to take advantage of the OData channel programming paradigm that you've learned about here.

Service development is one of the two main options for service creation. Although it's more complicated than its counterpart, service generation, it is also more flexible.

6   Service Development

This chapter explains the process of *service development*, which is the backend-side development of OData services using ABAP. After reading this chapter, you'll be able to develop services with the main development tool, the SAP NetWeaver Gateway Service Builder, making use of the OData channel as the development paradigm.

The steps described in this chapter are in line with the three main steps of service development (data model definition, service implementation, and service maintenance) as explained in Chapter 5. As you'll recall, data model definition, service implementation, and service maintenance don't necessarily have to be performed using a waterfall approach; the data model definition and the service implementation are iterative tasks that will be revisited frequently to let the OData service and its capabilities grow iteration by iteration. (This approach is very similar to other programming languages where you start with a first UI element and implement its functionality, and then add the next UI element and implement its functionality, and so on.)

In this chapter, we explain the steps of OData service development as they would occur in a real-world scenario. Figure 6.1 shows the steps of this development process.

Data model definition, service implementation, service maintenance

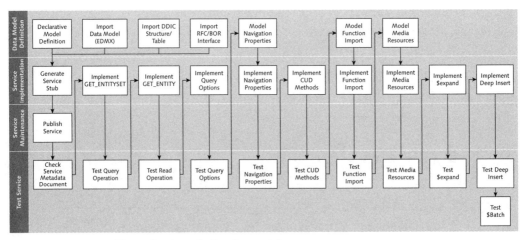

Figure 6.1 Example Development Process

6.1   Data Model Definition

Service Builder   As you've learned from the previous chapters, each OData service consists of a data model definition and a service implementation. At runtime, the model definition results in the service document and the service metadata document, and the service implementation results in the actual functionality of the SAP NetWeaver Gateway service. For an SAP NetWeaver Gateway OData service using the OData channel development paradigm, the model definition is provided via the model provider class (MPC). The service implementation is provided via the data provider class (DPC). The tool that performs both of these tasks is the SAP NetWeaver Gateway Service Builder.

> **Manual Service Creation**
>
> It's possible to manually perform the implementation of MPC and DPC by using the Class Builder (Transaction SE24) in ABAP. However, this process can be pretty time consuming and, especially in the case of the MPC, might be a bit error prone. Also on the DPC side, there are some recurring tasks (e.g., mapping of a data source and the creation of CRUD-Q methods for the different entity sets) that are easier with a tool.
>
> From the possible deployment options, you've seen that a remote call into another system out of the IW_BEP/SAP_GWFND component is also possible.

In this case, you need to consider that, for example, a certain data element might not be locally available on the IW_BEP/SAP_GWFND system.

There are two main steps in the data model definition: first, create a project, and second, define the actual data model. In this section, we'll walk you through both of these major steps.

Two steps in data model definition

6.1.1 Creating a Project

Before you can start with the model definition, you first need to start the Service Builder (Transaction SEGW) and create a new project. A project defines the brackets around all artifacts that are created during your OData service development. The Service Builder allows you to open and work on multiple projects in parallel. Figure 6.2 shows an example of a single Service Builder project.

Transaction SEGW

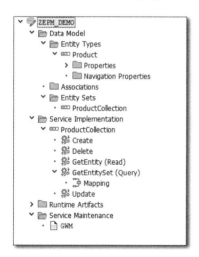

Figure 6.2 Example of a Service Builder Project

The root node is the project itself—in this case, ZEPM_DEMO. As the first subnode, you find DATA MODEL. This node takes care of your entire model definition. The SERVICE IMPLEMENTATION subnode actually injects life into your service by mapping data sources (e.g., RFCs or BAPIs) to your model. It also allows you to manually implement the respective methods using ABAP. RUNTIME ARTIFACTS summarizes all artifacts (or the most important ones) that are generated during your project lifecycle. And, finally, SERVICE MAINTENANCE allows you to register and activate your service on the SAP NetWeaver Gateway hub.

When starting the Service Builder the first time, you see an empty window (see Figure 6.3).

Figure 6.3 Service Builder Start Screen

Create project Choose the CREATE PROJECT button to create a new Service Builder project (see Figure 6.4).

Figure 6.4 Service Builder Create Project Button

Project details This opens the CREATE PROJECT dialog where you need to provide a project NAME, DESCRIPTION, GENERATION STRATEGY, PACKAGE, and PERSON RESPONSIBLE (see Figure 6.5), as described here:

▶ NAME
Special characters and spaces aren't allowed in project names, and they can't start with numbers. Individual words can be separated by underscores. The maximum length of the project name is 30 characters.

▶ DESCRIPTION
A 60-character, free-text field that should describe your project.

▶ GENERATION STRATEGY

Defaulted to STANDARD. There is currently only one generation strategy that can be chosen.

▶ PACKAGE and PERSON RESPONSIBLE

The default elements that you already know from other repository objects (e.g., ABAP reports, DDIC tables, etc.). $TMP is used for local development that you don't want to transport into any target system. If you want to transport the project and its content to any target system, you need to provide a transportable package. Such a package can be created by using the ABAP Development Workbench (Transaction SE80).

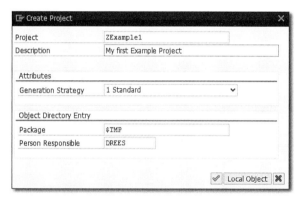

Figure 6.5 Create Project Dialog Screen

The project name becomes an ABAP repository entry, which is why the project name has to fulfill the typical SAP naming conventions (it has to start with a "Z" or a "Y"). In addition to that, you can also use a registered namespace surrounded by slashes (e.g., /MyNamespace/project) just as you also do when, for example, creating your own data element or function module by using the other standard SAP development tools. The object repository entry in this example is R3TR IWPR ZEXAMPLE1.

ABAP repository entry

IWPR refers to *Gateway Business Suite Enablement—Service Builder Project* and is of course transportable via a regular ABAP Workbench transport request. IWPR only transports the project as such—not the generated artifacts (e.g., MPC). Those will be separate entries in the transport request with their respective repository object types.

6.1.2 Creating the Data Model

Data model options

As soon as you have a project, you can start building your SAP OData service. The first thing you need to do is create the data model. As introduced in Chapter 5, there are multiple options to build a data model:

▸ Create a declarative data model.
▸ Import a data model via EDMX.
▸ Import a data model via DDIC.
▸ Import a data model via RFC/BOR.

The declarative model definition is typically chosen whenever you start from scratch with your data model definition, which means you have no source from which to derive your data model. Otherwise, you'll use whichever method is appropriate for the data source in question.

Let's discuss each of these options in more detail.

Creating a Declarative Data Model

Manual creation

A declarative data model is created manually. To create your first entity type via this method, right-click on DATA MODEL, and choose CREATE • ENTITY TYPE (see Figure 6.6).

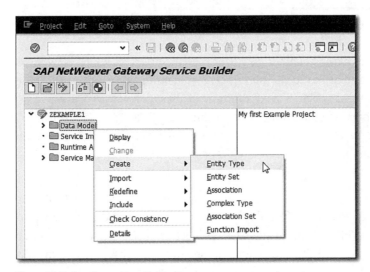

Figure 6.6 Creating a New Entity Type

In the CREATE ENTITY TYPE dialog, you can specify the name of your entity type. The name has to be unique inside your project.

Optionally you can also mark the CREATE RELATED ENTITY SET checkbox. This allows you to create a corresponding entity set with an assignment to this entity type in one step. Typically, there is a 1:1 relationship between an entity type and an entity set, but this isn't required; an entity type can be used in many entity sets. For example, a Business-Partner entity type might be used in entity sets with the name ShipTo-PartnerCollection, SoldToPartnerCollection, and so on.

Create related entity set

In the first example, you'll create a product entity type (see Figure 6.7) with a set of properties.

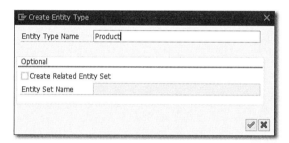

Figure 6.7 Creation of a New Entity Type

After the entity type has been created, the project tree is automatically updated, and the new entity type is highlighted and selected. On the right-hand side, you see all of the attributes of the entity type (see Figure 6.8).

Figure 6.8 Entity Type Attributes

One of the important attributes is the ABAP structure type name. Via this optional attribute, you can define a link of your entity type to a DDIC structure or table. This is quite important because it allows you to inherit your property definition (e.g., length and precision) from the underlying DDIC element. In addition to that, you also inherit any

labels, including their translations, from the DDIC. This is quite beneficial if you offer your application in multiple languages and want the
application to pick the labels from the exposed metadata (either once
during design time or dynamically during runtime via the metadata document) in the respective language. Even if you're running just a single
language, this link means that don't have to maintain your labels in multiple areas. (On the other hand, if the application dynamically fetches its
labels from the metadata document, you can't predict how things might
look in the final UI. It's entirely up to you which approach you prefer.)

So far, the entity type has no properties. This can be changed by expanding the project tree and double-clicking on PROPERTIES (see Figure 6.9).

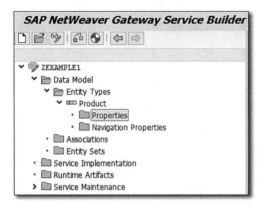

Figure 6.9 Properties Node in the Project Tree

On the right–hand side of the project window, the properties grid of the
current entity type is shown. Because there is no property so far, the
grid is of course empty after creating a new entity type. By clicking the
APPEND ROW or INSERT ROW buttons, you can create a new property for
the current entity type.

As mandatory information, you have to provide the name and the EDM
core type of the property (even if you provide a DDIC reference). Each
entity type also has to have at least one property marked as the key
property.

In the current example, you'll create three properties for the product   **Three properties**
entity type: `ProductID`, `Category`, and `Name`. They are all defined as
`Edm.String` with individual lengths (see Figure 6.10).

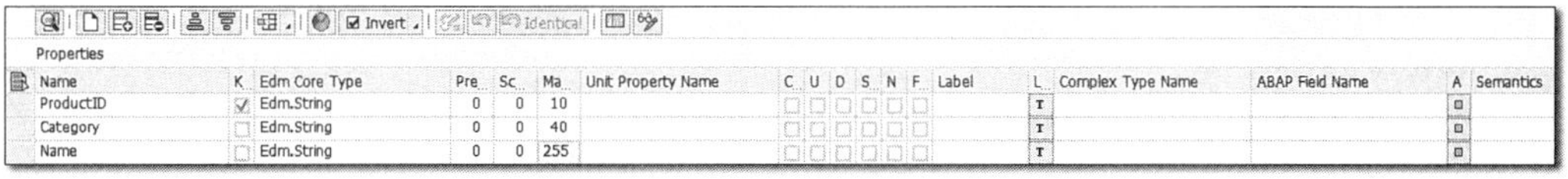

Figure 6.10 Entity Type Properties

The property `ProductID` is marked as a key property. So the primary key   **Key property**
of the product entity type consists of only one field. The max length
attribute is defined as 10 for the `ProductID`, 40 for the category, and 255
for the name in this example.

The attribute flags (see Figure 6.11) are described in Table 6.1.

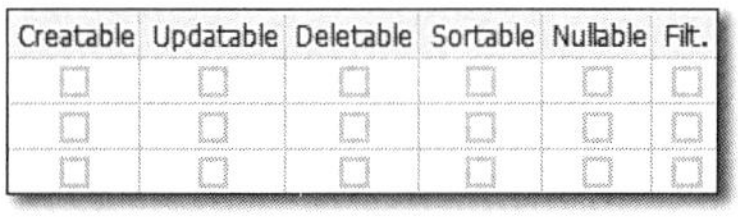

Figure 6.11 Property Attribute Flags

Letter	Meaning	Annotation	Description/Example
C	Creatable	`sap:creatable`	This property can be provided by an application when creating an entry resource of this entity type.
			Most of the properties typically have this flag set because they are supposed to be filled when an entry is being created (e.g., `CustomerName`).
			This flag is typically not set in cases where the backend provides the property when an entry is being created (e.g., `SalesOrderNumber` or `BusinessPartnerNumber`).

Table 6.1 Entity Type Attributes

Letter	Meaning	Annotation	Description/Example
U	Updatable	`sap:updatable`	This property can be provided by an application when updating an entry resource of this entity type. The updatable attribute is often in line with the creatable attribute. It's typically set whenever a property of an existing entry can be changed (e.g., `PhoneNumber`). It's typically not set whenever a property is calculated by the backend (e.g., `ChangeTimeStamp` or `NetSum`).
D	Deletable	`N/A`	This attribute has no relevance because individual properties can't be deleted (this has no effect on changing individual properties to their initial state).
S	Sortable	`sap:sortable`	The sortable annotation indicates to a consumer if the property can be used in an `$orderby` query option (e.g., `$orderby=CustomerName`).
N	Nullable	`Nullable`	The nullable annotation defines if a property can contain a `Null` value or not. This is very important for `Date` or `Time` fields (for example) if they don't contain a value on the ABAP side; as such, an empty field can't be rendered into an OData response if the nullable annotation isn't set. It's good advice to set the nullable attribute for all nonkey properties to make sure they can carry even empty ABAP values. Note that key properties may not contain nullable properties, that is, may not have the value `Null`.

Table 6.1 Entity Type Attributes (Cont.)

Letter	Meaning	Annotation	Description/Example
F	Filterable	`sap:filterable`	The filterable annotation indicates to a consumer if the property can be used in a `$filter` query option (e.g., `$filter=OrderNumber eq '1234'`).

Table 6.1 Entity Type Attributes (Cont.)

The annotations are rendered into the metadata document (see Figure 6.12).

```
- <EntityType Name="Product" sap:content-version="1">
  - <Key>
      <PropertyRef Name="ProductID" />
    </Key>
    <Property Name="ProductID" Type="Edm.String" Nullable="false" MaxLength="10" sap:creatable="false" sap:updatable="false"
      sap:sortable="false" sap:filterable="false" />
  </EntityType>
```

Figure 6.12 Property Metadata with All Flags Set

The creatable, updatable, sortable, and filterable attributes are only used in the metadata document to inform the consumer application about the intended behavior. There is no control via the SAP NetWeaver Gateway framework if a certain property is actually being used the way it's annotated via the metadata. Even if a property isn't marked as updatable, you can still provide the property along with an update request, and the property value will reach the data provider implementation. So it will not be—for example—filtered or handled via an error if you perform an operation that isn't allowed according to the annotations in the metadata document.

Creatable, updatable, sortable, filterable attributes

As a recommendation, the data provider implementation (DPC) should always behave the same way because the metadata is defining the model. But this isn't a must and unfortunately in many service implementations isn't considered, as most of the services are being developed for individual use cases. Whenever you develop an OData service for reuse, it's strongly recommended to define proper metadata; otherwise, the service consumers have to identify the service capabilities via trial and error, which is obviously not a good practice.

In this example, flag all attributes of the three properties (apart from the nullable attribute of the key field) and also provide some labels (see Figure 6.13).

Properties											
Name	K	Edm Core Type	Pre..	Sc..	Max Lngth	Uni..	Creatable	Updatable	Deletable	Sortable	Nullable	Filt.	Label
ProductID	☑	Edm.String	0	0	10		☑	☑	☑	☑	☐	☑	Product Identifier
Category	☐	Edm.String	0	0	40		☑	☑	☑	☑	☑	☑	Product Category
Name	☐	Edm.String	0	0	255		☑	☑	☑	☑	☑	☑	Product Name

Figure 6.13 Maintained Attributes and Labels

Now you're done with this small and simple entity type. The next step is to create an entity set, which is required because the service provisioning as well as the service consumption takes place based on entity sets. An entity set can be created by double-clicking the entity set node in the project explorer. This opens the entity set section on the right-hand side where you need to select the APPEND ROW or INSERT ROW buttons.

In this example, create an entity set with the name `ProductCollection` (see Figure 6.14).

Entity Sets											
Name	Entity Type Name	Label	L.	Semantics	C	U	D	P.	A	S.	S.	R.
ProductCollection	Product		I		☑	☑	☑	☑	☑	☑	☐	☐

Figure 6.14 Creation of Entity Set ProductCollection

Naming entity sets There are different approaches for naming an entity set for a given entity type. Some people prefer to add "Set" to the entity type name (in this example, `ProductSet`). Others prefer to use the plural (`Products`). In these examples, you'll add "Collection" to define the name of the resulting entity set. It's entirely up to you which approach you prefer and how to handle it in your own OData services; just be sure not to mix the approaches within a single OData service.

For each entity set, you also need to specify the underlying entity type name. This is mandatory information. The entity type name can either be typed in manually or chosen from an F4 help dialog. Optionally, you can also provide a label. This label is rendered into the metadata document and allows a consumer application to, for example, display a page title.

On the entity set level, there are again certain flags that annotate the capabilities of the related entity set. Similar to the flags on the entity type level, those flags are only part of the meta-information (in this case, in both the metadata as well as the service document). There is no handling via the framework, which means that, for example, if an entity set isn't annotated as creatable, you can still do a POST request and create the related entry resource. Again, make sure that the metadata of the OData service is in line with the actual service provisioning.

Flags

Table 6.2 describes the meaning of the entity set attributes.

Letter	Meaning	Annotation	Description/Example
C	Creatable	sap:creatable	Creation of entries of the related entity type is supported. Creates are handled via HTTP POST requests. For example, you can create a business partner entry.
U	Updatable	sap:updatable	Updates of entries of the related entity type are supported. Updates are handled via HTTP PUT requests addressing the entry resource you want to update. For example, you can update a product with the product ID "123".

Table 6.2 Entity Set Attributes

Letter	Meaning	Annotation	Description/Example
D	Deletable	sap:deletable	Deletions of entries of the related entity type are supported.
			Deletions are handled via HTTP DELETE requests addressing the entry resource you want to delete.
			For example, you can delete a sales order line item with the key OrderId='50000' Item='10'.
P	Pageable	sap:pageable	Client-side paging of this entity set is supported. Client-side paging works via the query parameter. The client can define the page size and the number of entries to be skipped.
A	Addressable	sap:addressable	This indicates whether the related entity set can be addressed directly via the URI (e.g., ProductCollection) or whether you have to use a navigation property to address it via a different entry, for example, SalesOrderCollection('1')/Items. SalesOrderItemCollection would not be directly addressable because it makes no sense to read all order items across all sales orders without the respective order header.

Table 6.2 Entity Set Attributes (Cont.)

Letter	Meaning	Annotation	Description/Example
S	Searchable	`sap:searchable`	Searchable indicates whether the service implementation (`QUERY` method) supports a search string. A search string doesn't filter on any properties as such but provides the search string via the URI search parameter, for example, `ProductCollection?search='box'`.
S	Subscribable	`N/A`	This attribute indicates if a consumer can subscribe to changes of the underlying entities. Subscription and notification handling require corresponding system configuration (bgRFC) as well as user exit implementations or event linkages to send a notification based on a backend event.
R	Requires Filter	`sap:requires-filter`	Indicates whether a query requires a filter or not. If a filter is required, you can't execute a query without a filter. For example, `Business-PartnerCollection` fetches all business partners available in the system, which can be quite a lot. Therefore, it makes sense to force a consumer to provide a filter.

Table 6.2 Entity Set Attributes (Cont.)

The entity set attributes are rendered into the metadata document (see Figure 6.15).

```
<?xml version="1.0" encoding="utf-8" ?>
- <edmx:Edmx Version="1.0" xmlns:edmx="http://schemas.microsoft.com/ado/2007/06/edmx"
    xmlns:m="http://schemas.microsoft.com/ado/2007/08/dataservices/metadata" xmlns:sap="http://www.sap.com/Protocols/SAPData">
  - <edmx:DataServices m:DataServiceVersion="2.0">
    - <Schema Namespace="ZTEST2_SRV" xml:lang="en" xmlns="http://schemas.microsoft.com/ado/2008/09/edm">
      - <EntityType Name="Product" sap:content-version="1">
        - <Key>
            <PropertyRef Name="ProductID" />
          </Key>
          <Property Name="Name" Type="Edm.String" MaxLength="255" sap:label="Product Name" />
          <Property Name="Category" Type="Edm.String" MaxLength="40" sap:label="Product Category" />
          <Property Name="ProductID" Type="Edm.String" Nullable="false" MaxLength="10" sap:label="Product Identifier" />
        </EntityType>
      - <EntityContainer Name="ZTEST2_SRV" m:IsDefaultEntityContainer="true">
          <EntitySet Name="ProductCollection" EntityType="ZTEST2_SRV.Product" sap:creatable="false" sap:updatable="false" sap:deletable="false"
            sap:pageable="false" sap:addressable="false" sap:content-version="1" />
        </EntityContainer>
        <atom:link rel="self" href="http://vegtwy1mst.wdf.sap.corp:50000/sap/opu/odata/sap/ZTEST2_SRV/$metadata"
          xmlns:atom="http://www.w3.org/2005/Atom" />
        <atom:link rel="latest-version" href="http://vegtwy1mst.wdf.sap.corp:50000/sap/opu/odata/sap/ZTEST2_SRV/$metadata"
          xmlns:atom="http://www.w3.org/2005/Atom" />
      </Schema>
    </edmx:DataServices>
  </edmx:Edmx>
```

Figure 6.15 Sample Metadata Document with Entity Set Attributes

This easy example just has a single entity type assigned to a single entity set. Because you don't have multiple entity types in this example, there is also no need to define any association yet (this will change later on).

Read on to see how to import a more sophisticated EDMX (entity data model XML) file with multiple entity types, entity sets, associations, and related navigation properties.

Importing a Data Model via EDMX

Entity data model XML — It is also possible to import an already existing EDMX (entity data model XML) file. This can be created via any toolset that is capable of modeling an entity data model and exporting it as an EDMX file. One example for such a toolset is the SAP NetWeaver Gateway Productivity Accelerator (GWPA) (explained in Chapter 8), which contains an OData Model Editor. Another source of EDMX files is any OData service that you have access to, as the metadata document ($metadata) provides a file that can be used as an input.

In this example, you'll use the metadata document of the SAP NetWeaver Gateway demo service. To do this, you need to temporarily store the metadata file in your file system. To import a data model from a file, you first create a new project.

Start by creating a new project for importing a data model from a file (see Figure 6.16).   **Create new project**

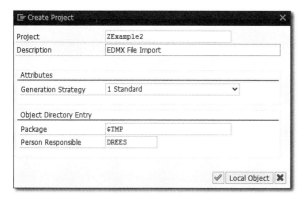

Figure 6.16 Creating a New Project for File Import

After you've created a new project, right-click on DATA MODEL, and choose IMPORT • DATA MODEL FROM FILE (see Figure 6.17). This opens up the SELECT A MODEL FILE FOR IMPORT dialog where you pick the metadata document or EDMX file that you've prepared (see Figure 6.18).

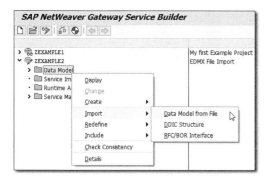

Figure 6.17 Importing a Data Model from File

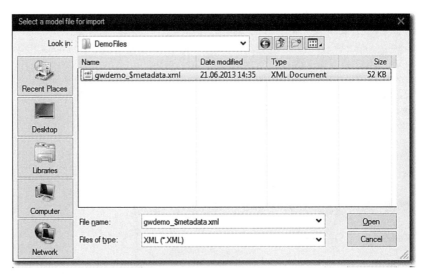

Figure 6.18 Select a Model File for Import Dialog

Depending on your local SAPGUI settings, you might get an SAPGUI security pop-up screen that prompts you to allow access to the specified file. You must allow this; otherwise, the import will be aborted.

File import successful
After the file import has finished, you get a success message: MODEL FILE IMPORTED SUCCESSFULLY. In some cases, the import might fail if the model file, for example, contains unsupported or unexpected tags or entity data model types. In this case, you have to adjust the data model file or choose a different one.

You can now expand the project tree and explore the imported elements (see Figure 6.19). For the SAP NetWeaver Gateway demo service, quite a number of entity types, entity sets, associations, and so on have been imported.

> **Note**
>
> The data model from file import only imports the meta-information into your service. No service provisioning is imported. This has to be done afterward either via the Service Builder or by implementing the related DPC methods in ABAP.

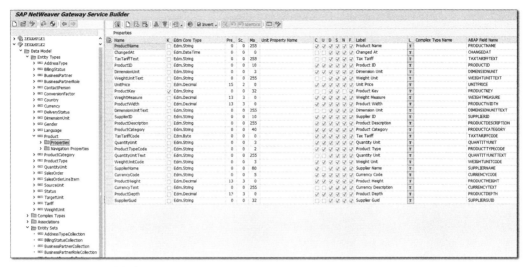

Figure 6.19 Data Model after File Import

After the data model has been imported, you can adjust the model to your needs. You can, for example, delete those elements you don't want to have in your final model. You can also add new elements (e.g., properties) to your model if required.

Importing a Data Model via DDIC

The third option to build up an OData model definition is to import a DDIC structure or table. For this, you create a new project (ZEXAMPLE3), right-click on DATA MODEL, and choose IMPORT • DDIC STRUCTURE (see Figure 6.20).

This opens the DDIC IMPORT window. This time, choose the database table SFLIGHT. After you provide the structure or table name, press Enter. This loads the definition from the DDIC and displays the fields with the attributes found. It also prepopulates the object name field with the name of the structure/table imported. This object name is the name of the resulting entity type and should be overwritten with a meaningful entity type name (e.g., SalesOrderHeader instead of VBAK). For this example, replace the defaulted value with "Flight".

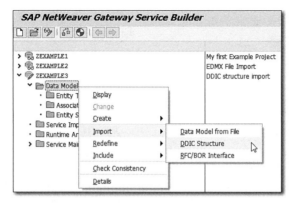

Figure 6.20 Starting the DDIC Structure Import Wizard

If you provide a database table, the DDIC import tool can identify the key information from the source. This isn't possible if you provide a DDIC structure, because structures don't have any key fields defined.

Client field Most of the DDIC tables that contain business data also have a client field as part of their primary key. The client field (sometimes called MANDT) isn't required in your model because, by default, your login takes place in a specific client, and the ABAP runtime adds the corresponding client information for each database operation.

The USAGE column defines whether a field will be ignored (IGNORE), set as a key (KEY), or used as a regular property (PROPERTY). In this example, set the MANDT field to IGNORE to keep it out of the data model (see Figure 6.21).

The second editable column, NAME, allows you to override the prepopulated name derived from the individual DDIC field name. This allows you to quickly rename the properties to provide more meaningful names to the developer of a consumer application. For example, field names such as CARRID (or Carrid) are hard to understand by any non-ABAP developer. Instead, you might want to provide CarrierID. In addition, rename CONNID to ConnectionID and FLDATE to FlightDate.

All other columns are read only and provide a preview of the properties that are going to be created (e.g., Edm Core Type, Scale, and Preci.).

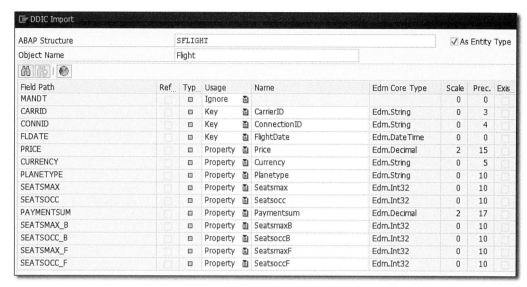

Figure 6.21 DDIC Import Wizard

When you're done, just press Enter again, and the corresponding entity type is created in your project. You can repeat these steps as many times as you want to add more entity types to your project (unlike the EDMX file import feature, which overwrites the entire model).

Entity type created

There is also the As Entity Type checkbox in the DDIC import wizard, which is selected by default. If you deselect this checkbox, you can create a complex type instead of an entity type. Complex types don't contain any key attributes. Therefore, the Usage dropdown only contains Ignore and Property in this case. The created entity type is automatically associated with the related DDIC structure/table that was used in the wizard (see Figure 6.22).

Figure 6.22 Entity Type with an Associated DDIC Table

As mention earlier, the DDIC structure/table reference allows the framework to pick the property definition from the underlying structure/table field. This includes the data type, length, and precision as well as labels for all installed languages.

Because the DDIC import only creates entity types and complex types, you have to create the corresponding entity sets yourself. In this example, create the entity set FlightCollection for the entity type Flight.

Importing a Data Model via BOR/RFC

Finally, the fourth option to import a data model is the BOR/RFC import. Business Object Repository (BOR) allows importing the interface of a BOR method (e.g., BusinessPartner.CreateFromData). *Remote function call* (RFC) is a more popular term and allows the import of an RFC interface. BOR methods often point to (remote) function modules, so BOR and RFC data sources are pretty similar from a Service Builder perspective.

BAPI_EPM_ PRODUCT_GET_ LIST

Let's create a new project and perform the import of the remote function module BAPI_EPM_PRODUCT_GET_LIST. Start the RFC wizard by right-clicking on DATA MODEL and choosing IMPORT • RFC/BOR INTERFACE (see Figure 6.23).

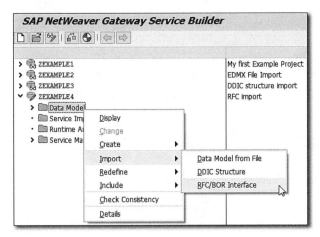

Figure 6.23 Start RFC/BOR Import Wizard

On the initial screen, specify the entity type name. In this example, enter "Product". Secondly, you specify whether the BOR/RFC interface you want to import resides in the local system (local from the perspective of the IW_BEP/SAP_GWFND component, which is typically the SAP ERP backend system) or is located in a remote system. In the latter case, you need to also provide the RFC destination to the corresponding system.

Then you need to tell the wizard if you want to import the interface of an BOR object or of an RFC module. Finally, you need to provide the name of the object you want to import. Based on the specified type, you get individual F4 help dialogs that allow you search for the object you're looking for. This also works in a remote scenario.

BOR or RFC

In this example, create the entity type "Product" from the LOCAL system by importing the interface of the RFC with the name BAPI_EPM_PRODUCT_GET_LIST (see Figure 6.24).

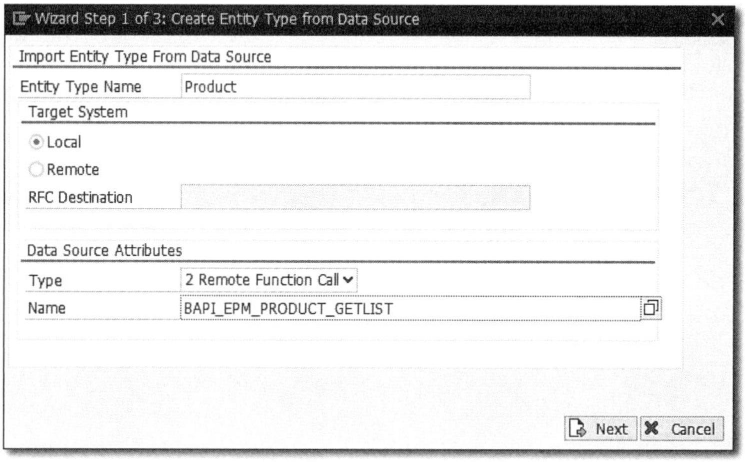

Figure 6.24 RFC Import Wizard: Step 1

Choose NEXT when you're done with the first page of the wizard. On the second page (see Figure 6.25), you initially see the collapsed interface of the RFC or BOR method.

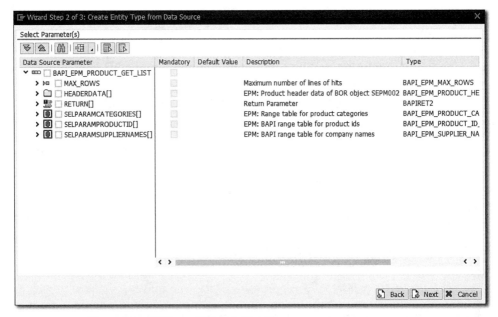

Figure 6.25 RFC Import Wizard: Step 2

Parameters

Each interface parameter has an individual icon that describes the type of the following parameters:

▶ Import parameter

▶ Export parameter

▶ Changing parameter

▶ Tables parameter

▶ BAPI return parameter

▶ Select options parameter

The first four parameters (import, export, changing, tables) are the typical parameters that function modules can have. The BAPI return parameter is a special tables parameter based on type BAPIRET2. This parameter has an individual icon because the Service Builder automatically handles the return table if you model the service provisioning with the Service Builder (e.g., Get_EntitySet method). There is no need to define a Return entity type in your data model to expose error information to the consumer; this is automatically done by reading the return table and throwing the related exception (e.g., there will be a business error exception thrown in case of an "E" message in the return table). This error results in a corresponding HTTP return code, along with the error long text in the response.

> **Note**
>
> This automatic error handling only takes place if you model the service provisioning via BOR/RFC mapping. If you implement the respective DPC methods yourself in ABAP, you need to verify any return code/return tables and throw the related exception.

Select options or ranges parameters are highlighted with a green icon that has square brackets. There is also no need to add ranges tables as entity types into your data model, because those should be mapped with corresponding filter parameters in the service implementation and not via individual entity types. Ranges tables are identified based on their DDIC structure with the typical SIGN and OPTION fields as well as a LOW and a HIGH field for the related filter parameter.

The RFC import wizard allows you to expand the collapsed interface to browse the underlying parameters, substructures, or nested tables. This example uses a BAPI, which, by definition, can't have a nested interface. Therefore, you only find "normal" fields in the import, export, and table structures. To define an entity type for products, mark the table parameter HEADERDATA[] (see Figure 6.26).

Data Source Parameter	Mandatory	Default Value	Description
∨ ▣▢ ☐ BAPI_EPM_PRODUCT_GET_LIST	▢		
› ▶▢ ☐ MAX_ROWS	▢		Maximum number of lines of hits
∨ ▭▢ ☑ HEADERDATA			EPM: Product header data of BOR object SEPM002
· ◈ ☑ PRODUCT_ID	▢		Product ID
· ◈ ☑ TYPE_CODE	▢		Product Type Code
· ◈ ☑ CATEGORY	▢		Product Category
· ◈ ☑ NAME	▢		Description
· ◈ ☑ DESCRIPTION	▢		Description
· ◈ ☑ SUPPLIER_ID	▢		Business Partner ID
· ◈ ☑ SUPPLIER_NAME	▢		Company Name
· ◈ ☑ TAX_TARIF_CODE	▢		Product Tax Tariff Code
· ◈ ☑ MEASURE_UNIT	▢		Quantity Unit
· ◈ ☑ WEIGHT_MEASURE	▢		Weight Measure
· ◈ ☑ WEIGHT_UNIT	▢		Quantity Unit
· ◈ ☑ PRICE	▢		Price
· ◈ ☑ CURRENCY_CODE	▢		Currency Code

Figure 6.26 RFC Import Wizard: Selection of a Table Parameter

After you're done with the selection of interface parameters, you can choose NEXT. This shows the final screen of the RFC import wizard (see Figure 6.27). This is the summary screen where you see which entity sets and/or complex types will be created.

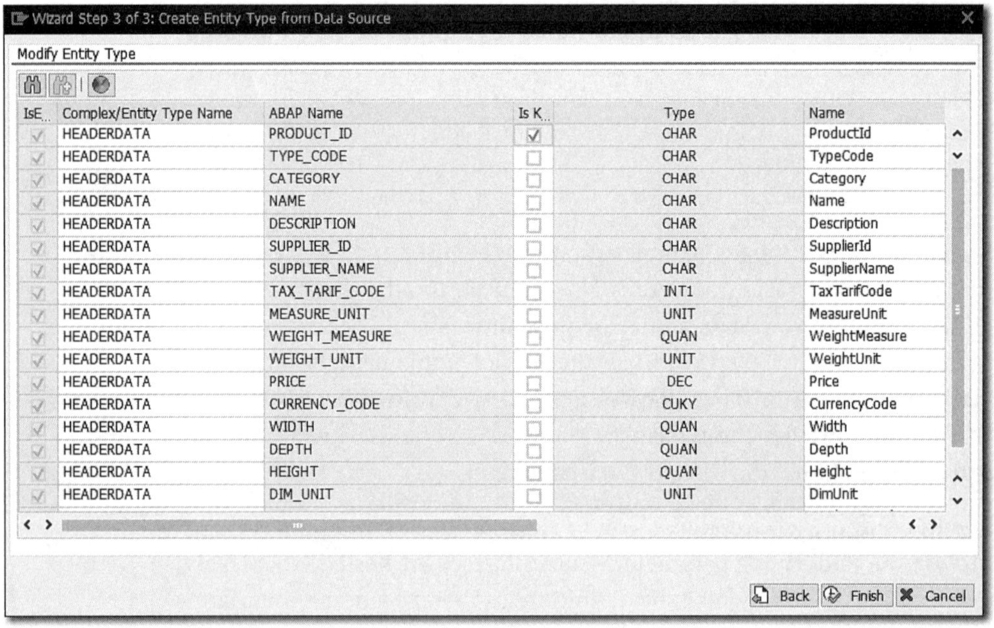

IsE	Complex/Entity Type Name	ABAP Name	Is K	Type	Name
✓	HEADERDATA	PRODUCT_ID	✓	CHAR	ProductId
✓	HEADERDATA	TYPE_CODE	☐	CHAR	TypeCode
✓	HEADERDATA	CATEGORY	☐	CHAR	Category
✓	HEADERDATA	NAME	☐	CHAR	Name
✓	HEADERDATA	DESCRIPTION	☐	CHAR	Description
✓	HEADERDATA	SUPPLIER_ID	☐	CHAR	SupplierId
✓	HEADERDATA	SUPPLIER_NAME	☐	CHAR	SupplierName
✓	HEADERDATA	TAX_TARIF_CODE	☐	INT1	TaxTarifCode
✓	HEADERDATA	MEASURE_UNIT	☐	UNIT	MeasureUnit
✓	HEADERDATA	WEIGHT_MEASURE	☐	QUAN	WeightMeasure
✓	HEADERDATA	WEIGHT_UNIT	☐	UNIT	WeightUnit
✓	HEADERDATA	PRICE	☐	DEC	Price
✓	HEADERDATA	CURRENCY_CODE	☐	CUKY	CurrencyCode
✓	HEADERDATA	WIDTH	☐	QUAN	Width
✓	HEADERDATA	DEPTH	☐	QUAN	Depth
✓	HEADERDATA	HEIGHT	☐	QUAN	Height
✓	HEADERDATA	DIM_UNIT	☐	UNIT	DimUnit

Figure 6.27 RFC Import Wizard: Step 3

In this example, only the tables parameter HEADERDATA is marked, which automatically selects all fields underneath. Therefore, the wizard only generates a single entity type with the name HEADERDATA and a property for each parameter of the interface table. The entity type name is derived from the node that you've selected.

HEADERDATA The name "Product" that you defined on the first screen of the wizard is ignored in this case because the HEADERDATA node has been selected. If you select all parameters (or a subset) under the node HEADERDATA, but not the HEADERDATA node itself, the wizard uses the entity type name defined on the first screen. The reason for this behavior is the capability of the RFC/BOR wizard to create multiple entity types out of multiple interface tables in one step. That's why the name of the interface element is used for the entity type name.

Prior to clicking the FINISH button, you should always verify that the very first column (ISENTITY) is marked as expected. In this example, this field is checked for all entries. This is correct and indicates that all properties will end up in an entity type and not a complex type. The name of the resulting entity type is shown in the next (editable) column COMPLEX/ENTITY TYPE NAME. If you want, you can change the name of the resulting entity type by changing all columns—but this isn't the recommended approach, as it takes time to adjust all properties one by one. It's a lot easier to let the wizard generate the entity type and then just change the name in the project.

Verify first column

If the ISENTITY column isn't marked, the properties will end up in a complex type (or in several complex types). This is, for example, the case if you select import or export structures (not tables) of RFC/BOR interfaces.

In addition, you should take a look at the KEY column and mark those properties that define the primary key of the resulting entity type (complex types don't have key fields). If you don't mark any property as KEY, you'll get a corresponding message, as a project check is automatically triggered when you finish the wizard and an entity type without a primary key is considered an erroneous entity type.

Key column

The next editable column, NAME, defines the name of each generated property in your model. This is what the outside world will see when consuming your OData service. Editing this list allows you to quickly change the name of all properties. Each property also has an ABAP name (see the ABAP NAME column), which isn't editable. The ABAP name is the field name you see on the ABAP side when processing a query or any other operation. This is important to distinguish because the ABAP name—especially when derived from an RFC interface or DDIC structure—sometimes looks a bit cryptic, whereas the property name can be defined in a more consumer-friendly way (e.g., `SalesOrderID` instead of `VBELN`).

In the last column, LABEL (you need to scroll to see it), you can define the label of your property. If an RFC/BOR object uses an underlying DDIC structure, the entity type is bound to the related DDIC element, and thus you don't need to change the label here. If you want to override a label

Define label

that comes via the DDIC link, you can do this by editing the properties in the properties overview by navigating to it via the project tree (after you've completed the wizard).

After you click the FINISH button, the property type(s) and/or complex type(s) will be created. A project check is executed (see Figure 6.28) to check if there are any problems with the current project definition.

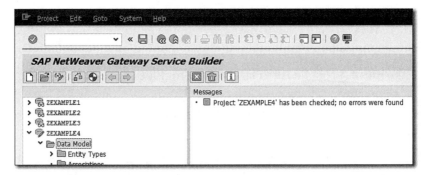

Figure 6.28 Project Check after the RFC/BOR Import

A typical error that is shown after this check is a forgotten primary key definition. If this happens, simply double-click on the error, and you'll be taken to the erroneous element.

In this example, the property type HEADERDATA was created although we've specified "Product" on the first page of the wizard. This is because we've selected the entire HEADERDATA table from the interface and not individual fields. You can easily change the entity type name by double-clicking on it in the project tree and changing it to "Product" in the ALV grid. Similar to the other examples, a corresponding entity set with the name ProductCollection must be manually created.

6.2   Service Registration in the SAP Business Suite System

Four projects   If you've followed the examples before, you now have four projects in your Service Builder:

- ▶ ZEXAMPLE1: manually created product entity type
- ▶ ZEXAMPLE2: imported data model from GWDEMO service
- ▶ ZEXAMPLE3: imported data model from SFLIGHT DDIC structure
- ▶ ZEXAMPLE4: imported data model from RFC BAPI_EPM_PRODUCT_GET_ LIST

You now have to generate the runtime artifacts and register them in the backend system. This is done by generating the project, which is triggered by clicking the GENERATE RUNTIME OBJECTS button (see Figure 6.29).

Figure 6.29 Generate Runtime Objects Button

The first time you click the GENERATE RUNTIME OBJECTS button, you get the model and service definition pop-up screen (see Figure 6.30). Typically, you keep the default values and just click the OK button. But it's important to understand the values that are defaulted as well as the meaning of the respective fields.

Model and Service Definition	
Model Provider Class	
Class Name	ZCL_ZEXAMPLE1_MPC_EXT
Base Class Name	ZCL_ZEXAMPLE1_MPC
Data Provider Class	
☑ Generate Classes	
Class Name	ZCL_ZEXAMPLE1_DPC_EXT
Base Class Name	ZCL_ZEXAMPLE1_DPC
Service Registration	
Technical Model Name	ZEXAMPLE1_MDL
Technical Service Name	ZEXAMPLE1_SRV

Figure 6.30 Model and Service Definition Pop-Up Screen

All ABAP classes that are generated are named with the pattern `<namespace>CL_<project_name>_<suffix>`. Typically, the namespace is just one of the default namespaces "Z". So in the ZEXAMPLE1 project, the names of the generated classes will start with `ZCL_ZEXAMPLE1`.

MPC
: As we explained in Chapter 5, the model provider class (MPC) is an ABAP class that provides the runtime representation of your model definition. As such, all model information that you've defined in your project will be generated into the MPC. As a consequence, you have to regenerate the MPC every time you change the model definition in your project.

Extension class and base class
: The model definition is generated into two classes. The extension class (with the suffix `_MPC_EXT`) and the base class (with the suffix `_MPC`). Technically the base class is derived from the `/IWBEP/CL_MGW_PUSH_ABS_MODEL` super class. The extension class has the base class as its super class. The extension class is the class that will be registered via the technical model name. This means that the extension class can define which methods to redefine and which methods to inherit from the base class.

DPC
: The same holds true for the data provider class (DPC). There you also find an extension class (suffix `_DPC_EXT`) and a base class (suffix `_DPC`). The DPCs are responsible for the runtime representation of your service implementation. For instance, the DPCs execute `CREATE`, `READ`, `UPDATE`, `DELETE`, `QUERY`, and many more operations.

The DPC base class inherits from the super class `/IWBEP/CL_MGW_PUSH_ABS_DATA`. The DPC extension class inherits from the DPC base class. The DPC extension class is the class that is registered via the technical service name. So the extension class is the class that is executed in your OData service.

The reason for having extension classes (`MPC_EXT` and `DPC_EXT`) is that they allow you to add your own coding into the model definition as well as the service implementation. This is necessary because there are certain use cases (e.g., consumption of complex RFC interfaces or handling of deep inserts) that can't be entirely defined by using the Service Builder.

The extension classes (`MPC_EXT` and `DPC_EXT`) can be changed via the typical development tools (e.g., the ABAP Class Builder), and the Service Builder won't overwrite those extension classes. The regeneration only adds new methods to the classes if necessary (e.g., if you add a new entity set to your project, corresponding CRUD-Q methods are generated into the DPC base class and thus inherited into the DPC extension class). So you're safe in performing your own development in the extension classes.

Note that the respective CRUD-Q methods (including any manually created redefinitions) are deleted from both the DPC base and the extension class if you remove the related entity set from your project. Therefore, you need to handle deletions of entity sets carefully, because they may result in the loss of your redefinitions and thus in the loss of your own ABAP coding.

CRUD-Q

Every OData channel service requires a technical model name and a technical service name on both the backend as well as the SAP NetWeaver Gateway hub server. The backend definitions of the technical model name as well as the technical service name are performed along with the generation of the MPCs and DPCs.

The technical model name basically just points to the MPC extension class. The definition of the technical model name is equal to the backend registration of the model, which can also be performed via the IMG (SAP NETWEAVER • GATEWAY SERVICE ENABLEMENT • BACKEND ODATA CHANNEL • SERVICE DEVELOPMENT FOR BACKEND ODATA CHANNEL • MAINTAIN MODELS). By default, each model is registered with version 1.

The technical service name points to the DPC extension class and is equal to your external service name (the name under which you'll consume your OData service). Additionally, the technical service name also points to the technical model name because the service implementation needs to have a model definition. The definition of the technical service name is equal to the registration of the service, which can also be performed via the IMG (path: SAP NETWEAVER • GATEWAY SERVICE ENABLEMENT • BACKEND ODATA CHANNEL • SERVICE DEVELOPMENT FOR BACKEND ODATA CHANNEL • MAINTAIN SERVICES). By default, each service is registered with version 1.

Package name

After you click OK in the model and service definition pop-up screen, you are prompted to provide the package name for the generated classes (see Figure 6.31). Typically, you assign your classes to the same package as the project.

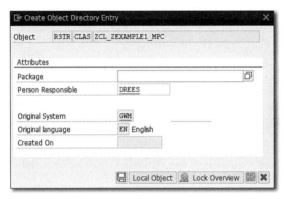

Figure 6.31 Object Directory Entry for the MPC Base Class

After you've provided all information, the generation and backend registration starts. Depending on the number of different RFC interfaces and, more importantly, the size of their interfaces you've defined in your service implementation, the generation might take some time. In the examples here, there is currently no service implementation, so the generation is performed pretty fast.

Messages window

After the generation has finished, the MESSAGES window appears (Figure 6.32). It should report only green traffic lights, which is your verification that the generation was successful. If the project check or project generation was not successful, you'll find corresponding information in the message window.

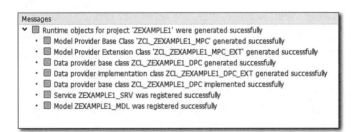

Figure 6.32 Messages Window after First Project Generation

After the project has been generated, you also see that the RUNTIME ARTIFACTS node in your project is populated. If you expand or double-click the RUNTIME ARTIFACTS node, you see all artifacts that have been generated. In this example, there are the two DPCs, the two MPCs, the model object, and the service object (see Figure 6.33).

Runtime Artifacts				
Name	Generated Artifact Type	Program ID	Object Type	Object Name
ZCL_ZEXAMPLE1_DPC	Data Provider Base Class	R3TR	CLAS	ZCL_ZEXAMPLE1_DPC
ZCL_ZEXAMPLE1_DPC_EXT	Data Provider Extension Class	R3TR	CLAS	ZCL_ZEXAMPLE1_DPC_EXT
ZCL_ZEXAMPLE1_MPC	Model Provider Base Class	R3TR	CLAS	ZCL_ZEXAMPLE1_MPC
ZCL_ZEXAMPLE1_MPC_EXT	Model Provider Extension Class	R3TR	CLAS	ZCL_ZEXAMPLE1_MPC_EXT
ZEXAMPLE1_MDL	Registered Model	R3TR	IWMO	ZEXAMPLE1_MDL
ZEXAMPLE1_SRV	Registered Service	R3TR	IWSV	ZEXAMPLE1_SRV

Figure 6.33 Runtime Artifacts of ZEXAMPLE1

If your project grows, you'll also find new entries in the RUNTIME ARTI-FACTS node. For instance, there will be an ABAP interface for each RFC module/BOR method that you use in the service implementation (e.g., an RFC module that you provide for the query execution). As mentioned before, the resulting model registration is accessible via the IMG (see Figure 6.34).

Runtime artifacts

Display Model	
🔒 Model	
Model Information	
Technical Model Name	ZEXAMPLE1_MDL
Model Version	1
Model Provider Class	ZCL_ZEXAMPLE1_MPC_EXT
Description	ZCL_ZEXAMPLE1_MPC_EXT

Figure 6.34 Model Definition of ZEXAMPLE1_MDL

The same holds true for the service registration (see Figure 6.35). The model registration and the service registration together is referred to as the backend registration of an OData channel service.

The generation of the MPCs and DPCs, as well as the backend registration of the model and service, concludes the registration of the OData service on the backend.

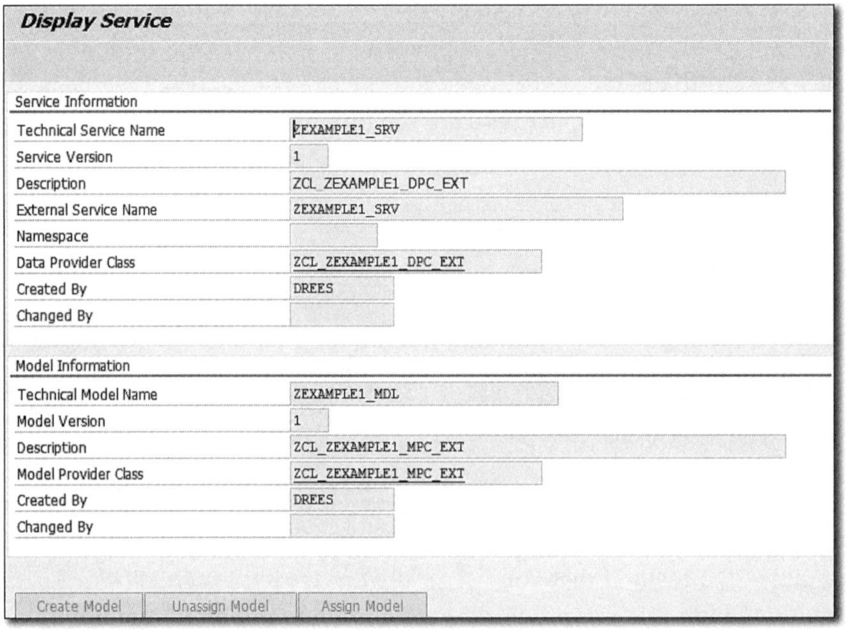

Figure 6.35 Service Definition of ZEXAMPLE1_SRV

6.3   Service Stub Generation

The service implementation actually injects life into the OData service. So far, you've just developed the data model of the OData service. The service implementation connects the data model with the underlying backend business logic (e.g., provided by an RFC function module or any other business logic). This will be explained in detail in Section 6.5.

According to Figure 6.1, shown earlier, at this point we'll only look at the generated service implementation stub that was generated by the Service Builder as part of the project generation step in Section 6.2. The reason for only briefly looking at the service implementation now is to consume the OData service to see the result of the metadata that was defined in Section 6.1. And because every OData channel service requires an MPC as well as a DPC to function, we also need to consider the service implementation prior to run the service.

To see the generated DPC, expand the RUNTIME ARTIFACTS node, right-click on ZCL_ZEXAMPLE1_DPC, and select GO TO ABAP WORKBENCH (see Figure 6.36). **DPC**

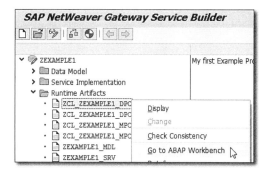

Figure 6.36 Displaying the Generated DPC Base Class Implementation

This opens up the ABAP Class Builder with the DPC base class. The methods shown in black have been redefined; this takes place every time you generate your project (see Figure 6.37). **ABAP Class Builder**

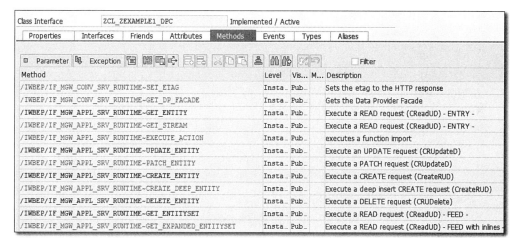

Figure 6.37 DPC Base Class

As an example, look at the redefined /IWBEP/IF_MGW_APPL_SRV_RUNT-IME~GET_ENTITYSET method by double-clicking the method name (see Figure 6.38).

Method	/IWBEP/IF_MGW_APPL_SRV_RUNTIME~GET_ENTITYSET	Active

```
 1 □method /IWBEP/IF_MGW_APPL_SRV_RUNTIME~GET_ENTITYSET.
 2 ⊟ *&-----------------------------------------------------------------*
 3   *&  Include              /IWBEP/DPC_TMP_ENTITYSET_BASE
 4   *&* This class has been generated by DREES on 03.08.2013 23:36:57 in client 800
 5   *&*
 6   *&*        WARNING--> NEVER MODIFY THIS CLASS <--WARNING
 7   *&*   If you want to change the DPC implementation, use the
 8   *&*   generated methods inside the DPC provider subclass - ZCL_ZEXAMPLE1_DPC_EXT
 9 └ *&-----------------------------------------------------------------*
10   DATA productcollectio_get_entityset TYPE zcl_zexample1_mpc=>tt_product.
11   DATA suppliercollecti_get_entityset TYPE zcl_zexample1_mpc=>tt_supplier.
12   DATA productconvfacto_get_entityset TYPE zcl_zexample1_mpc=>tt_productconvfactor.
13   DATA lv_entityset_name TYPE string.
14
15   lv_entityset_name = io_tech_request_context->get_entity_set_name( ).
16
17 □CASE lv_entityset_name.
18 ⊟ *-----------------------------------------------------------*
19   *            EntitySet - ProductCollection
20   *-----------------------------------------------------------*
21 ◇  WHEN 'ProductCollection'.
22   *   Call the entity set generated method
23       productcollectio_get_entityset(
24         EXPORTING
25           iv_entity_name = iv_entity_name
26           iv_entity_set_name = iv_entity_set_name
27           iv_source_name = iv_source_name
28           it_filter_select_options = it_filter_select_options
29           it_order = it_order
30           is_paging = is_paging
31           it_navigation_path = it_navigation_path
32           it_key_tab = it_key_tab
33           iv_filter_string = iv_filter_string
34           iv_search_string = iv_search_string
35           io_tech_request_context = io_tech_request_context
36         IMPORTING
37           et_entityset = productcollectio_get_entityset
38           es_response_context = es_response_context
39       ).
```

Figure 6.38 Generated GET_ENTITYSET Method of the DPC Base Class

Looking at the coding, you can see that there is a big case control structure. For each entity set, a separate submethod is called, which is also created as part of the generation step. This happens for all five CRUD-Q operations for each entity set.

Business exceptions

By default, those methods throw business exceptions (see Figure 6.39). This is because the actual service implementation hasn't yet taken place, so an exception is thrown to handle any service call to the respective operation.

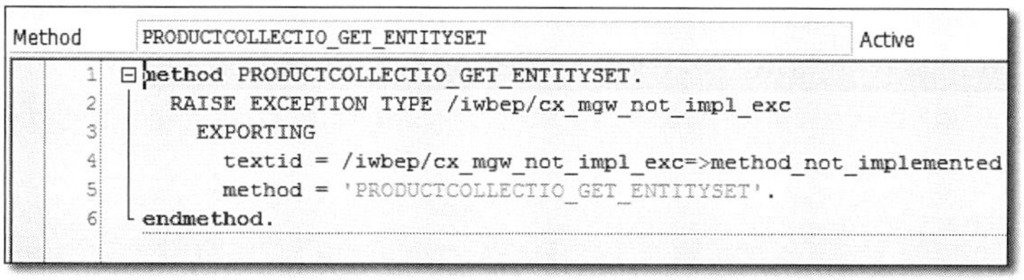

Method	PRODUCTCOLLECTIO_GET_ENTITYSET	Active

```
1   ⊟ method PRODUCTCOLLECTIO_GET_ENTITYSET.
2       RAISE EXCEPTION TYPE /iwbep/cx_mgw_not_impl_exc
3         EXPORTING
4           textid = /iwbep/cx_mgw_not_impl_exc=>method_not_implemented
5           method = 'PRODUCTCOLLECTIO_GET_ENTITYSET'.
6   ⌐ endmethod.
```

Figure 6.39 Generated PRODUCTCOLLECTIO_GET_ENTITYSET Method of the DPC Base Class

6.4 Service Maintenance

The next step is the registration and activation of the OData service on the SAP NetWeaver Gateway hub, otherwise known as the *service maintenance* phase. This can be done manually by executing Transaction /IWFND/MAINT_SERVICE and using the ADD SERVICE button on the SAP NetWeaver Gateway hub system; however, it's easier to perform the service registration and activation on the SAP NetWeaver Gateway hub right out of the Service Builder on the backend.

Registration and activation on hub

As a prerequisite, you have to maintain an SAP NetWeaver Gateway hub system in the IMG of the backend system. This is performed via the following IMG path: SAP NETWEAVER • GATEWAY SERVICE ENABLEMENT • BACKEND ODATA CHANNEL • CONNECTION SETTINGS TO SAP NETWEAVER GATEWAY • SAP NETWEAVER GATEWAY SETTINGS. In this IMG activity, you specify a name of the destination system, a client, an alias, and an RFC destination through which the hub system can be reached. For an embedded deployment (when the backend and SAP NetWeaver Gateway hub are on the same box), you still need to maintain a corresponding entry. In this case, you enter "NONE" as the RFC DESTINATION (see Figure 6.40).

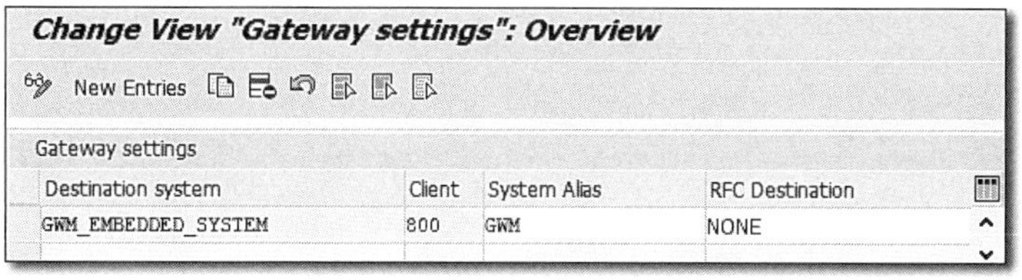

Maintain in IMG

Change View "Gateway settings": Overview

New Entries

Gateway settings

Destination system	Client	System Alias	RFC Destination	
GWM_EMBEDDED_SYSTEM	800	GWM	NONE	

Figure 6.40 Registered SAP NetWeaver Gateway System on the Backend

Make sure to enter an RFC destination for all entries you maintain. Otherwise, the corresponding entry won't show up in the Service Builder UI.

After you have your SAP NetWeaver Gateway hub system maintained in the IMG, you find a corresponding entry in each project under the SERVICE MAINTENANCE node. (Make sure to restart the Service Builder transaction each time you change the SAP NetWeaver Gateway settings in the IMG, because the Service Builder is caching these values.) The Service Builder shows detailed information on the right-hand side if you double-click the entry (see Figure 6.41).

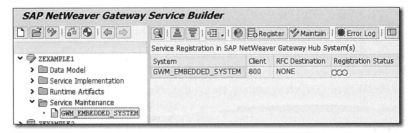

Figure 6.41 Service Registration Status on the SAP NetWeaver Gateway Hub

Now it's time to register and activate the service on the SAP NetWeaver Gateway hub. This is performed by marking the SAP NetWeaver Gateway hub system and clicking the REGISTER button.

The first time you do this, you get a pop-up screen to inform you that the activity will take place on the selected system (see Figure 6.42). That means the provided RFC destination will be used to jump into the target SAP NetWeaver Gateway hub system to register and activate your service there. (This is why each entry has to have an RFC destination.)

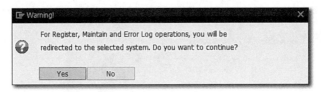

Figure 6.42 Redirect Warning

If you confirm the pop-up screen, you'll get the next pop-up screen to provide the system alias. This system alias is the alias defined on the SAP NetWeaver Gateway hub system that points to the backend system you're coming from. In an embedded deployment, you typically define an alias in the SAP NetWeaver Gateway IMG that is called LOCAL. This one also uses RFC DESTINATION NONE and makes sure that the call stays in the local system. After you've selected the system alias (see Figure 6.43), you can click the OK button.

System alias

Figure 6.43 Alias Definition for the Service Activation

The next pop-up screen has some more fields. It again comes from the SAP NetWeaver Gateway hub system, and is the same as running Transaction /IWFND/MAINT_SERVICE on the SAP NetWeaver Gateway hub system and clicking the ADD SERVICE button (see Figure 6.44).

On this screen, you define a technical service name as well as a technical model name on the SAP NetWeaver Gateway hub side. Those will be assigned 1:1 to the service name and model name on the backend system defined during the backend registration. The external service name is derived from the technical service name on the backend you've chosen earlier and can't be changed in this dialog.

Technical service and model name

You typically leave the default values as they are and only provide a package name for the repository objects that are created. After you click the OK button, the service registration and activation on the SAP NetWeaver Gateway hub system takes place, and you're taken back to the Service Builder on the backend system.

If the service registration and activation was successful, the system overview screen shown in Figure 6.45 will display a green traffic light.

Add Service	×

Service

Technical Service Name	ZEXAMPLE1_SRV
Service Version	1
Description	ZCL_ZEXAMPLE1_DPC_EXT
External Service Name	ZEXAMPLE1_SRV
Namespace	
External Mapping ID	
External Data Source Type	C

Model

Technical Model Name	ZEXAMPLE1_MDL
Model Version	1

Creation Information

Package	$TMP
	Local Object

ICF Node

⦿ Standard Mode   ◯ None
◯ Compatibility Mode for SP 02

☑ Set current client as default client in ICF Node

Figure 6.44 Add Service Dialog on the SAP NetWeaver Gateway Hub

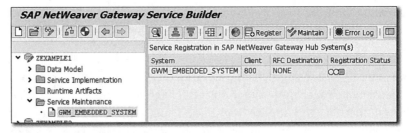

Figure 6.45 Status Change after Successful Service Activation

The OData service is now registered and active on the SAP NetWeaver Gateway hub system, which means that it can be consumed. The service name in the URI is the external service name that you've seen in the ADD

SERVICE dialog and is derived from the technical service name that you specified during the first generation of the project in the Service Builder.

You can use the SAP NetWeaver Gateway client (Transaction /IWFND/ GW_CLIENT) on the SAP NetWeaver Gateway hub system to consume the service. The URI is */sap/opu/odata/sap/ZEXAMPLE1_SRV*. If you execute this URI in the SAP NetWeaver Gateway client, you get the service document (see Figure 6.46).

Transaction /IWFND/GW_ CLIENT

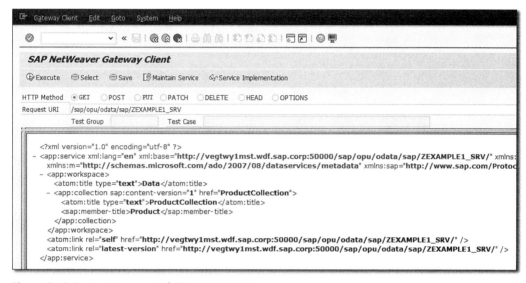

Figure 6.46 Service Document of ZEXAMPLE1_SRV

If you add /$metadata, you'll get the service metadata document of the example service (see Figure 6.47).

The service has a single collection (ProductCollection), which you can consume as well, but because you haven't done any service implementation so far, it would result in an error message. The service implementation is covered next.

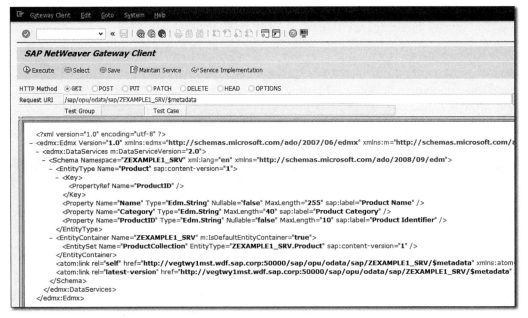

Figure 6.47 Metadata Document of ZEXAMPLE1_SRV

6.5 Incremental Service Implementation and Model Enhancement

Iterative approach

It's now time to implement the service in an iterative approach, as shown earlier in Figure 6.1. Whenever an OData service is consumed, a typical entry point is the execution of a query to fetch the collection/feed of, for example, business partners or products. That's why the get_entityset method is typically implemented first in most of the cases. This allows you to fetch a feed of an entity type and will be explained in detail in Section 6.5.1. From the feed, you receive links to each contained entry resource. That's why the single read (get_entity) is typically implemented after the get_entityset. The way a single read can be implemented is explained in detail in Section 6.5.2.

Query options

Enriching an OData service with powerful query options can be pretty important because it allows consumers to, for example, only request the required properties ($select), filter the result based on different criteria ($filter), perform client-side paging ($top/$skip), calculate the number of entries in a feed along with the feed itself ($inlinecount), or sort the feed according to your needs ($orderby). All of these query options are explained in detail with code examples in Section 6.5.3.

Navigation properties (also known as navigation links) are important elements of OData services because they define the allowed/foreseen navigations between OData elements. This can, for example, be the navigation from a sales order header (entry) to the corresponding list of sales order line items (feed). The definition and implementation of navigation properties is explained in detail in Section 6.5.4.

If you want to allow write access to your entity set, you also have to implement the create_entity, update_entity, and the delete_entity methods (CUD methods). The detailed implementation of the CUD methods is explained in Section 6.5.5.

In Section 6.5.6, we explain and provide an implementation example for function imports. Function imports are used whenever the known CRUD-Q operations aren't sufficient and a dedicated function (e.g., confirm-order or reject-delivery) is required in an OData service.

Media resources can be used to expose binary data such as, for example, graphics to consumers. In Section 6.5.7, we explain how an entity type can be defined as a media link entity type and what you need to consider in this case.

$expand is another powerful feature of OData services that allows you to retrieve multiple entries and/or feeds along the defined navigation properties by using a single service call instead of executing multiple services calls. This typically improves the performance significantly because, for example, less data needs to be determined on the backend. The detailed implementation is explained in Section 6.5.8.

A deep insert is basically the opposite of $expand. Instead of retrieving a nested structure, you can write a nested structure into the SAP NetWeaver Gateway server. This typically substitutes the need to perform several individual create calls. A deep insert can, for example, be used if you want to create a sales order header together with a list (feed) of sales order line items in one single create call. Section 6.5.9 explains in detail how a deep insert can be implemented.

And, finally, Section 6.5.10 provides an introduction into `$batch`, which is used to bundle multiple independent service calls into one batch call. It can, for example, be used to fetch customizing data that is provided via multiple independent collections.

Before you start to implement your own coding, you should re-generate your project to ensure that the MPCs and the DPCs are up to date and match the current state of your project definition. This also ensures that no definition errors are contained in your project (see Figure 6.48).

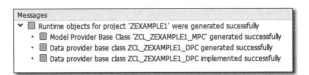

Figure 6.48 Successful Regeneration of the Sample Project

6.5.1 Feed (GET_ENTITYSET)

The `get_entityset` of the `ProductCollection` entity set is implemented via the Service Builder by expanding the SERVICE IMPLEMENTATION node and the PRODUCTCOLLECTION node. Then you right-click on GETENTITY-SET (QUERY) and choose GO TO ABAP WORKBENCH (see Figure 6.49).

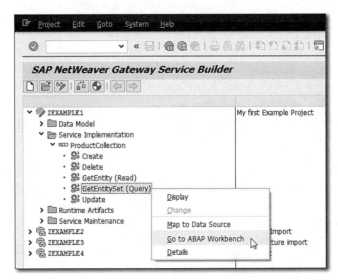

Figure 6.49 Navigate to Query Implementation in the ABAP Workbench

This opens a dialog informing you that the implementation of the respective method hasn't yet been performed (see Figure 6.50).

Figure 6.50 Information Screen: Method Not Yet Implemented

Confirming this pop-up screen opens the data provider extension class ZCL_ZEXAMPLE1_DPC_EXT in the ABAP Class Builder (Transaction SE24). Because no method has been redefined yet, all methods are displayed with a blue font. The blue font is an indicator that a method is inherited from the super class (in this case, the DPC base class) and will be executed there—if not redefined.

You'll find quite a number of methods derived from several interfaces in the data provider extension class. The one that we're indirectly looking at first is GET_ENTITYSET of the interface /IWBEP/IF_MGW_APPL_SRV_RUNT-IME. This method is handling all query calls (Get Entityset) of all entity sets of this OData service. That's why this method first needs to distinguish which entity set is being requested. This is where the Service Builder comes into play again; it generates a case structure into each of the five CRUD-Q methods (CREATE_ENTITY, GET_ENTITY, UPDATE_ENTITY, DELETE_ENTITY, GET_ENTITYSET) to handle the individual entity set requested by calling a separate method. In addition to the case structures, the Service Builder generates five separate CRUD-Q methods for each entity set into the DPC base class, which also end up in the extension class via inheritance.

Methods derived from interfaces

The separation of the generic five CRUD-Q methods into individual instance methods (protected) per entity set provides a clear distinction of the methods required to handle the OData requests. The name is concatenated out of the entity set name as well as the respective CRUD-Q method. If the resulting method name exceeds 30 characters, the name of the entity set will be truncated to still guarantee a unique name across the DPC.

Five methods   The five methods generated in the example project are listed here:

- ▶ PRODUCTCOLLECTIO_CREATE_ENTITY
- ▶ PRODUCTCOLLECTIO_DELETE_ENTITY
- ▶ PRODUCTCOLLECTIO_GET_ENTITY
- ▶ PRODUCTCOLLECTIO_GET_ENTITYSET
- ▶ PRODUCTCOLLECTIO_UPDATE_ENTITY

To implement the Get_Entityset method in the example, you need to redefine the PRODUCTCOLLECTIO_GET_ENTITYSET method.

Set the DPC extension class to edit mode Ctrl + F1 , and scroll down to PRODUCTCOLLECTIO_GET_ENTITYSET (make sure this line is selected). Now click the REDEFINE button. This opens up the ABAP editor and redefines the method PRODUCTCOLLECTIO_GET_ENTITYSET. By default, the Service Builder generates a code stub that consists of a commented call to the same super method. Replace the existing coding with the lines in Listing 6.1.

```
METHOD productcollectio_get_entityset.

  DATA: ls_headerdata TYPE bapi_epm_product_header,
        lt_headerdata TYPE STANDARD TABLE OF bapi_epm_product_
header,
        ls_product    LIKE LINE OF et_entityset.

  CALL FUNCTION 'BAPI_EPM_PRODUCT_GET_LIST'
*     EXPORTING
*       MAX_ROWS                 =
      TABLES
        headerdata               = lt_headerdata
*       SELPARAMPRODUCTID        =
*       SELPARAMSUPPLIERNAMES    =
*       SELPARAMCATEGORIES       =
*       RETURN                   =
        .

  LOOP AT lt_headerdata INTO ls_headerdata.
    ls_product-productid = ls_headerdata-product_id.
    ls_product-category  = ls_headerdata-category.
    ls_product-name      = ls_headerdata-name.
```

```
    APPEND ls_product TO et_entityset.
  ENDLOOP.

ENDMETHOD.
```

Listing 6.1 Product Collection, Get_Entityset Method

As you can see, the sample code performs a call to the underlying business logic (function module BAPI_EPM_PRODUCT_GET_LIST) to retrieve the list of products. This easy example neither supports any filter criteria nor any limitation of the number of items read; you simply fetch all existing EPM products from the database.

Calls function module

After retrieving the data, you need to map it to the export table. For the Get_EntitySet method, this table is always called ET_ENTITYSET. Looking at the signature, you see that the type of this export table is ZCL_ZEXAMPLE1_MPC=>TT_PRODUCT. This is a generated type in the MPC base class. This is important to know because whenever you add or change any property, you have to make sure to regenerate your project to see this change in the generated MPC.

The mapping of the product list (LT_HEADERDATA) to the export table (ET_ENTITYSET) is pretty straightforward. You could have used the ABAP statement move-corresponding if you had named the productid property with an underscore. Move-corresponding could also have been used if you had implemented the projects that have been generated using DDIC import or RFC-interface import, because in those cases ET_ENTITYSET would have been of the same data type as LT_HEADERDATA. Mapping is also needed if you use the EDMX import option, because then the export table would also have been a generated type as in the described case that works with the manually created entity type.

Whenever you encounter any problem in determining the result, you can raise a business exception /IWBEP/CX_MGW_BUSI_EXCEPTION. This terminates the processing and throws the related HTTP error code to the consumer along with the error statements you provide.

Raise business exception

When you're done with the coding, activate the changes by clicking the ACTIVATION button (or pressing Ctrl+F3 in the Class Builder). Make sure to activate all changes you've implemented (see Figure 6.51).

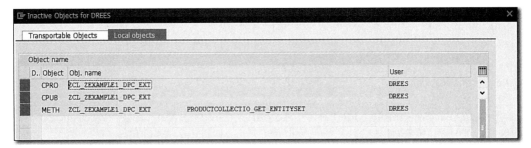

Figure 6.51 Activating All Changes of Your Implementation

The Service Builder project was already generated before, so there's no need to regenerate it.

Via the SAP NetWeaver Gateway client, you can now run the query by executing the URI */sap/opu/odata/sap/ZEXAMPLE1_SRV/ProductCollection*. As expected, you get the collection of product entities (see Figure 6.52).

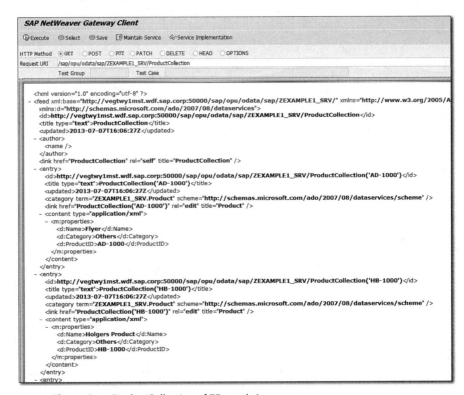

Figure 6.52 ProductCollection of ZExample1

As you can see from the result, the OData feed provides a link for each entry that allows you to navigate to the respective entry resource (see tag `entry-id`). Because you haven't yet implemented the single read method (`get_entity`), those links would result in an error if you execute them now.

6.5.2 Single Read (GET_ENTITY)

Similar to the `QUERY` method, you can easily develop the single read via the ABAP Class Builder. This time, expand the SERVICE IMPLEMENTATION • PRODUCTCOLLECTION node, right-click on GETENTITY (READ), and choose GOTO ABAP WORKBENCH. An information pop-up screen appears because the method hasn't yet been implemented.

This time, scroll down to the method `PRODUCTCOLLECTIO_GET_ENTITY`, put the cursor on it, switch to edit mode, and click the REDEFINE button.

Replace the generated code stub with the lines in Listing 6.2.

```
METHOD productcollectio_get_entity.

  DATA: ls_key_tab     TYPE /iwbep/s_mgw_name_value_pair,
        ls_product_id TYPE bapi_epm_product_id,
        ls_headerdata TYPE bapi_epm_product_header.

  LOOP AT it_key_tab INTO ls_key_tab.
    IF ls_key_tab-name EQ 'ProductID'.
      ls_product_id-product_id = ls_key_tab-value.
    ENDIF.
  ENDLOOP.

  CALL FUNCTION 'BAPI_EPM_PRODUCT_GET_DETAIL'
    EXPORTING
      product_id              = ls_product_id
    IMPORTING
      headerdata              = ls_headerdata
*   TABLES
*     CONVERSION_FACTORS      =
*     RETURN                  =
      .

  er_entity-productid = ls_headerdata-product_id.
```

```
      er_entity-category   = ls_headerdata-category.
      er_entity-name       = ls_headerdata-name.

ENDMETHOD.
```

Listing 6.2 Product Collection, Get_Entity Method

Pick key fields   The first thing you need to do in the coding is to pick the key fields from the input table. The `Get_Entity` method addresses a single entry resource from the collection. This is done by providing the key properties as part of the URI in parentheses right after the collection name (e.g., *ProductCollection('HT-1000')*).

The names of the key properties need to be provided as part of the URI if the entity type has more than one key property defined in its metadata. But there's no need to concatenate any URIs manually with property names and key values because the framework takes care of it by generating the respective links automatically.

Access key properties   You access the key properties by looping over the input table `IT_KEY_TAB`. This table provides the key properties with the external property name. This is the name the consumer sees. The internal (ABAP) name of the property can be different; this depends on the property definition in your metadata.

If you want to retrieve the list of key values with their internal representation, you can use the method `get_keys( )` of the `io_tech_request_context` object that is part of the method interface. In this example, the external name of the key property is `ProductID`. This name is case sensitive and has to be provided exactly the way it was defined in the metadata. If in doubt, you can set an external breakpoint in your DPC method and look at the content of the respective key table.

After you've looped over the key table and picked the primary key of the object you want to fetch, you can call the respective function to fetch the data. In this case, use the function module `BAPI_EPM_PRODUCT_GET_DETAIL` to read the product details. The result (`HEADERDATA`) is then mapped into the return structure `ER_ENTITY`. This is done field by field because the external and internal name of the primary key product ID is different. If the field names are identical, you can of course use the `move-corresponding` ABAP statement to fill the return structure as described earlier when implementing the `GET_ENTITYSET` method.

The return structure is of type `ZCL_ZEXAMPLE1_MPC=>TS_PRODUCT`, which is generated into the MPC base class.

After activating the changed DPC extension class, you can read the detail of, for example, product HT-1000 by executing the following URI via the SAP NetWeaver Gateway client: */sap/opu/odata/sap/ZEXAMPLE1_SRV/ ProductCollection('HT-1000')*.

Activate changed DPC class

As expected, you now get a single entry instead of an OData feed (see Figure 6.53).

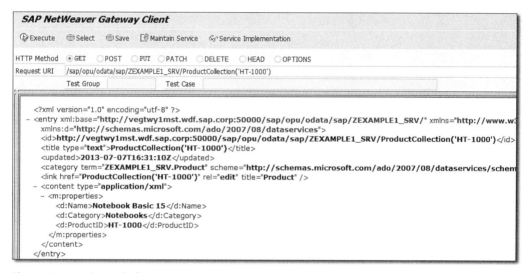

Figure 6.53 Single Read of Product 'HT-1000'

6.5.3 Query Options

Currently, the example service is able to provide an unfiltered list of products (feed/collection) as well as the related entries (get detail, single read).

In this section, we'll take a close look at the different query options such as `$select`, `$filter`, `$top`, `$skip`, `$inlinecount`, and `$orderby`. They allow you to only select the properties you want (`$select`), filter the result ($filter), perform a client-side paging ($top and $skip), count the number of records ($inlinecount), and/or sort them ($orderby).

$select

The $select query option allows you to select the properties you want to receive in your OData feed as well as in your single read. The $select is handled automatically by the framework. That means it automatically reduces the list of properties provided to the OData consumer—irrespective of what data the data provider has determined.

If you want to react on a $select query option in the way that you, for example, only read and determine the properties that have been requested, you have to do this in the DPC extension class (Get_Entity/ Get_EntitySet methods). You can access the $select properties by using the io_tech_request_context->get_select( ) method. The method provides you a table of all selected properties.

Reacting on a $select query option can have a significant performance improvement if you can, for example, avoid the calculation or determination of certain expensive properties (i.e., properties whose calculated values require significant effort, such as with price calculations, availabilities, etc.).

This example would not benefit from considering the $select statement anyway, because all properties are determined by the underlying function module.

$filter

The $filter query option is the most frequently used query option. It allows you to filter the result set of your Get_EntitySet implementation. By that, you can avoid providing an unfiltered list of all business partners or sales orders to the consumer (which can be quite a huge collection with many entries).

An entity set can also be annotated as requiring a filter. In this case, you have to provide a $filter query option in the URI. But as mentioned earlier, this is just an annotation, and no framework feature checks this.

The example service isn't yet able to handle any filter criteria because you haven't done anything in that regard so far. Looking at the interface of the `BAPI_EPM_PRODUCT_GET_LIST` function module, you see that it has range filter parameters for categories, product IDs, and supplier names (see Figure 6.54).

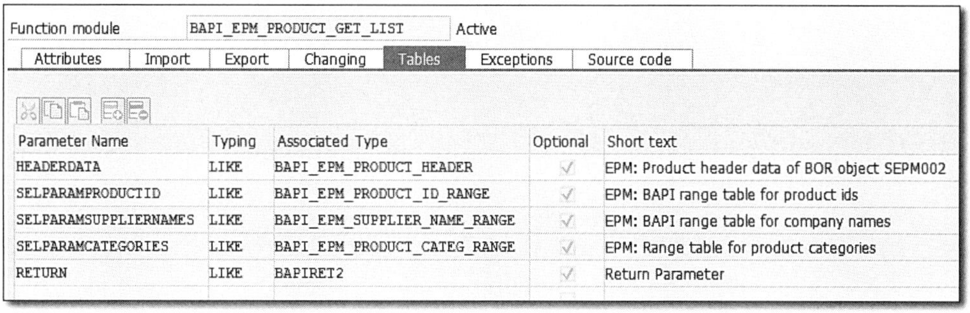

Function module	BAPI_EPM_PRODUCT_GET_LIST				Active		
Attributes	Import	Export	Changing	Tables	Exceptions	Source code	

Parameter Name	Typing	Associated Type	Optional	Short text
HEADERDATA	LIKE	BAPI_EPM_PRODUCT_HEADER	✓	EPM: Product header data of BOR object SEPM002
SELPARAMPRODUCTID	LIKE	BAPI_EPM_PRODUCT_ID_RANGE	✓	EPM: BAPI range table for product ids
SELPARAMSUPPLIERNAMES	LIKE	BAPI_EPM_SUPPLIER_NAME_RANGE	✓	EPM: BAPI range table for company names
SELPARAMCATEGORIES	LIKE	BAPI_EPM_PRODUCT_CATEG_RANGE	✓	EPM: Range table for product categories
RETURN	LIKE	BAPIRET2	✓	Return Parameter

Figure 6.54 Interface of BAPI_EPM_PRODUCT_GET_LIST

To make use of a filter parameter, you have to enhance the coding in the `Get_EntitySet` DPC extension class. Replace the `PRODUCTCOLLECTIO_GET_ENTITYSET` method with the lines in Listing 6.3.

Enhance coding

```
METHOD productcollectio_get_entityset.

  DATA: ls_headerdata TYPE bapi_epm_product_header,
        lt_headerdata TYPE STANDARD TABLE OF bapi_epm_product_
header,
        ls_product    LIKE LINE OF et_entityset.

  DATA: ls_selparamproductid    TYPE bapi_epm_product_id_
range,
        lt_selparamproductid    TYPE STANDARD TABLE OF bapi_
epm_product_id_range,
        ls_filter_select_options TYPE /iwbep/s_mgw_select_
option,
        ls_select_option         TYPE /iwbep/s_cod_select_
option.

  LOOP AT it_filter_select_options INTO ls_filter_select_
options.
    IF ls_filter_select_options-property EQ 'ProductID'.
```

```
        LOOP AT ls_filter_select_options-select_options INTO ls_
select_option.
            ls_selparamproductid-sign   = ls_select_option-sign.
            ls_selparamproductid-option = ls_select_option-option.
            ls_selparamproductid-low    = ls_select_option-low.
            ls_selparamproductid-high   = ls_select_option-high.
            APPEND ls_selparamproductid TO lt_selparamproductid.
        ENDLOOP.
      ENDIF.
    ENDLOOP.

    CALL FUNCTION 'BAPI_EPM_PRODUCT_GET_LIST'
*     EXPORTING
*       MAX_ROWS                    =
      TABLES
        headerdata                  = lt_headerdata
        selparamproductid           = lt_selparamproductid
*       SELPARAMSUPPLIERNAMES       =
*       SELPARAMCATEGORIES          =
*       RETURN                      =
                    .

    LOOP AT lt_headerdata INTO ls_headerdata.
      ls_product-productid = ls_headerdata-product_id.
      ls_product-category  = ls_headerdata-category.
      ls_product-name      = ls_headerdata-name.
      APPEND ls_product TO et_entityset.
    ENDLOOP.

  ENDMETHOD.
```

Listing 6.3 Product Collection, Get_Entityset Method with ProductID Filter

The changes introduced in this example take place at the beginning of the coding. Via the import table parameter it_filter_select_options, you receive the provided filter statement in a ranges-table-friendly way, so you can easily map it into a corresponding ranges table if the $filter parameter of the requested URI can be mapped into it. To do this, loop over the import parameter check for the external property name and copy the entries over into a local ranges table that is defined based on the function module interface. Then you also need to uncomment the `selparamproductid` parameter and provide the local ranges table.

Now you need to activate the DPC extension class to actually use the new filter criteria. As an example, you can execute the following URI to filter on products with the `product-id >= 'HT-1000'` and `product-id <= 'HT-1020'`:

/sap/opu/odata/sap/ZEXAMPLE1_SRV/ProductCollection?$filter=
ProductID ge 'HT-1000' and ProductID le 'HT-1020'

In addition to this, you can enrich the coding to also consider a filter on categories. Besides the data declaration and the mapping for the function module, add the code shown in Listing 6.4 into the loop.

Filter on categories

```
    ELSEIF ls_filter_select_options-property EQ 'Category'.
      LOOP AT ls_filter_select_options-select_options INTO ls_
select_option.
        ls_selparamcategories-sign   = ls_select_option-sign.
        ls_selparamcategories-option = ls_select_option-option.
        ls_selparamcategories-low    = ls_select_option-low.
        ls_selparamcategories-high   = ls_select_option-high.
        APPEND ls_selparamcategories TO lt_selparamcategories.
      ENDLOOP.
    ENDIF.
```

Listing 6.4 Product Collection, Get_Entityset Method Additional Filter on Category

In addition to the previous filter, the URI for filtering on `Category = 'Handhelds'` looks like the following:

/sap/opu/odata/sap/ZEXAMPLE1_SRV/ProductCollection?$filter=
ProductID ge 'HT-1000' and ProductID le 'HT-1020' and Category eq
'Handhelds'

As you can see, filter criteria can become quite complex.

The filter criteria are mapped into ranges tables by the framework. This allows you to easily process them and to assign them to the corresponding ranges-input table of your function module in your `Get_EntitySet` method. The OData framework provides them in a generic table in which each entry represents a property that is used in the filter query option.

Ranges tables

Note that the preparation of the ranges tables has certain limitations. Similar to defining an ABAP report with `select-options` fields, you can't cover all use cases. For example, a filter such as `FieldA eq 'A' or FieldB eq 'B'` can't be put into ranges tables because of the `or` operator. It would work if you use `and` instead of `or`, but that's of course a different statement and thus has a different result.

For these cases, the framework provides the import variable `IV_FILTER_STRING` that contains the actual filter string provided via the `$filter` query option (but not in a ranges tables style).

$top, $skip, and $inlinecount

Client-side paging
The `$top` and `$skip` query options are called client-side paging. It means that the client (consumer) defines how many entries to receive (`$top`) and how many entries to skip (`$skip`) by the SAP NetWeaver Gateway server. This enables the consumer to implement a paging functionality.

Let's assume the consumer is able to display three products per page. The following URI fetches the first page (products 1–3):

/sap/opu/odata/sap/ZEXAMPLE1_SRV/ProductCollection?$top=3&$skip=0

The following URI fetches the second page (products 4–6):

/sap/opu/odata/sap/ZEXAMPLE1_SRV/ProductCollection?$top=3&$skip=3

As you can see, the `$top` value (page size) remains stable if the page size doesn't change, whereas the `$skip` value provides the number of *entries* to be skipped—not the number of pages.

This allows you to implement quite efficient data accesses to the underlying database, because you only need to read the records that are relevant for the requested page. When you're fetching your data via any standard function module (as in this example), you can't really benefit from it because most of the function modules don't support input parameters for `top` and `skip`. What you typically find is a `MAX_ROWS` input parameter that at least limits the number of records returned. But you can only make use of this if no sorting has to be applied on the returned list.

Consider an example with default sorting by the function module and three products per page. To read the product entries for page 5, for example, you can calculate the MAX_ROWS parameter via the formula:

MAX_ROWS = <page_size> × <page> = 3 × 5 = 15

So you need to read the first 15 records from the database to provide the entries for page 5 (products 13–15). The entries for all other pages (products 1–12) are read by the RFC module but need to be ignored in the Get_EntitySet processing. This gets worse if the client keeps calling the SAP NetWeaver Gateway server for page 6, page 7, page 8, and so on, because more and more entries need to be fetched that are finally thrown away.

As you can see, client-side paging can cause significant load on the server. Ultimately, though, it all depends on how access to the underlying database tables has been implemented. If you're accessing your own Z-tables, you can significantly improve your SELECT statements to reduce the server load.

Server load

The values for $top and $skip are provided via the input structure IS_PAGING. This structure has two fields: top and skip. The calculation and filtering of the result table has to be done via your own coding. Prior to calling the BAPI_EPM_PRODUCT_GET_LIST function module, you can calculate the max-rows parameter like this:

```
lv_maxrows-bapimaxrow = 0.
IF ( is_paging-top IS NOT INITIAL ).
  lv_maxrows-bapimaxrow = is_paging-top + is_paging-skip.
ENDIF.
```

Lv_maxrows is declared as type bapi_epm_max_rows. Right after the function module, you can apply the $top and $skip options. For that, you need to calculate the start and the end of the table entries you want to copy over into the get_entityset export table, as shown in Listing 6.5.

```
lv_start = 1.
IF is_paging-skip IS NOT INITIAL.
  lv_start = is_paging-skip + 1.
ENDIF.

IF is_paging-top IS NOT INITIAL.
```

```
    lv_end = is_paging-top + lv_start - 1.
ELSE.
    lv_end = lines( lt_headerdata ).
ENDIF.

LOOP AT lt_headerdata INTO ls_headerdata
    FROM lv_start TO lv_end.
    ls_product-productid = ls_headerdata-product_id.
    ls_product-category  = ls_headerdata-category.
    ls_product-name      = ls_headerdata-name.
    APPEND ls_product TO et_entityset.
ENDLOOP.
```

Listing 6.5 Product Collection, Get_Entityset Method with External Paging

Max-rows parameter

As mentioned earlier, and as you can see from the coding, the only benefit comes by providing the `max-rows` parameter, which might reduce the number of records fetched from the database (we don't know that unless we investigate how the function module determines its data). Other than that, `$top` and `$skip` just ensure that a subset of the determined data is returned to the consumer.

The `$inlinecount` query option typically comes into play in combination with `$top` and `$skip`. Similar to `$count`, it's supposed to count the number of entries. But the difference is that the value of the inline count is provided along with the OData feed. That's why it's called "inline." The `$inlinecount` query option has to be provided with the value "allpages" in order to work. If you provide `$inlinecount=none`, it's handled as if no inline count was provided.

Entire number of entries

Inline count always counts the entire number of entries—even if the resulting collection contains less because of `$top` and/or `$skip`. So in this case, it destroys the option to use the `max-rows` input parameter of the function module because you need to receive all entries to be able to count them. You can use the method `has_inlinecount( )` of the input object `io_tech_request_context` to find out if the `$inlinecount` query option was provided. The adjusted coding before the function module call looks like the following:

```
lv_maxrows-bapimaxrow = 0.
IF ( is_paging-top IS NOT INITIAL ) and
```

```
    ( io_tech_request_context->has_inlinecount( ) EQ abap_
false ).
    lv_maxrows-bapimaxrow = is_paging-top + is_paging-skip.
  ENDIF.
```

And right after the function module call, you can provide the inline count by setting the value `inlinecount` of the export structure `ES_RESPONSE_CONTEXT`:

```
  IF io_tech_request_context->has_inlinecount( ) EQ abap_true.
    es_response_context-inlinecount = lines( lt_headerdata ).
  ENDIF.
```

Provides 3 entries, counts entire collection

As an example, the following URI only provides the first 3 entries (first page) but counts the entire collection (in this case, 42 entities):

/sap/opu/odata/sap/ZEXAMPLE1_SRV/ProductCollection?$top=3&$skip=0&$inlinecount=allpages

The inline count is contained in the OData response via the tag `m:count` (see Figure 6.55).

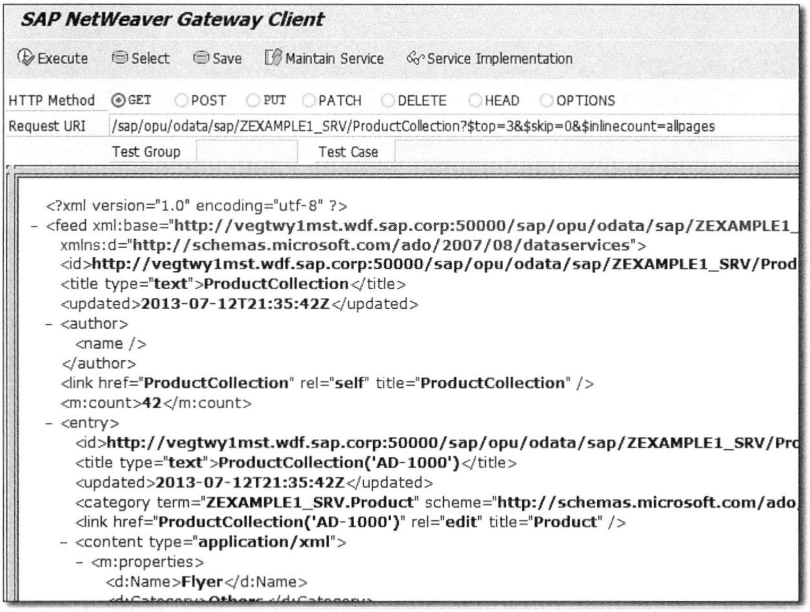

Figure 6.55 Query Result with $inlinecount

$orderby

The `$orderby` query option allows you to define the sorting of your result set. `Order-by` parameters are provided by the framework in your `Get_EntitySet` method via the import table `IT_ORDER`. The table contains an entry for each property provided in the `$orderby` clause.

If you want the collection to be sorted by category (first) and name (second), the URI would look like the following:

/sap/opu/odata/sap/ZEXAMPLE1_SRV/ProductCollection?$orderby=Category, Name

In this case, the table `IT_ORDER` contains the two entries shown in Table 6.3.

Property	Order
Category	asc
Name	asc

Table 6.3 Content of Table IT_ORDER

Correspondingly, you get `order = desc` if you provide the related `$orderby` query property with the descending option "`desc`". Ascending "`asc`" doesn't need to be provided because it's the default sort order.

In combination with `$top` and `$skip`, you should always first perform the sorting and secondly the paging. Otherwise, the result might be incorrect.

Server-side paging
If you combine those query options and also don't execute your own `SELECT` statement, it's even harder to perform an efficient database access; this is because RFC modules usually don't offer any sorting capabilities. This basically means that, for each page, you always have to read all records, sort them, and then pick the requested page from it. Such requests have to be handled carefully because they can significantly impact the performance of the server if there are many concurrent calls. In this case, it's more efficient to go for server-side paging, which typically requires the client to cache the entries that were already read.

6.5.4 Navigation Properties

Navigation properties allow you to navigate from one entry or collection to another entry or collection. A typical example is the navigation from a sales order header (entry) to the list of sales order line items (collection). Navigation properties are always based on associations (relationships) that also define the cardinality. In addition, you can optionally define a referential constraint to specify the foreign key relationship (if possible).

You can see a number of navigation property examples with associations and referential constraints in the ZEXAMPLE2 project into which the metadata of the GWDEMO sample service has been imported. To add a navigation property to the ZEXAMPLE1 project, you first need to enter the property "SupplierID" of type "Edm.String" with the MAX LENGTH "10" to the product entity type (see Figure 6.56). Then you have to regenerate the project and add a mapping line into the `Get_EntitySet` and `Get_Entity` methods.

Navigation property examples

Properties															
Name	K..	Edm Core Type	Pre..	Sc..	Ma..	U	C..	U	D	S..	N	F..	Label	L..	C..	ABAP Field Name
ProductID	☑	Edm.String	0	0	10	☑	☑	☑	☑	☐	☑		Product Identifier	T		PRODUCTID
Category	☐	Edm.String	0	0	40	☑	☑	☑	☑	☑	☑		Product Category	T		CATEGORY
Name	☐	Edm.String	0	0	255	☑	☑	☑	☑	☑	☑		Product Name	T		NAME
SupplierID	☐	Edm.String	0	0	10	☑	☑	☑	☑	☑	☑		Supplier ID	T		SUPPLIERID

Figure 6.56 Product Entity Type with New Property SupplierID

The `SupplierID` is provided via the output table/structure `HEADERDATA`. For the `Get_EntitySet` method (`PRODUCTCOLLECTIO_GET_ENTITYSET`), the required line needs to be added into the loop:

```
ls_product-supplierid = ls_headerdata-supplier_id.
```

For the `Get_Entity` method (`PRODUCTCOLLECTIO_GET_ENTITY`), the required line looks like the following:

```
er_entity-supplierid = ls_headerdata-supplier_id.
```

After activation of the DPC extension class, you can verify whether the `SupplierID` is properly exposed in the OData service (see Figure 6.57).

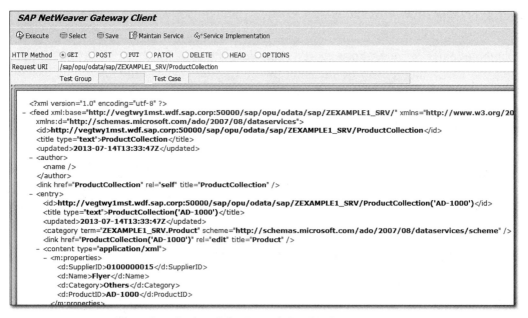

Figure 6.57 Product Collection with SupplierID

Supplier entity type

To be able to navigate from one entity to another, you need a new entity type in the model. For this, you create a new entity type called "Supplier" in the project ZEXAMPLE1 (see Figure 6.58).

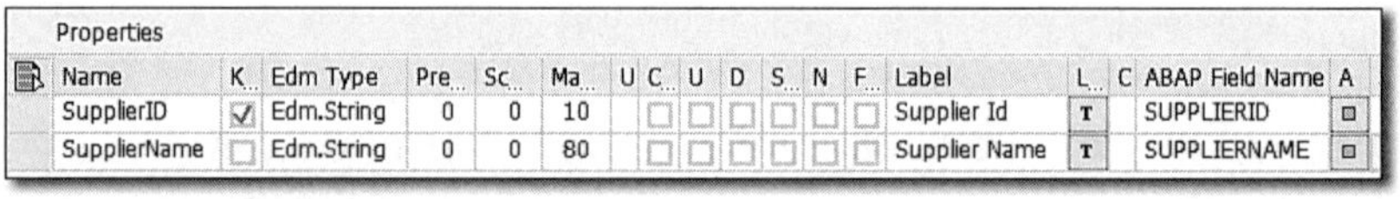

Figure 6.58 New Entity Type: Supplier

For the sake of simplicity, just define two properties SupplierID and SupplierName for the supplier entity type. Also, create a new entity set called SupplierCollection (see Figure 6.59).

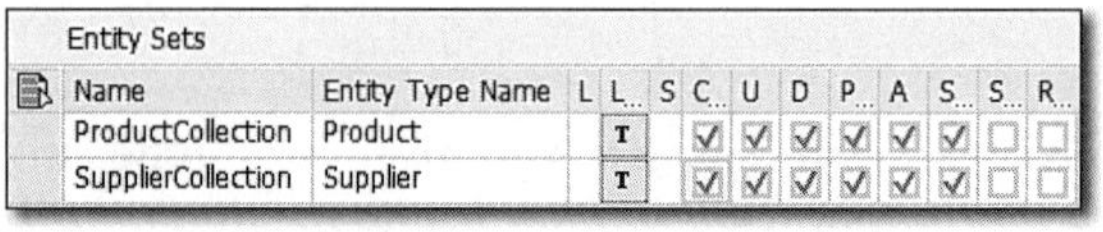

Figure 6.59 New Entity Set: SupplierCollection

The next step is to regenerate the project and redefine the new method SUPPLIERCOLLECTI_GET_ENTITYSET of the DPC extension class with the coding in Listing 6.6.

Generate and redefine

```
METHOD suppliercollecti_get_entityset.

  DATA: ls_bpheaderdata TYPE bapi_epm_bp_header,
        lt_bpheaderdata TYPE STANDARD TABLE OF bapi_epm_bp_
header,
        ls_supplier     LIKE LINE OF et_entityset.

  CALL FUNCTION 'BAPI_EPM_BP_GET_LIST'
    TABLES
      bpheaderdata = lt_bpheaderdata.

  LOOP AT lt_bpheaderdata INTO ls_bpheaderdata.
    ls_supplier-supplierid   = ls_bpheaderdata-bp_id.
    ls_supplier-suppliername = ls_bpheaderdata-company_name.
    APPEND ls_supplier TO et_entityset.
  ENDLOOP.

ENDMETHOD.
```

Listing 6.6 Supplier Collection, Get_Entityset Method

The SUPPLIERCOLLECTI_GET_ENTITY needs to be implemented with the coding in Listing 6.7 to fetch an entry based on the provided primary key.

```
METHOD suppliercollecti_get_entity.

  DATA: ls_key_tab     TYPE /iwbep/s_mgw_name_value_pair,
        ls_bp_id       TYPE bapi_epm_bp_id,
        ls_headerdata TYPE bapi_epm_bp_header.

  LOOP AT it_key_tab INTO ls_key_tab.
    IF ls_key_tab-name EQ 'SupplierID'.
      ls_bp_id-bp_id = ls_key_tab-value.
    ENDIF.
  ENDLOOP.

  CALL FUNCTION 'BAPI_EPM_BP_GET_DETAIL'
    EXPORTING
```

```
      bp_id      = ls_bp_id
    IMPORTING
      headerdata = ls_headerdata.

  er_entity-supplierid   = ls_headerdata-bp_id.
  er_entity-suppliername = ls_headerdata-company_name.

ENDMETHOD.
```

Listing 6.7 Supplier Collection, Get_Entity Method

Now you need to activate the changes in the DPC extension class. Via the SAP NetWeaver Gateway client, you can execute the following URI to fetch the list of suppliers (see Figure 6.60):

/sap/opu/odata/sap/ZEXAMPLE1_SRV/SupplierCollection

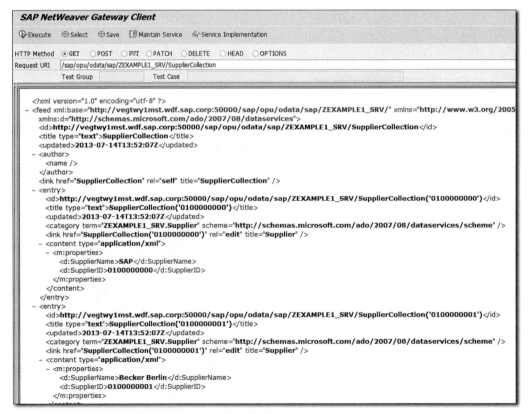

Figure 6.60 SupplierCollection of the ZEXAMPLE1_SRV Service

Also verify that the Get_Entity implementation is working by executing any of the provided URIs in the collection. So far, you've added a new entity type and a new entity set with an implementation for the Get_Entity and Get_EntitySet methods. Now let's define the navigation property. For this, you first need to create an association by double-clicking on DATA MODEL • ASSOCIATIONS in the project tree and clicking the CREATE button in the grid. Each association has to hava a name, principal entity type, principal entity cardinality, dependent entity type, and dependent entity cardinality (see Figure 6.61).

Define navigation property

Figure 6.61 Definition of Association Assoc_Product_Supplier

As each supplier can deliver 0...n products, set the DEPENDENT ENTITY CARDINALITY (supplier) to 1 and the PRINCIPAL ENTITY CARDINALITY (product) to M. Make sure to use the [F4] value help to see the possible cardinality values.

Now you can define the navigation property by navigating to DATA MODEL • ENTITY TYPES • PRODUCT • NAVIGATION PROPERTIES and clicking the CREATE button to define a navigation property for the product entity type. The navigation property requires a NAME and a RELATIONSHIP NAME (see Figure 6.62). The RELATIONSHIP NAME is the association you've defined before.

Figure 6.62 Navigation Property Definition

For the navigation property NAME, specify "ToSupplier" to use this navigation property to navigate from the product to the related supplier.

Now you can check and regenerate the project. After the regeneration, you'll see that the metadata has grown. This isn't only because of the newly added supplier entity type but also because of the association and the navigation property that you've defined.

Check and regenerate

The navigation property is also visible in the product collection (see Figure 6.63) as well as in each product entry. Each entry resource now contains a new link that ends with */ToSupplier*, which allows you to navigate to the related supplier entry.

```
<entry>
  <id>http://vegtwy1mst.wdf.sap.corp:50000/sap/opu/odata/sap/ZEXAMPLE1_SRV/ProductCollection('AD-1000')</id>
  <title type="text">ProductCollection('AD-1000')</title>
  <updated>2013-07-14T14:15:49Z</updated>
  <category term="ZEXAMPLE1_SRV.Product" scheme="http://schemas.microsoft.com/ado/2007/08/dataservices/scheme" />
  <link href="ProductCollection('AD-1000')" rel="edit" title="Product" />
  <link href="ProductCollection('AD-1000')/ToSupplier" rel="http://schemas.microsoft.com/ado/2007/08/dataservices/related
- <content type="application/xml">
  - <m:properties>
      <d:SupplierID>0100000015</d:SupplierID>
      <d:Name>Flyer</d:Name>
      <d:Category>Others</d:Category>
      <d:ProductID>AD-1000</d:ProductID>
    </m:properties>
  </content>
</entry>
```

Figure 6.63 Navigation Property in the Product Collection

This particular navigation property navigates to a supplier entry—not to the collection—because of the definition of the cardinality. In the EPM example, a product always has a unique supplier, whereas a supplier can deliver many products.

Error at execution   If you execute this navigation link for any product, you'll run into an error. This is because the URI with the navigation link only contains the primary key of the product, but the Get_Entity method of the supplier (which is invoked when executing the navigation link) requires the primary key of the supplier. That is the reason you need to enhance the previous coding a little bit.

The change that you need to implement now is to derive the SupplierID from the ProductID. This needs to be done in the supplier Get_Entity method SUPPLIERCOLLECTI_GET_ENTITY as shown in Listing 6.8.

```
METHOD suppliercollecti_get_entity.

  DATA: ls_key_tab    TYPE /iwbep/s_mgw_name_value_pair,
        ls_bp_id      TYPE bapi_epm_bp_id,
        ls_headerdata TYPE bapi_epm_bp_header.

  DATA: ls_product TYPE zcl_zexample1_mpc=>ts_product.
```

```
IF iv_entity_set_name EQ 'ProductCollection'.
  CALL METHOD productcollectio_get_entity
    EXPORTING
      iv_entity_name         = iv_entity_name
      iv_entity_set_name     = iv_entity_set_name
      iv_source_name         = iv_source_name
      it_key_tab             = it_key_tab
      io_request_object      = io_request_object
      io_tech_request_context = io_tech_request_context
      it_navigation_path     = it_navigation_path
    IMPORTING
      er_entity              = ls_product.
  ls_bp_id-bp_id = ls_product-supplierid.
ELSE.
  LOOP AT it_key_tab INTO ls_key_tab.
    IF ls_key_tab-name EQ 'SupplierID'.
      ls_bp_id-bp_id = ls_key_tab-value.
    ENDIF.
  ENDLOOP.
ENDIF.

CALL FUNCTION 'BAPI_EPM_BP_GET_DETAIL'
  EXPORTING
    bp_id      = ls_bp_id
  IMPORTING
    headerdata = ls_headerdata.

er_entity-supplierid   = ls_headerdata-bp_id.
er_entity-suppliername = ls_headerdata-company_name.

ENDMETHOD.
```

Listing 6.8 Supplier Collection, Get_Entity Method with Supplier Determination via the Product Entity

As you can see, the product detail is read by calling the method PRODUCTCOLLECTIO_GET_ENTITY. This provides the product entry that corresponds to the product key that is handed over via the navigation link.

The IF statement makes sure that this code snippet is only executed in the navigation property case. In the regular supplier Get_Entity case, this coding doesn't need to be executed.

Activate changes Activate the changes in the DPC extension class, and execute the following sample URI via the SAP NetWeaver Gateway client:

/sap/opu/odata/sap/ZEXAMPLE1_SRV/ProductCollection('AD-1000')/ ToSupplier

As a result, you see the supplier entry (with its key and name) that belongs to the product 'AD-1000' (see Figure 6.64).

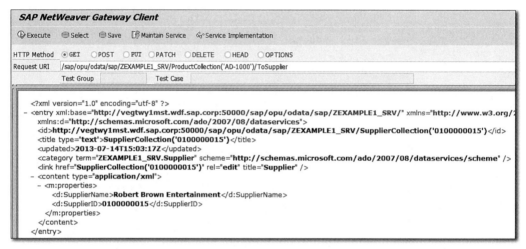

Figure 6.64 ToSupplier Navigation Result of Product AD-1000

According to the OData standard, you find a self-link to the retrieved supplier entry (.../SupplierCollection('0100000015')) in the navigation result.

6.5.5   CUD Methods

So far we've only read data from the underlying data source by executing the respective GET_LIST and GET_DETAIL function modules via the Get_EntitySet and Get_Entity methods. In contrast to read access, CRE-ATE, UPDATE, and DELETE (CUD) methods are *write access* operations because they typically change the underlying data.

Create

CREATE is used whenever you want to create a new entry into the respective collection. The CREATE operation for the product entity type is handled by the PRODUCTCOLLECTIO_CREATE_ENTITY method in the DPC.

Similar to the read methods, you need to redefine this method in the data provider extension class. As an example, use the coding in Listing 6.9.

Redefine in DPC
extension class

```abap
METHOD productcollectio_create_entity.

  DATA: ls_headerdata TYPE bapi_epm_product_header,
        ls_product    LIKE er_entity,
        lt_return     TYPE STANDARD TABLE OF bapiret2.

  io_data_provider->read_entry_data( IMPORTING es_data = ls_
product ).

  ls_headerdata-product_id    = ls_product-productid.
  ls_headerdata-category      = ls_product-category.
  ls_headerdata-name          = ls_product-name.
  ls_headerdata-supplier_id   = ls_product-supplierid.
  ls_headerdata-measure_unit  = 'EA'.
  ls_headerdata-currency_code = 'EUR'.
  ls_headerdata-tax_tarif_code = '1'.
  ls_headerdata-type_code     = 'AD'.

  CALL FUNCTION 'BAPI_EPM_PRODUCT_CREATE'
    EXPORTING
      headerdata        = ls_headerdata
*     PERSIST_TO_DB     = ABAP_TRUE
    TABLES
*     CONVERSION_FACTORS =
      return            = lt_return.

  IF lt_return IS NOT INITIAL.
    mo_context->get_message_container( )->add_messages_from_
bapi(
        it_bapi_messages         = lt_return
        iv_determine_leading_msg = /iwbep/if_message_con-
tainer=>gcs_leading_msg_search_option-first ).
```

```
      RAISE EXCEPTION TYPE /iwbep/cx_mgw_busi_exception
        EXPORTING
          textid              = /iwbep/cx_mgw_busi_excep-
tion=>business_error
          message_container = mo_context->get_message_
container( ).
    ENDIF.


    er_entity = ls_product.

ENDMETHOD.
```

Listing 6.9 Product Collection, Create Entity Method

Using the `read_entry_data` method of the import object reference `io_data_provider`, you can retrieve the data that was passed along the `POST` request in the HTTP body. The entry is retrieved in the format of the entity type definition. That's why the structure `ls_product` is of type ER_ENTITY.

To successfully call the function module `BAPI_EPM_PRODUCT_CREATE`, some values that are not part of the data model need to be defaulted (e.g., `measure_unit`). This is the specific logic of the underlying business function.

Error handling | In this example, we've also introduced error handling. For the sake of simplicity, we haven't done this in the `Get_EntitySet` and `Get_Entity` cases (which definitely makes sense there as well). The error handling consists of retrieving the return table from the function module call.

Assuming that only errors will be part of the return table, if the table isn't empty, you first use the member object reference `mo_context` to determine the message container (via `get_message_container( )`) and use the `add_messages_from_bapi` method to log the BAPI messages. Secondly, you raise a business exception `/iwbep/cx_mgw_busi_exception` that will abort the processing, send an HTTP 400 return code to the consumer, and provide the messages as part of the response body.

At the end of the method, you provide the newly created entry back to the framework (ER_ENTITY). Typically, you have to call the corresponding `Get-Detail` BAPI to fetch the detail of the newly created entry because some properties might have been changed or calculated. This isn't the case for this example, so you can pass the retrieved entry right back to the framework.

After you've performed the implementation of the CREATE method, again activate the DPC extension class. After that, use the SAP NetWeaver Gateway client to verify if the CREATE operation works as expected. The CREATE operation requires a proper HTTP body with the entry to be created. Instead of putting such an HTTP body together manually, you can use the USE AS REQUEST button in the SAP NetWeaver Gateway client. For this, you first need to execute a GET operation to receive a suitable source entry. Then click the USE AS REQUEST button to copy it over to the left-hand side of the SAP NetWeaver Gateway client (see Figure 6.65). The left-hand side is the REQUEST side, and the right-hand side is the RESPONSE side.

Activate DPC extension class

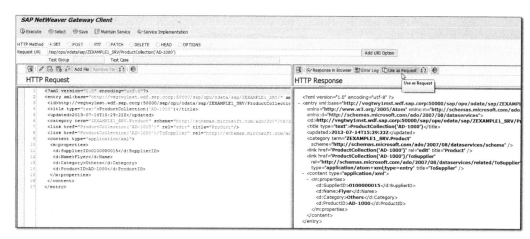

Figure 6.65 Use As Request Function in the SAP NetWeaver Gateway Client

Before you can execute the CREATE operation, you also need to change the HTTP method from GET to POST. In addition, you need to adjust the URI because the CREATE operation has to be executed on a collection and not on a single entry (make sure to remove the brackets with the primary key). And finally, of course, you may want to adjust the HTTP body, which contains the data of the entry to be created (e.g., make sure to change the product ID and the product name).

Depending on the underlying business logic, the primary key may not need to be provided in the HTTP request body if it's calculated by the function module that was mapped in the CREATE operation. In this example, you have to provide a unique/new product ID because there is no number range that calculates a new ID for you.

HTTP 201   If the CREATE operation was successful (see Figure 6.66), you get an HTTP 201 response. Furthermore, you get the newly created record. This is because the backend server might have determined the primary key of the new entry (not in this example case, however); therefore, the server has to provide the record or the client won't be able to access it without the key.

In addition, the client benefits from this if the server determines/calculates properties other than just the primary key, because those values are sent along with the response and the client doesn't need to execute another GET request. This pattern is different in the update case, as you'll see next.

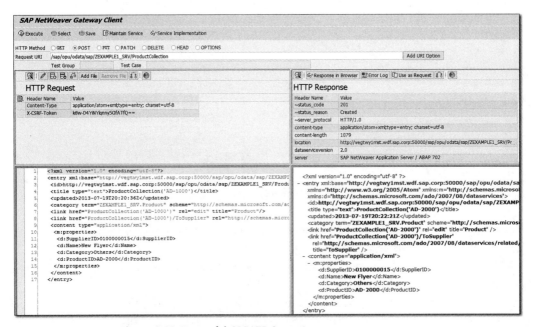

Figure 6.66 Successful CREATE Operation

Update

The UPDATE operation comes into play whenever an existing entry resource needs to be changed. So the URI needs to address the entry like in a Get-Detail case. The UPDATE operation for the product entity type is handled by the PRODUCTCOLLECTIO_UPDATE_ENTITY method in the DPC. Similar to the other methods that you've implemented, you redefine this method in the DPC extension class and apply the coding in Listing 6.10.

```
METHOD productcollectio_update_entity.

  DATA: ls_key_tab      TYPE /iwbep/s_mgw_name_value_pair,
        ls_product_id   TYPE bapi_epm_product_id,
        ls_headerdata   TYPE bapi_epm_product_header,
        ls_headerdatax  TYPE bapi_epm_product_headerx,
        ls_product      LIKE er_entity,
        lt_return       TYPE STANDARD TABLE OF bapiret2.

  io_data_provider->read_entry_data( IMPORTING es_data = ls_
product ).

  LOOP AT it_key_tab INTO ls_key_tab.
    IF ls_key_tab-name EQ 'ProductID'.
      ls_product_id-product_id = ls_key_tab-value.
    ENDIF.
  ENDLOOP.

  CALL FUNCTION 'BAPI_EPM_PRODUCT_GET_DETAIL'
    EXPORTING
      product_id              = ls_product_id
    IMPORTING
      headerdata              = ls_headerdata
*   TABLES
*     CONVERSION_FACTORS      =
*     RETURN                  =
          .

  ls_headerdata-category    = ls_product-category.
  ls_headerdata-name        = ls_product-name.
  ls_headerdata-supplier_id = ls_product-supplierid.

  ls_headerdatax-product_id = ls_headerdata-product_id.
```

```
     ls_headerdatax-category    = 'X'.
     ls_headerdatax-name        = 'X'.
     ls_headerdatax-supplier_id = 'X'.

     CALL FUNCTION 'BAPI_EPM_PRODUCT_CHANGE'
       EXPORTING
         product_id           = ls_product_id
         headerdata           = ls_headerdata
         headerdatax          = ls_headerdatax
*        PERSIST_TO_DB        = ABAP_TRUE
       TABLES
*        CONVERSION_FACTORS   =
*        CONVERSION_FACTORSX  =
         return               = lt_return.

     IF lt_return IS NOT INITIAL.
       mo_context->get_message_container( )->add_messages_from_
bapi(
         it_bapi_messages           = lt_return
         iv_determine_leading_msg = /iwbep/if_message_con-
tainer=>gcs_leading_msg_search_option-first ).

       RAISE EXCEPTION TYPE /iwbep/cx_mgw_busi_exception
         EXPORTING
           textid               = /iwbep/cx_mgw_busi_excep-
tion=>business_error
           message_container = mo_context->get_message_
container( ).
     ENDIF.

     er_entity = ls_product.

ENDMETHOD.
```

Listing 6.10 Product Collection, Update Entity Method

This implementation reuses certain elements from the other methods. First, use the `io_data_provider` input object reference to fetch the incoming data from the HTTP body. Then, pick the primary key from the key table. With the primary key, read the product instance with the function `BAPI_EPM_PRODUCT_GET_DETAIL` to fill the `ls_headerdata` structure. (A good practice is to check the return table for errors; this helps avoid situations where an incorrect key is provided. We've skipped this in our example for the sake of simplicity.)

After the product instance is read, apply the incoming properties. You also need to set the X flags in the corresponding X-structure to inform the BAPI of which attributes to update. Next, call the BAPI_EPM_PRODUCT_ CHANGE to actually perform the update. Similar to the CREATE method, you check the return table for existing messages and throw an exception in that case. Finally, there is also an ER_ENTITY export parameter that should be filled.

Incoming properties

After you're done with the implementation of the UPDATE method, you need to activate the DPC extension class. Now you must use the SAP NetWeaver Gateway client to verify whether the UPDATE operation works as expected. To do this, first perform a single read to get a proper HTTP response body that you can copy over to the request side by using the USE AS REQUEST button. The URI remains unchanged because the UPDATE operation is always performed on a single entry resource. You only need to switch the HTTP method from GET to PUT. If the update was successful (see Figure 6.67), you only get an HTTP 204 (no content) response.

Figure 6.67 Successful Update Operation

The HTTP code indicates that the response body is empty. This happens on purpose because the assumption is that the client has all information and thus sending the entry along with the response causes unnecessary overhead. The client can always perform a single read to fetch the entity again if the backend server has calculated any values that the client doesn't have.

Delete

The DELETE operation is typically very simple to implement. It requires redefining the PRODUCTCOLLECTIO_DELETE_ENTITY method of the DPC extension class. You can use the coding in Listing 6.11 as an example.

```
METHOD productcollectio_delete_entity.

  DATA: ls_key_tab     TYPE /iwbep/s_mgw_name_value_pair,
        ls_product_id  TYPE bapi_epm_product_id,
        lt_return      TYPE STANDARD TABLE OF bapiret2.

  LOOP AT it_key_tab INTO ls_key_tab.
    IF ls_key_tab-name EQ 'ProductID'.
      ls_product_id-product_id = ls_key_tab-value.
    ENDIF.
  ENDLOOP.

  CALL FUNCTION 'BAPI_EPM_PRODUCT_DELETE'
    EXPORTING
      product_id    = ls_product_id
*     PERSIST_TO_DB = ABAP_TRUE
    TABLES
      return        = lt_return.

  IF lt_return IS NOT INITIAL.
    mo_context->get_message_container( )->add_messages_from_
bapi(
      it_bapi_messages           = lt_return
      iv_determine_leading_msg = /iwbep/if_message_con-
tainer=>gcs_leading_msg_search_option-first ).

      RAISE EXCEPTION TYPE /iwbep/cx_mgw_busi_exception
        EXPORTING
```

```
        textid              = /iwbep/cx_mgw_busi_excep-
tion=>business_error
        message_container = mo_context->get_message_
container( ).
  ENDIF.

ENDMETHOD.
```

Listing 6.11 Product Collection, Delete Entity Method

First, again handle the primary key of the entry to be deleted. With this information, call the DELETE function BAPI_EPM_PRODUCT_DELETE right away. The return table is checked again for entries, and an exception is thrown if any entry exists—assuming that you don't receive any success messages in the return table. **Primary key**

After the activation of the DPC extension class, you can verify whether the implemented DELETE operation works properly. DELETE operations are always executed on a single entry. Therefore, you have to provide a URI that addresses a single-entry resource. The HTTP method has to be DELETE.

If the DELETE was successful, you get an HTTP 204 (no content) response (see Figure 6.68).

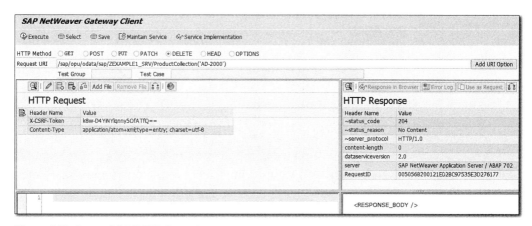

Figure 6.68 Successful DELETE Operation

6.5.6   Function Imports

Function imports or actions are supposed to be used whenever a function needs to be executed on a business object that doesn't fit into the default CRUD-Q operations. One example is the release of a sales order that might influence a number of properties and in addition also trigger some backend functionality (e.g., start a workflow). Function imports are defined on the service level, so a function isn't executed on a dedicated collection or entry.

Define function import

A function import can be defined by right-clicking on DATA MODEL and selecting CREATE • FUNCTION IMPORT. This opens up the CREATE FUNCTION IMPORT window, where you first need to provide a name of the function import (see Figure 6.69).

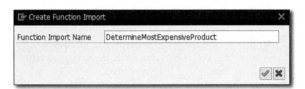

Figure 6.69 Create Function Import Dialog

For each function import, you can define a return kind of the function import. The values listed in Table 6.4 are supported.

Return Kind	Description
Complex type	Data returned as complex type
Entity type	Data returned as entity type
No return	No data returned

Table 6.4 Function Import Return Types

In this example, you want to implement a function import that determines the most expensive product. For that, you first need to enter the property "Price" and select type EDM.DECIMAL, PRECISION 23, and SCALE 4 for the product entity type. Make sure to adjust the Get_EntitySet, Get_Entity, CREATE, and UPDATE methods to also consider this new property.

The return type is an entity type because you want to receive the related product that is the most expensive one. Note that we don't consider the case in which multiple products are most expensive. In this case, you simply pick the first one (for the sake of simplicity, don't consider different currencies). If you set the return kind (RET. KIND field) to ENTITY TYPE, you can also specify the return type. In this case, this is the PRODUCT entity type. The return cardinality specifies how many of the defined return type can occur. The values in Table 6.5 are supported.

Cardinality	Description
0..1	No more than one instance occurs. Zero instances are also permitted.
1	Occurrence of exactly one instance.
0..n	Occurrence of zero or more instances.
1..n	Occurrence of one or more instances.

Table 6.5 Return Cardinalities

In this example, there should always be one single product that is the most expensive. However, if there is no product at all, the result can also be empty. Therefore, choose 0..1 for the RETURN CARDINALITY field.

If you choose a cardinality where many (n) entries can be returned (collection), you also need to define the return entity set. In this example, this field is set to READ-ONLY.

The HTTP method basically defines whether the function import is just reading any data (HTTP GET) or is also manipulating any data (HTTP POST). This is important because a GET may not change any data in the system. A POST method is always protected via a cross-site request forgery (CSRF) token, which isn't the case for GET accesses.

Finally, set the ACTION FOR ENTITY TYPE to PRODUCT to indicate that this function import is related to the product entity type.

After all attributes are specified, you have the function import definition shown in Figure 6.70.

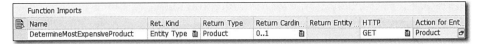

Figure 6.70 Definition of a Sample Function Import

Provide import parameter

You also need to provide an import parameter for the example function import. This parameter defines the product category of which you want to determine the most expensive product.

To define import parameters for function imports, you need to expand the new node FUNCTION IMPORTS • DETERMINEMOSTEXPENSIVEPRODUCT in the project tree and then double-click on FUNCTION IMPORT PARAMETERS. You can add entries into the grid by using the ADD/CREATE buttons.

In this example, enter a function import parameter called "Category". It has the same attributes as the category property in the product entity type (see Figure 6.71).

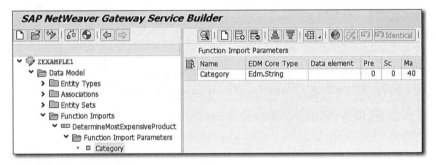

Figure 6.71 Definition of Function Import Parameter

That is all you need to do on the metadata side. You can now check and regenerate the project. The service provisioning (data provider) has to be done manually by redefining the respective method in the DPC extension class. For this, open ZCL_ZEXAMPLE1_DPC_EXT in the Class Builder, and put it to edit mode. The method you need to redefine is EXECUTE_ACTION (interface /IWBEP/IF_MGW_APPL_SRV_RUNTIME).

Listing 6.12 shows the coding we're using.

```
method /IWBEP/IF_MGW_APPL_SRV_RUNTIME~EXECUTE_ACTION.

data: lt_headerdata type TABLE OF BAPI_EPM_PRODUCT_HEADER,
```

```
        ls_headerdata type BAPI_EPM_PRODUCT_HEADER,
        lt_categories type TABLE OF BAPI_EPM_PRODUCT_CATEG_RANGE,
        ls_categories type BAPI_EPM_PRODUCT_CATEG_RANGE,
        ls_parameter  type /IWBEP/S_MGW_NAME_VALUE_PAIR,
        ls_product    TYPE ZCL_ZEXAMPLE1_MPC=>TS_PRODUCT.

    case iv_action_name.
      when 'DetermineMostExpensiveProduct'.
*       Put Category filter together
        read table it_parameter into ls_parameter index 1.
        if sy-subrc eq 0.
          ls_categories-low    = ls_parameter-value.
          ls_categories-option = 'EQ'.   "Equal
          ls_categories-sign   = 'I'.    "Including
          append ls_categories to lt_categories.
        endif.
*       Fetch filtered Products
        CALL FUNCTION 'BAPI_EPM_PRODUCT_GET_LIST'
          TABLES
            HEADERDATA        = lt_headerdata
            SELPARAMCATEGORIES = lt_categories.
*       Determine the most expensive one.
        sort lt_headerdata by price DESCENDING.
        read table lt_headerdata into ls_headerdata index 1.
        if sy-subrc eq 0.
          ls_product-productid = ls_headerdata-product_id.
          ls_product-name      = ls_headerdata-name.
          ls_product-category  = ls_headerdata-category.
          ls_product-supplierid = ls_headerdata-supplier_id.
          ls_product-price     = ls_headerdata-price.

          copy_data_to_ref(
            EXPORTING
              is_data = ls_product
            CHANGING
              cr_data = er_data ).
        endif.

    endcase.

endmethod.
```

Listing 6.12 Function Import for DetermineMostExpensiveProduct

In this method, first use a case control structure, because every function import of the OData service is handled via this single ABAP method (there is no submethod generated), and you need to distinguish which function import is supposed to be handled. The next step is to pull the import parameter (category) out of the list of function import parameters. In this case, simply assume that there is only one parameter provided. This one is being added to the category ranges table of the function module that you use.

Call function module   Then call the `BAPI_EPM_PRODUCT_GET_LIST` function module to provide the filtered list of products. Then you need to sort descending by price and pick the first record (ignoring the possibility that multiple products are most expensive and that prices may have different currencies; in other words, pick the one with the highest number). The found record is mapped to the data model (note that we've added the `Price` property to the model; if you don't do this make sure to comment the line where `ls_product-price` is assigned). Finally, copy the output structure `ls_product` to a data reference `er_data`, which is performed by the very helpful `copy_data_to_ref` method from the framework.

After you've activated the DPC extension class, you can execute the function import. The URI in the SAP NetWeaver Gateway client is the following:

/sap/opu/odata/sap/ZEXAMPLE1_SRV/DetermineMostExpensiveProduct?Category='Keyboards'

From the URI structure, you can see that every function import is executed based on the service itself and not based on a collection or single entry. Parameters are handed over in the regular way of using URL parameters. Multiple parameters are separated by &. Table parameters can't be used (though this functionality is planned for future versions).

From the result of the function import (see Figure 6.72), you can see that a product was found. The category filter was also used properly.

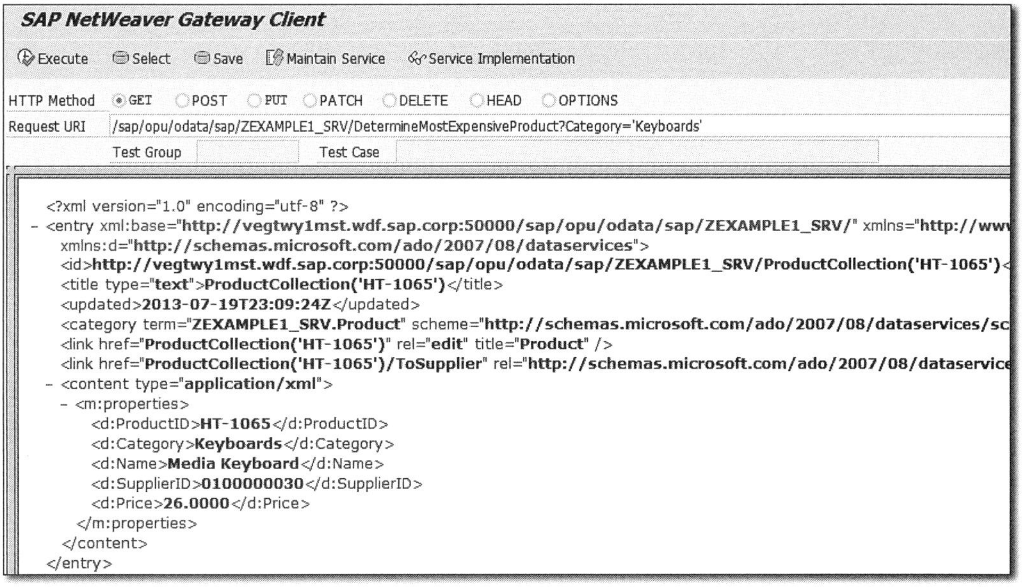

Figure 6.72 Result of Function Import Execution

6.5.7 Media Resources

Media resources are used to expose different binary data, such as graphics and videos, to consumers. A media resource is accessed via a media link entry.

To let a regular entity type become a media link entity type, you have to flag it as media via the Service Builder using the M checkbox on the entity type level. The same attribute can also be set manually via coding in the MPC extension class by using the set_is_media( ) method on the entity type level. As a result, the HasStream attribute in the metadata document of the entity type is set to true.

Flag as media

As soon as you define an entity type as a media type, you also have to consider two properties:

▶ **Source URI**
The source URI property can be used by the consuming application to retrieve the associated media resource itself from the respective location.

It is recommended to annotate the property that contains the source URI during runtime using the `set_as_content_source( )` method, but this is optional. The framework uses this information during runtime to provide a content tag that consists of the MIME-type (see next point) as well as the URI.

If no property is defined as the content source, or if the property value is empty at runtime, the framework automatically generates a source tag that uses the `$value` option. This allows the consumer to access the raw value of the entry.

▶ **MIME type**
The MIME type describes the type of the media resource (e.g., *image/ jpeg*). The property containing the MIME type has to be annotated by using the `set_as_content_type( )` method. It is mandatory to define this. If you don't, you'll get a runtime error when accessing any data.

If the source URI contains an absolute path to the media resource, the consumer can access the resource directly from its location (e.g., *<content-server>:<port>/path/subpath/.../picture.jpg*). But this requires that the consuming application has direct access to that media location, which might not be given by default due to, for example, required authentication or access via firewall.

$value   Instead of accessing the resource via an absolute URI, you can also access it via the SAP NetWeaver Gateway server by using the `$value` option to get the raw value of the corresponding entry. This requires implementing the `Get_Stream` method in the DPC extension class, which has to return the corresponding stream. This is very beneficial because a consumer application continues to communicate with the same server (SAP NetWeaver Gateway) instead of connecting/authenticating with multiple destinations.

To enhance the ZEXAMPLE1_SRV service, you first need to add two new properties: one for the source URI and one for the MIME type. As mentioned before, the source URI property is optional.

For our example, enter the property names "PictureURI" (`Edm.String`, length 255) and "PictureMIMEType" (`Edm.String`, length 128) to the product entity type (see Figure 6.73).

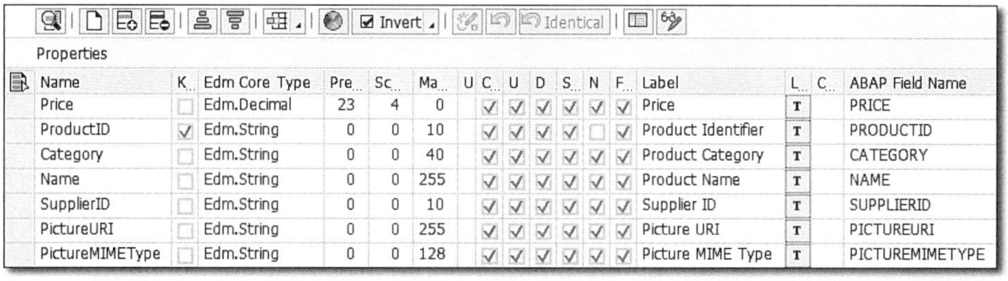

Name	K.	Edm Core Type	Pre..	Sc..	Ma..	U	C	U	D	S.	N	F.	Label	L.	C.	ABAP Field Name
Price	☐	Edm.Decimal	23	4	0	☑	☑	☑	☑	☑	☑		Price	T		PRICE
ProductID	☑	Edm.String	0	0	10	☑	☑	☑	☑	☐	☑		Product Identifier	T		PRODUCTID
Category	☐	Edm.String	0	0	40	☑	☑	☑	☑	☑	☑		Product Category	T		CATEGORY
Name	☐	Edm.String	0	0	255	☑	☑	☑	☑	☑	☑		Product Name	T		NAME
SupplierID	☐	Edm.String	0	0	10	☑	☑	☑	☑	☑	☑		Supplier ID	T		SUPPLIERID
PictureURI	☐	Edm.String	0	0	255	☑	☑	☑	☑	☑	☑		Picture URI	T		PICTUREURI
PictureMIMEType	☐	Edm.String	0	0	128	☑	☑	☑	☑	☑	☑		Picture MIME Type	T		PICTUREMIMETYPE

Figure 6.73 Properties for Media Resources

In the MPC extension class, you need to redefine the `define( )` method with the code shown in Listing 6.13.

```
method DEFINE.

  DATA: lo_entity_type TYPE REF TO /iwbep/if_mgw_odata_entity_
typ,
        lo_property    TYPE REF TO /iwbep/if_mgw_odata_prop-
erty.

  super->define( ).

  lo_entity_type = model->get_entity_type( 'Product' ).
  lo_entity_type->set_is_media( ).
  lo_property = lo_entity_type->get_property( 'PictureURI' ).
  lo_property->set_as_content_source( ).
  lo_property = lo_entity_type->get_
property( 'PictureMIMEType' ).
  lo_property->set_as_content_type( ).

endmethod.
```

Listing 6.13 Redefinition of Define Method

This code first calls the define method of the super class (MPC base class) where all definitions defined via the Service Builder take place. Then you make the entity type a media type by calling the `set_is_media( )` method. The `PictureURI` property is set to `content-source` and the `PictureMIMEType` property is set to `content-type`.

MPC base class

After you've regenerated the project and activated the MPC extension class, you'll find a new tag in the metadata document of your service: m:HasStream (see Figure 6.74).

```
<?xml version="1.0" encoding="utf-8" ?>
- <edmx:Edmx Version="1.0" xmlns:edmx="http://schemas.microsoft.com/ado/2007/06/edmx" xmlns:m="http://sche
  - <edmx:DataServices m:DataServiceVersion="2.0">
    - <Schema Namespace="ZEXAMPLE1_SRV" xml:lang="en" xmlns="http://schemas.microsoft.com/ado/2008/09/ed
      - <EntityType Name="Product" m:HasStream="true" sap:content-version="1">
        - <Key>
            <PropertyRef Name="ProductID" />
          </Key>
          <Property Name="ProductID" Type="Edm.String" Nullable="false" MaxLength="10" sap:label="Product Identifier"
          <Property Name="Category" Type="Edm.String" MaxLength="40" sap:label="Product Category" />
          <Property Name="Name" Type="Edm.String" MaxLength="255" sap:label="Product Name" />
          <Property Name="SupplierID" Type="Edm.String" MaxLength="10" sap:label="Supplier ID" />
          <Property Name="Price" Type="Edm.Decimal" Precision="23" Scale="4" sap:label="Price" />
          <Property Name="PictureMIMEType" Type="Edm.String" MaxLength="128" sap:label="Picture MIME Type" />
          <Property Name="PictureURI" Type="Edm.String" MaxLength="255" sap:label="Picture URI" />
          <NavigationProperty Name="ToSupplier" Relationship="ZEXAMPLE1_SRV.Assoc_Product_Supplier" FromRole="Fr
        </EntityType>
```

Figure 6.74 Media Entity Type

Next, you need to take care of the data provisioning. For this, again adjust the Get_EntitySet and Get_Entity methods to also map the PictureURI field into the result.

MIME type

The MIME type is unfortunately not part of the HEADERDATA structure and thus needs to be calculated manually. This is often necessary because there isn't always a suitable source field that can be taken from the return structure/table of a certain function. In this example, you'll add this determination to the product Get_EntitySet method of the DPC extension class.

Together with the previous examples, the PRODUCTCOLLECTIO_GET_ENTITYSET method has grown to what is shown in Listing 6.14.

```
METHOD productcollectio_get_entityset.

  DATA: ls_headerdata TYPE bapi_epm_product_header,
        lt_headerdata TYPE STANDARD TABLE OF bapi_epm_product_
header,
        ls_product    LIKE LINE OF et_entityset.

  DATA: ls_selparamproductid      TYPE bapi_epm_product_id_
range,
        lt_selparamproductid      TYPE STANDARD TABLE OF bapi_
epm_product_id_range,
```

```
        ls_selparamcategories      TYPE bapi_epm_product_categ_
range,
        lt_selparamcategories      TYPE STANDARD TABLE OF bapi_
epm_product_categ_range,
        ls_filter_select_options TYPE /iwbep/s_mgw_select_
option,
        ls_select_option           TYPE /iwbep/s_cod_select_
option.

  DATA: lv_maxrows TYPE bapi_epm_max_rows,
        lv_start   TYPE int4,
        lv_end     TYPE int4.

  DATA: lr_mr_api TYPE REF TO if_mr_api.

  lr_mr_api = cl_mime_repository_api=>if_mr_api~get_api( ).

  LOOP AT it_filter_select_options INTO ls_filter_select_
options.
    IF ls_filter_select_options-property EQ 'ProductID'.
      LOOP AT ls_filter_select_options-select_options INTO ls_
select_option.
        ls_selparamproductid-sign   = ls_select_option-sign.
        ls_selparamproductid-option = ls_select_option-option.
        ls_selparamproductid-low    = ls_select_option-low.
        ls_selparamproductid-high   = ls_select_option-high.
        APPEND ls_selparamproductid TO lt_selparamproductid.
      ENDLOOP.
    ELSEIF ls_filter_select_options-property EQ 'Category'.
      LOOP AT ls_filter_select_options-select_options INTO ls_
select_option.
        ls_selparamcategories-sign   = ls_select_option-sign.
        ls_selparamcategories-option = ls_select_option-option.
        ls_selparamcategories-low    = ls_select_option-low.
        ls_selparamcategories-high   = ls_select_option-high.
        APPEND ls_selparamcategories TO lt_selparamcategories.
      ENDLOOP.
    ENDIF.
  ENDLOOP.

  lv_maxrows-bapimaxrow = 0.
  IF ( is_paging-top IS NOT INITIAL ) AND
```

```
        ( io_tech_request_context->has_inlinecount( ) EQ abap_
false ).
      lv_maxrows-bapimaxrow = is_paging-top + is_paging-skip.
    ENDIF.

    CALL FUNCTION 'BAPI_EPM_PRODUCT_GET_LIST'
      EXPORTING
        max_rows              = lv_maxrows
      TABLES
        headerdata            = lt_headerdata
        selparamproductid     = lt_selparamproductid
*       SELPARAMSUPPLIERNAMES =
        selparamcategories    = lt_selparamcategories
*       RETURN                =
        .

    IF io_tech_request_context->has_inlinecount( ) EQ abap_true.
      es_response_context-inlinecount = lines( lt_headerdata ).
    ENDIF.

    lv_start = 1.
    IF is_paging-skip IS NOT INITIAL.
      lv_start = is_paging-skip + 1.
    ENDIF.

    IF is_paging-top IS NOT INITIAL.
      lv_end = is_paging-top + lv_start - 1.
    ELSE.
      lv_end = lines( lt_headerdata ).
    ENDIF.

    LOOP AT lt_headerdata INTO ls_headerdata
      FROM lv_start TO lv_end.
      ls_product-productid  = ls_headerdata-product_id.
      ls_product-category   = ls_headerdata-category.
      ls_product-name       = ls_headerdata-name.
      ls_product-supplierid = ls_headerdata-supplier_id.
      ls_product-price      = ls_headerdata-price.
      ls_product-pictureuri = ls_headerdata-product_pic_url.

      IF ls_product-pictureuri IS NOT INITIAL.
        CALL METHOD lr_mr_api->get
```

```
      EXPORTING
        i_url              = ls_product-pictureuri
      IMPORTING
        e_mime_type        = ls_product-picturemimetype
      EXCEPTIONS
        parameter_missing  = 1
        error_occured      = 2
        not_found          = 3
        permission_failure = 4
        OTHERS             = 5.
    ENDIF.

    APPEND ls_product TO et_entityset.
  ENDLOOP.

ENDMETHOD.
```

Listing 6.14 Product Collection, Get_Entityset Method with Filters, Client-Side Paging, Inline Count, and MIME Type Determination

In this specific example, the `PictureURI` contains an absolute path to the MIME repository. This is a special feature of the EPM product RFC modules. Therefore, you can use the MIME repository API to determine the MIME type of the picture. This can be done via the `GET` method.

As a result, you see the `PictureMIMEType` property filled for those entities in the collection that have a valid `PictureURI` (see Figure 6.75). In addition, you see that a `content` tag with the values `type` and `src` is rendered into the result. And there is also a new link that points to the entity's raw data (`/$value`).

```
- <entry>
    <id>http://vegtwy1mst.wdf.sap.corp:50000/sap/opu/odata/sap/ZEXAMPLE1_SRV/ProductCollection('HT-1000')</id>
    <title type="text">ProductCollection('HT-1000')</title>
    <updated>2013-08-03T20:18:08Z</updated>
    <category term="ZEXAMPLE1_SRV.Product" scheme="http://schemas.microsoft.com/ado/2007/08/schem
    <link href="ProductCollection('HT-1000')" rel="edit" title="Product" />
    <link href="ProductCollection('HT-1000')/$value" rel="edit-media" type="image/jpeg" />
    <link href="ProductCollection('HT-1000')/ToSupplier" rel="http://schemas.microsoft.com/ado/2007/08/dataservices/re
    <content type="image/jpeg" src="/SAP/PUBLIC/BC/NWDEMO_MODEL/IMAGES/HT-1000.jpg" />
  - <m:properties>
      <d:PictureMIMEType>image/jpeg</d:PictureMIMEType>
      <d:PictureURI>/SAP/PUBLIC/BC/NWDEMO_MODEL/IMAGES/HT-1000.jpg</d:PictureURI>
      <d:Price>0.0000</d:Price>
      <d:SupplierID>0100000000</d:SupplierID>
      <d:Name>Notebook Basic 15</d:Name>
      <d:Category>Notebooks</d:Category>
      <d:ProductID>HT-1000</d:ProductID>
    </m:properties>
  </entry>
```

Figure 6.75 Entity with Media Resource Information

Be sure to also adjust the product `Get_Entity` method (`PRODUCTCOLLECTIO_GET_ENTITY`) of the DPC extension class with the same logic to also determine the `PictureMIMEType` property. This ensures that `Get_Entity` and `Get_EntitySet` provide the same properties. The final coding is shown in Listing 6.15.

```abap
METHOD productcollectio_get_entity.

  DATA: ls_key_tab    TYPE /iwbep/s_mgw_name_value_pair,
        ls_product_id TYPE bapi_epm_product_id,
        ls_headerdata TYPE bapi_epm_product_header.

  DATA: lr_mr_api TYPE REF TO if_mr_api.

  lr_mr_api = cl_mime_repository_api=>if_mr_api~get_api( ).

  LOOP AT it_key_tab INTO ls_key_tab.
    IF ls_key_tab-name EQ 'ProductID'.
      ls_product_id-product_id = ls_key_tab-value.
    ENDIF.
  ENDLOOP.

  CALL FUNCTION 'BAPI_EPM_PRODUCT_GET_DETAIL'
    EXPORTING
      product_id              = ls_product_id
    IMPORTING
      headerdata              = ls_headerdata
*   TABLES
*     CONVERSION_FACTORS      =
*     RETURN                  =
    .

  er_entity-productid  = ls_headerdata-product_id.
  er_entity-category   = ls_headerdata-category.
  er_entity-name       = ls_headerdata-name.
  er_entity-supplierid = ls_headerdata-supplier_id.
  er_entity-price      = ls_headerdata-price.
  er_entity-pictureuri = ls_headerdata-product_pic_url.

  IF er_entity-pictureuri IS NOT INITIAL.
    CALL METHOD lr_mr_api->get
      EXPORTING
```

```
      i_url                = er_entity-pictureuri
   IMPORTING
      e_mime_type          = er_entity-picturemimetype
   EXCEPTIONS
      parameter_missing  = 1
      error_occured      = 2
      not_found          = 3
      permission_failure = 4
      OTHERS             = 5.
 ENDIF.

ENDMETHOD.
```

Listing 6.15 Product Collection, Get_Entity Method with MIME Type Determination

The content-src tag already provides an absolute path to the picture ⟶ Absolute path
itself. A consumer can call this one to retrieve the media resource. But in
this example, you want to provide the raw data of the entity that is
retrieved when the /$value option is used.

For this, you have to implement (redefine) the /IWBEP/IF_MGW_APPL_
SRV_RUNTIME~GET_STREAM method in the DPC extension class. Provide
the coding shown in Listing 6.16.

```
METHOD /iwbep/if_mgw_appl_srv_runtime~get_stream.

  DATA: ls_product TYPE zcl_zexample1_mpc=>ts_product.
  DATA: lr_mr_api  TYPE REF TO if_mr_api.
  DATA: ls_stream  TYPE ty_s_media_resource.


  CASE iv_entity_name.
    WHEN 'Product'.
      CALL METHOD productcollectio_get_entity
        EXPORTING
          iv_entity_name          = iv_entity_name
          iv_entity_set_name      = iv_entity_set_name
          iv_source_name          = iv_source_name
          it_key_tab              = it_key_tab
          io_tech_request_context = io_tech_request_context
          it_navigation_path      = it_navigation_path
        IMPORTING
          er_entity               = ls_product.
```

```
        IF NOT ls_product-pictureuri IS INITIAL.
          lr_mr_api = cl_mime_repository_api=>if_mr_api~get_
api( ).
          CALL METHOD lr_mr_api->get
            EXPORTING
              i_url                = ls_product-pictureuri
            IMPORTING
              e_content            = ls_stream-value
              e_mime_type          = ls_stream-mime_type
            EXCEPTIONS
              parameter_missing    = 1
              error_occured        = 2
              not_found            = 3
              permission_failure   = 4
              OTHERS               = 5.

        copy_data_to_ref(
          EXPORTING
            is_data = ls_stream
          CHANGING
            cr_data = er_stream ).
      ENDIF.
    ENDCASE.

ENDMETHOD.
```

Listing 6.16 Service Get-Stream Method

The coding first checks if the current entity type to be processed is a product (similar to the function import, there is no individual method generated, which is why these methods typically start with a case structure).

Execute method Next you execute the product Get_Entity method to fetch the product details. Because you've implemented the handling for the PictureURI property before, the ls_product-pictureuri field now contains the value that you need to determine the stream—at least for those products that have a URI. For this, you again use the MIME repository API GET method. It provides the actual content and the MIME type. Both need to be put into a specific structure of type ty_s_media_resource. At the end, you use the already known `copy_data_to_ref` method to copy the structure into a generic data container.

After activating the DPC extension class, you can run the following URI in the SAP NetWeaver Gateway client:

/sap/opu/odata/sap/ZEXAMPLE1_SRV/ProductCollection('HT-1000')/ $value

As a result, you get the picture of the product HT-1000 (see Figure 6.76).

Figure 6.76 Raw Value of Product HT-1000

6.5.8 Expand/Self-Expand

The `$expand` query option is very powerful and allows you to provide multiple entities and/or entity sets in one single service call, instead of performing several calls subsequently.

The `$expand` takes place along the defined navigation properties. It's handled by the SAP NetWeaver Gateway framework, which calls the respective `Get_Entity` and/or `Get_EntitySet` methods of the related DPC and puts the result together into a nested table or structure. The SAP NetWeaver Gateway framework knows the dependencies (associations) between each entity type as defined in the metadata and thus knows which methods to call and how to put the result together.

Handled by SAP NetWeaver Gateway framework

The only disadvantage you have when letting the SAP NetWeaver Gateway framework do the job is that certain RFCs might be unnecessarily called multiple times. This is because the framework knows the technical dependencies but not the business context of the data handled. To avoid this, you can redefine the DPC framework method `GET_EXPANDED_ENTITY` (interface `/IWBEP/IF_MGW_APPL_SRV_RUNTIME`) or `GET_EXPANDED_ENTITYSET`.

In this example, a navigation property has been defined between the product and the supplier. Instead of performing multiple service calls to first fetch the product and then fetch the supplier, you can use the `$expand` query option to provide both with a single service call. For this, you can, for instance, use the following URI in the SAP NetWeaver Gateway client to retrieve the details of product HT-1000 along with the supplier information:

/sap/opu/odata/sap/ZEXAMPLE1_SRV/ProductCollection('HT-1000')? $expand=ToSupplier

In the response, you see that the supplier is provided with an `m:inline` tag (see Figure 6.77).

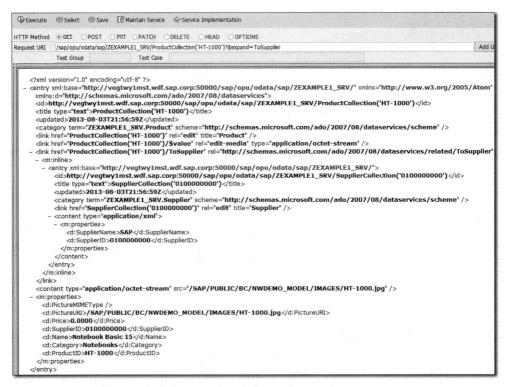

Figure 6.77 Product Details with $expand to Supplier

To demonstrate the redefinition of the GetExpandedEntity method, you first need to enhance the data model. Add another entity type with the name ProductConvFactor to the model. It has the following properties (see Figure 6.78).

Enhance data model

	Name	K.	Edm Core Type	Pre.	Sc.	Ma.	U.	C.	U	D	S.	N	F.	Label	L.	C.	ABAP Field Name
	ProductID	✓	Edm.String	0	0	10		✓	✓	✓	✓	☐	✓	Product Identifier	T		PRODUCT_ID
	SourceUnit	✓	Edm.String	0	0	3		✓	✓	✓	✓	☐	✓	Source Unit	T		SOURCE_UNIT
	TargetUnit	✓	Edm.String	0	0	3		✓	✓	✓	✓	☐	✓	Target Unit	T		TARGET_UNIT
	Numerator	☐	Edm.Int32	0	0	0		✓	✓	✓	✓	✓	✓	Numerator	T		NUMERATOR
	Denominator	☐	Edm.Int32	0	0	0		✓	✓	✓	✓	✓	✓	Denominator	T		DENOMINATOR

Figure 6.78 Properties of Entity Type ProductConvFactor

Create an entity set with the name ProductConvFactorCollection that uses the new entity type. Create an association with the NAME Assoc_Product_ProdConvFactor that defines a 1:M relationship between the PRODUCT and the PRODUCTCONVFACTOR entity types (see Figure 6.79).

	Name	E.	Principal Entity	Principal Entity Cardinality	Dependent Entity	Dependent Entity Cardinality
	Assoc_Product_Supplier		Product	M	Supplier	1
	Assoc_Product_ProdConvFactor		Product	1	ProductConvFactor	M

Figure 6.79 New Association Assoc_Product_ProductConvFactor

Double-click on REFERENTIAL CONSTRAINTS, and add a new entry for the ProductID (see Figure 6.80). Note that the read-only fields are filled as soon as you enter data into the other fields and press ⏎Enter.

	Principal Entity	Principal Key	Dependent Entity	Dependent Property
	Product	ProductID	ProductConvFactor	ProductID

Figure 6.80 Referential Constraint for ProductID

Create a navigation property for the product entity type with the name ToConvFactors that uses the newly created association (see Figure 6.81).

Create navigation property

	Name	Relationship Name	Label
	ToSupplier	Assoc_Product_Supplier	
	ToConvFactors	Assoc_Product_ProdConvFactor	

Figure 6.81 Navigation Property ToConvFactors

Generate the project to update the MPCs and the DPCs. Because you've added a new entity set to the model, there are five new methods (CRUD-Q) generated into the DPC base class, which are inherited to the extension class.

Redefine the conversion factor `Get_EntitySet` method `PRODUCTCONVFACTO_GET_ENTITYSET` in the DPC extension class, and provide the coding shown in Listing 6.17.

```
METHOD productconvfacto_get_entityset.

  DATA: ls_key_tab             TYPE /iwbep/s_mgw_name_value_
pair,
        ls_product_id          TYPE bapi_epm_product_id,
        ls_conversion_factors TYPE bapi_epm_product_conv_fac-
tors,
        lt_conversion_factors TYPE STANDARD TABLE OF bapi_epm_
product_conv_factors,
        ls_conv_factor         LIKE LINE OF et_entityset.

  LOOP AT it_key_tab INTO ls_key_tab.
    IF ls_key_tab-name EQ 'ProductID'.
      ls_product_id-product_id = ls_key_tab-value.
    ENDIF.
  ENDLOOP.

* Calling this method only makes sense via a navigation propert
y.
  CHECK ls_product_id IS NOT INITIAL.

  CALL FUNCTION 'BAPI_EPM_PRODUCT_GET_DETAIL'
    EXPORTING
      product_id              = ls_product_id
*   IMPORTING
*     HEADERDATA              =
    TABLES
      conversion_factors      = lt_conversion_factors
*     RETURN                  =
            .

  LOOP AT lt_conversion_factors INTO ls_conversion_factors.
    ls_conv_factor-product_id = ls_conversion_factors-product_
id.
```

```
    ls_conv_factor-source_unit = ls_conversion_factors-source_
unit.
    ls_conv_factor-target_unit = ls_conversion_factors-target_
unit.
    ls_conv_factor-numerator   = ls_conversion_factors-numera-
tor.
    ls_conv_factor-denominator = ls_conversion_factors-denomi-
nator.
    APPEND ls_conv_factor TO et_entityset.
  ENDLOOP.

ENDMETHOD.
```

Listing 6.17 Product Conversion Factors Collection, Get_Entityset Method

Activate the DPC extension class. Now you can execute the following URI to list all conversion factors of HT-1000:

Activate DPC extension class

/sap/opu/odata/sap/ZEXAMPLE1_SRV/ProductCollection('HT-1000')/ ToConvFactors

The corresponding expand statement to fetch the product and the conversion factors is the following:

/sap/opu/odata/sap/ZEXAMPLE1_SRV/ProductCollection('HT-1000')? $expand=ToConvFactors

As you can see, this is pretty straightforward and works fine. The only problem is that the preceding $expand statement executes the function module BAPI_EPM_PRODUCT_GET_DETAIL two times: first to fetch the product detail and second to fetch the list of conversion factors. In this little example, this might not be a problem, but in a real scenario accessing, for example, SAP CRM sales data over multiple entity types, that can have a significant performance impact.

Therefore, it's possible to redefine the framework methods GET_ EXPANDED_ENTITY and/or GET_EXPANDED_ENTITYSET as already mentioned earlier. In these methods, you can expand the data yourself and return the result in a nested table or structure. This gives you full flexibility on which expands you want to handle yourself and which you want the framework to handle. You can also handle the $expand partially if you want.

Redefine framework methods

In this example, you'll handle the $expand of the conversion factors, so navigate into the DPC extension class, and redefine the GET_EXPANDED_ENTITY method of interface /IWBEP/IF_MGW_APPL_SRV_RUNTIME. Provide the coding shown in Listing 6.18.

```
METHOD /iwbep/if_mgw_appl_srv_runtime~get_expanded_entity.

* Nested result type
  DATA: BEGIN OF ls_prod_convfactors.
          INCLUDE TYPE zcl_zexample1_mpc=>ts_product.
  DATA: toconvfactors TYPE STANDARD TABLE OF zcl_zexample1_
mpc=>ts_productconvfactor WITH DEFAULT KEY,
        END OF ls_prod_convfactors.

  DATA: ls_product_id    TYPE bapi_epm_product_id,
        ls_headerdata    TYPE bapi_epm_product_header,
        ls_conv_factors  TYPE bapi_epm_product_conv_factors,
        lt_conv_factors  TYPE TABLE OF bapi_epm_product_conv_
factors,
        ls_conv_factor   TYPE zcl_zexample1_mpc=>ts_productconv-
factor.

  DATA: lv_entityset_name              TYPE /iwbep/mgw_tech_
name,
        lv_source_entityset_name       TYPE /iwbep/mgw_tech_
name,
        lv_compare_result_prod_convfac TYPE io_expand->ty_e_
compare_result,
        ls_expanded_clause             LIKE LINE OF et_
expanded_tech_clauses,
        ls_key_tab                     TYPE /iwbep/s_mgw_name_
value_pair.

  lv_entityset_name              = io_tech_request_context-
>get_entity_set_name( ).
  lv_source_entityset_name       = io_tech_request_context-
>get_source_entity_set_name( ).
  lv_compare_result_prod_convfac = io_expand->compare_to_tech_
names( 'TOCONVFACTORS' ).

* Expand on Product/Conversion Factors?
  IF lv_entityset_name EQ 'ProductCollection' AND
```

```
      ( lv_compare_result_prod_convfac EQ io_expand->gcs_compare_
result-match_subset OR
        lv_compare_result_prod_convfac EQ io_expand->gcs_compare_
result-match_equals ).

      READ TABLE it_key_tab INTO ls_key_tab INDEX 1.
      ls_product_id-product_id = ls_key_tab-value.

      CALL FUNCTION 'BAPI_EPM_PRODUCT_GET_DETAIL'
        EXPORTING
          product_id        = ls_product_id
        IMPORTING
          headerdata        = ls_headerdata
        TABLES
          conversion_factors = lt_conv_factors.

      ls_prod_convfactors-pictureuri = ls_headerdata-product_pic_
url.
      ls_prod_convfactors-name        = ls_headerdata-name.
      ls_prod_convfactors-category    = ls_headerdata-category.
      ls_prod_convfactors-productid   = ls_headerdata-product_id.
      ls_prod_convfactors-supplierid = ls_headerdata-supplier_id.

      LOOP AT lt_conv_factors INTO ls_conv_factors.
        MOVE-CORRESPONDING ls_conv_factors TO ls_conv_factor.
        APPEND ls_conv_factor TO ls_prod_convfactors-toconvfac-
tors.
      ENDLOOP.

      copy_data_to_ref(
        EXPORTING
          is_data = ls_prod_convfactors
        CHANGING
          cr_data = er_entity ).

      ls_expanded_clause = 'TOCONVFACTORS'.
      APPEND ls_expanded_clause TO et_expanded_tech_clauses.
    ELSE.
      super->/iwbep/if_mgw_appl_srv_runtime~get_expanded_entity(
        EXPORTING
          iv_entity_name          = iv_entity_name
          iv_entity_set_name      = iv_entity_set_name
```

```
            iv_source_name              = iv_source_name
            io_expand                   = io_expand
            it_key_tab                  = it_key_tab
            it_navigation_path          = it_navigation_path
            io_tech_request_context     = io_tech_request_context
        IMPORTING
            er_entity                   = er_entity
            et_expanded_clauses         = et_expanded_clauses
            et_expanded_tech_clauses    = et_expanded_tech_clauses ).
    ENDIF.

ENDMETHOD.
```

Listing 6.18 Service Get-Expanded-Entity Method for Conversion Factors Expansion

This coding appears a little lengthy but is actually not too complex. The data declaration part defines a nested structure that can hold the product as well as the list of conversion factors. The conversion factors go into a table field with the name `ToConvFactors`, which always has to be equal to the name of the defined navigation property. Then you need some tables/structures to call the RFC module as well as some fields for some framework data.

The `lv_compare_result_prod_convfac` field based on `io_expand->ty_e_compare_result` is very important because it will be used in the `io_expand->compare_to_tech_names` call to determine where you are in the expand tree. As this is a fairly small tree, the comparison will result in match-equals. Inside the `IF` statement, you pick the primary key from the key table and with that call the `BAPI_EPM_PRODUCT_GET_DETAIL` function module only once—retrieving the product `HEADERDATA` along with the table of conversion factors in one shot.

Fill nested structure
Then you need to fill the nested structure that was defined at the beginning with the results of the function module call. The nested structure is copied to the data reference that you return. Lastly, you need to tell the framework that you've actually taken care of the `$expand` by adding a line to `et_expanded_tech_clauses` specifying the navigation property (`ToConvFactors`) that you've handled.

The `else` branch is for all other expands that you want the SAP NetWeaver Gateway framework to handle generically. Note that, for the sake of simplicity, we haven't addressed any error handling out of the function module call.

6.5.9 Deep Insert

A deep insert is the inversion of `$expand`. Instead of receiving a nested structure of entries and/or collections, a consumer is able to `POST` a nested structure to the SAP NetWeaver Gateway server. By doing this, you can, for example, create a sales order header together with the collection of line items with a single service call.

Inversion of $expand

In this example, you'll create a product together with the list of conversion factors by using a deep insert. A product is a single entry, whereas the list of conversion factors is a collection.

Similar to `$expand`, you need to implement the handling yourself in the DPC extension class. The deep insert is handled by the `CREATE_DEEP_ENTITY` method of the framework interface `/IWBEP/IF_MGW_APPL_SRV_RUNTIME`.

If you've followed the media resource implementation steps before, switch the entity type back from a media entity type to a regular entity type. Otherwise, the `CREATE_STREAM` method needs to handle the deep insert (which of course also works, but isn't the point of this discussion). The easiest way to switch the entity type back to a regular one is to comment the line `lo_entity_type->set_is_media( )` in the MPC extension class. After you've changed the MPC extension class, be sure to activate it.

In the DPC extension class, redefine the `CREATE_DEEP_ENTITY` method of the interface `/IWBEP/IF_MGW_APPL_SRV_RUNTIME`, and provide the coding shown in Listing 6.19.

```
METHOD /iwbep/if_mgw_appl_srv_runtime~create_deep_entity.

* Nested input/result type
  DATA: BEGIN OF ls_prod_convfactors.
          INCLUDE TYPE zcl_zexample1_mpc=>ts_product.
  DATA: toconvfactors TYPE STANDARD TABLE OF zcl_zexample1_
mpc=>ts_productconvfactor WITH DEFAULT KEY,
        END OF ls_prod_convfactors.
```

```
   DATA: lv_entityset_name TYPE /iwbep/mgw_tech_name,
         ls_headerdata      TYPE bapi_epm_product_header,
         ls_conv_factors    TYPE bapi_epm_product_conv_factors,
         lt_conv_factors    TYPE TABLE OF bapi_epm_product_conv_
factors,
         ls_conv_factor     TYPE zcl_zexample1_mpc=>ts_product-
convfactor,
         lt_return          TYPE TABLE OF bapiret2.

   lv_entityset_name = io_tech_request_context->get_entity_set_
name( ).

   CASE lv_entityset_name.
     WHEN 'ProductCollection'.
       io_data_provider->read_entry_data( IMPORTING es_
data = ls_prod_convfactors ).

       ls_headerdata-type_code      = 'AD'.
       ls_headerdata-tax_tarif_code = '1'.
       ls_headerdata-currency_code  = 'EUR'.
       ls_headerdata-measure_unit   = 'EA'.
       ls_headerdata-supplier_id    = ls_prod_convfactors-sup-
plierid.
       ls_headerdata-name           = ls_prod_convfactors-name.
       ls_headerdata-category       = ls_prod_convfactors-cate-
gory.
       ls_headerdata-product_id     = ls_prod_convfactors-pro-
ductid.
       ls_headerdata-price          = ls_prod_convfactors-price.

       LOOP AT ls_prod_convfactors-toconvfactors INTO ls_conv_
factor.
         MOVE-CORRESPONDING ls_conv_factor TO ls_conv_factors.
         APPEND ls_conv_factors TO lt_conv_factors.
       ENDLOOP.

       CALL FUNCTION 'BAPI_EPM_PRODUCT_CREATE'
         EXPORTING
           headerdata          = ls_headerdata
         TABLES
           conversion_factors = lt_conv_factors
```

```
        return                = lt_return.

    IF lt_return IS NOT INITIAL.
       mo_context->get_message_container( )->add_messages_
from_bapi(
          it_bapi_messages         = lt_return
          iv_determine_leading_msg = /iwbep/if_message_con-
tainer=>gcs_leading_msg_search_option-first ).

       RAISE EXCEPTION TYPE /iwbep/cx_mgw_busi_exception
          EXPORTING
            textid              = /iwbep/cx_mgw_busi_excep-
tion=>business_error
            message_container = mo_context->get_message_
container( ).
    ENDIF.

    copy_data_to_ref(
      EXPORTING
        is_data = ls_prod_convfactors
      CHANGING
        cr_data = er_deep_entity ).

  WHEN OTHERS.
    CALL METHOD super->/iwbep/if_mgw_appl_srv_runtime~create_
deep_entity
      EXPORTING
        iv_entity_name        = iv_entity_name
        iv_entity_set_name    = iv_entity_set_name
        iv_source_name        = iv_source_name
        io_data_provider      = io_data_provider
        it_key_tab            = it_key_tab
        it_navigation_path    = it_navigation_path
        io_expand             = io_expand
        io_tech_request_context = io_tech_request_context
      IMPORTING
        er_deep_entity        = er_deep_entity.
  ENDCASE.

ENDMETHOD.
```

Listing 6.19 Service Create-Deep-Entity Method for Product and Conversion Factors Creation with Error Handling

Define complex
data type First, you again define a complex data type `ls_prod_convfactors` that can carry the nested data that is retrieved with the POST call. In the case structure, make sure that this is a POST on the `ProductCollection` and not on any other collection. The `others` branch will actually end up in a technical exception because a deep insert isn't generically handled by the framework and thus has to be handled via the redefined `CREATE_DEEP_ENTITY` method.

Besides the product properties, the nested structure `ls_prod_convfactors` has a table field (`toconvfactors`) that contains the table of conversion factors. All of these properties are processed and put into the respective structure/table data fields to be able to call the `BAPI_EPM_PRODUCT_CREATE` function module. The error handling is done by checking whether the return table is empty. If the return table has entries, the log is saved, and a business exception is thrown.

Finally, the nested structure is copied to a data reference and by that handed back to the framework via the `er_deep_entity` parameter. This is necessary because a POST requires the return of the entity created to at least inform the consumer about the primary key of the created entity (and maybe some calculated fields). In this example, there is neither an internal number range that defines the next primary key nor an entity property that is defaulted. Therefore, you can return the same nested structure that you've received (if the BAPI `CREATE` was processed successful).

Via the SAP NetWeaver Gateway client, you can easily test the deep insert of your service. It's recommended to first perform an `$expand` on any source entity that you want to use as a pattern and to click the Use as Request button to copy the response body over to the request body.

Adjust product ID Next, adjust the data, because the product ID has to be unique. Also adjust the product ID for the conversion factor(s). Then you need to change the HTTP method to POST and change the URI to the `ProductCollection`. Finally, you can execute the call; if everything is successful, you get a nested structure of the created data back (see Figure 6.82). As verification, you can perform a GET on the newly created product with its conversion factors to see if the nested data was persisted successfully.

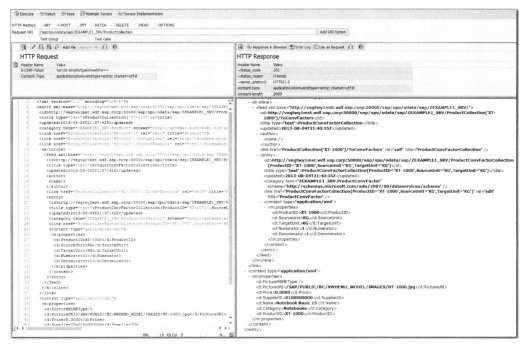

Figure 6.82 Successful Deep Insert of Product and Conversion Factors

6.5.10 Batch

An OData batch request is typically used whenever a consumer wants to perform multiple independent HTTP calls and wants to avoid multiple server roundtrips. A common example is the fetching of customizing data at application start, where you typically request the data of several independent collections.

Batch processing just batches up several independent OData service calls into a single (big) call. Those calls can combine read and write accesses. For write access, you need to define related `change-sets` in the request body to define logical units of work for everything that has to be executed either entirely or rolled back in case of any problem.

Combine read and write access

> **Note**
>
> Batch processing can't be used if the individual calls are dependent on each other (e.g., one call requires the results of a preceding call).

325

A batch call is always performed via the HTTP POST method. The URI for all $batch requests of an OData service is always the same; for example, the URI for this example in the SAP NetWeaver Gateway client looks like */sap/opu/odata/sap/ZEXAMPLE1_SRV/$batch*.

The individual steps to be executed need to be put into the request body. That has the positive side effect that the URIs are also secured if you use the HTTPS protocol.

The OData batch request is a multipart MIME v1.0 message in which each part may have a different content type. The easiest meaningful batch is probably the execution of two get_entity calls. Such a request body looks like the code shown in Listing 6.20.

```
--batch_zmybatch
Content-Type: application/http
Content-Transfer-Encoding: binary

GET ProductCollection('HT-1000') HTTP/1.1


--batch_zmybatch
Content-Type: application/http
Content-Transfer-Encoding: binary

GET ProductCollection('HT-1001') HTTP/1.1


--batch_zmybatch--
```

Listing 6.20 Sample $batch Request Body

An OData batch request also requires setting the Content-Type request header according to the boundary defined. In the preceding case, the Content-Type needs to be multipart/mixed;boundary=batch_zmybatch.

If you execute this batch request via the SAP NetWeaver Gateway client, you get the details of product HT-1000 and HT-1001 (see Figure 6.83).

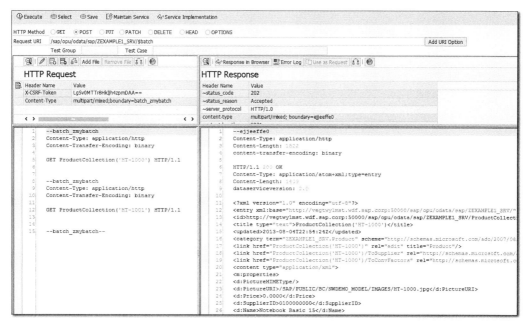

Figure 6.83 Simple Batch Request with Two Read Calls

Note that the boundary marker `batch_zmybatch` is set in the request header, as well as in front of each retrieve operation preceding with `--` in the request body. The `Content-Type` on the header level is set to `multipart/mixed`. Each operation needs to define its `Content-Type`, which in this example is `application/http`.

Boundary marker

Be sure to provide at least two blank lines between each batch operation. Otherwise, you get a malformed service request error. Don't forget to conclude the HTTP request body with the closing boundary marker with preceding double hyphens (`--`) as well as subsequent double hyphens (`--`). The batch operation itself (`GET ProductCollection('HT-1000') HTTP/1.1`) needs to define the HTTP operation (in this case, `GET`) as well as the resource and additional parameter, as in the URI.

Because this simple batch example only consists of retrieve operations, a `change-set` isn't necessary. Whenever a batch request contains any write operations, you have to provide a `change-set`.

You can use this, for example, in a regular UPDATE operation that—
according to the OData standard—doesn't return the entry resource
updated. But you can combine an UPDATE operation together with a GET
operation to fetch the details. A corresponding $batch request can look
like the code in Listing 6.21.

```
--batch_zmybatch
Content-Type: multipart/mixed; boundary=changeset_zmychangeset

--changeset_zmychangeset
Content-Type: application/http
Content-Transfer-Encoding: binary

PUT ProductCollection('HT-1001') HTTP/1.1
Content-Type: application/atom+xml

<atom:entry xmlns:atom="http://www.w3.org/2005/Atom">
<atom:content type="application/xml">
<m:properties xmlns:m="http://schemas.microsoft.com/ado/2007/
08/dataservices/metadata" xmlns:d="http://sche-
mas.microsoft.com/ado/2007/08/dataservices">
  <d:SupplierID>0100000001</d:SupplierID>
  <d:Name>Notebook Basic 17 - Test</d:Name>
  <d:Category>Notebooks</d:Category>
  <d:ProductID>HT-1001</d:ProductID>
</m:properties>
</atom:content>
</atom:entry>

--changeset_zmychangeset--


--batch_zmybatch
Content-Type: application/http
Content-Transfer-Encoding: binary

GET ProductCollection('HT-1001') HTTP/1.1


--batch_zmybatch--
```

Listing 6.21 Example Batch Call

This OData batch request first updates the product HT-1001 and then performs a GET request to read the updated entry resource. If there are multiple write operations (CREATE, UPDATE, DELETE) contained in a single change-set, no operation may perform a commit-work because otherwise the all-or-nothing paradigm can't be met. The framework is checking this and will trigger a short dump if this rule is violated. This check is deactivated if the change-set only consists of a single write operation.

The SAP NetWeaver Gateway framework executes a commit-work at the end of each change-set. At the beginning of each change-set, the SAP NetWeaver Gateway framework executes the CHANGESET_BEGIN method (interface /IWBEP/IF_MGW_APPL_SRV_RUNTIME). This method can be redefined if you want to implement your own handling. It has to be redefined if the change-set contains changes to more than one entity type.

Commit-work

In the change-set-begin method, you can, for example, set a member variable to indicate that a change-set processing is taking place. This information can be used inside an UPDATE method to only store changes in memory or to avoid a commit-work.

The change-set-begin method can also be used to verify if the change-set contains unsupported combinations of entity types. The method has an input table, it_operation_info, that lists all entity types contained in the current change-set. This allows you to react on combinations you don't want to support by throwing the corresponding exception.

At the end of each change-set, the CHANGESET_END method (same interface) is called. You can redefine it to perform your own change-set end handling where you reset the member variable and perform your database UPDATE and/or commit-work.

6.6 Summary

This chapter has given you an introduction to the OData service development using the SAP NetWeaver Gateway Service Builder toolset. Following a step-by-step approach, we've modeled, implemented, and executed the OData service.

The model definition was done in a declarative way by creating entity types, entity sets, properties, associations, referential constraints, navigation properties, and function imports. We also looked at the options to import a model definition from an EDMX file, from a DDIC structure/table, and from a BOR/RFC interface.

The service implementation part was entirely done by redefining/overwriting the related methods in the DPC extension class using ABAP. This works pretty well, although might sometimes appear to be a bit lengthy. That's why the Service Builder has the capability to generate the service implementation of the CRUD-Q methods by mapping the respective method to a corresponding data source (e.g., RFC module). This will be explained further in the next chapter.

Service generation is another way to create OData services using SAP NetWeaver Gateway. This chapter explains the end-to-end development tools and development cycle for this process.

7   Service Generation

In the last chapter, we taught you how to develop service implementation logic with custom ABAP code. However, it's also possible to leverage existing interfaces and business objects in the SAP Business Suite to generate OData services without the need to write a single line of code. This process is called *service generation*.

This chapter explains the generation of OData services using the SAP NetWeaver Gateway Service Builder. The generation of OData services from existing interfaces and business objects (such as remote function calls [RFCs], Business Application Programming Interfaces [BAPIs], GenIL objects, Service Provider Interface (SPI) building blocks, SAP NetWeaver BW Easy Queries, etc.) takes place by translating existing, predefined interfaces and SAP business objects into more compact and consumable new OData services.

We discuss three use cases:

▶ The first and most widely used use case is the RFC/BOR Generator.

▶ The second use case is to generate a service based on another SAP business object using redefinition.

▶ The third use case is to compose an OData service from already existing OData services in SAP NetWeaver Gateway.

The first option, service generation using the RFC/BOR Generator, doesn't require code writing but does require several manual steps. Like service development, the service generation using the RFC/BOR Generator takes place in the three main phases—data model definition phase,

RFC/BOR
Generator

service implementation phase, and service maintenance phase—as depicted again in Figure 7.1. However, in contrast to service development, where service implementation is performed via a code-based implementation, the developer has to map the interface of the RFC/BOR interface to the OData service. Though this process step requires detailed knowledge of the underlying RFC function modules, ABAP knowledge is only necessary to the extent required to understand the corresponding data types. (The exception for this rule is when there is no appropriate function module available and thus needs to be created, which is also explained and demonstrated in this chapter.)

Redefinition
Compared to using the RFC/BOR Generator, the second option, which is to generate a service using redefinition, is a much easier approach. This involves redefining an existing business object based on GenIL objects, SPI objects, and SAP NetWeaver BW Easy Queries or MDX queries. In contrast to the RFC/BOR Generator, the mapping process in these integration scenarios is more straightforward because the business objects in question are already similar to OData services. When using redefinition, the data model definitions of existing business object entities and methods are mapped to the entity types and sets of an OData service while the implementation is generated on the basis of mapped OData artifacts chosen by the developer.

Model composition
Finally, the third option is to compose an OData service from already existing OData services in SAP NetWeaver Gateway, which is called *model composition*. This method allows mashing up existing services in SAP NetWeaver Gateway to create a new OData service. It allows the reuse of existing services for new use cases without the need to change the existing ones. A possible use case is, for example, a business process that leverages an SAP NetWeaver BW Easy Query to retrieve customer data with certain sales key figures. Part of the business process is also that users can create or change sales orders for these customers. You can generate an OData service based on the existing query and perform a mashup between this read-only service and another OData service in SAP NetWeaver Gateway that allows changing or creating sales orders.

This chapter includes detailed coverage of the technical basics of selected integration scenarios as well as best practices for efficient OData service generation. The goal is to enable the reader to generate services with the main development tool, the SAP NetWeaver Gateway Service Builder. For this, we've provided examples that make use of the following:

❶ RFC/BOR interface

❷ Redefinition (of an SAP NetWeaver BW Easy Query, SPI building block, and an external OData service)

❸ Model composition

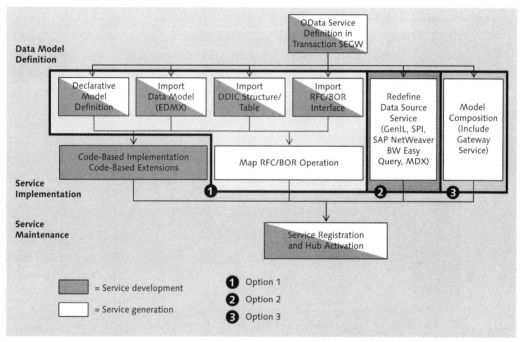

Figure 7.1 Service Generation in SAP NetWeaver Gateway Using the Service Builder (Transaction SEGW)

7.1 Generation via RFC/BOR Interface

In Chapter 6, we introduced the process of data model definition by importing the OData model from an RFC/BOR interface. This approach is commonly used because most SAP NetWeaver Gateway OData services are based on remote function modules. In this section, we'll show you how to implement the service by simply mapping the interfaces of the RFC function modules to the operations of the OData service (as opposed to the code-based approach taken in Chapter 6).

You'll start the service generation process by creating a new project, ZRFC1, in the Service Builder and defining a data model (Section 7.1.1). The model will consist of two entity types: `SalesOrderHeader` and `SalesOrderLineItem`. Both entity type definitions will be imported from the corresponding sample function modules that are part of the SAP *Enterprise Procurement Model* (EPM). EPM is a test application that serves as a proxy for SAP's real-world SAP Business Suite applications.

Next, you'll define a navigation property between the order header and the line items to navigate from a header entry to its collection of line items. This also allows you to perform an `$expand` call to retrieve the header information along with the corresponding line items in one single service call. The model is depicted in Figure 7.2.

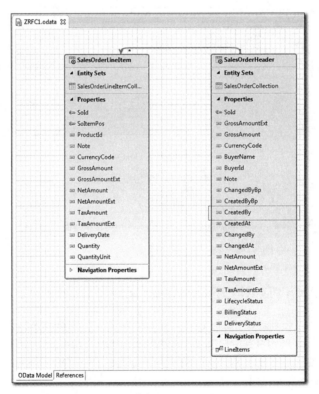

Figure 7.2 Entity Data Model: Service ZRFC1

As we mentioned in Chapter 5, in real-world development scenarios, the sequence in which data model definition, service implementation, and service maintenance are performed will vary and not always follow the waterfall model shown earlier in Figure 7.1.

After the data model is defined, repository objects are generated, and the service is registered in the backend by the Service Builder (Section 7.1.2). In this step, the model provider class is generated. Also generated is a stub for the data provider class with (empty) methods that have to be implemented by either code-based implementation (as described in Chapter 6) or by mapping (as described in this section). Because the basic service implementation (stub creation) has already been performed, you'll first continue with activating the service to test the service metadata document and to test the implementation of the different CRUD-Q methods (Section 7.1.3). This real-world service creation flow is depicted in Figure 7.3.

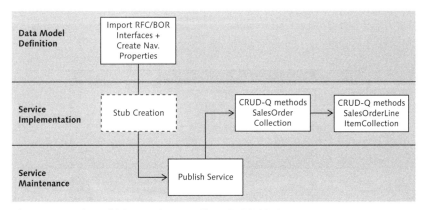

Figure 7.3 Real-World Service Creation Flow: RFC/BOR Generator

The final service implementation is described in Section 7.1.4 and Section 7.1.5. It is performed via the Service Builder by assigning the corresponding RFC function modules to the respective operation and by mapping the function module fields to the related entity set properties. This allows you to implement full CRUD-Q operations (CREATE, READ, UPDATE, DELETE, and QUERY) as well as navigation property support without writing a single line of ABAP code—at least as long as a corresponding RFC function module is available. In this example, you'll use a set of five EPM sales order function modules. You'll see that the CRUD-Q operations on the header level can be easily generated, whereas the operations on the item level need certain adjustments.

7.1.1 Data Model Definition

So let's get started. After creating the mentioned project, you first import the data model from the RFC module BAPI_EPM_SO_GET_LIST. This function module is used to retrieve the list of sales order headers. The interface also has an output table for the line items.

When defining a data model based on a function module, the interesting part of the function module is the interface; as such, you use the interface definition to derive the model definition for your entity types. The actual data provided by the function module comes into play when you do the service implementation.

Entity type: step 1   In this new project, right-click on DATA MODEL and choose IMPORT • RFC/BOR INTERFACE. This opens the CREATE ENTITY TYPE FROM DATA SOURCE screen (see Figure 7.4).

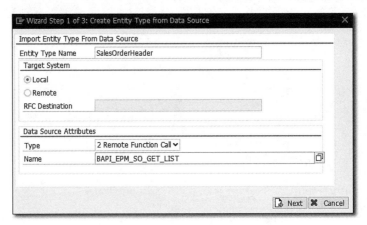

Figure 7.4 Step 1 of the RFC Import Wizard

For ENTITY TYPE NAME, enter "SalesOrderHeader". Note that this name will only be considered if you select individual fields from the interface in the subsequent step.

For TARGET SYSTEM, use LOCAL to fetch the interface from the local system. It's also possible to provide an RFC DESTINATION to fetch the function module interface from a remote system.

DATA SOURCE ATTRIBUTES specify what data source you're looking for. TYPE can be BOR OBJECT or REMOTE FUNCTION CALL. Note that regular function modules (nonremote) aren't supported. And finally, you have to name the RFC function module from which to fetch the interface. In this case, enter "BAPI_EPM_SO_GET_LIST" and choose NEXT.

The wizard now reads the interface definition of the provided data source and shows the result on the second screen of the wizard (see Figure 7.5). On this screen, you select the attributes you want to be created as properties in your entity type.

Entity type: step 2

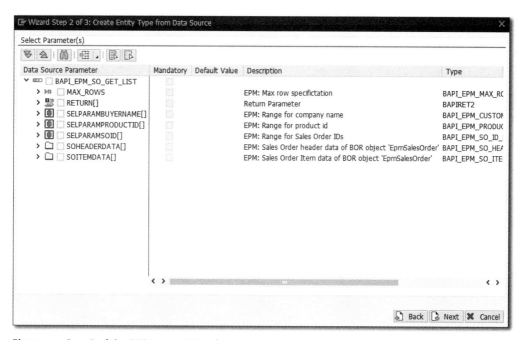

Figure 7.5 Step 2 of the RFC Import Wizard

Start by selecting the properties for the sales order header entity type. Note that the RFC/BOR import wizard can be used to create multiple entity types and/or complex types in one go. But for the sake of simplicity, we'll call the wizard one by one for each entity type we want to create.

To create the entity type for the sales order header, the corresponding interface table is SOHEADERDATA. You can select the entire table by marking the checkbox next to SOHEADERDATA. Although this is the easiest way, it has the minor disadvantage that the entity type name provided on the first page is ignored, and instead the entity type receives the name of the interface table (this is because you can select multiple tables to create multiple entity types in one go). Instead of selecting the entire SOHEADERDATA table, you can also select individual fields by expanding the tree.

Entity type: step 3 Select the entire table, and choose NEXT. On the subsequent screen, mark the primary key field(s) of the entity type you want to create. (If you don't, you'll get an error after completing the wizard; a project check is automatically triggered right after the wizard execution, and an entity type without a primary key is considered an erroneous entity type.)

In this example, mark SO_ID (sales order ID) as the primary key of the sales order header entity type (see Figure 7.6) and choose FINISH.

If you've marked the entire table, you need to change the entity type name from SOHEADERDATA to SalesOrderHeader. Also make sure that the entity type has the right ABAP structure assigned to it, that is, BAPI_EPM_SO_HEADER (see Figure 7.7). This is important because it ensures that the related entity properties and model provider class (MPC) type declarations are based on the correct Data Dictionary (DDIC) object.

Now perform the same steps to create an entity type for the sales order line items. The name of the entity type is SalesOrderLineItem. It can be imported by using the same function module, BAPI_EPM_SO_HEADER. The interface table is SOITEMDATA. The primary key consists of two fields: SO_ID and SO_ITEM_POS.

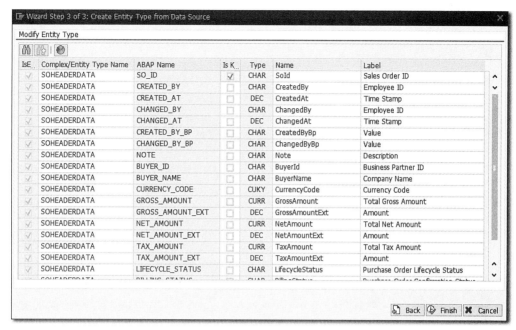

Figure 7.6 Step 3 of the RFC Import Wizard

Figure 7.7 ABAP Structure Assignment to Entity Type

Setting SAP Annotations

Make sure to set the respective SAP annotations (creatable, updatable, etc.) for each property imported. It's strongly recommended to set at least the nullable annotation for each nonkey property; otherwise, this might lead to problems when executing the service, especially with date/time fields.

After both entity types have been created, you need to create the corresponding entity sets. For each entity type, you create one entity set (see Figure 7.8).

Entity sets

Figure 7.8 Entity Sets for Sales Order Header and Line Item Entity Types

Association and referential constraint

The next step is to define an association with a referential constraint. This allows you to create a navigation property that can be used to fetch the line items related to a certain sales order header. The association can be created by navigating to the ASSOCIATION node under DATA MODEL in the project tree. It can also be created by right-clicking on DATA MODEL and selecting CREATE • ASSOCIATION. This opens the association wizard that allows you to create an association together with the referential constraint as well as the navigation property.

On the first screen of the association wizard, you specify the name of the association and the entity types contained with their respective cardinality (see Figure 7.9). You can also check the CREATE RELATED NAVIGATION PROPERTY checkbox to also create a corresponding navigation property. In this example, you're creating the navigation property `LineItems`.

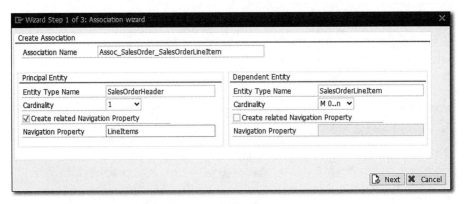

Figure 7.9 Step 1 of the Association Wizard

On the second screen, you specify the referential constraint by mapping the key fields of the principal entity type to the properties of the dependent entity. In this example, the PRINCIPAL ENTITY type is the `Sales-OrderHeader`, and the PRINCIPAL KEY only consists of a single field, `SoId`.

This property is mapped to `SoId` of the dependent entity type `Sales-OrderLineItem` (see Figure 7.10).

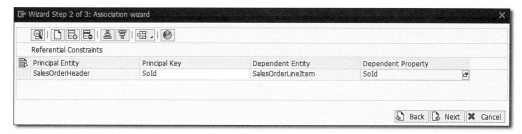

Figure 7.10 Step 2 of the Association Wizard

On the third screen, you provide the name of the association set to be created. The name is defaulted based on the name provided for the association. The corresponding entity sets are derived from the related entity types (see Figure 7.11).

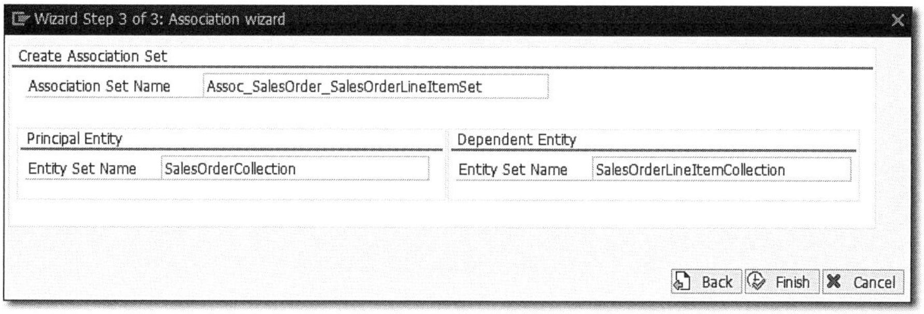

Figure 7.11 Step 3 of the Association Wizard

This concludes the model definition of the RFC example. The data model now consists of two entity types, two entity sets, an association with referential constraint, and a navigation property.

7.1.2   Service Registration: Stub Creation

You can now generate the runtime artifacts by clicking the GENERATE button. In the MODEL AND SERVICE DEFINITION pop-up, leave the default values as provided by the Service Builder. This step creates both MPC classes and both data provider classes (DPCs), as you've learned from

Model and service generation

previous chapters. Please note that while the MPC contains the model information, the DPC is created as an empty stub. The Service Builder also registers the service on the backend by creating a technical model and a technical service (see Figure 7.12).

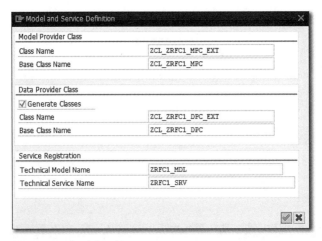

Figure 7.12 Model and Service Generation

7.1.3 Service Maintenance

Service activation on the hub

After the project has been successfully generated and registered on the backend, you can register and activate the OData service on the SAP NetWeaver Gateway hub so that it gets published. For this, you expand the SERVICE MAINTENANCE node in the example project, right-click on the hub entry you want the service to register and activate on, and select REGISTER from the context menu.

After confirming the warning pop-up, informing us about the fact that this step will be carried out on the SAP NetWeaver Gateway hub system, you provide the system alias that was created before on the hub system (here we choose LOCAL since we are using an embedded deployment).

This opens up the ADD SERVICE pop-up screen where you see the corresponding elements (service name, model name, etc.) that will be created on the SAP NetWeaver Gateway hub system (see Figure 7.13).

Again leave the default values as they are, and click the LOCAL OBJECT button, which sets the package to $TMP. If you want to transport the repository elements, you need to provide a transportable package.

Note the EXTERNAL SERVICE NAME field under which the service will be activated as an Internet Communication Framework (ICF) service. This name is derived from the technical service name provided during the first generation of the project where the registration of the OData service on the backend took place. It's not possible to change the external service name while registering and activating the service on the SAP NetWeaver Gateway hub.

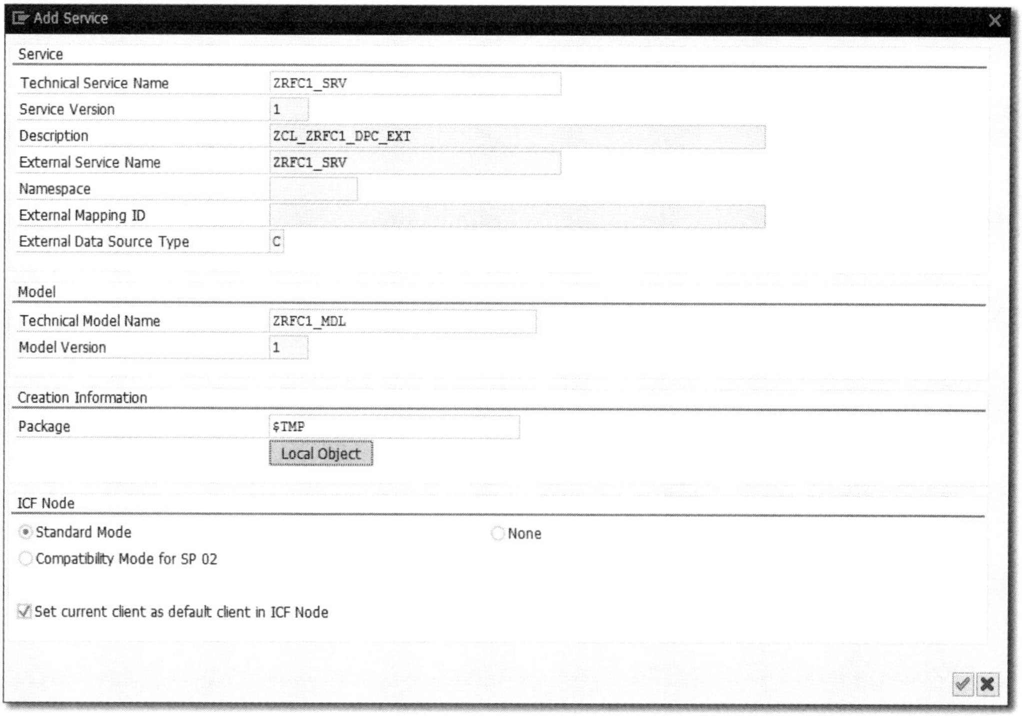

Figure 7.13 Add Service Dialog on the SAP NetWeaver Gateway Hub

After confirming the ADD SERVICE dialog, the OData service is activated on the SAP NetWeaver Gateway hub system. You can now use the SAP NetWeaver Gateway client to test the service—at least the metadata, as

Test metadata

343

only an empty stub has been generated for the DPC. The assignment of RFC methods has not yet been done.

The URI of the service is */sap/opu/odata/sap/ZRFC1_SRV* and provides the service document. Adding */$metadata* provides the metadata of the OData service. This allows you to verify whether all properties have been derived properly from the provided RFC function module. You also see the key fields, the association, the referential constraint, and the navigation property you've defined in the project (see Figure 7.14).

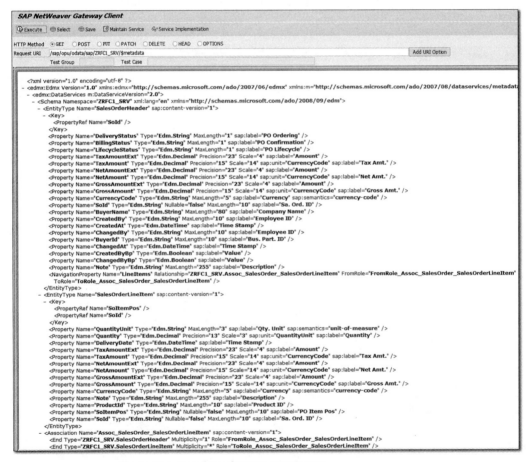

Figure 7.14 Metadata of ZRFC1_SRV Service

7.1.4   Service Implementation: SalesOrderCollection

After the runtime artifacts are generated, you can start with the service implementation. The Service Builder has generated (empty) methods for each CRUD-Q method of an entity set in the DPC as a stub. To start the mapping process, you have to select MAP TO DATASOURCE in the context menu of a CRUD-Q method of an entity set in the SERVICE IMPLEMENTATION folder (Figure 7.15). The built-in mapping tool of the Service Builder then allows you to define mappings between the interface parameters of a function module or BAPI and the properties of an entity set.

Next we'll walk through the mapping process for all CRUD-Q methods of the entity set SalesOrderCollection.

Query

Let's start with the SalesOrderCollection entity set. For this, you expand the SERVICE IMPLEMENTATION • SALESORDERCOLLECTION node in the project, right-click on GETENTITYSET (QUERY), and choose MAP TO DATA SOURCE (see Figure 7.15).

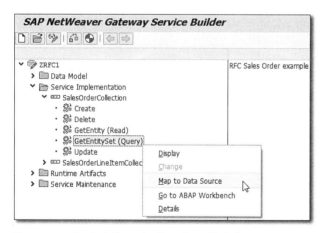

Figure 7.15 Context Menu for Mapping a Data Source

This opens a dialog where you first need to specify if the data source resides in the local system where IW_BEP or SAP_GWFND are installed, or if the data source is available in a remote system (see Figure 7.16). In

Local or remote system

345

the latter case, you need to provide the RFC DESTINATION to the remote system (which is the same as you provided when defining the data model out of an RFC interface).

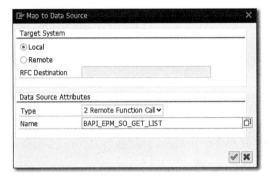

Figure 7.16 Map to Data Source Pop-Up Dialog

Mapping screen In the example, you call the EPM function module from the local system. In the DATA SOURCE ATTRIBUTES section, you first define the type of data source that you want to map to your OData service. The type can either be a BOR object/method or an RFC function module. Regular function modules (non-RFC) aren't supported.

In this example, you choose REMOTE FUNCTION CALL and BAPI_EPM_SO_GET_LIST for the module that you want to map. After clicking OK, you'll see the prepopulated mapping screen (see Figure 7.17). The grid in the middle shows the current mapping of the operation. On the right-hand side, you see the RFC function module that you've provided as well as its interface.

By default, nothing is mapped. Because the model is imported from an RFC interface, it's possible to use the PROPOSE MAPPING button to propose a mapping based on the origin of each property.

The proposal remains empty for those cases where the Service Builder isn't able to propose a mapping based on the property origin (e.g., in a case where you've manually added a property to the corresponding entity type not using the import from RFC). In such cases, you need to perform the mapping manually by dragging the wanted function module parameter from the right-hand side (data source) and dropping it to the entity set property line you want to map the parameter to.

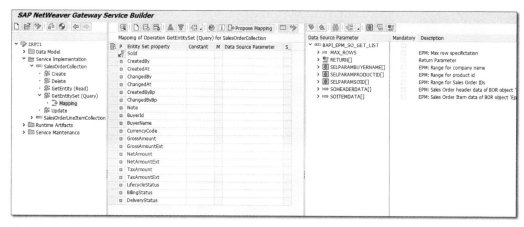

Figure 7.17 Mapping Screen of the GetEntitySet (QUERY) Operation

As soon as you map a parameter, the mapping direction is set. The mapping direction is visualized by an arrow pointing to the left (output) or pointing to the right (input) in the MAPPING DIRECTION column. If the mapping direction can't be defaulted, there will be a question mark icon. The mapping direction icon is a button that you can click to change the mapping direction, providing that the mapped RFC function module parameter supports this (e.g., a function module output parameter can't be mapped with an input direction).

Mapping direction

Output mapping direction means that the function module parameter is provided to the consumer (e.g., property value in an entry of a collection). Input mapping means that the property value is handed over to the function module call as an input parameter (e.g., a filter).

It's mandatory to map all primary key entity set properties with a data source parameter. Otherwise, the project check will display an error. Nonprimary key properties can remain unmapped. This has the same effect as if you deleted the line from the mapping grid, which, of course, doesn't delete the property itself.

Data source parameter

> **Note**
>
> The CONSTANT VALUE column isn't relevant for output values. It's relevant only for input values (e.g., an X flag that a certain RFC might require to provide the necessary data).

In this example, the mapping proposal can map all parameters to the corresponding entity set properties of the GetEntitySet (QUERY) operation (see Figure 7.18).

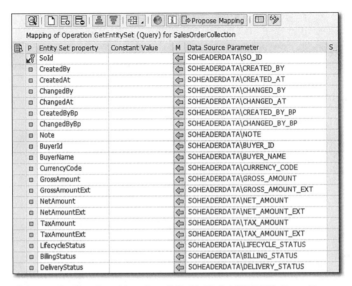

P	Entity Set property	Constant Value	M	Data Source Parameter	S
	SoId			SOHEADERDATA\SO_ID	
	CreatedBy			SOHEADERDATA\CREATED_BY	
	CreatedAt			SOHEADERDATA\CREATED_AT	
	ChangedBy			SOHEADERDATA\CHANGED_BY	
	ChangedAt			SOHEADERDATA\CHANGED_AT	
	CreatedByBp			SOHEADERDATA\CREATED_BY_BP	
	ChangedByBp			SOHEADERDATA\CHANGED_BY_BP	
	Note			SOHEADERDATA\NOTE	
	BuyerId			SOHEADERDATA\BUYER_ID	
	BuyerName			SOHEADERDATA\BUYER_NAME	
	CurrencyCode			SOHEADERDATA\CURRENCY_CODE	
	GrossAmount			SOHEADERDATA\GROSS_AMOUNT	
	GrossAmountExt			SOHEADERDATA\GROSS_AMOUNT_EXT	
	NetAmount			SOHEADERDATA\NET_AMOUNT	
	NetAmountExt			SOHEADERDATA\NET_AMOUNT_EXT	
	TaxAmount			SOHEADERDATA\TAX_AMOUNT	
	TaxAmountExt			SOHEADERDATA\TAX_AMOUNT_EXT	
	LifecycleStatus			SOHEADERDATA\LIFECYCLE_STATUS	
	BillingStatus			SOHEADERDATA\BILLING_STATUS	
	DeliveryStatus			SOHEADERDATA\DELIVERY_STATUS	

Figure 7.18 Complete Mapping of GetEntitySet (QUERY) Operation

After you're done with the mapping, you should verify that the project and mappings are technically correct and thus avoid runtime errors. The Service Builder checks whether, for example, the data types of the mapped function module fields are compatible.

Generate project   That's all you need to do to implement the QUERY method in this example. The only thing that is left is to generate the project. After you've done this, and the project is generated successfully, you can run the service by executing the following URI in the SAP NetWeaver Gateway client:

/sap/opu/odata/sap/ZRFC1_SRV/SalesOrderCollection

Executing this URI provides an unfiltered list of sales order headers provided by the function module BAPI_EPM_SO_GET_LIST.

So far, you haven't performed any input mapping. Therefore, the QUERY operation doesn't support any filtering capabilities. This can be changed by adding new lines to the mapping of the GetEntitySet

(QUERY) operation of the sales order header collection. This, of course, requires suitable input parameters of the RFC function module that is used.

The function module BAPI_EPM_SO_GET_LIST has three SELECT-OPTION input tables: SELPARAMSOID, SELPARAMBUYERNAME, and SELPARAMPRODUC-TID. The first two (sales order ID and buyer name) are based on header level; the third one (product ID) is on the line item level. To use the two SELECT-OPTION tables on the header level, you first have to add two new mapping lines to the mapping grid by clicking the APPEND ROW or INSERT ROW buttons.

The entity set property names can either be typed in manually or picked from the F4 value help. In this example, enter "SoId" and "Buyer-Name". Then you can drag and drop the wanted ranges tables from the function module interface to the data source parameter fields of the newly added lines. Because you aren't mapping regular input fields but SELECT-OPTION tables, you get a MAP RANGE pop-up for each SELECT-OPTION table you map (see Figure 7.19).

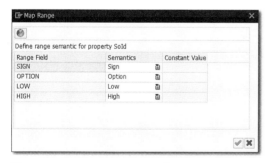

Figure 7.19 Map Range Pop-Up for Mapping SELECT-OPTION Filters

The Service Builder needs to know in which field of the ranges table the SIGN, OPTION, LOW, and HIGH values are located, which is why the pop-up is automatically shown each time you map a ranges table. Typically, the values in this pop-up are properly defaulted and just need to be confirmed.

After you've completed the mapping of the sales order ID and the buyer name SELECT-OPTION tables, the GetEntitySet mapping screen has two new input mappings (see Figure 7.20).

New input mapping

Figure 7.20 Input Mapping of SELECT-OPTION Filters

The green icon with the square brackets indicates that the mapping is based on a ranges table. By clicking on the respective icon, you can open the corresponding map range pop-up to verify the mapping and change it.

Now you need to regenerate the project to actually use the newly mapped filters. As an example, you can execute the following URI to filter on sales orders with the id >= '0500000010' and id <= '0500000020':

/sap/opu/odata/sap/ZRFC1_SRV/SalesOrderCollection?$filter=SoId ge '0500000010' and SoId le '0500000020'

In addition, you can filter on the buyer name. It's possible to add this to the already existing filter. The URI for filtering on buyer name = "Panorama Studios" in addition to the previous filter looks like the following:

/sap/opu/odata/sap/ZRFC1_SRV/SalesOrderCollection?$filter=SoId ge '0500000010' and SoId le '0500000020' and BuyerName eq 'Panorama Studios'

As you can see, the filter criteria can become quite lengthy.

Filter criteria — The filter criteria are mapped into ranges tables by the framework. This allows you to easily process them and to assign them to the corresponding RANGES-INPUT table of your RFC module in the GetEntitySet method. The OData framework provides them in a generic table in which each entry represents an entity set property that is used in the $filter query option.

Note that the preparation of the ranges tables has certain limitations. Similar to defining an ABAP report with SELECT-OPTIONS fields, you can't cover all use cases. For example, a filter such as FieldA eq 'A' or FieldB eq 'B' can't be put into ranges tables because of the or operand. It would work if you use and instead of or, but this of course has a different result.

Single Read

Similar to the QUERY operation, you can easily model the single read via the Service Builder. This time, you expand the node SERVICE IMPLEMENTATION • SALESORDERCOLLECTION, right-click on GETENTITY (READ), and choose MAP TO DATA SOURCE.

The target system remains the same (LOCAL), but can of course be different if needed (although it's unlikely that the query and the single read results are coming from different systems). This time, provide BAPI_EPM_SO_GET_DETAIL as the RFC function module from which you want to get your data. You again use the PROPOSE MAPPING button to perform the mapping of the function module parameters to the corresponding entity set properties.

Besides the output parameter, you also have to create an input mapping for all key fields (in this example, it's only one key field). This is something the check function of the Service Builder would report as an error if missing (see Figure 7.21).

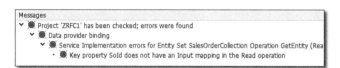

Figure 7.21 Missing Input Mapping Reported in the Message Window

The missing input mapping can easily be performed by adding a new line to the mapping screen and selecting SoId as the entity set property via the value help. Now you need to drag and drop the RFC input parameter SO_ID-SO_ID to the data source parameter column. Because this is an import parameter of the RFC module, the mapping direction is automatically set to input. There is no MAP RANGE pop-up and no green brackets shown as in the QUERY operation because you're not mapping a SELECT-OPTIONS table.

Missing input mapping

The project check now shows a green traffic light as the reported problem was corrected. After generating the project, you can read a single entry of the sales order header collection by executing, for example, the following URI via the SAP NetWeaver Gateway client:

/sap/opu/odata/sap/ZRFC1_SRV/SalesOrderCollection('0500000011')

As expected, you now get a single entry instead of an OData feed.

> **Problems with Conversion Exits in SP06**
>
> In SAP NetWeaver Gateway 2.0 SP06, the conversion exits are turned on for the entire data model by default. As a result, all values exposed are converted to their external representation first. For IDs, this typically results in cutting off leading zeros (e.g., sales order ID 0500000011 is exposed as 500000011).
>
> As a consequence, any converted value has to be converted back to the internal representation when, for example, used as a filter parameter or key field. This conversion can't of course be done by the consumer and has to happen on the backend system. The generated RFC coding in SP06 unfortunately doesn't provide this capability, and therefore the backend conversion needs to be done manually by redefining the respective DPC methods and implementing some of your own ABAP code. This issue has been fixed with SP07.
>
> A recommended workaround for this is to turn off the conversion handling for the entire model. This needs to be done in the define method of the model provider class. The corresponding coding of the MPC extension class for redefining the define method is the following:
>
> ```
> METHOD define.
>   super->define( ).
>   model->set_no_conversion( abap_true ).
> ENDMETHOD.
> ```
>
> After activating this coding, the conversion exit will no longer be called, and thus no backend conversion is necessary.

So far, the service is capable of fetching filtered and unfiltered collections of sales order headers as well as single sales order header entries. The next step is to implement create, update, and delete capabilities.

Create

The CREATE operation is used whenever you want to create a new entry into the respective collection. In the Service Builder, you can perform the service implementation for the SalesOrderCollection CREATE operation by expanding the node SERVICE IMPLEMENTATION • SALESORDER-COLLECTION, right-clicking on CREATE, and selecting MAP TO DATA SOURCE.

This opens up the MAP TO DATA SOURCE dialog where you specify the target system, the data source type, and the name of the data source. In this example, you again choose RFC as the data source, and enter the RFC function module BAPI_EPM_SO_CREATE.

Again, you use the PROPOSE MAPPING button to perform the mapping of the function module parameters to the respective entity set properties. This time, the default direction is input because all properties have to be moved from the request body to the corresponding input structure of the RFC function module.

The handling of the RFC return table is automatically done by the generated coding. In the case of an error, a corresponding business exception is thrown, and the error text is provided along with the corresponding HTTP code. This also takes place for the other operations, but typically comes into focus when writing data into the system.

If the mapping proposal is correct, you only need to manually add a new mapping line for the order ID that is returned by the Create RFC function module. If the mapping proposal isn't correct, the check function of the Service Builder reports an error, such as the missing input mapping that you saw in Figure 7.21.

In this example, this information is returned by the field SO_ID of the export structure SALESORDERID. It needs to be mapped to the primary key of the entity type. The mapping direction is automatically set to output. The complete mapping is shown in Figure 7.22.

After you're done with the mapping of the CREATE operation, check and regenerate the project again. After that, you use the SAP NetWeaver Gateway client to verify whether the CREATE operation works as expected (you can use any other REST client to test the service as well).

The CREATE operation requires the creation of a proper HTTP body with the sales order entry. Instead of putting such an HTTP body together manually, you can use the USE AS REQUEST button in the SAP NetWeaver Gateway client. For this, you first need to execute a GET operation to receive a suitable source entry. Then you click the USE AS REQUEST button to copy it over to the left-hand side of the SAP NetWeaver Gateway client (the left-hand side is the "request" side, and the right-hand side the "response" side).

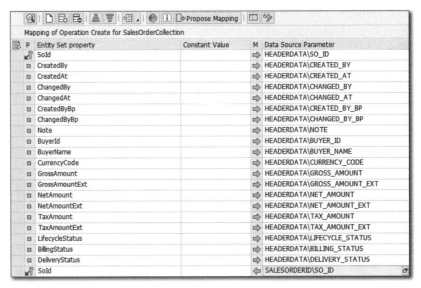

Figure 7.22 Mapping of the Create Operation

Before you can execute the CREATE operation, you first need to change the HTTP method from GET to POST. In addition, you need to adjust the URI, because the CREATE operation has to be executed on a collection and not on a single record (make sure to remove the brackets with the primary key).

Finally, you need to adjust the HTTP body and the property values. In this example, you need to remove all properties apart from Currency-Code, BuyerName, BuyerId, and Note. This is because the underlying RFC function module doesn't allow the other fields to be provided in the CREATE operation. You can also delete the mapping of these properties to make sure the fields aren't provided to the function module call, but then the consumer won't know that the properties are ignored. If you keep the mapping, corresponding error messages are provided to the consumer if those unallowed properties are still provided.

If the CREATE operation is successful (see Figure 7.23), you get an HTTP 201 response. Furthermore, you get the newly created record along with the calculated order number derived from the related number range. In addition, there are some other fields that have been calculated/ determined by the backend server (e.g., CreatedAt, CreatedBy, etc.).

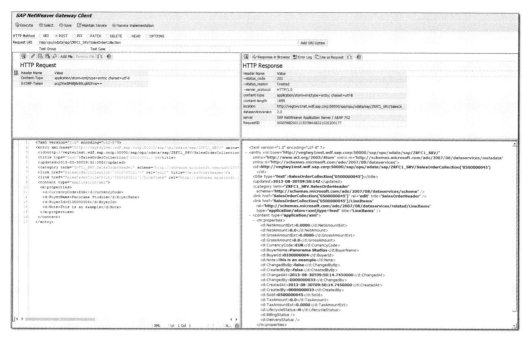

Figure 7.23 Successful CREATE Operation

You may wonder why the complete entry is returned after the creation, despite the fact that only the sales order ID was mapped as the output property before. This is because the RFC/BOR Generator automatically generates a `get_entity` call at the end of the `Create` method to retrieve the created entry.

Update

The UPDATE operation comes into play whenever an existing entry needs to be changed. In the Service Builder, you can perform the service implementation for the `SalesOrderCollection` UPDATE operation by expanding the node SERVICE IMPLEMENTATION • SALESORDERCOLLECTION, right-clicking on UPDATE, and selecting MAP TO DATA SOURCE.

This time, you provide `BAPI_EPM_SO_CHANGE` in the MAP TO DATA SOURCE dialog. Similar to the CREATE operation, you perform the mapping by using the PROPOSE MAPPING button.

Map to data source

You also have to inform the RFC function module about the fields you're going to change. This is based on the standard SAP BAPI behavior in which each import structure field has to have a corresponding X structure. This X structure has a flag for each field of the original structure indicating whether the field is to be considered.

In this example, this is the SOHEADERDATAX structure (note the X at the end). The fields of this structure have the same names as the original import structure; the difference is that only the primary key fields (in this example, just SO_ID) are based on the same data element. All other fields point to a default data element BAPIUPDATE, which is a character 1 field.

Each property in the OData service that you want to be able to change via the UPDATE operation has to contain an X in the field of the SOHEADER-DATAX structure. If there is no X, the field must be blank. For this, you can make use of the constant values on the mapping screen. To achieve this, you need to add one line for each constant you want to provide (see Figure 7.24). Constant values don't have an entity set property because they are a constant for the function module call (input mapping). It's not possible to provide a constant value for an output mapping (which wouldn't make much sense).

Finally, you also need to map the SoId entity set property to the SO_ID\SO_ID input structure of the RFC function module. When it's all said and done, you're mapping the sales order primary key property three times to be able to call this RFC function module.

After you're done with the mapping of the UPDATE operation, you can check and regenerate the project again. After that, you use the SAP NetWeaver Gateway client to verify whether the UPDATE operation works as expected. Similar to the CREATE operation, you first perform a single read to get a proper HTTP response body that you can copy over to the request side by using the USE AS REQUEST button. The URI remains unchanged, as the UPDATE operation is always performed on a single entry. You only need to change the HTTP method from GET to PUT. If the update was successful, you get an HTTP 204 (no content) response.

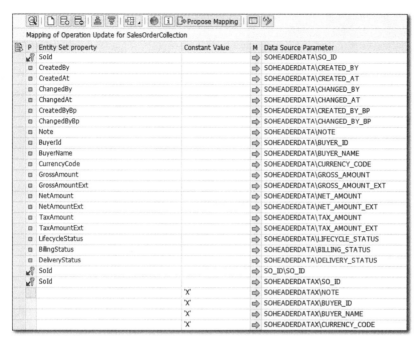

Figure 7.24 Mapping the UPDATE Operation with Constant Values

The HTTP return code indicates that the response body is empty. This is intentional, as the assumption is that the client has all information, and thus sending the entry along with the response causes unnecessary overhead. The client can always perform a single read to fetch the entry again in case the backend server has calculated any values that the client doesn't have.

Delete

In contrast to the UPDATE operation, the DELETE operation is rather simple to implement. In the Service Builder, you can perform the service implementation for the SalesOrderCollection DELETE operation by expanding the node SERVICE IMPLEMENTATION • SALESORDERCOLLECTION, right-clicking on DELETE, and selecting MAP TO DATA SOURCE.

The corresponding function module is BAPI_EPM_SO_DELETE. It only requires the primary key to be mapped (see Figure 7.25) as no request body and no X fields are required for this operation.

Primary key

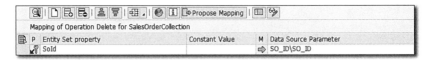

Figure 7.25 Mapping the DELETE Operation

After the regeneration of the project, you can verify if the implemented DELETE operation works properly. DELETE operations are always executed on a single entry; therefore, you have to provide a URI that addresses a single sales order. The HTTP method has to be DELETE. If the DELETE operation is successful, you get an HTTP 204 (no content) response.

7.1.5 Service Implementation: SalesOrderLineItemCollection

After you've performed the mapping for the entity set SalesOrderCollection, you'll do the same for the second entity set SalesOrderLineItemCollection. In this case, we'll show an example where no suitable EPM RFC function module is provided for each method, and explain how to circumvent this issue by developing your own wrapper RFC function model.

Query

For the sales order header, you were able to map all five CRUD-Q operations to the corresponding EPM RFC function modules. This was pretty straightforward because there are related function modules for each operation available.

No dedicated RFC function modules Next, you need to take care of the sales order line items (entity set SalesOrderLineItemCollection). For line items, there are no dedicated RFC function modules available in the EPM demo model. Instead, the line items information is provided as part of the corresponding sales order header function modules. That's the reason why the mapping can't entirely be done via the Service Builder. Instead, some of the operations have to be redefined with your own coding.

In the metadata, we've defined a navigation property LineItems that allows you to navigate from a sales order entry to its list of line items.

Such a navigation property is also required when using the `$expand` system query option or the deep insert capability described in Chapter 2.

The metadata of the `SalesOrderLineItemCollection` entity set has been annotated as not addressable. That means you don't allow any consumer to access the collection directly by, for example, executing the following URI:

/sap/opu/odata/sap/ZRFC1_SRV/SalesOrderLineItemCollection

Because you can't prevent the consumer from executing such an URI, you need to make sure that the service implementation is responding to this request appropriately.

The first operation you're going to map to the related data source provider is the `GetEntitySet` (`QUERY`) operation. Because there is no dedicated RFC function module for fetching the list of line items (`QUERY`), you need to use the sales order header detail function module `BAPI_EPM_SO_GET_DETAIL`, which also provides the list of line items via its table parameters. | Map operation

In the project tree, expand the node SERVICE IMPLEMENTATION • SALESORDERLINEITEMCOLLECTION, right-click on GETENTITYSET (QUERY), and select MAP TO DATA SOURCE. In the dialog pop-up, provide the function module `BAPI_EPM_SO_GET_DETAIL`. Again, make use of the mapping proposal.

Because the sales order header detail function module requires a sales order ID as an input parameter, you add a new mapping line where you map the entity set property `SoId` to the function module import parameter `SO_ID-SO_ID` (see Figure 7.26). Via the referential constraint that was defined in the metadata, the framework is able to provide the primary key from the principal entity type (`SalesOrderHeader SoId`) as filter criteria to the dependent entity type property (`SalesOrderLineItem SoId`). | New mapping line

After generating the project, you're able to use the navigation property to navigate from the sales order header to the list of line items. The list of line items is determined via the filter on the sales order ID. The following is a sample URI: */sap/opu/odata/sap/ZRFC1_SRV/SalesOrderCollection('0500000000')/LineItems*.

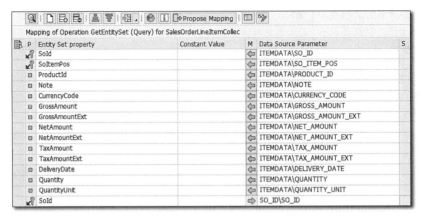

Figure 7.26 Mapping of the Line Item GetEntitySet (QUERY) Operation

Accessing the list of line items without any filter will result in an error because the RFC function module requires the sales order ID to be provided.

Single Read

Three options

Mapping the single read (GetEntity) operation is a little trickier now because there is no suitable EPM RFC function module that provides a single sales order line item. In such a case, you basically have three options. The first is to create your own (Z-)RFC function module that wraps a suitable standard RFC function module along with the missing ABAP logic that you need, and then map it using the Service Builder, as you've seen before. The second is to use the standard RFC function module and map the fields as well as possible, generate the coding, copy the entire method over to the DPC extension class, and adjust it. The third option is to implement the operation entirely from scratch, as we described in the previous chapter.

The second and the third options are somewhat similar because both implement the operation via the respective method (e.g., Get_Entity) in the extension class. However, the second option has the disadvantage that it suggests a present mapping done via the Service Builder, despite the fact that the generated method is actually not used anymore (because it was copied over to the extension class method and thus is disconnected from further changes and regenerations). Another disadvantage of the second approach is the following: Suppose you have a BAPI that performs a read request on a sales order. This will have the sales order ID as an input field, but will not necessarily have an output field that contains the sales order ID. In this case, it wouldn't be possible to map the sales order ID as an output field.

We'll focus on the first option, which is to develop a wrapper RFC function module, Z_BAPI_EPM_SO_ITEM_GET_DETAIL. For this example, we've created a function group via Transaction SE80 (e.g., ZRFC1).

Wrapper RFC function module

The interface of the wrapper function module consists of two import parameters, one for the sales order id (SO_ID) and one for the sales order line item position (SO_ITEM_POS). It has one export structure itemdata that can hold a single line item. The table parameter RETURN is for the BAPI return table. The coding is shown in Listing 7.1.

```
FUNCTION z_bapi_epm_so_item_get_detail.
*"----------------------------------------------------------------
*"*"Local Interface:
*"  IMPORTING
*"     VALUE(SO_ID) TYPE  SNWD_SO_ID
*"     VALUE(SO_ITEM_POS) TYPE  SNWD_SO_ITEM_POS
*"  EXPORTING
*"     VALUE(ITEMDATA) TYPE  BAPI_EPM_SO_ITEM
*"  TABLES
*"      RETURN STRUCTURE  BAPIRET2 OPTIONAL
*"----------------------------------------------------------------

  DATA: ls_so_id    TYPE bapi_epm_so_id,
        lt_itemdata TYPE STANDARD TABLE OF bapi_epm_so_item,
        ls_return   TYPE bapiret2.

  ls_so_id-so_id = so_id.
  CALL FUNCTION 'BAPI_EPM_SO_GET_DETAIL'
    EXPORTING
      so_id           = ls_so_id
*   IMPORTING
*     HEADERDATA      =
    TABLES
      itemdata        = lt_itemdata
      return          = return.
```

```
    CHECK return[] IS INITIAL.
    READ TABLE lt_itemdata INTO itemdata WITH KEY so_item_
pos = so_item_pos.
    IF sy-subrc NE 0.
      CALL FUNCTION 'BALW_BAPIRETURN_GET2'
        EXPORTING
          type   = 'E'
          cl     = 'SEPM_BOR_MESSAGES'
          number = '003'
          par1   = 'Item does not exist'
        IMPORTING
          return = ls_return.
      APPEND ls_return TO return.
    ENDIF.

ENDFUNCTION.
```

Listing 7.1 Coding of the Wrapper RFC to Retrieve Sales Order Item Details

As you can see, the standard EPM function module `BAPI_EPM_SO_GET_DETAIL` is used to retrieve the requested information. This function module returns the entire list of all line items for a given sales order. As a second step, you use the import parameter `SO_ITEM_POS` to pick the requested line item out of the determined line item list `lt_itemdata`. A corresponding message is added to the return table, in case a nonexistent item position was provided via `SO_ITEM_POS`.

After you've activated the Z-RFC function module, you can map it to the `GetEntity` (`READ`) operation for the `SalesOrderLineItemCollection` entity set (see Figure 7.27).

Propose mapping Note that the PROPOSE MAPPING button can still be used, even though the data model was derived from a different RFC function module. This is because the PROPOSE MAPPING functionality not only checks the function module name, but also considers the declaration of the respective fields. In other words, it's always worth trying the PROPOSE MAPPING button.

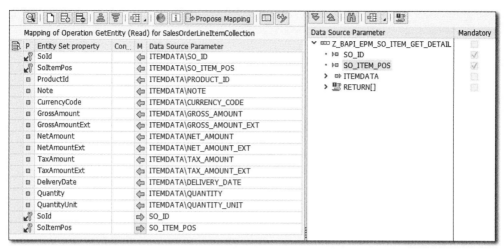

Figure 7.27 Mapping the Line Item GetEntity (READ) Operation

Also note that the RFC function module definitions are cached. So if you keep adjusting your function module interface, you may need to restart the Service Builder transaction or you might not see your interface changes. After generating the project, you can test the single read for the sales order line item with, for example, the following URI:

Cached RFC function module definitions

/sap/opu/odata/sap/ZRFC1_SRV/SalesOrderLineItemCollection(SoId= '0500000002',SoItemPos='0000000030')

Create

The CREATE operation for the SalesOrderLineItemCollection entity set can also be mapped using a wrapper function module. Similar to the single READ operation, you create a new Z-RFC function module Z_BAPI_ EPM_SO_ITEM_GET_CREATE. The interface consists of an import parameter for the sales order id (SO_ID) and import structures for the line item data (SOITEMDATA) as well as the known X-structure (SOITEMDATAX) with the flags indicating what to do. The PERSIST_TO_DB import parameter defines whether the data should be persisted to the database or just kept in memory. The parameter also defines whether a COMMIT WORK is executed. By default, this parameter is set.

Wrapper function module

Via the export parameter SO_ITEM_POS, you return the created line item position back to the caller. The coding is shown in Listing 7.2.

```
FUNCTION z_bapi_epm_so_item_get_create.
*"----------------------------------------------------------------
*"*"Local Interface:
*"  IMPORTING
*"     VALUE(SO_ID) TYPE  SNWD_SO_ID
*"     VALUE(SOITEMDATA) TYPE  BAPI_EPM_SO_ITEM
*"     VALUE(SOITEMDATAX) TYPE  BAPI_EPM_SO_ITEMX
*"     VALUE(PERSIST_TO_DB) TYPE  BAPI_EPM_
BOOLEAN DEFAULT ABAP_TRUE
*"  EXPORTING
*"     VALUE(SO_ITEM_POS) TYPE  SNWD_SO_ITEM_POS
*"  TABLES
*"      RETURN STRUCTURE  BAPIRET2 OPTIONAL
*"----------------------------------------------------------------

  DATA: ls_so_id        TYPE bapi_epm_so_id,
        lt_soitemdata   TYPE STANDARD TABLE OF bapi_epm_so_
item,
        lt_soitemdatax  TYPE STANDARD TABLE OF bapi_epm_so_
itemx,
        ls_itemdata_new TYPE  bapi_epm_so_item,
        lt_itemdata_new TYPE STANDARD TABLE OF bapi_epm_so_
item.

  ls_so_id-so_id = so_id.
  APPEND soitemdata  TO lt_soitemdata.
  APPEND soitemdatax TO lt_soitemdatax.
  CALL FUNCTION 'BAPI_EPM_SO_CHANGE'
    EXPORTING
      so_id         = ls_so_id
      persist_to_db = persist_to_db
    TABLES
      soitemdata    = lt_soitemdata
      soitemdatax   = lt_soitemdatax
      return        = return.

  CHECK return[] IS INITIAL.
  CALL FUNCTION 'BAPI_EPM_SO_GET_DETAIL'
    EXPORTING
```

```
      so_id    = ls_so_id
   TABLES
      itemdata = lt_itemdata_new.

 SORT lt_itemdata_new BY so_item_pos DESCENDING.
 READ TABLE lt_itemdata_new INTO ls_itemdata_new INDEX 1.
 so_item_pos = ls_itemdata_new-so_item_pos.

ENDFUNCTION.
```

Listing 7.2 Coding of the Wrapper RFC to Create Sales Order Item Details

This time, the EPM function module BAPI_EPM_SO_CHANGE is used, as the creation of a line item is a change to the related sales order instance. The SOITEMDATAX table has an ACTIONCODE field that is used to indicate that this is an insert operation. The actual value I is set as a constant value via the mapping of the CREATE operation in the Service Builder (see Figure 7.28).

EPM function module

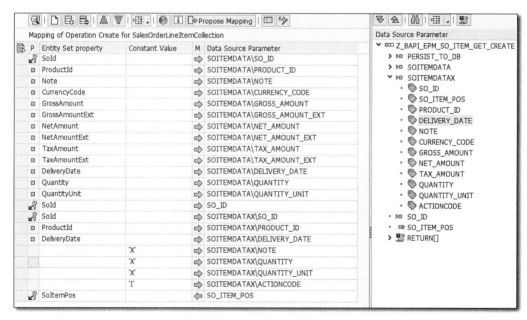

Figure 7.28 Mapping of Line Item CREATE Operation

After the successful creation of the line item (verified by checking if the return table is empty), read the entire list of line items by using BAPI_EPM_SO_GET_DETAIL; this is the only way to identify the newly created line item position.

After generating the project, you can test the sales order line item CREATE operation via the SAP NetWeaver Gateway client by performing a POST on the following URI:

/sap/opu/odata/sap/ZRFC1_SRV/SalesOrderLineItemCollection

Similar to the other POST requests that you executed before (using the SAP NetWeaver Gateway client), it's recommended to first perform a GET on a line item detail and to click the USE AS REQUEST button as a starting point for the HTTP request body. Adjusting such a defaulted HTTP request is a lot easier than manually creating the request from scratch.

Update

Standard RFC function module

The UPDATE operation can even be mapped using the standard RFC function module BAPI_EPM_SO_CHANGE. There is no need to implement a wrapper function module in this specific case. This is because of the interface and the ability of the RFC/BOR Generator to handle even table parameters.

The ACTIONCODE in this case is U, because you want to update the record (see Figure 7.29).

After generating the project, you can test the sales order line item UPDATE operation via the SAP NetWeaver Gateway client by performing a PUT request on, for example, the following URI:

/sap/opu/odata/sap/ZRFC1_SRV/SalesOrderLineItemCollection(SoId= '0500000011',SoItemPos='0000000020')

If everything goes smoothly, the HTTP response will be empty and the HTTP return code is 204 (no content).

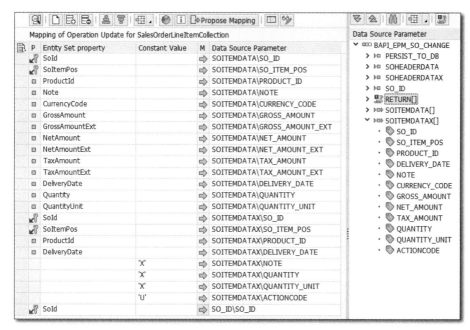

Figure 7.29 Mapping of Line Item UPDATE Operation

Delete

Last but not least, the line item `DELETE` operation again requires a wrapper RFC function module. This is because a line item isn't just uniquely identified by its item position, but also requires the product ID as well as the delivery date, which is an EPM-specific logic. Accordingly, you must again develop a wrapper Z-RFC function module `Z_BAPI_EPM_SO_ITEM_GET_DELETE` that first reads the line item detail and then prepares the call to the `BAPI_EPM_SO_CHANGE` standard function to delete the line item entry.

Wrapper RFC function module

The coding looks like Listing 7.3.

```
FUNCTION z_bapi_epm_so_item_get_delete.
*"----------------------------------------------------------------
---------
*"*"Local Interface:
*"  IMPORTING
*"     VALUE(SO_ID) TYPE  SNWD_SO_ID
*"     VALUE(SO_ITEM_POS) TYPE  SNWD_SO_ITEM_POS
```

```
*"     VALUE(PERSIST_TO_DB) TYPE  BAPI_EPM_
BOOLEAN DEFAULT ABAP_TRUE
*"  TABLES
*"     RETURN STRUCTURE  BAPIRET2 OPTIONAL
*"------------------------------------------------------------
---------

  DATA: ls_so_id     TYPE bapi_epm_so_id,
        ls_itemdata  TYPE bapi_epm_so_item,
        lt_itemdata  TYPE STANDARD TABLE OF bapi_epm_so_item,
        ls_itemdatax TYPE bapi_epm_so_itemx,
        lt_itemdatax TYPE STANDARD TABLE OF bapi_epm_so_itemx.

  CALL FUNCTION 'Z_BAPI_EPM_SO_ITEM_GET_DETAIL'
    EXPORTING
      so_id      = so_id
      so_item_pos = so_item_pos
    IMPORTING
      itemdata    = ls_itemdata
    TABLES
      return      = return.

  CHECK return[] IS INITIAL.
  APPEND ls_itemdata TO lt_itemdata.

  ls_itemdatax-so_id        = so_id.
  ls_itemdatax-so_item_pos  = so_item_pos.
  ls_itemdatax-product_id   = ls_itemdata-product_id.
  ls_itemdatax-delivery_date = ls_itemdata-delivery_date.
  ls_itemdatax-actioncode   = 'D'.
  APPEND ls_itemdatax TO lt_itemdatax.

  ls_so_id-so_id = so_id.
  CALL FUNCTION 'BAPI_EPM_SO_CHANGE'
    EXPORTING
      so_id       = ls_so_id
*     SOHEADERDATA  =
*     SOHEADERDATAX =
      persist_to_db = persist_to_db
    TABLES
      soitemdata  = lt_itemdata
      soitemdatax = lt_itemdatax
```

```
        return         = return.

ENDFUNCTION.
```

Listing 7.3 Function Module to Delete a Sales Order Line Item

After generating the project, you can test the sales order line item DELETE operation via the SAP NetWeaver Gateway client by performing a DELETE request on, for example, the following URI:

/sap/opu/odata/sap/ZRFC1_SRV/SalesOrderLineItemCollection(SoId='0500 000011',SoItemPos='0000000020')

Upon success, this also leads to an HTTP 204 (no content) return code.

7.1.6 Conclusion

As you've seen from the provided example, the Service Builder helps you significantly in modeling your metadata as well as defining your service provisioning. However, there are also situations where you either need to adjust the generated coding or implement some wrapper functions, because the RFC/BOR Generator isn't able to cover all possible use cases.

7.2 Generation via Redefinition

As you saw in Section 7.1, creating an OData service using the RFC/BOR Generator has much in common with the manual development process described in Chapter 6. In both cases, it's necessary to use an entity data model as a basis for the service implementation. Although the RFC/BOR Generator doesn't require the developer to write his own code, the mapping process can become tedious if there is no suitable RFC function module available. On the other hand, the generated services provide a lot of out-of-the-box functionality such as the support of filtering and client-side paging that otherwise has to be implemented manually.

Obviously, it would be nice to be able to generate OData services with a minimized need for manual action—and this is where the integration scenarios supported by the SAP NetWeaver Gateway Service Builder come into play. SAP has invested greatly in sophisticated frameworks that allow the modeling of business objects for various use cases. In addition, customers themselves have implemented their business scenarios based on these frameworks or have adapted existing objects delivered by SAP. Fortunately, these business objects can be used to generate OData services—a process known as *redefinition*.

Redefinition

The term redefinition stems from the inheritance concept that is available in ABAP objects. ABAP objects allow a method of a superclass to be redefined in a subclass to implement extended functionality while still being able to leverage the functionalities of the base class. An OData service that has been created through the Service Builder using redefinition inherits the functionality of the business object that has been used as a data source.

Redefinition frameworks

Redefining a service from an existing business object is available for the following frameworks:

- SAP NetWeaver Business Warehouse (SAP NetWeaver BW)
- Service Provider Interface (SPI)
- Generic Interaction Layer (GenIL)
- SAP HANA

These business objects already have much in common with OData services. Because they support similar concepts, such as entity sets and query methods, it's possible to map these concepts to the entity sets and CRUD-Q methods of an OData service.

In addition, it's possible to create a service via redefinition from the following:

- OData services built with SAP NetWeaver Gateway
- OData services built with third-party tools

The support of these integration scenarios has been implemented within different software components that have been built on top of IW_BEP and are shipped in separate add-ons. While the integration scenario for SPI requires the deployment of the IW_SPI add-on, the integration with GenIL requires the IW_GIL add-on. The integration with SAP

NetWeaver BW objects and OData services is already included in IW_
BEP and SAP_GWFND. Depending on the add-ons that are installed in
your system, the redefinition option in the Service Builder will offer
different submenu options. You'll find the options CREATE FROM SPI,
CREATE FROM GENIL, and CREATE FROM BW QUERY SERVICE as shown in
Figure 7.30, depending on the installed add-ons just mentioned.

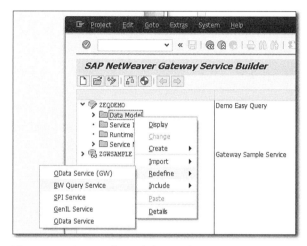

Figure 7.30 Options for Redefinition (in SP07)

Selecting one of these options starts a wizard that will guide you through
the following three steps:

Wizard

1. Select the business object.

2. Perform service registration in the backend and deal with transport-
   related issues.

3. Select artifacts of the data source.

A hands-on description of the generation of an OData service is almost
identical for all integration scenarios mentioned earlier. The steps that
have to be performed to generate an OData service based on existing
services from external frameworks and from existing OData services
from SAP NetWeaver Gateway mainly differ in the third dialog, which
shows the artifacts of the data source that can be selected.

After having shown in depth in Section 7.1 how a service can be generated based on the RFC/BOR Generator, we now provide step-by-step

**Redefinition
examples**

instructions on how OData services can be generated based on two business objects and one external OData service:

▸ SAP NetWeaver BW Easy Query (Section 7.2.1)

▸ Service Provider Interface (Section 7.2.2)

▸ External OData Service (Section 7.2.3)

7.2.1 SAP NetWeaver BW Easy Query

SAP NetWeaver BW Easy Queries provide an external interface for accessing analytic queries in SAP NetWeaver BW. Unlike other external query interfaces in SAP NetWeaver BW, SAP NetWeaver BW Easy Queries intentionally limit the flexibility of data processing to provide an easy way to consume queries. SAP NetWeaver BW Easy Queries thus reduce complexity in certain areas.

Business case
Let's look at a use case for the generation of a service based on an SAP NetWeaver BW Easy Query. Suppose that a company wants to offer an application that can be used to provide data about the sales numbers of its products in various countries. The reporting data will be dynamically filled with the query data from the company's SAP NetWeaver BW system.

In this example, we'll use the SAP demo content for features. Each sample scenario of the SAP demo content contains predefined objects, such as InfoProviders, queries, and workbooks, with prepopulated data. Part of the SAP demo content is a sample scenario based on the SAP NetWeaver Demo Model, which contains several queries—we'll use the one that is called 0D_FC_NW_C01_Q0001. (For more details about the SAP demo content, see *http://help.sap.com/saphelp_nw74/helpdata/en/47/addc08e04b1599e10000000a42189c/frameset.htm*.)

> **Note**
>
> The SAP demo content of SAP NetWeaver 7.40 SP02 that has been used for this book doesn't contain SAP NetWeaver BW Easy Queries. Therefore, the existing query mentioned above has been copied, marked as an SAP NetWeaver BW Easy Query, and saved with a new technical name: Z0D_FC_NW_C01_Q0001. This will change with SP06 of SAP NetWeaver Gateway

7.40, where several queries of the demo content have been marked as SAP NetWeaver BW Easy Queries.

Follow these steps in SAP NetWeaver BW:

1. Before you start to use SAP NetWeaver BW Easy Query, there are certain system settings that have to be performed in your SAP NetWeaver BW system. These settings are described in SAP Note 1944258.
2. Use the BEx Query Designer (which allows you to look up an existing or create a new query model) to create or locate the analytic query to be used.
3. Release the analytic query for external access as an SAP NetWeaver BW Easy Query. Here you have to comply with rules for SAP NetWeaver BW Easy Query design. A tabular layout has to be selected, and you have to keep in mind that only single-valued and interval variables are supported, and no conditions or exceptions can be used. In addition, there is no support for input-enabled queries used in planning contexts.

The generation of a corresponding OData service for an existing SAP NetWeaver BW Easy Query has to be performed in a system where the IW_BEP add-on has been deployed or in a system that runs on top of at least SAP NetWeaver 7.40 SP02. This can either be in the SAP NetWeaver BW system or in the SAP NetWeaver Gateway hub system.

As a prerequisite, the SAP_BW component must be based on SAP_BW 7.30 SP08 and above or SAP_BW 7.31 SP05 and above.

For this chapter, we're using client 001 of an SAP NetWeaver 7.40 ABAP Trial system (*www.sap.com/abaptrial*) where SAP NetWeaver BW sample content has been activated.

In the remainder of this section, you'll perform the steps described in the following:

Process steps

1. Generate an OData service based on the SAP NetWeaver BW Easy Query using redefinition. This encompasses the data model definition and service implementation phases.

2. Publish the service on the SAP NetWeaver Gateway system (service maintenance).

3. Use the BEAUTIFICATION option to rename the properties of the generated entity set. This is part of the data model definition phase.

4. Regenerate the service that belongs to the service implementation phase.

The steps and their assignment to the three phases of service creation have been depicted in Figure 7.31.

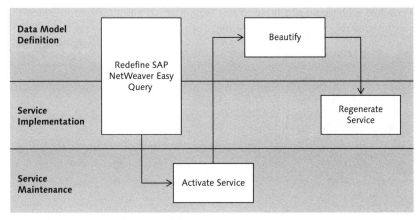

Figure 7.31 Sequence of Steps Redefining an SAP NetWeaver BW Query Service

Redefine SAP NetWeaver BW Easy Query

Create a project
After the SAP NetWeaver BW Easy Query is created, you can now start to generate an OData service by creating a project in the Service Builder that is called ZEQDEMO.

Redefine
Here you right-click on the DATA MODEL node, select REDEFINE, and then choose BW QUERY SERVICE as shown in Figure 7.32.

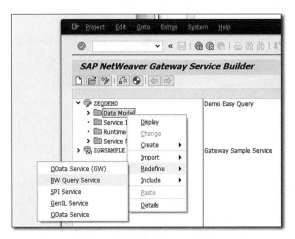

Figure 7.32 Redefine SAP NetWeaver BW Query Service

This starts the wizard for the redefinition of an SAP NetWeaver BW query service, as shown in Figure 7.33. In the first of three screens of the wizard, you have to enter several input parameters. In the ACCESS TYPE field, specify which kind of SAP NetWeaver BW query to use. You can choose from the two options CONTROLLER FOR MDX (SAP BW) or CONTROLLER FOR EASY QUERIES (SAP BW). For this scenario, choose the latter. In the RFC DESTINATION field, specify the name of the RFC destination pointing to the SAP NetWeaver BW system. For our example, choose NONE, because the SAP NetWeaver BW Easy Query is accessed in the same system and client. Leave the CATALOG NAME field blank. For the QUERY NAME field, enter the name of the SAP NetWeaver BW Easy Query ZOD_FC_NW_C01_Q0001, which was created beforehand.

Wizard: Step 1

Figure 7.33 Redefining SAP NetWeaver BW Query Service: Step 1 of 3

On the second screen of the wizard, shown in Figure 7.34, you provide a description for the technical model and the technical service that is being created.

Wizard: Step 2

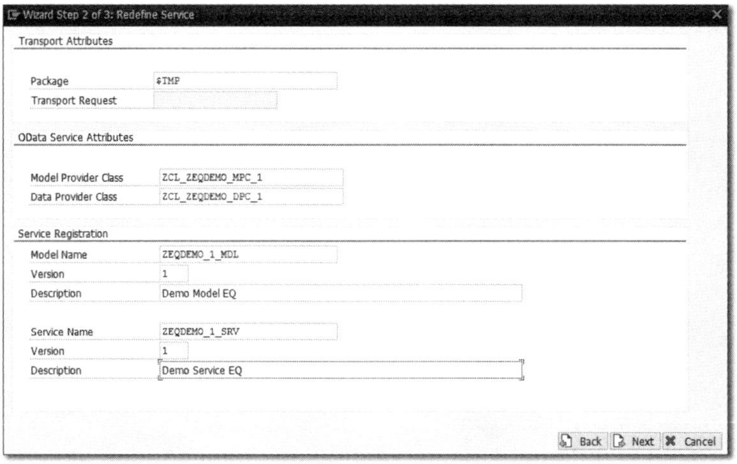

Figure 7.34 Redefining SAP NetWeaver BW Query Service: Step 2 of 3

On the final screen of the wizard, be sure to select all options, as shown in Figure 7.35, and click FINISH.

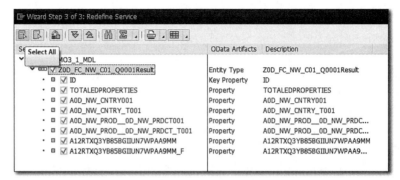

Figure 7.35 Redefining SAP NetWeaver BW Query Service: Step 3 of 3

The only activity that is left for the developer is to click the GENERATE button to generate an OData service based on an SAP NetWeaver BW Easy Query through redefinition, as shown in Figure 7.36.

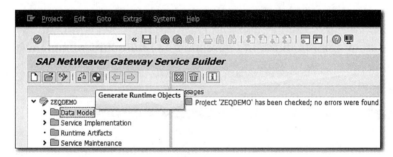

Figure 7.36 Generation of the Redefined Service

In the MODEL AND SERVICE DEFINITION dialog box shown in Figure 7.37, select the OVERWRITE EXTENDED SERVICE checkbox to overwrite the existing service, and click CONTINUE. This step creates both MPC classes and DPC classes, as you've learned from the previous examples. It also registers the service on the backend side by creating a technical model and a technical service.

In the CREATE OBJECT DIRECTORY ENTRY window, click the LOCAL OBJECT button, which sets the package to $TMP. If you want to transport the repository elements, you need to provide a transportable package.

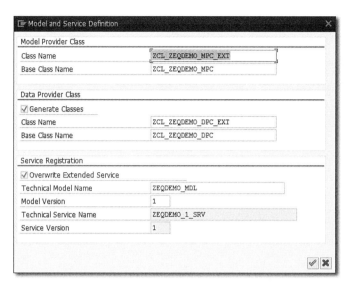

Figure 7.37 Model and Service Generation: SAP NetWeaver BW Easy Query

Activate Service

After the project has been successfully generated and registered on the backend, the service must be registered and activated on the SAP NetWeaver Gateway hub system. For this, you expand the SERVICE MAINTENANCE node in the project, right-click on the hub entry you want the service to register and activate on, and select REGISTER from the context menu.

Service activation

After confirming the warning pop-up, which informs you that this step will be carried out on the SAP NetWeaver Gateway hub system, you provide the system alias that was created before on the hub system that points to the SAP NetWeaver BW system (this pop-up only appears if several system alias entries have been created).

In the ADD SERVICE dialog on the hub, click LOCAL OBJECT to select $TMP as the package for the repository objects of the service that you're now going to generate, and click OK. If you want to create repository objects that can be transported, you have to choose an appropriate package.

Test the service

Afterward, it's possible to test the access to the newly created service. Expand the SERVICE MAINTENANCE node in the project, right-click on the hub entry used to publish the service, and select MAINTAIN from the context menu. Here you can click GATEWAY CLIENT to start the SAP NetWeaver Gateway client as shown in Figure 7.38.

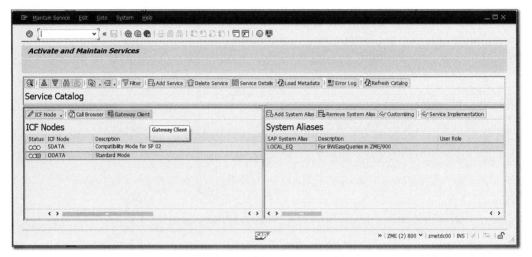

Figure 7.38 Testing the Activated Service with the SAP NetWeaver Gateway Client

If the service is working properly, the browser or SAP NetWeaver Gateway client displays the service document as shown in Figure 7.39.

```
<app:service xml:lang="de" xmlns:atom="http://www.w3.org/2005/Atom"
xmlns:app="http://www.w3.org/2007/app"
xml:base="http://wdflbmd6865.dummy.nodomain:50000/sap/opu/odata/sap/ZEQDEMO_1_SRV/">
 - <app:workspace>
     <atom:title type="text">Data</atom:title>
   - <app:collection xmlns:sap="http://www.sap.com/Protocols/SAPData"
     href="ZOD_FC_NW_C01_Q0001Results" sap:content-version="1" sap:deletable="false"
     sap:updatable="false" sap:creatable="false" sap:label="ZOD_FC_NW_C01_Q0001">
       <atom:title type="text">ZOD_FC_NW_C01_Q0001</atom:title>
       <sap:member-title>ZOD_FC_NW_C01_Q0001</sap:member-title>
     </app:collection>
   </app:workspace>
   <atom:link
   href="http://wdflbmd6865.dummy.nodomain:50000/sap/opu/odata/sap/ZEQDEMO_1_SRV/"
   rel="self"/>
   <atom:link
   href="http://wdflbmd6865.dummy.nodomain:50000/sap/opu/odata/sap/ZEQDEMO_1_SRV/"
   rel="latest-version"/>
</app:service>
```

Figure 7.39 Test Service Document

You can retrieve the result of the query by entering the following URI in the SAP NetWeaver Gateway client:

/sap/opu/odata/sap/ZEQDEMO_1_SRV/Z0D_FC_NW_C01_Q0001Results

The service responds with a set of entries as shown in Figure 7.40.

```
<entry>
  <id>http://wdflbmd6865.dummy.nodomain:50000/sap/opu/odata/sap/ZEQDEMO_1_SRV/Z0D_FC_NW_C01_Q0001Results('2.3_DEMOB')</id>
  <title type="text">Z0D_FC_NW_C01_Q0001Results('2.3_DEMOB')</title>
  <updated>2013-09-17T15:07:24Z</updated>
  <category scheme="http://schemas.microsoft.com/ado/2007/08/dataservices/scheme" term="ZEQDEMO_1_SRV.Z0D_FC_NW_C01_Q0001Result"/>
  <link title="Z0D_FC_NW_C01_Q0001Result" href="Z0D_FC_NW_C01_Q0001Results('2.3_DEMOB')" rel="self"/>
- <content type="application/xml">
  - <m:properties>
      <d:ID>2.3_DEMOB</d:ID>
      <d:TotaledProperties/>
      <d:A0D_NW_CNTRY>DE</d:A0D_NW_CNTRY>
      <d:A0D_NW_CNTRY_T>DE</d:A0D_NW_CNTRY_T>
      <d:A0D_NW_PROD__0D_NW_PRDCT>MOB</d:A0D_NW_PROD__0D_NW_PRDCT>
      <d:A0D_NW_PROD__0D_NW_PRDCT_T>Mobile Devices</d:A0D_NW_PROD__0D_NW_PRDCT_T>
      <d:A12RTXQ3YB85BGIIUN7WPAA9MM>14706156.00000000000000</d:A12RTXQ3YB85BGIIUN7WPAA9MM>
      <d:A12RTXQ3YB85BGIIUN7WPAA9MM_F>14.706.156,00 EUR</d:A12RTXQ3YB85BGIIUN7WPAA9MM_F>
    </m:properties>
  </content>
</entry>
```

Figure 7.40 Single Entry: Query Result

Log on to the SAP NetWeaver BW client of the ABAP trial system to have a look at the query results that can be retrieved using Transaction RSRT. Enter the name of the query, and choose the query display option HTML. The result is shown in Figure 7.41 for the drilldown of COUNTRY and PRODUCT CATEGORY.

SAP NetWeaver BW query results

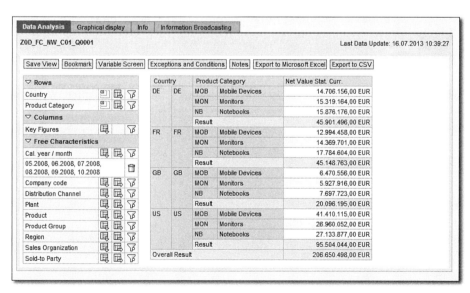

Figure 7.41 Transaction RSRT: Query Monitor

Beautify

As you may have noticed (refer to Figure 7.40), the properties of the entity set Z0D_FC_NW_C01_Q0001Results that return the query result aren't very easy to grasp. They are defined by the technical names found in the original SAP NetWeaver BW query. However, the properties of the entity set can be renamed and beautified so that they are easier to understand by the non-SAP developer. To do so, start the Service Builder, and open the project ZEQDEMO. Navigate to the entity type Z0D_FC_NW_C01_Q0001Result, and choose REDEFINE ATTRIBUTES as shown in Figure 7.42. Replace the value in the NAME column with values that are derived from those you find in the LABEL column. These are the same that can be found in the sap:label annotations in the service metadata document.

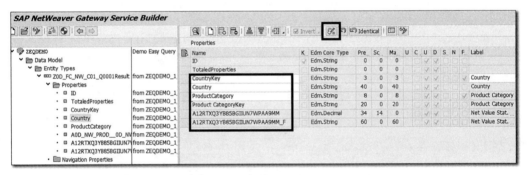

Figure 7.42 Redefining Attributes

No special characters

Note that properties must not contain special characters such as white spaces. You thus create property names following a *CamelCase* notation by removing any special characters such as white spaces or points. Perform the following changes in the NAME column:

▶ Change A0D_NW_CNTRY_T to Country.

▶ Change A0D_NW_CNTRY to CountryKey.

▶ Change A0D_NW_PROD__0D_NW_PRDCT_T to ProductCategory.

▶ Change A0D_NW_PROD__0D_NW_PRDCT to ProductCategoryKey.

▶ Change A12RTXQ3YB85BGIIUN7WPAA9MM to NetValue.

▶ Change A12RTXQ3YB85BGIIUN7WPAA9MM_F to NetValueText.

In addition to the property names in the generated entity type, you can redefine the name of the entity type `Z0D_FC_NW_C01_Q0001Result` and the entity set `Z0D_FC_NW_C01_Q0001Results` to `NetValueResult` and `NetValueResults` respectively and click SAVE.

Regenerate Service

After performing all changes, you can now regenerate the OData service by clicking the GENERATE button. Then you can retrieve the beautified query result in the browser or the SAP NetWeaver Gateway client.

The generated service supports filtering out of the box. This is because the properties used in the row have been marked in the underlying SAP NetWeaver BW Easy Query such that they are provided as text and keys. This is why you're able to filter on the entity set `NetValueResults` using the filter string `$filter=CountryKey eq 'US'` to limit the result set using the following URI in the SAP NetWeaver Gateway client or in a browser:

/sap/opu/odata/sap/ZEQDEMO_1_SRV/NetValueResults?$filter=Country Key eq 'US'&$select=ProductCategory,NetValueText&$format=json

Compare the result shown earlier in Figure 7.41 with the result retrieved with Transaction RSRT shown in Figure 7.43.


```
{
 - d: {
   - results: [
     - {
       + __metadata: {...},
         ProductCategory: "Mobile Devices",
         NetValueText: "41.410.115,00 EUR"
       },
     - {
       + __metadata: {...},
         ProductCategory: "Monitors",
         NetValueText: "26.960.052,00 EUR"
       },
     - {
       + __metadata: {...},
         ProductCategory: "Notebooks",
         NetValueText: "27.133.877,00 EUR"
       },
     - {
       + __metadata: {...},
         ProductCategory: "Overall Result",
         NetValueText: "95.504.044,00 EUR"
       }
     ]
   }
}
```


Figure 7.43 Filtered and Beautified Result

7.2.2   Service Provider Interface (SPI)

A second example of an integration scenario is the SPI. In contrast to SAP NetWeaver BW, query services based on SPI also allow you to create, update, and change data in the backend system. Because the SPI is remote-enabled, the IW_SPI add-on can also be deployed on the SAP NetWeaver Gateway hub system. As a result of the redefinition process, the nodes, data structure, and ID structure in the SPI model are mapped to the corresponding entity types in an OData model.

In this section, we'll use a sample SPI object based on the enterprise procurement model that is shipped as part of the SAP Business Suite foundation software component (SAP_BS_FND 731 SP06). This business case is that you want to build an OData service for an application that allows a user to list the business partners of the fictional company ITelo. The application will allow the user not only to list business partners, but also to create new business partners and to update existing ones as well as retrieve the contacts of a business partner. To take advantage of the work already invested in building this business partner service using the SPI framework, you can reuse this service to generate an easy-to-consume OData service.

To run this example, you need an SAP NetWeaver Gateway hub system or SAP backend system where the add-ons in Table 7.1 have been deployed.

Software Component	Release	Level	Description
IW_BEP	200	0006	Backend Event Provider
IW_SPI	100	0002	Service Provider Infrastructure
SAP_BS_FND	731	0006	SAP Business Suite Foundation

Table 7.1 Add-Ons Needed to Generate OData Services Based on SPI

The system in this example is using an embedded deployment. In the remainder of this section, you'll perform the steps required to generate an OData service based on an SPI service:

1. Generate an OData service based on a service provider service using redefinition (encompasses the phases data model definition and service implementation).

2. Publish the service on the SAP NetWeaver Gateway system (service maintenance).

In contrast to the redefinition of an SAP NetWeaver BW Easy Query, it's not necessary to jump back to the data model definition phase because the names of the entity types, entity sets, and their properties are already readable.

The steps and their assignment to the three phases of service creation are depicted in Figure 7.44.

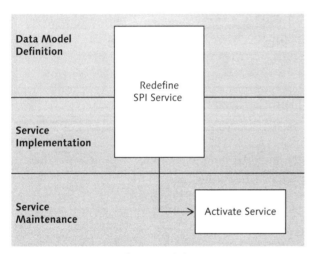

Figure 7.44 Sequence of Steps Redefining an SPI Service

Redefine SPI Service

Create project

Start by creating a new project in the Service Builder (Transaction SEGW) that is called ZSPIDEMO. In the project tree, you right-click on the DATA MODEL node, select REDEFINE, and then choose SPI SERVICE as shown in Figure 7.45.

On the first screen of the wizard (see Figure 7.46), you have to specify the SPI object that should serve as a data source, as described in Table 7.2.

Redefine SPI service

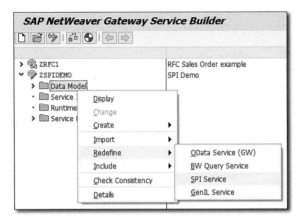

Figure 7.45 Starting Service Generation Based on SPI Objects

Wizard: Step 1 of 3

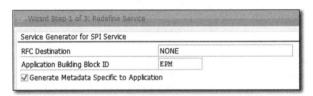

Figure 7.46 Selecting the Application Building Block ID

Field Name	Value
RFC DESTINATION	Specify the name of the RFC destination pointing to the backend system where the SPI object resides. Choose NONE.
APPLICATION BUILD-ING BLOCK ID	Enter the name of the SPI object, which is called the *Application Building Block ID*. Enter the value "EPM".

Table 7.2 Input Fields (Screen 1 of 3): Redefining Service Wizard for SPI Objects

Wizard: Step 2 of 3
On the second screen of the wizard, enter meaningful descriptions in the DESCRIPTION fields of the technical model and the technical service that will be generated by the Service Builder. All other values that are suggested by the Service Builder can be left unchanged, as shown in Figure 7.47.

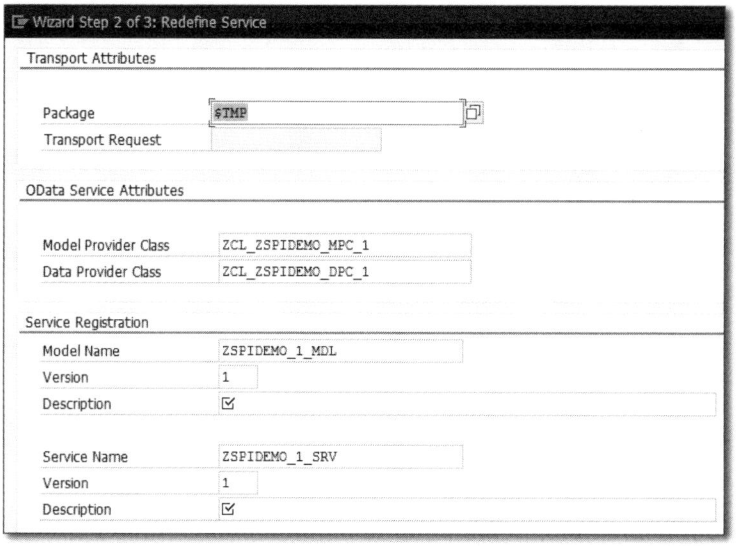

Figure 7.47 Service Registration in the Backend

On the third screen of the wizard, you finally have to choose the SPI service artifacts, which will be mapped and become part of the OData service.

Wizard: Step 3 of 3

In this example, select the entity types `Business_Partner` and `Contact` and the association `ContactofBusiness_Partner` as shown in Figure 7.48. Click FINISH.

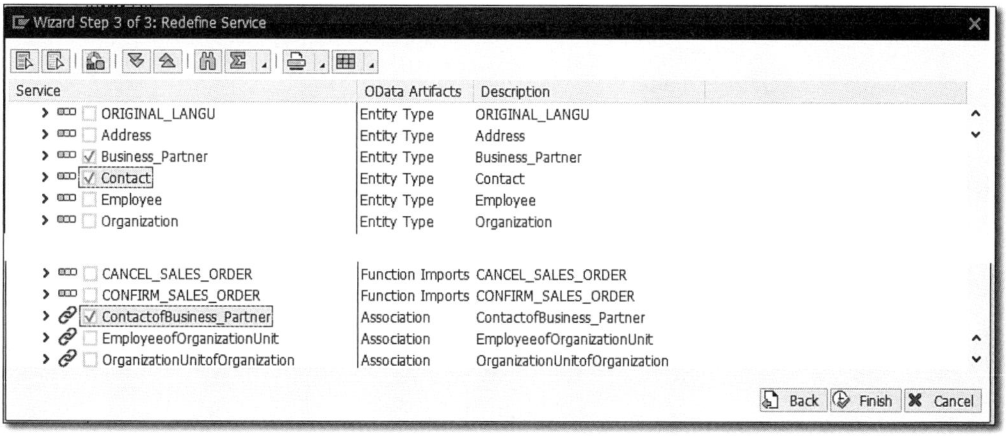

Figure 7.48 Selecting OData Artifacts: Step 3 of 3

Generate In the Service Builder, you now have to choose from the menu PROJECT •
GENERATE or click the GENERATE button. In the following MODEL AND
SERVICE DEFINITION dialog box, select the OVERWRITE EXTENDED SERVICE
checkbox to overwrite the existing service, and click CONTINUE as shown
in Figure 7.49. In the CREATE OBJECT DIRECTORY ENTRY dialog box, enter
"$TMP" as the package name, and click SAVE, or click the LOCAL OBJECT
button.

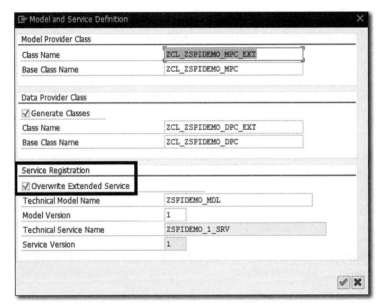

Figure 7.49 Model and Service Definition

Activate Service

After the service has been generated, you need to register and activate
the service in the SAP NetWeaver Gateway hub. To do so, expand the
SERVICE MAINTENANCE node in the project, right-click on the hub entry
you want the service to activate on, and select REGISTER from the context
menu.

In the SELECT SYSTEM ALIAS (HUB TO BACKEND) dialog, select the system
alias LOCAL_SPI that has been configured for this SPI service redefinition
scenario. Because we're using a system that contains the software

component SAP_BS_FND 731 SP03, the software version of the system alias entry has been set to /IWSPI/BSFND_731 as shown in Figure 7.50.

Change View "Manage SAP System Aliases": Overview							
New Entries 🗋 🗟 ⟲ 🗟 🗟 🗟							
Manage SAP System Aliases							
SAP System Alias	Description	Local GW	For Local App	RFC Destination	Software Version	System ID	Client
LOCAL_SPI	For SPI service generation	☑	☐	ZME_800	/IWSPI/BSFND_731	ZME	800

Figure 7.50 System Alias Configuration

In the ADD SERVICE dialog, you have to specify the package being used.

SAP System Alias Definition for SPI Integration Scenario

The implementation of the integration scenario for SPI was changed in the past. As a result, it's necessary to specify a software version for the SAP system alias that points to the backend system where the SPI service resides. That's why you have to make sure that you've created an appropriate SAP system alias before activating the service.

While creating an SAP system alias, the software version must be selected depending on the version of the software component SAP_BS_FND that is used in the backend system:

▶ If the SPI is used in an SAP_BS_FND 702 SP09 system, choose DEFAULT as the software version.

▶ If the SPI is used in an SAP_BS_FND 731 SP03 system, choose /IWSPI/ BSFND_731 as the software version.

Now you're ready to test the service. To do so, expand the SERVICE MAINTENANCE node in the project, right-click on the hub entry on which you've registered and activated the service, and select MAINTAIN from the context menu.

Test service

Using the SAP NetWeaver Gateway client, you can show that the generated service allows for retrieving a list of business partners, the details of one business partner, and a list of contacts via a navigation property (Figure 7.51). The service even supports the use of filtering options. Therefore, you can perform the following requests using the SAP NetWeaver Gateway client:

- Show a list of business partners by entering the following relative URL in the SAP NetWeaver Gateway client:

  /sap/opu/odata/sap/ZSPIDEMO_1_SRV/Business_PartnerCollection

- Show the details of one business partner:

  /sap/opu/odata/sap/ZGW100_XX_SPI_1_SRV/Business_PartnerCollection (binary'0050561C01C71ED284BB80D90161152B')/

- Show the contacts of the selected business partner using the navigation property `ContactCollection`:

  /sap/opu/odata/sap/ZSPIDEMO_1_SRV/Business_PartnerCollection (binary'0050561C01C71ED284BB80D90161152B')/ContactCollection? $select=FIRST_NAME,LAST_NAME,EMAIL_ADDRESS&$filter=FIRST_ NAME eq 'Karl'&$format=json&sap-ds-debug=true

```
{
 - d: {
   - results: [
     - {
       + __metadata: {...},
         FIRST_NAME: "Karl",
         LAST_NAME: "Muller",
         EMAIL_ADDRESS: "karl.mueller@sap.com"
       }
     ]
   }
}
```

Figure 7.51 Query Result of Generated Service, Based on SPI Integration

7.2.3 Generation via External OData Services

odata.org   Finally, a third way to generate an OData service is by basing it on an external OData service. To explain this process, let's have a look how the sample OData service on the *odata.org* site for Microsoft's Northwind database can be consumed with SAP NetWeaver Gateway. The URL of this service is *http://services.odata.org/Northwind/Northwind.svc/* where *Northwind.svc* is the service name and *Northwind* is the service namespace. (You might have to use the query option `$format=xml` to be able to display the service document in a browser properly: *http://services.odata.org/Northwind/Northwind.svc/?$format=xml*.)

To access the OData service from the system where IW_BEP is deployed, an appropriate HTTP destination *ODATAORG* has to be created that points to the OData server *http://services.odata.org*, as shown in Figure 7.52. If needed, appropriate proxy settings have to be configured when, for example, calling the service from a company network.

HTTP destination

Figure 7.52 RFC Destination Used for OData Services Consumption and Integration

Define Data Model and Implement Service

Because the integration scenario for external OData services isn't implemented into the Service Builder with SP06 of SAP NetWeaver Gateway 2.0, you have to start Transaction /IWBEP/OCI_SRV_GEN. This will change with SP07. The data that has to be entered in Transaction /IWBEP/OCI_SRV_GEN is shown in Figure 7.53.

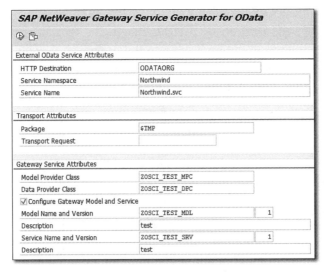

Figure 7.53 OData Services Consumption and Integration Using Transaction /IWBEP/OCI_SRV_GEN

Activate Service

After registering the service in the backend, it has to be registered and activated on the hub using Transaction /IWFND/MAINT_SERVICE. Note that an appropriate system alias entry has to be created (OCI_NORTH in the SAP SYSTEM ALIAS field, as shown in Figure 7.54) that is based on the same RFC destination (here: ODATAORG) that has been used for the generation of the service. Because the service has been deployed on the hub itself but is calling a service on a remote server (*odata.org*), the LOCAL GW and FOR LOCAL APP flags have to be activated for the SAP SYSTEM ALIAS entry. This is because the logic (MPC and DPC) that is calling the external service was generated on the local SAP NetWeaver Gateway hub server.

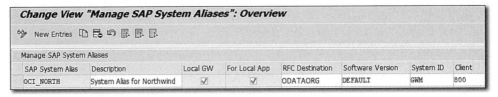

Figure 7.54 System Alias Configuration for OData Services Consumption and Integration

7.3   Model Composition: Include Gateway Service

As explained in Chapter 5, the idea behind model composition is to create mashups between multiple services that are leveraging generated services based on SAP NetWeaver BW, GenIL, SPI, and custom-built services. As you've seen in the previous sections, the integration scenarios allow you to easily generate services that leverage the power of the underlying business object or service. These generated services are limited to the scope of the underlying data source, however.

As an example for a use case of model composition, you can take the services generated using redefinition in Section 7.2.1 and Section 7.2.2. Both services allow that their entity sets (sales numbers or the business partners) be filtered by country. It is thus beneficial to have enhanced versions of theses OData services, which, in addition, have an entity set of countries from which a user can choose. From a country that has been selected, it should be possible to use a navigation property to navigate to the business partners or the sales numbers of that country. This is where model composition comes into play. Starting from a simple service that returns a collection of countries and their details, you can include a generated service (e.g., based on the SPI) or another existing service to create a service that will show all business partners of a selected country.

Use case

In the example in this section, you'll start by creating a service that publishes a list of countries using code-based implementation. In a second step, you'll include the sample service GWDEMO into this service, rather than integrating one of the generated services from the previous sections. You do this because the GWDEMO service that is available in every system in which the software components IW_BEP or SAP_GWFND have been deployed contains, among others, a business partner entity set. As a result, this how-to section can be performed in any system without the need to have SPI or SAP NetWeaver BW-based services in place.

The process of service creation for this example of model composition is shown in Figure 7.55.

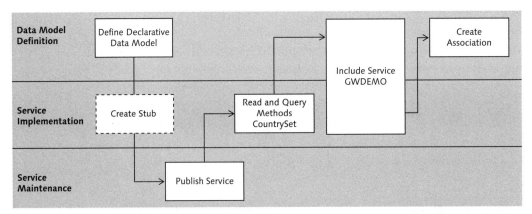

Figure 7.55 Sequence of Steps Redefining Creating a Service Using Code-Based Implementation and Model Composition

Define Declarative Data Model

List of countries and country codes

In this step, you create a simple service using code-based implementation that provides the consumer with a list of countries and country codes. The data model will have an entity type Country and an entity set CountrySet. The entity type Country has the properties listed in Table 7.3.

Name	Key	Edm Core Type	Precision	Scale	Maximum Length
CountryKey	X	Edm.String	3	0	3
CountryName		Edm.String	40	0	40

Table 7.3 Entity Type Country

Activate/Publish Service

After the project has been generated and the repository objects have been generated where the service has been registered in the backend, you can proceed to activate the service in the SAP NetWeaver Gateway system so that you can test the service metadata document. For this, you expand the SERVICE MAINTENANCE node in the project, right-click on the hub entry you want the service to register and activate on, and select REGISTER from the context menu.

After confirming the warning pop-up that this step will be carried out on the SAP NetWeaver Gateway hub system, you select the appropriate system alias (this pop-up only appears if several system alias entries have been created).

In the ADD SERVICE dialog on the hub, click LOCAL OBJECT to select $TMP as the package for the repository objects of the service that you're now going to generate, and click OK. If you want to create repository objects that can be transported, you have to choose an appropriate package.

Choose package

Implement Read and Query Methods

You can now implement the two methods COUNTRYSET_GET_ENTITYSET and COUNTRYSET_GET_ENTITY. Because the service has already been activated, you can test the service while performing the service implementation rather than following the sequential waterfall development approach. The coding of these methods is shown in Listing 7.4 and Listing 7.5.

```
method COUNTRYSET_GET_ENTITYSET.
  DATA: ls_data LIKE LINE OF et_entityset.
  data:
  " Structure for one country
  ls_country type t005t,
  " Table of countries
  lt_countries type standard table of T005t.

  select distinct land1 landx
    into corresponding fields of table lt_countries
    from t005t
    where spras = SY-Langu.

  LOOP AT lt_countries INTO ls_country.
    CLEAR ls_data.
    move ls_country-land1 to ls_data-countrykey.
    move ls_country-landx to ls_data-countryname.
    APPEND ls_data TO et_entityset.
  ENDLOOP.
endmethod.
```

Listing 7.4 COUNTRYSET_GET_ENTITYSET

```
method COUNTRYSET_GET_ENTITY.
  DATA: lt_keys TYPE /IWBEP/T_MGW_TECH_PAIRS,
        ls_key TYPE /IWBEP/S_MGW_TECH_PAIR,
        ls_product_id type BAPI_EPM_PRODUCT_ID,
        COUNTRYKEY type C length 3.
  data:
        " Structure for one country
        ls_country type t005t,
        " Table of countries
        lt_countries type standard table of T005t.
  lt_keys = IO_TECH_REQUEST_CONTEXT->GET_KEYS( ).
  READ TABLE lt_keys with key
  name = 'COUNTRYKEY' INTO ls_key.
  COUNTRYKEY = ls_key-value.
  select single land1 landx
    into corresponding fields of  ls_country from t005t
      where spras = SY-Langu and
            land1 = ls_key-value.
  move ls_country-land1 to er_entity-countrykey.
  move ls_country-landx to er_entity-countryname.
endmethod.
```

Listing 7.5 COUNTRYSET_GET_ENTITY

Include Service GWDEMO

In this project, right-click on DATA MODEL and choose INCLUDE • ODATA SERVICE (GW) as shown in Figure 7.56.

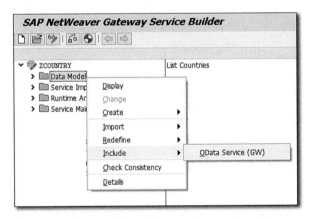

Figure 7.56 Include SAP NetWeaver Gateway Sample Service GWDEMO

This opens the INCLUDE MODEL FROM SERVICE wizard (see Figure 7.57). Choose SERVICE IN CURRENT SYSTEM, and select the TECHNICAL SERVICE NAME from the input help. In this example, choose /IWBEP/GWDEMO, and then click CONTINUE. Note that the version of the service is automatically populated.

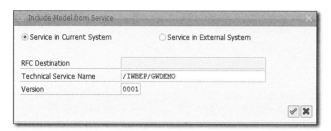

Figure 7.57 Include Model from Service GWDEMO

After this step, you'll find an entry for the model references in the tree view of your Service Builder project, as shown in Figure 7.58.

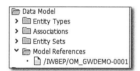

Figure 7.58 Model Reference

Create Association

Next you have to create an association between the entity type Business_Partner that stems from the included model of the service GWDEMO and the entity type Country that is part of the model of the service ZCOUNTRY that you've just created. Because this association is created between an entity type that is part of the Service Builder project and an entity type that has been included, it's referred to as an *external association*.

First, double-click on ASSOCIATIONS, and switch to change mode. Now you can choose to append or insert a new row for a new association with the name CountryToBP. Next, click on the EXTERNAL ASSOCIATION EDITOR button in the mass maintenance view. In the CREATE EXTERNAL ASSOCIATION windows that is shown in Figure 7.59, ensure that EXTERNAL is

Change mode

395

selected in the ASSOCIATION TYPE field. Here, the entry /IWBEP/OM_
GWDEMO-0001 is automatically populated or has to be selected from
the input help in the MODEL REFERENCE field.

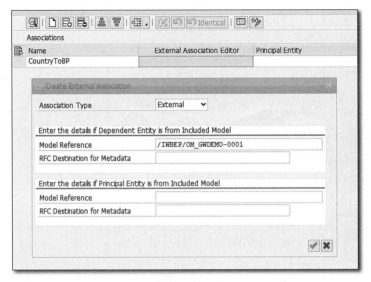

Figure 7.59 Creating an External Association

After creating the settings for the external association to the model
/IWBEP/OM_GWDEMO-0001, you can add the entity type Business-
Partner from the included model as the DEPENDENT ENTITY. The PRINCI-
PAL ENTITY is the entity type Country that you created in the first step.
The association should look as shown in Figure 7.60. The PRINCIPAL
ENTITY CARDINALITY is set to 1, and the DEPENDENT ENTITY CARDINALITY
of the BusinessPartner is set to M (because there can be none or several
business partners in the country chosen from the list of countries).

Figure 7.60 External Association CountryToBP

Referential
constraint

Now that you've created an association, you can create a referential
constraint and then create a navigation property in the entity type. The

referential constraint is needed so that the framework will later handle any call to the entity set BusinessPartners that is performed via the navigation property that you're going to create.

Double-click on REFERENTIAL CONSTRAINTS, and select CountryKey as the PRINCIPAL KEY. The DEPENDENT PROPERTY CountryCode can be selected from the input help as shown in Figure 7.61.

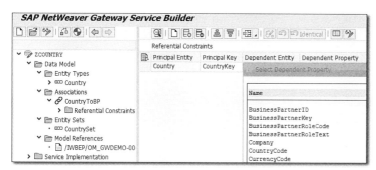

Figure 7.61 Creating Referential Constraint between the Entity Types Country and BusinessPartner

Based on the referential constraint, you can now create a navigation property ToBP for the entity type Country. To do so, expand the entity type Country to view the NAVIGATION PROPERTIES folder. Double-click the NAVIGATION PROPERTIES folder, and switch to change mode. Here you create a navigation property ToBP based on the association Country-ToBP as shown in Figure 7.62.

Change mode

Figure 7.62 Creating Navigation Property ToBP

To persist the changes, you have to generate the project, which will regenerate the DPC and MPC. You can now run the following URI in the Service Builder to retrieve all business partners from the US region:

Generate project

/sap/opu/odata/sap/ZCOUNTRY_SRV/CountrySet('US')/ToBP

The result of this query is shown in Figure 7.63.

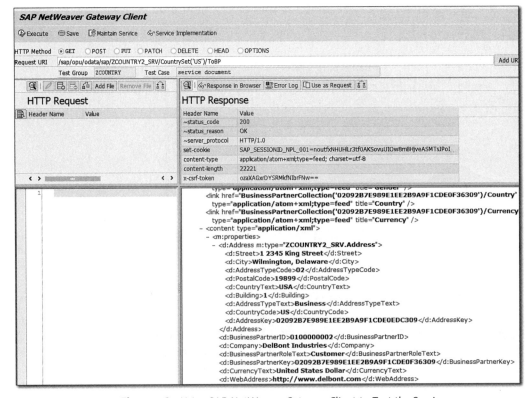

Figure 7.63 Using SAP NetWeaver Gateway Client to Test the Service

7.4   Summary

In this chapter we've shown the three different ways to generate OData services in SAP NetWeaver Gateway:

▸ RFC/BOR interface
▸ Redefinition
▸ Model composition

You've learned that by using the RFC/BOR Generator, it's possible to create an OData service in SAP NetWeaver Gateway based on existing RFC function modules without writing a single line of code. But we also showed what needs to be done if no suitable RFC function module is available for each method of your OData service, and how to circumvent this issue by developing your own wrapper RFC function model. In addition, generating OData services using redefinition was shown for the following integration scenarios:

▶ SAP NetWeaver BW Easy Query

▶ Service Provider Interface (SPI)

▶ Generation via external OData services (OSCI)

Finally, you learned that the third approach, model composition, allows you to combine existing services with newly created services without the need to change the existing ones.

PART III
Application Development

Application development can be optimized by different SAP tools. This chapter walks through the installation and use of the main tool: the SAP NetWeaver Gateway Productivity Accelerator.

8   SAP NetWeaver Gateway Productivity Accelerator

Application development has become an increasingly important topic in recent years in both the consumer and business sectors. In addition to the specific situation, the target platform, and the corresponding development language, the supported development tools play a crucial role.

To make the entry into the world of application development as easy as possible, SAP provides some useful standalone plugins, and in addition, a new Eclipse plugin called SAP NetWeaver Gateway Productivity Accelerator (GWPA). These toolkits are optimized for the needs of any application developer and offer an easy and fast consumption of any available OData service. This generates either a complete small sample application, including a simple user interface (UI) and the coding for the consumption of the given OData service, or the needed proxy classes without a default UI for more experienced application developers.

Proxy classes are very common design patterns used to shift the control for another object to a substituting class. This optimizes the handling of complex processes because the generated methods provide all of the needed functions for the service communication, such as the HTTP connection to the OData service or the authentication process. You can find all basic information and the download URL in the developer center at the SAP Community Network (SCN) at *http://scn.sap.com/community/developer-center/netweaver-gateway* (Figure 8.1).

Proxy classes

This chapter focuses on the available GWPA plugins and functions.

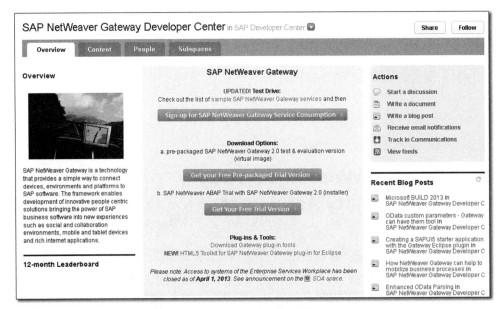

Figure 8.1 SAP NetWeaver Gateway Developer Center

GWPA for Microsoft

SAP published the SAP NetWeaver Gateway Productivity Accelerator for Microsoft during the writing of this book. It's a Visual Studio 2010/2012 add-on, and works very similarly to the normal GWPA Eclipse plugin. You can find further information at *http://help.sap.com/nwgwpam*.

Chapter overview

Specifically, we explain which consumption toolkits are available (Section 8.1) and how to install these toolkits as an Eclipse plugin (Section 8.2). Also part of this chapter is a short introduction to the available OData sample services from *www.odata.org*, the available sample SAP NetWeaver Gateway services provided by SAP, and how to get free access to those (Section 8.3). Finally, we'll use the Eclipse-based graphical OData Model Editor for creating and changing OData models (Section 8.4).

Note

For specific development instructions about using the iOS and Android plugins for mobile development, see Chapter 9.

8.1 Consumption Toolkits

To download any plugin provided by SAP, look in the PLUGIN & TOOLS area at the SAP NetWeaver Gateway developer center on the SCN (*http://scn.sap.com/community/developer-center/netweaver-gateway*), where you can find the SAP GWPA download link. As mentioned, there are also some standalone plugins for different platforms and the specific development environments available, such as the SAP NetWeaver Gateway Developer Tools for Xcode.

These standalone plugins for development systems can only be used in the specific environment in question (e.g., iOS or Android). Based on the standalone plugins, GWPA provides Eclipse-based developer tools, which are available for the same scenarios, such as provisioning and consumption of OData services or the OData Model Editor (Figure 8.2).

Environment-specific

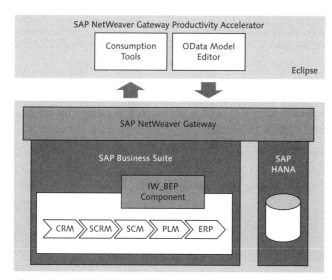

Figure 8.2 SAP NetWeaver Gateway Productivity Accelerator (GWPA)

The following toolkits are part of GWPA:

▸ Toolkit for Android

▸ Toolkit for HTML

▸ Toolkit for iOS

▸ OData Toolkit for Java Platform (SE)

▸ Toolkit for PHP

The iOS and Android toolkits use the SAP mobile client SDKs to generate applications that allow direct communication to either SAP NetWeaver Gateway or to the SAP Mobile Platform. This provides a seamless upgrade story from an application connecting directly to SAP NetWeaver Gateway to an application connecting to the SAP Mobile Platform.

8.2   Installation

Installation
process

You can install the GWPA toolkit as follows:

1. Start Eclipse (Juno or Kepler, if you want to use Kepler, replace *juno* with *kepler* in the URL in a later step).

2. From the main menu, choose HELP • INSTALL NEW SOFTWARE.

3. In the WORK WITH field, enter the update site URL where the features are available for installation: *https://tools.hana.ondemand.com/juno*.

The update site lists the features available for GWPA together with their name and version. The option ODATA MODELER AND TOOLS CORE FOR SAP (GWPA) must be installed; all other options are available for optional installation depending on your chosen service consumption platform. In Chapter 9, we'll show you the detailed required installation process for an Android starter application, so mark the checkbox next to TOOLKIT FOR ANDROID (GWPA) in addition to installing the needed plugin (Figure 8.3). If you want to go on with the development process for another platform (e.g., HTML5/SAPUI5, which we'll discuss in Chapter 10), also mark the corresponding checkboxes.

You can find the full installation document on the SAP website:

*https://help.hana.ondemand.com/gateway_gwpa/pdf/SAP_NetWeaver_
Gateway_Productivity_Accelerator_Inst_Guide_en.pdf*

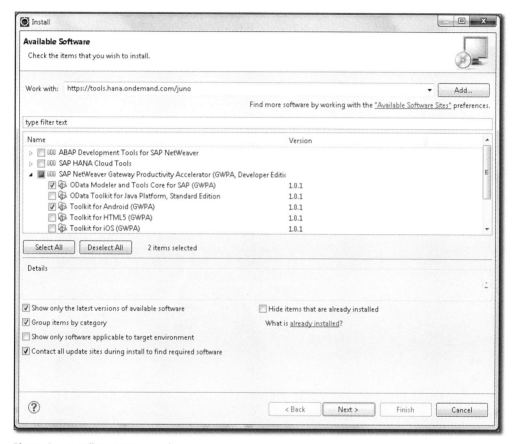

Figure 8.3 Installing GWPA in Eclipse

Click NEXT, and you'll see an overview of the selected items to be installed. Click on the NEXT button again, and read and accept the terms of the license agreement by choosing the radio button and clicking on FINISH. The installation process starts, and you have to confirm a security warning due to unsigned software by clicking the OK button twice. On completion, Eclipse prompts you to restart. Restart Eclipse.

Now you can enable a wizard to provide you with a list of the SAP NetWeaver Gateway hosts from which you can choose the SAP service you want (requires SAP NetWeaver Gateway 2.0 SP05 or higher). When configuring the SAP NetWeaver Gateway connection, you can specify which one is the default connection. In addition to the connection settings, you can choose another SAP OData mobile client SDK if you don't want to use the default one, which is automatically installed with the GWPA Eclipse plugin. The iOS and Android toolkits use the SAP mobile client SDKs to generate applications that allow direct communication to either SAP NetWeaver Gateway or SAP Mobile Platform.

To configure the connection settings for an SAP NetWeaver Gateway host in Eclipse, choose WINDOW • PREFERENCES from the Eclipse main menu. Select ODATA DEVELOPMENT • SAP NETWEAVER GATEWAY • CONNECTIONS. Choose ADD to enter a new connection to an existing SAP NetWeaver Gateway system (Figure 8.4).

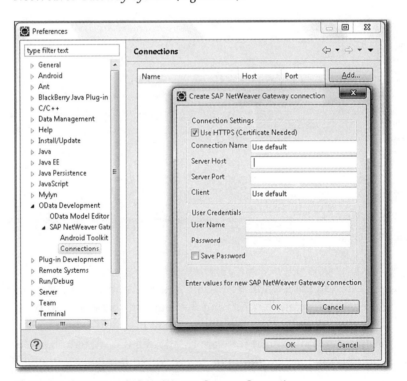

Figure 8.4 Creating an SAP NetWeaver Gateway Connection

Enter the connection settings—Server Host, Server Port, User Name, Password—for SAP NetWeaver Gateway. Click OK.

In Section 8.3, we'll show you how to get access to the SAP NetWeaver Gateway service test drive. Afterwards, Section 8.4 will give you a quick overview of the possibilities of the GWPA OData Model Editor and how to use the tool.

8.3   OData Sample Services

If you don't have an SAP NetWeaver Gateway system available but want to start with your first development steps directly and consume an OData service or just to get a first impression, you can register for the free SAP NetWeaver Gateway sample service test drive. You can get access to the SAP test drive for SAP NetWeaver Gateway services on the main page of the SAP NetWeaver Gateway Developer Center (refer to Figure 8.1) or directly on the SCN page at *http://scn.sap.com/docs/DOC-40986*.

First, you have to sign up for an account with your SCN user data (*https:/ /supsignformssapicl.hana.ondemand.com/SUPSignForms*). After you're registered for the system, you should receive an email with your user name and password. From now on, you can connect to the system via WebGUI, SAPGUI Windows, or SAPGUI Java. You'll have read and write authorizations and access to the development tools, but you're not allowed to develop yourself. Debugging with viewing permissions is possible, however.

SAP test drive

> **Warning**
>
> The Enterprise Service Workplace (ESW) services are no longer available.

SAP provides a number of typical scenarios to help you become familiar with the technology. Each available OData service provides at least the following functionalities:

- Metadata document
- Consumption model

- Sample query operation
- Sample read operation

SAP sample services

You're free to use your preferred development environment or web browser to connect to the demo services via the following list of URIs:

- **Flight example** (read only)
  Access information about the famous SAP flight data:

  https://sapes1.sapdevcenter.com/sap/opu/odata/IWFND/RMTSAMPLE FLIGHT/?$format=xml

- **Bank example** (read only)
  Access information about bank data:

  https://sapes1.sapdevcenter.com/sap/opu/odata/sap/Z_BANK/?$format =xml

- **Sales order example** (read only)
  Access sales order information such as header and line item data:

  https://sapes1.sapdevcenter.com/sap/opu/odata/sap/ZCD204_EPM_ DEMO_SRV/?$format=xml

- **Enterprise Procurement Model** (read only)
  Access information about business partner, address data, and more:

  https://sapes1.sapdevcenter.com/sap/opu/odata/IWBEP/GWDEMO/ ?$format=xml

SAP will continuously offer additional services covering more and more use cases. A complete list of all available SAP NetWeaver Gateway sample services is available on SCN at *http://scn.sap.com/docs/DOC-31221*.

OData.org sample services

OData.org also provides three useful example services:

- **Northwind service** (read only)
  Access the famous Northwind database:

  http://services.odata.org/Northwind/Northwind.svc/

- **OData sample service** (read only)
  Access categories, products, and suppliers data:

  http://services.odata.org/OData/OData.svc/

▶ **OData sample service** (read/write)
Access categories, products, and suppliers data with write functionalities (during a session, identified by the URL):

http://services.odata.org/v3/odata/odata.svc

The complete list of OData sample services is available at *www.odata.org/ecosystem/.*

You're now able to familiarize yourself with the technology and the OData services. Let's now take a look at an OData model.

8.4   SAP Gateway Productivity Accelerator OData Model Editor

GWPA isn't just a helpful tool for application development; it also enables you to create new OData models within an Eclipse-based OData Model Editor. You can also change existing OData models and view a relationship model in an easy-to-use graphical modeler.

The ease and efficient use of the tools allows people with no ABAP development skills to create/change an OData model. The OData Model Editor gives you the opportunity to speed up the development process, addressing non-SAP developers who want the freedom to concentrate on the data they require in a given business context. After you finish the model creation, you can export the model, so the ABAP developer can use the export file to generate the service on top of that with the SAP NetWeaver Service Builder. The provided OData perspective in Eclipse is one of the core elements of the GWPA and is installed as a Basis function during the installation process (refer to Section 8.2). The perspective is a customized view to give you all of the comfort you need during the model creation process.

No ABAP development skills required

To create or edit your OData model, start the GWPA Model Editor by opening Eclipse and choosing the NEW PROJECT wizard. Open the ODATA DEVELOPMENT node, and select ODATA MODEL in the displayed window (Figure 8.5).

OData model

Figure 8.5 GWPA OData Development

Click NEXT. On the following screen, SAP NetWeaver Gateway OData Model Editor provides multiple options to create an OData model project:

- BLANK ODATA MODEL
- ODATA SERVICE METADATA URL
- ODATA SERVICE METADATA FILE
- SERVICE CATALOG

Select a service   To set up a model based on an existing service, click BROWSE, and choose an existing Eclipse project (if you don't have a project available, create a new one first). Enter a MODEL NAME, and choose ODATA SERVICE METADATA URL from the model content options. Click NEXT.

The NEW ODATA MODEL page is displayed as shown in Figure 8.6, where you have to enter a SERVICE URL of your OData service, which will be created as an OData model. Click GO to receive the service details, including the available entities. Click FINISH.

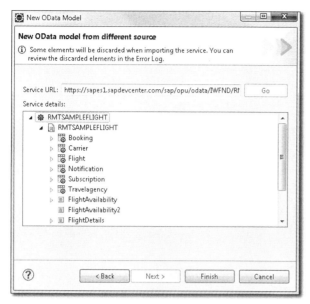

Figure 8.6 New OData Model from Service URL

The GWPA OData Model Editor starts to import the metadata from the service URL and generates a new OData model (Figure 8.7).

Display OData model

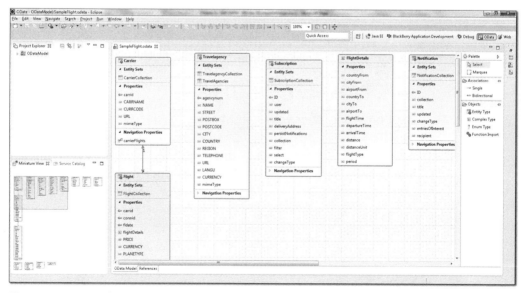

Figure 8.7 Generated Model from Existing OData Service

Edit the OData model

Now you can access different options to edit the model by right-clicking on the object you want to edit (Figure 8.8). You can do the following:

- Add new entity sets.
- Delete existing entity sets.
- Add new properties to an existing entity set.
- Delete properties from an existing entity set.

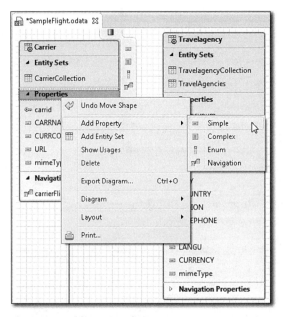

Figure 8.8 Adding a Simple Property to an Existing Entity Set

Export the OData model

Save the model after you've finished the editing process. To export the modified OData model, go to FILE • EXPORT • ODATA DEVELOPMENT • ODATA MODEL, and click NEXT. In the next window, click BROWSE, select the OData model (file type .odata) inside your project, and choose an export format (OData version) from the dropdown menu. Finally, you have to choose an export path by clicking the associated BROWSE button. Click FINISH to export the OData model as an XML file to your file system. Now you're able to reimport the enhanced OData model within the Service Builder.

8.5   Summary

The SAP NetWeaver Gateway Productivity Accelerator tool provides a lot of functions, such as the service consumption and application generation for different platforms and the OData Model Editor to optimize the entire development process. GWPA is very easy to use and will have a huge impact on the development time and improve the quality of your future application development projects.

Next, in Chapter 9, we'll introduce you to the process of developing mobile applications using OData and SAP NetWeaver Gateway. Specifically, we'll focus on the two main types of mobile applications: native applications and hybrid applications. Platform-independent HTML5/SAPUI5 applications will be described in Chapter 10.

The chapter walks you through mobile application development with the SAP NetWeaver Gateway development tools. You'll learn more about needed software for the different operating systems and get introduced to the technical basics for mobile development.

9   Mobile Application Development

The procession of smartphones and tablet computers in recent years has significantly affected the development of mobile applications. For example, in the early days of mobile phones, small applications such as calendars or calculators were a revolutionary part of an operating system, but were permanent and not able to be removed or replaced by the owner of the device. Now, this is no longer the case. Since these early days, mobile applications have become much more flexible, and now play a huge role in the consumer and business sector—and their importance continues to grow.

The change from a consumer world to a global business world, where fast changes are necessary for the success of a company, makes mobile applications more and more important every day. The PC market is shrinking, while the number of mobile applications downloaded rises every year by a huge amount. One of the reasons is the enormous speed of innovation inside the mobile world and the corresponding increased frequency and capabilities of mobile devices.

Before you start developing mobile applications, you should answer the following questions to make the right decisions for your future mobile applications:

First questions for mobile applications

▶ Do we need more than one specific hardware provider?

▶ Do we need OData plugins, or can we create our coding from scratch?

▸ Should we use hybrid applications, and do we have web application developers in-house?

Chapter overview

In this chapter, we introduce the topic of developing mobile applications using SAP NetWeaver Gateway. In Section 9.1, we discuss mobile development, including its three main approaches: native development, hybrid development, and HTML5 development. In the rest of the chapter, we concentrate on the details of native mobile applications (Section 9.2) and on hybrid development (Section 9.3). HTML5 isn't only for mobile applications (you can use it as a normal website for your desktop PC/Mac), so we concentrate on this special topic in Chapter 10.

9.1   Introduction to Mobile Development

Apple, Google, BlackBerry, and Microsoft are leading IT companies that push the market and consumers with new ideas and hardware enhancements. As a consequence, the growing options for business processes, development, and mobile device management will enable enterprises to manage and secure their mobile devices and optimize their business processes for the challenges of a globalized world.

Hybrid versus native applications

This basketful of different approaches is also one reason why cross-platform mobile application development is becoming more and more important. Using this approach, you have the ability to reduce development costs and deploy a functionality at the same time to many different devices. These cross-platform applications are normally web applications that run on almost every modern mobile platform in the same way, but have no access to the native Application Programming Interface (API) of the specific platform. This is the main reason that hybrid container applications, which combine the power of native APIs and the freedom of operating system choice, are becoming more and more popular in the consumer and business world.

SAP Mobile Platform

The whole application market is growing every day, and every company has to decide which horse they want to saddle. SAP provides the SAP Store for all existing SAP applications that have been developed by SAP or partners. All of these applications are based on the SAP Mobile Platform approach (Figure 9.1).

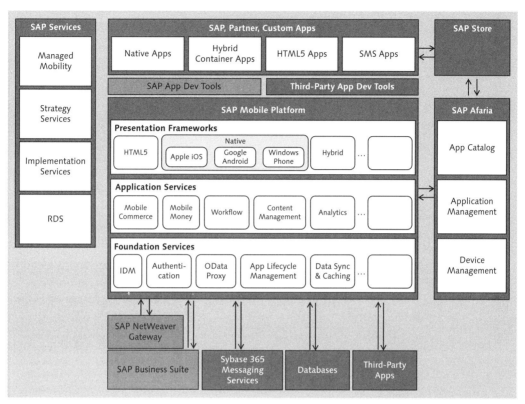

Figure 9.1 SAP Mobile Platform

Before a company's decision makers decide which application to buy or to develop, they have to ask themselves some questions about the use case, the existing system landscape, and the necessary devices (and therefore the platform).

Generally you can distinguish between three different approaches, which are all usable with the SAP Mobile Platform:

Different application approaches

► Native applications

► Hybrid container applications

► HTML5 applications (also known as web apps)

The major characteristics of these three approaches are outlined here:

▶ **Native development**

    ▷ Reuses investments/assets from HTML/hybrid development

    ▷ Provides access to robust device and middleware services such as database/data object store and replication services

    ▷ Uses SAP Afaria to help with application lifecycle, deployment, and management

    ▷ Works well for applications requiring robust graphics and complex offline transactions

▶ **Hybrid development**

    ▷ Provides access to native device capabilities

    ▷ Utilizes encrypted/secure data store

    ▷ Has a robust data messaging layer

    ▷ Supports application lifecycle management (ALM)

    ▷ Allows data integration with complex SAP and non-SAP data sources

▶ **HTML5 development**

    ▷ Takes advantage of web development resources

    ▷ Takes advantage of industry-standard development tools and tool chains

    ▷ Allows for easy cross-platform build, support, and deployment

    ▷ Works well for rapid development of simple applications accessing web services

With that high-level introduction, let's get into more details about native and hybrid applications. As we mentioned, HTML5 applications will be discussed in more detail in Chapter 10.

9.2 Native Mobile Applications

Benefits of native applications

This section shows why native application development is still important for the business world. Native applications in general offer the best performance and options for graphic design. They are based on *software development kits* (SDKs), which are created especially for the corresponding platform and fitted to the needs of a specialized developer. You have total control over the user experience and have access to the local device-specific capabilities, such as camera, GPS, or storage. But that is also one reason why developing native applications can be more complex and costly than developing mobile websites. Native application development also involves selecting a specific platform, which will always exclude some people. The application distribution is handled in most cases over the central store (e.g., Apple App Store, Google Play).

The high-level pros and cons of native application development are outlined in Table 9.1.

Pros	Cons
Good performance	Platform-specific development
Local API access	Development costs
Store distribution	License costs
Offline functionality	Application store approval

Table 9.1 Native Applications: Pros and Cons

In this section, we'll explain how to use SAP NetWeaver Gateway to develop applications for the most common platforms: Apple iOS (Section 9.2.1), Google Android (Section 9.2.2), Microsoft Windows Phone 8 (Section 9.2.3), and BlackBerry (Section 9.2.4).

9.2.1 Apple iOS

iOS is a mobile operating system developed and distributed by Apple Inc. iOS was originally called the iPhone OS, but was changed during the years since the 2007 release. The newest iOS 7.x version was released on September 18, 2013. The Apples iOS SDK offers *Xcode*, which is a very comfortable environment for native iPhone/iPad development. You need fundamental knowledge of Objective-C to create your own application.

> **Warning: Xcode Plugin Outdated**
>
> Although we discuss Xcode in this section, the Xcode plugin from SAP became outdated during the writing of this book. It can be used for test scenarios, but we recommend using the Eclipse-based GPWA tool for your future Apple iOS projects.

Standalone Eclipse plugin

The standalone SAP NetWeaver Gateway developer tool for iOS is an application for Macintosh-computers with the MacOS operation system. It generates an Xcode integrated development environment (IDE) project, which allows you to simply choose an SAP NetWeaver Gateway service, define UI screens, and create a mobile application.

> **MacOS Required**
>
> You need a Macintosh computer with MacOS to use the SAP NetWeaver Gateway developer tool for iOS. It doesn't run on other environments (for example, a Windows environment) for technical and legal reasons.

The developer tool enables you to create an iPhone starter kit application with an OData service connection. This starter kit application is a minimal version with all necessary functionalities to consume an OData service. The generated code, including the useful proxy classes (see the introduction of Chapter 8 for a short description), can be used as a basis to create your first iOS app. The proxy classes include the functionalities to execute read/write calls with a small amount of additional development. The generated user interface (UI) supports read-only scenarios only, but can be enhanced to your needs.

As described, you can use the developer tool to do the following:

- Browse through the SAP NetWeaver Gateway OData service.
- Utilize the SAP OData Mobile Client SDK client libraries.
- Create a minimal starter kit application.

iOS: Minimum Requirements   Requirements

- SAP NetWeaver Gateway 2.0
- Xcode 4.2 or higher
- MacOS 10.6.8 or higher
- iPhone/iPad iOS5 or higher
- SAP OData Mobile Client SDK client libraries for iOS 2.1.2 and 2.1.3

Next we'll explain the development process of your iOS application consuming OData. First, you have to download the Developer Tool for Xcode and the SAP OData Mobile SDK from the SAP Community Network (SCN) download area:

http://www.sdn.sap.com/irj/scn/downloads?rid=/webcontent/uuid/60486c42-3c56-2f10-43b6-c5fe6f696dd7   Download SDK

Next to the plugin, you can find detailed documentation for the installation process. Accept the license agreement first, and download the two ZIP files to your MAC computer. Next, unpack the ZIP files and start the *SAPNetWeaverGatewayDeveloperToolForXcode.pkg* file. The wizard is displayed and guides you through the installation process. After the installation is finished, you can start the application.

To get started developing, go to the FINDER, and select APPLICATIONS. Double-click SAP NETWEAVER GATEWAY DEVELOPER TOOL FOR XCODE. The SAP NetWeaver Gateway developer tool for Xcode is displayed.   Development

Now you can select the desired mode for running the tool from the two options provided (Figure 9.2):

- APPLICATION generates a full Xcode project with screens
- PROXY generates only proxy classes

Figure 9.2 Choice of Desired Modes for Running the Tool

Before you can continue, you have to add one or more SAP systems to the plugin settings. These systems indicate from where you want to receive your OData services.

Connection preferences

To set up the application preferences, go to MENU • SAP NETWEAVER GATEWAY DEVELOPER TOOL FOR XCODE • PREFERENCES. The PREFERENCES window is displayed (Figure 9.3).

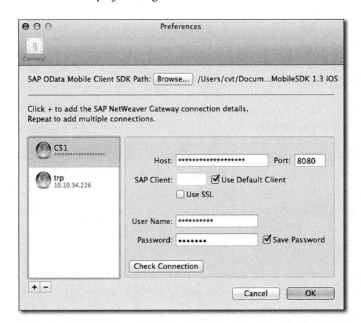

Figure 9.3 SAP NetWeaver Gateway Developer Tool for Xcode Preferences

SAP OData Mobile Client SDK

Click BROWSE, and then select the path to the SAP OData Mobile Client SDK libraries (i.e., select the iOS folder under the OData folder in the Mobile SDK hierarchy). Enter the details of the SAP NetWeaver Gateway server(s) to which you want to connect. Click the + button on the lower-left corner of the page to add a connection. (You can add as many connections as you wish.) In the CONNECTION NAME field, enter a name for the connection. You'll use this name to select the desired connection in the browser window later on. Click CREATE. In the PREFERENCES window, enter the HOST name, the PORT number, and the SAP CLIENT number for the specific connection.

If relevant, select the USE DEFAULT CLIENT CHECKBOX (default). Enter your USER NAME and PASSWORD. If relevant, select the SAVE PASSWORD checkbox. Click CHECK CONNECTION. A message appears stating whether the connection was successful or not. If it's not successful, try one of the troubleshooting options displayed.

To create a complete project, click the APPLICATION button. You can enter an APPLICATION NAME, select a project type—LIST/DETAILS (UNIVERSAL) or WORKFLOW (IPHONE)—and click BROWSE to choose an SAP NetWeaver Gateway service required for the application (Figure 9.4).

Create List/Details app

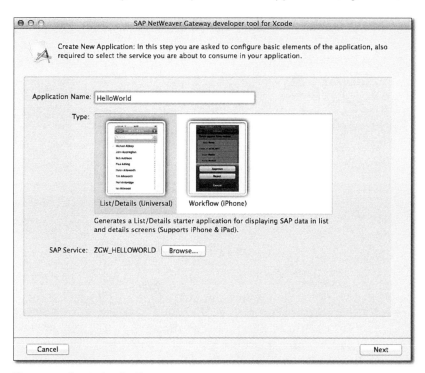

Figure 9.4 Create Application

To navigate to the view settings, click NEXT. For each view, you must select one of the following types:

▶ LIST
The UI generated from this type of view is a table.

▶ DETAILS
The UI generated from this type of view is a two-columned table.

The relationship between the views is based on the association between the entity sets. After you've selected an entity set for the first view, you can only select an entity set that is associated to it in the second view, or you can choose to display the details of the entity set you selected for the first view. Configure the first view of the application as it will be displayed in the UI. In the TITLE field, enter a name for the view. From the TYPE dropdown list, the A-Z LIST option is selected automatically (Figure 9.5). Change the selection to LIST for creating a nonindexed list view.

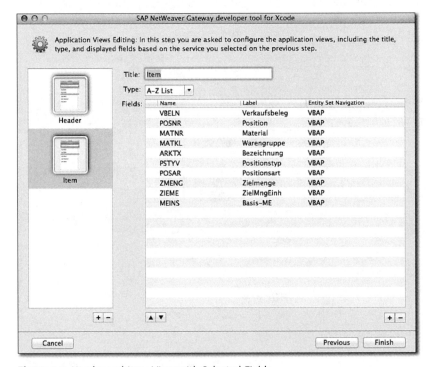

Figure 9.5 Header and Item View with Selected Fields

Click to see the fields available for the selected entity set. The ADD
FIELDS TO THE APPLICATION VIEW page is displayed.

Add new fields

> **Note**
>
> The DETAILS option isn't available for the first view because a detail view
> always references to a main view, which has to be created first.

From the ENTITY SET NAVIGATION dropdown list, select the desired entity
set to be displayed. Select the checkboxes of the desired fields for the
view. Click OK. Repeat the previous steps for configuring more views.
Every time you finish editing a view, you return to the overview page of
all existing views shown earlier in Figure 9.5.

Finish your work on the views and click FINISH to create the complete
Xcode project with all necessary files (Figure 9.6).

Finish application
development

Figure 9.6 Generated Xcode Project

Xcode Emulator   The created example application can be tested inside the Xcode Emulator. In runtime, you need to enter a user name and a password for login. Just enter the same credentials you used to login to your SAP system.

You can see an example of a generated iPhone application in Figure 9.7.

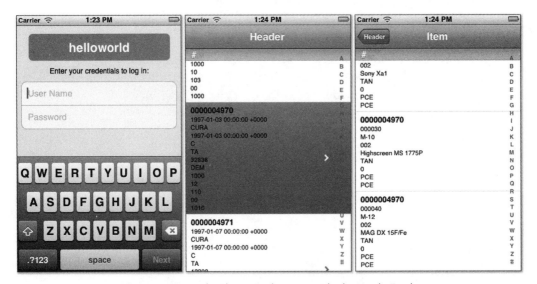

Figure 9.7 Example iPhone Application inside the Xcode Emulator

The generated coding also provides methods to connect to the Sybase Unwired Platform in *RequestHandler.m* and *Services/Framework/SDM-ConnectivityHelper.m*.

9.2.2   Google Android

Android is an open mobile platform that was developed by Google and, later, by the Open Handset Alliance. Google defines Android as a "software stack" for mobile phones. Android is based on the Linux operating system (kernel 2.6), and all of its applications are written using Java.

Google Android is the fastest growing mobile platform for smartphones and tablet PCs. That's only one of the reasons that SAP provides its own specific plugin-wizard for easy creation of simple Java projects with OData consumption capabilities.

We'll now show you how to generate a starter application with the SAP NetWeaver Gateway Productivity Accelerator (GWPA) toolkit for Eclipse. The application you create in the framework plugin can retrieve, and interact with, data from your existing SAP systems through SAP NetWeaver Gateway.

Android application with GWPA

Android: Minimum Requirements

▶ SAP NetWeaver Gateway 2.0

▶ Installed Eclipse 3.6.2 or higher

▶ Android SDK tools (version 18)

▶ Installed Android Developer Tools (ADT) for Eclipse

▶ Windows XP, Linux kernel 3.0, Mac Snow Leopard 10.6.8

You first need to install the ADT Eclipse plugin (*http://developer. android.com/sdk/installing/installing-adt.html*) before you start with the installation process of the SAP NetWeaver Gateway plugin for Eclipse. After the ADT installation process is finished, install the GWPA toolkit (refer to Section 8.2 in Chapter 8). GWPA provides wizards that obtain user actions and data to generate code suitable for the specific installed extension.

Further Resources

Further information for all Android SDKs is available at *http://developer. android.com/sdk/index.html*.

Now that we're done with the formalities, you can go ahead and use the plugin to create an Android application. Start by opening the NEW PROJECT wizard and selecting STARTER APPLICATION PROJECT under the ODATA DEVELOPMENT node (refer back to Figure 8.5 in Chapter 8). Click NEXT, choose your project name, select ANDROID from the dropdown of available target platforms, and enter the Android project-specific attributes. Click NEXT again.

Create an Android application

Available templates

You can choose from the following three templates:

▶ BASIC APPLICATION
Generates an application structure with entry points for custom development.

▶ LIST/DETAILS APPLICATION
Generates an application for displaying SAP data in list and details screens.

▶ WORKFLOW APPLICATION
Generates an application for displaying workflow task items that require user decision.

Select the LIST/DETAILS APPLICATION template from the templates page of the wizard, and click NEXT.

Choose service via catalog

There are several ways to select the service on which to base your application. We've entered an SAP NetWeaver Gateway system in the connection settings, so we can use the catalog functionality to explore the SAP NetWeaver Gateway service catalog. Clicking the CATALOG button opens the service catalog of your defined SAP system. You can browse or search for any services provided by the specified system and have a deep look into the different entities, properties, associations, and descriptions inside the different services. Choose one service, and click OK. The service URL is selected and insert into the matching field on the previous screen. Click NEXT to continue.

Modeling application pages

The final step of the LIST TEMPLATE is to model the application pages (Figure 9.8). The modeling is quite intuitive. You start with a LIST activity that displays data from a selected collection of the service in a list manner. Choose a few fields to appear on each entry in the list. Then add a new page by clicking the + button on the bottom-left side and choosing the fitting entity set in the navigation dropdown.

Finish application development

Click the FINISH button of the wizard, and a new Android project is generated containing a semantic proxy for the service. Also, the SAP OData Mobile SDK libraries are copied into the project under the *libs* folder. Now you can run the application in an emulator (Figure 9.9) or on a real Android device and check it out. In runtime, you need to enter a user name and a password for login.

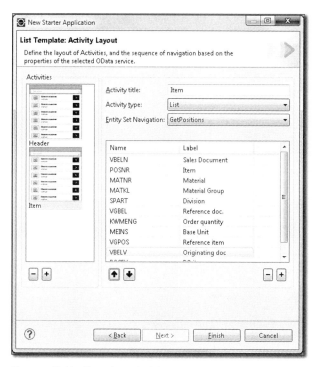

Figure 9.8 List Template: Activity Layout

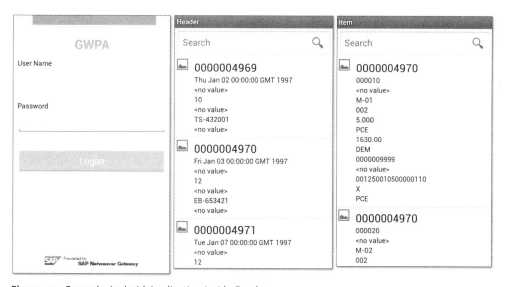

Figure 9.9 Example Android Application inside Emulator

The generated coding of the header call, for example, looks like the code shown in Listing 9.1.

```
    public List<VBAK> getSalesDocHead(String data) throws SDMPa
rserException
    {
        List<VBAK> returnList  = new LinkedList<VBAK>();
        List<ISDMODataEntry> list  = parser.parseSDMODataEntrie
sXML(data, "SalesDocHead", schema);

        for (ISDMODataEntry isdmoDataEntry : list)
        {
            returnList.add(new VBAK(isdmoDataEntry, parser, sch
ema));
        }
        return returnList;
    }
```

Listing 9.1 Method for Retrieving Entity Set

9.2.3   Windows Phone 8

Microsoft Windows 8 is the current version of Microsoft Windows and was developed in 2007. The UI, called Surface, makes a standard concept possible for representation on mobile phones, tablets, and desktop computers.

Microsoft Windows Phone 8, formerly known as Apollo, is the current version of Microsoft's phone operating system. In contrast to Windows Phone 7, it's no longer based on Windows CE but on the Windows NT kernel, which is the same as Windows 8.

Let's now use Windows Phone 8 to develop another simple OData application. We only show the phone development process here because the code, development process, and requirements on the Windows Phone application and Windows 8 application are very similar.

Microsoft OData plugin

SAP doesn't provide an OData plugin for Visual Studio because Microsoft already delivers two different plugins for Windows 8 and Windows Phone, which can be downloaded from the official Microsoft website at *http://msdn.microsoft.com/en-us/jj658961.*

Windows Phone 8: Minimum Requirements

- Microsoft Windows 8
- Microsoft .NET Framework 4.5
- Windows Phone SDK 8.0
- Microsoft Visual Studio 2012 or Microsoft Visual Studio Express 2012
- OData Client Tools for Windows Phone Apps
- NuGet Package Manager v2.1

We'll discuss the following tasks in this section:

- How to create a new Windows Phone application
- How to add an OData service to the project
- How to query the added service and show the results

First, install the Windows Phone SDK and then the OData Client Tools for Windows Phone Applications. These tools add the support to your Windows Phone projects for OData services.

Start the Visual Studio application in your Windows 8 system. Select FILE • NEW • PROJECT. Select WINDOWS PHONE from the INSTALLED TEMPLATES pane (depending on your preferred language) in the ADD NEW PROJECT dialog box, and then select the WINDOWS PHONE APP template. Choose C#.

Start new project

Next, enter a name for the project, and then click OK. Select the Windows Phone 8, which is the target for this application, and click OK again. The new project is created (Figure 9.10).

To add an OData service reference to the project, right-click the project name on the right side, and click ADD SERVICE REFERENCE. Enter the URI of your SAP NetWeaver Gateway OData service, and click GO. This downloads the metadata document from your OData service. Now enter a name in the NAMESPACE text box, and then click OK (Figure 9.11).

Add OData service

The data classes are generated into a new code file, which is added to the created project structure. These data classes are used to access the OData service resources as local objects with `Create`, `Read`, `Update`, and `Delete` (CRUD) functionalities.

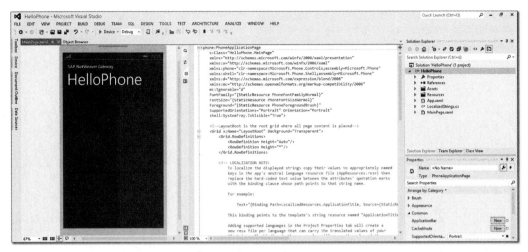

Figure 9.10 Windows 8 Phone Application Project

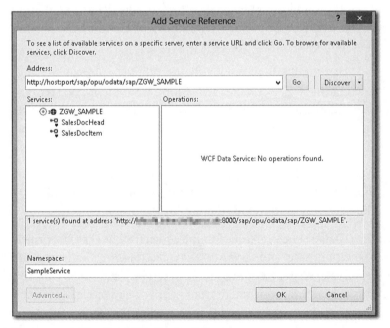

Figure 9.11 Adding the OData Service Reference

User interface To define the Windows Phone application UI, you can edit the *MainPage.xaml* file. Double-click on the file to open the XAML markup for the `MainPage` class that is the UI for the Windows Phone application.

Go to the *MainPage.xaml.cs* file, and add the `using` statements in Listing 9.2 to bind the OData service data to controls in the Windows Phone application.

```
using System.Data.Services.Client;
using HelloPhone.SampleService;
```

Listing 9.2 Used Libraries

Next, add the private declarations in Listing 9.3 to the `MainPage` class.

```
private ZGW_SAMPLE context;
private readonly Uri SampleServiceUri = new
Uri("http://host:port/sap/opu/odata/sap/ZGW_SAMPLE/");
private DataServiceCollection<VBAK> vbak;
```

Listing 9.3 Private Declarations

Add the `MainPage_Loaded` method to the `MainPage` class as shown in Listing 9.4.

```
private void MainPage_Loaded(object sender, RoutedEventArgs e){
    // Initialize
    context = new ZGW_SAMPLE(SampleServiceUri);
    vbak = new DataServiceCollection<VBAK>(context);
    // Define a LINQ for all Sales Document Header
    var query = from vbeln in context.SalesDocHead
                select vbeln;
    // Register LoadCompleted event
    vbak.LoadCompleted += new EventHandler<LoadCompletedEventArg
s>(vbak_LoadCompleted);
    // Load Sales Document Header feed
    // by executing the LINQ query
    vbak.LoadAsync(query);
}
```

Listing 9.4 Windows Phone Projects: MainPage_Loaded Method

When the main page is loaded, this code initializes the binding collection and content, and creates an event handler for the `LoadComplete()` event.

Add the `vbak_LoadCompleted` method in Listing 9.5 to the `MainPage` class.

```
void vbak_
LoadCompleted(object sender, LoadCompletedEventArgs e)
{
    if (e.Error == null)
    {
        // Handling for data feed
        if (vbak.Continuation != null)
        {
            // next page
            vbak.LoadNextPartialSetAsync();
        }
        else
        {
            // Set the data context to the sample data
            this.LayoutRoot.DataContext = vbak;
        }
    }
    else
    {
    MessageBox.Show(string.Format("An error occurred: {0}", e.E
rror.Message));
    }
}
```

Listing 9.5 Windows Phone Projects: LoadCompleted Method

When the `vbak_LoadCompleted()` event is handled, and the request is successfully returned, the `LoadNextPartialSetAsync()` method is called to load the following results pages, while there is a next `vbak` page. When the `Continuation()` property returns no value, the collection of loaded `vbak-objects` is bound to the `DataContext` property of the `Lay-outRoot`.

Now you can run the application in an emulator or on a real Windows Phone device and check it out. In runtime, you need to enter a user name and a password for login.

9.2.4   BlackBerry

All BlackBerry equipment by the Canadian Research in Motion (RIM) company uses its own proprietary binary system. For a long time, the operation was possible through a thumbcaster, but the new equipment uses a touchscreen. RIM's BlackBerry smartphones offer extensive client-server-software and is widely spread within the range of business. Applications for BlackBerry are written in Java; because of this, the development of applications for BlackBerry is nearly identical to Android development, which is also done in Java.

The standalone SAP NetWeaver Gateway for Eclipse plugin for BlackBerry was removed from SCN because it was using RIM's BEAM server, which is no longer supported.

New OData Library for BB10

During the writing of this book, there was an OData library for BlackBerry 10 published. Further information is available on GitHub: *https://github.com/blackberry/OData-BB10.*

Because the SAP plugin for BlackBerry is no longer available, we can't use an existing native development toolkit for BlackBerry. However, we can provide a small native code example to help you get started with the consumption of an OData service in your existing BlackBerry project, as provided in Listing 9.6.

```
public String getCarrierName(String carrname) throws IOExceptio
n
{
// SAP NetWeaver Gateway OData collection
String requestUrl = "https://sapes1.sapdevcenter.com/sap/opu/
odata/IWFND/RMTSAMPLEFLIGHT/
CarrierCollection(carrname='" + carrname + "')";

// HTTP connection
HttpConnection httpConnection = (HttpConnection) Connector.open
(requestUrl);
httpConnection.setRequestProperty("Content-Type","text/xml");
httpConnection.setRequestMethod(HttpConnection.GET);

// Basic authentication header
httpConnection.setRequestProperty("Authorization", "Basic " +
Base64OutputStream.encodeAsString(userpassword.getBytes(), 0,
userpassword.getBytes().length, false, false));
```

```
// Response
intstatus = httpConnection.getResponseCode();

// Exception
if (status != HttpConnection.HTTP_OK)
{
throw new RuntimeException("Error code: " + status);
}

// Read input stream
InputStream inputStream = httpConnection.openInputStream();
httpConnection.close();

// Converting
String resultAsString = new String(IOUtilities.streamToBytes(in
putStream),"UTF-8");

return resultAsString;
}
```

Listing 9.6 BlackBerry Code Snippet

Further Resources

For more information about consuming SAP NetWeaver Gateway services from Blackberry applications, we recommend the following:

http://wiki.sdn.sap.com/wiki/download/attachments/250646828/Blackberry +-+How+to+Guide.pdf?version=1&modificationDate=1323340162991

9.3 Hybrid Mobile Applications

Hybrid applications are a mix of web and native applications with the aim of balancing advantages and disadvantages of both. Hybrid frameworks are usually based on web technologies and enable the development of cross-platform applications that aren't distinguishable from native apps.

Access to native APIs

Hybrid frameworks offer a native container for web applications with several functions for the specific platforms. In this way, it's possible for an application to—for example—access the calendar of the specific platform or make the phone vibrate, which isn't possible within a pure web application. Using these effects, hybrid applications are compiled as "native packages" and can be offered at platform-specific app stores. To lay the groundwork for hybrid technologies, the *web view* is embedded in a native application and renders the user interface of the web application using the native browser engine.

Because the range of web applications is expanding quickly, it's inevitable that there will eventually be the capability for more more functions that are currently reserved for native applications. For this reason, we believe that hybrid applications are a temporary solution that will ultimately be replaced by pure web applications. For example, with the latest update of iOS, Apple expanded the support of new HTML5 functions, and it is now possible for an HTML5 web application to—for example—access a phone's native acceleration sensors.

Hybrid versus web applications

That being said, as it is currently, hybrid applications can be very valuable. A connection from a web application inside a hybrid container to the native API is the key benefit of hybrid applications, because this means that developers can code their own API bridge or take advantage of existing and well-documented solutions, such as Adobe PhoneGap or the SAP-owned Hybrid Web Container (HWC). Next we'll introduce these two most commonly used hybrid application development solutions.

9.3.1   PhoneGap

PhoneGap is a freely available tool to develop applications using JavaScript, HTML5, and CSS3, instead of device-specific languages such as Objective-C. It's not a platform-specific SDK, but rather an interface that enables access to the browser or equipment functions. It results in hybrid applications, which, as we discussed, use a development approach that combines a mix of native development and web development. All layout rendering is done via web views, as opposed to the platform's native UI framework (this is the web part), but they are packaged as applications for distribution and have access to native device APIs (this is the native part).

> **PhoneGap: Minimum Requirements**
> ▶ SDK for HTML development of your choice
> ▶ Web browser for packaging process of Adobe PhoneGap Build

Native interfaces   While waiting on real standardized specifications, you don't have the choice—you need to create some bridges between JavaScript and the native code of the targeted platform to have access to its capabilities. The idea is to take the native languages of each platform (C#, Objective-C, or Java) and create a framework with these languages that will expose interfaces to the JavaScript developer.

HTML, CSS, and   In the early days of PhoneGap, developers had to create every applica-
JavaScript   tion in particular native development environments. This wasted time because the main development part is the UI development in HTML, JavaScript, or CSS, and only the export of the native compiled file is part of the special SDK. Now, however, there is a cloud-based service called PhoneGap Build (Figure 9.12) on top of the PhoneGap framework.

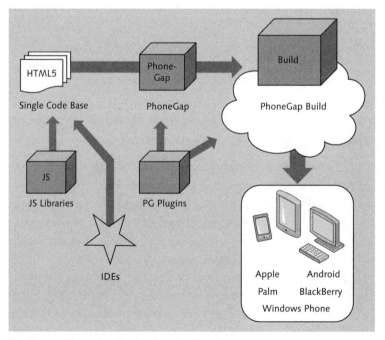

Figure 9.12 PhoneGap Application Creation Process

This service reduces the service development time, providing a wizard to build your own mobile application with the help of SDKs for many different platforms.

For the web OS and Symbian platforms, you'll get back a binary that is ready for submission and distribution. For Android, iOS, and BlackBerry, you'll need to provide the correct certificates and/or signing keys to allow distribution. See additional documentation for more details at *http://html.adobe.com/edge/phonegap-build/faq.html*.

You don't need to install anything for a local conversion because the processing takes place completely in the cloud. Instead, start by opening an account with PhoneGap cloud. To do this, go to the PhoneGap Build website at *https://build.phonegap.com/plans/free*.

Installation process

Simply upload your HTML, CSS, and JavaScript files for your HTML5 web application packed in a ZIP file to the PhoneGap Build cloud service or point to a repository on GitHub. If you don't have an HTML5 application available, you can have a look at Chapter 10 or use the example *HelloWorld.html* file in the downloads available on the book's website at *www.sap-press.com*. PhoneGap Build undertakes the compilation and packaging for you. In minutes, you'll receive the download URLs for all supported mobile platforms (Figure 9.13).

Figure 9.13 PhoneGap Build: Application Builds

In addition to the iOS application, you can—after a successful upload and generation process—install all compiled applications on several platforms.

To install PhoneGap Build applications directly on your device without connection to a PC, you just need to launch your favorite QR code reader, point your device at your application's code, and follow the link. This will even work for iOS. As an alternative, you can also download the application as a file and start it in the locally installed SDK-emulator or transfer it to your device.

To export iOS files, you need to deposit the Apple developer key. When you upload a new application to PhoneGap Build, if you don't have a default certificate-profile pair attached to your account, you'll be alerted that the iOS build can't be completed.

> **Further Resources**
>
> For more information about Adobe PhoneGap, we recommend the following link: *http://docs.phonegap.com/en/3.0.0/index.html*.

9.3.2   Hybrid Web Container

A similar product to PhoneGap is the *Hybrid Web Container* (HWC). HWC is a native application that is installed on the mobile device. The container application includes some of the SAP Mobile Platform local data store and embeds the WebKit runtime from the native operating system's SDK. It also embeds a browser that allows developers to build mobile applications using their web development skills, while maximizing the power of native device services.

The SAP Mobile Platform development tools enable you to use Mobile Business Objects (MBOs) and also OData sources.

> **Further Resources**
>
> You can use MBOs and OData sources in hybrid applications together. Go to the following web page to find more information about MBO-based hybrid applications: *http://infocenter.sybase.com/help/index.jsp?topic=/com.sybase.infocenter.dc01920.0232/doc/html/vhu1281977425220.html*.

Now we show you how to develop an OData-based hybrid application with the Sybase Unwired Platform Mobile SDK. The Sybase Unwired Platform Mobile SDK is the development environment for Sybase Unwired Platform applications and is based on Eclipse and distributed as a complete installer.

Install Mobile SDK

You can download the needed Sybase Unwired Platform Mobile SDK from the SAP Service Marketplace or *http://www.sdn.sap.com/irj/scn/go/ portal/prtroot/docs/webcontent/uuid/f00164c9-bcb7-2f10-d2b3-ac79a6faf 833* and install it on your computer.

> **HWC: Minimum Requirements**
>
> ▶ Windows XP
> ▶ Sybase Unwired Platform Mobile SDK Developer Edition 2.20 SP04

The following features will be installed:

▶ Native Object API

▶ HTML5/JS Hybrid Application API

▶ OData SDK

▶ Mobile Analytics Kit

The basic steps for developing an OData-based hybrid application are the following:

Create hybrid application

▶ Use the packaging tool to generate the *manifest.xml* file and hybrid application ZIP package.

▶ Use the DEPLOY WIZARD in the SAP Control Center to deploy the hybrid application ZIP file.

After the installation process is finished, navigate to the *\HybridApp\PackagingTool* folder inside the Mobile SDK, and double-click the *packagingtool.bat* file to start the packaging tool. First, you have to choose an OUTPUT DIRECTORY, where the output of the tool will be generated. After you've entered a path, click OK. The HYBRID APP PACKAGING TOOL window opens (Figure 9.14).

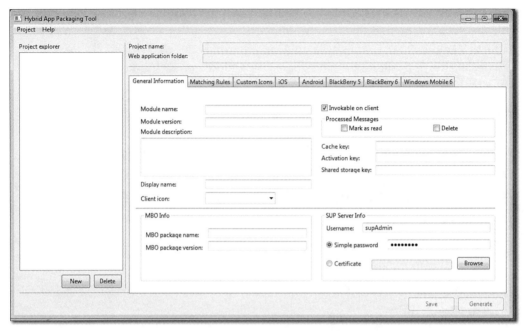

Figure 9.14 Hybrid App Packaging Tool

Click NEW to create a new project. Enter a PROJECT NAME, and choose the WEB APPLICATION folder, where you've stored your already developed web application (Figure 9.15). Click OK.

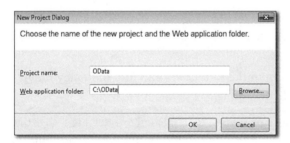

Figure 9.15 Creating a New Project

If you don't have a web application yet, you can create a small sample application in only a few minutes. Create a folder and create a new file inside the folder. Name the file *index.html,* and edit the file with the Notepad editor. Paste in the code shown in Listing 9.7.

```
<html>
<head>
<script src="datajs-1.1.1.min.js"></script>
<script>
function successCallback(data, response) {
    document.writeln("<table><tr><th>CARRID</th><th>CONNID</
th><th>PRICE</th><th>CURRENCY</th></tr>");
    for (var i = 0; i < data.results.length; i++) {
        document.writeln("<tr><td>" + data.results[i].carrid +
"</td><td>" + data.results[i].connid+ "</
td><td>" + data.results[i].PRICE+ "</
td><td>" + data.results[i].CURRENCY+ "</td></tr>");
    }
    document.writeln("</table>");
}
function errorCallback(e) {
    alert("An error occurred");
    alert(e);
}
</script>
</head>
<body>
<script>
    OData.read("https://sapes1.sapdevcenter.com/sap/opu/odata/
IWFND/RMTSAMPLEFLIGHT/
FlightCollection", successCallback, errorCallback);
</script>
</body>
</html>
```

Listing 9.7 Datajs and OData Service

You need access to the SAP NetWeaver Gateway sample services as described in Chapter 8, Section 8.3. Once you have this, download the actual version of the *datajs* JavaScript file from *http://datajs.code plex.com/*, place it in the same folder as the *index.html* file, and, if necessary, adjust the script line with the downloaded version using the code shown in Listing 9.8.

```
<script src="datajs-1.1.1.min.js"></script>
```

Listing 9.8 Datajs Including

445

The datajs JavaScript library provides a Read method to fetch the data from the OData service and return it as JavaScript objects.

Cross-Site HTTP Requests

You won't be able to test the created application inside your browser by default because of cross-site HTTP requests. Modern browsers won't allow connection to any server that isn't the initial server that hosted the page. In our case, the page is being hosted from our local file system and is attempting to connect to the external OData service.

As a workaround for our development, Google Chrome can be started with a flag: --disable-web-security. Right-click the desktop icon of Google Chrome, select PROPERTIES, and add the flag to the target, separated by a space, to the *chrome.exe*.

After you've created a new project inside the package tool, you have to specify the platform(s). Select the tab strip and click on the SUPPORT PLATFORM checkbox. Also enter the START-UP HTML FILE as "index.html". You can select multiple platforms to be supported (Figure 9.16).

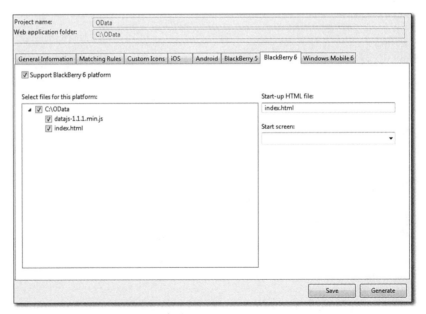

Figure 9.16 Selecting Supported Platforms

Click the GENERATE button when you're finished. The package tool packs all needed files into a ZIP file and stores this file inside the selected OUT-PUT DIRECTORY from the first step (Figure 9.17).

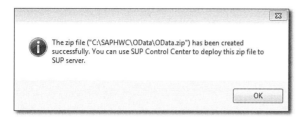

Figure 9.17 Successful HWC Package Creation

The typical content of a hybrid application package is listed in Table 9.2.

Files	Task
Web application files (HTML, JavaScript, and CSS)	HTML5, JavaScript, and CSS. Provides UI and business logic.
Manifest (XML)	Describes the content of the ZIP file.
Workflow client (XML)	Provides metadata information for MBO operations and object queries.
Look and feel (XML)	Uses a reference inside a `<File>`...`</File>` tag to specific device platforms.

Table 9.2 Hybrid Application Package Content

Finally, you can deploy the generated ZIP file and assign it to any device using the SAP Control Center.

Further Resources

For more information about developing OData-based applications with the HWC, we recommend *http://infocenter.sybase.com/help/index.jsp?topic=/ com.sybase.infocenter.dc01920.0230/doc/html/vhu1343081102033.html.* For more information about SAP Mobile Platform development in general, we recommend the book *Mobile Development for SAP* (2013, SAP PRESS).

9.4 Summary

In this chapter, you've learned the difference between native and hybrid applications and the corresponding development of these kinds of applications. In this context, we developed different sample applications for well-known operating systems such as Apple iOS, Google Android, Windows Phone, and BlackBerry. We used the existing plugins for the native SDKs, the SAP NetWeaver Gateway Productivity Accelerator, and some code examples to give a brief introduction to the development of native mobile applications. Finally, we explained two of the important hybrid application development tools: Adobe PhoneGap and Hybrid Web Container. You've learned how to generate the wrapper for web applications with access to the native API.

If you need further information, you can find more details on SCN or on the different manufacturer developer websites. It remains to be seen how customer demand will develop in the future, and which technology will take the lead in the race of mobile application development. Today, it's not possible to give a final recommendation as to which technology should be used.

Develop once and use it on different platforms—this dream can come true with the development of HTML5 applications. We show you the easy development of a new HTML5 application with SAPUI5 and give you a short introduction to SAP Fiori.

10 SAPUI5 Application Development

There are three important building blocks for web application development: HTML, CSS, and JS. HTML defines the structure and layout of a web document and is the main language of nearly all web content. The visual formatting of that content is normally done with the declarative language for style sheets, Cascading Style Sheets (CSS). Finally, JavaScript (JS) is a scripting language for validating user input or communication with web servers; it expands the capabilities of HTML and CSS.

The latest release of HTML, HTML5, has new features such as the ability to play video or audio within web pages, and, in combination with CSS or JS, animation and interactivity. HTML5 is not only for mobile applications—it can also be used as a normal website for desktop computers or laptops. Although HTML5 is platform-independent, it's not browser independent—it is not yet an official standard, and no browsers have full HTML5 support today. However, all major browsers, including Internet Explorer, Firefox, Chrome, Safari, and Opera, continue to add new HTML5 features to their latest releases. Before you start with the development of your new HTML5 application, you have to think about who will benefit from this and which browsers are available for these specific use cases. You can use the *http://html5test.com/* website to test your browser to see which HTML5-specifications are supported.

HTML5 Browser Recommendation	Browser

We currently recommend the Google Chrome browser for HTML5 development because, as of today, it supports more HTML5 features than Internet Explorer or Mozilla Firefox. At the end of 2012, the World Wide Web Consor-

449

tium (W3C) said they would provide a stable HTML5 browser recommendation by the end of 2014.

Web applications The new features in HTML5 also include mobile device support. Due to its advanced features in this respect, the phrase "HTML5 applications" has become a synonym for *web applications*. In this chapter, we're talking about the creation of web applications. Usually, these are always-online applications that have direct access to your server, where the data is stored.

We'll start the chapter by introducing you to SAP Fiori and SAPUI5 (Section 10.1). *SAP Fiori* is an example of a group of HTML5 applications provided by SAP. They were created with the *SAP User Interface Development Toolkit for HTML5* (SAPUI5).

SAP Fiori/SAPUI5

The SAPUI5 JavaScript library is growing very fast. Because all SAP Fiori applications and all how-to guides in this chapter are based on SAPUI5, remember to use these tutorials as a first step into the SAPUI5 world. If you are going to plan a production application, look at the official SAP web pages (or references in this chapter), to see whether there is a newer version or a newer how-to guide available.

After introducing you to the basics of SAPUI5 and how HTML5, Java-Script, and CSS fit together, we'll walk you through the steps in SAPUI5 development. In Section 10.2, we'll show you the three different options you have to create a new application. In Section 10.3, we'll show you the Eclipse-integrated deployment option. Finally, in Section 10.4, we'll show you two examples of enhancing SAPUI5 applications.

OpenUI5

SAPUI5 is now nearly completely open source, and often referred to as *OpenUI5* (though we will continue to use the term "SAPUI5" in this chapter). OpenUI5 is the free version of SAPUI5, which is available under the Apache 2.0 Open Source license. One important reason to open the main functions of SAPUI5 was the growing HTML5 developer community and the corresponding development process of SAPUI5 itself. While the UI development process is totally decoupled from the backend system, it was an important step to open the UI side to the community. (However, not everything is opened. There are still some control libraries that are only available in the SAPUI5 version.)

For more information, we recommend the following sources:

▶ *http://sap.github.io/openui5/index.html*

▶ *https://openui5.hana.ondemand.com/#content/Overview.html*

10.1   Introduction to SAP Fiori and SAPUI5

The best example of SAPUI5 currently in use is a series of applications known as SAP Fiori. In this section, we'll start by briefly introducing you to these applications and their SAPUI5 architecture. Then we'll move on to a more general discussion of SAPUI5, including an explanation of how to install the SAPUI5 development toolkit.

10.1.1   SAP Fiori

SAP Fiori was developed in close cooperation with more than 250 customers. Along with them, the most-used software functions in everyday business challenges were identified. SAP Fiori is intended to increase employee productivity, reduce work completion time, and increase the adoption of business processes. Applications from SAP Fiori can be used with any browser that supports HTML5—desktop as well as mobile devices.

SAP Fiori applications provide a simple UI and intuitive user experience. The consistent and responsive design automatically adapts to the UI of the calling device and adjusts the layout to fit to the screen size.

The slogan *"keeping simple things simple"* rings true with SAP Fiori. SAP Fiori can be implemented either as a collection of applications on a single platform or as multiple web applications. At the time of this writing SAP Fiori applications have been released in two waves. In Wave 2, the

Keeping simple things simple

Launch Pad was enhanced with more personalization (i.e., search and favorites functionality). You're able to start all existing applications via the Launch Pad that is optimized for the device in use (Figure 10.1).

Figure 10.1 SAP Fiori Launch Pad

First and second wave The first release of SAP applications for SAP Fiori included 25 applications for common functions such as workflow approvals, information lookups, and self-service tasks. These applications address four user roles: managers, employees, sales representatives, and purchasing agents (see Table 10.1). The second wave is officially called *SAP Fiori for SAP Business Suite 7 Innovations 2013* and extends the total number of available SAP Fiori applications to 206.

Role	Applications
Manager	▶ Approve Requests
	▶ Approve Leave Requests
	▶ Approve Timesheets
	▶ Approve Travel Requests
	▶ Approve Travel Expenses
	▶ Approve Shopping Carts
	▶ Approve Purchase Orders
	▶ Approve Requisitions
	▶ Approve Purchase Contracts
	▶ My Spend

Table 10.1 SAP Fiori: First 25 Applications

Role	Applications
Employee	▶ My Leave Requests
	▶ My Timesheet
	▶ My Travel Requests
	▶ My Paystubs
	▶ My Benefits
	▶ My Shopping Cart
	▶ Track Shopping Cart
Sales Representative	▶ Check Price and Availability
	▶ Create Sales Orders
	▶ Track Sales Orders
	▶ Change Sales Orders
	▶ Track Shipments
	▶ Customer Invoices
Purchasing Agent	▶ Track Purchase Orders
	▶ Order from Requisitions

Table 10.1 SAP Fiori: First 25 Applications (Cont.)

Note

You can find the complete catalog of SAP Fiori apps on the following website:

http://help.sap.com/fiori_bs2013/helpdata/en/99/e464520e2a725fe100000 00a441470/content.htm?frameset=/en/29/9a5652d8c3725fe10000000a441 470/frameset.htm

As mentioned before, the look and feel of SAP Fiori applications are optimized and changed dynamically for the different screen sizes of each device. While the desktop and tablet views offer all information in one screen, the smartphone view is optimized for smaller screens, and has a totally different, but intuitive, way of navigation. It will remind you of your own native smartphone applications.

Look and feel

The general architecture for SAP Fiori is really simple and relies on the following components (Figure 10.2):

Architecture

453

- SAPUI5 for SAP NetWeaver add-on
- SAP NetWeaver Gateway (OData service connection)
- SAP Business Suite (content and business logic)

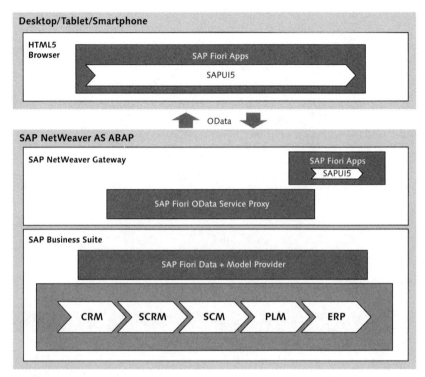

Figure 10.2 SAP Fiori Architecture

From a technical point of view, each SAP Fiori application consists of a data-providing component and a UI component. The SAP Fiori UI component is a normal SAPUI5 application built by SAP, and the data-providing component contains the business logic and the SAP NetWeaver OData service. The SAP Fiori UI component is normally installed on the same system as the SAP NetWeaver Gateway components to avoid the same origin policy issues. Using a shared reverse proxy, you can also install the SAP Fiori UI component on any other SAP NetWeaver ABAP AS with an installed SAPUI5 for SAP NetWeaver add-on.

Further Resources

For more details about architecting an SAP Fiori deployment, we recommend the following: *http://scn.sap.com/community/developer-center/front-end/blog/2013/05/16/architecting-an-sap-fiori-deployment*.

Enhancing the functionality of any SAP Fiori application can be done by changing the SAP Business Suite, SAP NetWeaver Gateway, and/or SAPUI5 layers. You don't have to enhance all of the layers each time, so we want to give you a short overview of the criteria for determining which layer has to be enhanced (see Table 10.2).

Enhancing SAP Fiori applications

Application Layer	Enhancement
SAP Business Suite	Required content/business logic doesn't exist on the backend side.
SAP NetWeaver Gateway	Required content/business logic exists on the backend side but isn't exposed as an OData service by SAP NetWeaver Gateway.
SAPUI5	Required content/business logic exists on the backend side and is exposed as an OData service by SAP NetWeaver Gateway but isn't consumed by the frontend SAPUI5 application.

Table 10.2 Application Layers for SAP Fiori

A future option to enhance the SAPUI5 layer is the SAP App Designer, which is currently available in a trial version on the SAP HANA Cloud Platform. You can get access to the SAP App Designer by creating a free SAP HANA Cloud Platform developer account on the *https://account.hanatrial.ondemand.com/* website.

SAP App Designer

After the registration process is finished, you can start the SAP App Designer trial from *https://appdesigner.hanatrial.ondemand.com/* and

455

open the only available MY LEAVE REQUESTS demo application by clicking the OPEN button in the right corner (Figure 10.3).

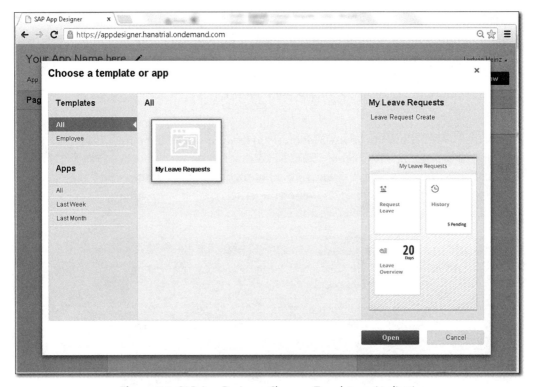

Figure 10.3 SAP App Designer: Choose a Template or Application

The selected application layout and pages open quickly (Figure 10.4),
and you're able to change the layout by adding or removing UI elements.

Because only the trial version with limited functionality is available
today, we'll focus on the enhancement of the UI layer of an existing SAP
Fiori application in Section 10.4.2 with Eclipse support. If also you want
to enhance your OData service from SAP NetWeaver Gateway (second
layer), refer to our discussion of service development in Chapter 6.

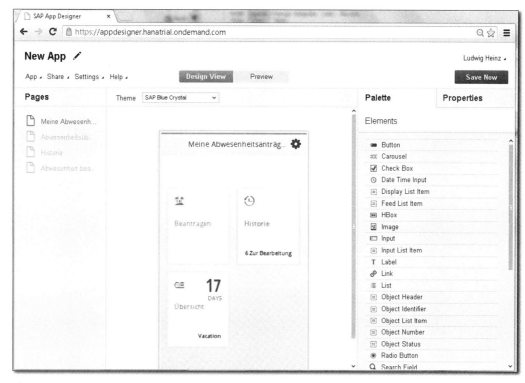

Figure 10.4 SAP App Designer: Change Mode

10.1.2 SAPUI5

SAPUI5 supports application developers in creating easy-to-use UI applications based on HTML5 and JavaScript. The SAPUI5 runtime is a client-side HTML5 rendering library with a set of UI controls for building both desktop and mobile applications. SAPUI5 is an Eclipse-based plugin and provides a lightweight programming model, is based on JavaScript, and can be used together with any other JavaScript library. The UI design is managed with *Cascading Style Sheets Level 3* (CSS3), which allows you to adopt themes to your own branding in a very effective way. SAP uses the *jQuery* library as a foundation and to add all additionally needed elements to the already proven open source library.

> **Further Resources**
>
> For more information how to get started with SAPUI5 development, we recommend:
>
> *https://sapui5.netweaver.ondemand.com/devguide.html*

Model-View-
Controller

SAPUI5 development is based on the *Model-View-Controller* (MVC) concept (Figure 10.5). MVC is a pattern for structuring software development in the three independent units:

▸ **Model**
Application data, business rules, functions, logic.

▸ **View**
Rendering, UI, layout.

▸ **Controller**
Application behavior, user actions/input, converting.

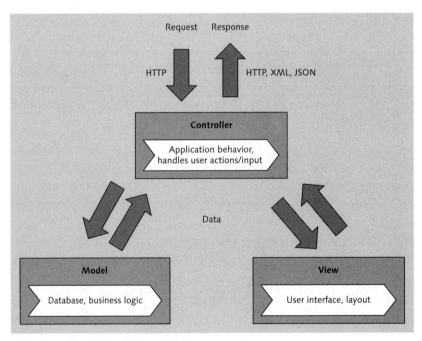

Figure 10.5 Model-View-Controller Concept

According to the MVC paradigm, the coding relevant for the view (UI) is distinguished from the coding for the controller. This makes it easier to connect to non-SAP backends.

SAPUI5 Eclipse Plugin: Minimum Requirements	Requirements

> ► Eclipse Juno (version 4.2 or higher); for Kepler (version 4.3), the ABAP Repository Team Provider isn't yet available
>
> ► Windows OS (XP, Vista, or 7) 32- or 64-bit
>
> ► JRE version 1.6 or higher, 32-bit or 64-bit
>
> ► For deployment with SAPUI5 ABAP Repository Team Provider SAPGUI for Windows 7.20, patch level 9 or higher Microsoft VC Runtime DLLs VS2010

The SAPUI5 development toolkit is a set of Eclipse-based tools, editors, and wizards that helps you create new projects and supports the development process with code snippets and code completion. A good point to start is on the Demo Kit web page at *https://sapui5.netweaver.ondemand.com/sdk/* (Figure 10.6).

Figure 10.6 SAPUI5: Demo Kit

The first step in the SAPUI5 application development process is, of course, to create an application. We discuss the following three options for this in Section 10.2:

▶ Without the help of any SDK, that is, manual creation (Section 10.2.1)

▶ With SAPUI5 (Section 10.2.2)

▶ With support of the SAP NetWeaver Gateway Productivity Accelerator (GWPA) (Section 10.2.3)

Any web application that has been developed by using the SAPUI5 framework can run on the following platforms:

▶ SAP NetWeaver ABAP Server

▶ SAP NetWeaver Java Server

▶ SAP HANA Cloud Platform

▶ Open Source Java Application Server

▶ Static Open Source Web Server

Choosing one of the SAP platforms, there are two options for the deployment process, depending on the release version of SAP NetWeaver:

▶ **SAP NetWeaver 7.03/7.31**
Eclipse-integrated deployment process with the ABAP Repository Team Provider plugin.

▶ **SAP NetWeaver 7.00, 7.01, 7.02, and 7.03/7.31 < SPS04**
Manual deployment process with report /UI5/UI5_REPOSITORY_ LOAD.

Before we get any further, it's time to download and install the development toolkit for SAPUI5. The installation steps are very easy and similar to the installation process of the GWPA (refer to Chapter 8, Section 8.2). The steps are as follows:

Eclipse Juno 1. Start Eclipse. (Juno is recommended because Kepler has some limitations. However, if you want to use Kepler, replace *juno* with *kepler* at the end of the URL given in step 3.)

2. From the Eclipse main menu, choose HELP • INSTALL NEW SOFTWARE.

3. In the WORK WITH field, enter the update site URL where the features are available for installation: *https://tools.hana.ondemand.com/juno*.

OData and SAPUI5

If you want to consume any OData service and generate a starter application with OData, make sure you also install the GWPA toolkit for HTML5 as described in Section 8.2 of Chapter 8. This will support your SAPUI5 development with the needed OData consumption.

The update site lists the features available for SAPUI5 together with their name and version (Figure 10.7).

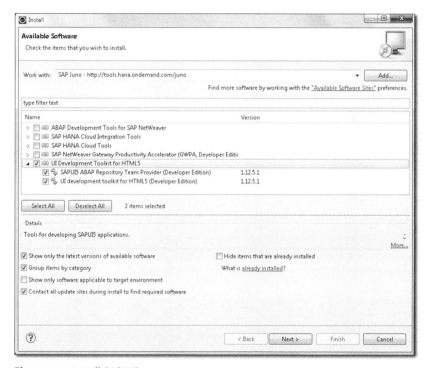

Figure 10.7 Install SAPUI5

4. Select the UI DEVELOPMENT TOOLKIT FOR HTML5 checkbox, and all child elements are selected automatically. The SAPUI5 ABAP REPOSITORY TEAM PROVIDER (DEVELOPER EDITION) checkbox is important for the integrated deployment process to the ABAP Repository.

5. Click NEXT. Eclipse downloads the needed plugins, and you'll see an overview of the selected items to be installed.

461

6. Click Next again, and read and accept the terms of the license agreement by choosing the radio button and clicking on Finish.

7. The installation process starts, and you have to confirm a security warning because of unsigned software by clicking the OK button twice. On completion, Eclipse prompts you to restart. Restart Eclipse.

Now you're able to use the plugin to create or enhance your SAPUI5 applications.

10.2 Creating an SAPUI5 Application

Now that you have a general idea of how SAPUI5 application development works and have seen an example of it in SAP Fiori, let's dive into the technical details a bit more. In this section, we'll walk through the three options for creating SAPUI5 applications.

10.2.1 Manually

Hello World example

The first option is the *Hello World* example provided by SAP, which takes only a few minutes. You can use any computer to create this sample application and use nearly every browser to test the created application. The important thing is to know where you can refer to SAPUI5 on one server.

> **SAPUI5 JavaScript File**
>
> The SAPUI5 JavaScript file in the script tag *https://sapui5.netweaver.ondemand.com/resources/sap-ui-core.js* is prefilled at least as far as possible at the time of writing this document. Try to call this URL in your browser first. If it doesn't work, you need to find another SAPUI5 installation, or you can deploy SAPUI5 directly on one of your own servers.
>
> You can find this JavaScript file at *https://sapui5.hana.ondemand.com/sdk/docs/guide/HelloWorld.html*.

To create your first SAPUI5 application on your Windows computer, create a new "text document" (i.e., right-click on your desktop, and select NEW • TEXT DOCUMENT) and name the file, for example, "HelloWorld.html". The important part is the file extension *html*, which you have to use. Therefore, accept the change warning of the change from *txt* to *html,* and open the newly created file with the Windows Notepad editor (don't use Microsoft Word).

Type the HTML code shown in Listing 10.1 into the editor, and save the file when you're finished:

```
<html>
<head>
    <meta http-equiv="X-UA-Compatible" content="IE=edge" />
    <meta http-equiv="Content-Type" content="text/html;char-
set=UTF-8"/>
    <title>SAPUI5</title>

    <script id="sap-ui-bootstrap"
        src="https://sapui5.netweaver.ondemand.com/resources/
sap-ui-core.js"
        data-sap-ui-theme="sap_goldreflection"
        data-sap-ui-libs="sap.ui.commons"></script>

    <script>
        $(function(){
            $("#uiArea").sapui("Button", "btn", {
                text:"Hello World!",
                press:function(){$("#btn").fadeOut();}
            });
        });
    </script>

</head>
<body class="sapUiBody">
    <div id="uiArea"></div>
</body>
</html>
```

Listing 10.1 SAP HelloWorld Sample Application

That's it! To test your first SAPUI5 application, open the completed HTML file in your preferred browser. You'll see the implemented

463

button with the given label inside your created SAPUI5 application (Figure 10.8).

Figure 10.8 SAPUI5: Hello World Application Button

Hello World
Now you can click SAPUI5: HELLO WORLD, and it will fade out (Figure 10.9).

Figure 10.9 SAPUI5: Hello World Application after Clicking the Button

This manual procedure is optimized by SAPUI5 for Eclipse, which we discuss next.

10.2.2 With SAPUI5

You can now go ahead and start Eclipse. To create a new SAPUI5 project, start by opening the NEW APPLICATION PROJECT wizard and selecting APPLICATION PROJECT under the SAPUI5 APPLICATION DEVELOPMENT node.

Click NEXT, and enter your PROJECT NAME (Figure 10.10).

Create new view
Keep the CREATE AN INITIAL VIEW checkbox selected to create a new view (you're also able to create additional views later on). In addition, you can choose your target device: DESKTOP or MOBILE (in this scenario, keep DESKTOP selected). Click NEXT again.

To create a new view (Figure 10.11), you have to specify the view-related data, such as the FOLDER (keep the default), the view NAME of your choice, and the DEVELOPMENT PARADIGM (keep JAVASCRIPT selected).

Figure 10.10 Creating an Application Project for SAPUI5

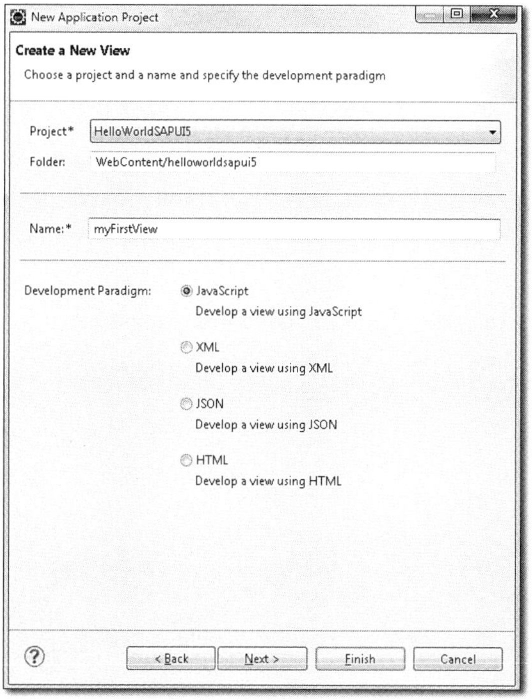

Figure 10.11 Creating a New View

Click NEXT to see the confirmation page with a summary of the selected data on the previous pages. Check the information, and click FINISH if everything is correct. The wizard creates a new SAPUI5 project and opens the file *index.html*, the controller (*myFirstView.controller.js*), and the view (*myFirstView.view.js*) JavaScript files in the preview view (Figure 10.12).

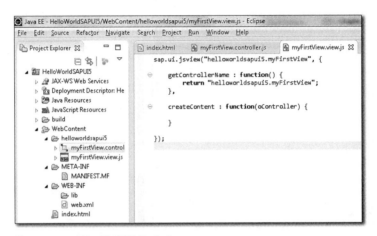

Figure 10.12 New SAPUI5 Project

Add buttons

We've already shown how to create a new SAPUI5 application with one button implemented. To add a similar function inside the created Eclipse project, follow these steps:

1. To add a new button to your SAPUI5 application, open the JavaScript view file (*myFirstView.view.js*), and add the code in Listing 10.2 to the existing `createContent` function.

```
createContent : function(oController) {
var aControls = [];
var oButton   = new sap.ui.commons.Button({
id    : this.createId("MyFirstButton"),
text : "HelloWorld"
});
aControls.push(oButton.attachPress(oController.display-
Text));
return aControls;
}
```

Listing 10.2 View Function

2. Handle the event `displayText`.

3. Open your JavaScript controller file (*myFirstView.controller.js*), and add the code in Listing 10.3.

```
displayText : function(oEvent) {
    alert(oEvent.getSource().getId() + "works!");
}
```

Listing 10.3 Controller Function

Note

The shown coding works for JavaScript only. If you've selected a different development paradigm, visit the SAP help site to get the right source code:

https://help.sap.com/saphelp_nw74/helpdata/en/07/d2bdc3ad0e4c62b1412 3e6f80dca56/content.htm

You can test your new SAPUI5 application in an embedded Jetty server by right-clicking on the project node and choosing RUN AS • WEB APP PREVIEW (Figure 10.13).

Web app preview feature

Figure 10.13 Test SAPUI5 Application in Web App Preview

Everything is configured automatically, and a new tab opens next to the existing ones inside Eclipse. You can also open the URL inside a browser of your choice (Figure 10.14).

Figure 10.14 Web App Preview with the SAPUI5 Button

To check that the method is working, click the created HELLOWORLD button. An alert pop-up appears with the internal button ID and the defined text message (Figure 10.15).

Figure 10.15 Alert Message Inside SAPUI5

If you change anything inside your SAPUI5 project, you have to refresh the application preview with the REFRESH button (the icon with two arrows on the left-hand side of the location bar). You can also test the application in your external default browser by choosing the OPEN IN EXTERNAL BROWSER button (the globe icon on the right-hand side of the location bar).

Further Resources

For more information about how to develop your first application using SAPUI5, we recommend:

https://help.sap.com/saphelp_nw74/helpdata/en/51/0d6eeed849447fbf497c fa5b640514/content.htm

10.2.3 With SAP Gateway Productivity Accelerator and OData Connection

The two SAPUI5 applications created previously work without any connection to your SAP system or any other system. In the following pages, we show you how to create your first SAPUI5 application with a connection to an OData service provided by SAP NetWeaver Gateway.

Start Eclipse, and install the ODATA MODELER AND TOOLS CORE FOR SAP
(GWPA) and the TOOLKIT FOR HTML5 (GWPA), as described in Section
8.2, Chapter 8. After the installation process is done, you can use the
plugin to create an SAPUI5 application. Start by opening the NEW
PROJECT wizard and select STARTER APPLICATION PROJECT under the
ODATA DEVELOPMENT node (refer back to Figure 8.5 in Chapter 8). Click
NEXT, choose your PROJECT NAME, and select HTML5 from the drop-
down of available target platforms (Figure 10.16).

Figure 10.16 Create New Starter Application Project for HTML5

Click NEXT again. Now you have to choose the template on which you
want to base your starter application (Figure 10.17). Choose LIST/
DETAILS APPLICATION (SAPUI5), and click NEXT.

Choose templates

Now you have to choose your OData service location. Enter the URL of
your preferred service, and click GO to retrieve all available service collections (Figure 10.18).

SAPUI5 application

469

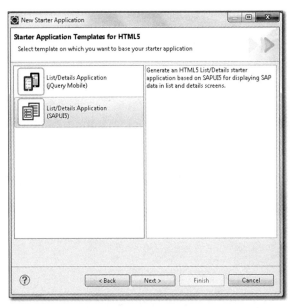

Figure 10.17 Starter Application Templates for HTML5

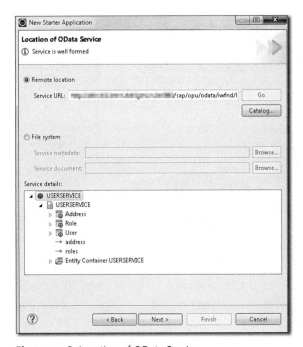

Figure 10.18 Location of OData Service

Click NEXT to navigate to the last window of the NEW STARTER APPLICA-
TION wizard. You're now able to enter a view title and select an entity set
navigation from the available service collections in the dropdown menu
(Figure 10.19). To add additional fields to a view, click the + button in
the bottom-right corner. You can select and add any existing properties
to the view. With the help of the arrows, you can change the order of
the attributes in the table.

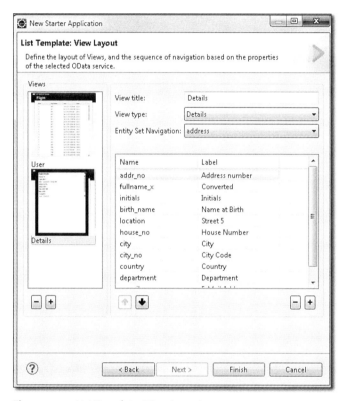

Figure 10.19 List Template: View Layout

You can also add another view with, for example, the DETAILS view, by
clicking the + button in the bottom-left corner. You have to do the same
configuration steps as in the main view. The VIEWS frame always gives
you a short preview of the added views that are created.

Add another view

After you're finished, click FINISH to start the view generation. The wizard creates all necessary files and folders for a complete SAPUI5 project (Figure 10.20).

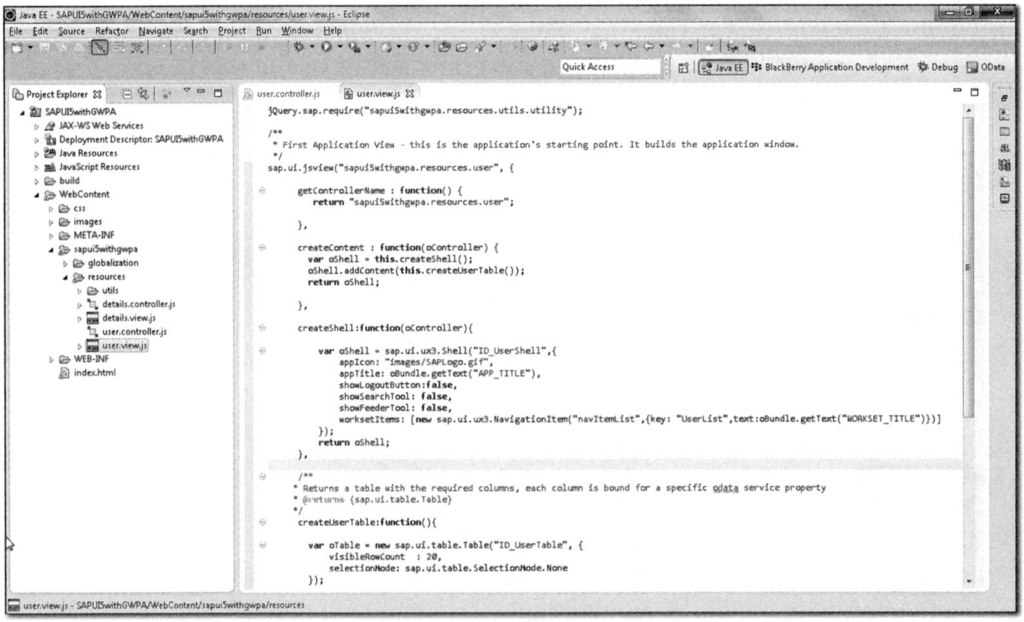

Figure 10.20 SAPUI5 Project with OData Connection

10.3 Deploying an SAPUI5 Application to SAP NetWeaver AS

Now that you've created an SAPUI5 application, you can deploy it on the SAP NetWeaver Gateway system.

Developer

You need a developer key/license to deploy your project.

You can deploy the application created in Section 10.2.3 by right-clicking on the project node and choosing TEAM • SHARE PROJECT (Figure 10.21).

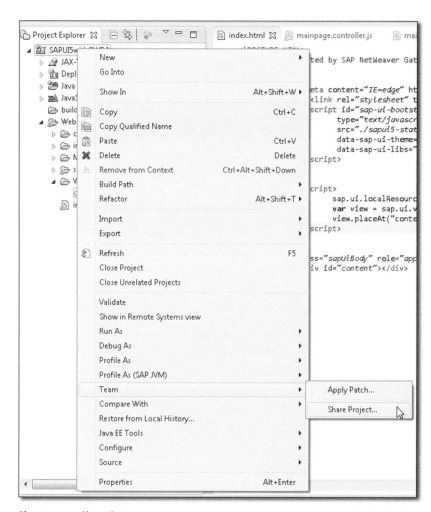

Figure 10.21 Share Project

Choose SAPUI5 ABAP REPOSITORY in the following window, and click NEXT. Search the system connection inside your *Saplogon.ini* file by clicking on the BROWSE button. Make sure the needed system is inside the *saplogon* file, because you can't select the target system (Figure 10.22). In addition, add the system properties to the SAPGUI launch pad, and then select the new entry with the help of the wizard.

SAPUI5 ABAP
Repository

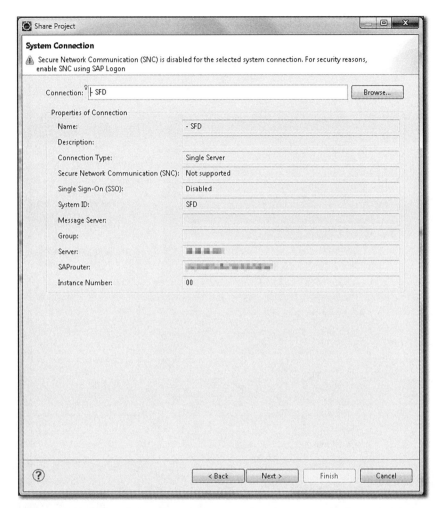

Figure 10.22 System Connection

Click NEXT, and enter your logon credentials, including the CLIENT and LANGUAGE, in the following window. Click NEXT again and then select or create a Business Server Pages (BSP) application, where your SAPUI5 project files will be stored. (The only reason for this is to create a better structure on the server side; that is, the SAPUI5 application isn't transformed into a real BSP application.) Enter a NAME (starting with customer namespace "Z" or "Y") and a DESCRIPTION, and then choose a PACKAGE (Figure 10.23).

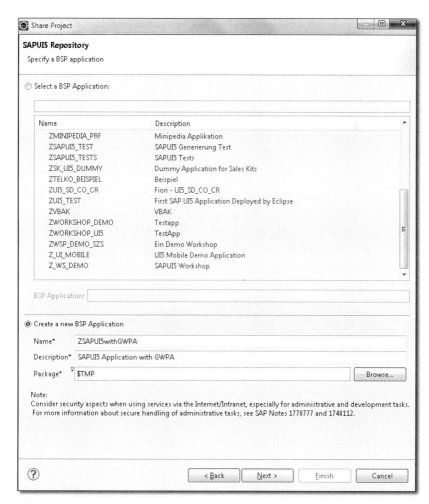

Figure 10.23 SAPUI5 Repository

To create a first demo scenario, choose $TMP as the PACKAGE, and click NEXT. Because of this, you don't have to create or select a transport request in the next window and can click NEXT again.

The connection between the Eclipse server and your selected server is established. After this process has finished, you'll see the server details such as system ID, client, and user next to the project title (Figure 10.24).

Established connection

475

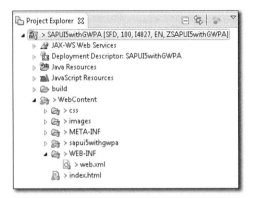

Figure 10.24 SAPUI5 Project with Connection to an ABAP Server

Submit files
The next step is to submit all of the project files to the created BSP repository. Right-click on your project, and choose TEAM • SUBMIT (Figure 10.25).

Figure 10.25 Submit SAPUI5 Project Files

Inside the upcoming window, all files are selected, so you can click FINISH to start uploading the files. Submitting changes from your local Eclipse to the SAP NetWeaver AS takes up to one minute.

Run application
After everything is submitted to the server, you can run your SAPUI5 application directly on the server by right-clicking your project and choosing RUN AS • RUN ON ABAP SERVER (Figure 10.26).

The SAPUI5 application runs on the SAP NetWeaver AS and fetches the content with the implemented OData service (Figure 10.27).

> **Further Resources**
>
> You can find further information about how to synchronize your SAPUI5 repository on the SAPUI5 web page at *https://sapui5.hana.ondemand.com/sdk/#docs/guide/UI5BSPRepository.html*.

Figure 10.26 Run on ABAP Server

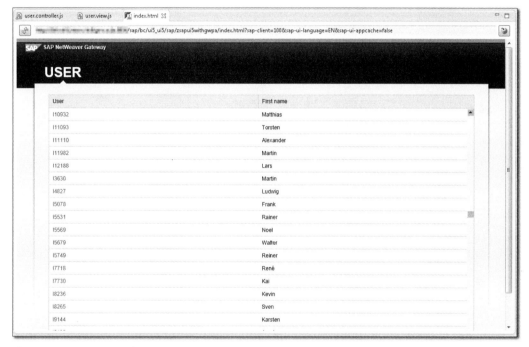

Figure 10.27 SAPUI5 Application

10.4 Enhancing an SAPUI5 Application

Finally, let's look at two examples of enhancing SAPUI5 applications.

10.4.1 Using SAPUI5 Code Snippets

SAPUI5 provides some code snippets to enhance your application with predefined coding. These are examples and templates showing how to use the runtime and controls. You have to install SAPUI5 (refer to Section 10.2.2) to use these snippets. The snippets are available as prepared HTML5 pages with no separation in the MVC files.

Start Eclipse   Working with the code snippets is very easy. First you have to start Eclipse and navigate to WINDOW • SHOW VIEW • OTHER. The SHOW VIEW window appears, and you can easily enter "snippets" in the search bar field, or you can navigate to the SNIPPETS element inside the GENERAL node manually (Figure 10.28).

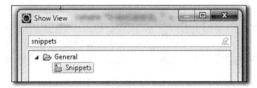

Figure 10.28 Show Snippets View

Select the SNIPPETS element, and click OK. The snippets view opens on the bottom of Eclipse (Figure 10.29).

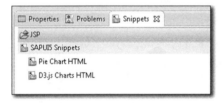

Figure 10.29 Snippets View

Sometimes, you can't see the SNIPPETS view, so you have to open another Eclipse perspective. You can insert some coding from the snippets to your created project; alternatively, you can create a new project. Open your project in the PROJECT EXPLORER, and navigate to the *index.html* file inside the WEBCONTENT folder. Double-click the file to open it, and delete all of the content inside.

Insert snippets   You can insert the new code from the snippet by double-clicking the snippet or using drag and drop to move the selected element into the empty area of the editor of the open *index.html* file (Figure 10.30).

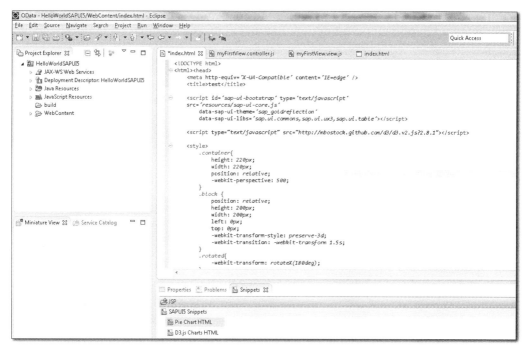

Figure 10.30 SAPUI5 Code Snippets

Save your project, right-click the project node, and choose RUN AS • WEB
APP PREVIEW (Figure 10.31) to test your changed application.

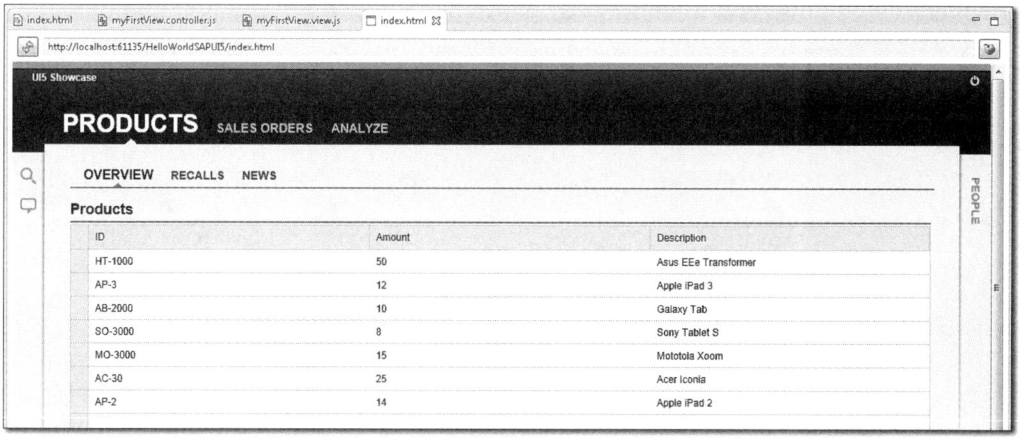

Figure 10.31 Web App Preview Code Snippet

Make sure your *index.html* preview page isn't open; otherwise, you have to click the REFRESH button to see the new content.

Further Resources

For more details, including step-by-step documentation, we recommend the following:

https://help.sap.com/saphelp_nw74/helpdata/en/b4/3514f9e7a94650a7affd dd9056fb35/content.htm

---

10.4.2 Existing SAPUI5/SAP Fiori UI Layer

You can also enhance the existing SAPUI5 UI layer. Let's do this using SAP Fiori as an example.

Modification-Free Extensions

The second wave of SAP Fiori applications provides an extensibility concept to create modification-free extensions. We will show the enhancement via modification, because the modification-free version is not available for every use case. You can find further information here:

http://help.sap.com/fiori_bs2013/helpdata/en/e5/115d520f101357e100000 00a445394/content.htm

---

To do this, the first step is to download the original SAP Fiori project resources to your Eclipse environment. Start the SAP Logon, choose the system where the SAP Fiori files are installed, and log on with your credentials.

Developer

You need a developer key/license to upload the changed project later on.

Technical SAP Fiori name

You need the technical name of the SAP Fiori application you want to change. Follow these steps to find the names of all installed SAP Fiori financial applications:

1. Start the ABAP Development Workbench with Transaction SE80.

2. Select BSP APPLICATION in the dropdown menu on the left side.

3. Enter "UI5_FI*" in the input field, and start the search by pressing
   Enter (Figure 10.32).

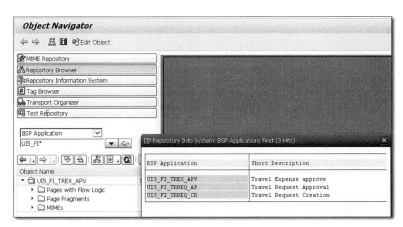

Figure 10.32 Installed FI SAP Fiori Applications: Technical Names

You'll get a list of all installed SAP Fiori applications on your system. For this example, you want to enhance the SAP Fiori manager application Travel Expenses Approve (technical name UI5_FI_TREX_APV).

To download the corresponding project files, start the ABAP Editor with Transaction SE38. On the initial screen of the ABAP Editor, enter the report name "/UI5/UI5_REPOSITORY_LOAD", and start the report by pressing F8 or clicking the Execute button (Figure 10.33).

Download SAP Fiori files

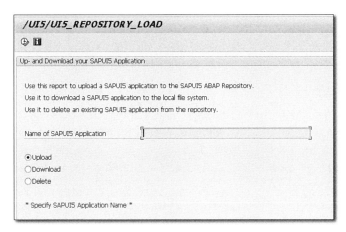

Figure 10.33 Report /UI5/UI5_REPOSITORY_LOAD

> **Further Resources**
>
> You can find further information about manual deployment in SAP Note 1793771.

From the report's main menu, enter the name of the SAPUI5 application "UI5_FI_TREX_APV", and select the DOWNLOAD radio button. Press F8 or click the EXECUTE button, and specify a target dictionary on your local computer. Click the OK button to confirm the selected folder. The selection of all necessary files starts immediately. You'll receive a list of all selected files and folders and have to start the download by clicking the green text CLICK HERE TO DOWNLOAD at the end of the list. Click the CONTINUE button on the following pop-up for the external codepage, and leave the CODEPAGE field empty to use the built-in default. The download process is started and will take some time. After the download is finished, you get a green success message on the bottom of the report with the amount of transferred bytes.

> **Further Resources**
>
> For more details on how to extend SAP Fiori applications, we recommend the following:
>
> *http://help.sap.com/saphelp_fiori/fiori10_extend_en.pdf*

Create an SAPUI5 project

The next step is to create an initial SAPUI5 project inside Eclipse. Start Eclipse, and create a new SAPUI5 project by clicking FILE • NEW • SAPUI5 APPLICATION DEVELOPMENT • APPLICATION PROJECT. Click NEXT, and enter your PROJECT NAME. Deselect the CREATE AN INITIAL VIEW checkbox, and click FINISH to create the empty project (refer to Section 10.2.2 for a similar process).

The final step is to copy all downloaded files and folders from the SAP Fiori application to the WEBCONTENT folder of your created SAPUI5 application project. Navigate to the dictionary on the file system where you've downloaded the SAP Fiori resources, and select all content (press Ctrl+A) and copy it (press Ctrl+C) to the clipboard. Switch back to

Eclipse again, right-click on the WEBCONTENT folder, and paste the files. Confirm the dialog that appears to overwrite the existing content by clicking YES TO ALL.

Now that you've added the SAP Fiori content to your project, you can start to enhance the layout inside Eclipse. For example, you can add a button with additional information. Expand the folder WEBCONTENT • VIEWS • MASTER at the tree menu, and double-click on the *Home.view.html* file to open the edit mode.

Insert the lines of code from Listing 10.4 after the closing tag of `data-sap-ui-type="sap.m.PullToRefresh"` in line 5 (Figure 10.34).

Change view

```
<div data-sap-ui-type="sap.m.Button" data-
press="openInfoDialog" data-text="Information" data-
width="100%"></div>
```

Listing 10.4 Enhance View Layout

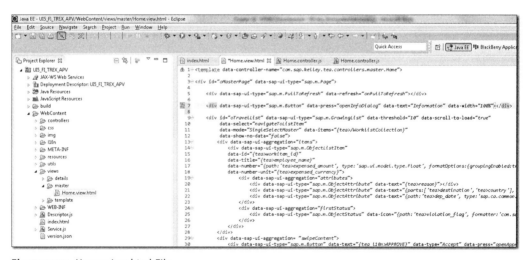

Figure 10.34 Home.view.html File

Save your changes. This adds a button with the text INFORMATION to the home screen of the SAPUI5 application. Now you have to implement the `openInfoDialog` function in the controller JavaScript file. Expand the folders CONTROLLERS • MASTER above the already opened VIEWS folder, and double-click on the *Home.controller.js* file to open this file in edit mode.

Change controller   Insert the lines of code from Listing 10.5 after the closing comma in line 64 (Figure 10.35).

```
openInfoDialog:function(){
    sap.m.MessageBox.show("Please visit http://www.sap-
press.com",sap.m.MessageBox.Icon.INFORMATION,"",[])
    },
```

Listing 10.5 Enhance Controller Functions

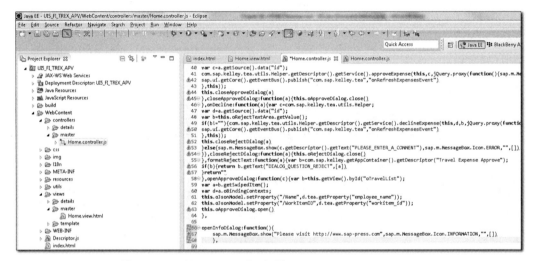

Figure 10.35 Home.controller.js File

After you've saved the changes again, you have to deploy it on the SAP NetWeaver AS. Right-click on the WEBCONTENT folder, and select COPY. Navigate to drive D, and paste the folder, including all content, by pressing `Ctrl`+`V` (you can use any other directory of your choice instead of drive D).

Start the report /UI5/UI5_REPOSITORY_LOAD, and specify a new SAPUI5 name in the customer namespace (to create a new SAPUI5 application), or use the existing name to modify the SAP Fiori default application.

To create a new SAPUI5 application, enter "ZUI5_TREX_APV" in the input field (the new name has a maximum of 15 characters). Next, select the UPLOAD radio button. Press 𝐅𝟖 or click the EXECUTE button, and specify the source target as "D:\WebContent" for this example.

Click OK to confirm your choice. The content of the folder is inspected, and you get an overview of all folders and files, including additional information in the left column if the file or folder will be created, changed, or deleted. Navigate to the end of the list, and click the green text CLICK HERE TO UPLOAD. The files are inserted in the project structure of a BSP application. A pop-up appears (Figure 10.36) where you enter a DESCRIPTION and enter "$tmp" as the PACKAGE (in addition, the TRANS-PORT REQUEST field is also required).

Figure 10.36 BSP Application Parameters

Click the CONTINUE button or press 𝐄𝐧𝐭𝐞𝐫 to start the upload process. After the upload is finished, you'll get a green success message and can start testing your enhanced SAPUI5/SAP Fiori application.

Open the SAPUI5 application with a URL similar to this (replace *system:port* with your server specific information): *http://system:port/sap/bc/ui5_ui5/sap/zui5_trex_apv/index.html.*

The added INFORMATION button is shown on the navigation bar on the left side of the SAPUI5 application. Clicking the button opens a static information window with your defined text message (Figure 10.37).

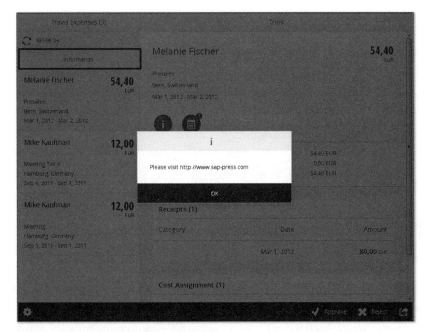

Figure 10.37 Enhanced SAP Fiori Application

10.5 Summary

After reading this chapter, you should understand the benefits of HTML5 and how to create a new SAPUI5 application inside the Notepad editor, how to create your first application with SAPUI5 support, how to consume an OData service with support of the SAP NetWeaver Gateway Productivity Accelerator, and how to generate an SAPUI5 application with the LIST view. You can use the SAPUI5 code snippets to speed up your development process. You should also know how to deploy any SAPUI5 application to SAP NetWeaver AS and how to extend an existing SAP Fiori application.

HTML5 isn't a final standard yet, so the use of the correct browser has a big influence on the look and feel of your application. Take a look at the supported browsers by SAPUI5 on the following webpage to make sure you take the right one to test and develop your SAPUI5 application: *https://sapui5.hana.ondemand.com/sdk/docs/guide/BrowserSupport.html.*

If you need further information, you can find more detailed information on SCN. The central place to start with your SAPUI5 development career is the demo kit on the SAP HANA Cloud Platform at *https://sapui5.hana.ondemand.com/sdk*.

Social media is everywhere. In this chapter, we'll show you the available possibilities with OData for some of the biggest social media platforms in the world.

11   Social Media Application Development

We're in a data-driven economy. Web Application Programming Interface (API) designers need to define what and how to expose data from a variety of applications, services, and stores. Even if platforms such as Facebook, Twitter, or Sina Weibo (the Chinese microblogging site and a hybrid of Twitter and Facebook) don't offer OData services themselves, this chapter explains how you can connect an OData service to any available social media platform to provide your selected data to the outside world.

Today, social media is the basis for social communication and information. Social media platforms enable people to swap ideas, exchange state of minds, or pick up information that expands beyond their own culture and society. Most people also post and tell the community about their loves and interests, so it's easy for companies that do market research to turn this information into valuable knowledge about consumers. In fact, social media is not only a platform for gathering information, but also for improving services based on feedback from customers. Via feedback from social media platforms, companies can provide better products or customer-tailored services.

An effective use of social media platforms also offers the possibility of proactive contact with consumers. This is the point where SAP NetWeaver Gateway comes into action by providing information directly out of your SAP system and placing it into well-considered different social media channels.

The Hypertext Processor (PHP) is the basis for any social media application development. In this chapter, we'll start by creating a PHP web page based on the OData SDK for PHP (Section 11.1) and use this as a basis for the subsequent sections, where we'll enhance this file and connect to the APIs of the social media platforms Facebook (Section 11.2), Twitter (Section 11.3), and the famous Chinese microblogging site Sina Weibo (Section 11.4), which is a hybrid of Facebook and Twitter.

Obsolete OData Plugins

OData.org displays many different client or server tools to consume or create OData services. Unfortunately, there are two plugins for the content management system Drupal described in the context of social media that are out of date and no longer work with the current version of the main software component:

► Views Module (*https://drupal.org/project/odata*)
► Custom Module (*https://github.com/mindtree/ODataDrupal*)

The other still available content management system OData plugin for Joomla (*http://joomlacode.org/gf/project/odata/*) also won't work on the actual Joomla release for versions 2.5.14 or 3.1.5.

11.1 PHP

Hypertext Preprocessor (PHP) is a server-side scripting language designed for web development. It was created in 1994 by Rasmus Lerdorf and can be used to connect to a database or web service. Because PHP is a server-side scripting language, you need a web server that supports PHP to see the results of the developed applications in this chapter. If you don't have a web server, we recommend XAMPP. It's an easily installable Apache distribution that also includes MySQL, PHP, and Perl. To install XAMPP, you only need to download and extract a ZIP file.

PHP is a one of the most-used languages for creating websites, and is also preinstalled on most web hosts. In the following pages, you'll see how to create an OData-consuming web page with the help of the available OData software development kit (SDK) for PHP.

The SDK enables you to easily consume an existing OData service and use the data inside your functions. The OData SDK for PHP is based on the *DataSvcUtil* file, which is used to generate a proxy class based on the metadata exposed by the selected OData service. These classes can be used later on in your PHP application to connect to your OData service and execute the available `Create`, `Read`, `Update`, and `Delete` (CRUD) methods. This makes it very easy and fast to start with your web application development, because you don't need to write the code that handles the calling of the service or the data parsing. The SDK doesn't have any dependency on the web server operating system.

OData SDK for PHP

Getting Started with PHP

You can find all necessary download links here:

▶ XAMPP: *http://sourceforge.net/projects/xampp/files/*.

▶ OData SDK for PHP: *http://odataphp.codeplex.com/*.

▶ Aptana Studio: *http://www.aptana.com/products/php/*. We recommend this open-source, Eclipse-based IDE for building your web applications.

Getting started with PHP

After you've downloaded the SDK, you have to install and configure it correctly. First, create a folder named *odataphp*. Extract all files and folders inside the *framework* folder from the downloaded ZIP file to the newly created folder. To make sure PHP can execute the SDK functions, add the path to the *odataphp* folder to the `include_path` directive in the *php.ini* configuration file. For example: `include_path = ".; C:\xampp\ php\odataphp"`.

Next create a variable called `ODataphp_path` in the *php.ini* file beneath the previously added line, and set it to the path where the PHP toolkit was installed. For example: `ODataphp_path = "C:\xampp\php\odataphp"`.

In addition, make sure the PHP-XML module is installed and *php_xsl.dll* and *php_curl.dll* functions in *php.ini* are enabled. If you're using XAMPP, everything is preconfigured correctly.

Generate the proxy class After the installation process is completed, you can generate the proxy class for your selected OData service. Open the command-line tool on your operation system, and navigate to the folder where your OData SDK *odataphp* folder is located. The command to create the proxy class with the help of the *PHPDataSvcUtil.php* file is well explained in the available SDK documentation.

In this example scenario, you'll create the proxy class of your OData service into the *C:\PHPODataSample* folder, so enter the following command (replace the placeholder *youruser* and *yourpassword* with your credentials, if needed, or remove them):

```
php odataphp\PHPDataSvcUtil.php /uri=https://sapes1.sapdev-
center.com/sap/opu/odata/IWFND/RMTSAMPLEFLIGHT /out=C:\
PHPODataSample /auth=windows /u=youruser /p=yourpassword
```

The utility file creates a proxy file in the specified output folder and gives a confirmation message in the console (Figure 11.1).

Figure 11.1 Generate OData PHP Proxy File

After a few seconds, the proxy class for the OData service is created. The generated file contains the definition of a class that can be used to execute the available functions of the OData service.

Consume OData You'll use the newly created proxy class file to consume the OData service in a simple list view. Navigate to your output folder, where the proxy class file is now located. Create an empty *index.php* file inside this folder. Copy the complete folder to your web server (e.g., into the XAMPP *htdocs* folder). Next, the created proxy class needs to be included in your *index.php* file. For example: `require_once "RMTSAMPLE-FLIGHT.php";`.

> **Note**
>
> The field names of the proxy class are case sensitive and have to be used just as they are displayed in the metadata document. In our example, all of the key fields are lowercase, while the PRICE and CURRENCY fields are uppercase.

Insert the code in Listing 11.1 to consume all available data sets of the entity `CarrierCollection` and to display the fields `carrid` and `CARRNAME`. Replace *youruser* and *yourpassword* with your logon credentials.

```php
<?php
require_once "RMTSAMPLEFLIGHT.php";
// Connect
$OData = new RMTSAMPLEFLIGHT('https://sapes1.sapdevcenter.com/
sap/opu/odata/IWFND/RMTSAMPLEFLIGHT/');
$OData->Credential = new WindowsCredential('youruser',
'yourpassword');
echo "------ Carrier list ------ <br/>";
try {
    $OData->addHeader('X-Requested-With', 'XMLHttpRequest');
// Execute
    $flights= $OData->Execute("CarrierCollection")->Result;
// Output
    foreach ($flights as $flight){
        echo "ID: " . $flight->carrid . "<br/>";
        echo "Name: " . $flight->CARRNAME . "<br/><br/>";
    }
    }catch(DataServiceRequestException $exception)
    {
        echo $exception->Response->getError();
    }
?>
```

Listing 11.1 PHP OData Consumption

Save your changes, and open the file in your browser. The result of our example is shown in Figure 11.2.

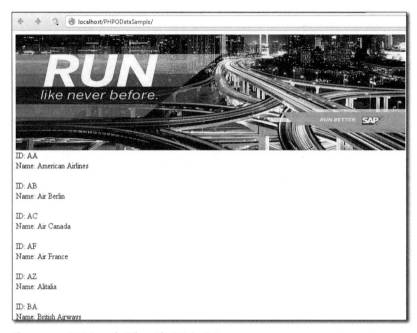

ID: AA
Name: American Airlines

ID: AB
Name: Air Berlin

ID: AC
Name: Air Canada

ID: AF
Name: Air France

ID: AZ
Name: Alitalia

ID: BA
Name: British Airways

Figure 11.2 PHP Sample File with OData Data

Now you can implement the logic to connect to the OData service and execute the necessary functions with PHP. These functionalities are the basis for all the following sections in this chapter, so make sure this works correctly.

11.2 Facebook

Facebook is the biggest free online social networking service, and it's still growing. It was founded in February 2004 by Mark Zuckerberg and some other students of Harvard University. Facebook has over one billion active users.

Create application   If you don't already have a developer account, visit *https://developers.facebook.com/* and create an account. After the creation process is finished, log in, click APPS on the top toolbar, and click CREATE NEW APP.

The CREATE NEW APP window appears where you have to enter the APP NAME and choose an APP CATEGORY (Figure 11.3).

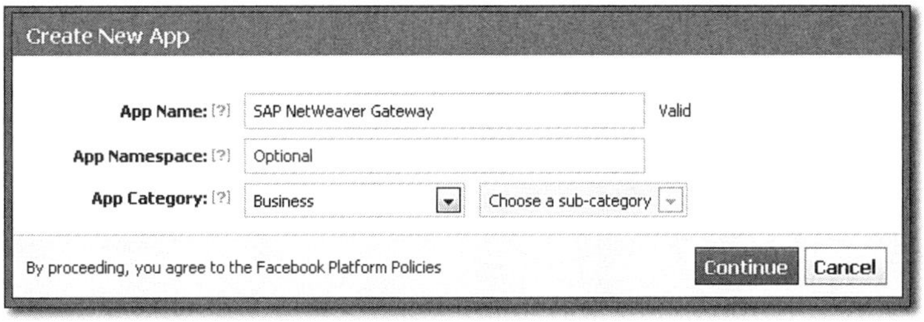

Figure 11.3 Create Facebook Application

Click CONTINUE, enter the CAPTCHA on the following page, and click CONTINUE again. You'll be forwarded to the BASIC application settings page. Enter a NAMESPACE where the application will be available later, which for this example is "sapnetweavergateway". The direct URL will be *http://apps.facebook.com/sapnetweavergateway*.

Namespace

Select WEBSITE WITH FACEBOOK LOGIN and APP ON FACEBOOK to define how your application integrates or connects with Facebook. Enter your application SITE URL where the PHP files will be stored—for this example, *http://localhost/facebook/*. Mark the CANVAS WIDTH radio button as FLUID to adjust the width automatically (Figure 11.4). Click SAVE CHANGES.

In the next step, you need to allow the application to post new entries on your profile and add additional permissions. Click on PERMISSIONS on the left menu bar, and enter "publish_actions" in the USER & FRIEND PERMISSIONS field. Click SAVE CHANGES, and navigate back to the BASIC settings page, where the APP ID and the APP SECRET are stored for getting access to the Facebook API.

Permissions

For this part of application development, there is a Facebook PHP SDK available, of course. (You can find a tutorial for Facebook PHP at the following website: *https://developers.facebook.com/docs/php/gettingstarted/*.) Create an empty folder called FACEBOOK, and download the Facebook PHP SDK from *https://github.com/facebook/facebook-php-sdk*.

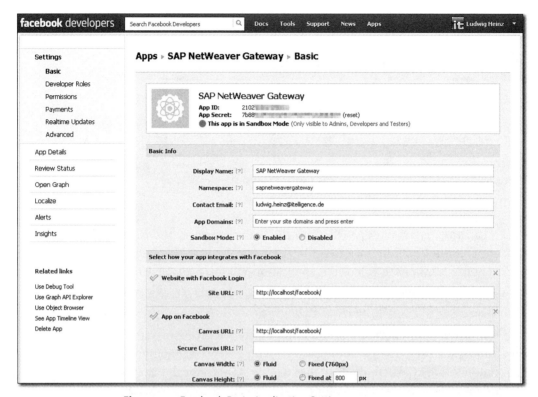

Figure 11.4 Facebook Basic Application Settings

Extract the folder FACEBOOK-PHP-SDK-MASTER and all included files from the already downloaded *facebook-php-sdk-master.zip* file into the newly created FACEBOOK folder. Also copy the *RMTSAMPLEFLIGHT.php* file from the created PHP folder (explained in Section 11.1) to the FACEBOOK folder.

Create a new file called *index.php,* and open the file in an editor. Enter the coding block from Listing 11.2 into the *index.php* file, and replace the appId, secret, and OData service username and password:

```
<html xmlns="http://www.w3.org/1999/xhtml" xmlns:fb="http://
www.facebook.com/2008/fbml">
<head>
<title>SAP NetWeaver Gateway</title>
<?php
require_once "RMTSAMPLEFLIGHT.php";
```

```php
require 'facebook-php-sdk-master/src/facebook.php';

$facebook = new Facebook(array(
'appId'  => 'yourappid',
'secret' => 'yoursecret',
'perms' => 'publish_stream',
'cookie' => true,
));

// User ID
$user = $facebook->getUser();

if ($user) {
  try {
    $user_profile = $facebook->api('/me');
  } catch (FacebookApiException $e) {
    error_log($e);
    $user = null;
  }
}
// Login or logout
if ($user) {
  $logoutUrl = $facebook->getLogoutUrl();
} else {
  $loginUrl = $facebook-
>getLoginUrl($params = array('scope' => "publish_stream"));
}
?>
</head>
<body>
<div id="fb-root">
<?php if ($user): ?>
    <img src="https://graph.facebook.com/<?php echo $user; ?>/
picture">
<?php echo "Welcome " . $user_profile['name'];?>
<?php else: ?>
    <div>
        You are not logged in and couldn't post any update!
        <a href="<?php echo $loginUrl; ?>">Login with Facebook<
/a>
    </div>
<?php endif ?>
```

```php
<?php
// Connect
$OData = new RMTSAMPLEFLIGHT('https://sapes1.sapdevcenter.com/
sap/opu/odata/IWFND/RMTSAMPLEFLIGHT/');
$OData-
>Credential = new WindowsCredential('youruser', 'yourpassword')
;
try {
    $OData->addHeader('X-Requested-With', 'XMLHttpRequest');
// Execute
    $flights= $OData->Execute("CarrierCollection")->Result;
//  Output
    foreach ($flights as $flight){
        echo '    <form action="" >
                  <input type="text" name="text" style="width
:300px" value="Carrier:' . $flight->carrid . '" />
                  <input type="submit" />
            </form>';
        echo "Name: " . $flight->CARRNAME . "<br/><br/>";
    }
    }catch(DataServiceRequestException $exception)
    {
        echo $exception->Response->getError();
    }

// Post Facebook update
if( isset($_REQUEST['text']) ) {

    $params = array(
    'message' => $_REQUEST['text'],
    'name' => 'OData!',
    'caption' => "SAP NetWeaver Gateway",
    'link' => 'http://sap.com',
    'actions' => array(
        array(
            'name' => 'SAP',
            'link' => 'http://www.sap.com'
        )
    )
);
$ret_obj = $facebook->api('/me/feed/', 'POST', $params);
var_dump($ret_obj);
```

```
}
?>
</body>
</html>
```

Listing 11.2 Facebook PHP OData Consumption

Save all your changes, copy all of the files to your web server, and open
https://apps.facebook.com/sapnetweavergateway/ with your browser (Figure 11.5).

Figure 11.5 Facebook Runs OData

Log in with your Facebook credentials, right-click the LOGIN WITH FACE-
BOOK link, and click OPEN LINK IN NEW TASK. Two separated OAuth per-
mission windows appear. First, you have to confirm that the application
is allowed to receive YOUR PUBLIC PROFILE AND FRIEND LIST. Click OK.
The next window asks for permission to POST TO YOUR FRIENDS ON YOUR
BEHALF. Click OK again. Close the open window and refresh your original

Test application

web page. You'll see your profile image and a personal welcome message. Now you can post a new entry from the OData service data to your Facebook profile. Click one of the Submit buttons. You'll see a response on the bottom of your created PHP page with information about the successful creation of your entry. Your Facebook profile will look like the screen shown in Figure 11.6.

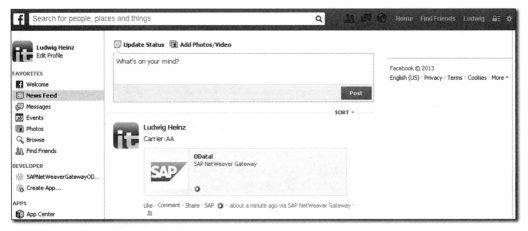

Figure 11.6 Updated Facebook Profile

You can now directly post any content from an SAP OData service of your choice to your Facebook profile.

11.3 Twitter

Twitter is an online social networking and microblogging service founded in 2006. It enables users to send and read 140-character tweets. Twitter currently has around 240 million users. One of the reasons Twitter is so popular is the huge number of developers who have built so many applications for it over the years.

Twitter SDKs To start developing OData applications for Twitter, visit *https://dev. twitter.com*, and create your personal account. Like many other social networks, Twitter has its own API that programmers can work with. You can find a complete list of all available SDKs for the different programming languages at *https://dev.twitter.com/docs/twitter-libraries*.

Open *https://dev.twitter.com/apps* to create a new application and sign in with your user credentials. Click the CREATE A NEW APPLICATION button, and enter the application details such as NAME, DESCRIPTION, WEBSITE, or CALLBACK URL, which is where the user should be returned after successfully authenticating. Accept the DEVELOPER RULES OF THE ROAD, enter the CAPTCHA, and click the CREATE YOUR TWITTER APPLICATION button to create your first Twitter application. You are redirected to the application details, where you can find the CONSUMER KEY and CONSUMER SECRET (Figure 11.7).

Access level

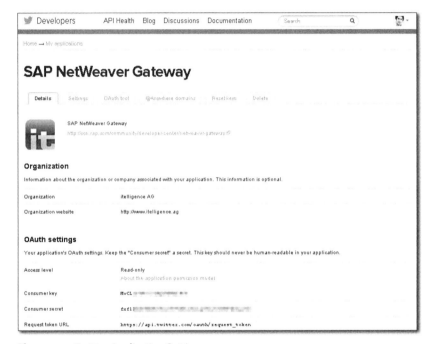

Figure 11.7 Twitter Application Settings

To make sure you're able to post messages over the API, you have to change the ACCESS LEVEL. Switch to the SETTINGS tab, and change the APPLICATION TYPE to READ, WRITE, AND DIRECT MESSAGES. Click UPDATE THIS TWITTER APPLICATION'S SETTINGS.

As already stated, there are many different PHP libraries available for Twitter. For this example, you'll use the TwitterOAuth-library, which you can download from *https://github.com/abraham/twitteroauth.*

Extract all of the files from the already downloaded *TwitterOAuth-master.zip* file, and rename the folder TwitterOAuth-master to "twitter". Copy the *RMTSAMPLEFLIGHT.php* file from the created PHP folder (explained in Section 11.1), rename the *Example.php* to "index.php", and open the file in an editor.

OAuth token
Add your OAuth tokens provided by Twitter to the `config` array as shown in Listing 11.3.

```
$config = array(
    'consumer_key' => 'CONSUMER_KEY',
    'consumer_secret' => 'CONSUMER_SECRET',
    'oauth_token' => 'AUTH_TOKEN',
    'oauth_token_secret' => 'AUTH_SECRET',
    'output_format' => 'object'
);
```

Listing 11.3 Twitter API Keys

Replace every single line behind the coding line

```
$tw = new TwitterOAuth($config);
```

with the coding block given in Listing 11.4.

```
// Post
require_once "RMTSAMPLEFLIGHT.php";
// Connect
$OData = new RMTSAMPLEFLIGHT('https://sapes1.sapdevcenter.com/
sap/opu/odata/IWFND/RMTSAMPLEFLIGHT/');
$OData-
>Credential = new WindowsCredential(youruser, yourpassword);
try {
    $OData->addHeader('X-Requested-With', 'XMLHttpRequest');
// Execute
    $flights= $OData->Execute("CarrierCollection")->Result;
// Output
    foreach ($flights as $flight){
        echo '   <form action="" >
                    <input type="text" name="text" style="width
:300px" value="Carrier:' . $flight->carrid . '" />
                    <input type="submit" />
            </form>';
        echo "Name: " . $flight->CARRNAME . "<br/><br/>";
```

```
    }
    }catch(DataServiceRequestException $exception)
    {
        echo $exception->Response->getError();
    }
// Post Twitter update
if( isset($_REQUEST['text']) ) {

    $params = array(
        'status' => $_REQUEST['text'],
    );
    $response = $tw->post('statuses/update', $params);
    var_dump($response);
}
?>
```

Listing 11.4 Twitter PHP OData Consumption

Save all your changes, copy the files to your web server, and open the   Twitter application
index.php file with your browser. Log in with your Twitter credentials.
After logging in, you are prompted to approve the application. Click the
AUTHORIZE application to connect. You'll see a list of available carriers
(Figure 11.8).

Figure 11.8 Custom Twitter Update Page

Click one of the Submit buttons to post the content from the input form in your Twitter account. You'll see a response on the bottom of your created PHP page with information about the successful creation of your tweet. Your Twitter account will look like the screen shown in Figure 11.9.

Figure 11.9 OData Tweet

You can now directly post any content from an SAP OData service of your choice to your Twitter account.

11.4 Sina Weibo (新浪微博)

Sina Weibo (*weibo* is the Chinese word for microblog) is a Chinese hybrid of Twitter and Facebook and is also one of the most popular websites in China. It was launched by SINA Corporation in August 2009 and has more than 500 million registered users. We'll use this unique example to show you how easy it is to provide your SAP data for any available social media platform in the world.

Not every Weibo page is available in English, so we'll show you a translation for Mandarin words as necessary. You may want to use a browser with built-in page translation, such as Google Chrome. To enable the translation bar, click on the Chrome menu on the browser toolbar and select Settings. Click Show Advanced Settings, and navigate to the Languages section. Mark the Offer to translate pages that aren't in a language I read checkbox to activate the translation feature. Because not everyone will be able to use Google Chrome, we'll show the default screen with no browser-based translation.

You need a normal Sina Weibo user account before you can create your first application. To create your new account, just open *www.weibo.com/signup/signup.php* in your browser. Normally, the language will be automatically set to English. Otherwise, you can do this manually by opening the dropdown menu on the bottom-right corner and selecting ENGLISH (Figure 11.10). **Account**

Figure 11.10 Switch Language to English

Click the 确定 (DETERMINE) button on the following message window to confirm that you want to switch to the English language.

Due to the very strict enterprise verification requirements (e.g., a signed enterprise application letter), we suggest that you create a personal account for your first test application. Enter your EMAIL, PASSWORD, NICKNAME, and VERIFICATION CODE, and then click SIGN UP NOW (Figure 11.11).

Figure 11.11 Creating a Personal Account

> **Note**
>
> Sometimes, you're prompted to verify your login data with phone verification. To avoid this, you can try the last step again with a different email address.

You are redirected to the next page, where you have to enter some further details, such as your LOCATION (美国 = USA), GENDER, and BIRTHDAY. All other information is optional (Figure 11.12).

Click NEXT. You can choose up to five of your interests. Click ENTER when you're finished. You are redirected to your user profile, where you have to click the NEXT STEP button twice and the GOT IT button once to close the WHAT'S NEW WITH YOU window. You'll see a reminder to activate your account, with an email sent to your email address. Make sure to confirm your email address.

Create developer account

To start, navigate to the developer web page at *http://open.weibo.com/development,* and create a new developer account. Click the 创建应用 (CREATING APPLICATIONS) button, which is the leftmost button on the screen (Figure 11.13).

Figure 11.12 Account Detail Information

Figure 11.13 Creating a Developer Account

If you need to log in, use your email account as the user name. Next, you have to choose the kind of application you want to create. For this example, you'll create a web application, so click in the middle on 网页应用 (the computer monitor icon).

You are prompted to enter further personal data. Table 11.1 lists the information that has to be entered.

Mandarin	English
开发者类型	DEVELOPER TYPE (个人 = PRIVATE, 公司 = COMPANY)
开发者名称	DEVELOPER NAME
所在地区	COUNTRY (美国 = USA)
详细地址	ADDRESS
邮编	ZIP
企业邮箱	EMAIL
企业电话	BUSINESS PHONE
聊天工具	CHAT TOOL
网站	WEBSITE
紧急联系人姓名	EMERGENCY CONTACT NAME
紧急联系人电话	EMERGENCY CONTACT PHONE

Table 11.1 Personal Data

Click the blue 提交 (SUBMIT) button to submit the data.

You have to confirm your email address once again by email. Confirm the opening window by clicking the blue 确定 (DETERMINE) button to confirm the email will be sent to the right address. After approximately five seconds, you should be redirected to the initial Sina Weibo user page, and your progress bar on the left side should show 20% (Figure 11.14).

Figure 11.14 Sina Weibo User Account: Progress 20%

Make sure to confirm your email address; otherwise, you won't be able to post anything. Check your email inbox, and activate your account with a click on the activation link inside or copy the link to your browser. A new browser window opens, and you should be redirected to the initial web page. The progress bar on the left should show 30% now. To register your application, click the 应用开发 (APPLICATION DEVELOPMENT) button, which is the third button from the left on the top bar (Figure 11.14).

Next, click on the green 创建应用 (CREATING APPLICATIONS) button to finally create the application. You have to choose the kind of application again. Click the 网页应用 (WEB APPLICATIONS) button, which is the button in the middle, and fill in the form with information for your application, as listed in Table 11.2.

Create application

Mandarin	English
应用名称	NAME
应用地址	URL (application address)

Table 11.2 Application Data

Mandarin	English
应用简介	DESCRIPTION (SHORT)
应用介绍	DESCRIPTION (EXTENDED) (Enter 20 words or more.)
应用分类	CATEGORY
标签	TAGS (CHOOSE 其他 – OTHER)

Table 11.2 Application Data (Cont.)

Keep the checkbox next to 我已阅读并接受《新浪微博开发者协议》to confirm that you've read and accept the SINA WEIBO DEVELOPER AGREEMENT.

After filling in the form, click the 创建 (CREATE) button, which is the leftmost button (Figure 11.15).

Figure 11.15 Creating a Weibo Application

Application key and secret You're redirected to your application's main page. Now you need the APP KEY and APP SECRET (similar to a password token) to get access to the Weibo API. Click the 应用信息 (APPLICATION INFORMATION) button, which is the second button on the left side (Figure 11.16).

Figure 11.16 Application Settings

In the already opened submenu on the left side, click the 高级信息 (ADVANCED INFORMATION) button (second button in the submenu; it has an exclamation point icon) to set a redirect URL (Figure 11.17).

Figure 11.17 Creating OAuth Redirect Settings

OAuth callback page Click the 编辑 (EDIT) button on the right side of the OAUTH2.0 授权设置 bar, and fill the two empty fields with your callback pages as shown in Table 11.3.

Mandarin	English
授权回调页	AUTHORIZATION CALLBACK PAGE
取消授权回调页	DEAUTHORIZE CALLBACK PAGE

Table 11.3 Callback Pages

Enter the authorization callback page as *http://yourwebserver/callback.php*. Click the green 提交 (SUBMIT) button to confirm your input.

Additional test account To create an additional test account, click on the third button (测试帐号 TEST ACCOUNT) in the submenu that should be still open. To edit this, click on the 编辑 (EDIT) button on the right side of that bar again. Add a NICK-NAME (用户昵称) for a new test account (添加测试帐号), and click the green 提交 (SUBMIT) button to confirm your input. Click the green 提交 (SUBMIT) button to confirm your input again. Now you've added a new test account successfully.

Sina Weibo SDK Sina Weibo also offers many SDKs for different languages. You can find a detailed list at *http://open.weibo.com/wiki/SDK/en*. As mentioned in Section 11.1, we want to develop every social media application based on PHP, so go to *http://code.google.com/p/libweibo/downloads/list* and download the latest version of Weibo PHP SDK.

Download the *weibo-phpsdk-v2-2013-02-20.zip* file. Next duplicate the already created PHP folder (Section 11.1), and rename it to "weibo". Extract all of the files from the Weibo PHP SDK to the *weibo* folder, and overwrite the *index.php*. Start editing the *config.php* file, and insert your application key, application secret, and the callback URL. Replace the information in Listing 11.5 with your created Sina Weibo application information.

```
// Replace it with your key
define( "WB_AKEY" , '12345678910111121314');
// Replace it with your key
define( "WB_SKEY" , '9999999999999999999');
```

```
define( "WB_CALLBACK_URL" , 'http://yourwebserver/
callback.php' );
```

Listing 11.5 PHP Weibo API Configuration

Make sure the `WB_CALLBACK_URL` is exactly the same in both the Weibo
settings and the authorization callback page.

Next you have to edit the *saetv2.ex.class.php* file to avoid warning messages. Replace

SSL option

```
curl_setopt($ci, CURLOPT_SSL_VERIFYHOST, 1);
```

with

```
curl_setopt($ci, CURLOPT_SSL_VERIFYHOST, 2);
```

> **Note**
>
> Option 1 is to check the existence of a common name in the Secure Sockets
> Layer (SSL) peer certificate. Option 2 is to check the existence of a common
> name and also verify that it matches the hostname provided.
>
> In production environments, the value of this option should be kept at 2.

Now you have to edit the *weibolist.php* file to implement your OData
connection. Open this file and replace the coding block in Listing 11.6
with the coding block in Listing 11.7.

weibolist.php

```
<form action="" >
<input type="text" name="text" style="width:300px" />
<input type="submit" />
</form>
```

Listing 11.6 Weibo PHP Block to Replace

```
<?php
require_once "RMTSAMPLEFLIGHT.php";
// Connect
$OData = new RMTSAMPLEFLIGHT('https://sapes1.sapdevcenter.com/
sap/opu/odata/IWFND/RMTSAMPLEFLIGHT/');
$OData->Credential = new WindowsCredential(
  'youruser', 'yourpassword');
try {
    $OData->addHeader('X-Requested-With', 'XMLHttpRequest');
```

```
//  Execute
    $flights= $OData->Execute("CarrierCollection")->Result;
//  Output
    foreach ($flights as $flight){
        echo '    <form action="" >
                    <input type="text" name="text" style="width
:300px" value="Carrier:' . $flight->carrid . '" />
                    <input type="submit" />
            </form>';
        echo "Name: " . $flight->CARRNAME . "<br/><br/>";
    }
    }catch(DataServiceRequestException $exception)
    {
        echo $exception->Response->getError();
    }
?>
```

Listing 11.7 Weibo PHP OData Consumption

Save all your changes, copy the files to your web server, and open the *index.php* file with your browser. Log in with your Sina Weibo credentials. You are prompted to authorize the application accesses to your profile information (Figure 11.18).

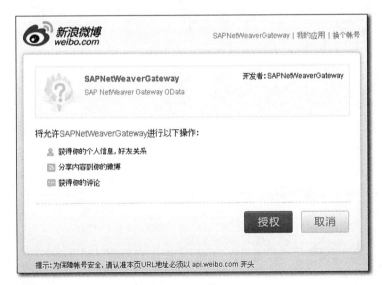

Figure 11.18 Granting Access to User Profile

Click the red 授权 (AUTHORIZE) button to authorize access. The default *index.php* web page appears, in which you have to click the red weibo login 点击进入授权页面 (CLICK TO ENTER) button. You are redirected to your callback page with an authentication code as a parameter. After authorization is complete, click the 进入你的微博列表页面 (ENTER YOUR MICROBLOGGING PAGE) link to enter your microblogging page. You'll see a list of available carriers (Figure 11.19) and a list of all related updates to your account below the carriers.

Authorize access

Figure 11.19 Custom Weibo Update Page

Click one of the SUBMIT buttons to post the content from the input form to your Sina Weibo account (Figure 11.20).

Post content

You can now directly post any content of your choice from an SAP OData service to your Sina Weibo account.

Figure 11.20 Sina Weibo Custom Message

11.5 Summary

Social media is important for your daily business. In this chapter, you've learned how to enable your different user groups to access and deliver data from the SAP system into the social media world via PHP and SDKs. Specifically, you've used the existing PHP SDK for OData to create a basic application with OData access. Based on this, you've created an application for Facebook, for Twitter, and for the Chinese microblogging platform Sina Weibo.

This last chapter of Part III is focused on the topic of enterprise application development and provides examples of OData service development for Microsoft SharePoint, Microsoft Excel, and more.

12   Enterprise Application Development

Enterprise business applications are the fourth pillar of the possible options for you and your company's daily business (Figure 12.1). Though developing applications for today's enterprises is normally not a simple task, this chapter enables you to create applications on the business side with the data you need to solve your business problems on your own. Using SAP NetWeaver Gateway, your business can centralize data from different sources into one enterprise application.

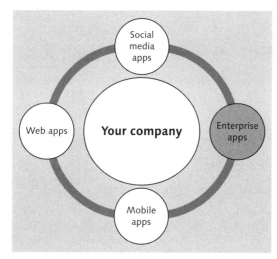

Figure 12.1 Enterprise Applications

Microsoft Corporation was founded in 1975 and is the largest computer technology firm in the world, developing software and software-related services and solutions. This wide range of computing solutions makes Microsoft the most popular computing platform in the business world today. This is why some of the most common tools from Microsoft, such as SharePoint, LightSwitch, and Excel, are used here to show you how to consume SAP-provided OData services inside your existing business system landscape.

GWPA for Microsoft

SAP published the SAP NetWeaver Gateway Productivity Accelerator for Microsoft during the writing of this book. It's a Visual Studio 2010/2012 add-on, and works very similarly to the normal GWPA Eclipse plugin. You can find further information at *http://help.sap.com/nwgwpam*.

At the beginning of this chapter, we introduce the application development for Microsoft SharePoint (Section 12.1). Then we'll show you how you can easily consume any OData service with the Microsoft Excel plugin Power Pivot (Section 12.2), how to build a Microsoft LightSwitch application (Section 12.3), and help you with code snippets for Microsoft ASP.NET (Section 12.4).

12.1 Microsoft SharePoint/Office 365

The Microsoft SharePoint server offers your enterprise business new functionalities for data access, collaboration, and document management. Developing applications for Microsoft SharePoint widens the range of possible programming languages and technology stacks, which can be consolidated with Microsoft SharePoint.

Note

We'll use the term *Microsoft SharePoint* in this chapter to describe the process of development for both Microsoft SharePoint and Office 365.

To start, register a new Office 365 account if you don't have your own Microsoft SharePoint server for testing purposes. There is a 30-day trial account available. You can find a how-to guide to start building your applications for Microsoft Office and Microsoft SharePoint on the

Microsoft development center page: *http://msdn.microsoft.com/en-US/library/office/apps/fp161179*.

The range of options depends on the type of hosting and application pattern you choose (mixing is also possible). We show you how to create a Microsoft SharePoint application with Visual Studio 2012, retrieving data from an existing OData service. This is a very convenient option for providing your SAP data to your existing Microsoft SharePoint server, which can be accessible from the web.

Microsoft Office 365: Minimum Requirements

▶ Microsoft Office 365 (trial) account

▶ Office Developer Tools for Visual Studio 2012

▶ SharePoint Client Components

Start Visual Studio 2012, and select FILE • NEW • PROJECT to create your first Microsoft SharePoint application. Expand the VISUAL C# node, and select APP FOR SHAREPOINT 2013, which is located under the OFFICE/SHAREPOINT template node (Figure 12.2).

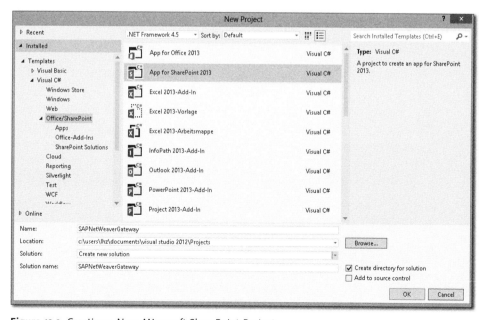

Figure 12.2 Creating a New Microsoft SharePoint Project

Settings
Enter the project NAME and click OK. Next, you need to specify the Microsoft SharePoint settings. There are three different options for how to host your application, as shown in Table 12.1.

Option	Description
Microsoft SharePoint-hosted applications	All components are hosted on either an on-premise or Office 365 Microsoft SharePoint farm.
Provider-hosted applications	This includes components that are deployed and hosted outside the Microsoft SharePoint farm.
Autohosted applications	This includes provider-hosted applications whose remote components are provisioned and deployed for you on Windows Azure.

Table 12.1 Hosting Options for Microsoft SharePoint Applications

Enter a name for your Microsoft SharePoint application, and enter the URL of the Microsoft SharePoint server that you'll be debugging against. The URL will be in the form *https://YOURUSERNAME.sharepoint.com*. After you enter the URL, select SHAREPOINT-HOSTED from the dropdown menu (Figure 12.3).

Add OData service
Click FINISH. When the project generation process is done, a popup appears, and you have to enter your Microsoft SharePoint credentials. After the validation is successfully finished, right-click on the created project, and choose ADD • CONTENT TYPES FOR AN EXTERNAL DATA SOURCE to add a new OData service to the project (Figure 12.4).

> **Note**
>
> When using an OData service with required log-in credentials, Visual Studio uses the domain as part of the authentication header. You can add a backslash at the beginning of your user name (such as "\myuser") to ignore the domain. To avoid any problem with the authentication method on your side, we'll show the OData consumption process with the help of a free sample service from *odata.org* (we first introduced this in Chapter 8, Section 8.3).

Figure 12.3 Creating a New Application for Microsoft SharePoint

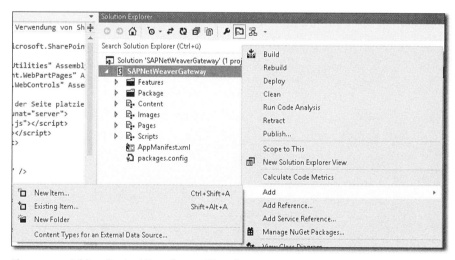

Figure 12.4 Adding Content Type for an OData Source

Make sure the OData service is reachable from your Microsoft Share-Point server. Enter your OData service URL and a name for the new data source (Figure 12.5).

Figure 12.5 Specifying the OData Source

Choose entities   Click NEXT. In the next step of the wizard, you have to select the entities that you want to use in order to generate external content types. Choose the entities you want to work with by clicking on the checkbox for each entity (Figure 12.6).

Click FINISH to start the generation process.

> **Note**
>
> To create an external list, leave the field CREATE LIST INSTANCES FOR THE SELECTED DATA ENTRIES (EXCEPT SERVICE OPERATIONS) checked so the tools can create your external list automatically.

After a few seconds, the generation process is finished, and the tool creates an external content type and external list instances in your Visual Studio project.

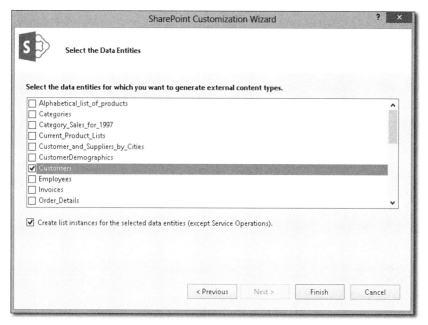

Figure 12.6 Selecting OData Service Entities

To deploy your solution, choose Debug • Start (or press [F5]). Visual Studio builds the application and deploys it to your Microsoft SharePoint server (and if you change something in an existing application, the old version is automatically reinstalled). After this deployment process is finished, the default browser window opens, and you have to log in with your credentials again. Your newly created application is shown. Although you haven't configured the layout of the page, you can see some basic information, and you have to adjust the URL to show the result of the consumed OData service: */yourappname/Lists/yourentity name*.

In our example the URL will look like this:

https://odata.sharepoint.com/SAPGateway/Lists/Customers

You can also access your application from the home page of Office 365. When you're logged in, go to the developer site, and click the Site Content link on the left side. You'll see your deployed applications in the application list (Figure 12.7).

Deploy

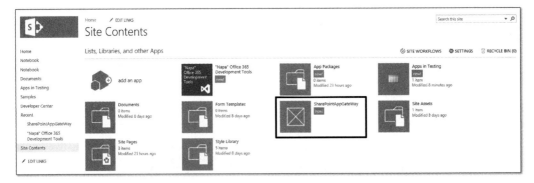

Figure 12.7 Site Contents Office 365

You'll also see your newly created Microsoft SharePoint application on the home page on the APPS IN TESTING list.

As a result, you'll get a page like the one shown in Figure 12.8, including the data from the OData service in a simple table-view layout.

CustomerID		CompanyName	ContactName	ContactTitle	Address	City	Region	PostalCode	Country	Phone	Fax
ALFKI	...	Alfreds Futterkiste	Maria Anders	Sales Representative	Obere Str. 57	Berlin		12209	Germany	030-0074321	030-0076545
ANATR	...	Ana Trujillo Emparedados y helados	Ana Trujillo	Owner	Avda. de la Constitución 2222	México D.F.		05021	Mexico	(5) 555-4729	(5) 555-3745
ANTON	...	Antonio Moreno Taquería	Antonio Moreno	Owner	Mataderos 2312	México D.F.		05023	Mexico	(5) 555-3932	
AROUT	...	Around the Horn	Thomas Hardy	Sales Representative	120 Hanover Sq.	London		WA1 1DP	UK	(171) 555-7788	(171) 555-6750
BERGS	...	Berglunds snabbköp	Christina Berglund	Order Administrator	Berguvsvägen 8	Luleå		S-958 22	Sweden	0921-12 34 65	0921-12 34 67
BLAUS	...	Blauer See Delikatessen	Hanna Moos	Sales Representative	Forsterstr. 57	Mannheim		68306	Germany	0621-08460	0621-08924
BLONP	...	Blondesddsl père et fils	Frédérique Citeaux	Marketing Manager	24, place Kléber	Strasbourg		67000	France	88.60.15.31	88.60.15.32
BOLID	...	Bólido Comidas preparadas	Martín Sommer	Owner	C/ Araquil, 67	Madrid		28023	Spain	(91) 555 22 82	(91) 555 91 99
BONAP	...	Bon app'	Laurence Lebihan	Owner	12, rue des Bouchers	Marseille		13008	France	91.24.45.40	91.24.45.41
BOTTM	...	Bottom-Dollar Markets	Elizabeth Lincoln	Accounting Manager	23 Tsawassen Blvd.	Tsawassen	BC	T2F 8M4	Canada	(604) 555-4729	(604) 555-3745
BSBEV	...	B's Beverages	Victoria Ashworth	Sales Representative	Fauntleroy Circus	London		EC2 5NT	UK	(171) 555-1212	
CACTU	...	Cactus Comidas para llevar	Patricio Simpson	Sales Agent	Cerrito 333	Buenos Aires		1010	Argentina	(1) 135-5555	(1) 135-4892
CENTC	...	Centro comercial Moctezuma	Francisco Chang	Marketing Manager	Sierras de Granada 9993	México D.F.		05022	Mexico	(5) 555-3392	(5) 555-7293

Figure 12.8 Microsoft Office 365 Application with OData

12.2 Microsoft Excel

Microsoft has published the tool Power Pivot to consume OData services directly from Microsoft Excel. You can use the installable Excel
plugin as a data mashup and data exploration tool to create analytical
reports or business graphics and update these with real data from SAP
with just one click.

Power Pivot: Minimum Requirements

▶ Microsoft Excel 2010 or above

▶ .NET Framework 4.0

▶ Visual Studio 2010 Tools for Office Runtime

▶ Microsoft Power Pivot plugin

Power Pivot enables you and your employees to use OData to consume
centralized data from different sources, such as SAP NetWeaver Gateway, and integrate it in one place (Figure 12.9).

Power Pivot

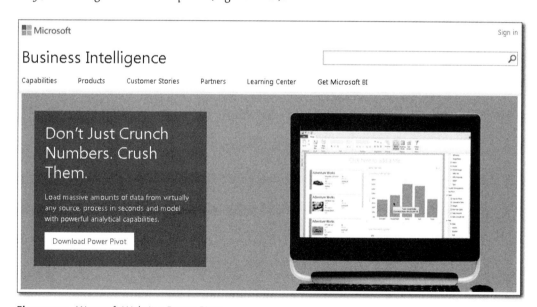

Figure 12.9 Microsoft Website: Power Pivot

You can find a detailed requirements list and the necessary download links at the Microsoft website *http://www.microsoft.com/en-us/bi/power pivot.aspx*.

> **Note**
>
> Whether to use the 32- or 64-bit version of the Power Pivot tool depends on the version of your installed Excel, not on your operating system.

After you've downloaded (and installed) all necessary prerequisites, you can install and configure Power Pivot for Excel. First, open the folder where you downloaded Power Pivot for your Excel version, double-click the *PowerPivot_for_Excel.msi* file, and follow the steps in the wizard.

After the installation process is complete, click FINISH. Start Microsoft Excel. The PowerPivot tab bar appears in the Office 2010 ribbon (Figure 12.10).

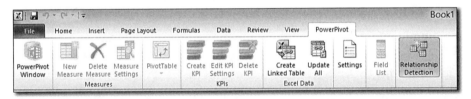

Figure 12.10 Power Pivot Ribbon

Consume data feed   To get started using Power Pivot, click the POWERPIVOT WINDOW button on the left-top corner of the bar. In the new window that appears, click on the small GET EXTERNAL DATA FROM A DATA FEED button to enter your OData service (Figure 12.11).

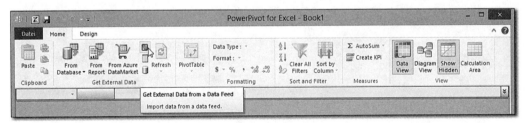

Figure 12.11 External Data Source

Enter your service URL in the following window, and click ADVANCED. Scroll down to the security options and change the INTEGRATED SECURITY method, USER ID, and PASSWORD to your needs (Figure 12.12).

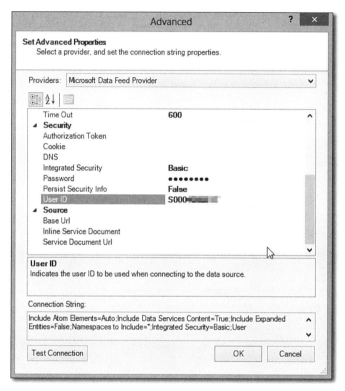

Figure 12.12 Security Credentials

Confirm your changes by clicking OK. Click TEST CONNECTION to test your settings. If the connection is successful, you can continue by clicking CONTINUE. You can select the available collection in the next screen by checking them and close the wizard by clicking FINISH (Figure 12.13).

The Power Pivot plugin fetches all of the data from the selected collections into Microsoft Excel. You'll be informed of the amount of rows for each entity received in an additional window. After the import is finished, you can close this window by clicking CLOSE. The plugin creates a sheet for each entity collection (Figure 12.14).

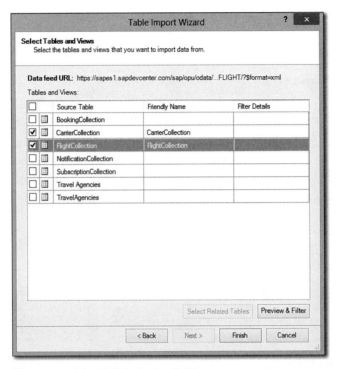

Figure 12.13 Select OData Service Entities

Figure 12.14 Power Pivot Data View

Model
You can also see an overview of the entire model of the consumed OData service. Click DIAGRAM VIEW on the right corner of the Power Pivot ribbon. The model is displayed, including all fields (Figure 12.15).

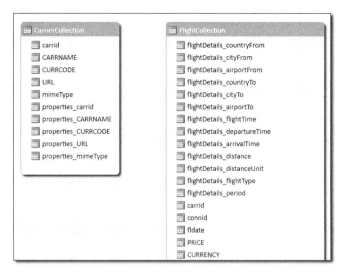

Figure 12.15 Power Pivot Data Model

Now you're able to fetch all required data directly to Microsoft Excel without copying or downloading manually from the source. You now have lots of possibilities for creating analytic reports or diagrams based on your SAP data.

12.3 Microsoft LightSwitch

Microsoft LightSwitch is a Visual Studio product for creating business enterprise applications. The applications are built on Microsoft platforms and .NET technologies, and the UI runs on Microsoft Silverlight and an HTML5 client, or as a Microsoft SharePoint 2013 application. It supports data sources such as Microsoft SharePoint, OData, and Windows Communication Foundation (WCF) services. The business logic can be written in Visual Basic or Visual C#, and the design of entities, relationships, and user interface screens is managed with an included graphic designer.

Microsoft LightSwitch: Minimum Requirements

▸ Visual Studio 2012
▸ .NET Framework

Create the
application

To start a new LightSwitch project, start Visual Studio 2012, and select FILE • NEW • PROJECT. Choose LIGHTSWITCH on the left menu bar, and select the programming language of your choice. You'll create a new Visual Basic project in this example (Figure 12.16).

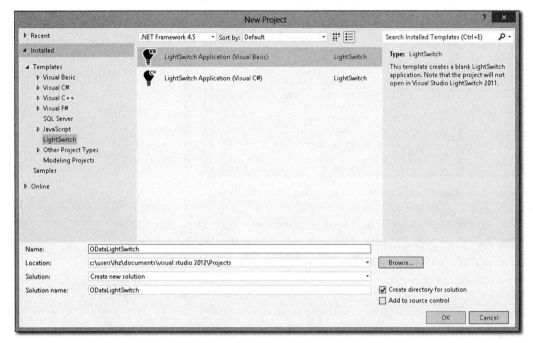

Figure 12.16 Creating a LightSwitch Project

Data source

Enter a project name, and click OK. After your project is created, Visual Studio opens a START WITH DATA screen. Click the ATTACH TO EXTERNAL DATA SOURCE link to open the data source wizard. First, you have to choose the data source, which is an ODATA SERVICE (Figure 12.17) in our scenario.

Click NEXT, and you'll be asked to specify the OData service endpoint.

> **Warning**
>
> The data type Media Element isn't supported by LightSwitch (this is a general issue, not an SAP-specific issue). Microsoft LightSwitch simply ignores these elements if they're included.

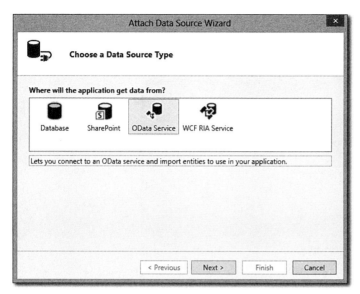

Figure 12.17 Data Source Type: OData Service

Specify the SAP NetWeaver Gateway service URL with the authentication type set to OTHER, and enter your credentials (Figure 12.18). OData service

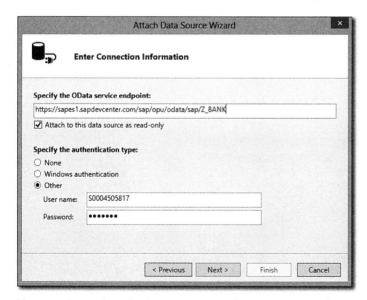

Figure 12.18 Attaching the Data Source Wizard: OData Service Endpoint

Select entities Click NEXT, and the plugin fetches the available entities and displays them in a selectable tree view. You can mark the necessary entities by clicking on their checkboxes (Figure 12.19).

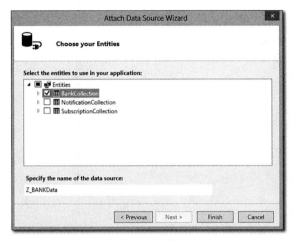

Figure 12.19 Choose OData Entities

The name of the data source is the OData service name by default, but this can be changed if you want. Click FINISH.

The tool then generates the corresponding data source and shows the selected entities on the designer screen as a table (Figure 12.20).

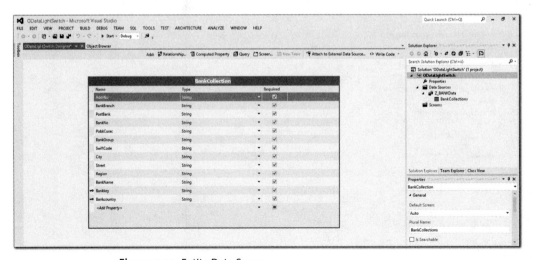

Figure 12.20 Entity Data Source

This table isn't a screen element, so you have to add a new screen manually to display the datasets from the OData service. Right-click the Screens folder in the Solution Explorer on the right side, and click the Add Screen button.

A popup appears where you select the screen template Editable Grid Screen. Select your screen data source from the dropdown menu on the right side, and enter a screen name into the Screen Name field (Figure 12.21).

Add screen

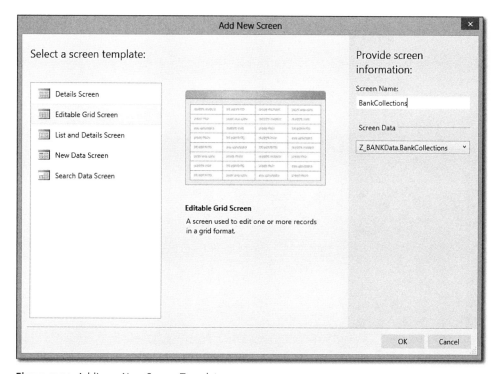

Figure 12.21 Adding a New Screen Template

Click OK. The ODataLight Designer opens with the selected collection and the default screen layout with all available attributes. Add, delete, or rearrange the attributes in the data grid row (Figure 12.22).

When you're finished, press F5 to build and start the application. The created data grid appears, and the fetched data from the OData service is shown (Figure 12.23).

OData LightSwitch application

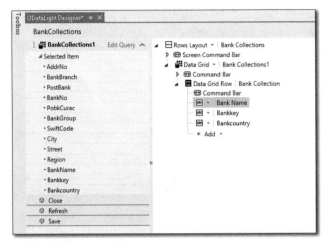

Figure 12.22 LightSwitch Designer: Layout

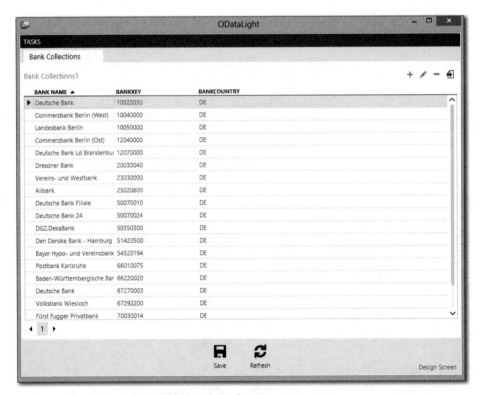

Figure 12.23 OData LightSwitch Application

Now you've created a simple Microsoft LightSwitch application with OData as the data source, which is the basis for further development.

12.4 Microsoft Active Server Pages (ASP) .NET

Microsoft ASP.NET is a server-side web application framework. It's part of the .NET Framework, so when coding ASP.NET applications, you have access to classes in the .NET Framework. In addition, you can code applications in any language compatible with the common language runtime (CLR). This includes Microsoft Visual Basic and C#.

If you're still using Visual Studio 2010, you can take a look inside SCN, where you can find a guide on how to install and use the SAP NetWeaver Gateway Developer Tool for Visual Studio.

> **Warning**
>
> There is a separate standalone plugin called SAP NetWeaver Gateway Developer Tool for Visual Studio available on SCN, but the tool supports only Visual Studio 2010. The statement in the SAP documentation that states that the plugin is compatible with "Visual Studio 2010 or *higher*" is wrong.
>
> SAP published the SAP NetWeaver Gateway Productivity Accelerator for Microsoft during the creation process of this book. It's a Visual Studio 2010/2012 add-on and works very similarly to the normal GWPA Eclipse plugin. You can find further information at *http://help.sap.com/nwgwpam*.

Because the SAP plugin for Microsoft ASP.NET doesn't work for Visual Studio 2012, Listing 12.1 shows you how to consume an OData service with any version of Visual Studio.

```
private static void GetCarrierByID()
{
    // Carrier ID for search
    string carrierId = "AA"; //American Airlines

/** SAP NetWeaver Gateway OData service **/
string serviceUrl = "http://<Gateway_Host>:<Gateway_Port>/sap/
opu/odata/iwfnd/RMTSAMPLEFLIGHT/";
```

```
RMTSAMPLEFLIGHT.RMTSAMPLEFLIGHT service = new RMTSAMPLEFLIGHT.R
MTSAMPLEFLIGHT(
    new Uri(serviceUrl));
    service.Credentials = new NetworkCredential(username, passw
ord);

/** Execute **/
var carrier = (from Carrier c in service.CarrierCollection
          where c.carrid == carrierId
          select c).FirstOrDefault();

/** Write result to console **/
Console.WriteLine(String.Format("Carrier ID = {0}",carrier.carr
id));
Console.WriteLine(String.Format("Carrier Name = {0}",carrier.ca
rrname));
}
```

Listing 12.1 .NET Application Code Snippet

12.5   Summary

After reading this chapter, you should be able to provide data to consumers such as Microsoft SharePoint and Microsoft Excel. Even if you
aren't a technical expert, with the SAP NetWeaver Service Builder functionalities discussed in earlier chapters and, for example, the Power
Pivot plugin, you can provide and consume data from SAP by yourself.
In this context, we also developed a LightSwitch sample application and
gave you sample coding for Microsoft ASP.NET. The examples in this
chapter explore only a small amount of possible options for enterprise
application development with SAP NetWeaver Gateway.

PART IV
Administration

This chapter highlights a number of topics not directly linked to SAP NetWeaver Gateway development but still important for a production environment.

13 Lifecycle Management: Testing, Service Deployment, and Operations

Like all software developments, SAP NetWeaver Gateway-based software developments follow a certain lifecycle. Typically, it starts with the identification of a business need and the analysis of user requirements, which is then followed by designing a solution for the specific need with both the SAP Business Suite and the frontend specialists. Then the actual implementation, testing, documentation, and deployment of the SAP NetWeaver Gateway services takes place, followed by the rollout of the frontend developments for the different platforms and, finally, maintenance and operations. Usually, this process doesn't stop, but is incremental and looks like a spiral; as soon as new business needs come up, the process phases are executed once again (Figure 13.1). Compared with the first time, however, it starts on top of what is already there, building on the existing foundation.

SAP NetWeaver Gateway solution lifecycle

In this chapter, we focus on three selected SAP NetWeaver Gateway solution lifecycle phases: *testing*, *deployment*, and *operating* an SAP NetWeaver Gateway environment. The other phases (*design* and *implementation*) have been addressed throughout Chapter 5, 6 and 7. What the phases covered in this chapter have in common is that they aren't directly related to development. However, they are very important for the success of your SAP NetWeaver Gateway project.

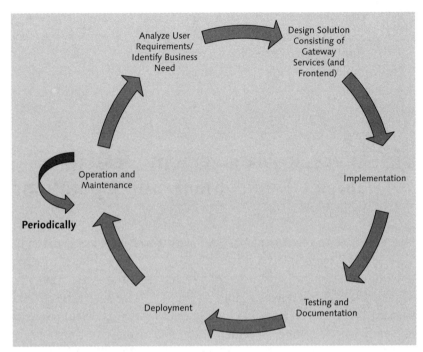

Figure 13.1 SAP NetWeaver Gateway Solution Lifecycle

13.1 Testing

Three-tier
architecture

SAP NetWeaver Gateway's three-tier architecture (SAP Business Suite tier, SAP NetWeaver Gateway tier, and consumer tier) on the one hand facilitates testing by providing obvious and straightforward interfaces to be tested; on the other hand, it can create new challenges due to the different technologies used (ABAP, client technology) and the fact that people with different know-how that belong to different departments in the organization have to be involved.

In general, it's easy to give test recommendations for the SAP NetWeaver Gateway/ABAP side of things, because this technology stays the same in all projects. For the client side, it gets a lot harder because the multiple possible client technologies might require different test approaches. Just think of a mobile application that should ideally be tested on the device and not only in an emulator, which could result in a bigger test setup—meaning that these tests are only worth performing after the application has reached a certain maturity level. At the same time, a simple HTML5 application can easily be tested very early during development, potentially even with agile/test-driven development methods.

This is especially true for applications based on the SAP UI Development Toolkit for HTML5 (SAPUI5), which can be deployed on the SAP NetWeaver Gateway hub system. These applications have a lifecycle similar to OData services based on SAP NetWeaver Gateway, because SAPUI5 applications are technically deployed on an ABAP system as a Business Server Page (BSP).

In this section, we'll introduce you to the process of testing both SAP NetWeaver Gateway services and client applications. We'll end the section with some general best practices for testing.

13.1.1 Testing SAP NetWeaver Gateway Services

Testing OData services that have been developed with SAP NetWeaver Gateway can be done independently of the target platform from which the service will be used. SAP provides several tools as part of the SAP NetWeaver Gateway platform that facilitate the testing services. The two main tools are the *SAP NetWeaver Gateway client* and the *service validation tool*. Both are described in detail in this section.

Main test tools

SAP NetWeaver Gateway Client

The SAP NetWeaver Gateway client (Transaction /IWFND/GW_CLIENT) is a powerful tool that provides the freedom to test any OData service. This enables you to test your OData services proactively and run a quality assurance test before a service is used. The SAP NetWeaver Gateway client allows you to do the following:

▶ Create test cases for OData services.

▶ Save the created test cases and replay them at any time.

▶ Simulate a service at runtime to identify and resolve potential issues.

▶ Reproduce runtime situations that led to a particular error.

▶ Run several test cases in a sequential order to test more complex scenarios of creating, updating, reading, and deleting data.

The SAP NetWeaver Gateway client is fully integrated with other SAP NetWeaver Gateway tools such as Transaction /IWFND/MAINT_SERVICE (Maintain Service) or Transaction /IWFND/ERROR_LOG (Error Log) to allow for following up on identified problems efficiently. It acts as an HTTP client and enables the testing of HTTP requests and responses as they would arise at runtime. The SAP NetWeaver Gateway client is started using Transaction /IWFND/GW_CLIENT, and its UI is shown in Figure 13.2.

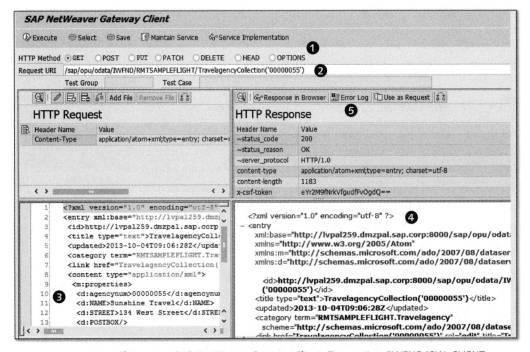

Figure 13.2 SAP NetWeaver Gateway Client: Transaction /IWFND/GW_CLIENT

You can perform GET, PUT, POST, PATCH, DELETE, HEAD, and OPTIONS HTTP methods, as shown in ❶. The tool provides an area for entering the request URI (shown in ❷) and a screen area for the actual HTTP request (shown in ❸). This HTTP request area can be filled with the service data (request payload) either directly or by uploading from a local file. After you've executed the request, the response is displayed in the HTTP response frame as shown in ❹. If an error arises as a result of the test, the HTTP status and value are displayed. You can then display details of the HTTP response, display the response in an additional browser window, or navigate to the ERROR LOG transaction tab (as shown in ❺) to analyze and correct the error.

To facilitate repeated testing, the SAP NetWeaver Gateway client is integrated with an underlying database allowing for accessing request data already stored in that database or for storing your own test cases in that database. Stored test cases can then be executed repeatedly. Test cases can be grouped into test groups so that they are easier to retrieve. It's especially possible to store the expected HTTP return code(s) for each test case. If the return code differs from the one that has been specified as the expected one in the test case, the test case is shown as erroneous, as shown in ❶ of Figure 13.3.

Test cases and groups

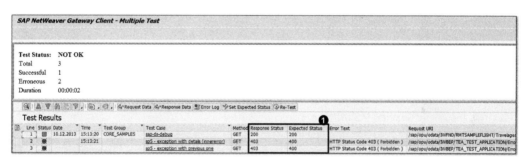

Figure 13.3 Gateway Client: Multiple Test Screen

To further facilitate testing, SAP delivers the test group CORE_SAMPLES that already contains sample data for your testing. You can enable these test cases for usage by selecting GATEWAY CLIENT • CREATE CORE_SAMPLES from the menu in your SAP NetWeaver Gateway client. Existing test cases can be adapted to your needs, or you can define and save your own.

Test cases delivered by SAP

After running your test cases, the results are displayed on the SAP NETWEAVER GATEWAY CLIENT – MULTIPLE TEST screen as shown in Figure 13.3. At a glance, you can see the status of the test indicated by a traffic light icon, the HTTP method, HTTP response, expected status or statuses, descriptive error text, a request URI, and the test group. In case of errors, you can jump to the error log by clicking the ERROR LOG button, and after fixing the problem that led to the error, you can click the RE-TEST button to run a retest.

CSRF
The SAP NetWeaver Gateway client also supports you when performing WRITE operations. Here the cross-site request forgery (CSRF) token that is needed for such operations is acquired automatically. (This is opposed to the approach of using a third-party REST client. In that case, you first have to perform a separate GET request to fetch a CSRF token for any subsequent Update, Create, or Delete operation.)

Note that the SAP NetWeaver Gateway client requests a new CSRF token for every READ operation. As a result, the token displayed in the transaction changes all of the time, although it has a certain lifetime.

> **Further Resources**
>
> More details on the SAP NetWeaver Gateway client can be found here:
>
> *http://help.sap.com/saphelp_gateway20sp06/helpdata/en/2e/389be03ca745 34a254569cd4a1a018/frameset.htm*

Service Validation Tool

Runtime validation
SAP NetWeaver Gateway offers a validation tool that validates the runtime for all SAP NetWeaver Gateway services. Runtime validation ensures that the runtime is behaving as intended with no issues (such as syntax errors in programs, RFC authorization issues, etc.). It involves executing READ and QUERY operations on the collections exposed via the service document and checking the HTTP response code. For READ operations, the tool also takes care of executing the self-links for all of the collections and all of the navigation properties in a recursive manner. No user intervention is required during this process.

To validate a service, go to Transaction /IWFND/SRV_VALIDATE, and enter the service document identifier. Select VALIDATE SERVICE, and choose EXECUTE. After a validation run, you can select DISPLAY LAST RUN RESULTS and choose EXECUTE to look at the detailed results.

> **eCATT Based Test Automation For OData Service**
>
> The Extended Computer Aided Test Tool (eCATT) is one of the main tools used by customers to create and execute functional tests. Its primary goal is the automated testing of business processes in SAP. Test APIs have been published as a project on Code Exchange on the SAP Community Network (SCN) to allow for eCATT-based test automation of OData services exposed through SAP NetWeaver Gateway. You can find these test APIs here:
>
> *http://scn.sap.com/docs/DOC-41875*

13.1.2 Testing a Client Application

Testing the client application is a complex topic because there are so many client platforms that could be used to call SAP NetWeaver Gateway services. Therefore, providing you with detailed recommendations on how to test your specific client application on your specific technology is beyond the scope of this book.

What is possible, however, is to look at the three main categories of SAP NetWeaver Gateway projects and identify commonalities of the three project categories as well as some differences that you need to take into account for your test strategies:

Project categories

▶ **Mobile**
This category contains all SAP NetWeaver Gateway projects in which applications are deployed on mobile devices (e.g., smartphones, tablets, notebooks) and use SAP NetWeaver Gateway to access SAP Business Suite systems. Examples of mobile applications include Android applications, iPhone applications, and BlackBerry applications.

▶ **Desktop**
This category contains all projects in which an application using SAP NetWeaver Gateway services is developed for a stationary device, typically a PC. Examples for desktop applications include, for example, an application built using Microsoft .NET.

▶ **Web**
This category contains all projects that use SAP NetWeaver Gateway for web-based access to SAP Business Suite systems. Examples include

Facebook applications, browser applications using HTML5 and Java-Script, and browser-based applications based on PHP.

Most other use cases and architectures are subcategories of these three main categories. The type of an SAP NetWeaver Gateway project has a significant impact on its lifecycle. A lot of things can be addressed very similarly, whereas other topics differ to a major extent from one type to another. In respect to an impact on testing, the following are some commonalities of the three categories of SAP NetWeaver Gateway projects just defined:

▶ Clients consume SAP NetWeaver Gateway services and rely on their accuracy. It's hard for the client application to identify incorrect data (although not impossible). Test cases should be created in the SAP NetWeaver Gateway client containing all requests that are planned to be issued by the consumer applications.

▶ It's hard to decide in which direction to test. In an ideal world, you would start bottom up, meaning that you would first verify the accuracy of the SAP NetWeaver Gateway services. Only then would the client application developers start their development. Unfortunately, the world isn't perfect, and for cost or availability reasons, the work of both teams (i.e., the SAP NetWeaver Gateway service team and the client application team) may significantly, if not completely, overlap each other.

▶ To make things even worse, it may be that team members are not experienced in both the client and the SAP Business Suite side, which has the potential to make communication between the two teams difficult. Fortunately, the OData protocol helps here, because the entity data model serves as a contract between the SAP and the non-SAP developers. SAP NetWeaver Gateway certainly facilitates the process of bringing the client developers and the SAP Business Suite developers together a lot better than traditional approaches; however, there are still some gaps between these two worlds that need to be bridged.

There are additional factors that come into play when testing SAP NetWeaver Gateway client applications. These factors are project-category specific and therefore don't come into play for every single client application you develop. However, if they do come into play, they have a strong impact on testing. These factors are:

- **Online versus offline**
  In almost all cases, web and desktop clients are used in always-online production environments. Therefore, a loss of connection should be looked at as a test case to see how your application reacts. At the same time, this will only result in a few test cases in your test plan. For some mobile applications, this might be different; that is, business-critical applications might have to run offline (i.e., when the connection is lost or the network connection is poor or unreliable). This does require additional development and testing effort.

- **Additional solutions**
  Additional solutions or technical mechanisms can influence application behavior and need to be taken into account for tests. Examples include the use of SAP Mobile Platform together with SAP NetWeaver Gateway or the impact of security mechanisms for web applications.

As stated earlier, from an SAP NetWeaver Gateway perspective, we can only briefly mention these topics. In the end, these are development and quality assurance topics on the client side. From an SAP NetWeaver Gateway perspective, the main testing concern is how best to synchronize the client application development with the SAP NetWeaver Gateway service development.

13.1.3 Best Practices for Testing in SAP NetWeaver Gateway

The focus of this best practices section lies on assuring and verifying the quality of the developed SAP NetWeaver Gateway services and on a working setup for the development project in respect to early usage of verified SAP NetWeaver Gateway services in client application development. Consider the following best practices for testing:

Testing best practices

- Before your project starts, make sure that the two development teams (client application, SAP Business Suite) talk to each other and verify that the planned SAP NetWeaver Gateway services deliver the right data for the client application. Unused data transferred via SAP NetWeaver Gateway services lowers performance levels. A missing field in the client application can result in some overhead (e.g., testing, communication). So some kind of dry testing pays off; in other words, check on whether your specifications fit the client and SAP NetWeaver Gateway side early.

▶ SAP NetWeaver Gateway service development usually starts first. There is no need for a major head start; a few days should be enough. Give the team sufficient time, though.

▶ Services should be grouped according to their use in the client application. Ideally, parts of the client application can already be based on developed and working SAP NetWeaver Gateway services. That way, client application developers can test their development against the real services at development time; no need for stubs on the client side, which saves time and improves quality. Overall, this results in an incremental approach. A good recommendation here in case of a tight project schedule is to use stubs on the SAP NetWeaver Gateway side to cater for the early consumption of services.

▶ Developed SAP NetWeaver Gateway services should be thoroughly tested using test tools, for example, the SAP NetWeaver Gateway client. When services have reached a certain maturity, these can then be handed over to the client application development. Additional tests can then be executed using the client application when it's ready to further improve the overall quality.

▶ Perform tests in the production environment early. That is, make sure that no surprises can come up with respect to the technical environment (e.g., reverse proxies, ports) or to the hardware you'll run the client application on (e.g., the development took place using an emulator only). Obviously, these early tests can't always be performed end-to-end at a very early stage. You can, however, run selected tests—it doesn't matter whether you call an SAP NetWeaver Gateway service using a browser or the client application. You detect the same problems between the browser and SAP NetWeaver Gateway as you would between the client application and SAP NetWeaver Gateway.

▶ Technically, using the query option `sap-ds-debug=true` facilitates improved testing with the browser because the XML or JSON response is rendered as an HTML page. Because of this, any browser can be used for testing, and the test results don't depend on the browser being used. In addition, using the query option `sap-ds-debug=true` shows many additional details that can be of interest during troubleshooting.

Overall, both OData and SAP NetWeaver Gateway have been designed for early and easy testing. This shows and should result in a great service and application quality.

13.2   Service Deployment

After both the developed SAP NetWeaver Gateway services and the client application have reached the required maturity level, it's time for the rollout. A *classic rollout* is one where you take some piece of ready-to-use software to its future users. This type of rollout is appropriate for the client application in mobile and desktop categories, but for SAP NetWeaver Gateway services, this description only partially fits. The services simply have to be deployed on the SAP NetWeaver Gateway server or the SAP Business Suite system using the change and transport system. An explanation of how to rollout client applications is a broader topic beyond the scope of this book. Instead, we'll focus on the SAP NetWeaver Gateway part, which is more of a deployment than a rollout.

As you saw in Chapter 5, Chapter 6, and Chapter 7, several repository objects, such as ABAP classes, have to be created when building an OData service. It's important to note that repository objects have to be created not only on the SAP Business Suite system, but also on the SAP NetWeaver Gateway server system. In addition to repository objects, you need to create customizing entries on the SAP NetWeaver Gateway server system as well. All of these repository objects and customizing entries have to be transported at the customer site using the change and transport system so that they can finally be used in production.

Repository objects

In the following, we'll take a closer look at the lifecycle management of an SAP NetWeaver Gateway service by first describing which repository objects have to be transported between the SAP Business Suite systems. Then we'll dive into the lifecycle management activities that have to take place on the SAP NetWeaver Gateway servers. Here we'll describe which repository objects have to be transported between the SAP

Versioning

NetWeaver Gateway servers in a system landscape and how customizing settings have to be transported. At the end of this section, we'll explain the concept of versioning that is supported by SAP NetWeaver Gateway services and investigate the different capabilities of Transaction /IWFND/MAINT_SERVICE (Activate and Maintain Services), which is used for service maintenance on SAP NetWeaver Gateway server systems. Versioning as a feature can be of interest if changes are performed in SAP NetWeaver Gateway services that aren't compatible with an already rolled out client software. In this case, multiple versions of clients and services have to be supported in parallel.

Deployment Options and Lifecycle Management

Of the different deployment options discussed in Chapter 4 (hub deployment with development in the SAP Business Suite system, hub deployment with development on the hub, and embedded deployment), one option needs special attention. In the case of hub deployment with development in the SAP Business Suite system, the transport of repository objects and customizing entries has to be synchronized between the SAP NetWeaver Gateway hub and the SAP Business Suite system—or at least you must ensure that the SAP Business Suite system transports are transported first so that the artifacts are available when registering and activating the service on the SAP NetWeaver Gateway hub.

The other two deployment options are easier to handle because all development artifacts and customizing entries are created in and transported to only one system, where both the SAP NetWeaver Gateway server and SAP NetWeaver Gateway backend enablement components are installed.

13.2.1 Transport of Repository Objects between SAP Business Suite Systems

In this section, the backend system we refer to is the system in which the development of an OData service takes place. Depending on the deployment option being chosen, this can also be on the SAP NetWeaver Gateway hub system if IW_BEP is deployed or, if the hub system runs on top of 7.40 SP02, the system on which the software component SAP_GWFND is present.

As a result of the development of an SAP NetWeaver Gateway service using the SAP NetWeaver Gateway Service Builder, the following repository objects are created:

Repository object examples

▶ Four ABAP classes:

▷ Data provider class

▷ Data provider extension class

▷ Model provider class

▷ Model provider extension class

▶ Service object

▶ Model object

▶ Service Builder project

These repository objects (listed in Table 13.1) have to be transported into the quality and the production systems, as depicted in Figure 13.4.

Short Description	Program ID	Object Type	Example of an Object Name
Service Builder Project	R3TR	IWPR	Z_PRODUCT
Class	R3TR	CLAS	ZCL_Z_PRODUCT_MPC
Class	R3TR	CLAS	ZCL_Z_PRODUCT_MPC_EXT
Class	R3TR	CLAS	ZCL_Z_PRODUCT_DPC
Class	R3TR	CLAS	ZCL_Z_PRODUCT_DPC_EXT
Model object	R3TR	IWMO	ZPRODUCT_MDL
Service object	R3TR	IWSV	Z_PRODUCT

Table 13.1 Repository Objects of an SAP NetWeaver Gateway Service in the Backend System

When importing these repository objects in the quality- or production backend system, the service is automatically registered in that system. To be able to consume the OData service, it has to be registered and activated in the SAP NetWeaver Gateway hub system. This process is described in Section 13.2.2.

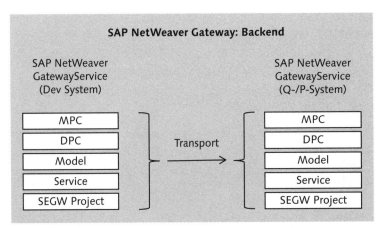

Figure 13.4 Repository Objects to Transport between SAP Business Suite Backend Systems

Transporting Service Builder project not mandatory

To use the service in other systems of the transport system landscape, transporting the Service Builder project isn't mandatory—it's enough to only transport the runtime components. You may find it convenient, however, to also have the Service Builder project available, because you can then open and use it as an entry point for Transaction SEGW if needed for troubleshooting.

13.2.2 Transport of Repository Objects and Customizing Entries between SAP NetWeaver Gateway Server Systems

In addition to the service implementation in the backend, the service has to be activated in the SAP NetWeaver Gateway hub, and might have to be registered for additional backend systems. As a result (as described in Chapter 5, Chapter 6, and Chapter 7), there are several repository objects and customizing entries created during development in the SAP NetWeaver Gateway hub system that then need to be transported. The administrator has to maintain some customizing settings directly in the quality and production system, however, rather than transporting them, for reasons we'll explain next.

In the SAP NetWeaver Gateway hub development system, only three repository objects are created:

▶ Service model
▶ Service
▶ ICF node

In addition, the following customizing settings are created:

▶ System alias (which might have already existed)
▶ Assignment of the system alias to the activated service

These objects are depicted in ❶ of Figure 13.5. In addition, the repository objects that have to be transported are listed in Table 13.2.

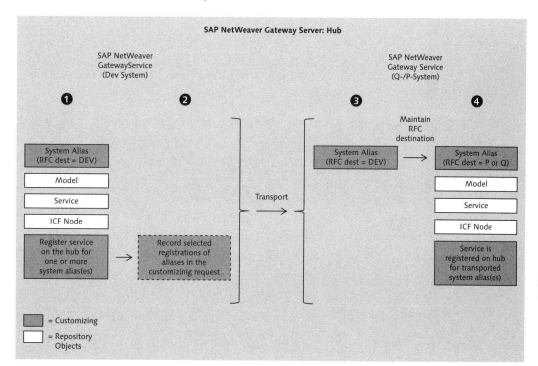

Figure 13.5 Repository Objects and Customizing Settings to Be Transported between the SAP NetWeaver Gateway Server Systems

Short Description	Program ID	Object Type	Example of an Object Name
Service	R3TR	IWSG	ZPRODUCT_SRV_0001
Model	R3TR	IWOM	ZPRODUCT_MDL_0001_BE
ICF node	R3TR	SICF	00O2TMQPDL0AXGC2ZZH2Y8XW1

Table 13.2 Repository Objects of an SAP NetWeaver Gateway Service in the SAP NetWeaver Gateway Hub System

Customizing entries

The customizing entries that are created as part of the service creation process on the SAP NetWeaver Gateway server development system need special attention. Some customizing settings have to be manually included in a customizing request, because they aren't recorded automatically. In addition, it's necessary to perform certain customizing steps on the SAP NetWeaver Gateway production system, because these can't be transported. We'll discuss these processes next.

Transporting the Assignment of System Aliases

When using Transaction /IWFND/MAINT_SERVICE (Activate and Maintain Services) to activate a service on the SAP NetWeaver Gateway hub and to assign it for one or more backend systems, the customizing settings that are being created are *not* recorded automatically. You have to record these settings *manually* in a customizing request instead. The reason for this is that it can't be taken for granted that a system alias entry does exist in other systems of the SAP NetWeaver Gateway system landscape. This step is depicted in ❷ of Figure 13.5.

This sometimes leads to the issue that the customizing settings that are necessary for the service to be correctly activated aren't transported. In turn, this leads to an error message in the target system if a client tries to consume the incorrectly activated service.

The transport of services is usually not performed by the developer, but by the system administrator—so this shouldn't be an issue, as long as this behavior is known to the system administrator, and the customizing settings are being manually recorded and transported. The manual recording of the customizing settings should not be overlooked though.

Transporting System Aliases

In an implementation done on SAP NetWeaver Gateway as a hub, there is the need to access SAP Business Suite systems or third-party systems via RFC, web services, or the OData protocol. The content provider connectivity abstracts from such protocol specifics by means of a system alias, which can be configured by the administrator to point to the desired RFC, web service, or HTTP destination. Due to their importance, the handling of these system alias entries needs special attention in a production SAP NetWeaver Gateway landscape.

What makes this very useful concept sometimes a little bit tricky is the fact that in development and production systems, destinations usually have different names. The reason for this is that often (customer) naming conventions for RFC destinations might, for example, contain the logical system name of the target system or other means that let the user conclude to which system the destination points. As a result, it's unfortunately required to maintain these system-specific settings in the system alias entries in every SAP NetWeaver Gateway hub system that is part of an SAP NetWeaver Gateway landscape (development, quality assurance, and production).

Destinations with different names

Technically, the settings for a system alias entry are stored in customizing tables that can be maintained using the view /IWFND/V_DFSYAL. Because clients in a production system are usually locked to prevent customizing changes, it's by default not possible to maintain the view /IWFND/V_DFSYAL unless the system is opened. Obviously, opening up a production system for this task is out of the question because of legal requirements, unless exceptional circumstances do require such changes (e.g., during an upgrade). What is possible, though, is to use a concept called *current settings* that has been introduced to address similar situations.

Table maintenance is started via a customizing task in the IMG, which is classified to allow such changes by having been declared as a current setting. With SP06, the customizing task for system alias maintenance is configured accordingly. As a result, you can maintain a system alias if the maintenance dialog is opened via the IMG. For this, you have to start Transaction SPRO and navigate to SAP NetWeaver • Gateway • OData

CHANNEL • CONFIGURATION • CONNECTION SETTINGS • SAP NETWEAVER GATEWAY TO SAP SYSTEM.

Using this concept of current settings, customers can now create system aliases once in the development system and then transport the system aliases to the production system. In the production system, the system administrator is able to maintain the RFC, web service, or HTTP destination that is actually used by a system alias in the target system.

13.2.3 Versioning

SAP NetWeaver Gateway provides versioning to allow for keeping older and newer SAP NetWeaver Gateway service versions separate. This is essential in order to enable different versions of a service to be available for consumption in parallel.

Version numbers

By default, every initial SAP NetWeaver Gateway service is registered and activated with version number 1. If the service is developed further and if any changes are incompatible to the consumers that already use the service, you can register and activate the SAP NetWeaver Gateway service with an increased version number (e.g., 2 or 3, etc.). This version number is a four-digit value, so you can potentially create 9,999 versions of your service.

When consuming this service, the consumer has to add, for example, *;v=2* to the URI to access version 2 of the service. For example:

http://<host>:<port>/sap/opu/odata/iwfnd/catalogservice;v=2/

Technically, each new version of a service is very similar to a completely new service. Each version has its own model provider class as well as a data provider class. This allows for keeping the entire logic of, for example, version 1 (which might be in production already), and defining everything independently for version 2.

13.2.4 Activate and Maintain Service Transaction

OData services need to be maintained and activated in the SAP NetWeaver Gateway hub system. To perform this task, you have to start Transaction /IWFND/MAINT_SERVICE on the SAP NetWeaver Gateway hub system.

On the first screen, the service catalog is displayed that contains a list of services that have been activated in the current system. Note that this list can also be retrieved using *http://<server>:<port>/sap/opu/odata/ iwfnd/CATALOGSERVICE/*.

A service can be tested by selecting it from the list and choosing either CALL BROWSER or GATEWAY CLIENT in the ICF NODES section. The ACTIVATE AND MAINTAIN SERVICES screen lets you perform the following tasks as shown in Figure 13.6:

❶ Register and activate a new service in the hub.

❷ Start the error log for the selected service.

❸ Test the selected service using a browser.

❹ Test the selected service using the SAP NetWeaver Gateway client.

❺ Add additional system alias entries for the selected service.

❻ Delete the system alias assignment for the selected service.

❼ Inspect service implementation.

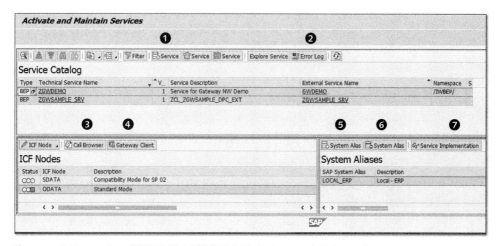

Figure 13.6 Transaction /IWFND/MAINT_SERVICE: Activate and Maintain Services

SAP wanted to make the process of activating a service on the development SAP NetWeaver Gateway hub system as convenient as possible for the service developer. Therefore, it's possible to start the service registration and activation on the SAP NetWeaver Gateway hub from within the Service Builder by right-clicking on the SAP NetWeaver Gateway hub entry you want to register your service to and activate on. Then, select REGISTER from the context menu.

13.3   Operations

Running tasks   The operations phase of the SAP NetWeaver Gateway lifecycle primarily consists of recurring tasks that shouldn't be neglected. Because operations isn't a one-time event but an ongoing task, operating your environment in a smart way is crucial. In this section, we'll first take a brief look at some periodic cleanup tasks before taking a deep dive into SAP NetWeaver Gateway-related monitoring. We'll wrap this section up with some troubleshooting best practices.

13.3.1   Periodic Cleanup Tasks

After rollout, periodic tasks need to be performed frequently to ensure that SAP NetWeaver Gateway runs smoothly and the performance stays optimal. Specifically, you need to clean up jobs on the SAP NetWeaver Gateway server system(s) that are executed on a regular basis. The frequency of running the different services depends on the load of your system and may vary.

Daily Jobs for Usage Data

When activating SAP NetWeaver Gateway, two daily jobs are scheduled that aggregate usage data and delete outdated usage data:

▶ SAP_IWFND_METERING_AGG is scheduled as a daily job that aggregates data based on the report /IWFND/R_MET_AGGREGATE.

▶ SAP_IWFND_METERING_DEL is scheduled as a daily job that deletes data older than two years based on the report /IWFND/R_MET_DELETE.

Application Log

With respect to the application log, there is a flag that controls what is written into the application log (e.g., only errors or also warnings). Make sure this flag is set appropriately. Otherwise, over time, the application log might amass a lot of entries. Nevertheless, even with limited settings, you need to periodically clear the application log. To limit the amount of data stored, the application log should only store one entry per request as a default. In addition, there is no need to store these entries for more than a few days.

In an SAP NetWeaver Gateway server, the application log can be cleared in the SAP NetWeaver Gateway IMG structure by following the navigation path Transaction SPRO • SAP NetWeaver • Gateway • OData Channel • Administration • Logging Settings • Clear Application Log.

In an SAP Business Suite system IMG, follow the navigation path Transaction SPRO • SAP NetWeaver • Gateway Business Suite Enablement • Backend OData Channel • Logging Settings • Clear Application Log.

It's recommended to carry out the activity, plan a job, and use report SBAL_DELETE to clear the application log.

13.3.2 Monitoring Overview

SAP NetWeaver Gateway comes with an optimized set of tools to first identify issues in your SAP NetWeaver Gateway environment (i.e., monitoring) and then, in a second step, allow you to dig deeper into the issue to solve it (i.e., troubleshooting). This set of tools is connected in several ways to allow you to jump from one tool to another when appropriate, saving time and making it easier to follow up on potential errors. The goal is for you to be able to concentrate on finding the problem and not on the tooling.

SAP NetWeaver Gateway tackles the monitoring and troubleshooting topic from several sides:

▶ **Computing Center Management System (CCMS)**
Monitors the SAP NetWeaver Gateway system environment and alerts the system administrator if it detects potential issues.

- **Error log**
  Provides detailed information about SAP NetWeaver Gateway runtime errors and allows for root cause analysis. Use this tool to analyze errors that have occurred and led to a termination of an OData request or notification processing (push channel). The error log can be accessed via Transaction /IWFND/ERROR_LOG on the SAP NetWeaver Gateway hub system or via Transaction /IWBEP/VIEW_ LOG on the SAP Business Suite system.

- **Application log**
  Enables viewing of the SAP NetWeaver Gateway application logs. This tool is recommended to check on more technical error details. Access the application log via Transaction /IWFND/APPS_LOG on the SAP NetWeaver Gateway system and Transaction /IWBEP/ERROR_ LOG on the SAP Business Suite system.

- **SAP Solution Manager**
  Monitors an SAP NetWeaver Gateway system landscape end-to-end. SAP Solution Manager delivers various monitors that raise alerts if certain error conditions are met. For example, an alert is raised if the number of errors in the error log exceeds a certain threshold.

- **Performance trace tool**
  Offers detailed information on the performance behavior of SAP NetWeaver Gateway service calls. It's the tool of choice for service calls showing performance problems. You can access it via Transaction /IWFND/TRACES.

Next, we'll discuss each of these tools in more detail. We'll conclude with some troubleshooting tips related to monitoring.

Monitoring via CCMS

Transaction RZ20   SAP NetWeaver Gateway is automatically monitored within the Computing Center Maintenance System (CCMS). The CCMS is provided in SAP NetWeaver and can be used immediately after installation. CCMS allows for collecting all monitoring information within your system landscape in the central monitoring system. Collected information about SAP NetWeaver Gateway can be viewed via Transaction RZ20. The information available here is updated on an hourly basis and includes which applications are in use and how often these are called.

Alerts are one central concept of the CCMS. These alerts are generated by the Alert Monitor if the status of a monitored system deviates from the norm. This deviation is identified by threshold values and rules. Alerts attract attention to critical situations and should be addressed by the system administrator. For SAP NetWeaver Gateway, this means that SAP NetWeaver Gateway-specific alerts point the system administrator to potential issues and greatly facilitate the monitoring of a production SAP NetWeaver Gateway environment.

Logging and Tracing via Error Log

The SAP NetWeaver Gateway error log is a very useful addition to the standard SAP NetWeaver application log viewer. We actually recommend the error log as the central point for logging in SAP NetWeaver Gateway. The tool can be accessed via Transaction /IWFND/ERROR_ LOG. It can be used both on an SAP NetWeaver Gateway hub system and in an SAP Business Suite system. There you have to use Transaction /IWBEP/ERROR_LOG instead. The tool provides detailed context information about errors that have occurred at runtime by providing information in two screen areas: an overview area and an error context area.

The SAP NetWeaver Gateway error log allows for identifying where exactly in the source code errors occur, seeing how often errors occur, reproducing errors, performing a root cause analysis, and in the end helping you fix the errors.

To facilitate this process, the error log is organized in an overview section (OVERVIEW area of the screen) and a detail section (ERROR CONTEXT area of the screen) (Figure 13.7). The OVERVIEW area lists all error IDs, their attributes, and the date and time at which the particular errors occurred. Error information and descriptive error texts can be displayed to obtain more detailed information about a particular error. You can also execute searches on the error list.

Alerts

Overview and details

561

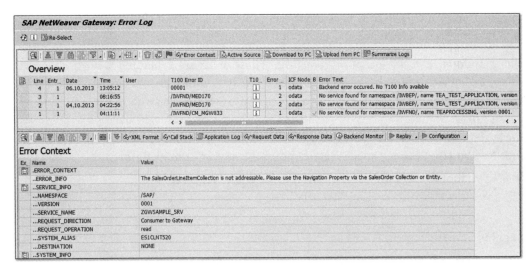

Figure 13.7 SAP NetWeaver Gateway: Error Log

Error context   The ERROR CONTEXT area can be accessed by selecting an error in the OVERVIEW area and then double-clicking on the error information. After you've done this, the relevant context information about an error is displayed in the ERROR CONTEXT area where further investigations are possible by expanding the information. The ERROR CONTEXT area provides you, among other things, with the following relevant information:

▶ XML FORMAT
Displays the error in context in an XML format, allowing you to see all information unfiltered.

▶ REQUEST DATA
Displays the request XML that was sent from an external consumer. This call contains HTTP request headers and payload.

▶ RESPONSE DATA
Displays the response XML sent from SAP NetWeaver Gateway. It contains the HTTP response headers and payload.

▶ REPLAY
Allows for two replay options (SAP NetWeaver Gateway client and web browser) to reproduce and correct errors.

▶ APPLICATION LOG
Allows for navigating to the corresponding entry in the application log.

Further Resources

Detailed information on the SAP NetWeaver Gateway error log can be found in the SAP NetWeaver Gateway technical operations guide at *http://help.sap.com/saphelp_gateway20sp06/helpdata/en/2e/389be03ca74534a254 569cd4a1a018/frameset.htm*.

Application Log Viewer

A specific tool allows you to view SAP NetWeaver Gateway application logs, as shown in Figure 13.8. To access this tool, go to Transaction /IWFND/APPS_LOG in the SAP NetWeaver Gateway hub system or Transaction /IWBEP/VIEW_LOG in the SAP Business Suite system. In the selection screen of this viewer, you can search log protocols by object, subobject, log ID, content ID, request direction, and date. The amount of logs that are created can be adjusted to best serve your individual needs. This adjustment takes place in the SAP IMG in the logging settings.

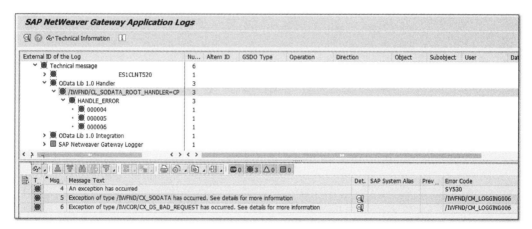

Figure 13.8 SAP NetWeaver Gateway Application Logs

Over time, the application log amasses a lot of entries, which periodically need to be cleared. As a default, it should only store one entry per request. In addition, it isn't necessary to store these entries for more than a few days.

> **Further Resources**
>
> More details on the SAP NetWeaver Gateway application log can be found here:
>
> *http://help.sap.com/saphelp_gateway20sp06/helpdata/en/d8/8afed0c41e4c4 593b5ecd48e8f2f76/content.htm*

SAP Solution Manager

Technical monitoring in SAP Solution Manager also provides content for SAP NetWeaver Gateway. In addition to the content provided for ABAP systems in general, additional monitoring metrics have been added for the performance of SAP NetWeaver Gateway service requests and number of exceptions per time frame (5 minutes) in the SAP NetWeaver Gateway log as shown in Figure 13.9.

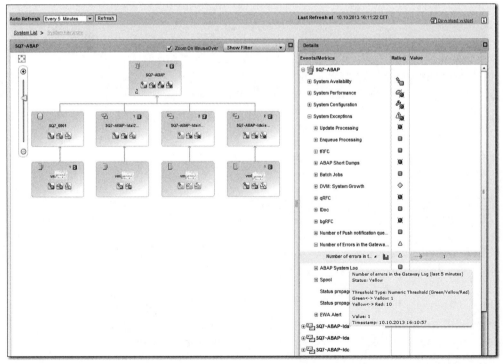

Figure 13.9 Technical System Monitoring of SAP NetWeaver Gateway in SAP Solution Manager

Performance Trace Tool

The SAP NetWeaver Gateway performance trace tool is a support utility for SAP NetWeaver Gateway that allows for monitoring system performance at a service call level. It's directed toward both developers and administrators of SAP NetWeaver Gateway services and enables tracing the performance of both the SAP Business Suite system and the SAP NetWeaver Gateway server (depending on the specific deployment).

> **Further Resources**
>
> More details on the SAP NetWeaver Gateway performance trace tool can be found in Appendix A, as well as at this link:
>
> *http://help.sap.com/saphelp_gateway20sp06/helpdata/en/9d/da3a2ceca344c f85568ae927e9858d/content.htm*

Before you can use the performance trace tool, you need to configure it according to your needs and activate it. To do the required configuration, go to Transaction /IWFND/TRACES (alternatively, you can go to Transaction SPRO, open the SAP Reference IMG, and then navigate to SAP NETWEAVER • GATEWAY • ODATA CHANNEL • ADMINISTRATION • SUPPORT UTILITIES • TRACES). There you can configure the tool according to user name or URI prefix.

Configuration

> **Note**
>
> To configure the performance trace tool for all OData service calls, enter the URI prefix "/sap/opu/".

After a successful configuration, the next step is to activate the performance trace, which actually takes place under the CONFIGURATION tab of the performance trace tool. Select ACTIVE from the dropdown list next to the PERFORMANCE TRACE field. It's important to choose SAVE CONFIGURATION to save your settings and immediately activate the performance trace. The active trace is started and runs for two hours as a default. You can check the duration of the trace in the ACTIVE TRACE IS VALID UNTIL field. Figure 13.10 shows how the performance trace is activated for a single service ZGWSAMPLE_SRV by specifying the following URI:

/sap/opu/odata/sap/ZGWSAMPLE_SRV/BusinessPartnerCollection

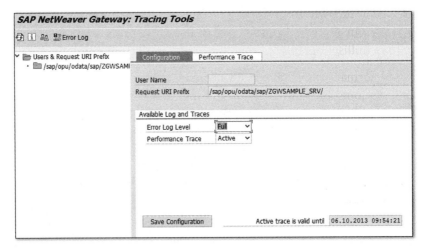

Figure 13.10 Activating Performance Trace

Tabular overview

If you now call any service according to the defined filter, the performance trace will generate information that you can display and analyze. To do so, go to the PERFORMANCE TRACE tab. You receive a tabular overview in which all service calls (after activation) are listed in chronological order.

The service call information is listed together with the ICF node, the date and time of the call, its expiry date, and the success of a specific service call execution, as shown in Figure 13.11.

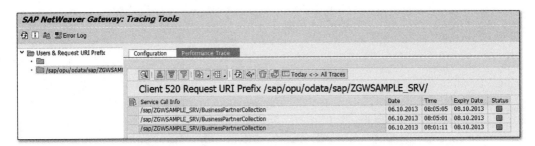

Figure 13.11 Performance Test Data

Additional information can be displayed for one or more service calls on demand. This information includes, for example, the number of subcalls, the location of a service call (i.e., in the SAP NetWeaver Gateway system or the SAP Business Suite system), class, method, and, most important in a trace, the total duration and the net time of a service call (both in milliseconds).

The performance trace tool is well connected to other SAP NetWeaver Gateway tools and allows for an easy follow up on detected shortcomings. By selecting a service and clicking a button, you can dig deeper into a topic either using SAP NetWeaver Gateway's error log tool or by directly jumping to the corresponding source code in the ABAP Workbench, as shown in Figure 13.12.

SAP NetWeaver Gateway: Performance Trace

Client 520 User   Status OK

Line No	Subcalls	Level	Location	Agent	Class	Method	Duration (ms)	Net Time (ms)
1	3	1	Gateway	OData Lib 1.0 Int	/IWFND/CL_SODATA_ROOT_HANDLER	DISPATCH	225	9
2					>Response Size	87816 Bytes		
3		2	Gateway	Metadata access	/IWFND/CL_MED_MDL_PROVIDER	GET_SERVICE_GROUP	3	3
4	3	2	Gateway	OData Lib 1.0 Int	/IWFND/CL_SODATA_PROCESSOR	READ	213	
5		3	Gateway	Data Provider: Ge..	/IWFND/CL_MGW_PROV_DELEGATOR	GET_DATA_PROVIDER	1	1
6	1	3	Gateway	OData Channel R..	/IWFND/CL_MGW_RUNT_RCLNT_PRXY	Call Remote BEP - NONE	196	6
7	1	4	BEP	OData Channel R..	REMOTE_FUNCTION_MODULE	/IWBEP/FM_MGW_READ_ENTITYSET	190	5
8		5	BEP	Data Provider	ZCL_ZGWSAMPLE_DPC_EXT	GET_ENTITYSET	185	185
9		3	Gateway	OData Lib 1.0 Int	/IWFND/CL_SODATA_MAPPER	GET_ENTITY_PROV_BY_FEED_DATA	16	16
10		2	Gateway	OData Lib 1.0 Int	/IWFND/CL_SODATA_PROC_DISPTCHR	Lib Serialization - write_to		

Figure 13.12 Performance Trace Data Single Request

> **Note**
>
> Performance trace log items have an expiration date. As a default, log items are stored for a duration of two days starting from the trace activation. It's possible to adjust these settings to your own needs.

Overall, the performance trace tool allows for an efficient and easy analysis of SAP NetWeaver Gateway service performance behavior and, as a result, enables you to identify time-consuming services efficiently. Using the integrated toolset, you can then follow up and improve the performance of service calls when needed.

Troubleshooting Tips

Troubleshooting is a science or an art depending on whether you take a more scientific, structured approach, or you let your experience and gut feeling guide you. To facilitate your search for the root cause of a problem in your SAP NetWeaver Gateway environment, consider the following tips:

▶ **Pair testing**
If your problem involves both the frontend and SAP NetWeaver Gateway/the SAP Business Suite, it helps to choose a pair of testers that represent and know both worlds.

▶ **Incremental exclusion**
Make sure you exclude all infrastructure topics first. For example, verify using a browser that OData service calls make it through the firewall. Then exclude other potential problems one by one.

▶ **Trace the steps**
Trace the steps the service request performs by using the tools explained in this chapter. Try to find the step where the problem occurs by, for example, using external breakpoints on the ABAP side.

13.4 Summary

This chapter introduced you to the lifecycle of a typical SAP NetWeaver Gateway project and how to manage selected phases. You've received insights into a number of nondevelopment topics such as testing, error handling, and service deployment. Because every project is different, in most cases you'll have to adjust and/or develop strategies for the test plan of your own SAP NetWeaver Gateway project or the operation of an SAP NetWeaver Gateway environment. The chapter has provided you a foundation that you can build on and that you can extend for your own project and specific environment.

In this chapter, we'll discuss the various security mechanisms that can be put in place to prevent unauthorized and unauthenticated use of data that has been published via SAP NetWeaver Gateway.

14 Security

SAP NetWeaver Gateway extends the reach of SAP business applications by offering easy access via the OData protocol through various channels. Of course, while taking advantage of this, it's necessary to control who is allowed to consume this data. Obviously, no CIO wants to risk the security of a company's internal or external data.

The fundamental aspects of *information security* (confidentiality, integrity, and availability) have to be taken into account for the whole lifetime of data, through all the different layers of SAP NetWeaver Gateway—from the OData client to the SAP Business Suite backend system. In this chapter, we provide an overview of some of the most important security concepts in SAP NetWeaver Gateway.

Confidentiality, integrity, availability

14.1 Network and Communication Security

A secure network infrastructure is of utmost importance when it comes to system protection. Opening up your system for easy access via OData and preventing unauthorized access to your business data have to be accomplished at the same time. A well-defined system architecture can eliminate many security threats, such as *eavesdropping*. Figure 14.1 shows the SAP NetWeaver Gateway's three-tier architecture (business layer, SAP NetWeaver Gateway, consumer) together with the communication protocols that are used between the different layers.

Three-tier architecture

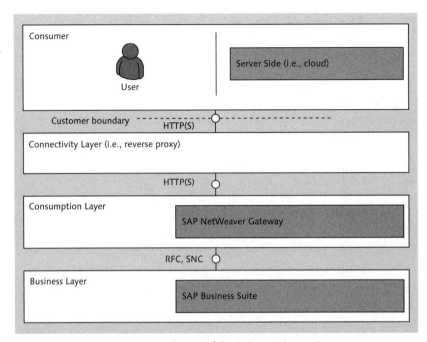

Figure 14.1 Technical System Landscape of the SAP NetWeaver Gateway

Maintaining the security of these three different layers involves two main processes: transport protection and input validation. *Transport protection* is the process of securing the data that is transported between these layers to ensure its confidentiality and integrity. *Input validation* is the process of validating input on the consumption layer before sending it to the backend system on the business layer—because even if the data is secured while in transport, there are other threats based on sending the OData service malicious data. Input validation encompasses but isn't limited to validating syntactical correctness of the incoming data based on formats of OData types (length, ranges, white list values), rejecting invalid input, and so on.

We'll discuss both of these security measures in more detail next.

14.1.1 Transport Protection

SSL/TLS   To ensure transport protection for data confidentiality and integrity, the network communication between the different components has to be secured. As a standard measure, the communication between the consumer and SAP NetWeaver Gateway in the consumption layer is secured by means of using secure sockets layer/transport layer security (SSL/TLS).

In external-facing scenarios, a common security measure is to put a reverse proxy in between the consumers coming from the Internet and the resource that will be published to the outside world. If the HTTP(S) requests are terminated by a reverse proxy (i.e., SAP Web Dispatcher), the proxy and SAP NetWeaver Gateway should implement certificate forwarding in the HTTP header. (Certificate forwarding isn't an SAP-proprietary approach; it is also supported by common reverse proxies.) The reverse proxy acts as a server-side proxy and is used to avoid same-origin policy restrictions.

Reverse proxy

In HTTP(S) communication, at one end of the "wire" you have an application (e.g., a browser or a native application), and on the other, you have a web server. Only the server and port number of the URL are visible on the wire, so as long as HTTP(S) is secure, you have no problem. However, a web server typically uses log files to log all of the traffic, so it is possible for someone to find the request URLs. If access to the log files isn't secured, or if you don't trust your web server system administrator, you have an issue. (Another location for spotting such information is at an intermediary server; i.e., access logs on the reverse proxy.)

HTTP(S) isn't enough

Consider a situation where the application at one end of the wire is a browser. A browser typically stores URLs in the browser history and also sends URLs around in the `Referrer` header field. This is a standard behavior and can't be avoided or influenced. If you write your own native application, you can control that end of the wire. However, this doesn't mean that the entire setup is secure, which is a common assumption by consumers. While it's true that the content—the body of an HTTP request—is secured when using HTTP(S), the URL and its parameters may still be accessible via web server log files or the browser cache.

OData uses parameters in URLs quite frequently, such as filter parameters or key fields when retrieving a single entity. For the reasons we just explained, this has the potential to result in threats. For example, one

Problem URL parameters

possible threat is that confidential data such as credit card numbers might be extracted from stored URLs in the browser history on the client side, or stored as part of web server logs. For example, suppose a banking service offers an entity set `CreditCardSet` that is based on the following entity type `CreditCard` shown in Figure 14.2.

Figure 14.2 Entity Type CreditCard: Unsecure

Key fields In this case, the credit card number is part of the key of the entity type `CreditCard`. Suppose the application retrieves the credit card details using the following request:

https://<server>:<port>/<rootURL>/CreditCardSet('1234 5432 1234 6543')

In this case, the credit card number is part of the URL and can be disclosed because of the reasons outlined earlier. However, there are ways to address this problem. Specifically, transfer of confidential data as part of a URL can be avoided if the entity key fields contain values such as GUIDs, rather than using the actual data in the entity data modeling. Thus, the first step to avoid the usage of confidential data as part of the key is to change the entity set so that a GUID is used as a key field. This is acceptable from a security perspective, as shown in Figure 14.3.

Query parameters However, if an OData client sends a query to the entity set `CreditCard-Set` to retrieve an entry by filtering the credit card number, the following HTTP request is sent to the server, resulting in sending the credit card number unsecured because query parameters are part of the URL:

https://<server>:<port>/<rootURL>/CreditCardSet?$filter=CardNumber eq '1234 5432 1234 6543'

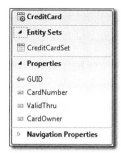

Figure 14.3 Entity Type CreditCard: Secure

A countermeasure against this threat is to send the query using the `$batch` endpoint. This way, the HTTP request is sent as part of a payload of an HTTP request and is thus secured by HTTP(S).

Countermeasure
$batch

In addition to the measures just discussed, it is also important that the communication between the SAP NetWeaver Gateway server and the connected backend systems is secured via Secure Network Communications (SNC). As of today, a trusted remote function call (RFC) is the only way to transfer user context between two ABAP systems. Trusted RFC connections are used in other scenarios as well, such as Central User Administration (CUA) and SAP Solution Manager. Because a trusted RFC connection allows the user to seamlessly connect from one system to the other system by using single sign-on (SSO), there is a threat when an unauthorized user manages to have access to the SAP NetWeaver Gateway hub system. The risk can be mitigated from two directions:

Backend
communication

▶ Protect the access path to the SAP NetWeaver Gateway server via implementation of the preceding protections.

▶ Protect the backend systems by withdrawing the authorization for remote logon based on the authorization object S_RFCACL from users and functions that don't require remote access (such as DDIC, SAP*, and other administrative users).

14.1.2 Input Validation

Application layer input validations are done by SAP NetWeaver Gateway on the consumption layer. For external-facing scenarios, SAP recommends keeping systems with business functions separate from those that are used for input validation. In a production environment, customers should therefore choose the hub deployment where the SAP NetWeaver Gateway system is installed on a separate system and not on the SAP Business Suite backend system (refer back to Chapter 4 for a full discussion of the SAP NetWeaver Gateway deployment options). Employing this best practice means that you can monitor the communication between the hub and the backend systems, allowing any protection against overloading and attacks. In addition, if SAP NetWeaver Gateway is attacked, the backend systems remain safe behind the protection layer of SAP NetWeaver Gateway. If you choose an embedded deployment of SAP NetWeaver Gateway in the SAP Business Suite backend system, you must have third-party systems on separate servers in front of the co-deployed system that perform the appropriate validation checks.

Next, we'll explain in more detail how SAP NetWeaver Gateway helps you secure your business scenario from the most prominent threats to input validation: namely *cross-site scripting* (XSS) attacks and *cross-site request forgery* (CSRF) attacks. In addition to these checks, which are included as part of SAP NetWeaver Gateway, there are other checks that can be configured separately, for example, virus scanning systems for file verification. We discuss all of these checks next.

Protection against Cross-Site Scripting (XSS)

Cross-site scripting

In a *cross-site scripting* (XSS) attack, the trust of a user in a website is exploited (Figure 14.4). XSS enables attackers to inject client-side script into web pages viewed by other users. Although all modern browsers have implemented a "same-origin" policy, XSS attacks are still in the top 10 of web application security issues.

Countermeasures

As a countermeasure against XSS attacks, SAP NetWeaver Gateway offers the validation of the syntactical correctness of incoming data based on formats of OData types (length, ranges, white list values). If any invalid input is detected, it's rejected by the framework. In addition, XSS protection is achieved through escaping HTML markup (e.g., `<br>` as `&lt;br&gt;`) according to Atom content processing rules (RFC 4287).

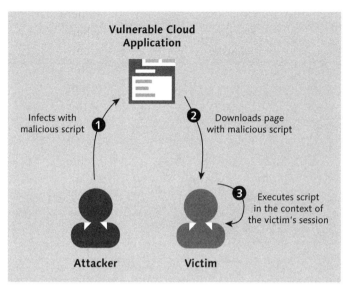

Figure 14.4 Cross-Site Scripting (XSS)

Protection against Cross-Site Request Forgery (CSRF)

Cross-site request forgery (CSRF) is almost the opposite of XSS. In XSS, an attacker exploits the trust of a user in a website; in CSRF, an attacker exploits the trust of a website in its consumer (Figure 14.5). In other words, CSRF is an attack that forces an end user to execute unwanted actions on a web application in which he is currently authenticated. The attack starts by an attacker luring a user to access a malicious OData service URL. The success of the CSRF attack depends on the predictability of the request URL to the vulnerable application.

Cross-site request forgery

Consider an example where a user is logged on to—for example—the HTML5 website of his bank that communicates to the backend using OData, as shown in Figure 14.5. While working on his bank account, suppose the user visits a different site that contains, for example, blog entries that contain unsafe content. Or perhaps the user receives an email with a manipulated link.

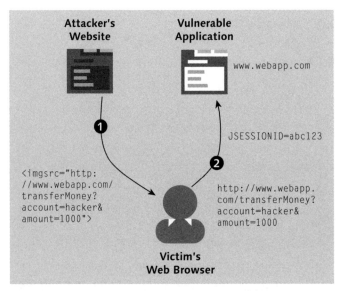

Figure 14.5 Cross-Site Scripting Forgery Attack (CSRF)

If the user clicks on the link in the email or clicks on a link in the blog (refer to ❶), the victim's browser follows this URL that references an action on the vulnerable web site (refer to ❷) together with the cookies that are used for authentication. In other words, CSRF exploits the trust that a site has in a user's browser. Notice that the URL that the victim's browser follows points to the vulnerable site, not to the malicious site. This is the "cross-site" part of CSRF.

Countermeasure The first way to protect against CSRF attacks is to refrain from making modifications via an HTTP GET request that is in any way part of the REST paradigm. An additional way to protect against CSRF attacks is to require a secret, user-specific token if the client wants to perform a modifying request using one of the HTTP verbs (POST, PUT, or DELETE). This so called CSRF token has to be retrieved by the client using a non-modifying request that is sent to the server beforehand. Therefore, as a first step, the client has to send a GET request with the header field X-CSRF-Token and the value Fetch. In a second step, the ICF runtime sends back the randomly generated CSRF token in the header field X-CSRF-Token as well as in the cookie sap-XSRF_<SID>_<client>. In a third step, this

CSRF token must be included by the client in the HTTP header X-CSRF-Token in any subsequent modifying requests. Since the client also sends back all cookies, the ICF runtime can validate the CSRF token found in the HTTP header X-CSRF-Token against the token from the cookie sap-XSRF_<SID>_<client>.

Because the tokens are generated randomly, an attacker can't guess their values and the attacker's site cannot put the right token in its submissions. Note that due to same-origin policies, the attacker isn't able to read the user's tokens. It's thus not possible for the attacker to craft an HTTP request that also contains the randomly generated X-CSRF-Token.

Tokens generated randomly

To demonstrate this more practically, let's start with the following sample request:

```
HTTP GET ... /BusinessPartnerCollection('0100000002')
```

The client adds the HTTP header X-CSRF-Token to the value Fetch. As a result, the client receives the X-CSRF-Token in the HTTP header of the HTTP response. If successful (HTTP 200), you'll find an X-CSRF-Token in the HTTP response headers.

```
Status Code: 200 OK
Content-Type: application/atom+xml;type=entry; charset=utf-8
...
X-CSRF-Token: oZipsu2chxoh2YMLNo9gRg==
Set-Cookie: {client MUST store cookies set by the server}
...
```

The X-CSRF-Token then has to be sent by the client in any subsequent modifying request such as PUT, POST, PATCH, or DELETE. The following update request

```
HTTP PUT ... /BusinessPartnerCollection('0100000002')
```

then has to contain the X-CSRF-Token in the HTTP header:

```
Content-Type: application/atom+xml;type=entry; charset=utf-8
...
X-CSRF-Token: oZipsu2chxoh2YMLNo9gRg==
Cookie: {client MUST return cookies set by the server}
...
```

In this case the update request is successful, the HTTP response body is empty, and the HTTP header contains status code 204 (no content).

When using the SAP NetWeaver Gateway client for testing, as shown in Figure 14.6, it isn't necessary to first request an X-CSRF-Token via a GET request and then to send it with a subsequent modifying request. This is because the SAP NetWeaver Gateway client does this automatically for you.

Figure 14.6 CSRF Token Handling in the SAP NetWeaver Gateway Client

Virus Scan Interface

In the SAP NetWeaver Gateway framework, virus scanning is available for incoming update and create requests on binary data for SAP NetWeaver Gateway services. Binary data can, for example, be handled using *media links* as described in Section 6.5.7 of Chapter 6.

The activity to maintain profiles for virus checking is available in the SAP NetWeaver Gateway Implementation Guide (IMG). To activate or deactivate virus checking, start Transaction SPRO, and open the SAP Reference IMG. Navigate to SAP NETWEAVER GATEWAY • ODATA CHANNEL • ADMINISTRATION • GENERAL SETTINGS • DEFINE VIRUS SCAN PROFILES. Here you can activate or deactivate the VIRUS SCAN SWITCHED OFF checkbox.

More information about the SAP Virus Scan Interface and the configuration in SAP NetWeaver Gateway can be found in the online documentation. Go to *http://help.sap.com/nwgateway*, and select SECURITY GUIDE • DATA PROTECTION AND PRIVACY • VIRUS SCAN.

14.2 User Management and Authorizations

Because SAP NetWeaver Gateway is based on the SAP NetWeaver ABAP Application Server (ABAP AS), it uses the local ABAP user management. Users can be created via the standard mechanisms. To facilitate user management, the SAP NetWeaver Gateway server can be connected to a central user management system landscape as an additional child system, or it can be managed using an identity management tool such as SAP NetWeaver Identity Management.

User management

The user accounts that have to be created in the SAP NetWeaver Gateway hub must show the same user name as in the connected backend systems. This is because the SAP NetWeaver Gateway hub system is connected to the backend systems using a trust relationship where SSO is accomplished via SAP assertion tickets. If the embedded deployment option has been chosen, it's then not necessary to create users in an additional system, because the users in the backend system that also serves as the SAP NetWeaver Gateway hub already exist.

User accounts

If an OData service is called, an authorization check is performed in the SAP NetWeaver Gateway server to check whether the user has the authorization to call that service, which is based on the authorization object S_SERVICE. It's thus possible to define ABAP authorization roles in the SAP NetWeaver Gateway system that lets you use a whitelist approach to control access to the SAP NetWeaver Gateway services. If this first authorization check is successful, the framework calls the service implementation in the backend via RFC. Even if access has been granted at the service level in the hub, the SAP user authorizations in the backend are checked as well. Appropriate authorization checks should be in place in the service implementation in the SAP Business Suite backend system. This is to ensure that a user won't be able to retrieve any business data via an OData call that he isn't allowed to see via SAPGUI or Web Dynpro UIs in the SAP Business Suite backend.

Authorizations

Because a trust relationship is used between the hub and the SAP Business Suite backend, users in the SAP Business Suite backend that will consume data via OData services must have an additional authorization based on the authorization object S_RFCACL allowing such remote calls.

The backend systems have to be protected by withdrawing the authorization for remote logon based on the authorization object S_RFCACL from users and functions that don't require remote access (such as DDIC, SAP*, and other administrative users). Otherwise, it would be possible for a hacked administrative user account to log on from the SAP NetWeaver Gateway hub into the backend.

In certain scenarios, external user credentials need to be mapped to the user credentials used in SAP NetWeaver Gateway and the connected SAP Business Suite backend systems. You have to distinguish here between scenarios where mapping takes place externally and scenarios where mapping takes place internally in SAP NetWeaver Gateway.

User mapping in SAP NetWeaver Gateway

Scenarios with user mapping on SAP NetWeaver Gateway's side are the following:

▶ The `NameID` attribute value in the Security Assertion Markup Language (SAML) assertion is mapped to the SAP NetWeaver Gateway user name.

▶ The X.509 client certificate's subject is mapped to the SAP NetWeaver Gateway user name.

▶ The SAP NetWeaver Gateway user is mapped to an attribute value in the SAML assertion.

External user mapping

There are other scenarios where user mapping has to be performed externally. An example for this setup is a scenario where the user name is an SAP NetWeaver Gateway user defined in the user store of SAP NetWeaver Portal. Another example is a scenario where an Identity Provider (IdP) is configured to issue SAML tokens so that the name of the SAP NetWeaver Gateway user is identical to the `NameID` attribute value in the SAML assertion.

14.3 Single Sign-On and Authentication Options

The most efficient way to facilitate simplified user authentication in an enterprise is via single sign-on (SSO), which refers to the mechanisms for enterprise users to authenticate themselves by a single authentication authority once and then gain access to other protected resources without reauthenticating. With the SSO functionality, users only need to authenticate once and are afterwards automatically authenticated when accessing systems that trust this initial authentication.

A nice analogy to this process is the cross boundary travel process. A German citizen receives a passport from the German authorities based on an initial authentication because the citizen presented his ID card. The passport that has been issued by the German authorities is in turn accepted by the US immigration office because the US authorities trust the German authorities (Figure 14.7).

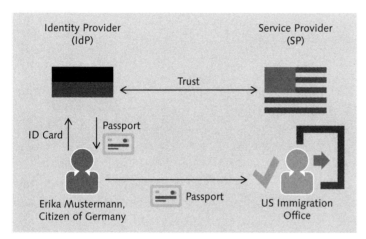

Figure 14.7 Cross Boundary Travel: An Analogy for Single Sign-On and Identity Federation

Because the process of cross boundary travel is easily understood, it's a great help to explain the basic terms of SSO that we'll use in the remainder of this chapter. Figure 14.8 shows the fundamental roles that participate in the process of SSO and identity federation.

The *Identity Provider* (IdP) is an authoritative site that is responsible for authenticating an end user and asserting his identity in a trusted fashion to trusted partners. For the cross boundary travel scenario, the German authorities play the role of the IdP because they issue a passport as proof of an initial identification based on the ID card that Erika Mustermann presented to them.

Identity Provider

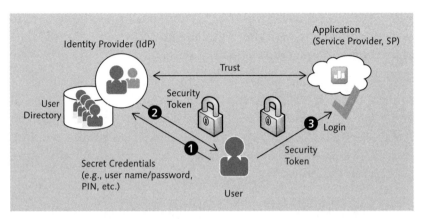

Figure 14.8 Single Sign-On Fundamentals

Service provider   The *service provider* (SP) has a trust relationship with an IdP to accept and trust (i.e., vouch for) information provided by the IdP on behalf of a user (without direct user involvement). Identity and access management are transferred to the IdP. In the cross boundary travel scenario, the US immigrations office plays the role of the SP. The only difference here is that the traveler has to present his passport to the representatives of the immigration office, whereas in an SSO scenario, the client (e.g., the browser) presents the token issued by the IdP to the SP without bothering the end user.

For SSO to SAP NetWeaver Gateway, SAP NetWeaver Gateway plays the role of the SP. The user has to present a security token issued by an IdP to SAP NetWeaver Gateway, which is seamlessly accepted by the SAP NetWeaver Gateway server. Therefore, first you must look at the authentication options that are supported by SAP NetWeaver Gateway as well as the different consumers or user agents (desktop application, HTML5 application, mobile client, etc.) that are involved to decide the best way to achieve SSO for a certain scenario.

> **Note**
>
> None of the authentication methods described here provide transport layer security (TLS) out of the box. We recommend that you use TLS mechanisms such as SSL/TLS to have increased security for the OData communication with the SAP NetWeaver Gateway server.

SAP NetWeaver Gateway supports the same authentication options offered by the underlying SAP NetWeaver ABAP runtime for browser-based communication. This is because communication via the OData protocol that is offered by the SAP NetWeaver Gateway hub is facilitated via the *Internet Communications Manager* (ICM) process using handlers in the *Internet Communication Framework* (ICF).

In this section, we explain the different authentication options that are available for SAP NetWeaver Gateway, including whether they enable SSO.

> **Note**
>
> Some of these authentication options require a certain release and might require additional software components from SAP or a third party that have to be licensed separately.

14.3.1 Basic Authentication

Basic authentication is the simplest form of authentication. The consumer application just provides a user name and a password when calling the OData service in SAP NetWeaver Gateway. Basic authentication isn't an option that allows SSO, because it requires the consuming application to store the user's credentials in a secure location and requires the application to cope with initial and expired passwords.

Using basic authentication also bears the risk that the system becomes vulnerable for distributed denial-of-service (DDoS) attacks. Users can be locked out because attackers have performed too many login attempts using the wrong credentials.

Basic authentication is, however, a valid option for the following scenarios:

► During design time, so developers can test their applications by using different credentials to impersonate users having different roles.

► In B2C scenarios where user self-service is used (see Section 14.4.7 for more details about this functionality).

14.3.2 SAP Logon Tickets with SAP NetWeaver Portal

SAP logon tickets are session cookies that are stored on the client browser. In the past, SAP had to rely on a proprietary SSO mechanism that is based on SAP logon tickets because common standards such as SAML or OAuth were not available at that time.

SAP logon tickets
The ticket-issuing instance for SAP logon tickets in SSO scenarios is usually taken over by the SAP NetWeaver Portal system that has the role of an IdP. SAP NetWeaver Portal issues an SAP logon ticket to a user after successful initial authentication at the portal against a user persistence specified in the portal user management engine (UME).

Because SAP logon tickets are cookie-based, technical and security limitations apply. Logon tickets are only sent to SAP NetWeaver Application Servers that are located in the same DNS domain as the SAP NetWeaver Portal server that issued the ticket. Therefore, SAP logon tickets aren't well suited for cross-domain scenarios. However, they can be used to achieve SSO for all SAP applications inside a single domain tree using domain relaxation.

SAP NetWeaver Portal itself offers SSO using different authentication options such as X.509 certificates or Integrated Windows Authentication. SAP NetWeaver Portal users can thus automatically be authenticated against the portal by reusing their Windows credentials. SSO to all SAP applications and also SAP NetWeaver Gateway is then achieved by using the SAP logon ticket that has been issued because the user has logged on successfully using his Windows credentials.

Integrated Windows Authentication
Note that Integrated Windows Authentication is now also supported for the ABAP stack using HTTP access, as described later in Section 14.3.6. This is especially of interest to desktop clients that can't leverage SAP logon tickets that have been issued by SAP NetWeaver Portal out of the box.

14.3.3 X.509 Client Certificates

An X.509 certificate is a signed data structure that binds a public key to a person, computer, or organization. Certificates are issued by certification authorities (CAs). Issuing public key certificates and private keys to users and computers in an organization is the task of a public key infra-structure (PKI).

When using authentication with client certificates, each user needs to possess a key pair, consisting of a public key and a private key. The public key is contained in the X.509 client certificate and can be made public. However, the user's private key needs to be kept safe.

Key pairs

One of the major benefits of using X.509 client certificates is that they are supported by many applications. The use of X.509 certificates is a widely accepted standard, and its stability is proved in numerous implementations. X.509 certificates can be used to achieve SSO for browser-based access, for the most recent version as well as for older releases of SAP NetWeaver ABAP, such as SAP NetWeaver ABAP 7.0. (Strictly speaking, this isn't a pure SSO solution because a user authenticates independently into each and every system.)

As a result, besides basic authentication and SAP logon tickets, X.509 certificates are the only authentication method that is supported for all releases of SAP NetWeaver ABAP (7.0 to 7.4) for which SAP NetWeaver Gateway has been released.

The one drawback to X.509 certificates is that their use usually requires customers to implement and run a PKI. Running and maintaining a PKI isn't as common as you might expect because it is seen as a cumbersome and expensive task. Fortunately, there is an alternative. Instead of implementing a full-fledged PKI, customers can implement the product *SAP NetWeaver Single Sign-On (SAP NetWeaver SSO)*. SAP NetWeaver SSO can, for example, leverage the Windows credentials of a currently logged-on user. Based on this authentication, which happens seamlessly, and the fact that the user has already logged on to his workstation by using his Windows user name and password, the secure login server issues a short-lived client certificate that is pushed to the user certificate store. This certificate can then in turn be used for SSO to SAP NetWeaver Gateway. Because you can choose very short lifetimes for the certificates, there is no need to bother with certificate revocation lists (which is necessary in a PKI).

SAP NetWeaver
Single Sign-On

Another way to seamlessly roll out X.509 certificates in an existing infra-structure is to leverage the auto-enrollment feature of Microsoft Active Directory. With this feature, the certificate is automatically copied to the user certificate store on a user's client. This local store is an encrypted store for certificates on Windows clients and contains personal and public root certificates.

User mapping Whereas the initial setup in the ABAP AS is a one-time effort to accept X.509 certificates, the need to map the client certificates subject to the SAP user accounts is an ongoing task. Mapping a certificate to the end user can be accomplished automatically by using an identity management tool such as SAP NetWeaver ID Management or by direct maintenance of table VUSREXTID using Transaction EXTID_DN, which also offers the option of a file upload.

14.3.4 SAML 2.0 Browser Protocol

Security Assertion Markup Language (SAML) is a standard for SSO and identity federation. The SAML 2.0 browser protocol specifies a profile that describes how the different roles (IdP, SP, and user) interact if the user is using a web browser to access the service provider.

In a scenario that uses the SAML browser protocol 2.0, SAP NetWeaver Gateway acts as a service provider. Several IdPs that issue the SAML token based on an initial authentication are supported. Depending on the scenario, different initial authentication options can be used by the client. The advantage of using the SAML 2.0 browser protocol is that there is no need to deploy anything on the client side; this is in contrast to solutions that use X.509 certificates, which have to be distributed to the clients.

Because the SAML 2.0 browser protocol is the recommended option for various scenarios (e.g., for the SAP Fiori applications), we'll explain the authentication flow in more detail (Figure 14.9 and Figure 14.10).

Reverse proxy
server The client sends an unauthenticated request to SAP NetWeaver Gateway via a reverse proxy server, as shown in ❶. The request issued by the client refers to an external URL for the OData service that is, for example, consumed by an SAP Fiori application. The SAP NetWeaver Gateway

server responds to the unauthenticated request with a redirect to the IdP (refer to ❷) as if to say "I don't know who you are; go talk to the SAML 2.0 IdP server." The client follows the HTTP 302 redirect URL, and sends the request to the SAML 2.0 IdP server, as shown in ❸. The SAML 2.0 IdP server challenges the client to identify itself, as shown in ❹. At this point, the SAML 2.0 IdP server can be configured to use any form of authentication appropriate for the customer's system infrastructure, for instance, basic authentication against a Microsoft Active Directory. The client supplies the required credentials, for instance, Windows user name and password (refer to ❺).

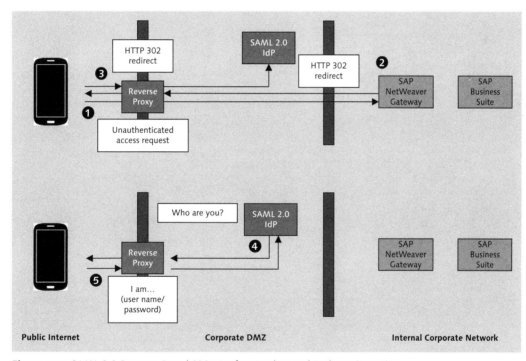

Figure 14.9 SAML 2.0 Browser-Based SSO: Artifact Binding and Redirect (Part 1)

If the SAML 2.0 IdP server determines the user credentials to be valid, it responds with another HTTP 302 to redirect the client back to the SAP NetWeaver Gateway server; however, this response now carries the required SAML artifact, as shown in ❻ of Figure 14.10. The client follows the HTTP 302 redirect URL and, in so doing, passes the SAML artifact back to the SAP NetWeaver Gateway server, as shown in ❼. The SAP NetWeaver Gateway server sends the SAML artifact to the SAML 2.0 IdP server for resolution as a back-channel web service (SOAP) request, as shown in ❽. The SAML 2.0 IdP server resolves the artifact and returns an assertion that SAP NetWeaver Gateway validates, as shown in ❾. If validation is successful, an ABAP session is created for the now authenticated user, as shown in ❿. The OData service in SAP NetWeaver Gateway now starts and sends data to the client, as shown in ⓫.

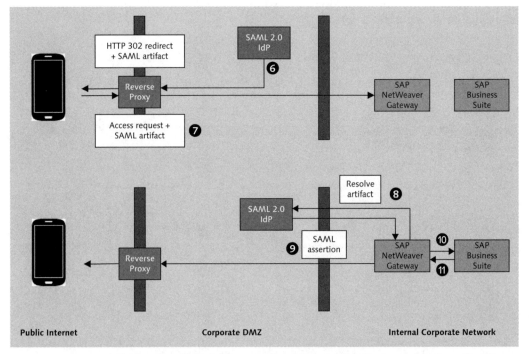

Figure 14.10 SAML 2.0 Browser-Based SSO: Artifact Binding and Redirect (Part 2)

14.3.5 OAuth

OAuth 2.0 is a protocol that allows users to grant a web-based client application access to resources that are owned by the user. The application that is authorized by the resource owner accesses the resources on behalf of the user. Strictly speaking, OAuth is not an authentication option, but a protocol to delegate authorization. From an end-user perspective, however, OAuth enables single sign-on for a wide range of scenarios, such as mobile applications, web sites, and more.

The advantage of OAuth is that it offers constrained access to services without the requirement to pass or store credentials. This makes it a good fit for cloud-based services and mobile services, where constrained access is of special interest.

One of the standard examples for OAuth, which is also used in the OAuth 2.0 Internet-Draft (*http://tools.ietf.org/html/draft-ietf-oauth-v2-10*), is a photo printing service. Assume that you've uploaded photos from your vacation on some cloud service. Now you want to print some photos and want to use another cloud service for this task. When you access the pictures, you have to authenticate by providing your user name and password. Because any access to your pictures requires authentication, this is also the case for the printing service. Obviously, you don't want to share your credentials with the printing service because you have limited trust to the printing service. Providing your credentials to the printing service allows the printing service to act on your behalf and, for example, allows it to even delete pictures. In addition, you have to change your password for the cloud service hosting your pictures to prevent the printing service from accessing this resource in the future.

Standard example

The idea of OAuth is thus to provide the printing service with a time-constrained security token that only allows limited read access to the pictures you've selected. In this example, you, as an owner of the images, fulfill the role of the OAuth resource owner.

Why is OAuth also relevant for scenarios in the enterprise? In an enterprise environment, you usually configure SSO because the systems are operated by one organization. However, even here, OAuth can make sense because it allows restricting the access to a system when being accessed via a mobile device rather than using, for example, SAPGUI. Take for example a mobile application for entering leave requests. When entering the data, the application only needs access to the leave request resources, and doesn't require access to the user's payroll data. In this case, OAuth ensures that the user and the leave request application *only*

Enterprise scenario

have permission to access the leave request resources, and do not have access to payroll resources.

OAuth is supported as part of the SAP standard as of SAP NetWeaver ABAP 7.40 and, by applying some SAP Notes, also for some releases lower than 7.40 (see SAP Note 1797103).

14.3.6 Kerberos: Integrated Windows Authentication

The most straightforward way to perform SSO in a Microsoft environment is to reuse the authentication information from Windows, that is, by using Integrated Windows Authentication, which is based on Kerberos.

When a user has successfully logged on to a Windows workstation with his credentials, a (Kerberos) session ticket is issued by the domain controller of Active Directory to access a resource that is offering Integrated Windows Authentication. SAP NetWeaver Application Server (SAP NetWeaver AS) ABAP supports Kerberos with Simple and Protected GSS API Negotiation Mechanism (SPNego) to enable authentication with web clients such as web browsers. In this case, the domain controller of the Windows domain acts as the IdP.

> **Note**
>
> To use SPNego with SAP NetWeaver AS ABAP, it requires SAP NetWeaver SSO 2.0 and higher as well as additional software licenses. SAP NetWeaver SSO 2.0 requires SAP NetWeaver ABAP 7.31 SP06 and higher as a runtime. With SAP NetWeaver ABAP 7.40, the required ABAP add-ons are part of the standard, although usage still requires licensing this functionality.

14.4 Recommended Authentication Options

The choice about which authentication method to use depends on the scenario and the user agent. In Table 14.1, we provide an overview of the scenarios and the recommended authentication options. In the rest of the section, we go into a bit more detail about each of these types of applications. We will explain which of the authentication options described in Section 14.3 are feasible for achieving single sign-on for a specific type of application, we will discuss the pros and cons of each authentication option, and we will provide a recommendation for one or more authentication options for each scenario that is listed in Table 14.1.

Scenario	Recommended Authentication Option
Web (HTML5) Application	▶ SAML 2.0 browser SSO for extranet scenarios ▶ Kerberos for intranet scenarios
Desktop application	▶ SAML 2.0 browser SSO for extranet scenarios ▶ Kerberos for intranet scenarios
Mobile applications (direct access)	SAML 2.0 browser SSO or OAuth
SAP Mobile Platform	X.509 certificates
SAP HANA Cloud Platform	SAML 2.0 browser SSO
Web server side	X.509 certificates
Business-to-consumer (B2C)	▶ Basic authentication when using user self service ▶ SAML browser protocol when mapping SAML authenticated users to service users

Table 14.1 Recommended Authentication Options for Different Integration Scenarios

14.4.1 HTML5 Web Application

The web application scenario (Figure 14.11) applies to HTML5, Internet, and intranet scenarios. (Other frontend technologies for web applications such as Silverlight and Flex are considered outdated and aren't recommended.) The scenarios usually require a separate web server for content hosting. In the case of SAPUI5, however, the SAP NetWeaver Gateway server itself can be used for deployment.

591

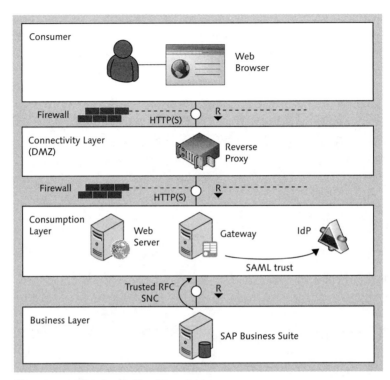

Figure 14.11 Web Application Scenario

In the web application scenario, multiple authentication options can be used. The recommended option for extranet scenarios is to use SAML 2.0 Browser SSO because it doesn't require the distribution of X.509 certificates and leverages existing user identities in a customer's identity management system. SAML 2.0 Browser SSO requires an IdP that can, for example, be based on SAP NetWeaver SSO or Microsoft Active Directory Federation Services (ADFS).

A second option is to use X.509 client certificates that require either a PKI or the usage of SAP NetWeaver SSO. If the HTTP(S) requests are terminated by a reverse proxy (i.e., SAP Web Dispatcher), the proxy and SAP NetWeaver Gateway should implement certificate forwarding in the HTTP header. Certificate forwarding isn't an SAP proprietary approach but is also supported by common reverse proxies. The reverse proxy acts as a server-side proxy and is used to avoid same-origin policy restrictions.

A third option for intranet scenarios is Kerberos. This is also the recommended option, because it is the most straightforward one.

14.4.2 Desktop Application

The consumer in this scenario can be any desktop application performing direct communication with the SAP NetWeaver Gateway system (Figure 14.12). As a standard measure, the communication between the desktop application and the SAP NetWeaver Gateway system is secured via HTTP(S). From a technical point of view, there are several options that can be used for authentication.

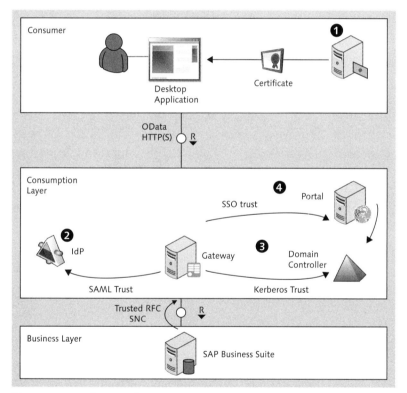

Figure 14.12 Desktop Application Scenario

The recommended option for intranet scenarios is the use of Kerberos tickets issued by a Windows domain controller (as shown in ❸). The use of X.509 client certificates can also be considered (as shown in ❶). This

Kerberos and X.509

requires, however, that you have a PKI or distribute X.509 certificates using SAP NetWeaver SSO. The end user has direct access to these tokens.

As shown in ❷, *SAML 2.0 Browser SSO* can also be used, because there are IdPs such as SAP NetWeaver SSO or ADFS that support Kerberos-based authentication. The use of the SAML tokens for SSO is, however, not straightforward. In contrast to a web application, where a browser handles HTTP redirects, parses HTML forms, and processes cookies, a desktop application does not support this behavior out of the box. The developer would have to ensure that the client code behaves like a browser when performing these actions. While for extranet scenarios this would be still the way to go, for intranet scenarios, Kerberos-based authentication should be chosen instead.

The same is true if you want to use the SAP NetWeaver Portal as a ticket-issuing instance for SAP logon tickets that can be used for authentication against the SAP NetWeaver Gateway system (refer to ❹). The developer also has to deal with a proper handling of cookies (MYSAPSSO2). Although the SAP NetWeaver Portal supports SSO using Integrated Windows Authentication as well as using the SPNego Login Module, it's recommended to use the native implementation of Kerberos support in SAP NetWeaver AS ABAP provided with SAP NetWeaver SSO 2.0 and higher. The use of SAP NetWeaver Portal to achieve SSO using Kerberos for HTML5-based applications is an option, however.

When using a trusted RFC connection between the SAP NetWeaver Gateway server and the backend, a successful authentication against SAP NetWeaver Gateway allows for a subsequent SSO to the SAP Business Suite systems.

14.4.3 Mobile Application (Direct Access)

If using mobile devices, a direct access to OData services published by SAP NetWeaver Gateway is supported but requires additional security measures to be in place (Figure 14.13). When using SAP Mobile Platform, this is offered by the platform out of the box.

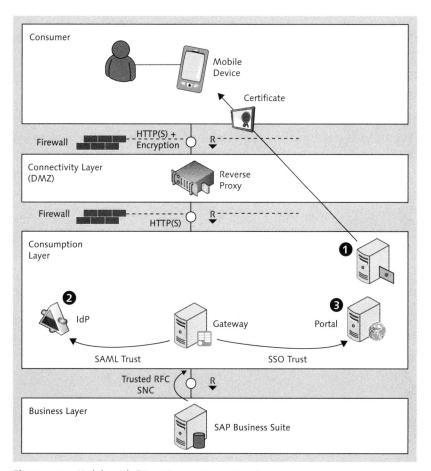

Figure 14.13 Mobile with Direct Access Integration Scenario

Communication between the SAP NetWeaver Gateway server and the consumer in the Internet is secured by using a reverse proxy, which is a common security measure in any data center. The reverse proxy allows restricting the access from the Internet to only certain services. As mentioned in Section 14.3.1, basic authentication isn't recommended because it requires handling and storing of passwords on mobile devices. Also, the handling of X.509 certificates can be tricky on certain mobile platforms because they don't offer an application-specific storage for X.509 certificates (refer to ❶). In addition, the rollout of certificates to the mobile devices has to be managed. Both functionalities are

Reverse proxy

595

part of the offering of the SAP Mobile Platform. Using SAP Logon Tickets is also not recommended because it requires the developer to handle the request from SAP Logon Tickets manually (refer to ❸). In the end, this leaves you with either SAML 2.0 browser protocol or OAuth 2.0 as the recommended authentication options for this scenario (refer to ❷).

The advantage of both approaches is that they don't require any installation of any additional components on the mobile device. It's possible to use an IdP, such as SAP NetWeaver SSO or ADFS, which offers authentication using the Windows user name and password. Using OAuth offers the additional benefit that the token issued for authentication (access token) only allows restricted access and enhancing security.

Note that the code of your mobile application must behave like a browser to handle HTTP redirects, parsing HTML5 forms, and processing cookies if the SAML 2.0 browser protocol is to be used. Similarly, OAuth requires the developer to implement an appropriate behavior of the mobile client.

As in other scenarios involving access by named users with SSO to the SAP Business Suite backend, any handling is facilitated via a trusted RFC connection between the SAP NetWeaver Gateway server and the backend.

14.4.4 SAP Mobile Platform

SAP Mobile Platform offers support for the development of mobile applications for various mobile devices based on Android, Blackberry, and iOS (support for Windows 8 is also planned). It offers several out of the box features that developers can implement for direct consumption of OData services published by SAP NetWeaver Gateway.

Out-of-the-box features

SAP Mobile Platform offers a device registration that is two-factor authenticated. As a result, the platform knows which user is using which device and thereby enables push notifications from SAP NetWeaver Gateway to the mobile device (see Appendix A for more information about this). The initial provisioning, including X.509 client certificate distribution, can be accomplished by using SAP Afaria, as shown in Figure 14.14. Part of the SAP Mobile Platform is also a relay server that facilitates outside connection to the SAP Mobile Platform server. Instead of using the relay server, customers can also use third-party reverse proxy servers, allowing a seamless integration into any existing security system landscape.

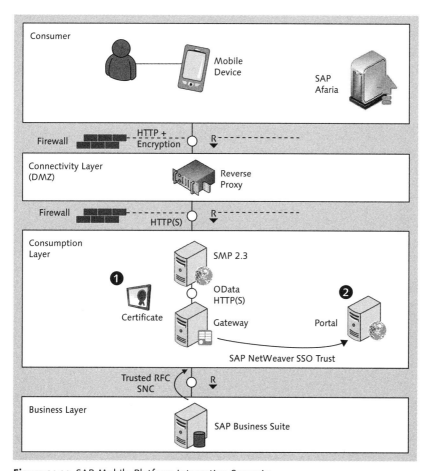

Figure 14.14 SAP Mobile Platform Integration Scenario

SAP Mobile Platform terminates client requests, handles device validation against known device lists, and offers the following two authentication options:

▶ Certificate forwarding between SAP Mobile Platform and SAP Net-Weaver Gateway, as shown in ❶ of Figure 14.14.

▶ SAP Mobile Platform request for SAP logon ticket from SAP NetWeaver Portal, which is then forwarded to SAP NetWeaver Gateway, as shown in ❷).

X.509 or SAP logon tickets

From a security point of view, the recommended authentication option is to use X.509 certificates. However, if certificates aren't planned or can't be distributed to the mobile devices, the use of SAP logon tickets issued by SAP NetWeaver Portal can be used. Note that SAP NetWeaver Portal supports Microsoft Active Directory as a data source for its UME. As a result, the mobile user is able to authenticate using his Windows user name and password.

14.4.5 Cloud

In a cloud-based scenario (Figure 14.15), the customer can federate user authentication from an on-premise IdP or from a public IdP to a cloud application. As an example, SAP runs such a public IdP in the cloud: the SAP ID Service. Many social media websites can also be used; it is convenient for users to be able to reuse existing accounts from Facebook, Google, etc. The application then accesses SAP NetWeaver Gateway on behalf of the consumer leveraging one of the authentication methods supported by SAP NetWeaver Gateway (for example, certificate-based logon). It can leverage an existing SAML token or request a new one from a local issuer. A reverse proxy acts as a connectivity solution for external consumers. SAP NetWeaver Gateway trusts the issuer of the SAML token in two authentication scenarios:

▶ Issuing a SAML 2.0 assertion for an unsolicited request

▶ Issuing a SAML 2.0 bearer assertion proving user's identity for OAuth 2.0 flow

Then SAP NetWeaver Gateway uses a trusted RFC connection to access services in the backend with named users.

As an example, consider a scenario based on the SAP HANA Cloud Platform, which is SAP's Platform-as-a-Service (PaaS) solution for building extensions for on-demand and on-premise solutions. To securely connect from the SAP HANA Cloud Platform to on-premise systems, applications can use a platform-provided connectivity service. The SAP HANA Cloud connector establishes a secure SSL VPN connection between the SAP HANA Cloud Platform and on-premise systems. The connectivity is created by an on-premise agent that initiates the secure tunnel from the internal network to the SAP HANA Cloud Platform. The SSL VPN connection supports different communication protocols such as HTTP(S) and RFC. SAP HANA Cloud Platform supports SAML2-based user propagation to enable single sign-on to the on-premise SAP NetWeaver Gateway server.

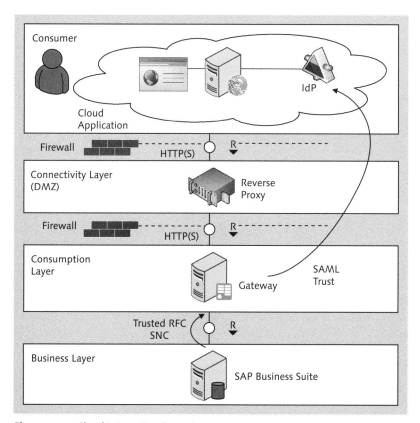

Figure 14.15 Cloud Integration Scenario

14.4.6 Web Server

In the web server scenario (Figure 14.16), the consumer has access to a web application that is hosted on a web server based on a framework such as PHP or ASP.NET. The application connects to the SAP NetWeaver Gateway server behind the scenes. Authentication can best be achieved using short-lived X.509 client certificates that can easily be generated on the fly for the current user. The user identity is part of the certificate's subject.

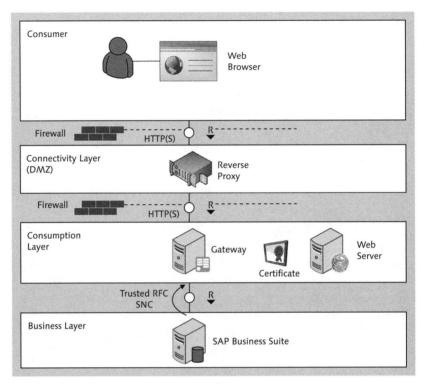

Figure 14.16 Web Server Integration Scenario

14.4.7 B2C Scenario

In B2C scenarios, customers access the business services provided by a company or organization that have typically no named user in the backend (Figure 14.17).

To accomplish this type of scenario, Gateway can support the following access configurations:

▶ Anonymous access

▶ User self-service to create named users

▶ Map SAML authenticated users to service users

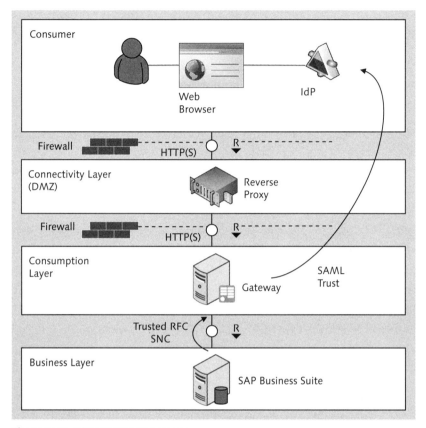

Consumer

Web
Browser

IdP

Firewall
HTTP(S)

R

Connectivity Layer
(DMZ)

Reverse
Proxy

Firewall
HTTP(S)

R

Consumption
Layer

Gateway

SAML
Trust

Trusted RFC
SNC

R

Business Layer

SAP Business Suite

Figure 14.17 B2C Integration Scenario

Anonymous Access

The first option is that SAP NetWeaver Gateway provides services with
anonymous access to all consumers. This requires some measures to be in
place that prevent a denial of service (DoS) attack. An example of an
application that uses anonymous access is the mobile application SAP
Citizen Connect. With SAP Citizen Connect, citizens can report public-
facing issues quickly and conveniently.

User Self-Service

The second option is to use the new *user self-service* that allows your customers to create named users in your SAP Business Suite backend. This

was delivered with SP07 of SAP NetWeaver Gateway 2.0, and allows your customers to do the following:

► Create users in your SAP Business Suite system

► Manage their user profiles

► Reset their password

Using named users rather than anonymous users is very beneficial for B2C scenarios because it facilitates storage of data and controlled access to data, auditing, and troubleshooting. This is the recommended option if customers should be able to view and pay bills, as in, for example, the new SAP Multichannel Foundation for Utilities software.

The user self-service process is depicted in Figure 14.18. The whole B2C process starts with a customer that is requesting a user ID in your SAP Business Suite and SAP NetWeaver Gateway hub system. The first request is calling the service /IWEP/USERREQUESTMANAGEMENT using a service user context. Here a POST request is performed on the entity set UserRequestCollection.

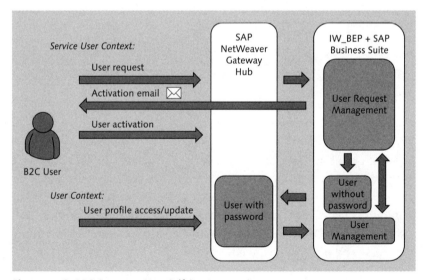

Figure 14.18 B2C Customer User Self-Service

Upon successful creation, the B2C customer receives an email notification that contains an activation URL. Here the B2C customer can enter a password that he will use in the future to log on to the system. B2C customers are also able to reset and change their passwords themselves without the need to involve any manual user management.

The big advantage of user self-service is that you can leverage named users in the backend system. With named users in place in the backend system, authorizations can be checked properly using the user context of the currently logged on user. Data can be easily stored for each user separately. Also, troubleshooting is much easier because any call from a mobile device can be tracked for a user.

Advantages

If one technical user is used (as opposed to having multiple named users), the application has to perform the authentication and send the backend information about the customer that is currently using the service. In addition, business logic has to be built in the backend to ensure that bookings performed by the technical user are stored in the correct context. Using one technical user is a large security risk. If, for example, the password isn't secret anymore, an attacker can access *all* customer data in the backend. When this happens with named users, only a single customer account is jeopardized.

The new self-service functionality is already used by some SAP solutions, such as the SAP Multichannel Foundation for Utilities. This solution allows customers to register and manage their accounts and perform several actions using a mobile device, such as view and pay bills and report problems and outages to their supplier.

Map SAML Authenticated Users to Service Users

The third option is to map SAML authenticated users to service users. This scenario is officially called *identity federation with transient name identifiers*. In this case, SAP NetWeaver Gateway acts as a service provider and trusts an (external) IdP for performing user authentication.

Identity federation with transient name identifiers

Identity federation with transient name identifiers enables you to provide authenticated users with access to your system. However, you don't need to create named users for them in your system; you can leverage technical users instead.

In contrast to anonymous access, users first have to authenticate at an IdP as an additional security measure. (The name "transient" comes from the fact that the user name already contained in the SAML token isn't actually used in this scenario.) Instead, you only determine how the attributes contained in the SAML2 token are mapped to technical users in your system. While the IdP handles the management of the users and their authentication without your intervention, you only have to bother about mapping the rules, which is a one-time effort.

As an example for a B2C scenario that can leverage identity federation with a transient name identifier, let's take a small retail company called ITelo that is selling IT equipment to its customers and thereby offering an e-procurement OData service. The employees of its customers are able to access the product catalogue, and cost center owners can place orders with ITelo through an HTML5-based application that consumes the OData service provided by ITelo.

This scenario is feasible because the employees of ITelo's customer have been authenticated by the IdP of the customer that has issued a SAML token containing the following attributes:

- Company name
- Cost center
- Role (cost center owner or employee)

ITelo trusts the SAML tokens that have been issued by the IdP of the customer, and ITelo's SAP NetWeaver Gateway hub has been configured to accept those SAML tokens. In addition, ITelo's IT department has created technical users for each cost center owner of the customer and one for all employees of the customer in the SAP NetWeaver Gateway hub and in ITelo's enterprise resource planning backend—rather than performing this task for each employee of the customer. (User creation has to take place in the SAP NetWeaver Gateway hub and the SAP NetWeaver Gateway backend because both use a trusted RFC connection.) Employees that aren't cost center owners are mapped instead to users in ITelo's SAP NetWeaver Gateway hub and backend that have only the authorization to display the product catalogue.

In our example, which is depicted in Figure 14.19, Dagmar Schulze (with the company Becker Berlin) is the owner of the cost center 10001234 and has authenticated at the IdP of her company. The IdP has issued a SAML token that contains the information about her role and her cost center assignment. When accessing the e-procurement service, she is mapped to the service user P123456 that has the authorization to place orders for the customer Becker Berlin. A normal employee would be mapped to the service user P123457, which has only read access to ITelo's backend system.

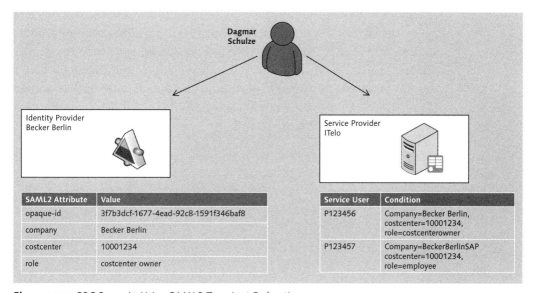

SAML2 Attribute	Value
opaque-id	3f7b3dcf-1677-4ead-92c8-1591f346baf8
company	Becker Berlin
costcenter	10001234
role	costcenter owner

Service User	Condition
P123456	Company=Becker Berlin, costcenter=10001234, role=costcenterowner
P123457	Company=BeckerBerlinSAP costcenter=10001234, role=employee

Figure 14.19 B2C Scenario Using SAML2 Transient Federation

The great advantage of using identity federation with transient name identifiers is that it enables you to grant controlled access to external users. Even if, for example, the role of an employee of ITelo's customer changes, ITelo doesn't have to maintain the users and rules on its side. This is especially true if an employee leaves the customer, because it's the task of the customer's IT department to make sure to delete the user account of that employee.

> **Note**
>
> B2C scenarios that don't use named users in the SAP Business Suite backend require the customer to license the usage of SAP NetWeaver Gateway.

14.5 Summary

In this chapter, we've provided an overview of the most important security-related topics with respect to SAP NetWeaver Gateway. We touched on the basics of network-related topics and provided a sound introduction to the various authentication options, together with a recommendation on how these can be leveraged to achieve SSO. Having a better understanding about which authentication option is best suited for the various scenarios that we've outlined will help you make an informed decision for you own use case.

PART V
Roadmap

The closing chapter of the book looks at different trends that might be relevant for future developments of SAP NetWeaver Gateway.

15 Recent and Future Developments

By now, you should have a good understanding of what SAP NetWeaver Gateway is all about. With this understanding comes the realization that SAP NetWeaver Gateway exists in a somewhat volatile environment due to ever-changing market situations, new technology, and new business trends.

For this reason, it's necessary for SAP NetWeaver Gateway to adjust and grow in order to meet constantly changing requirements. In this chapter, we'll give you an overview of some new technologies and trends and how they relate to SAP NetWeaver Gateway, and also look to what we can expect in the future. We'll finish the chapter with a final look at SAP NetWeaver 7.40, which includes SAP NetWeaver Gateway in the standard installation. If you read through the book, you already know most of the relevant information on release 7.40; the information contained in this chapter is simply a concise summary.

Disclaimer
Note that this chapter is about *possible* future developments. It's an attempt to foresee some of the trends, scenarios, and technologies that will be important in the future. This chapter is *not* meant to be a roadmap for SAP products. It simply offers some outlook on possible future developments based on today's information.

15.1 General Trends

Let's start with a look at some of the general trends we see in the industry right now.

15.1.1 Cloud Computing: Gateway as a Service

IaaS, PaaS, SaaS

Before we look at SAP NetWeaver Gateway and the cloud, let's quickly consider cloud computing in general. As we already discussed in Chapter 1, cloud computing is about effectively using resources, either hardware or software, provided by or through a network. What makes the approach special is that these resources are provided as services. In general, there are three main types of cloud services: Infrastructure as a Service (IaaS), Platform as a Service (PaaS), and Software as a Service (SaaS). (For details on the different approaches, refer back to Section 1.1.2 in Chapter 1.)

So what are the benefits of cloud computing, and does it justify a shift from on-premise solutions? For most companies, the main argument for moving into the cloud is eliminating the capital expense of procuring hardware and perpetual licenses, while at the same time reducing operating expenses for maintaining the systems. But this isn't the only benefit of cloud computing. Cloud computing allows flexible, fast, and comparatively cheap access to resources on demand. The newly-won agility companies achieve by moving into the cloud can be translated into acceleration of innovation cycles and increased business agility—a necessity in today's market.

It's important to understand that most companies don't plan to move completely into the cloud; they still prefer some systems to be on-premise (e.g., due to security concerns or legal restrictions). Fortunately, systems in the cloud easily integrate with on-premise systems, and this integration allows an extension of on-premise systems that increase their value.

With respect to SAP's cloud strategy, we can distinguish different areas:

- Applications
- Platform

- Business network
- Infrastructure and lifecycle management

Cloud Applications

Applications in the cloud come with many benefits. They are faster to deploy and easy to adopt, and they can be updated without interruption, which allows for nondisruptive innovation. SAP is offering more than 30 applications and suites in the cloud as of today. The applications focus on critical assets of companies such as customers, suppliers, and employees.

Cloud Platforms

SAP also offers Platform as a Service (PaaS): SAP HANA Cloud Platform (Figure 15.1). As the name suggests, the SAP HANA Cloud Platform is based on SAP HANA, which allows the combination of the benefits of cloud computing and the benefits—and speed—of SAP's in-memory database.

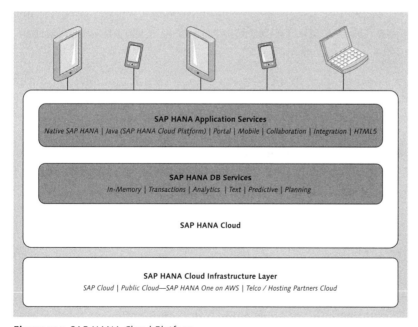

Figure 15.1 SAP HANA Cloud Platform

SAP HANA Cloud Platform

The SAP HANA Cloud Platform provides a standards-based development and runtime environment leveraging SAP HANA—and thus its speed— as a persistency service. It provides features such as a scalable document service or connectivity service enabling seamless integration with SAP and other systems; furthermore, the SAP NetWeaver Identity Management service can be used to implement federated identity management with the SAP HANA Cloud Platform.

An important aspect of the SAP HANA Cloud Platform is that it integrates seamlessly with on-premise installations through SAP HANA Cloud Integration (HCI) technology. In the context of other trends mentioned in this chapter, it comes with built-in functionality to create mobile, social, and analytical applications. Those applications can be managed and monitored via a web-based account page.

Business Networks

Using cloud computing as a technical solution for dedicated business scenarios is one way of leveraging the technology to save money and solve problems in specific setups. However, to gain the best out of the new possibilities, going a step further makes sense. Instead of using distinguished cloud installations with no further connection, you can benefit from business networks.

Ariba Business Network

A business network is a business collaboration community. The Ariba Business Network connects 730,000 businesses in 186 countries around the world—all connected through the cloud. Not only does this network allow customers to work efficiently and cost-effectively across the complete value chain, it also allows customers to implement automated processes between companies, thus offering completely new and extended business processes.

Infrastructure and Lifecycle Management

SAP virtualization and cloud management solutions

One of the challenges of cloud computing is leveraging the investment made in on-premise installations. SAP provides a scalable approach to cloud computing. With SAP virtualization and cloud management solutions, it's possible to take a step-by-step approach into the cloud. This approach allows you to get the most out of existing investments while at the same time profiting from virtualization cloud computing. As an additional benefit, SAP offers the possibility to take complete existing on-premise test installations and deploy them into public clouds. With this approach, it's possible to test at a minimum cost and keep critical on-premise systems safe.

To stress the importance of flexibility, SAP provides SAP HANA Cloud Integration (HCI) technology. This technology not only allows the integration of cloud applications and on-premise installations from SAP and third party vendors, but is also a new holistic cloud-based integration technology. SAP HCI offers both process and data integration capabilities and provides a kind of layer on top of a multitenant cloud infrastructure, creating a unified view of the data in that company. Customers who do not have an on-premise SAP NetWeaver installation can quickly get started using HCI via prepackaged integration and content. In addition, new custom content can be built easily using open APIs. The deployment choice (on-premise or on-demand) remains with the customer.

Overall, it's important to note that SAP offers a very flexible approach to cloud computing. Customers who want to deploy their SAP HANA-based applications in the cloud can choose from a wide variety of hosting capabilities provided by SAP and SAP partners, offering choices of how and with whom they step up into the cloud. Furthermore, a scalable approach allows moving into the cloud with the speed the customer sees fit for his company.

How does SAP NetWeaver Gateway fit into this picture? For the mentioned approach, it's essential that the benefits of SAP NetWeaver Gateway are made available in the cloud context as well. To this end, SAP has introduced *Gateway as a Service* (GWaaS). GWaaS runs in the SAP HANA Cloud Platform and can connect to SAP Business Suite systems that are SAP NetWeaver Gateway-enabled through SAP Cloud Connector. In combination, this setup allows you to take advantage of the benefits of SAP NetWeaver Gateway from within the cloud. Figure 15.2 shows what this setup can look like (just as an example).

Gateway as a Service

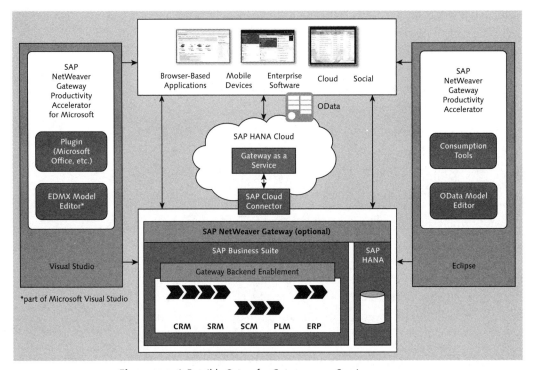

Figure 15.2 A Possible Setup for Gateway as a Service

15.1.2 Simplified UI: SAP Fiori

The importance of simple and intuitive UIs can't be stressed enough. For this outlook chapter, we mention it one last time because—even though not new—it's still a trend that SAP is following closely.

For SAP, it's important to allow access to SAP applications through simple UIs. One way to achieve this goal is by integrating existing technologies and products already in use by end users (see Section 15.1.6 for one example). Another approach is by providing SAP's own solution—SAP Fiori.

As discussed In Chapter 10, SAP Fiori is a set of applications that allows easy access to SAP software through simple UIs. In addition to the simple UI, it's important to understand that SAP Fiori supports multichannel scenarios; that is, you can use the applications on your desktop PC, your tablet, your smartphone, and more.

In terms of outlook, you can expect to see a lot of additional applications, offering functionality from more general scenarios to industry-
specific scenarios; these have the potential to be more functionally complex (but still simple from a UI perspective). Most importantly for our
purposes, you can expect a tighter integration between SAP NetWeaver
Gateway and SAP Fiori, especially for development tools.

Outlook for SAP Fiori

15.1.3 Gamification

So what is gamification all about? It may seem a bit odd to introduce
games and game mechanics in a business context—but if we take a closer
look at the mechanics, it turns out the approach makes sense. (Before we
do this, understand that gamification is somewhat of a new trend; that
is, it's hard to predict its development and impact in the future.)

One of the main challenges companies face today is the engagement of
their employees, customers, and end users in general. How can you
motivate your employees to work more efficiently? How can you convince your customers to visit your product pages more often, for a
longer time, and eventually buy your services? Gamification isn't the
entire solution for this problem, but it may be part of the solution.

Gamification as motivation

This may seem a bit abstract, so let's briefly walk through an example of
a help desk scenario involving a customer and the help desk employee.
In a classic scenario, the customer calls or writes to the help desk person
for assistance (e.g., "the display driver doesn't support 3D"). The help
desk person then provides a solution (e.g., "update the driver") and
eventually, perhaps after several iterations, the problem is fixed, the customer gives up, or the issue escalates.

With gamification, the motivation of the help desk employee can be
increased and thus may lead to a satisfied customer. One simple way to
do this is to add an experience level to help desk employees. Every piece
of positive feedback from a customer increases this experience level. To
enhance the effect, it makes sense to label specific levels (e.g., novice,
senior, expert). Furthermore, it may make sense to introduce leader-
boards or missions (e.g., solve 10 issues in a row with positive feedback). Those missions could then be combined with badges to increase
motivation even further.

Depending on the scenario, the kicker might be to combine those ideas with social media, so that the players—in our example, the help desk employees—can post their achievements. (Admittedly, this is a much better kicker when customers are in the player role.)

Gamification as innovation

Before we take a look at gamification at SAP, let's consider another important aspect of gamification—as innovation. The mentioned mechanics can easily be used to increase innovation within a company. To enable innovation, motivation is essential—preferably motivation of stakeholders and involved people. Here gamification can be the difference between getting involved and not getting involved. In combination with social media and the community, it's possible to access a knowledge pool that wasn't available before. All this together may lead to a completely new level of innovation.

SAP Community Network (SCN)

SAP understood the potential of gamification quite early, and was in a unique position to provide gamification and enterprise readiness with its applications. After years of using some gamification mechanics, and then officially implementing them on the SAP Community Network (SCN), it's now time to offer a platform that can be used in enterprises. Right now, we are in a very early phase. However, even as of today, you can find information on SAP's gamification platform on the web (SCN, LinkedIn, etc.).

Although we know information in this early phase is changing rapidly, let's look at what you can expect. SAP's gamification system is a standalone platform powered by SAP HANA cloud technologies that allows for introducing low risk gamification features into companies. Some key features you can expect include the following:

- Enterprise-level performance and scalability
- Single sign-on (SSO)
- Rule management for gamification mechanics
- SAPUI5 integration
- Developer API

As of today, SAP NetWeaver Gateway integration with the gamification platform is mainly through SAP Business Suite; i.e., you have to integrate features through development on the backend. However, the developer API will ultimately allow easy integration of gamification features into SAP NetWeaver Gateway applications.

An SAP NetWeaver Gateway component for gamification would allow easy usage of gamification features (e.g., game triggers) from consumer applications as well. Because the (OData) consumer applications have SAP NetWeaver Gateway as a common denominator, the features would be available directly to all application developers. In addition, because the gamification platform and SAP NetWeaver Gateway will support on-demand scenarios, as well as on-premise and on-device scenarios, customers can be extremely flexible in how they introduce gamification in their companies and how they eventually use it.

To sum it up, we see a natural fit between SAP NetWeaver Gateway and SAP's gamification platform. As of today, both can be used together to offer a flexible yet enterprise-ready approach to gamification for companies. With social media (see Section 15.1.4) as a kicker, gamification may be a literal game changer for engagement and innovation in companies.

15.1.4 Social Media

An outlook chapter would not be complete without at least mentioning social media as an ongoing trend. Although there are already real development possibilities for social media today (see Chapter 11), it's important to understand that social media is still a new trend, and will continue to evolve. One huge challenge today and in the near future will be the integration of social network mechanics into your enterprise. The SAP development team and, more specifically, the SAP NetWeaver Gateway team, is aware of those developments and is working on social media concepts to be built into the product in the future.

15.1.5 Internet of Things

What exactly is this Internet of Things? On a very basic level, it's the addition of physical objects into the Internet. For example, a lot of physical objects today are available for representation (e.g., tagged with an RFID chip), are more sophisticated and even aware of their surroundings through sensors (e.g., mini cameras), or can influence their surroundings via actuators. All of these objects communicate with their surroundings (including humans) or each other via *Machine to Machine (M2M) communication*, using communication protocols such as Internet Protocol (IP).

Interaction with end users A basic and current example of the Internet of Things is in the interaction with end users buying consumer products. Potential buyers can use their mobile phones in combination with RFID chips (or sometimes simple QR codes) on products to get additional information on the product (where does it come from? is it an original? is it "green"?). This information can be critical for the decision of the potential buyers to buy or not to buy a product. In a more sophisticated scenario, it's even possible to imagine situations in which the product automatically changes its price to convince the buyers to buy it.

From an enterprise perspective, the Internet of Things can make it easier to track products from the production site, through shipment, to the shop, and eventually to the consumer. In addition to all of the opportunities this may offer in the production process, it can help a company identify buyer patterns and track products—in some cases, even to the individual consumer.

The business scenarios are endless. For SAP, they were reason enough to come up with a joint announcement with Ericsson at the Mobile World Congress on February 25th, 2013, on a new combination of cloud-based M2M solutions to enhance enterprise efficiency. And this is just the beginning.

With solutions such as SAP HANA and its real-time capabilities, SAP is in a perfect spot to come up with its own end-to-end solution—the SAP Internet of Things Solution. The necessities to handle, analyze, and calculate with high volumes of data in real-time is a perfect use case for SAP HANA.

Further Resources

For more information on the Internet of Things at SAP, we recommend *http://www.sap.com/pc/tech/mobile/software/solutions/overview/internet-of-things.html*.

As mentioned, the SAP Internet of Things Solution provides an end-to-end solution, including the integration of various devices (in other words, M2M) and tools for managing those devices. Furthermore, it provides the tools required to easily and rapidly develop applications in this context.

Although we don't yet know the details of how SAP NetWeaver Gateway will integrate with SAP Internet of Things Solution, the applications we're talking about are for multichannel scenarios—so it's very likely to play a big role.

15.1.6 Microsoft Interoperability: SAP NetWeaver Gateway Productivity Accelerator for Microsoft (GWPAM)

Many customers of SAP are also customers of Microsoft. Understandably, those customers expect SAP and Microsoft to come up with a solution to integrate SAP and Microsoft in the best possible way.

Figure 15.3 shows a day in the life of a fictional employee who has both SAP and Microsoft solutions. Our imaginary user gets up early in the morning and checks his email on his Windows Phone 8. Instead of getting only regular email, the user also gets email about all relevant information from SAP backend systems (e.g., workflow items). At 8:30, our user schedules an SAP CRM appointment via Outlook 2013; that is, he is conducting an SAP task from within Microsoft Outlook 2013. At 10:00, he checks his sales pipeline—again, SAP information—via his Windows 8 Surface. At 11:30, he updates his budget via Excel 2013 and approves a workflow item at 12:00 using a Windows 8 native application. At 12:30, he conducts an online meeting with a customer using Lync 2013—which would not normally be extraordinary, except that he can also record it as an SAP CRM activity. As you can see, the integration between SAP and Microsoft isn't only about Microsoft technology consuming SAP data, but also about writing data back into SAP systems. At 3:00, he makes use of a SharePoint online application to create an SAP CRM lead. Finally, at 5:30, he records his time in SAP via Microsoft Outlook 2013 Web, which is part of Office 365, using cloud technology.

Integration with Windows devices

This day may look constructed, but in one way or another, it's true for many users out there today.

Duet Enterprise

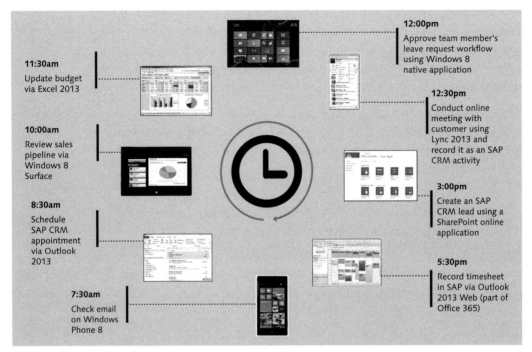

Figure 15.3 A Day with SAP and Microsoft

GWPAM   To continue this journey, SAP NetWeaver Gateway offers the Gateway Accelerator Productivity Application for Microsoft (GWPAM). GWPAM is a product that simplifies the integration of SAP NetWeaver Gateway-based services into Microsoft products. In terms of infrastructure, GWPAM offers an interoperability layer that ensures secure, reliable, and scalable communication between GWPAM applications and SAP backend systems. To create GWPAM applications, the SAP Business Suite provides an add-in for Visual Studio that allows sophisticated OData browsing. To support the developer even further, the SAP Business Suite provides a set of templates for contact, calendar, and workflow scenarios for Microsoft Outlook. For any Visual Studio C# project, there is a special treat: generic service generation. Generic service generation can be used for code-free development—the project is used as-is—or the project can be used as a template and can be extended and modified according to specific requirements.

Every project generated with the GWPAM add-in can instantly use enterprise-ready functionalities such as security, SSO, centralized configuration, or logging. SSO supports standards such as X.509 and SAML 2.0. For the developer, those functionalities are available out of the box and don't require any additional effort or knowledge.

When it comes to Microsoft Excel, the GWPAM add-in enables usage of data from SAP systems. For this, it leverages SAP NetWeaver Gateway to connect to the SAP backend. It's possible to both consume data from the SAP backend and update and create data in the backend, all from within Excel.

15.2 Development Trend: API Management

The trends discussed so far are general trends that have a direct or indirect implication on developing applications for SAP NetWeaver Gateway. However, there are also development trends worth discussing. For this discussion, we'll focus on one development trend around the management of Application Programming Interfaces (APIs)—API management.

API management is everything from planning APIs through implementing them to publishing them. In most cases, API management refers as well to the infrastructure and the tools needed in this context. To understand API management and related requirements a bit better, it makes sense to think of APIs as a kind of product. For this product, you want to know how it's used, by whom it's used, and if it's used correctly. In addition, you want to make sure its quality is guaranteed.

Most API management solutions allow you to control the usage of your APIs through any applications that use this API. Those solutions can even monitor specific activities and traffic to the level of an individual application. In addition to bug-fixing, performance optimization, and so on, this is also the basis of one of the most important aspects of API management, which is preventing misuse of your APIs. To prevent misuse, most API management solutions offer built-in features for security and governance.

Monitor API usage

API management solutions combine well with the cloud trend, offering enterprises the opportunity to choose between on-premise and on-demand solutions. There are two scenarios in which SAP NetWeaver Gateway may come into play here. In an on-demand scenario, GWaaS could be extended for API provisioning. In an on-premise scenario, SAP NetWeaver Gateway could be used on a Lean Java Server (LJS) for API provisioning.

15.3 SAP NetWeaver Gateway in SAP NetWeaver 7.40

Add-ons   As we discussed in the previous section, it's easy to see that SAP NetWeaver Gateway fits in smoothly with many current IT trends. Underscoring the preceding statement is the fact that SAP NetWeaver Gateway is now part of SAP NetWeaver 7.40. Although we've discussed release 7.40 throughout the book, we want to briefly highlight the most important release changes in this last chapter.

The necessary SAP NetWeaver Gateway add-ons can be divided into the following:

- Core components
- Business Enablement Provisioning (BEP) component
- Content adapter components
- Content components
- Screen scraping components

Let's take a closer look at these components for release 7.40.

15.3.1 Core Components

For SAP NetWeaver 7.40 and higher, SAP_GWFND (SAP NetWeaver Gateway Foundation) is the core component for SAP NetWeaver Gateway. It's part of standard SAP NetWeaver 7.40 installations.

SAP_GWFND for SAP NetWeaver 7.40 (SAP_GWFND 740) provides the functionality of IW_FND 250, GW_CORE 200, IW_BEP 200, and IW_HDB 100.

With the core component being part of the standard, there is no additional installation necessary to use SAP NetWeaver Gateway with an SAP NetWeaver 7.40 installation.

No additional installation

> **Note**
>
> There is one exception to the rule. If you created services for the generic channel, and you want to keep using them, you'll have to install the component IW_FNDGC 100. This is only necessary if services for the generic channel are still in use. In general, it's advised to consider solutions where the generic channel isn't used anymore.

With SAP NetWeaver 7.0 and 7.01, the core components are GW_CORE 190 and IW_FND 240. With SAP NetWeaver 7.02, 7.03, and 7.31, the core components are IW_CORE 200 and IW_FND 250.

15.3.2 Business Enablement Provisioning (BEP) Component

In SAP NetWeaver 7.0, 7.01, 7.02, 7.03, and 7.31, the component IW_BEP 200 was needed. IW_BEP enables the OData channel programming paradigm. For SAP NetWeaver Gateway Service Builder, it's required to build OData services. IW_BEP is an optional component. If you plan to install the content adapter components, you have to install it, however. Installation can be done either in the SAP Business Suite backend system or the SAP NetWeaver Gateway system.

IW_BEP may be optional, but it's a very important component, which is why SAP_GWFND 740 contains the complete functionality of IW_BEP 200. In other words, there is no additional installation necessary for SAP NetWeaver 7.40.

No additional installation

15.3.3 Content Adapter Components

The content adapter components are the following:

- IW_HDB
- IW_SPI
- IW_PGW
- IW_GIL

For SAP NetWeaver Gateway with SAP HANA, IW_HDB functions as the business content adapter enabling OData exposure of SAP HANA views. SAP_GWFND 740 includes the functional scope of IW_HDB 100, thus an installation on SAP NetWeaver 7.40 systems and higher isn't necessary.

On the Service Provider Infrastructure (SPI), IW_SPI provides a generic OData adapter. IW_SPI 100 has to be installed on SAP NetWeaver 7.40 systems to be used.

Requires installation of IW_GIL 100 IW_PGW is the bridge from SAP NetWeaver Gateway to SAP NetWeaver Business Process Management (BPM). In particular, it enables the exposure of BPM and Process Observer Task for BPM as well as SAP NetWeaver Business Workflow. Installation of IW_PGW 100 is necessary on SAP NetWeaver 7.40 to use its functionality.

A generic OData adapter for GenIL is provided by IW_GIL. The installation of IW_GIL 100 is necessary on SAP NetWeaver 7.40 systems to use this functionality.

> **Note**
>
> IW_SPI 100, IW_PGW 100, and IW_GIL 100 require the installation of SAP_GWFND 740 on an SAP NetWeaver 7.40 system. As mentioned before, SAP_GWFND 740 is part of the standard installations for SAP NetWeaver 7.40, so it comes down to making sure that SAP_GWFND 740 was installed correctly.
>
> For all SAP NetWeaver releases lower than SAP NetWeaver 7.40, the installation of the content adapter components (IW_HDB 100, IW_SPI 100, IW_PGW 100, and IW_GIL 100) require the installation of IW_BEP 200.

15.3.4 Content Components

The content components are the following:

▶ IW_CNT

▶ IW_CBS

Example content is provided via the content components. Example content includes customers, accounts, and leave requests grouped under SAP Customer Relationship Management (SAP CRM).

In general, it's possible for third-party vendors (e.g., SIs) to provide this kind of content as well. Other SAP departments and products may provide content components as well.

For SAP NetWeaver 7.40, the components are not preinstalled. IW_CNT 200 and IW_CBS 200 have to be installed and require the installation of IW_FNDGC 100.

Requires installation of IW_CNT 200, IW_CBS 200, and IW_FNDGC 100

> **Note**
>
> For SAP NetWeaver releases 7.02, 7.03, and 7.31, the installation of the content components (IW_CNT 200, IW_CBS 200) requires the installation of IW_FND 250.

15.3.5 Screen Scraping Component

With SAP NetWeaver Gateway, it's still possible to use screen scraping. To use the screen scraping generator, you have to install IW_SCS in the SAP Business Suite backend system. SAP NetWeaver 7.40 requires the installation of IW_SCS 200.

Table 15.1 shows the supported combinations of SAP NetWeaver Gateway components and SAP NetWeaver.

> **Note**
>
> Note that all components beyond server (GW_CORE, IW_FND, SAP_GWFND) are optional. For details on those components, refer to the preceding subsections.

The SAP NetWeaver 7.40 column is relevant from SAP NetWeaver Gateway 2.0 SP06 on.

	SAP NetWeaver 7.00	SAP NetWeaver 7.01	SAP NetWeaver 7.02	SAP NetWeaver 7.03/7.31 (SP01)	SAP NetWeaver 7.40 (SP01)
Server (GW_CORE, IW_FND, SAP_GWFND)	X (SP25)	X (SP10)	X (SP07)	X	Delivered with SAP NetWeaver 7.40
IW_CBS	N/A	N/A	X (SP07)	X	X
IW_CNT	N/A	N/A	X (SP07)	X	X
Screen Scraping (IW_SCS)	X (SP18)	X (SP03)	X (SP06)	X	X
Business Enablement Provisioning (IW_BEP)	X (SP18)	X (SP03)	X (SP06)	X	Delivered with SAP NetWeaver 7.40
IW_GIL		X (SP03)	X (SP06)	X	X
IW_SPI	X (SP18)	X (SP03)	X (SP06)	X	X
IW_HDB		X (SP03)	X (SP09)	X	Delivered with SAP NetWeaver 7.40
IW_PGW	X (SP18)	X (SP03)	X (SP06)	X	X

Table 15.1 Supported Combinations of SAP NetWeaver Gateway 2.0 SP04 and Higher

15.4 Summary

In this final chapter, we discussed some of the relevant trends we see in today's IT and enterprise world. We took a closer look at the different implications and possibilities related to these trends and SAP, including SAP NetWeaver Gateway in particular. As mentioned earlier, our intent was to outline possible future developments, as well as the importance of the role SAP NetWeaver Gateway might play in them. We concluded the chapter with a brief summary of SAP NetWeaver Gateway in SAP NetWeaver 7.40.

A   Advanced Topics

In this appendix, we'll cover some advanced topics that might be useful for your SAP NetWeaver Gateway project. This includes both advanced SAP NetWeaver Gateway features as well as advanced operations topics.

First, we'll take a closer look at scenarios in which multiple SAP Business Suite systems are connected to a single SAP NetWeaver Gateway server (hub) system. Then we'll look into an SAP NetWeaver Gateway feature that allows for sending notifications from SAP NetWeaver Gateway to consumers. Next, there will be an in-depth look at handling and analyzing errors and performance problems, including an introduction to the performance trace tool (which allows for analyzing the performance behavior of your services and identifying potential improvement areas). Finally, we'll look into the options you have if you need an application to run online and offline.

A.1   Connecting Multiple SAP Business Suite Systems

Routing, multiple origin composition (MOC), and throttling are advanced and very useful features of SAP NetWeaver Gateway. They were introduced with SAP NetWeaver Gateway 2.0 SP05 and address the use case of SAP NetWeaver Gateway connecting to multiple SAP Business Suite systems.

A classic example of a company that would have use for routing, MOC, or throttling is one that operates three identical SAP Business Suite systems in separate regions. Figure A.1 shows the structure of an example company with three data centers: one in the Americas, one in APJ, and one in Europe. We'll talk more about these three topics next.

629

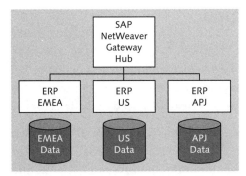

Figure A.1 Multiple Backend System Support

A.1.1 Routing

Routing is used to route a consumer request to a dedicated SAP Business Suite system if multiple system alias entries are assigned to a service. Using routing, it's possible, for example, to use a single service for all employees in a global setup that is made up of different regions. In this case, depending on user roles, a system call is redirected to the SAP Business Suite system that is located in the employees' region. A US employee, for example, only retrieves data from the US SAP Business Suite system while employees from the EMEA region only retrieve data from the SAP Business Suite system that serves the EMEA region.

Routing is performed in the SAP NetWeaver Gateway hub by the *destination finder* component. To execute the routing, it calls the class /IWFND/CL_MGW_DEST_FINDER. The destination finder performs the routing for OData services based on the customizing settings for the system aliases. For every system alias, it's possible to maintain a user role and the hostname of the OData client as additional optional parameters to configure the routing to a system alias entry.

The destination finder compares the role assignment of the current user. These settings are stored in maintenance view /IWFND/V_MGDEAM, which can be maintained via IMG by starting Transaction SPRO and navigating to SAP NETWEAVER • GATEWAY • ODATA CHANNEL • CONFIGURATION • CONNECTION SETTINGS • SAP NETWEAVER GATEWAY TO SAP SYSTEM. In addition, the value for the hostname that can optionally be maintained in the configuration is compared to the OData request's HTTP header field Host (e.g., 'myserver.mycompany.com:50055'). Based on the roles assigned to a user in the SAP NetWeaver Gateway hub and the hostname of the OData client, the destination finder then determines which SAP Business Suite system to call. If a service is registered for more than one system alias, as shown in Figure A.2, there must be exactly one entry flagged as default. That system alias is used for all standard requests.

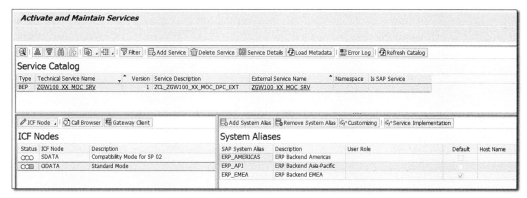

Figure A.2 Assignment of Multiple System Aliases

In some customer deployments, however, SAP roles aren't sufficient to determine the correct SAP Business Suite system. Because of this, SAP allows the implementation of customer-specific routing rules that can't be implemented via role assignment based on a BAdI. Customers that want to leverage this enhanced functionality can implement the enhancement spot /IWFND/ES_MGW_DEST_FINDER. This enhancement spot is described in more detail in Section A.1.3 because it can also be used to shield an SAP Business Suite system from being overloaded.

A.1.2 Multiple Origin Composition (MOC)

Multiple origin composition (MOC) allows a single service to connect to multiple SAP Business Suite systems in parallel and collect data from all of these systems. This data is then aggregated in that single service. MOC allows for READ, CREATE, QUERY, DELETE, and UPDATE operations on this data. As a result, a single service can be made available to access data from several system aliases. For example, the CFO of the company might need to be able to retrieve financial data from all regions.

Calling several SAP Business Suite systems at the same time using MOC obviously raises a few questions. The first question is how the result sets from the different SAP Business Suite systems can be distinguished. The framework achieves this by adding a new key field SAP__ORIGIN to each entity that is returned as an entry in the result set when the service is called using the MOC option ;mo, as shown in Listing A.1. Consequently, the service metadata document of a service that is called using the MOC option changes as well. Each entity type has an additional key field "SAP__ORIGIN". So, technically speaking, calling a service via MOC lets the framework create a different version of the service. For the consumption side, this has the consequence that calling an OData service with the MOC option probably requires adjustment of the client application because the OData interface has changed (if there was already an existing service without MOC).

```
Request:
/sap/opu/odata/sap/ZCD204_EPM_DEMO_SRV;mo/BusinessPartners
results": [
{
"SAP__Origin": „ERP_EMEA",
"BusinessPartnerID": "0100000000",
"CompanyName": "SAP"},
{
"SAP__Origin": „ERP_EMEA",
"BusinessPartnerID": "0100000001",
"CompanyName": "Becker Berlin"},
{
"SAP__Origin": „ERP_AMERICAS",
"BusinessPartnerID": "0100000027",
"CompanyName": "Developement Para O Governo"},
{
"SAP__Origin": „ERP_AMERICAS",
"BusinessPartnerID": "0100000028",
"CompanyName": "Brazil Technologies"}
]
```

Listing A.1 Response of a Request That Uses Multiple Origin Composition

Another important aspect when using MOC is the impact with respect to performance. Calling the SAP Business Suite systems in a sequential order might result in increased response times that can lead to timeout errors on the consumption side—remember, the SAP Business Suite systems might be located on different continents. Therefore, SAP NetWeaver Gateway allows for certain settings to be made to adjust MOC in such a way that several SAP Business Suite systems can be called in parallel. You can then tailor the level of parallel calls to your specific system environment. The performance can be checked with the help of the performance trace tool, which is discussed in Section A.4 of this chapter.

The two configuration parameters MINIMUM NUMBER OF BACKEND SYSTEMS and MAXIMUM NUMBER OF PARALLEL BACKEND CALLS are the most relevant. Both of these configuration settings have a major effect on the parallelization of service calls, which again has a major impact on performance.

With MINIMUM NUMBER OF BACKEND SYSTEMS, you basically define whether there is parallelization. If you put 0 for a value, no parallelization takes place. If you put a number n, parallelization will only be done from n SAP Business Suite systems onward.

MAXIMUM NUMBER OF PARALLEL BACKEND CALLS can be used to limit the number of parallel backend calls. This results in putting a ceiling on the use of SAP NetWeaver Gateway hub system resources.

As for the effect of these settings and the use of parallelization on the overall performance, keep the following in mind:

▶ For serialized calls, the duration of a service call in the SAP NetWeaver Gateway hub is the sum of all calls to the SAP Business Suite.

▶ For parallel calls, the duration of a service call is the duration of the single call that takes longest.

In conclusion, configuring MOC typically results in a major performance improvement.

A.1.3 Throttling

Throttling helps when the SAP Business Suite system needs to be shielded from being overloaded by too many client requests. To facilitate the implementation of throttling, SAP offers a BAdI that can be implemented by customers. This is the same BAdI that customers have to implement if they want to overrule the standard role-based routing.

The enhancement spot /IWFND/ES_MGW_DEST_FINDER is part of the SP05 shipment of SAP NetWeaver Gateway 2.0. This BAdI serves two use cases:

▸ To overwrite or enhance the standard routing for a service

▸ To control the traffic from the SAP NetWeaver Gateway hub to an SAP Business Suite system in order to limit the load on that SAP Business Suite system

The BAdI has the following input parameters:

▸ User ID

▸ Service Document Identifier, which is a concatenated string of the technical service name and the version (e.g., ZTEA_TEST_APPLICATION_0001)

▸ A table of system alias entries that contains the result of the standard routing

▸ A list of HTTP request parameters

The output of the BAdI is a table of system aliases. The BAdI may also leave the table unchanged; in this case, the default routing is applied.

As we said, the BAdI can be used not only to implement customer-specific routing, but also to shield the SAP Business Suite system from being overloaded by too many client requests. In Listing A.2, you can find sample code that can be used in such a BAdI implementation. This code raises an error message if a potential overload is discovered.

```
    ...
    RAISE EXCEPTION TYPE /iwfnd/cx_mgw_dest_finder
      EXPORTING
        textid           = /iwfnd/
cx_mgw_dest_finder=>backend_load_too_high
        http_status_code = /iwfnd/
cx_mgw_dest_finder=>gc_status_service_unavailable
        system_alias     = lv_system_alias.
```

Listing A.2 Sample Implementation to Throw an Exception Due to System Overload

When a BAdI implementation throws an exception as shown in Listing A.2, the OData client gets the HTTP error response as shown in Listing A.3.

```
HTTP Status          503 - Service Unavailable
<?xml version="1.0" encoding="utf-8" ?>
<error xmlns="http://schemas.microsoft.com/ado/2007/08/
dataservices/metadata">
<code>/IWFND/CM_COS/071</code>
<message xml:lang="en">The load on backend system 'ERP_GBC_100'
 is too high. Try again later.</message>
      </error>
```

Listing A.3 HTTP Error Response

A.2   Configuring Notifications in SAP NetWeaver Gateway

The use of notifications in mobile scenarios is very common. Getting notified if a comment is posted on your Facebook site or if somebody replied to a tweet you posted is a must-have feature that users expect from any social media application. The important thing here is that the user not only gets notified, but can also perform an action using the Facebook or Twitter client. Similar functionalities are useful in business scenarios. Managers appreciate being able to approve leave requests or purchase orders using their mobile device without having to switch to their laptop or PC after having been notified that something has happened that needs their attention.

This functionality is provided by the SAP NetWeaver Gateway Subscription and Notification framework, which is contained in the IW_BEP add-on or included in SAP NetWeaver 7.40 SP02. Notifications in SAP NetWeaver Gateway work as follows: to notify a user about a change that has happened in the SAP Business Suite system, the end user has to inform the SAP Business Suite system of which changes he's interested in and wants to be notified about. This is done via a *subscription*. For this, an entity set is marked as `sap:subscribable` in the SAP NetWeaver Gateway Service Builder, as shown in Figure A.3. When regenerating the project, the entity data model contains two new collections called

`NotificationCollection` and `SubscriptionCollection`. These entity sets get activated after the entity set has been marked as `sap:subscribable`.

Figure A.3 Entity Set Marked as Subscribable in the Service Builder

You can create, update, delete, read, and query the `SubscriptionCollection` like any other entity set of an OData service using an appropriate URL and payload.

At this point, we now have to distinguish between push-oriented and pull-oriented scenarios:

▶ In a *push-oriented scenario,* a notification is sent from the SAP Business Suite via SAP NetWeaver Gateway directly to the consumer.

▶ In a *pull-oriented scenario,* the notifications are only sent from the SAP Business Suite to the SAP NetWeaver Gateway hub. Here they are persisted until the client pulls for the changed business objects.

If a user wants to get notified through a push notification about changes in a certain entity set, the user has to send an appropriate post request to the `SubscriptionCollection` of the service (Figure A.4: ❶, ❷). The `persistNotifications` parameter has to be set to `false`. The request for the subscription is then sent via RFC (shown in ❸) from the SAP NetWeaver Gateway system to the SAP Business Suite system. In the SAP Business Suite system, the developer has to implement appropriate business logic, for example, in a BAdI that will check for subscriptions if an update has been performed. If a change occurred in the SAP Business Suite system, information about it is first sent to the SAP NetWeaver Gateway server (shown in ❹) via a background RFC (bgRFC), where it's queued and sent to the receiving HTTP endpoint (shown in ❺) that was specified in the subscription.

In a push-oriented mobile scenario, you typically need an intermediate server as a receiving HTTP endpoint that facilitates the communication between the mobile device and the SAP NetWeaver Gateway server. The intermediate component recommended by SAP is the SAP Mobile

Platform. Among other functionalities offered by a mobile platform, the SAP Mobile Platform holds the information concerning which device belongs to which user and is therefore able to send any notifications to the right person and device.

If the SAP Mobile Platform is used, it listens to a selected service for incoming notification requests. The information where this listener is located is sent by the mobile application to the SAP NetWeaver Gateway, where an appropriate HTTP destination has to be defined that points to the listener.

The intermediate server, such as the SAP Mobile Platform system, finally sends the notification to the user's device (shown in ❻).

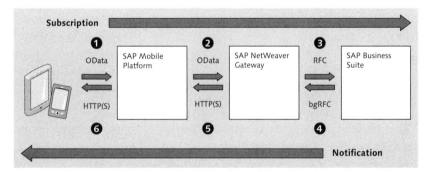

Figure A.4 Subscription and Notification in SAP NetWeaver Gateway: Push Scenario

In a pull-oriented scenario, the `persistNotifications` element in the original subscription payload `Create` request sent to the `Subscription-Collection` has to be set to `true`. The pull-oriented scenario is shown in Figure A.5. After the request has been sent from the client directly to the SAP NetWeaver Gateway (shown in ❶), it's sent from the SAP NetWeaver Gateway to the SAP Business Suite system (shown in ❷). Like in the push scenario, appropriate business logic, for example, in a BAdI, has to be implemented to check for changes in the SAP Business Suite system that will then send those changes (shown in ❸) via bgRFC to the SAP NetWeaver Gateway system. In a pull-oriented scenario, these notifications are then stored in the SAP NetWeaver Gateway system (shown in ❹).

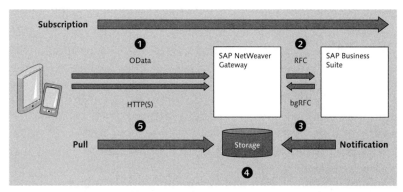

Figure A.5 Subscription and Notification in SAP NetWeaver Gateway: Pull Scenario

The client can pull the notifications using the NOTIFICATIONSTORE service provided with SAP NetWeaver Gateway. The notifications can actually be retrieved from the NotificationCollection as shown in the following GET request:

http://<hostname>:<port>/sap/opu/odata/iwfnd/NOTIFICATIONSTORE/
NotificationCollection

Although a pull-oriented scenario isn't a notification scenario in the strictest sense, it nevertheless helps to reduce the load on the SAP Business Suite side. Instead of querying the SAP Business Suite system for changes, this information can be retrieved from the NotificationCollection on the SAP NetWeaver Gateway system.

Further Resources

A detailed description on how to implement a service with push notifications can be found on the SAP Community Network (SCN), together with a video on YouTube describing the process: *http://wiki.sdn.sap.com/wiki/pages/viewpage.action?pageId=318672261*.

A.3 Using the Error Log

In this hands-on section, we'll walk you through the process of analyzing an error that occurred in the SAP Business Suite system. The process flow for the error analysis is shown in Figure A.6.

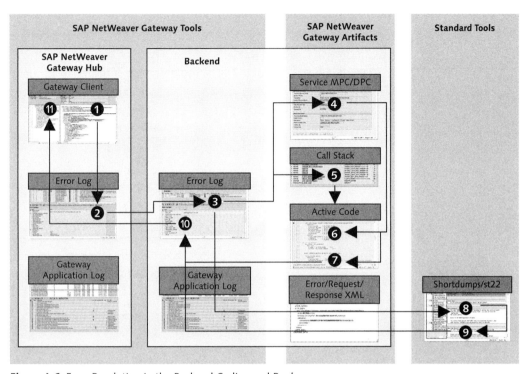

Figure A.6 Error Resolution in the Backend Coding and Replay

This process starts with a client executing a request (shown in ❶) that leads to an error. This error can be found in the error log (shown in ❷) on the SAP NetWeaver Gateway server. From there, the next step is to analyze the error in the SAP Business Suite error log (shown in ❸). Here you can investigate the service implementation (shown in ❹) or find the error location in the call stack (shown in ❺) to finally open the active coding (shown in ❻). The next step is then to either correct the coding or to set an external breakpoint to investigate the error situation (shown in ❼). If the error has led to an ABAP short dump, Transaction ST22 is used instead (shown in ❽), and breakpoints are set there (shown in ❾). After the error has been corrected, it's possible from within the error log (shown in ❿) to replay the request with SAP NetWeaver Gateway (shown in ⓫).

In this walkthrough, we follow, for the most part, the process outlined in Figure A.6 and start in the SAP NetWeaver Gateway hub. There we use the SAP NetWeaver Gateway client to perform an HTTP request to mimic the consumption of a service by an OData client. We use a sample service ZPRODUCT_SRV that retrieves demo product data from the SAP NetWeaver demo data model. This sample service is intended to make the error processing visible. In this specific scenario, the requested query method hasn't been implemented so that the generated code throws an error when it's called by the service.

By executing the request

/sap/opu/odata/sap/ZPRODUCT_SRV/Products

an exception is thrown as shown in Figure A.7. This exception holds several details (shown in ❶) that can be inspected in the error log.

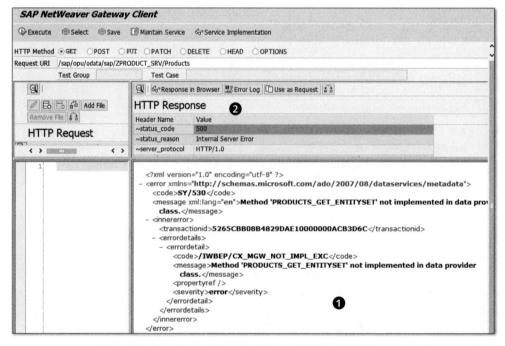

Figure A.7 Error When Calling the Service ZPRODUCT_SRV

Selecting ERROR LOG (❷ of Figure A.7) takes you to the error log. By double-clicking the error message, the error context appears (❶ of Figure A.8). Here, you can take a closer look at the system information, service information, and other details.

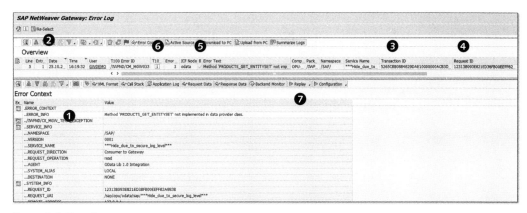

Figure A.8 Error Log

In the OVERVIEW section (shown in ❷), you can see the TRANSACTION ID of the request (shown in ❸) and the REQUEST ID of the client (shown in ❹). The TRANSACTION ID is important to know in case you want to search for this request in any standard SAP NetWeaver transaction. The TRANSACTION ID is also part of the SAP passport.

The next important information is the BACKEND ERROR flag (shown in ❺). This flag tells you that the root cause of this error appeared in the backend and not in the SAP NetWeaver Gateway hub system. (Backend system here refers to the system on which the implementation of the service based on IW_BEP has been performed.)

The next important information is the T100 long text, which is displayed if you click on the icon (shown in ❻) in the T100 ERROR INFO column. This long text might contain additional information about the error that has occurred, as shown in Figure A.9.

Figure A.9 T100 Error Information

When you click on BACKEND MONITOR, you're taken to the backend error log (Figure A.10) that can also be accessed using Transaction /IWBEP/ERROR_LOG on the backend system. It shows the error log in the SAP Business Suite system. This log looks very similar to the error log on the SAP NetWeaver Gateway server, so everything should look very familiar to you.

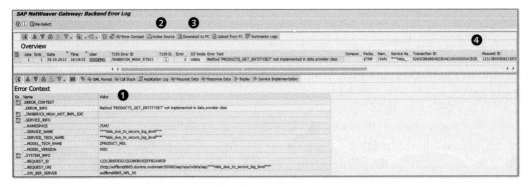

Figure A.10 Backend Error Log

Now you need to find out where exactly in the coding the exception was thrown. You have two options to find this information. The first option is to select CALL STACK (shown in ❶), and the second option is to select ACTIVE SOURCE (shown in ❷). CALL STACK helps you see the flow of the application. The option ACTIVE SOURCE brings you directly into the coding as shown in Figure A.11.

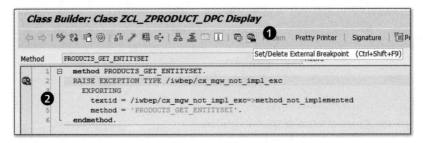

Figure A.11 ABAP Code Error Location

Here, you can set an external breakpoint (shown in ❶ and ❷). You either go back to the SAP NetWeaver Gateway client to perform the HTTP request again, or navigate back to the error log on the SAP

NetWeaver Gateway hub (as shown in Figure A.12) where you can choose REPLAY (shown in ❶) to run the request again.

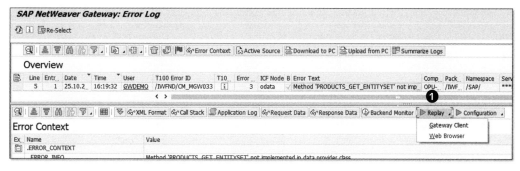

Figure A.12 Replaying a Request

The request is run in the SAP NetWeaver Gateway client again. In this example, however, an error message occurs that tells you a replay can't be performed due to security reasons (Figure A.13).

Figure A.13 Error Message: Secure Log Level

The error log level can be configured directly in the error log transaction. As shown in Figure A.14, from the menu shown in ❶, select ERROR LOG • GLOBAL CONFIGURATION. On the SAP NETWEAVER GATEWAY: GLOBAL CONFIGURATION page, you can set the error log level to FULL (shown in ❷).

Run the request in the SAP NetWeaver Gateway client again. Because you've set an external breakpoint, the system stops at the same location, as shown in Figure A.15.

In Figure A.15, you can see that a standard error message is generated for each method in the data provider class (DPC). It is executed if the corresponding method in the DPC extension class is called when the method in the extension class has not been implemented.

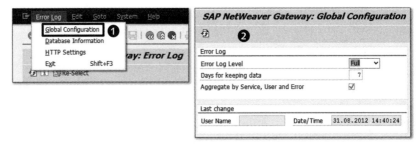

Figure A.14 Error Log Level Configuration

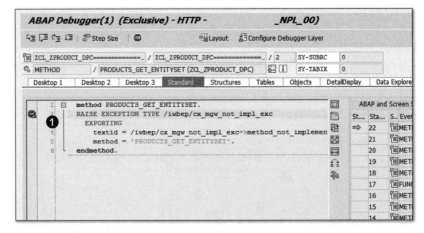

Figure A.15 Stop at Breakpoint

After implementing the GET_ENTITYSET method in the DPC extension class, you can try out the replay functionality again; this time, you've changed the settings of the error log as described earlier. As shown in Figure A.16, the request now runs successfully with an HTTP return code 200.

If you don't know how to solve a problem, choose DOWNLOAD TO PC in the error log to download the error message to your desktop.

The XML shown in Figure A.17 contains all of the information you saw in the UI of the error log, error data (shown in ❶), error context (shown in ❷), service info (shown in ❸), system info (shown in ❹), and even request data (shown in ❺).

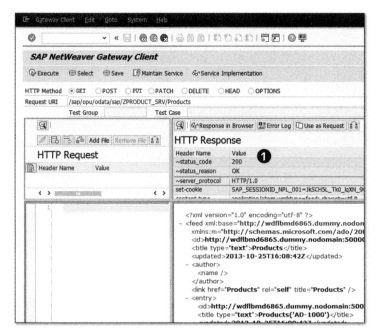

Figure A.16 Result after Implementation

```
<?xml version="1.0" encoding="UTF-8"?>
<SAPGW_BEP_ERROR_LOG>
  - <item timestamp="20131025160246">
      + <ERROR_DATA>
      - <ERROR_CONTEXT>
          <ERROR_INFO>Method 'PRODUCTS_GET_ENTITYSET' not implemented in data
          <_-IWBEP_-CX_MGW_NOT_IMPL_EXC/>
        - <SERVICE_INFO>
            <NAMESPACE>/SAP/</NAMESPACE>
            <SERVICE_NAME>***Hide_due_to_secure_log_level***</SERVICE_NAME>
            <SERVICE_TECH_NAME>***Hide_due_to_secure_log_level***</SERVICE_T
            <MODEL_TECH_NAME>ZPRODUCT_MDL</MODEL_TECH_NAME>
            <MODEL_VERSION>0001</MODEL_VERSION>
          </SERVICE_INFO>
          + <SYSTEM_INFO>
        </ERROR_CONTEXT>
      + <CALL_STACK>
      + <REQUEST_DATA>
        <RESPONSE_DATA>***Hide_due_to_secure_log_level***</RESPONSE_DATA>
    </item>
</SAPGW_BEP_ERROR_LOG>
```

Figure A.17 Error XML

A.4   Using the Performance Trace Tool

Every HTTP request coming from an OData consumer takes a certain path in an SAP NetWeaver Gateway system, as shown in Figure A.18. When a request is placed, the HTTP request first enters the HTTP framework on the hub, is then handled by the REST and OData library (shown in ❶), and finally ends up in the SAP NetWeaver Gateway framework (shown in ❷). From the SAP NetWeaver Gateway framework on the hub, a RFC call (shown in ❸) takes place to the SAP NetWeaver Gateway framework in the SAP Business Suite (shown in ❹). Finally, the application in the SAP Business Suite (shown in ❺) is called. This application consists of the service model that defines the metadata and the runtime.

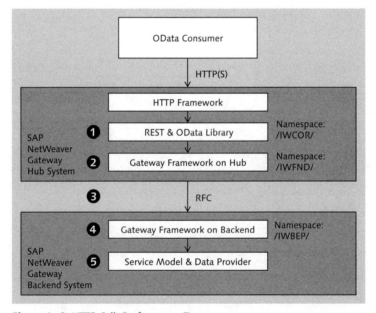

Figure A.18 HTTP Call: Performance Trace

From a performance point of view, you not only want to know the total response time but also what time a request takes in the different components mentioned earlier.

For a performance analysis, you want to know details about the time it took for the request to pass the SAP NetWeaver Gateway framework on the hub compared to the network overhead that results from the RFC from the hub to the SAP Business Suite for transfer of the data. In the SAP Business Suite, you want to know about the overhead of the backend framework and the processing time of the application Although it's mostly the backend implementation of a service that causes performance problems, it's also possible that a bad network connection between the hub and the SAP NetWeaver Gateway backend can result in bad response times.

To better understand the performance trace tool results, which are grouped by the namespace of the involved software components, it's good to know to which namespaces the components belong. While the REST and OData library components belong to the namespace /IWCOR/ and are contained in the GW_CORE add-on, the SAP NetWeaver Gateway framework components in the hub belong to the namespace /IWFND/ and are contained in the IW_FND add-on. The framework components in the SAP Business Suite belong to the namespace /IWBEP/ and are contained in the IW_BEP add-on. Note that as of 7.40, all components (GW_CORE, IW_FND, and IW_BEP) will be contained in only one add-on called SAP_GWFND, as discussed in Chapter 2.

With SP07 of SAP NetWeaver Gateway 2.0 and the corresponding SP level of SAP NetWeaver AS ABAP 7.40 (SP04), the performance trace tool has been enhanced so that analysis of response times is easier. Figure A.19 shows the performance trace tool available with SP07. In the following list, we've depicted how these values correspond to the response time components of the HTTP request shown in Figure A.18:

- Request processing time = ❶ + ❷ + ❸ + ❹ + ❺
- SAP NetWeaver Gateway hub system = ❶ + ❷
- RFC and network overhead = ❸
- SAP NetWeaver Gateway framework backend overhead = ❹
- Application (data provider) = ❺

Further Resources

More details on the SAP NetWeaver Gateway performance trace tool can be found here:

http://help.sap.com/saphelp_gateway20sp06/helpdata/en/9d/da3a2ceca344c f85568ae927e9858d/content.htm

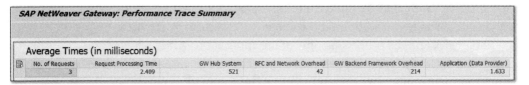

Figure A.19 New Performance Trace Summary Screen Available in SP07

A.5   Delta Query Support in Offline Scenarios

The scenarios that we have looked at so far covered the use of SAP NetWeaver Gateway in online production environments. However, there are, of course, use cases that require an application to run offline. For this reason, SAP NetWeaver Gateway offers a *delta query protocol*, which is supported as of SP07. The delta query protocol allows a client to retrieve data from an OData service that has been created, changed, or deleted since the client last checked. The delta query protocol supports synchronizing data from a single store to multiple clients. In addition, you have the ability to submit updates from the client to the server. This provides a solution for keeping a client's local data in sync with a single store.

In this section, we will take a look at the protocol specifics of delta queries via a sample service that is delivered as part of SAP NetWeaver Gateway. Then we'll describe the different options for implementing a service that supports delta queries.

A.5.1   Delta Query Protocol

The whole process starts with an initial request that is sent by a client to an entity set of an OData service that supports the delta query protocol. The server responds with a list of entities, just as a normal OData service does. In addition, a delta token link is returned at the end of the response for the entity collection.

The sample service RMTSAMPLEFLIGHT contains the entity set TravelAgencies_DQ, which supports the delta query protocol. Using the SAP NetWeaver Gateway client, we can send the following HTTP(S) request to the sample service to retrieve all travel agencies in an initial call:

/sap/opu/odata/IWFND/RMTSAMPLEFLIGHT/TravelAgencies_DQ

Toward the end of the XML document, you will find a relative link marked with `rel="delta"`. This has to be stored by the client and has to be used for a subsequent request to retrieve newly created, changed, or deleted data.

```
<feed>
    <entry>
    ...
    </entry>
<entry>
...
</entry>
<link rel="delta" href="TravelAgencies_DQ?
!deltatoken='005056B2190B1ED396FE518A3FCB83A6_20131203081145'"/
>
</feed>
```

Listing A.4 Delta Query Protocol — Delta Token

Suppose that one or more new travel agencies have been created or one or more existing travel agencies have been updated after the initial call. By sending the following request to the server, which contains the delta token, the client retrieves only a list of those newly created or changed travel agencies:

/sap/opu/odata/IWFND/RMTSAMPLEFLIGHT/TravelAgencies_DQ?!delta token='005056B2190B1ED396FE518A3FCB83A6_20131203081145'

If no data has been changed or created, the response of the service would be empty. In both cases, however, the response would contain a new delta token link.

In addition to handling newly created and updated entities, the delta query protocol also supports the handling of deleted entities. For this, the XML response is extended with the `<deleted-entry>` tag(s) that contain deleted entries, which are called *tombstones*.

```
<at:deleted-entry ref="http://myserver.mycompany.com:50000/sap/
opu/odata/IWFND/RMTSAMPLEFLIGHT/
TravelAgencies_DQ('00001761')" when="2013-12-03T08:12:36Z" />
<at:deleted-entry ref="http://myserver.mycompany.com:50000/sap/
opu/odata/IWFND/RMTSAMPLEFLIGHT/
TravelAgencies_DQ('00001762')" when="2013-12-03T08:12:36Z" />
<link rel="delta" href="TravelAgencies_DQ?!deltatoken='005056B2
190B1ED396FE518A3FCB83A6_20131203081236'" />
</feed>
```

Listing A.5 Delta Query Protocol—Tombstones

A.5.2 Service Implementation Options

Implementing delta query support requires the detection of changes that have been made to your business objects. There is no standard approach you can follow that works for each and every scenario. SAP currently offers two options:

- Use of a delta determination at request time using the *delta request log component*.
- Use of the *Agentry SAP Framework*.

The first approach calculates the deltas at request time. The second approach requires that changes to the business objects be tracked in a persistent database table, which is called the *exchange table*, with the help of the *Exchange Framework*.

Delta Request Log

When using the delta request log component, the implementation for the developer is fairly easy. Before passing the entity set back to the client in the GET_ENTITYSET method, it is passed to the framework, which calculates a hash value for each entity and stores the hash values in two application tables, (/IWBEP/D_QRL_HDR and /IWBEP/D_QRL_ITM).

If the client is requesting changed data at a later point in time using the delta token in the HTTP(S) request as a query parameter, the GET_ENTITYSET_DELTA method, as opposed to the GET_ENTITYSET method, is called. (However, it is necessary to perform the same query in the backend as in the `GET_ENTITYSET` method, and it is also necessary to perform the same calculation of hash values.)

Based on the data that is stored in tables `/IWBEP/D_QRL_HDR` and `/IWBEP/D_QRL_ITM`, it is now possible to compare the results of the second query with the results that were retrieved with the previous call. The method will compare both result sets and only send back those entities that have been newly created, changed, or deleted.

Further Resources

For a detailed description of an actual implementation of a service using the delta request log, we recommend the following:

http://scn.sap.com/docs/DOC-47043

Although the use of the delta request log component is straightforward and easy from an implementation perspective, the downside is that the load of the SAP Business Suite system is not reduced at all. For an alternative to this method, read on.

Agentry SAP Framework

If performance is an issue, managing deltas should be handled via the Agentry SAP Framework, which uses a persistent database table to track changes. This framework is part of the SAP Mobile Platform and is implemented as an ABAP add-on. The change detection concept of the Agentry SAP Framework is depicted in Figure A.20.

The changes that are detected by the Agentry SAP Framework implementation are processed by the framework in a persistent database table, the *exchange table*. At the very least, this table contains basic information such as last changed timestamp, change action (insert/update/delete), the user that performed this action, and—most important—the object key. In addition, the Agentry SAP Framework can also store additional information such as the actual values that have been changed (to avoid additional read requests to the backend by the client to retrieve those values), and offers filtering capabilities that allow you to track only those changes that meet certain, customized filter criteria.

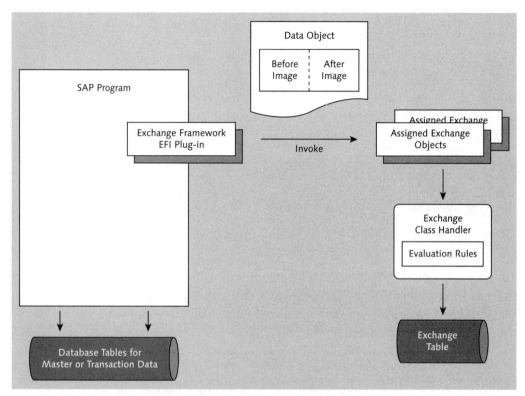

Figure A.20 Agentry SAP Framework Change Detection Concept

Further Resources

A detailed description of the Agentry SAP Framework components, an imple-mentation guideline, and a step-by-step example of how to create a delta query implementation can be found here:

https://scn.sap.com/docs/DOC-49290

A.6 Summary

This appendix has provided you with some insights into advanced topics related to SAP NetWeaver Gateway. Needless to say, this has been a high-level look at these topics, so consider this appendix a starting point only.

B   The Authors

Carsten Bönnen received his M.A. in Computer Linguistics and Artificial Intelligence in Germany in 2001 and started working at SAP that same year. Initially a Java developer and trainer, he soon became a consultant and led strategic projects in the then-new field of enterprise portals. By the end of 2002, he became a product manager for SAP NetWeaver Portal. A year later, he took on responsibility for a new product, which later became known as Visual Composer; subsequently, he managed the complete UI topic in this area. Looking for a new challenge in 2008, he joined the Microsoft Strategic Alliance Management group, which oversees the strategic alliance between SAP and Microsoft. Carsten remained in this role for four years before he joined the SAP NetWeaver Gateway product management team in 2012. Beyond his business-specific activities at SAP, he founded the first SAP karate group in 2005, which he continues to lead today.

Volker Drees studied electrical engineering at Fachhochschule in Wiesbaden, Germany and holds a degree in communications engineering (Nachrichtentechnik). He began his SAP career in 1998 in the consulting department, and has experience in a number of areas: ABAP development, R/3 implementations, mySAP CRM, mobile sales, mobile asset management, and mobile infrastructure. He recently worked as a regional group expert for mobile applications in the Business User and Information Worker Division at SAP. Currently, Volker works as a product expert for SAP NetWeaver Gateway in the HANA Platform I/O Gateway Division.

André Fischer has worked in product management for SAP NetWeaver Gateway since the launch of the product in 2011. After finishing his physics degree at RWTH Aachen University and Heidelberg University, Germany, he started his professional career in 1995 as a technology consultant for an SAP partner. From 1999 to 2000 he was responsible for setting up a data center as the co-managing director for a newly founded joint venture outsourcing company, and his technical expertise contributed to the company becoming a certified SAP hosting partner. As of 2002, André specialized in SAP security consulting and in 2004 he joined the newly created Collaboration Technology Support Center Microsoft at SAP AG. Over the last ten years at SAP, André has focused on the interoperability of SAP NetWeaver and Microsoft technologies, SAP Enterprise Search, SAP NetWeaver Single Sign-On, and SAP NetWeaver Gateway. André is a frequent speaker at conferences, including SAP TechEd, and has published a multitude of articles and blogs on the SAP Community Network. In 2013, he became SCN Topic Leader 2012-2013 for the SAP NetWeaver Gateway category. He is co-author of the SAP PRESS book *SAP NetWeaver/.NET Interoperability*. With almost 20 years of experience in various SAP technologies, André is a trusted advisor for many SAP customers and partners.

Ludwig Heinz studied business informatics at the University of Applied Sciences FHDW in Bergisch Gladbach, and has worked as an ABAP and mobile developer at itelligence AG since 2006. Ludwig has been a member of the SAP Design Partner Council for SAP NetWeaver Gateway since 2011. In addition, he works as a college lecturer and supports students working on bachelor's theses with focuses on mobile UI technologies.

 **Karsten Strothmann** is the global head of SAP NetWeaver Gateway CPS at SAP AG in Walldorf, Germany. He has 15 years of experience in the software industry, 13 of those at SAP. Before joining SAP NetWeaver Gateway in 2010, he worked on diverse topics such as mobile, SAP SRM, and SAP NetWeaver Portal. During his career he has applied himself to highly varied roles in product management, development, quality assurance, and consulting, which has enabled him to acquire a holistic view of both software creation and its usage. Karsten holds a master's degree in Computer Science from Dortmund University, Germany.

Index

■ Master the concepts and
principles behind EDI and IDocs

■ Explore EDI business processes,
architecture, and administration

■ Configure IDocs for B2B
integration and information
exchange

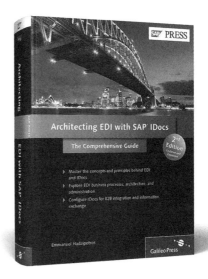

Emmanuel Hadzipetros

Architecting EDI with SAP IDocs

The Comprehensive Guide

Watch and learn how the fictitious Acme Pictures movie company uses EDI and
IDocs to make and sell its biggest flick yet. This extensive case study showcases
the requirements, standards, and capabilities you'll encounter as you build an
SAP EDI system and optimize electronic information exchange between
businesses via IDocs.

910 pp., 2. edition 2014, 79,95 Euro / US$ 79.95
ISBN 978-1-59229-871-6
www.sap-press.com

Galileo Press

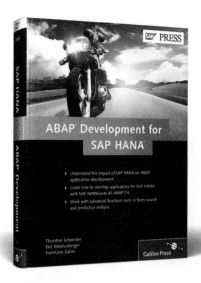

■ Understand the impact of SAP HANA on ABAP application development

■ Learn how to develop applications for SAP HANA with SAP NetWeaver AS ABAP 7.4

■ Work with advanced functions such as fuzzy search and predictive analysis

Thorsten Schneider, Eric Westenberger, Hermann Gahm

ABAP Development for SAP HANA

They say there's nothing new under the sun—but every once in a while, something novel comes along. With SAP HANA, even the most seasoned ABAP developers have some learning to do. Newbie or not, this book can help: install the Eclipse IDE, brush up your database programming skills, perform runtime and error analysis, transport old ABAP applications to HANA—and more. Expand your horizons!

609 pp., 2014, 69,95 Euro / US$ 69.95
ISBN 978-1-59229-859-4
www.sap-press.com

■ Explore hundreds of the most commonly-used function modules in ABAP

■ Learn about each function module's purpose and parameters, and see an example of each

■ Navigate by category or use the index to easily find the function module you need

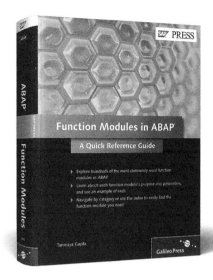

Tanmaya Gupta

Function Modules in ABAP

A Quick Reference Guide

Spending too much time on fruitless searches for the function module you need? In this compilation of the most-used function modules, you'll find essential information such as a description, parameters, prerequisites, and an example of each function module's use. Navigate this logically organized reference with the utmost ease—use different search options in the index to find the function module that will offer the most help.

977 pp., 2014, 69,95 Euro / US$ 69.95
ISBN 978-1-59229-850-1
www.sap-press.com

■ Implement SAP HANA as a
standalone data warehouse

■ Integrate SAP Data Services and
the SAP BusinessObjects BI tools
with SAP HANA

■ Benefit from step-by-step
instructions, technical details, and
downloadable data for every step

Jonathan Haun, Chris Hickman, Don Loden, Roy Wells

Implementing SAP HANA

You know what SAP HANA is—now you need to see it in action. Look no
further than this book, which will steer you through a real-life implementation
of the standalone version of SAP HANA. You'll find step-by-step instructions
and screenshots that show you how to implement real data in a real system,
from concept to go-live.

837 pp., 2013, 69,95 Euro / US$ 69.95
ISBN 978-1-59229-856-3
www.sap-press.com

■ Develop hybrid apps using MBOs and SAP Mobile Platform tools

■ Learn how to customize hybrid app functionality and user interfaces

■ Build native apps for Android and iOS

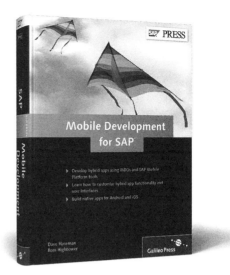

Dave Haseman, Ross Hightower

Mobile Development for SAP

Developers, developers, developers: SAP is calling you! With this book, get the whole picture on building mobile applications for SAP: from installation of Sybase Unwired Platform and its components, to complete explanations of building both hybrid and native applications for iOS and Android. After learning the steps, solidify your understanding with a case study that details the building of a live CRM mobile application. Aided by detailed instructions and screenshots, you'll find yourself building and customizing SAP mobile apps in no time at all.

617 pp., 2013, 69,95 Euro / US$ 69.95
ISBN 978-1-59229-448-0
www.sap-press.com

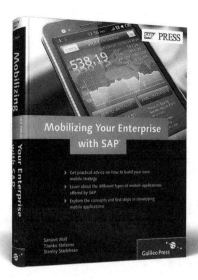

- Get practical advice on how to build your own mobile strategy

- Learn about the different types of mobile applications offered by SAP

- Explore the concepts and first steps in developing mobile applications

Sanjeet Mall, Tzanko Stefanov, Stanley Stadelman

Mobilizing Your Enterprise with SAP

The mobile revolution is everywhere, and now's the time to learn about how you can apply it to SAP. Whether you're a manager or an SAP consultant/developer charged with mobilizing an enterprise, this is the book you need to get started right now. Discover the different types of mobile solutions that SAP offers, and get detailed, expert insights on the concepts and technologies involved in the development of mobile applications. With this introduction, you'll be ready to make your way in an unwired world.

409 pp., 2012, 69,95 Euro / US$ 69.95
ISBN 978-1-59229-419-0
www.sap-press.com

Interested in reading more?

Please visit our website for all new
book and e-book releases from SAP PRESS.

www.sap-press.com